Land of Desire

ALSO BY WILLIAM LEACH

True Love and Perfect Union:
The Feminist Reform of Sex and Society

LAND OF
DESIRE

Merchants, Power, and the Rise of
a New American Culture

William Leach

Pantheon Books

NEW YORK

Library of Congress Cataloging-in-Publication Data
Leach, William R.
Land of desire : merchants, power, and the rise of a new American
culture / William Leach.
p.   cm.
Includes index.
ISBN 0-394-54350-5
1. Commercial   culture—United   States—History.   2.
Department stores—United States—History.   3. Sales
promotion—United   States—History.   4. Department
stores—Social   aspects—United   States—History.   5.
Consumer   behavior—United   States—History.   6.
United States—Commercial policy—History.   I. Title.
HF5465.U5L4   1993
381'.141'0973—dc20   92-50785
CIP

BOOK DESIGN BY CATHYRN S. AISON

Manufactured in the United States of America

FIRST EDITION

9 8 7 6 5 4 3 2 1

TO W.I.S. (1927–1985)
AND E.S.B.

THE BROKEN BALANCE

The people buying and selling, consuming pleasures, talking
    in the archways,
Were all suddenly struck quiet
And ran from under stone to look up at the sky: so shrill and
    mournful,
So fierce and final, a brazen
Pealing of trumpets high up in the air, in the summer blue over
    Tuscany.
They marveled; the soothsayers answered:
"Although the Gods are little troubled toward men, at the end
    of each period
A sign is declared in heaven
Indicating new times, new customs, a changed people; the
    Romans
Rule, and Etruria is finished;
A wise mariner will trim the sails to the wind."

                                I heard yesterday
So shrill and mournful a trumpet-blast,
It was hard to be wise. . . . You must eat change and endure;
    not be much troubled
For the people; they will have their happiness.
When the republic grows too heavy to endure, then Cæsar will
    carry it;
When life grows hateful, there's power . . .

Robinson Jeffers, "The Broken Balance," 1929, from *Rock and Hawk: A Selection of Shorter Poems by Robinson Jeffers*, Robert Haas, ed. (New York, 1987).

Contents

———————————◆———————————

ix

Preface

Whoever has the power to project a vision of the good life and make it prevail has the most decisive power of all. In its sheer quest to produce and sell goods cheaply in constantly growing volume and at higher profit levels, American business, after 1890, acquired such power and, despite a few wrenching crises along the way, has kept it ever since. From the 1890s on, American corporate business, in league with key institutions, began the transformation of American society into a society preoccupied with consumption, with comfort and bodily well-being, with luxury, spending, and acquisition, with more goods this year than last, more next year than this. American consumer capitalism produced a culture almost violently hostile to the past and to tradition, a future-oriented culture of desire that confused the good life with goods. It was a culture that first appeared as an alternative culture—or as one moving largely against the grain of earlier traditions of republicanism and Christian virtue—and then unfolded to become the reigning culture of the United States. It was the culture that many people the world over soon came to see as *the* heart of American life.

This book deals with the crucial formative years of this culture, 1880 to 1930. It seeks to illuminate its power and appeal as well as the tremendous ethical change it brought to America. Today, as mass consumer capitalism seems to be spreading across all frontiers, it is urgent for us to understand how it first came into being and what was gained or lost or repressed in that process. It is urgent for us to see this culture as a time-bound historical creation, especially if we have any misgivings about it, want to change it, or aim to reject it altogether.

Modern American consumer society has not been wanting for historians, and a good deal of their current work has been useful and informative; without it, in fact, *Land of Desire* could not have been written. At the same time, however, most of the new literature has either so damned consumer society as to make incomprehensible why it emerged at all or so praised and affirmed it as to imply that only fools, puritans, or masochists could have resisted or found fault with it. Today, the tendency is largely in the latter direction—toward praise and adulation—and even people who purport to be socialists or radical culture critics have embraced the idea that consumer capitalism has been (and is) basically and positively liberatory, the best system yet devised with the potential for meeting the "real" needs and desires of all human beings.

This book attempts a fuller assessment of the culture of consumer capitalism. It discusses the economic reality that ushered it into being—the national corporations, the mass market retailers, and the banks. The book deals with the advertisers and promoters, the display artists and fashionists, and the huge number of brokers and confidence men and women who devised the riveting enticements to serve business. But the book goes well beyond an economic analysis to see the culture as a whole, as a complex set of relations and alliances among different kinds of people and groups—cultural and noneconomic, religious and political—that worked together to create what merchant John Wanamaker called the "land of desire." The first part of this book is devoted to merchants and their enticements; the second and third parts show how those merchants cooperated with educators, social reformers, politicians, artists, and religious leaders to bring into existence the new economy and culture.

I want to warn the reader that *Land of Desire* does not focus on issues of popular consent and reception. Behavior is not the key subject of the book, although plenty of behavior is described in these pages, plenty of people affirming the new culture, opposing or hating it, celebrating it. Still, my subject is not consent but the *creation* of this culture. Consent, to be sure, played some kind of role, but it was not decisive. This idea sounds like a contradiction, since we know that defenders of capitalism have always claimed that capitalism has been (and is) the most democratic of economic systems; it has not only required but also begged for popular consent in order to function. Capitalist markets cannot perform, many economists claim, unless they respond well to the "real" needs and desires or to the consent of consumers.

Yet, I do not believe that consent was key to the creation and perpetuation of this new phenomenon. Indeed, the culture of consumer capitalism may have been among the most nonconsensual public cultures ever created, and it was nonconsensual for two reasons. First, it was not produced by "the people" but by commercial groups in cooperation with other elites comfortable with and committed to making profits and to accumulating capital on an ever-ascending scale. Second, it was nonconsensual because, in its mere day-to-day conduct (but not in any conspiratorial way), it raised to the fore only one vision of the good life and pushed out all others. In this way, it diminished American public life, denying the American people access to insight into other ways of organizing and conceiving life, insight that might have endowed their consent to the dominant culture (if such consent were to be given at all) with real democracy.

This book was built on extensive research carried on over many years. I am grateful to have been able to interview Dana O'Clare, display manager of Lord & Taylor in New York City in the 1930s; Fred Yost, retired senior vice-president and display expert at Wanamaker's in Philadelphia; retired retail buyers Marjorie Pleshette, Elizabeth Hamil, and Dora Sanders; Adolphina Mazur, wife of the late Paul Mazur, investment banker; the late Richard Bond, former president of Wanamaker's in Philadelphia; and Edward L. Bernays, pioneer creator of the science of public relations.

I was the first person in over six decades to have access to the archives of John Wanamaker's department store in Philadelphia, an unforgettable and fortunate experience since Wanamaker was America's most influential merchant of the early twentieth century. Although Robert Harrison, then senior vice-president of Wanamaker's, believed that I would find little of value in the store archives, he was wrong. All John Wanamaker's bound letterbooks were there, along with hundreds of unbound letters to and from Wanamaker and his son Rodman. Many newspaper scrapbooks, personal notebooks and pieces of diaries, and countless documents covering every aspect of the growth and evolution of the business were available. It was a rich archive indeed (now housed but still unprocessed in the Pennsylvania Historical Society), and I am extremely grateful to have been able to use

it. It is because of the almost five months I spent there that the first half
of this book is as much a biography of John Wanamaker as it is a study of
the culture he helped to create.

The resources of six other institutions also made crucial contributions
to the scope of this book: the New York Public Library, the New-York
Historical Society, the Library of Congress, the National Archives, the
National Museum of American History, and Bobst Library of New York
University. I would also like to thank the archivists and librarians of the
following institutions: the George Baker Library, Harvard Business School,
Cambridge, Massachusetts; the Metropolitan Museum of Art, New York
City; the American Museum of Natural History, New York City; the Brook-
lyn Museum, Brooklyn, New York; the Worcester Antiquarian Society,
Worcester, Massachusetts; the New York Municipal Archives and Record
Center; Pratt Institute in Brooklyn, New York; the Chicago Historical Society, Chicago, Illinois; the Newberry Library, Chicago, Illinois; the Brook-
lyn Historical Society, Brooklyn, New York; the Manuscripts Room of the
Butler Library, Columbia University, New York City; and the University
Archives and Tamiment Library of New York University. Also of value
were the archives of Marshall Field's in Chicago, Strawbridge and Clothier
in Philadelphia, and Woodward and Lothrop in Washington, D.C. I would
like to thank especially George Rinder, senior vice-president at Marshall
Field's, for his kind assistance when I visited there in the summer of 1985.
I owe thanks as well to Homer Sharp, archivist at Marshall Field's, to Henry
Adams, director of the Nelson Atkins Museum in Kansas City, Missouri,
and to Philip Cronenwett of Dartmouth College Library for their prompt
help with photographs.

Fellowships from the Guggenheim Foundation, the National Endowment for the Humanities, the Woodrow Wilson International Center for
Scholars in Washington, and the New York Institute for the Humanities
at New York University were indispensable in making the research of this
book possible. My thanks also go to Stanley Marcus of Dallas, Texas, whose
great generosity early on in this study opened many doors for me and helped
secure the direction of my work.

This book was built on more than research and with more than financial
aid, however. It benefitted from the generosity of friends and from the help
of scholars whose scrutiny saved me sometimes from errors of fact and
judgment. I would like to thank Elizabeth Gray Kogen and Mrs. Warren
I. Susman for their help. I am in debt to Michael Patrick Hearn for knowl-

edge regarding the life and times of L. Frank Baum, author of *The Wonderful Wizard of Oz*, which plays a major role in this study. Richard Fox's reading of one chapter on religion also made me deepen my discussion.

Christopher Lasch and William R. Taylor read the second draft of the book, freeing me, in turn, to meet the challenge of third and fourth drafts. I am indebted to these men, as I am to Donald Meyer and Mary O. Furner, who plowed through the manuscript twice. Furner and Meyer were direct and sharp, making me aware of many wrong turns, many excesses. Although both disagreed with me in places, the book is stronger because I addressed their arguments. The same goes for Roy Rosenzweig, whose full, detailed response to an early draft was a model of its kind.

My editor, Jeannette Hopkins, worked hard on the manuscript over many months. She much improved it and I thank her for that. I thank also Fred Jordan, Susan Norton, and others at Pantheon who helped bring this project to conclusion.

Elizabeth Blackmar has contributed to the making of this book in ways no one else has, not only by reading and critiquing it countless times, but by tolerating my limitations and reinforcing my strengths. Her much needed companionship helped get me through some very hard times.

My final thoughts are for Warren Susman, who died in 1985. This man, voracious for nearly everything in life and nourishing beyond words, set me on the road to history years ago. He stood in a line of great historians by the power with which he expressed his ideas as a teacher and by what he wrote. He had the most sustained passion for ideas of any person I have ever known. He made the study of history seem at times like the most thrilling and rewarding of occupations. His memory, almost more than anything else, kept this book alive and made certain it would be completed.

Land of Desire

THE LAND OF DESIRE AND

THE CULTURE OF

CONSUMER CAPITALISM

In 1906 the merchant John Wanamaker wrote that "everyone who starts a new thing has to stand where Columbus did when he set sail. Few had faith that he could ever reach the Land of Desire." Wanamaker announced the emergence of a new culture coming to dominate American life. At the heart of it was the quest for pleasure, security, comfort, and material well-being. "It speaks to us," said another merchant, "only of ourselves, our pleasures, our life. It does not say, 'Pray, obey, sacrifice thyself, respect the King, fear thy master.' It whispers, 'Amuse thyself, take care of yourself.' Is not this the natural and logical effect of an age of individualism?"[1]

In the decades following the Civil War, American capitalism began to produce a distinct culture, unconnected to traditional family or community values, to religion in any conventional sense, or to political democracy. It was a secular business and market-oriented culture, with the exchange and circulation of money and goods at the foundation of its aesthetic life and of its moral sensibility. This book is about the growth of that culture, about its character, and about the people and groups that brought it into being.

The cardinal features of this culture were acquisition and consumption as the means of achieving happiness; the cult of the new; the democratization of desire; and money value as the predominant measure of all value in society.

By World War I, Americans were being enticed into consumer pleasure and indulgence rather than into work as the road to happiness. The roots for this enticement lay deep in American and European history. For generations, America had been portrayed as a place of plenty, a garden in which all paradisiacal longings would be satisfied. Many Protestant settlers even thought that the millennial promise—the Second Coming of Christ—was destined to be fulfilled here and that the New Jerusalem would bring not only salvation and spiritual bliss but also temporal blessings and the end to poverty.[2] By the early 1900s this myth was being transformed, urbanized and commercialized, increasingly severed from its religious aims and focusing ever more on personal satisfaction and even on such new pleasure palaces as department stores, theaters, restaurants, hotels, dance halls, and amusement parks. These institutions still carried much of the former mythic message—the message that said Americans can be renewed and remade—but where the old ideas often conceived of America as a millennial land in which many different kinds of dreams might come true (spiritual, vocational, and political as well as material), this new era heralded the pursuit of goods as the means to all "good" and to personal salvation. Thus, pioneer advertiser Artemas Ward dropped the older religious dimension but kept the paradise. "This world," he wrote in 1892, "seems real only when it answers to our individual touch. Yet, beyond our touch, beyond our waking, beyond our working, and almost in the land of dreams, lie things beyond our present thought, greater, wider, stronger, than those we now lay hold on. To each a world opens; to everyone possibilities are present."[3]

A cult of the "new" belonged to this new culture. Here again Americans had been prepared by their own history. Phrases like the "New World," "new heaven on earth," and "new nation" were common currency; and everyone seemed to boast of the country's "innovative ways," as did Unitarian minister William Ellery Channing when he spoke glowingly in 1830 of America as "a new continent" of "new freedom," of "new social institutions," of "new paths," and of "new harvests." Newness and change themselves had become traditional in America. "The world and the books are so accustomed to use the word 'new' in connection with our country," wrote Mark Twain in *Life on the Mississippi*, "that we early get and permanently retain the impression that there is nothing old about it."[4] It was hard under these circumstances to defend any tradition, any inherited custom or belief, when the past itself was hostage to the new.

Emerson and Whitman expressed a profound side to this cult, inviting men and women to plunge into new experiences, to embrace the full range of expressiveness, to pursue the new on their own terms and not because it was thrust on them by others. One should seek the new, Emerson wrote, not for its own sake, nor for the "squalid contentment" and "excessive concern for comfort" often associated with material ventures but for the spiritual rebirth, insight, and virtue that might be discovered or encountered there.[5] The quest for the new was also fostered by the Western pursuit of knowledge, liberated for both good and ill by the Enlightenment and by the scientific revolution.

By the end of the century, however, commercial capitalism had latched on to the cult of the new, fully identified with it, and taken it over. Innovation became tied to the production of more and more commodities. Fashion and style were at the center, appropriating folk design and image, reducing custom to mere surface and appearance. The cult of the new was, perhaps, the most radical aspect of this culture, because it readily subverted whatever custom, value, or folk idea came within its reach. Science, too, was radical but not intrinsically hostile to custom or tradition or religion. Market capitalism *was* hostile; no immigrant culture—and, to a considerable degree, no religious tradition—had the power to resist it, as none can in our own time. Any group that has come to this country has had to learn to accept and to adjust to this elemental feature of American capitalist culture.

The democratization of desire emerged alongside the cult of the new and the unfolding of the consumer paradise. It, too, had roots—in the great movement in the United States toward democracy. For at least the first half of the nineteenth century, most American white men were self-employed voters, owners of landed property, and producers of foodstuffs and raw materials for a prosperous Atlantic trade largely free from the dangers of manufacturing that relied on disciplined work rhythms and a dependent work force to churn out goods. Americans rejoiced in their widely diffused prosperity. America was "the Land of Comfort" for all.[6]

But after 1885, in the wake of the rapid industrializing of the country, the idea of democracy, like the idea of the new and the idea of paradise, began to change radically. Gradually, wealth lay less in land and more in capital or in the money required to produce new goods. This pecuniary wealth was owned by a small minority; but at the same time, growing numbers of Americans were losing control over their work, becoming dependent on others—on the owners of the capital—for their wages and well-being. In this context a new conception of democracy developed, fostered by growing incomes and a rising standard of living and espoused alike by capitalists and many progressive reformers, a democracy at once more inclusive and more confining than before.

This highly individualistic conception of democracy emphasized self-pleasure and self-fulfillment over community or civic well-being. As the older grounds for economic and political freedom were eroding (ownership of property and control of work), newer and "better" grounds were coming into being. The concept had two sides. First, it stressed the diffusion of comfort and prosperity not merely as part of the American experience as heretofore, but instead as its centerpiece. Thus, progressive Herbert Croly, inspirer of President Theodore Roosevelt, wrote that the "promise of American life" consisted foremost in a "promise of comfort and prosperity for an ever-increasing majority of good Americans"; and business supporter and influential economist John Bates Clark argued that despite the "vast and ever-growing inequality" of wealth in America, democracy could be ensured through the benign genius of the "free" market, which allocated to Americans an infinitely growing supply of goods and services.[7] Second, the new conception included the democratizing of desire, or, more precisely, equal rights to desire the same goods and to enter the same world of comfort and luxury. American culture, therefore, became more democratic after 1880 in the sense that everybody—children as well as adults, men and women, black and white—would have the same right as individuals to desire, long for, and wish for whatever they pleased. The Land of Comfort was becoming the Land of Desire.

This new definition of democracy did not emerge without political opposition. Indeed, following the Civil War, a fierce conflict swept over the country, setting farmers and workers against businessmen over how democracy in industrial America should be organized. By the 1880s and 1890s a vocal populist and union movement had grown up that harkened back to the older republican America and that argued that democracy must be based on the ownership of property and work resources, not merely on the possession of goods. Democratic life and the virtue of the republic rested, they claimed, on independent families owning their own land and tools and producing themselves much of what they consumed. Social reformers and a new breed of economist echoed these ideas and even demanded that something be done to ensure the democratization of property and, thereby, the autonomy of ordinary Americans. "Either you must establish a more equitable division of property and produce," warned progressive economist Henry Carter Adams in 1879, "or the fatal end of democracy will be despotism and decadence."[8]

But the new market notion of democracy had many advocates and quickly rose to prominence. Democratizing individual desire—rather than wealth or political or economic power—was perhaps one of the new culture's most notable contributions to modern society, and this achievement had many consequences. It acted as a spur to effort, forcing people to compete, discipline themselves, and deny present comfort for future pleasures. At the same time, it often set husbands against wives, children against parents, and friend against friend. It fostered anxiety and restlessness and, when left unsatisfied, resentment and hatred. And because of its association with the new and its attachment to fantasy, it tended to reinforce the American refusal to face death as a fact of life, to divorce desire from death, longing from dread. In most cultures, acceptance of desire and longing has ordinarily been intermingled with acceptance of dread, the passage of time, and mortality. But in the United States, and especially in this cultural context, many of the writers who tried to set the tone took the dread and fear—or as the country's foremost writer of children's stories, L. Frank Baum, would say, the "heartache and nightmare"—out of desire, and gave life a happy face that would never grow old.

Through this culture ran another current that reinforced the anxiety and longing brought on by desire: the influence of money. Historian Perry Miller has written that pecuniary values were already the reigning values in America by 1815.[9] Nevertheless, after 1880, money was entering into the American economy and culture in a way it had never done before. In the past, men and women often made their own goods, relied on different currencies as mediums of exchange (at least before 1865), and sometimes bartered. Gradually, however, more and more Americans, no longer owning land or tools, were compelled to rely on money incomes—on wages and salaries—for their security and their well-being; at the same time, they became dependent "on goods made by unknown hands," as economist Wesley Clair Mitchell, the country's first authority on the business cycle, long ago pointed out.[10]

Such a transformation put money into a position of eminence in the lives of Americans. From now on pecuniary values (or market values) would constitute for many people the base measure for all other values, even for "the dim inner world by which men judge what is for them worthwhile," as Mitchell put it.[11] Charles Cooley, pioneer founder of modern sociology, worried about this trend, viewing it as an excrescence that had formed almost overnight. "Pecuniary values," he wrote in 1912, were not "natural" or "normal"; they were the historical outgrowth of a new economy and culture and "by no means the work of the whole people acting homogeneously." In the past, values had taken their "character from . . . the church"; now they were deriving it from "business and consumption." Increasingly, the worth of everything—even beauty, friendship, religion, the moral life—was being determined by what it could bring in the market.[12]

Consumption as a means to reach happiness, the cult of the new, democratization of desire, and pecuniary value had not been dominant in earlier decades (or anywhere else, for that matter, although Enlightenment philosophers had urged them on states and cultures as early as the late eighteenth century). Before 1880, the United States was largely an agrarian economy, with most Americans living and working on farms. As late as 1870 the average number of workers in any given factory was still fewer than ten.[13] Most markets were local or regional, and the majority of businesses were individually owned and managed. The culture was largely agrarian, republican, and religious; and most people—white people—controlled their own property or land.

This book examines how this older culture was challenged and was gradually superseded by the newer culture. It deals with the new national corporations and the investment banks as they moved almost overnight into the everyday lives of Americans. It focuses on mail order houses, on chain stores and dry goods houses, on hotels and restaurants, and especially on department stores, and it does so in part because most historians have for too long looked down on them—indeed, on the entire field of marketing, distribution, and merchandising—as subjects of only secondary importance compared to the fields of agricultural and industrial production and, therefore, as subjects unworthy of detailed study.[14] But this approach is mistaken; these institutions were—and are—indispensable to the capitalist economy. They brought the reality of capitalism—the dream life of capitalism, that is—directly, concretely home to generations of men and women. They, along with the other institutions, were the shapers of the Land of Desire. Without them, the new corporate economy could not have functioned and the Land of Desire would not have been born.

Land of Desire deals with three other matters central to an understanding of why and how the culture of consumer capitalism emerged in the way it did: the development of a new commercial aesthetic, the collaboration among economic and noneconomic institutions, and the growth of a new class of brokers. After 1880, American business began to create a new set of commercial enticements—a commercial aesthetic—to move and sell goods in volume. This was the core aesthetic of American capitalist culture, offering a vision of the good life and of paradise. Cultures must generate some conception of paradise or some imaginative notion of what constitutes the good life. They must bring to life a set of images, symbols, and signs that stir up interest at the very least, and devotion and loyalty at the most.[15] After 1880, American commercial capitalism, in the interest of marketing goods and making money, started down the road of creating just such a set and system of symbols, signs, and enticements, just such a vision of the good life. From the 1880s onward, a commercial aesthetic of desire and longing took shape to meet the needs of business. And since that need was constantly growing and seeking expression in wider and wider markets, the aesthetic of longing and desire was everywhere and took many forms. After 1880 this aesthetic appeared in show windows, electrical signs, fashion shows, advertisements, and billboards; as free services and sumptuous consumer environments; and as the artifacts or commodities themselves.

At the heart of the evolution of this commercial aesthetic were the visual materials of desire—color, glass, and light. Used for centuries by royal courts and by the military to excite devotion, loyalty, and fear, and by religions to depict otherworldly paradises, these materials were now mobilized in the United States and other industrialized countries to suggest a *this*-worldly paradise that was stress-free and "happy." "Coloured glass," wrote German architectural utopian Paul Scheerbart, who influenced Mies van der Rohe and Frank Lloyd Wright, among others, "destroys hatred." "Light softened by color, calms the nerves."[16] By 1910, American merchants, in their efforts to create the new commercial aesthetic, took command over color, glass, and light, fashioning a link so strong between them and consumption that, today, the link seems natural. By the 1920s so many commercial institutions and people had exploited "color" that, according to *The New York Times*, the word itself had been "worn to a frazzle."[17]

The new consumer direction of American culture was also the consequence of alliances among diverse institutions, noneconomic and economic, working together in an interlocking circuit of relationships to reinforce the democratization of desire and the cult of the new. National corporations, department stores, investment banks, hotel chains, and the entertainment industry joined this circuit, but so did the Metropolitan Museum of Art and the Brooklyn Museum, the Harvard Business School and the Wharton School, Cornell University, New York University, Pratt Institute, and the New York School of Design. Even the nation's most radical labor union, the Industrial Workers of the World, participated inadvertently in the building of this new culture.

American religious institutions, and the spiritual culture transmitted by them, were transformed by the new mass economy and culture and aided in their creation. It is one of the goals of this book to illuminate the character of that change, its spiritual as well as institutional character, its impact on consciousness. By 1900 mainstream Protestant denominations were beginning to bend and redefine their institutional missions in compliance with the new cultural perspective, and, in time, many Catholics and Jews went down a similar road. New religious or quasi-religious groups—the mind curers and positive thinkers like gurus Orison Swett Marden and Helene Blavatsky, and writers such as Eleanor Porter (author of *Pollyanna*) and L. Frank Baum (creator of *The Wonderful Wizard of Oz*) arrived on the scene, offering an outlook in comfortable harmony with the priorities and perspectives of the business world.

After about 1910, the federal government, too, joined the chorus of support and, with the expansion of the U.S. Department of Commerce under Herbert Hoover, placed a capstone on it in the 1920s.

Cultures of any endurance rest on strong relations among different institutions. After 1895, stores, museums, churches, and government agencies were beginning to act together to create the Land of Desire, redirecting aspiration toward consumer longings, consumer goods, and consumer pleasures and entertainments. A new group of brokers worked at the center of this circuit to facilitate the movement of images, money, and information. In the process they helped change the culture. I use the term "broker" here broadly, to encompass not only the obvious real estate brokers and stockbrokers but also any individual or group committed to helping business in a mediating capacity, among them investment bankers, corporate lawyers, and credit experts; urban museum curators and art school instructors who taught commercial and industrial "art" to up-and-coming designers; university professors who trained business leaders; economists who redefined the goals of the industrial order to include greater consumption; advertising agents and travel agents; "specialists" who created the "light and color" for places like Times Square; and professional model agencies (such as John Powers Incorporated in Manhattan) that brokered female bodies.

Journalist Samuel Strauss observed in the 1920s that brokers had the distinctive "talent" of being able to "adjust themselves to the time's changing demands."[18] Since time immemorial, they served as dispassionate go-betweens, bringing people together, arranging deals, negotiating contracts, and, most important, lending money. While earlier on the fringes of economic life, brokers—especially moneylenders—were regarded with contempt and fear for exploiting the resources of others but, as the market grew and new kinds of brokers appeared (jobbers, real estate agents, commodity and stock traders, and so forth), such prejudices began to weaken, although brokering's marginal character held on.[19]

After 1895 or thereabouts, the brokering class took on unprecedented size and began to fill a place in American life that turned the twentieth century into a century of intermediaries, and cities like New York into huge havens for brokering. The brokering style—repressing one's own convictions and withholding judgment in the interest of forging profitable relationships—is among the most modern of styles. It occupies a preeminence in today's political and moral economy. Brokers are now busy in nearly every sphere of activity, and they have helped inject into American culture a new amoralism essentially indifferent to virtue and hospitable to the ongoing inflation of desire. As with the merchants and the manufacturers, they were and are interested in expanding markets and volume turnover, in the movement of commodities from producer to consumer, in money, not people, and in the future, not the past. Don't worry about the past, advised one such broker, Emily Fogg Mead, an advertising expert and mother of Margaret Mead, in 1901, in an economics journal. "Accompanying all the early stages of innovation," she reassured businessmen, "is a fear of wrong-doing, of disloyalty to ideals, and of the coming destruction of the foundation of society; but the next generation has no conscientious misgivings."[20]

No country, it seems to me, developed the kind of commercial aesthetic, the type of brokering class, the form of institutional circuitry, or the variety of spiritual accommodations as those that emerged in the United States. The United States was the first country in the world to have an economy devoted to mass production, and it was the first to create the mass consumer institutions and the mass consumer enticements that rose up in tandem to market and sell the mass-produced goods. More effectively and pervasively than any other nation, America (or, more precisely, the dominant business class in America) forged a unique bond among different institutions that served to realize business aims. This book traces the history of these institutions and shows why they, along with the commercial establishments themselves, along with the Wanamakers, the Fields, and the Strauses, helped initiate and perpetuate the world's most powerful culture of consumption.

The culture of consumer capitalism, which became over time the very culture of America, did not appear without resistance or opposition—nothing this new or of this magnitude could have simply waltzed in and taken over. Nor were its effects felt everywhere in the same way. There were still many places—rural towns, religious communities, even urban enclaves—untouched to some degree by consumer capitalist culture. At the very time, moreover, that this culture was unfolding, another institutional complex was also emerging—the new public schools, the public universities, and the private colleges—which were not connected closely to the commercial system and which offered countless numbers of young Americans other paths to success and fulfillment (although, as we shall see, these institutions, too, yielded to the educational priorities of business). And, as I hope this book demonstrates, many groups and individuals raised their voices against the new cultural changes taking place and rebelled against them. These included farmers and workers who fought the large corporations; the small, independent merchants of the era who took part in the "retail wars" against the big department stores; religious believers and leaders as well as Congressional democrats and municipal socialists; insurgent economists and literary intellectuals; and numerous "ordinary" citizens. Many of these people were principally loyal to the older democratic producing tradition, a powerful tradition that claimed people themselves should determine the fate of their culture, the shape of their politics, and the conditions of their labor. Others simply feared the impact of capitalist culture on spiritual and creative life. And the very newness of this culture disturbed and alienated many men and women who lived through its creation and who felt, toward the end of their lives, like strangers in their own country. But despite this opposition and dissent, the culture did take hold and came to dominate and to reshape the American experience.

I

Strategies of Enticement

Chapter 1

THE DAWN OF
A COMMERCIAL EMPIRE

"They have emerged," wrote economist Edward Mead, husband of Emily Fogg Mead, of the new business corporations, in 1910, "like the trees in the primeval forest, wide and deep in the desires and necessities of mankind."[1] From meat-packing firms like Armour and Swift to giant U.S. Steel, corporations overshadowed the economy and took the collective American breath away. They belonged to a large array of economic groups and firms that altogether populated the new primeval forest with a host of trees, from such mass consumption companies as Sears, Roebuck, Woolworth's, and the hotel chain of Ellsworth Statler to such department stores as Marshall Field's of Chicago, Siegel-Cooper's of New York, and John Wanamaker's of Philadelphia, each run by aggressive merchants who invented the sometimes dreamlike, sometimes nightmarish world of modern merchandising.

By the turn of the century, the retail dry goods houses of the past—even Alexander Turney Stewart's white Marble Palace in downtown Manhattan—had been surpassed by the huge department stores that appeared virtually everywhere in America. Led by men who took risks and occasionally ended up bankrupt or even in prison, the mass retail businesses plunged into an extraordinary whorl of competitiveness. The department stores in particular, symbolic of the very essence of the consumer revolution, rose to dominance through a multitude of means. They sold a vast range of goods under single roofs and controlled masses of capital (their own and other people's), thus attempting to eliminate their small-scale competition. When this failed, they crushed their enemies in the retail wars of the 1890s, using, among other means, the arm of the state.

Growth was fast and furious, and often too dangerous or intense for many men accustomed to old-fashioned forms of quiet marketing and selling. By the late 1890s so many goods, in fact, were flowing out of factories and into stores that businessmen feared overproduction, glut, panic, and depression. A crisis in distribution struck the new economy, menacing the gains achieved in production. And out of the turmoil (the threat of which, however, would never disappear), businessmen would turn to new kinds of merchandising. Out of the turmoil would come a steady stream of enticements—display and decoration, advertising, fashion, style, service, and so forth—to break up the logjam of goods and to awaken Americans, as Emily Fogg Mead wrote, to "the ability to want and choose."

"The Master Institutions of Civilized Life"

At the center of the creation of the new economy and culture was a revolution in the production of industrial and agricultural goods and the advent of the profit-driven corporation. This revolution begot the brokers and was the principal cause behind the creation of America's new institutional circuitry. In just six years, between 1899 and 1905, American food output grew by nearly 40 percent. The quantity of cheap artificial jewelry doubled between 1890 and 1900, as did the amount of men's and women's ready-wear clothing. Production of glassware and lamps jumped from 84,000 tons in 1890 to 250,563 tons in 1914, and Americans were walking on more rugs by the end of the nineteenth century—so it was claimed—than were all other people in the world combined.[2] A multitude of goods were produced to satisfy needs that no one knew they had. Now "we have pickle and olive forks," Emily Fogg Mead wrote, "strawberry and ice cream forks, oyster and fish forks; we have also berry spoons, sugar spoons, soup spoons, salt spoons, mustard spoons in ever-increasing variety."[3] In 1890 a total of 32,000 pianos were marketed; by 1904 it was 374,000. There was an equally voluminous output of cheap sheet music. Today, only one or two American

piano firms survive (most successfully, Steinway), but in 1900 there were
perhaps hundreds of "name" pianos—among them Chickering, Baldwin,
Kranich and Bach, Mason and Hamlin, Emerson, Vose, Kimball, and
Brewster, most flooding the middle-class market with relatively cheap
instruments.[4]

All this production was the result of the addition of new tools and
"continuous-process" machines, and of the discovery of new energy sources
such as coal, steam, gas, oil, and—crucially—electricity. The machines
and energy speeded up and increased output to mass-production levels,
allowed businessmen to build factories and offices in any direction anywhere
in the country, and created the potential for what Fogg Mead called a
"never-ending scale of expansion."[5] Major railroad trunk lines, as we know
them today, were completed by 1895, and telephones and telegraph connected voices across great distances, increasing the rapid movement of goods
and money.[6] Reserves of labor to operate the machines also grew, consisting
of a vast army of immigrants and of native unemployed workers from the
countryside and small towns. So, too, business had at its disposal, for the
first time ever, huge amounts of capital for investment, capital pooled by
new commercial and state banks and, above all, by the new insurance
companies.[7]

In the vanguard were the large business corporations or combinations,
which superseded the typical mid-nineteenth-century firm in economic
importance. The earlier firm was small-scale and low volume and strove
for success through product differentiation or by manufacturing a single
unique product in a secure, relatively noncompetitive niche. The newer
corporations cared little for differentiation, everything about high volume,
full capacity production, and domination of mass markets. They came on
the scene (especially after 1895) in response to a rapid fall in prices, high
labor costs, and market volatility—all caused by intense competition. Corporations sought to end this competition by getting "control over prices,
labor, and middlemen"—but above all, as Edward Mead insisted, "control
over prices." "The essence of competition," he wrote, "is the sacrifice of
prices to the buyer, and the essential principle of combination is the control
of supply by the seller." Corporations wanted to be free, with intervention
from no one, to "charge what the traffic will bear" and to "get from the
buyer all that the buyer can be induced to pay."[8]

Unlike entrepreneurial firms, which were (and are) owned and conducted by individuals or partners, corporations were legal entities designed

to provide limited liability and to ensure continuity of ownership beyond the lifetime of the original owners. They were social organizations marked by administrative hierarchies, managing machines, tools, and labor. But they were above all economic institutions, created to generate capital through private and public stock ownership and, through consolidation and often mergers, to seize market control in behalf of making profits. "The modern industrial corporation," wrote Harvard economics professor Arthur Hadley in 1907, admiringly, "was developed as a means of meeting the need for capital by large industries," capital "far beyond the power of any one man or any small group of partners to furnish."[9]

Modern business corporations were profit-driven machines. By 1900, many of them, in alliances with promoters and investment bankers who helped form the consolidations and mergers, were remaking the economy into a system preoccupied with "making profits" rather than with "making goods." The investment bankers especially—as Thorstein Veblen was perhaps the first to note—were directing economic life along a largely pecuniary path; these men, who were little concerned about the intrinsic value or utility of goods, supplied corporations with credit to expand, merge, and control markets, often sitting on their boards of directors and even managing the businesses themselves. They brought into play a new form of capital— "business capital," as Veblen called it. By 1895 "investment for gain" had begun to "supersede commitment to industry and workmanship," a shift in outlook Veblen described as "one of the most significant mutations in man's history."[10]

Corporations carried out on a grand scale what Robert Heilbroner has argued is the essence of the capitalist process—"the continuous transformation of capital-as-money into capital-as-commodities, followed by a re-transformation of capital-as-commodities into capital-as-money." (Edward Mead again: "Great corporate beings grow continuously" and are "constantly adding to [their] equipment in order to increase [their] profits").[11] It was this potentially convulsive process that gave to the American economy and society its dynamic, innovative, thrusting-forward character—more goods this year than last, more next year than this, profit on profit. It led, inexorably, to the amassing of more and more capital in the hands of the owners of productive resources and capital, and conferred on those owners the power to decide who should be or should not be employed and the character of the work itself. The process endowed them with the power to direct the activities of society and to control access to wealth, goods, and happiness.[12] In the words of Veblen, the corporation had by 1900 "come not only to dominate the economic structure but to be the master institution of civilized life."[13]

Not all businesses adopted the corporate form—not the building and garment industries, for instance, both of which consisted of many individually operated firms that eluded incorporation (often to be free to rely on subcontracting and to employ the cheapest labor).[14] But corporations became preponderant in both the producer and consumer sectors of the economy. In record-breaking time, as business historian Alfred Chandler has shown, they took over the production and distribution of goods in the United States, displacing in importance small employer-owned businesses. Giant producer-goods firms were built, from E. I. Dupont, maker of explosives, to U. S. Steel and Standard Oil. Close behind or at the same time were the big consumer-goods corporations: soap companies like Procter & Gamble; tobacco conglomerates like R. J. Reynolds and P. Lorillard; and meat businesses like Gustavus Swift, Inc., with its "full line" of lamb, pork, beef, and poultry, its numerous branch meat packing houses, and its branch marketing outlets spanning the country by 1890.[15]

Americans also witnessed a great surge forward after 1895 in the expansion of the service industry. The hotel and restaurant business was virtually nonexistent throughout most of the nineteenth century, mostly small-scale, confined to a few cities. After the Civil War, the new railroads changed all this, building or helping to build plush hotels and restaurants in cities coast to coast that catered to traveling wholesale buyers and sellers, politicians, traveling actors and circus troupes, swelling numbers of tourists, and con artists of all stripes. The greatest growth came after 1900, marked by the arrival of the first "skyscraper hotel" and of the first chains of large hotels, multistory monoliths run like factories and staffed by thousands of workers toiling from dawn to dusk.[16]

Merchandising underwent a similar burst in development, including dry goods houses, chain stores, mail order and specialty houses, and, most spectacularly, department stores. Although many of these businesses, as Chandler has argued, remained independently owned and operated (as many are today), merchandising as a whole experienced the same impulse toward expansion, concentration, and even incorporation that overtook the rest of the economy.[17]

From Marble Palaces to Masses of Goods and Capital

Before 1880 businesses like department stores did not exist; what did exist were neighborhood dealers, small dry goods firms, and large wholesalers that fanned out through distributing outlets into cities, towns, and villages. In the next twenty years, however, cities throughout the country would be filled with large retail establishments—multifloored, multiwindowed buildings of great concentrated selling power. In England, Japan, France, and Northern Europe, department stores had also gained a foothold but only in capital cities (none existed in Rome or Madrid, however).[18] The great French stores for "popular trade" that also influenced American merchandising—Galeries Lafayette, Les Printemps, and Bon Marché—appeared only in Paris (a city, in any case, known principally for its luxurious specialty shops).[19] In Japan, just one large store commanded interest—Mitsukoshi of Tokyo.[20] English retailing, although highly evolved in terms of both small and large consumer cooperatives and multiple specialized shops, had major middle-class department stores—for instance, Whiteley's, Harrod's, and Selfridges—only in London. Significantly, Selfridges, the very *first* commercial building in England built on a steel frame and from reinforced concrete, was founded by an American, H. Gordon Selfridge.[21] There were department stores in Germany but these sold largely cheap goods to a "lower class" clientele (only Berlin's Wertheim, which catered to foreigners, boasted a middle-class character).[22]

American department store merchandising was different in its scope, size, and prolific middle classness. Substantial middle-class stores were constructed in many cities and even in small towns at such a rate as to outpace anything comparable going on elsewhere in the world. "You find stores of this category not only in New York, in Chicago, and in Philadelphia," observed one startled Swiss merchant during a visit to the United States in 1915, "but also well-known stores of enormous dimension in many other cities throughout the United States."[23]

Department stores overshadowed the scene through the sheer rapidity and size of their expansion, which started in earnest, if chaotically, in the early 1890s as merchants began to tack new wings onto older stores, often creating "shreds and patches without unity or dignity," as one architect complained.[24] They, along with retailing chains and mail-order businesses of all kinds, dominated merchandising after 1895. And they did so because they contributed to the creation of a new powerful universe of consumer enticements. The mass market merchants succeeded as well because they sold a world of new goods under one roof, concentrated ownership and controlled large capital sums (like other corporations), crushed or absorbed their competitors, and demonstrated great individual skill.

Of the few big early merchants, only the Scotch-Irish immigrant Alexander Turney Stewart, who possessed the nation's biggest stores in New York in the 1860s and 1870s, could have come close to what we think of as a modern mass retailer. Stewart was certainly a phenomenon, said to be the man who brought the one-price system to America, so successful by the late 1860s that President Ulysses S. Grant tried, to no avail, to appoint him secretary of the treasury. He made most of his money in the lucrative business expansion in New York City during and after the Civil War. His five-story cast-iron retail dry goods store, the Marble Palace, commanded the full block at Astor Place and Broadway in downtown Manhattan. Majestic on its white Corinthian columns and illuminated by gaslight and hundreds of windows, the store stood until a fire destroyed it in the 1950s. It was the largest building in New York City in the 1860s.[25] On the fourth floor, where manufacturing took place, stooping women and children labored at sewing machines in row upon row. Downstairs, ladies shopped, inspecting the high fashion and fancy dry goods on display—the Belfast laces, the silk gowns, the $1,000 camel-hair shawls.[26]

Stewart was one of the country's first great subjects of fantasy and myth about what wealth could give Americans, a man pursued and dreamed of by thousands who thought him "famed for his world renowned generosity . . . and great abundance," as one of his many doting correspondents wrote.[27] His very regal existence, strange in a land of republicans, gave birth to absurd ideas of benevolence and invited extraordinary appeals. One Brooklyn woman wrote to offer him her body: "I must have money and to get it am willing to sell myself. I come to you because you are a Gentleman and I feel safe in trusting you. I am conversant with what the world terms refined society. I am thirty years of age and good figure—will you make the purchase?" A man from Ohio begged Stewart to "send me fifty thousand dollars. I want to buy land and start a nursery. Send it at once for time is money." An eighteen-year-old boy from Florida pleaded "for a Velocipede. I have been trying to save money enough to buy one for some time but would not do so. I would not ask you sir if I thought *for one moment* you would not give it to me." "I would like to have you send me $3," wrote another boy, a fourteen-year-old from Belleville, New York, "you being the Wealthiest man I know.[28]

Stewart was condemned by some as a "social vampire" and his "whole system of business" reviled "an oppression."[29] But even after he died in 1876 and was buried in a casket of satin and gold, Stewart's hold over fantasy was lasting. Gail Hamilton, popular columnist and editor of *Harper's Bazaar*, wrote that he had freed Americans, at last, from the guilt of having wealth and desiring money. "We all want money and luxury," she said. "We only decry it when we cannot get it." Stewart told us that "we ought to enjoy wealth" and to "cease our idle carping against money."[30]

Yet, for all of this, Stewart did mostly a wholesale business (in the 1870s and 1880s, the only large merchandising was wholesale), and his retail store sold only fancy dry goods. "The only great store in existence" before 1876, John Wanamaker wrote a friend in 1908, "was the A. T. Stewart store, which was limited to dry goods."[31] By the midnineties, new unified mass retail institutions were being built, the first erected—according to many accounts—by the audacious Henry Siegel of New York City. Siegel started out as an independent merchant in Chicago, collaborated with Dutch-born Frank Cooper in 1887 to create the first Siegel-Cooper store, and then, flushed with success, marched off to New York. With help from the investment banking house of Goldman, Sachs, which issued bonds for him in the sum of $2 million, he bought up enormous chunks of Manhattan real estate. He opened the new Siegel-Cooper's in 1896 at Eighteenth Street and Sixth Avenue. It was a steel-framed stone building, six stories high, topped by a giant greenhouse, a roof-garden restaurant, and a two-hundred-foot tower—the first self-contained store "covered by a single roof in the world," according to Siegel's architects, Delemos and Cordes.[32]

By the early part of the new century, John Wanamaker wrote, "500-watt tungsten lamp" stores had overtaken the "candles" of the past, rising twelve to twenty-five stories and together covering millions of acres of selling space.[33] Many of the most famous firms began to assume their familiar shapes in these years: Marshall Field's in 1902 and 1912, and Carson, Pirie, Scott in 1903, both in Chicago; Macy's in 1902 in Manhattan; Filene's in Boston in 1912; and the white Famous-Barr department store in St. Louis in 1913, a magnificent structure that still overlooks the city's downtown retail district. In 1913, the "old conglomerate bunch of buildings" that had made up the Lazarus store in Cincinnati was torn down and replaced by a full-block integrated department store.[34]

More than other businesses, department stores revealed the totality of what the American economy was producing and importing. In the 1880s, most stores had only fifteen small departments, but by 1910, many offered upward to 125. Siegel-Cooper's sold in the late 1890s not only staples, yard goods, notions, ready-made clothing, machine-made furnishings, and hundreds of name-brand pianos but also photographic equipment in the largest photographic gallery anywhere, and monkeys, dogs, cats, birds, lion and panther cubs, and tropical fish in its huge pet department. In 1910 Macy's was conducting the largest domestic rug business in the country, at Thirty-fourth Street and Seventh Avenue in Manhattan, and Wana-maker's in Philadelphia had the "finest bookstore in the United States," soon to be surpassed by Marshall Field's of Chicago, which would exceed in volume and sales any other such business "in the world."[35]

Stores from Bloomingdale's and Siegel-Cooper's in New York to The Fair in Chicago sold huge quantities of preserved and refrigerated meats, canned foods, fresh vegetables, cheeses, breads, candies, numerous coffees and teas, and gourmet specialties.[36] Macy's, the first large retail store to merchandise kosher foods, according to the store's food buyer, William Titon, by 1914 was selling "all the rare tropical fruits and vegetables, irrespective of season."[37] Its food department had dietetic foods (granola, wheat bran, wheat flakes, peanut butter, whole wheat foods, yogurt, and so forth); 265 different kinds of wine, claret, and champagne; also an assortment of beers, gins, brandies, rums, whiskies, and liquors of "all descriptions," and, under Macy's own label, Red Star Brand cocktails (pre-mixed manhattans and martinis).[38] The "grocery" business in department stores paid well, but some merchants refused to engage in it: "Our firm has declined the grocery business," wrote John Wanamaker to an inquiring customer in 1899, "because it could not be done profitably without wines and liquors, the use of which we are opposed to on principle."[39]

Besides selling goods in great array, the mass retailers secured the capital to enlarge their facilities continually as well as to buy and sell more and more goods. Many merchants, for instance, tried to integrate all the elements of the economic process, from raw materials and manufacturing to distribution and marketing, as well as wholesale and retail merchandising. To be sure, by 1900—and certainly by the 1920s—this kind of integration was rapidly disappearing, as mass retailers dropped their manufacturing units and wholesale divisions to concentrate exclusively on retailing, leaving the other functions to be carried out more efficiently by others. But before this time, merchants like A. T. Stewart—even in the 1870s—exercised such control (with factories abroad and even in his own store). So did Marshall Field's until the early 1930s, with its far-flung system of mills, factories, and branch wholesale offices (thirty, even in 1932); John Wanamaker to some degree (in candies, pillows, cosmetics, ice cream, and toothpaste); and Macy's, with a textile factory in Ireland, a fine china plant in France, and a glassware outlet in Bohemia.[40] Bloomingdale's was not only making its own underwear in 1909 but its own pianos as well, in a four-story building at Sixty-third Street in Manhattan, employing "hundreds of expert piano builders." Mandels on State Street in Chicago manufactured a "better class of mattresses and box springs and overstuffed furniture."[41]

Many merchants took the first steps toward the creation of national chains, part of a pattern of consolidation already under way in manufacturing. In 1906 Wall Street investment bankers financed the expansion of Sears, Roebuck and Company, the mail-order house first incorporated in 1892 and serving the still enormous farmer-country market; the banks offered millions of dollars' worth of Sears stock on the public securities market to get the company the capital needed to expand. "For the first time," a historian of the company writes, "Sears, Roebuck had a solid financial footing," with "plenty of working capital to support its rapid increase in sales volume."[42] This was a trend with notable implications for the shaping of this country's economy and culture. Historian Allan Nevins has written that "down to 1906, very little of the public money market was open to entrepreneurs in the mass-merchandising field."[43] But the investment bankers, seeing handsome financial rewards before them and their clients, helped reverse this trend. In 1912, the same cooperating banking firms that served Sears—Lehman Brothers and Goldman, Sachs—financed and reorganized F. W. Woolworth Co., increasing its stores from the eighteen of 1892 to six hundred, both in America and Europe.[44]

Other retailers expanded by absorbing their competitors. As early as 1901 John Claflin, son of Horace B. Claflin, who founded the nation's biggest wholesale business, tried to incorporate a chain of department stores into his now deceased father's business. John Claflin had restructured the firm, which had already been functioning as a holding company over an ample number of retail stores, into a corporation in 1890, and, with the financial aid and advice of investment banker J. P. Morgan, Claflin expanded farther. Between 1901 and 1909 Morgan advised him to create two new holding companies whose securities would be sold on the public market. By 1910 Claflin's business as a whole owned nearly forty retail stores, including such well-known firms as Lord & Taylor and McCreery's in New York and Hahne's in Newark.[45]

May Department Stores of St. Louis, Missouri, which would become one of America's longest-lived department store chains, was incorporated in 1910 in New York City. By 1914 the May company owned a Denver shoe and clothing company, a real estate and investment business, a Cleveland department store, Boggs and Buhl department store in Pittsburgh, the M. O'Neill and Co. store in Akron, Ohio, and, above all, the Famous-Barr department store in St. Louis, claimed by a store promoter in 1913 as the "biggest office building in the world."[46]

Henry Siegel also had dreams of creating a merchandising empire. With help from investment bankers, he formed a syndicate of stores in 1901, the Siegel-Cooper stores (of which he was by now the sole owner), the Simpson-Crawford-Simpson store in Manhattan, and the Schlesinger and Mayer store in Chicago.[47] A few years later, he bought the old Macy's store at the corner of Fourteenth Street and Sixth Avenue (the Straus brothers, whose family bought the Macy store in 1877, having moved uptown to Thirty-fourth Street by this time), called it the Fourteenth Street Store (designed to "cater to the masses," as he put it), and also built another Siegel store, in Boston. Siegel's stores had fifty to a hundred departments as well as such "services" as restaurants, parlor rooms, dental facilities, and banks for regular deposits and withdrawals. His customers put millions of dollars in his banks, posing a temptation that would prove to be his undoing.[48]

Now head of Henry Siegel Corporations, Siegel was capitalized at more than $10 million and backed by Manhattan lawyer and financier Henry Morgenthau, Sr., a member of Siegel's board of directors. Morgenthau, who would later serve as U.S. ambassador to Turkey at a critical historical moment, catered to the growth needs of the big merchants and helped consolidate the New York real estate business.[49] Because of his assistance in 1893, Isidor and Nathan Straus won a bidding war for possession of the Wechsler & Abraham department store in Brooklyn when that partnership decided to split up. As Wechsler's lawyer, Morgenthau persuaded Wechsler to sell out on the grounds that he "was unwise to run the business alone and should not risk securing it." The result was Abraham & Straus. In 1896, as lawyer to Judge Henry Hilton, owner at the time of A. T.

Stewart's Astor Place store whose expenses were outrunning his profits, Morgenthau "advised [Hilton] that he should sell out the business and take his loss." This, in turn, made it possible for John Wanamaker of Philadelphia to acquire and remake Stewart's into the biggest department store in the country.[50] In 1909, Lincoln and Edward Filene of Filene's in Boston, on the verge of relying on investment bankers to help finance the building of their new store, heard from Morgenthau that "there is no chance of failure, if you have plenty of capital."[51]

Success was not a foregone conclusion, however, as Morgenthau would soon learn in his dealings with Siegel. Between 1913 and 1914 both the Siegel and Claflin businesses collapsed. Claflin's self-destructed because the old wholesale firm had failed to control many of its retail stores, which had exceeded the firm's credit by millions of dollars (five-thousand banks were involved) and had refused to do business with the wholesale division, thus setting the company at odds with itself. Once again, J. P. Morgan stepped in, and this time he reorganized the business into a new firm, the Associated Dry Goods Corporation, still one of the nation's leading retail corporations. He demanded and got Claflin's resignation.[52] Siegel went down ingloriously in 1914 after making the wild blunder of accepting from major New York bankers loans he knew he probably could not pay back— all his stores but one were operating without profits and were greatly overcapitalized. To stay afloat, he took money from his own store banks (in other words, from his customers) to cover the heavy losses. He was found out, and in February 1914, twenty thousand creditors descended on him but with no prospect of repayment; within the year he was behind bars, convicted of grand larceny and serving a nine-month sentence at the Monroe County Penitentiary in Rochester, New York. The event might have stunned Morgenthau had he not been in Turkey by this time and probably too busy with the Turkish slaughter of Armenians to pay much attention to Siegel's downfall.[53]

The Retail Wars of the 1890s

The success of the mass market retailers was due to more than their capacity to summon large amounts of capital or to offer a huge assortment of goods under one roof or through a single catalog. There were other, more direct means, which included alliances among merchants, reformers, and state governments to defeat the opposition. In the 1890s, retail wars, emblematic of the turmoil involved in what Alan Trachtenberg has called the "incorporation of America," erupted (especially in the western states) to challenge even the legality of department stores.[54] "The all-devouring monsters" were destroying the "little man," some New York City grocers said in anguish.[55] Even earlier, small merchants began to organize against bigger merchants to resist extermination, reflecting a process underway in Paris and London as well, where, as historian W. Hamish Fraser has written, it seemed as if "retailing were passing out of the hands of the small vendor into those of larger firms."[56] In America, however, the resistance of small dealers against bigger merchants unfolded on a larger canvas.

"This is a free country," said the president of a small traders' group in Kansas City in 1891, "but if this city is to have two or three big stores that are to do all the business, all the little ones must perish." "I am being victimized by three department houses, and street peddlers," complained a Kansas City dry goods dealer in that same year.[57] In the wake of the 1893 depression, small retailers blamed their miseries on the department stores. The "big store," one retailer argued, "removes much in the matter of independence for men and women in small ways, and compels a dependence which, while it may give more money to the fortunate ones, renders them subject to a central power which in time becomes a tyranny which will leave no boundless America offering homes to the oppressed."[58] Laws were introduced in state capitals from California to New York to tax "the octopus which has stretched out its tentacles in every direction, grasping in its slimy folds the specialist or one-line man"—the florist, the shoeman, the grocer, the jeweler, the furniture dealer, and the like. Butchers and liquor dealers often led the fight.[59]

The struggle was especially heated in Chicago, where, in the wake of the 1893 depression, hundreds of firms went bankrupt.[60] Stores like Marshall Field's on State Street weathered the storm and even prospered, having straddled the center of the Chicago business district, driven up real estate values to levels unaffordable to small competitors, and cut deeply into the small firms' clientele by selling the whole range of goods. Since the 1880s, Marshall Field (and his smart second-in-command, H. Gordon Selfridge, later founder of Selfridges in London) had been at pains to persuade all the leading Chicago retailers—John V. Farwell and Co., the Boston Store, Mandels, and even Field's archenemy, Carson, Pirie, Scott—to cluster closely together on State Street so they could function like an irresistible unified magnet of selling power. "He wanted to build up State Street," a Field's executive later recalled of his boss; he "went a long way to get Mandels established and then to keep them there," and also "helped set up the Boston Store."[61]

Marshall Field was accustomed to crushing his adversaries. He set his teeth against all labor unions, dismissed any employee who had any ties whatever with unions, and time and again enlisted "professional toughs" or heavily financed the National Guard out of his own pocket to break up strikes.[62] For years he symbolized for Chicago working people, as one Chicago paper put it, the "united capital" behind the war against "organized labor," or as Field himself described it, "the people of Chicago" against the "tyranny of lawless strikers."[63]

The big Chicago merchants gained perhaps surprising support from a new group of middle-class liberal reformers—"progressive" men and women who hated and feared the labor conflict of the day and who looked to the emergence of some centralizing agency to combat "local and particularistic forces."[64] These people belonged mostly to the professional class of lawyers, doctors, and ministers, or to a newer group of engineers and managers who believed department stores and such were the wave of the future, convinced that it was the duty of small retailers and workers alike to resign themselves inevitably to this change.[65] Many reformers admired the utopian novelist Edward Bellamy, whose popular 1886 novel *Looking Backward* had put the department store at the epicenter of American society and whose Nationalist movement (an indigenous Socialist movement) attacked all forms of "particularism." Nationalists, Bellamy explained, considered the "crushing of the country rivals" and the "absorption of the city rivals" into a "whole quarter concentrated under one roof" a great historical achievement.[66] They dreamed of integrating all Americans into a centralized system of mass consumption that guaranteed everybody, in exchange for acceptance of a disciplined industrial regime, instantaneous access to the same consumer goods and services. The goal was to have what Bellamy called "a homogeneous world-wide social system" along militaristic lines, free of class conflicts, local nuances, and sectarian differences.

Ranged against this formidable alliance of merchants and reformers was a coalition of small retailers, skilled and unskilled workers, small real estate men operating on the city's margins, and labor leaders who viewed the stores as exploiters of women and children. Together they launched a movement to drive the department stores out of the city. Behind the insurgents stood the "local" political bosses; the machine; the recently elected Democratic mayor, Carter Harrison; and also, briefly, the Democratic City Council. "Real estate values," said City Council members and the mayor in February 1897, "have been unreasonably and enormously enhanced by the centralization" of the big stores "into one giant retail district." A group of local women also tried to galvanize support for the small retailers, seeking to undermine public sentiment for the big stores.[67] When The Fair, a substantial store then undergoing a major expansion, applied for a license in August to sell meats, the city refused it.[68] In November the mayor took the department store merchants to court to compel them to abide by provisions of a city ordinance forbidding them to sell meat and liquor. The City Council itself passed a resolution to enforce a graduated scale of license fees to be paid by merchants who vended more than a single line of merchandise.[69]

The rise of department stores aroused a similar discontent and even opposition in many other cities, and some store officials in those cities felt obliged publicly to defend large-scale merchandising. In New York City, for instance, the Downtown Business Men's Association on Fulton Street, organized explicitly to oppose "trusts and monopolies and the encroachments of the department stores upon all branches of business," provoked Robert Ogden, head of Wanamaker's New York store on Broadway and Astor Place, to counterattack. In a lecture he delivered in New York and elsewhere, Ogden maintained—in language close to Bellamy's—that department stores were in the vanguard of progress, that they gave jobs to thousands, and that the "ideas" of the small dealers were hopelessly "backward." "The implication of the criticism [against department stores]," he said, "is that the Department Store destroys the livelihood of the small competitors." That was "true to a degree," he conceded, but dwelling on it would miss the real point that the department store

> conserves opportunities for a livelihood and makes them more abundant. Sympathy for persons who, refusing to recognize existing conditions, have pursued a hopeless venture to a disastrous end is constantly in demand. But the judgment should recognize the fact that the result comes from ignorance or obstinacy, or both. If the suffering individual had simply adapted *himself to actual conditions*, and had sought his livelihood through some of the large

concerns, he would have been in the enjoyment of a fair compensation, and would not appear as a sympathy-seeking mendicant.

Ogden saw little in the claim that the small dealers had as much right to
exist as the department stores did. Nor did he mention the role capital
played in deciding who would win. "History" shows, Ogden affirmed, that
"before the advent of the Department Store," the "small storekeeper belonged to a failing class—not five per cent of the retail merchants of the
former days permanently achieved success. If, therefore, failure was then
the rule, the coming of the great retail store has proved a blessing to a great
industrial class.[70]

By 1900 or thereabouts, the wars to vanquish department stores began
to peter out, although there were still sporadic, unsuccessful attempts in
New York and Massachusetts to impose special taxes on them.[71] The department stores had prevailed. State legislatures turned back the proposed
laws, or state supreme courts declared them unconstitutional. The result,
wrote a trade spokesman, "has dispelled the idea that the great emporium
is a monster created by some mysterious agency for the destruction of the
small trader."[72] The states—some uneasily, perhaps—had sided with department stores, thus legitimizing their economic existence. The Massachusetts Bureau of Labor Statistics published a report "showing" that while
"there was some danger that the department stores will establish a monopoly
in the handling of some of certain kinds of goods," the large retailers had
"encroached upon the business of 'single line stores' much less than the
public [had been] disposed to believe."[73] Meanwhile, the federal Industrial
Commission in Washington, D.C., released a report in 1901 claiming that
department stores had "materially widened the field for specialty stores"
and that they "*must* be located in the trade centers of our cities." It commended the big merchants for making the United States "a nation of large
consumers in the way of comfortable wearing apparel, comforts and decorations for our homes as well as of luxuries of all kinds."[74] With the waning
of the depression of the 1890s, moreover, many small retailers did rebound,
thereby contributing to the weakening of resistance against the merchants
in Illinois and elsewhere.

In Chicago, as a sign of what the merchants had achieved, thousands
of Chicagoans swamped the new twelve-story Marshall Field's store when
it opened in 1902 as a transformed business intended not only to serve "the
swagger rich" or the "fine silk business," as heretofore, but also "masses of

shoppers." "We have built this great institution for the people," announced Selfridge in his public statement at the opening, "—to be their store, their downtown home, their buying headquarters."[75] Containing more than one million square feet of selling space, the store was decked with "cut flowers on every counter, shelf, showcase, and desk," blooming plants, palms, and ferns, and banners and streamers. "It seemed as if there were a million American beauty roses," reported a young Chicago woman to a member of Wanamaker's management in Philadelphia, who inquired what was going on there. "Great bowls or bulbs of electricity," she wrote, "were strangely and remarkably made." Six string orchestras, on various floors, filled the store with music. Nothing was permitted to be sold the first day. In the new downstairs "basement," which sold "bargains" and duplicated the upstairs goods at "less expensive qualities," "the mass of Chicago"—"the Italian woman, with a basket of fish, a Pole, or Hun, and the street boy"— viewed the scene. "Now, the business is no doubt very much increased, but more cosmopolitan."[76]

Many merchants in the district even closed up shop to let their employees visit Field's. In other cities, merchants kept tabs on the progress and impact of the opening. "I have read everything that I could see in print about your opening," wrote John Wanamaker, Field's biggest national rival, to Selfridge, "and confess that I feel more interest in what you are doing than in any other business except our own. I hope to make a visit to see with my own eyes."[77] Mayor Carter Harrison of Chicago was so impressed by the outpouring of interest that he invited Field's to prolong the show for another week. "The opening was one of the grandest events that has ever been known in Chicago," concluded the above young woman, ". . . in a word, simply Wonderland."[78]

As the last shred of resistance to the big merchants seemed to vanish, American commercial business entered a critical phase. In no other time in their history, perhaps, had merchants more freedom to do what they pleased with their property or the property of others. In New York City, in the course of only ten years or so, the entire downtown retail district from Fourteenth to Twenty-third streets, between Broadway and Sixth Avenue (historically known as "the ladies' mile" because so many women shopped there), was abandoned for choicer properties uptown so merchants could be near the new transportation depots, the emerging entertainment district, and a prosperous middle class that had fled immigrant-packed lower Manhattan. Between 1900 and 1915 not only Macy's but also Altman's, Lord

& Taylor, Stern's, Arnold Constable, McCreery's, and Saks, perhaps nearly twenty-five major stores altogether, took possession of the uptown retail district, east and west, between Thirty-fourth and Fifty-second streets.

"The Greatest Merchant in America"

If merchants like Henry Siegel flared up in a brilliant flash of success, only to descend, from greed and undisciplined ambition, into the depths of imprisonment, others were more clever, perhaps more virtuous, and far more consistent and enduring. The most significant was John Wanamaker of Philadelphia, by all accounts "the greatest merchant in America." (See plate 17.) He himself boasted in 1909 that he "had revolutionized the retail business in the United States."[79]

Born in 1838 in a small rural neighborhood just twenty-five miles from downtown Philadelphia, John Wanamaker was the son of a bricklayer and builder who came, like John's mother, from a mix of German, Scotch, Dutch, and French ancestries. Both parents were devout Presbyterians who reared John to be just as devout, just as loyal to his faith and his Bible. He was to read the Bible over and over again throughout his life. By 1860, when he was twenty-one, merchandising was just beginning to offer young men promising careers. Torn between evangelical religion and the new world of commerce, he veered toward commerce. He wanted to be another Alexander Turney Stewart, but a "retailing" Stewart, a merchant prince of retail. His career began in earnest during the Civil War (due to ill health, he eluded the draft), when he exploited the opportunities presented by the enormous demand for army supplies and uniforms. He grew rich in the process, and this wealth led to the enlargement of his first business: clothing for men and boys.[80]

In 1876 three events propelled Wanamaker on the way to becoming America's leading merchant. Alexander Stewart died that year, which must have sent a shiver of anticipating excitement through Wanamaker. The Centennial Exposition opened in Philadelphia, then the principal manufacturing center in the United States. It was the country's first world's fair and probably the most influential of all the fairs because it unlocked the floodgates to what became a steady flow of goods and fantasies about goods. "It was like lifting a veil," wrote a contemporary, "in revelation of the size, the variety, and the beauty of the world." "It was the cornerstone," Wanamaker himself would later say, "upon which manufacturers everywhere rebuilt their business to new fabrics, new fashions, and more courageous undertaking by reason of the lessons taught them from the exhibits of the nations of the world."[81] The last event of 1876 (actually begun in December 1875) was the most profound for Wanamaker: It was a major religious revival, and it was held on Wanamaker's own property. At Wanamaker's invitation, the leading evangelist of the day, Dwight L. Moody, conducted the revival on Market Street, in the abandoned Pennsylvania Freight Station, a place that Wanamaker planned to transform immediately from an "Old Depot" into the "Grand Depot," or what he would call a "new kind of store." (See plate 1.)

In Wanamaker's mind, at least, the revival consecrated what he was doing. Months after it occurred, he wrote Moody, then preaching the gospel in Chicago: "Whilst I cannot come to you, we pray for you and especially in these anniversary days of the making of the Old Depot. How I lived yesterday a year ago and how my heart today yearns for the days that are past. Every corner of the building is still fragrant with the sweet spices of other days."[82] Although Dwight Moody tried to get Wanamaker to leave his business (I will have more to say about this in a later chapter), Wanamaker rebuffed him.[83] By the mid-1890s he had become the greatest bearer of Alexander Stewart's legacy, his Philadelphia store perhaps the city's central institution.[84] And, as if to prove his right to the Stewart legacy, Wanamaker bought Stewart's own "Marble Palace" on Broadway and Astor Place in New York. This was a bold move, not only because Stewart's had languished, repeatedly changing hands, but also because it was clear—even in 1896—that the movement of commercial growth in New York was uptown, not downtown. But Wanamaker, as long as he lived, beat the odds. He made Robert Ogden superintendent of the store, and breathed new life into it, remaining himself in Philadelphia. Six years later, he built a "modern" store across the street from the old Palace, and joined the two by an overhead bridge passageway. Designed by the Chicago architect Daniel Burnham, the new building quickly became one of the "sights" of New York and remained so until the 1940s.[85] (See plate 3.)

Wanamaker was thrilled by the processes of acquiring the real estate and of demolishing the old structures that preceded the building of the New York store, which the store managers would later claim had more square footage and more windows than the Empire State Building. "When

I get possession of the Astor Place premises," he wrote Alexander Orr, president of the Rapid Transit Commission in 1903,

> I hope to be successful in getting the Broadway Trust Co. to accept this new location in place of where they are at the present time. This of course will enable me then to complete quickly the entire building on the block bounded by Eighth and Ninth Streets, Broadway and Fourth Ave., and when I secure all of the Snug Harbor Astor Place holdings, I will take down the Sinclair Building, and possibly the other building, thus making a handsome improvement. The development of the three blocks and the small piece at the corner of Fourth Ave. and Tenth Street, which practically embraces all of the real estate of the Sailor Snug Harbor east of Broadway and south of Tenth Street, will make a very great change in the architectural condition of the neighborhood.[86]

According to Henry Morgenthau, who negotiated the purchase of the leaseholds and the buildings for Wanamaker, it was the "greatest real-estate bargain ever made in New York."[87]

A few years later, in 1911, Wanamaker told a business group that "it is a tremendous thing to live—dying is next to nothing. Beasts and birds die—living is everything. The universe is sensitive to the merest touch and therefore it is possible to set wheels in motion that shall outrun the world."[88] In 1912 he opened a twenty-four-story department store in the heart of Philadelphia that still stands and that, according to its architect, Daniel Burnham, "[was] the most monumental commercial structure ever erected anywhere in the world."[89]

Wanamaker is all the more interesting for his personal tensions and for the way these tensions shed light on the commercial economy and culture he was helping to create. He translated the new economy into a new culture for many Americans—we might call him one of this country's domesticators of commercial culture, a man who not only "revolutionized retailing," as he said himself, but who also legitimated fashion, fostered the cult of the new, democratized desire and consumption, and helped produce a commercial environment steeped in pecuniary values. But, like many other Americans, he seemed to be of two minds about this culture. A very religious man, he went so far as to build Christian institutions—Bible schools, churches, domestic and international missions—that he hoped, on some level, would reconcile the world of consumption with traditional religious beliefs and practices. He tried to integrate Christianity into the new culture, although, as we shall see, what he did in the end was to marginalize religion and doom it to irrelevance.

Wanamaker began his life in the outskirts of a still rural Philadelphia, and he ended it at the helm of an urban commercial empire: Rural and urban, country and commerce, would always compete in him. He was the most ardent exponent of fashion, but he championed the "simple life" movement. He commanded large sums of capital but was contemptuous of brokers, real estate agents, and financial capitalists. At a time when he was amassing capital to build his new stores, he refused—as he wrote in his diary—to rely on "any financial help outside of ourselves." "I am sure," he wrote in another entry, "I shall be better for learning to depend on myself, humanly, rather than on the financial system of our country that now operates by the might and money power of a few men."[90] Asked whether he was a "capitalist," he said he wasn't. Though he owned factories and was about to transform his stores from a "partnership" into a "corporation," "I am only a merchant," he said.[91]

For a fleeting moment, during the 1907 panic, Wanamaker, one of the wealthiest men in America, was, in his eyes and those of other businessmen, one of the poorest. All his money was tied up in his investments. He survived that panic (with the help of friendly creditors), and not without, once again, taking the high ground. "We have had the iron age and the stone age and this is the business age," he told General William Booth, founder and commander of the Salvation Army, in 1907, "and all over the world men are worshipping the most helpless god of all that is in or out of heathen temples—MONEY—the dumb god without eyes to see, or ears to hear, or power to add a handbreadth to a man's life."[92]

The Crisis of Distribution

John Wanamaker, Marshall Field, Henry Siegel, Percy and Jesse Straus, and similar merchants were at the forefront of a redirection of American life. They contributed to the creation and expansion of the Land of Desire, as did the national corporations and commercial and investment banks. But they were not in themselves decisive in transforming America into a consumer society or Americans into dependable consumers. Other conditions had to come into play, including the assistance of noneconomic institutions, the accommodations of religion, and the emergence of a new group of intermediaries (all of which will be examined in due course in this book). Another propelling condition had to appear as well: the impact of fear, fear about consumer reception (or resistance), fear about the movement of goods, fear about distribution.

As the corporations and commodities multiplied, it became clear that consumption—and distribution and marketing—could not be taken for granted. After 1875, many economists, merchants, and manufacturers feared that the business economy would be so committed to more and more productivity, so money-mad, that it would cause glutting, overproduction, and economic crisis. The fear may have been unwarranted (at least in some industries, there appears to have been minimal overproduction), but whether true or false, it was widely and persistently held. "If there has not been overproduction, then why is it that the warehouses of the world are filled with goods?" a merchant asked in 1877.[93] "The country is suffering from overproduction," asserted another merchant in 1912. "The goods must be moved." "While we are but on the threshold of efficiency in production, the progress thus far made has outstripped the existing system of distribution. If our possibilities are to be fully utilized, the problems of distribution must be solved."[94] Even Theodore Dreiser tried to join the chorus in a 1902 essay, "Problem of Distribution" (never published), in which he claimed that the large cities were not moving fruits and vegetables in time enough to forestall spoilage and waste.[95]

The crisis of distribution meant different things to different people. For some, mainly defenders of workers and the poor, it meant the distribution of wealth or the equalization of income. Historian Dorothy Ross writes that the "distribution of wealth" was the "core issue" for the generation of reformers and economists after 1870.[96] For others, above all for businessmen, this crisis was one of goods or the movement of goods from producers to consumers. Both crises, of course, were related: To increase incomes meant that one would, perhaps inevitably but not necessarily, increase consumption and thus help remove the snags that blocked the flow of goods. Indeed, the relationship between these two "crises"—one of wealth, the other of commodities—was heatedly debated from the 1880s to 1910 (it is still debated today). On the left were native socialists such as

Edward Bellamy, who urged that the state provide guaranteed annual incomes to every adult so that everyone would have equal access to the same things. On the right, economists such as John Bates Clark argued that labor and capital "got exactly what they deserved" and that the market, left to its own devices, would yield the most just distribution of incomes and goods.

Clark's voice, on the whole, won out, accepted by businessmen who defended the idea that the market would be—had to be—the prime medium for resolving the crisis in the distribution of wealth. But when it came to the crisis in the distribution of goods, businessmen who ran full-capacity, high-volume firms looked in another direction. Here, something beyond dependence on the "natural laws" of supply and demand was called for to ensure turnover. Businessmen would have to intervene more aggressively, not only by controlling prices, output, and labor or by establishing alliances with others (above all, as we shall see, with the state), but also by persuading and changing minds, by producing a new consumer consciousness, by transforming the imagination. The challenge was a big one, wrote Emily Fogg Mead in 1901. It required the diffusion of "desire" throughout the entire population, not just through the "elite," which was already able to "utilize the new goods at once." And money income was not the decisive factor in building desire. "We are not concerned with the ability to pay," Fogg Mead insisted in her widely quoted 1901 article defending advertising methods (even Thorstein Veblen admired and used it), "but with the ability to want and choose" and to open up the "imagination and emotion to desire." "*Without imagination, no wants,*" wrote another ad expert, Katherine Fisher, in 1899. "Without wants, no demand to have them supplied."[97]

So, business pursued the imagination in a way no other group in U.S. history had ever done. It turned rapidly to new methods of marketing and to the dissemination of strategies of enticement—advertising, display and decoration, fashion, style, design, and consumer service. It reshaped the structure and character of the work force as well, introducing not only new brokers but a new class of service workers (salespeople, waiters and waitresses, bellhops and deskclerks, etc.), at the beck-and-call of consumers and growing at a rate far in excess of any other workers. It affected women as well as men, employing a minority of women at higher and higher salaries (especially in the fashion industry) and a majority in the lowest paid and most degraded occupations. The new business economy and culture affected children, too, by abstracting them as *individual* consumers out of the family, and by constructing a separate child world, independent of the adult world and competitive with it as a source of profit. And business, in collaboration with other groups and in its drive to break up the distributive logjam, flooded American culture with new symbols and images. A whole new aesthetics of color, glass, and light appeared on the American scene.

Chapter 2

FACADES OF COLOR,
GLASS, AND LIGHT

"Our minds are full of windows," wrote John Wanamaker in 1916. Wanamaker's own buildings had thousands of windows, not only office windows but also almost a hundred large show windows that occupied the circumference of his New York and Philadelphia stores. "Show windows are eyes to meet eyes," he said. Today, people take show windows for granted and scarcely observe the surfeit of glass shapes and surfaces on nearly every city street. But in the early 1900s many were disoriented by the images and goods displayed behind the glass, even by the glass itself.[1]

On a return visit from England in 1904, Henry James was disturbed by the "towers of glass" that had been erected almost overnight in Manhattan. In *The American Scene*, he compared the tower windows to the stained glass windows of artist John La Farge, just installed in Ascension Church on Fifth Avenue. He saw the church windows—the "loveliest of images"—as endangered by "windows that speak loudest for the economic idea." The La Farge windows, though "new," were doomed by "those invidious presences"—the business windows—which "were going to bring in money, and was not money the only thing a self-respecting structure could be thought of as bringing in?" James, comparing the church window with the "invidious" kind, and a formal aesthetic with a pecuniary or commercial aesthetic, feared an impending tragedy of "removal," an inevitable disappearance of the older "beauty." "Window upon window, at

any cost, is a condition never to be reconciled with any grace of building,"
he said. "The building can only afford lights, each light having a superlative
value as an aid to the transaction of business and the conclusion of sharp
bargains. Doesn't it take in fact acres of window-glass to help even an expert
New Yorker to get the better of another expert one, or to see that the other
expert doesn't get the better of *him*."[2]

When Willa Cather visited New York City in the winter of 1903, she
was surprised to see fresh flowers displayed in small glass cases at corner
flower stands, "seeming somehow more lovely and alluring," she said, than
they would have been in a natural setting. Edna Ferber wrote angrily of a
Chicago show window in the winter of 1911, "It is a work of art that
window, a breeder of anarchism, a destroyer of contentment, a second feast
of Tantalus." "It boasts peaches, downy and golden, when peaches have
no right to be, strawberries glow therein when shortcake is a last summer's
memory."[3] In the spring of 1902 Theodore Dreiser had toured Fifth Avenue
in New York and peered into the newly designed and decorated show
windows: "What a stinging, quivering zest they display," he said, "stirring
up in onlookers a desire to secure but a part of what they see, the taste of
a vibrating presence, and the picture that it makes."[4]

James, Cather, Ferber, and Dreiser were reacting to something almost
wholly new in American life—the spread of an aesthetic to serve business
needs. At the heart of it was the desire to show goods off day and night
through all possible means. Showing off was not entirely new to American
business; in some form or another, it had been going on in cities such as
Philadelphia and Boston since the late colonial period. What *was* new was
the volume of showing off, the quantity of selling materials, and the management of visual space in behalf of the movement of goods. What was
new was the intermingling and application of color, glass, and light to create
an extensive public environment of desire.

In the late 1890s new visual media were invented, including the "cut"
or the ad picture, the artistic poster, the painted billboard, the electrical
sign, and most alluring of all, the show window. At the same time, specialists, skilled in promoting goods and in creating just the right images,
just the right combinations of color, glass, and light, were doing business.
Among them were advertising genius Elbert Hubbard; Wanamaker's partner
who believed that department stores were destined to destroy small retailers,
Robert Ogden; and Maxfield Parrish, America's most influential commercial artist. The author of *The Wonderful Wizard of Oz*, L. Frank Baum,

was also among this group; indeed, long before he grew famous as a writer of children's books, Baum was a nationally recognized authority on window display, advising thousands of other window trimmers on what he called the "arts of decoration and display." Along with other window experts, Baum helped create a remarkable landscape of glass, perhaps the most powerful field of desire yet to appear in American cities.

By 1910 mass market businessmen, with the aid of men like Baum, Parrish, Ogden, and Hubbard, were seeking to occupy visual space through an onslaught of pictures. Together they helped change not only the way many people saw and understood goods but also how they lived in their society.

Elbert Hubbard and Eye Appeal

Elbert Hubbard, an influential advertising man and promoter, built his career around his own personal image. Hubbard was a publicity counsel for hundreds of advertisers, as well as the manager of the "Roycrofters," a well-known arts and crafts business in upstate New York that tried to blend mass-production and mass-selling styles with the handcrafted and "the Renaissance" in a "modern" American way. He made a fortune writing "publicity preachments" for retail businesses and national corporations and for "everything from toothpicks to motor trucks." His promotional one-liners—the soundbites of his generation—shaped the way a generation or more of Americans thought about business and commodities.

Before Hubbard drowned in 1915, when the *Lusitania* went down, he had been photographed "in almost every conceivable position and condition," an admirer said. Photographers captured him playing golf with John D. Rockefeller, dancing the one-step with Eva Tanguay, chatting with Elbert H. Gary, confiding in Thomas Edison, riding a favorite horse, "Garnet," around his country estate, straddling a motorbike, shaving with a new safety razor, and posing near an electric fan or in a fur coat in the middle of August. The photograph of this rather weird-looking tall man with long hair, a big Quaker hat, and a Byronic tie hung in each room of his offices and workshops. His face was engraved on his business stationery and could be seen on a huge electric sign outside his workplace, or hung as an imposing painted sign at his hometown train station in East Aurora, New York. In

The Philistine, a magazine published by Hubbard, almost every issue contained several photographs of him. Friends were said to lament that "his last advertisement [the last photograph ever taken of him] sank with him in the cabin of the ill-fated *Lusitania*."[5]

Hubbard's "life was an advertisement." "Everybody," he announced, "should advertise while they are alive." "The man who does not advertise," he said before a 1911 meeting of advertising men, "is a dead one, whether he knows it or not." He argued time and again that people should push themselves and their "services and commodities" forward into the public space, push and push, and that the best way to do that was through pictures. "Life is too short for you to hide yourself away mantled in your own modesty."[6]

One of Hubbard's friends observed that he "deified commerce" and "religionized his business." Although he had grown up in the 1870s in the Midwest with the Protestant church at "the center of all our social life," inch by inch he left the church for his new faith.[7] "There is room in business for all your religion, all your poetry, all your love. Business should be beautiful and it is fast becoming so." "When I want to hear really good sermons nowadays, we attend a weekly lunch of the ad club, and listen to a man who deals in ways and means and is intent upon bringing about paradise, here and now."[8] He rejoiced in what he called the "multiple markets" of capitalism. He was convinced that only constant publicity could break down barriers between goods and people; his business slogan was "economic salvation lies in closer relation between the producer and consumer."[9]

Before the late 1880s, visual advertising was looked down on as linked to circuses and P. T. Barnum hokum. Newspapers and magazines, in fact, offered little or no advertising, and what they did print was small-scale and with small-agate type, visually unappealing, words jammed closely together into single columns, and with scant illustration and display. The few existing advertising agents wrote no ads themselves but, as "space brokers," simply acquired space in newspapers and journals so that others might announce their own goods.[10] After 1885, as merchandise flowed out of factories, national manufacturers and large retailers began to transform advertising's character and scope. In 1880 a total of $30 million was invested in advertising; by 1910, new big businesses such as oil, food, electricity, and rubber were spending more than $600 million or 4 percent of the national income (a percentage that remained unchanged for the next sixty years). The very existence of the first mass market newspapers and mass market magazines of the 1890s and early 1900s—*Cosmopolitan, The Saturday Evening Post, The Ladies' Home Journal,* and *Comfort Magazine*—was made possible by the advertising investments of large retailers and corporations.[11]

National corporations, from Procter & Gamble to the Colgate Company, sought for the first time to reach consumers directly through national advertising campaigns. The big retailers demonstrated the value of "continuous advertising," of advertising throughout the year, of the "everyday advertisement." "The newspaper of today," one retailer said in 1904, "is largely the creation of the department store." "The time to advertise is all the time," said John Wanamaker.[12]

The first nationally renowned advertising agents, such as Elbert Hubbard, practiced their trade, as did the national agencies employing many specialized advertising men or women (the percentage of advertising women in the agencies, small at first, would increase after 1910). In the 1880s there were only two copywriters of any consequence in the country; by the late 1890s there were hundreds, by 1915 thousands. In 1904 the Advertising Federation of America was established.[13] Advertising "experts" no longer limited themselves to selling space; they *invented* advertising words and images.

Though often at odds with one another in these early years over who should control the advertising, manufacturers and retailers had methods and style in common. Both relied on new sales promotion campaigns and on coordination through a range of instruments—magazines, direct mail advertising, newspapers, door-to-door demonstrations, free samples, and billboards.[14] They agreed on the central place of the picture, the image, the photograph in persuading consumers to buy goods and services.

By the late 1890s "eye-appeal" had begun to rival copy for prominence. "Color, form, and visualization," said one early proponent, is "indispensable" to advertising's success.[15] Another marketeer, in 1905, advised stores to "appeal to the imagination," and "induce buying" through "artistic cuts" and said that advertising should be full of "living, speaking things." "Pictures are first principles," said another. "You may forget what you read—if you read at all. But what you see, you know instantly!"[16] A billposter advertiser put it this way: "It is hard to get mental activity with cold type, *YOU FEEL A PICTURE.*"[17]

"We recognized their value," recalled one of Wanamaker's staff in 1904 of advertisements in the 1880s, "but didn't know how to produce enough interesting pictures to supply the daily demand. Now I can suggest 300 pictures for one of those ads, but you must remember that we were entirely on new ground then." In one of his personal memorandum books for 1911, which he labeled "Things to Remember," John Wanamaker recorded: "Pictures are the lesson books of the uneducated." And two years later, he wrote one of his buyers, recommending above all the kind of advertising "picture that has motion in it, or that creates emotion in the man or woman looking at it."[18]

Perhaps the first popular images to emerge were the "advertising cards" of the 1880s and 1890s, given out free by circuses, theaters, dry goods houses, department stores, and cigar companies to customers at the door or by mail. These brightly colored cards depicted varied activities and scenes—swimming at Coney Island, Jumbo the Elephant at the opera, fluttering butterflies, clowns cartwheeling in the streets, and Alice in Wonderland topsy-turvy dreamlike renderings. The cards failed to show the actual goods or services on sale (thus not really showing off in pictures and signs), but many carried price lists on the back, and—most important— each attempted to associate its business with games, luxury, pleasure, fantasy, or faraway mystery. Adults and children everywhere collected them and filled countless albums with them, such as the album Louise Kummer of Washington kept in the 1880s of cards mostly from dry goods houses and now in a Washington, D.C., museum.[19]

At the height of this card craze, other forms of visual advertising began to portray goods clearly, especially the mail-order catalogs of Sears, Roebuck and Company, Montgomery Ward's, and the catalogs of the larger retail stores. As far back as the late 1860s a few dry goods houses had used catalogs to sell goods by mail, but few were visual. Even in the 1890s, they lacked reliable visual material, similar to the illustrations in fashion magazines that only hinted at what the goods really looked like.[20] At the turn of the century, an important representational change was under way. By this time almost 1,200 mail-order concerns were competing for the patronage of more than 6 million customers "in the most obscure and remote localities, raking the country as with a fine-tooth comb."[21] Specialized catalogs were printed, from Wanamaker's *Baby Coaches* and *Bicycles* to *Good Eating Magazine* of Simpson, Crawford, Simpson on Sixth Avenue in New York or Siegel-Cooper's *Modern Housekeeping and Food News*.[22] At the same time, catalog covers began to be imaginatively conceived (often by well-known artists) and as skillfully lithographed in a palette of colors as the advertising cards. (See plate 4.)

Inside these catalogs, some hundreds of pages long, lively, precise drawings and many attractive photographs were replacing copy and the stilted images of the past. Catalogs everywhere were full of "beautifully clear and distinct half tones and line cuts" and excellent "artwork." "We never saw a catalog so thoroughly illustrated," wrote an impressed advertiser in 1907 of the most recent addition to the catalog business, "nearly every item is pictured. A woman can buy almost as satisfactorily from one of these plates as from the counters."[23] The 1898 Christmas catalog of the Irishman Hugh O'Neill's department store on Sixth Avenue in New York had a scenic cover and, as a harbinger of things to come, four pages in color on finely coated paper, showing, among other things, golden lamps and blue smoking jackets. A year later a Wanamaker catalog advertised a rose-pink corset.[24]

One can only guess at the impact this flood of color in advertising had on customers, an impact advertisers did everything to orchestrate. Artemas Ward, pioneer advertiser and editor of *Fame* who beckoned Americans into a new "land of dreams" and who owned the most lucrative franchise for selling advertising on buses and trains in the nation, defended color in subway advertising. From the first days of the New York subways before the First World War, he exhorted business to use color because it showed "strikingly the grain, the texture, the juiciness, the savoriness" of the goods for sale. It is the "priceless ingredient," he said. "It *creates desire for the goods displayed.*" "It imprints on the buying memory." It "speaks the universal picture language," reaching "foreigners, children, people in every station of life who can see or read at all."[25]

The iconographic trend marked newspapers as well. In 1894 "the advertising shift from columns into full pages" was formally announced in the trade press. Increasingly, the small, bunched, antivisual copy of the past, confined in half columns and corners of pages, was being superseded by full-page display advertising, with bolder headlines, wider margins, varied typescript, and, above all, distinct pictures of the goods for sale.[26]

Attractive packaging came into vogue as well, along with colorful circulars and trademark labels for national corporate brand goods and for locally sold retail commodities alike. Such labels, in effect, committed businesses to producing and selling standardized products. By 1905 there were ten thousand registered trademarks, for everything from fountain pens to soft drinks, each reaching out in a visually enticing way for consumer attention and loyalty. Systematically building the reputations of corporations, trademarks appeared everywhere, as historian Susan Strasser has written, "stamped onto sides of beef, crackers, and bedposts, prominent in advertisements, and emblazoned on company letterheads."[27]

Signs of the Times

Even more far-reaching was the growth of the American outdoor advertising industry. Between 1890 and 1915 countless posters, signboards, billboards, and electrical images had appeared in the United States. The first American colored posters, designed for theaters, amusement parks, and dry goods houses, were circulated after 1895, inspired in large measure by the work of French poster artists such as Jules Cheret and Eugene Grasset who injected into commodities a new *joie de vivre*. When the English poet Rupert Brooke toured Wanamaker's in Philadelphia in 1913, he was astonished to learn that "leading young 'post-impressionist' painters" from Paris had been "designing posters for this store for years," and he also "watched with awe" as a young American artist "did entirely Matisse-like illustrations to some summer suitings." At Wanamaker's, as Brooke discovered in an interview with "the very intelligent lady in charge," all the "artists were given a free hand, except, of course, for nudities . . . or people smoking."[28]

Advertisers tacked posters up in street transportation, at railroad stations, and—from the very moment the first subways were operating—in the same spots still allotted for them today. "It was a poster that sent me to Coney Island," wrote one of New York's culture critics, Joseph Huneker, of a 1914 poster of a bandmaster conducting a "succulent symphony" of crabs, fish, lobster, fruit, watermelons, cantaloupes, and clams. "I had sworn never to tread again" to Coney Island, Huneker said. "But that poster! Ah! If these advertising men only knew how their signs and symbols arouse human passions they would be more prudent in giving artists full swing with their suggestion-brushes . . . I was in haste to be off. I *mentally saw* that gustatory symphony."[29]

Across America billboards pictured national trademarks or products—

Gillette razors, Kodak cameras, Colgate toothpaste, Wrigley chewing gum, and Budweiser beer. A giant Coca-Cola sign blocked the view of Niagara Falls, while Mennen's Toilet Powder was suspended over the gorge. "From the entrance to the Capitol grounds on Pennsylvania Avenue" in Washington, D.C., wrote a tourist, "one must see a great right-angled line of signs," and "there is no way to view the nearby Garfield Monument without taking in a background of billboards."[30]

A profitable sideline of the outdoor advertising business—electrical sign advertising—evolved rapidly after 1900. New trade journals were published to meet the needs of this aggressive industry, among them *Signs of the Times: A Journal For All Interested in Better Advertising*, published initially in about 1910 in Cincinnati, Chicago, and New York. Still available today, this periodical coopted an old religious phrase, "signs of the times" as its title, a phrase used for hundreds of years by evangelical Protestants who saw in certain "signs" the impending end of the world and the "Second Coming of Jesus Christ." Indeed, in the first year this journal was delivered to customers, ferment swept through American churches, stirred up by an apparent decline of religion and by a wave of "modernism" (or by that religious perspective that accepted Darwinism, scientific advances of all kinds, and a historical approach to the Bible). In New York City, evangelical leaders like Baptist minister Isaac Haldeman compiled the "most comprehensive" volume of premillennial prophesies of decline yet to appear, *Signs of the Times*, based on what Haldeman believed were "signs" of "business corruption and greed." The advertisers' *Signs of the Times*, of course, foretold a different future and worshiped quite different gods.[31]

"Electrical advertising," a spokesman said, "is a *picture medium*. Moreover, it is a *color* medium; still again, electrical advertising is a medium of motion, of action, *of life, of light*, of compulsory attraction."[32] Whole new districts of commercial white light, which Americans and others have long associated with the consumer core of cities, now appeared. In the mid-1890s, merchants employed the first "spectacular" electrical displays, mounted on skeletal steel frames with flashing devices. Broadway in Manhattan became well known for such signs, from the forty-five-foot Heinz pickle in green bulbs at Madison Square in 1900 to the illuminated Roman chariot race (seventy-two feet high and nine hundred feet wide) atop the Hotel Normandie at Thirty-eighth Street and Broadway in 1910.[33]

One broker of commercial light, O. J. Gude, "known as the Napoleon of publicity," coined the phrase "the Great White Way." Gude saw in light a commercial niche no one else had yet seen. He invented the permament signboard for painted advertising, upgraded the traditional bill-posting business into a corporate enterprise, and created the first large electric advertising signs. His "work," he claimed, expressed the best in American aesthetics. "Outdoor advertising," Gude said, "has felt and shown the effects of the artistic spirit of the people in this country; it is beautiful, rather than brutally dominant."[34]

Gude was delighted that these signs "literally forced their announcements on the vision of the uninterested as well as the interested passerby." He echoed almost verbatim what Emily Fogg Mead had argued in 1901— that such obtrusiveness was a necessity if "new habits were to be opened." "The successful advertisement," Fogg Mead had said, "is obtrusive. It continually forces itself upon the attention. It may be on sign boards, in the street-car, or on the page of a magazine. Everyone reads it involuntarily. It is a subtle, persistent, unavoidable presence that creeps into the reader's inner consciousness."[35] "Sign boards are so placed," repeated Gude, "that everybody must read them, and absorb them, and absorb the advertiser's lesson willingly or unwillingly. The constant reading of 'Buy Blank's Biscuits' makes the name part of one's sub-conscious knowledge."[36]

The first "talking" signs operated along Broadway and elsewhere (although not yet concentrated in Times Square, which was largely a World War I and postwar creation), followed, after 1912, by panoramic and moving signs, known as "sky signs," allowing merchants to move copy swiftly along the boards from left to right and to change reading matter daily. Varied colored lacquers covered the moving lights. Electricians redesigned the marquees of theaters and hotels, stores and other businesses, putting the names of people, companies, and goods "up in lights." Thousands of tourists in sightseeing coaches visited the commercial districts to view what Gude called "the phantasmagoria of the lights and electric signs."[37]

Not everyone was pleased by these intrusions. Reform groups in many cities saw the signs as aesthetic nuisances and as threats to real estate values. "The abuses," admitted Emily Fogg Mead, "are much in evidence." "The weary traveler becomes impatient at the staring street-car 'ads,' at the gaping signs and, above all, at the desecration of rocks and cliffs and beautiful scenery."[38] One such traveler was the sociologist Edward Ross, who, on a railroad trip through the Pacific Northwest in 1912, saw a sign—"Mrs. Scruber's Tooth Powder"—displayed against a background of shaggy pines. "Had we passengers felt proper resentment, we would have avoided that tooth powder to the end of our days," he wrote. "But, idolators of 'enterprise' that we are, we never think of boycotting those who fling their business in our faces at inopportune moments." Urban businesses, he continued, seem to have carte blanche to do what they wish with the public space: "In the city, every accessible spot where the eye may wander, frantically proclaims the merits of somebody's pickles or Scotch Whiskey." But "why," Ross asked, "should a man be allowed violently to seize and wrench my attention every time I step out of doors, to flash his wares into my brain with a sign?"[39]

The impact of these protests were mixed, to say the least, as billboard advocates took refuge in the First Amendment and argued, to the satisfaction of many, that aesthetics was a matter of taste and, therefore, could not be legislated or regulated.[40] By World War I, municipal restrictions did begin to restrict billboards to certain areas but most often as a result of business lobbying. In many cities, a movement by upscale retailers was set in motion to pass zoning laws to prevent the erection of billboards in affluent shopping districts. Wealthy neighborhoods also exercised obvious clout in zoning out signs. But in poorer districts, in the mass market commercial centers of cities, and on a growing number of highways and roads, a determined billboard industry continued to "force" its "announcements" on Americans.

The Careers of Robert Ogden and Maxfield Parrish

Several conditions hastened business's embrace of pictorial advertising. One was the creation of professional organizations to manage the quantity and placement of signs. The billboard industry, chaotic and unregulated throughout most of the nineteenth century, was marked by indiscriminate posting in cities, towns, and the countryside; nothing prevented circuses and theaters in particular from hoarding choice advertising spots or from easily shutting out other firms. By 1910 a new leasing law, instigated by the outdoor advertisers, governed the competition. Clients were now assured "listed and protected showings," which meant that no other signs would be permitted in those spaces during a contract's duration. The result was a greater variety of showings, since advertising displays from many companies were now given equal treatment. (At the same time, however, many sign advertisers, representing the most powerful corporations, began to buy up costly leases with no intention of advertising, thereby finding a new way of excluding the competition.)[41]

Another factor in the advance of pictorial advertising was the availability of new kinds of color and light. Goods could now be vividly conceived and projected. American business, after 1880, had at its fingertips an unrivaled supply of new colors—more than one thousand separate shades and hues, according to a count by colorist Louis Prang. These artificial colors (such as mauve and chrome yellow) were made from aniline coal-tar dyes, and some exceeded in brilliance anything in nature. So many colors had been invented by the turn of the century that color standards were created to make clear to everybody in business, from Berlin to Chicago, what different reds or blues actually looked like. (The most popular standard was devised by Albert Munsell in 1900 and is still in use today.)[42]

New varieties of light also had appeared by 1910—gaslight, arc light, prismatic light (efficiently targeted daylight), carbon-burning electrical light, light from tungsten filaments, floodlights, and spotlights. "The sheer abundance of light," writes historian Reyner Baynam of business architecture, "effectively reversed all established visual habits by which buildings were seen. For the first time it was possible to conceive of buildings whose true nature could only be perceived after dark, when artificial light blazed out through their structures."[43]

The introduction of phototechnology and color lithography at century's end allowed businessmen and commercial artists to reproduce all kinds of images cheaply and abundantly. The graphic arts and photography, as historians of the visual arts have demonstrated, ushered in a new era in the representation of visual information between 1880 and 1910, making it more eye-catching. Any article, any painting, any photograph could be readily converted by new technical processes into attractive halftone illustrations. The technology introduced a different way of generating images and compelled nonphotographic artists, too, to render objects and people with greater authenticity. The "fashion plate" industry, for example, was irrevocably changed: It was no longer possible to rely on the old stereotypic pictures of the earlier magazine days. "Even fashion pictures which are drawn now," wrote one retailer in 1902, "must be much truer to life than they were made formerly. Photography has, in this respect, at least done good service for beauty."[44]

The evangelical commitment of certain merchants helped energize this

new advertising pictorialism. One such merchant was Robert Ogden, Wanamaker's partner and superintendent of the New York store in the late 1890s.
Ogden spoke publicly about the use of pictorial advertising long before most
other businessmen (Wanamaker included) conceded the power of pictures.
In the 1880s he "persistently advocated the use of illustrations" to Wanamaker's advertising staff; "he was an enthusiast," remembered Manly Gillam, a nationally known copywriter who worked for Wanamaker's at the
turn of the century.[45]

Ogden was zealous about other matters as well. He was, for instance,
widely known as a champion of racial justice. Born in 1836 in Philadelphia
and reared in part by a "black mammy," he led the fight for black education
in the South along lines set by Booker T. Washington. Ogden was president
of the Board of Trustees of Hampton Institute in Virginia, one of the first
industrial labor colleges for blacks.[46] Wanamaker greatly admired Ogden,
whom, he said, "I loved as truly as I loved any man outside of my own
family." "It is not such an easy thing for a man to love another man," but
"there was a magnificence about him." When Ogden died in 1913, Wanamaker wrote his own son, Rodman, that "we shall not have his like again.
He was a miracle of goodness."[47] Ogden shared Wanamaker's Presbyteri-
anism, although he was not orthodox in his views, detested "pious Christian
cant," and saw nothing basically wrong with card-playing, the theater, or
billiards.[48] But as Ogden became rich, he worried about his growing inability
to reconcile his "practical affairs" with "Christian ideals," especially about
the self-indulgence of his two teenage daughters who were "coming out"
in Philadelphia. He told a friend, too, that he "really doubted at times
whether he had the right to deal in all the finery on display at
Wanamaker's."[49]

To Rodman Wanamaker, his right-hand man in running the New York
store in the late 1890s, Ogden wrote something rather different. "I have
ideals," he wrote in 1898, "at the center of which is the fundamental
principle, the power to make money which I want to push." The retail
business "added to the sum of human happiness by increasing the power
of money to supply the comforts of life." Money was at the heart of it all—
money through goods, money through other people's dreams, money
through service, money through pictures. And he lectured John Wanamaker himself in letters about the importance of advertising: "It is the centre
and inspiration of this business, the vitalizing force for all else that we
do. . . . It is a science that cannot be trifled with."[50]

In an 1897 speech in New York City before the Sphinx Club, the country's first advertising club, Ogden explained why "hot pictures" were superior to "cold type." They held the attention like no other advertising. Where "printing fails, the hot picture rouses the curiosity, touches the sense of humor, appeals to the refined taste, and commands unconsciously the attention of the average beholder. The advertiser must command involuntary attention." He saw a mission here, a mission to bring "beauty" to ordinary people. "I have no doubt whatever that the high priests of art would sneer at the statement that art in advertising is art for humanity's sake; but, nevertheless, such is the case, and humanity benefits by the art that is expended upon advertising, and the benefits include the artist himself and the audience to which he appeals." Get rid of the precious notion that "art is for art's sake; art belongs to commerce; it must be connected with 'practical things,' " he said.[51]

Merchants like Ogden and Wanamaker hired trained artists to prepare their ads, another reason pictorial advertising came to be so extensive and so sophisticated. By the end of the century, mass market corporations and retailers were able to choose among an ever-swelling group of commercial artists to design billboards, posters, catalogs, and display advertising in newspapers and magazines.

The most famous of the artists whose talents were enlisted to sell goods was Maxfield Parrish, regarded throughout the first half of the twentieth century as America's greatest commercial artist. Parrish designed for nearly every conceivable promotional medium. He painted murals for hotels, restaurants, and barrooms—for example, the "legendary" Old King Cole mural for New York's Knickerbocker Hotel in 1906; the mural was later transferred to the King Cole Room in the St. Regis Hotel. He designed billboards for automobile companies, advertising panels like the Rubaiyat and Cleopatra designs for Crane's Chocolates, and magazine illustrations like the Arabian Nights paintings in *Collier's Magazine*. In one such ad a courtier serves raspberry Jell-O to a Renaissance king and queen, each in purple robes on a golden throne. His work achieved a distribution that was the envy of many other artists, thanks, in part, to Rushing Wood, a Manhattan advertising agency which, on demand, converted his designs into billboards, calendars, posters, and window cards for department stores and specialty houses. People clipped his pictures out of magazines and put them in their kitchens and bedrooms.[52]

A handsome man, Parrish often posed in the nude for the male and also for the female figures in his own posters. He was born in Philadelphia in 1870 and benefited greatly from the revolt of his agnostic Quaker father, Stephen, who, one account has it, turned against the "drab view of life" to become a part-time artist (and owner of a successful stationery store).[53] The young Parrish came to public attention in the late 1890s with his illustrations for children's books, including the color drawings for *Mother Goose in Prose* by L. Frank Baum. Parrish did the pictures in Edith Wharton's popular *Italian Villas and Their Gardens*, to Wharton's own considerable satisfaction. He prepared various publicity designs for corporate businesses and consumer institutions; linen labels and catalog covers for Wanamaker's in the 1890s; menus for Philadelphia's Bartram Hotel; and posters for such national manufacturers as Royal Baking Powder, Colgate Toothpaste, Santa Claus Soap, and Improved Welsbach Light. He attempted to heighten the appeal and modernity of the goods (and of the corporations that made them) by setting old against new to accentuate the virtues of "the modern." He placed the new goods in Renaissance, medieval, or ancient settings, with flamboyantly garbed boys in doublets and tights taking snapshots with Adlake Cameras, or with fairies in Aladdin-like caves using factory-made soaps.

Parrish often connected a commodity or a company with a whimsical atmosphere. He was called, in fact, the Peter Pan of illustrators. He seemed fascinated by what one contemporary described as the "magic of surfaces"; by using repeated glazes over a single design, he often got luminous effects with color. The special blue colors that endowed his pictures with a brilliant enamel-like appearance were widely known as "Parrish blues."[54] Parrish collaborated in 1915 with another commercial colorist, Louis Tiffany, in the construction in Philadelphia of "Dream Garden," an iridescent mosaic mural fifty feet long and fifteen feet wide, commissioned by the Curtis Publishing Company. Parrish designed the mural, which Tiffany translated into glass. Recently restored and still viewable at the Curtis Center in Philadelphia, it was intended to convey a sense of "mystery" that, as its creators said, might "even find its way to the comparatively uneducated eye." Parrish conceived the picture with waterfalls, purple mountains, lush flora, golden canyons, and abundant flowers, all intermingling into a vague and polymorphous mass of color. The mural made no demands on the viewer; it was a piece of mass commercial art whose purpose was to please with pretty colors and the play of lights upon the mosaic.[55]

Parrish's calendars for the Mazda Lamps of the Edison Electric Company became famous, each calendar devoted to facets of what Parrish called the mythic history of light. Parrish found here his trademark image—a radiant natural setting, with youths and maidens garbed in blues and golds, each looking longingly into the distance. Sometimes the visual "radiance" of his pictures—the automobile billboards, for instance, which he did in the late teens—were so effective that, as one observer put it, "the public stopped and stared and delighted but forgot to notice what the pictures advertised."[56] (See plate 5.)

Parrish preferred to paint pictures that merely "suggested" the power of a corporation or the appeal of a commodity rather than those that openly showed the goods or companies themselves. "I would much rather do things like ideal gardens, spring, autumn, youth, the spirit of the sea, the joy of living (if there is such a thing)," he wrote one of his clients, the chocolate manufacturer Clarence Crane. "I kind of wish you had seen the one [Dreamlight] I did for the General Electric people, a sort of calendar they are to bring out in the fall to remind the public that they make a good lamp. I think I got a little of the *spirit of the thing*. Do you know what I mean by the spirit of the thing? I mean the spirit of the things in which we take the most joy and happiness in life. The spirit of out of doors, the spirit of light and distance . . . that is a quality not lost on the public, I feel sure."[57]

Parrish insisted that his work carried no special message or purpose beyond the one of giving pleasure to everybody and of offending nobody. "You know and I know," he told his agent, Rushing Wood, "that what people like is a beautiful setting with charming figures clothed or otherwise, and probably no one special feature. Whatever it is, it's elusive." My "paintings [are] calculated to appeal, as reproductions, to the widest possible audience." Parrish took advertising picture-making to its limits in animistic fetish, saturating landscapes in light and color, trying to link businesses and goods with life-giving warmth and renewal, with innocence and child life, and with a faraway transcendence.

Parrish and other advertisers discovered, just as other groups in the past had discovered, that pictures can attract attention, inspire a measure of loyalty, and excite desire. Striking pictures, advertisers knew, succeeded because they gave "life" and "meaning" to otherwise meaningless or lifeless objects; they imparted to goods a potency the goods lacked. "No more stiff relics from the past," said one marketeer, "only *character, life, color, action, and human interest in drawings*—and above all the *natural*, something to arrest the attention and concentrate it on the *merchandise* or some other feature of the goods to be sold." "Color, sparkle, contrast, atmosphere, pleasing inequalities of space and mass" are absolutely indispensable.[58]

L. Frank Baum and The Show Window

Show windows, of course, showed the goods most enticingly of all, arranging them in "pleasing inequalities of space and mass" in a way unmatched by any other pictorial medium. Today, after years of television advertising, show windows have lost their key place in the repertoire of enticements, so much so that we cannot even imagine how they could have shocked such people as Henry James or Edna Ferber or how they might have served as central, eye-level devices for capturing consumers. Nothing competed with them for selling power, not the advertising cards, not the posters or billboards, not even the early electrical signs. They belonged to a constantly expanding landscape of glass, perhaps the most graphic indication that a new economy and culture of desire of extraordinary dimensions was in the works.

Before 1885 or so, window display in the modern sense barely existed. Trimmers crowded goods together inside the windows or, weather permitting, piled them outside on the street. Many stores exhibited nothing at all in the windows; some avoided display as tasteless; and most simply did not know how to exhibit the manufactured goods that inundated their shelves. The resources and settings were shoddy. By and large, from store to store, the lighting was poor, the glass of inferior quality, and the display fixtures makeshift (often cheesecloth, boxes, piece goods, or random materials dredged up from back rooms).[59] (See plate 2.)

Modern display style can be traced specifically to 1889, when *The Dry Goods Economist*, the most influential voice in late-nineteenth-century merchandising, shifted its interest from finance to retailing. This New York-based organ, from its founding in 1858 into the 1880s, had published little for merchants on retailing methods, reporting instead on money markets, the brokerage business and real estate, and commodities trading. It featured a weekly column on Christian evangelical activities, appealing to merchants to pursue "selfless and Spartan paths." In 1889, in a climate growing markedly more secular and more commercially competitive, it decisively embraced merchandising. "Show your goods," it told merchants, "even if you show only a small quantity, for the sale of goods will certainly be in proportion to the amount of goods exhibited."[60] By the end of the century, with a sharp upswing in the business cycle, new vistas had opened in visual merchandising.

Among the first significant converts to new methods was not an obvious business type but L. Frank Baum, America's best-known writer of children's books. (See plate 17.) Baum's work in retailing was almost as important to the development of American culture as were his Oz stories and fantasies. Like Parrish, he honed new skills attuned to the needs of merchants. His magazine and manual on the "arts of decoration and display" (as he called them) were among the first published anywhere in the world.[61] The manual soon predominated in window display, passing through several editions over the years, and his journal emerged as the most enduring of all such journals. He called it *The Show Window*, which after 1900 evolved into *The Merchants Record and Show Window*, then into *Display World* in the 1920s, and finally into today's *Visual Merchandising*.

Baum was born on a handsome estate, Rose Lawn, in upstate New York in 1856. The last of seven children in a rich, mostly German-American family, he was lovingly cared for by his parents, especially by his devout mother, Cynthia Baum, who tried to bring him up (but to no avail) by strict Methodist principles.[62] Just to the south of the Baum home were the oil fields of Pennsylvania, whose dark green oil—almost as green as the emeralds of Oz—first gushed their riches in the 1850s. Baum spent his childhood and youth in the shadow of oil. His father, Benjamin, made fast money in the oil fields, skimming crude oil off the river that flowed through the fields, refining the oil, and selling it at a good profit; one of his employees may have been John D. Rockefeller, who was soon to transform his own refining firm, Standard Oil, into the first giant business corporation in history.[63] Later, Benjamin founded and directed the Second National Bank of Syracuse, another indication of the economic development overtaking the region, then invested in dairy land and retail properties.[64]

L. Frank Baum himself was not greatly attracted by his father's industrial and banking world. What he liked was the other side of capitalism, the entertainment and consumption side, the "dream life" side. Baum wanted to lift taboos from the expression of desire. "To gain all the meat from the nut of life," he said, "is the essence of wisdom, therefore, 'eat, drink, and be merry'—for *tomorrow* you die."[65] He preferred spending to saving.

Insofar as he had a religion at all, it was the new American mind-cure therapy of "theosophy," one drawn to the here and now and to freeing its followers from any guilt about enjoying life, goods, or money. He married Maud Gage, daughter of Matilda Joslyn Gage, a leading nineteenth-century feminist, and he, too, defended women's rights on the grounds that women, as well as men, should be free to do whatever they wanted. "The key to success of our country," he said, "is tolerance." "Live and let live."[66] Baum wrote children's stories as well—above all, *The Wonderful Wizard of Oz*— tailored to the spiritual aspirations of commercial America. (I will have more to say about Baum's fairy tale and his philosophy of life in Chapter 8.)

As a young man Baum fell in love with the theater, directing to it much of the energy that in some earlier time he might have channeled into religion. Barely out of his teens, he plunged into the theater and by 1880 was writing and producing his own plays, performing lead roles, and touring the Midwest with his wife. He simultaneously took up a career in merchandising that quickly became the moneymaking focus of his professional life. He worked as a traveling salesman and founded his own business, "Baum's Castorine Company," making axle grease out of crude oil.[67] In the late 1880s he traveled to Aberdeen, South Dakota, where his wife's homesteading family had staked their claim, and there he built a retail store, Baum's Bazaar, modeled after F. W. Woolworth's chain store in Utica, New York, a city Baum had visited on one of his many selling tours.

Increasingly accustomed to hype and humbug, Baum gave away gifts of "Gunther's Candy" to all the women who came to his store on the first day. A steady stream of advertisements poured from his pen into the neighborhood press. Baum's Bazaar, he said, had something for everyone, including new commodities such as Chinese lanterns, tinware, factory-made crockery and candy, cigarettes, bicycles, ice cream, and solid brass cuspidors. Children peered through the big plate-glass window that fronted Baum's store.[68]

While Baum was getting this enterprise going, however, a depression struck the region, businessmen were thrown into debt and bankruptcy, and Baum's Bazaar collapsed. Forced to find work elsewhere, he turned to journalism, scraping together enough capital to buy a defunct local newspaper, *The Aberdeen Saturday Pioneer*. He wrote nearly everything for this paper, including the advertising, and though chastened by penury, he remained a fervent booster of Aberdeen's growth. He wanted "manufac-

turing to ensure year-round trade" and urged merchants to do whatever
was needed to promote consumption.[69]

Always an actor above all else, he got a special kick out of the tricks
of display that merchants were beginning to master in the 1890s. Once,
he wrote, "there were no such things as a 'show window.' " Now, in places
as unlikely as South Dakota, merchants were learning how to mass and
assemble goods in the windows. "Even the male mind, naturally obtuse
upon such matters, is forced to marvel at the beauty of the display."[70] He
heaped praise on one "gorgeous Carnival" conducted by local merchants
to show off domestic and imported wares, with booths erected on the main
avenue, each containing "live" female mannequins who "wore" the goods
being sold, some women covered with strawberries, oranges, and nuts and
crackers, others adorned with diamonds, silks, and satins, Haviland china,
and even miniature typewriters. Today such a carnival might well be attacked as an affront to women. But Baum saw nothing strange here; indeed,
he might have joined the two developments—the growth of merchandising
and the advancement of women—positively in his own mind. The costumes, Baum reported, were "simply exquisite, and gorgeous, dainty and
rich enough to grace the court of any medieval queen." The whole thing
was a "dazzling spectacle," a "peep into Elysium."[71]

In the spring of 1891 everything seemed to fall apart in Aberdeen.
Economic crisis blighted the city; Baum went broke and lost his property.
He set out again to find still another job, and this time he struck gold,
choosing Chicago, the biggest boom town of them all, then preparing for
what would prove to be the greatest world's fair in American history.[72] In
Chicago goods in great variety were marketed and sold—from the first
manufactured candy kisses (invented in Chicago in the 1890s) and an
abundance of out-of-season fruits to many kinds of oriental rugs and name-
brand grand pianos. Even prostitutes—as the German sociologist Max
Weber would be shocked to discover on a visit to Chicago at the turn of
the century—were sold on "side streets" in "show windows" under electric
light and with the "prices . . . displayed!"[73] It was here that the greatest
midwestern department stores bestrided the city's center and that Marshall
Field periodically called out the National Guard to crush the unions.

For a few months Baum worked for *The Chicago Evening News*; then
he got a full-time job with Pitkin and Brook, a leading crockery and glass
wholesaler in Chicago, selling goods on the road. Baum soon emerged as
the company's top salesman and, by the mid-1890s, was secure enough to

buy a large house, with bathroom and gaslight, on Chicago's North Side. He and his wife stinted at nothing for their four children, especially at Christmastime, when, as one of his sons remembered, there were often "four Christmas trees . . . in a blaze of different colors—one for each of the four boys—in the four corners of the room," with "wonderful presents" set beneath them. Any holiday, in fact, was to Baum an excuse for indulging his family and himself.[74]

In time Baum wearied of selling on the road and sought work that would allow him to support his family at home. He began writing down the children's stories that would make him famous. He also hit upon an idea that perfectly matched the needs of Chicago's retailers: the creation of show windows.

An obvious change was under way in Chicago's merchandising, just as it had been in Aberdeen. But here the changes were on a monumental scale, symbolized by the grim retail wars of the decade, by the struggle between unions and stores, and by the inexorable growth in inventories of manufactured goods which few merchants seemed able to whittle away. Baum was far more interested in the inventories than he was in retail wars or labor strife. In fact, he had a plan, a method, a new display strategy that would show merchants how to move their goods and increase profits. Most merchants, he was convinced, were ignorant about display; they still left merchandise in heaps in windows and on shelves. He sensed that the goods demanded a new treatment that would produce a new kind of drawing power.

With his years of experience in merchandising and in the theater, no one was better equipped than Baum to instruct merchants on the new display strategies. No one was more sure, as well, that people could be persuaded or tricked by windows into buying goods. "It is said," Baum wrote, expressing a conviction he shared with P. T. Barnum, "that people are not as readily deceived by window display, but we all know better than this. There seems to be no way to protect people from imposition, even supposing they desired to be protected." In any case, "without advertising, the modern merchant sinks into oblivion."[75]

In 1898 Baum founded the National Association of Window Trimmers, a first-of-its-kind trade organization whose object was "the uplifting of mer- cantile decorating to the level of a profession."[76] There were soon two hundred members. Baum was its secretary. A year earlier he published the first issue of *The Show Window,* a medium-sized "monthly journal of decorative art," usually sixty or more pages in length, heavily illustrated with drawings and photographs, and packed with advertising for everything from "dowager corsets" to "Frink's window reflectors." By 1900 it was bedecked in colors—rose, pink, yellow, green, tan, blue, and brown. "I conceived of the idea of a magazine devoted to window trimming," Baum informed a family member, "which I know is greatly needed and would prosper if ever we would get it together." Marshall Field's right-hand man, superintendent H. Gordon Selfridge, who was just then building bigger windows and enlarging his display staff, hailed *The Show Window* as "an indispensable organ" for department stores. In a few months circulation grew into the tens of thousands.[77]

The Show Window was at the forefront of a new movement in merchandising designed to foster year-round consumer desire. In the process it helped change the face of display. In page after page it recommended new tactics to attract consumer attention, especially Baum's strong personal preference, "spectacular" moving electrical displays of revolving stars, "vanishing ladies," mechanical butterflies, revolving wheels, incandescent lamp globes—anything to get the customer to "watch the window!" "People will always stop to examine anything that moves," he said, "and will enjoy studying out the mechanics or wondering how the effect has been obtained."[78]

The Show Window's most radical message, however, concerned the merchandise itself: Use the best art to "arouse in the observer the cupidity and longing to possess the goods," as Baum put it. Baum seemed tolerant of greed. After all, didn't any successful business depend on other people's greed? Nor did he seem very interested in the inherent worth of the goods on sale (as many merchants might have been); he concentrated, rather, on the way the goods "looked" and hence on their "selling" power. What mattered was getting people to buy. As long as the goods "are properly displayed," he predicted, "the show window will sell them like hot cakes, even though [the goods] are old enough to have gray whiskers."[79]

Baum exhorted merchants not to crowd goods in the windows, as in the past, but to single them out. Don't let the lamps and tin pots sit there, Baum said; make them "come alive" as if they were figures on the stage.[80] *The Show Window* dwelled repeatedly on theatrical themes. Look for the "possibilities lying dormant in the beautiful goods." "Tastefully display a single apron." Adjust the electric lighting and widen and deepen the show windows. "Suggest possibilities of color and sumptuous display that would delight the heart of an oriental." Bring the "goods out in a blaze of glory." Make them look like jewels.[81]

A Maze of Glittering Crystal

Baum left retailing two years later, in 1900, when *The Wonderful Wizard of Oz* was published, and the number of show windows greatly multiplied. Businessmen, once forced to import good plate glass from France, now had plenty, with domestic factories marketing tremendous amounts of manufactured glass. Fifteen years later, Americans were consuming about half all the plate glass produced throughout the world. The glass was cheaper and clearer, too, stronger and larger; windows were varied in depth, shape, and finish to accommodate the increasing diversity and volume of merchandise. Each of the show windows in Wanamaker's new 1906 New York store was "about the size of the average dwelling room," able to carry libraries, drawing rooms, bedrooms, and dining rooms, "following one another in a series." The new Scruggs, Vandervoort, and Barney store in St. Louis was "practically glass throughout," its three lowest stories all of "immense plates."[82] Soon "all glass fronts" were commonplace in prosperous retail districts; and, with the addition of mirrors, windows reflected the light, as well as the objects within and without, in a "splintering maze of glittering crystal," as one retailer described it. Unlike the midnineteenth century, when it was still thought indiscreet and vulgar to stare into windows, by the beginning of the twentieth century, people were being invited—even baited—to look. Merchants hired professional "window gazers" to encourage gawking.[83]

The new exterior glass environment began to change the way people related to goods. In the past—even in the most recent past—people shopped in the town markets (or in Europe and elsewhere, in the market squares, halls, and bazaars) in the midst of the goods themselves. Whitechapel district of London in the 1850s, for instance, served the working class and poor; an extensive open-air market with few fixed shops, it overflowed with hawkers and itinerant street peddlers who sold everything from poultry, fish, flowers, and mince pies to oysters, lemonade, coffee, watercress, and goldfish. Working-class housewives elbowed their way through the rough and tumble of Whitechapel, bargaining for their bacon and cheese, their tea and sugar, even their firewood. The same pattern was replicated to some degree in the United States (although, perhaps, never in such a totally class-segregated fashion or to such an extent).[84] In late antebellum Philadelphia, a city ranked at the top in commercial development at the time, shoppers still strolled among open-air stalls along Market Street, the city's central artery, where they could touch, smell, and examine the goods (as well as enjoy the social context, the people) all at once. There was access and movement from all sides; contact between customers and goods "flowed on undisturbed," as one commentator described it.[85]

Such open-air shopping persisted in the countryside and in working-class neighborhoods well into the 1920s.[86] Even today, in many cities, ephemeral street fairs are common occurrences. There also seems to be a resurgence of more fixed open-stall marketing in such cities as New York and Los Angeles, especially in the newer and heavily populated immigrant communities. Canal Street in New York, for instance, is filled with open-air shops. But from the late 1890s, this form of shopping was increasingly superseded for many people by something quite different. Massive volumes of goods in all price ranges, housed in permanently constructed large buildings and attracting complex populations, now induced merchants to control the flow and exhibition of goods. On the one hand, the goods—or, more correctly, the merchant's capital investment in them—had to be protected not only from pilfering hands but also from the weather and street grime. On the other hand, there had to be a way to foster the impression of intimacy, some way to get the goods out of confinement. Indeed, the pressure to move goods in quantity and at expanding profit levels—to "break down the barriers separating customers and merchandise," as Frederick Kiesler, Austrian émigré artist and show window expert later put it—was greater than ever. Just as one answer had been the creation of two-dimensional advertising pictures and signs, so there were also three-dimensional show windows.

Reliance on glass for display had several significant consequences: It contributed to the formation of a new culture of class—that is, it helped to demarcate more clearly the affluent from the poorer buying public. From the late 1890s, uptown shopping in cities like New York became connected with glass and affluence, whereas downtown shopping remained linked with open-air stalls for immigrants, for the working poor, and for bargain hunters of all classes. Glass also closed off smell and touch, diminishing the consumer's relationship with the goods. At the same time, it amplified the visual, transforming the already watching city person into a potentially compulsive viewer. It must have altered the character of the relationship between goods and people by permitting everything to be seen yet rendering it all beyond touch. In the 1830s Ralph Waldo Emerson wrote lyrically of the primary role of the visual sense in his essay "Nature." "I became a transcendent eyeball; I am nothing; I see all," he said. Emerson, of course, was writing about the woods, about nature, but by 1910 the Emersonian shopper was being born, burdened by a growing desire that might grow ever greater in the imagination—all eyes, no nose, no fingers.[87]

Glass was a symbol of the merchant's unilateral power in a capitalist society to refuse goods to anyone in need, to close off access without being condemned as cruel and immoral (as he might have been condemned in a precapitalist feudal society when it was expected that powerful personages, even as they extracted payments from peasants, had an obligation to give something in return).[88] At the same time, the pictures behind the glass enticed the viewer. The result was a mingling of refusal and desire that must have greatly intensified desire, adding another level of cruelty. Perhaps more than any other medium, glass democratized desire even as it dedemocratized access to goods. There it is, you see it as big as life—you see it amplified everywhere, you see everything revealed—but you cannot reach it. Unless you shatter the window or go in and pay for it, you cannot have it. In such a context, the breaking of glass could have easily become a class act.

By 1910 show windows were above and also below the ground at subway station stops in many major American cities. The placing of these windows, unavoidable to riders who passed by in subway cars or who stood on platforms, made them among the most desirable and costly of windows; merchants fought over the rights from local city governments to acquire space to build them. "Show window privileges are extremely valuable," Filene's real estate agent reported in 1909, and "it looks as though we are going to secure exceptional privileges." Filene's on Washington Street in Boston had "splendid" underground windows, the management boasted. According-ing to trade journal accounts so did the stores along Market Street in Philadelphia—Snellenberg's, Wanamaker's, Lit's, Strawbridge and Cloth-ier, and Gimbels—each with windows presenting "gorgeous displays" ex-tending the length of the subway platforms. Chicago underground windows were built in 1905 for Field's, Mandels, and Carson, Pirie, Scott. In 1902, after the construction of New York's IRT, which soon reached from Manhattan into Brooklyn, store after store in New York City claimed long stretches of brightly illuminated underground windows on display night and day.[89]

Form out of Chaos

The arsenal of merchandising display and decoration expanded with the proliferation of windows. The concept of the "enclosed window," with background and ceiling paneled in wood, became popular in retail stores for the first time. "Enclosed windows," wrote one decorator, "keep out the dust and flies," "prevent damage to stock," and "furnish a background from which to drape."[90] By 1910, such contained visual spaces, constructed from oak or mahogany, offered city stores much opportunity to exploit consumer fantasy. The displayman's repertoire also opened to embrace colored glass caps, sheets of colored glass, and projectors to flood the windows with color. Independent display companies supplied merchants with pedestals, millinery stands, velours and silks, decorative backgrounds, and a remarkable new store fixture: the mannequin.[91]

Throughout most of the nineteenth century, people saw full-bodied mannequins mostly in dime museums, places well known for their displays of freaks, "rare" animals and birds, and wax figures of dead kings and queens and notorious criminals. After 1875, more "refined" mannequins could be viewed as "grouped figures" in the anthropological exhibits of the world fairs in Philadelphia and Chicago.[92] In merchandising, however, the commonest dress forms were "headless dummies"—no arms, heads, or feet. Then, by 1912, with the rise of ready-to-wear clothes and the production of fully prepared garments, complete mannequins gained a "wonderful popularity." Even Marshall Field's, long a holdout for the headless dummy, began to pose them in the windows to show goods.[93] The first "new" mannequins were primitively made, mostly female, doll-like static wax figures that tended to melt in the heat, very similar to the images in magazines like Godey's Lady's Book. In time merchants put them into temperature-controlled window spaces and molded them from a more reliable blend of papier-mâché and wax. And, challenged by the rise of photography, which affected all forms of image production, mannequins were made with authentic-looking hair, adjustable limbs, natural facial features, and "animated attitudes." "As many types of wax figures exist, as there were human beings," said one retailer.[94]

Armed with mannequins and other display materials, merchants had much greater liberty to manipulate goods in their windows. Although many handicaps remained until well into the 1920s—unwieldy lighting, window glare, the presence of too many goods and too much decorative "busy-ness" in the windows—department store owners pushed the entire display profession in a new direction.[95] And, by attempting to stimulate desire for all goods, they even aided the cheap chain merchants such as Woolworth's, who did no display or decorating whatsoever.

Displaymen "drenched" their goods in color to increase their appeal. After Edmund Rostand's play *Chanticleer* was performed on Broadway in 1910 with brightly colored birds in leading roles, a stream of red flowed through New York City windows. Hats, slippers, parasols, hosiery, and slippers were shown in ensembles of chanticleer red; brilliant red drapes hung on window backs; and in one B. Altman window on Thirty-fourth Street, a trimmer covered a dress form with scarlet silk and black chanticleer lace in a rooster design. A different color "dramatized" every window at Gimbels on Broadway at Thirty-fourth Street in February 1916: purple light on silverware, green on silk, blue on furniture, and red on a bedroom set inspired by Japanese designs.[96]

Displaymen also foregrounded and singled out objects in the Baumian show window manner. Although most displaymen would not overcome their desire to crowd the windows until the 1920s, many were beginning to do so. (See plate 7.) "Form must come from chaos," urged one retailer in 1905, "separate lines" and "even individual items" should be "given prominence." "One feature of the display" must "dominate all the rest," said another. To the degree possible and sensible, all commodities, including everyday manufactured articles and food, were treated in similar ways. Strategic use of light helped, producing an illusion of depth and energy—"a vibrating presence," as Theodore Dreiser had described it in 1902.

Mannequins especially helped in extracting form from chaos, their purpose to "rivet" the eyes to a few goods, contribute to the making of centered ensembles, and "create an atmosphere of reality that aroused enthusiasm and acted in an autosuggestive manner." Displaymen even "dramatized" women's underwear on full-bodied mannequins in the show windows, a practice that departed radically from nineteenth-century methods, when merchants tended to pile up such goods on shelves or mass them into architectural cones or arches. The novelist John Dos Passos was so impressed by these that he used them in his novel *1919* to show how a man's sexual desire could be stirred in this new urban setting. "All kinds of things got him terribly agitated," Dos Passos wrote of one of his characters, "so that it was hard not to show it. The wobble of the waitresses' hips and breasts, while they were serving meals, girls' underwear in store windows."[97]

Some of these underwear displays were shocking enough to cause street crowding and sometimes even street rioting. In Spokane, Washington, the police were called in to break up a crowd that had "jammed" up around a window with "living mannequins" wearing revealing "Directoire" gowns. One young man who "refused to move from the store window" had to be dragged away forcibly by the "bluecoats"—the first such arrest, a retailer boasted, "in the Northwest as the result of an exhibit of the Directoire."[98]

But these windows did not take hold without resistance. As early as 1899, when such displays first appeared, women's clubs crusaded against them as "immoral"; there were similar periodic if ever-weakening yearly assaults. Benjamin Altman, who died in 1913, detested the full-bodied mannequin and, indeed, all mannequin displays on moral grounds; out of homage to his memory, Altman's had no mannequins until the late 1920s. Yet for reasons that probably reflected general public acceptance as well as the "pressures" of merchandising for mass markets, most of the big stores remained committed to these displays. "If the trade demands underwear," one spokesman for the display industry wrote in 1919, "the house that does not show it will lose out."[99]

By the 1910s American business was beginning to alter the meaning of goods through dramatic treatment, investing them with a significance that set them off and above other things. But merchants did more than visually focus goods; they attempted to give goods "associative" power as well. "Associate the goods with people and events," one retailer said, and not with "the idea of buying and selling: in this manner you command attention." Glamor, "riotous color schemes," luxury, escape, adventure, and leisure activities were invoked in the windows to attract customers to the goods.[100]

The associational style worked differently for men and for women. The display of men's wear was low-keyed, unassuming, connected with dark colors, always simple, muted, and undecorative in the "masculine" manner.

"Simplicity should be the keynote in every display of men's clothing and furnishings" was a typical merchant's advice. "Most men are averse to gay colors even in their ties. . . . The average man is inclined to look upon elaborate decorative effects as 'useless frills.' " It was one of the cardinal rules of early-twentieth-century display that men's wear never be shown in "excessively animated" ways and never be visually reinforced by bright colors. Certainly no male mannequins in underwear appeared in windows. Nor were male mannequins used much at all, except as foils for other displays or to illustrate male dress in the most nonanimated way.[101]

For women, matters were quite different. In 1911 in Philadelphia, a simple Wanamaker's millinery display organized around a portrait of a beautiful woman painted in the manner of John Singer Sargent was meant to convey the idea of luxury or of abandon to sensual desires. Trimmings placed in velveteen settings at Greenhut's on Fourteenth Street in New York City were designed to "bring constantly to mind" the impending "excitement of the evening activities." Macy's 1914 spring window opened with a "radical departure" for the store: an entire ballroom scene to show off evening gowns, with "a reproduction of a promenade on the Riviera" displaying other luxuriously dressed mannequins.[102]

Arthur Fraser's Temple

Many of the men who did these displays—and they were all men at this time—treated the work as a business and nothing more. Others tried to transform it into an art form, and still others were confused over the ethics of what they were doing. One ambivalent trimmer was Walter F. Allert, whose career at Macy's was a seesaw between celebration and condemnation of visual merchandising. Allert set up new interior "display fixtures" at Macy's, in the "main center portion of the store," which had never functioned before as a display space, and he introduced mannequins in furnished bedrooms in the show windows. He championed a new technology that eliminated window glare and reflections.[103] On one occasion he said that "the whole business world is waking up to the beautiful way of doing things." Yesterday the window dresser put "a cartload of hats into a display"; today he "stages those hats in a way that will make every woman in town *stop, look, and listen*—and, what is more, *buy*." Allert even urged city governments to hire "municipal display managers" so that the cities, too, might be as "beautiful as department stores." He spoke of his "dream" of a "City inspired by the word DISPLAY, built up . . . on the principle of Display."[104]

But three years after joining Macy's in 1910, he also began to caution against too much reliance on "elaborate shows and demonstrations" to "induce people to spend their money on things they cannot afford." For the moment, he was defending "value" and "economy" over excess and waste, and, four years later, was even attacking fancy show windows. "We are not theatrical producers," he said. "We are not setting a stage. Think of putting an article in the window with such surroundings as to create a *false* desire or anticipation on the part of the customer."

Sometime in 1916 Allert had what one of his friends called a "crisis." He quit his job and became a Christian Scientist.[105] Other displaymen were dismayed, although the most respected of them, Herman Frankenthal of Altman's, who had himself survived a "personal crisis" and returned, was convinced that Allert, too, would survive. Frankenthal, a German émigré who worked in Philadelphia in the early 1870s, then at Stern's in downtown Manhattan, and finally at Altman's on Thirty-fourth Street, was the first display man to drape dress forms in show windows, an art he brought "to a high degree never attempted before," with twenty-five thousand or more yards of silk sold as a consequence at Altman's in a single day. In about 1910 he had a nervous collapse and left Altman's, but he was back in a few months. "There is a fascination with the window," Frankenthal said, "such a fascination as has kept me working at Altman's for nineteen years. Such a peculiar profession is this art of the window . . . that they all come back. . . . Allert, too, will come back."[106] Frankenthal was right: Allert did come back, but he failed to regain his former status, a sign of which was the disappearance of his name from the trade press.

Other displaymen—such as Arthur Fraser of Marshall Field's, America's "leading display director" before 1920 (and for many years after)—seemed never to have been at odds with themselves over display. Fraser, a Quebec-born Catholic, carried the "associational style" to a point unequaled by any other window trimmer before him. Fraser had followed his brother to the United States, ending up as a dry goods clerk in his teens in Creston, Iowa, in the mid-1890s. He might have stayed in Creston forever had it not been for a visit by a representative of Harry Selfridge, the driven superintendent of Marshall Field's who was now charting new paths in retailing.

"Learn to forget the past," Selfridge told his staff repeatedly, "and deal more and more with the present."[107]

Selfridge was doing business in a way that even bewildered Marshall Field, who was a wholesaler at heart. "It was like a high wind hitting the place," one Field's executive said of Selfridge's influence: He was "a fine talker, straight as a ramrod, and all over retail." In the late 1890s Selfridge added the first show windows to Field's, along with low shelving, telephones, display fixtures, revolving doors, and the first window trimmers. "Every day is Show Day in this establishment," he told his staff in 1902. In that year the store had the "largest windows of highly polished plate glass of any other building" in Chicago.[108] It was Selfridge who helped get Baum's *The Show Window* off the ground as the principal American trade journal on display.

One of Selfridge's agents recruited Arthur Fraser for display work in 1895 when Fraser was still very young. In 1897 he was reportedly the first displayman to project single bursts of color (no goods included)—in this case, red in all its shades and tints—through the windows. By the early 1900s, now head of display, Fraser was setting precedents by cutting down the "clutter" in the windows and by reducing the quantity of goods on display by 75 to 90 percent. He introduced full-bodied mannequins to Field's in 1913, highly realistic papier-mâché figures he claimed to have invented and, according to *Women's Wear Daily*, he was the first trimmer (although this is a claim—like so many others made in this promotion-driven field—difficult to confirm) to "accessorize mannequins." "I tried to get the mannikins so real," he said, "that the woman would feel it was she wearing it." By 1916, he commanded a staff of fifty men and women—painters, sculptors, and craftsmen.[109]

Fraser was utterly theatrical in his methods. "We would dramatize our merchandise—really stage work," he recalled in an interview. "I went to New York to the theater a lot. I derived more from the theater than anything else."[110] In the early 1900s the New York theater was going through a reform in scenic design; sets were more realistic, better built, and more in harmony with the ideas of the play and with the performers. Fraser picked up these changes and, about 1907, when the store windows were deepened and widened, he began to experiment, usually placing his goods within expensive message-oriented settings intended to trigger instant desire.[111] "If the dress showed the influence of the Louis XIV style," wrote a Fraser admirer, "then the setting was formed correctly along the lines of the period, or if what were known as Empire fashions were in favor and were displayed, then the background, the hangings, and the furniture and all other accessories recalled the splendid simplicity of the ancient classic Greece and Rome." When the motif or "central idea" was Japanese, as it was in the fall of 1913, Fraser installed in his windows Japanese landscape paintings, against which he foregrounded goods inspired by Japanese motifs. "The soft, hazy tones and vague lines, with the faint, snow-capped Fujiyama in the distance," wrote a display "expert," "gave wonderful perspective to the whole setting. This is real Japanese art."[112]

Judged by the photographs of his show windows that remain to us, and when considered in relation to what was to follow in display, Fraser's "artistry" hardly seems as impressive today as it was to people in the 1910s. His display "work" (and that of his numerous imitators) was showy, often stilted and formulaic, and dependent on scenic painting as background. In time his style would greatly improve, and even by 1915 or 1916 the effects he began to achieve were remarkable. But whatever the year his aim never changed. Like all big-store displaymen, he wanted women—above all women—to look into his windows and imagine, "There is an idea that I could have worked out in my home" or "That dress is just the right combinations of materials and colors." He "hoped to create in the mind of the viewer a psychological harmony," as he would later say, "a sort of a 'glimpse into the interior of the temple' that is an inherent desire in all of us."[113] (See plate 8.)

Until the 1930s, all the show windows at Marshall Field's were covered on Sundays, out of respect, it was said, for the "puritanism" of the store's founder.[113] But such a strategy also had the planned effect of building up anticipation for the weekly revelations, as countless customers came to look over Fraser's "artwork." In the fall of 1916, when gold curtains opened to reveal the displays, thousands of women were waiting to get a look. And men, too, looked into show windows, into Field's windows and into the windows of other fanciful trimmers as well. "We go across 34th and 5th Avenue, and up to 42nd," Theodore Dreiser wrote in his diary, of a shopping trip in New York City, "looking in windows. Wonderful display. . . . We visit Arnold Constable, Franklin Simon and Co., Lord and Taylor, and Macy. It is getting colder. . . . These stores are so fascinating in the winter."[115]

Chapter 3

INTERIORS

In January 1879 Sophie Hall, the wife of an Episcopalian minister from New York City, began her diary with comments on prayer meetings and upcoming missionary work. "Death only for a season," she recorded, "must rise again." About a week later, on Sunday, she heard a sermon at a Congregationalist church in lower Manhattan, and was impressed by the preacher's warning: "If Christianity or Religion interferes in any way with your business be assured it is not a legitimate business." But on the next day Mrs. Hall went shopping with a friend at Macy's retail store on Fourteenth Street, staying much longer than she had planned. "Got to Macy's Emporium," she writes, "and saw so many beautiful things that we found it a trying matter to get out."[1]

Forty years later, Fannie Schmertzler, teenage daughter of middle-class New Yorkers, was caught stealing at the same store. "She is not vicious," wrote her lawyer to Percy Straus, Macy's vice president, in a leniency appeal, but "bears every evidence of refinement and general good character." Eight months before "the occurrence," she even worked at Macy's, and, since leaving the store, has

> promoted charitable work, being associated with the Israel Orphan Asylum. In an unguarded moment, during the height of Christmas

purchasing when the desire to possess articles is the greatest, and
the display of articles in stores is so alluring, and so easy to take,
the psychological effect upon her rendered her susceptible to
nonresistance to temptation, and impulsively, but not deliberately,
she wavered from her moral resolve and committed a wrong.[2]

In 1879, Sophie Hall suffered minor moral distress, a mere smidgen of
guilt, at lingering in the store and being tempted by the goods. In 1920,
Fannie Schmertzler, too, dawdled at Macy's, tempted as much by the
"alluring display" of goods as by the goods themselves, and, of course, she
did not get out in time.

Between Hall's visit and Schmertzler's thievery, a new era in interior
merchandising had dawned. Customers encountered new interior spaces
organized by merchants to promote consumption. Merchants added technologies and fixtures, from escalators to glass cases, to facilitate physical
movement and shopping. They structured the social character of interiors,
dividing them along class lines, creating bargain basements for the "masses"
and elegant little "salon rooms" for "the classes" (as merchants themselves
used these terms). Distinct children's departments with carnival atmospheres (especially toy departments) began to appear in retail stores, symptomatic of an emerging child world, quite separate from the adult world,
that had never existed before in the United States. Merchants worked on
an imaginative canvas, relying on color, glass, and light and on theatrical
strategies—or on what they called "central decorative ideas"—to transform
interior spaces. What was happening on the outside, in other words, was
occurring on the inside as well.

Dismantling Doorsteps and the New Intimacy with Goods

Before 1880, most businesses did little to arrange goods and spaces to appeal
to shoppers; and even those merchants presumably most likely to care—
the large retail merchants—were displaying goods clumsily inside the stores,
piling them up on wooden counters and bunching them together. (See
plate 9.) A mark of decorative skill—even into the 1890s—was to hang
goods on walls and pillars, from the transept domes, and over railings.[3]

Merchants decorated the walls with goods or hid them on shelves and in drawers, where they could be protected from dust and the dirty fingers of customers.[4] Many retailers continued to do business this way even after 1885, but change was in the air, with the advent of new methods of interior display and decoration.

Gradually, the imperative of "don't touch" gave way to an insistence to "get closer." Merchants invited customers in by dismantling doorsteps, imitating, according to a writer for The Dry Goods Economist, "saloon architecture," which had proven the effectiveness of this little architectural detail. "A step at the entrance is a mistake," the article advised. "No hindrance should be offered to people who may drift into the store."[5] Merchants also replaced their old-fashioned "swinging doors" with "revolving doors," to speed up movement. "Swinging doors," it was asserted, "are a constant menace to the careless crowds always coming and going," whereas "revolving doors" allow for "easier access."[6] They constructed subway entrances into basement departments and increased the number of entrances to the stores as a whole. Aisles were widened. "So far as I know," John Wanamaker boasted of his Philadelphia store to a friend, "there are no large stores in any city in the world so well supplied with entrances and exits to the street as this Store, nor is there any with as much aisle space."[7] Bigger aisles were first introduced in the mid-1890s, when Henry Siegel of Siegel-Cooper's transformed the principal artery of his New York store into an "immense street" of "ample open spaces" by which customers were attracted into the store. "In the middle of the store," the architect explained, "this corridor will widen out into an ample court"; the shoppers could recover equilibrium, relax, and look around.[8]

Elevators and escalators also made circulation easier and faster. Omnipresent in big stores by 1900, elevators were grouped along with the "quick selling" bargains far away from the store entrances, thus compelling customers to "move through" the stores past the costly goods on the main floor. Retailers arranged individual floors and departments according to the same principle. For example, in 1916 the Abraham & Straus store in Brooklyn completely altered its floor-covering department by displaying the expensive oriental rugs near the elevators and hustling the cheaper grades and carpet yardage to the rear.[9]

When John Wanamaker first became aware of escalators in 1898, he knew he had to have them; by 1912, with the completion of his second "big store," "moving stairways" were carrying customers up and down, to the wonder of many.[10] "Oh, happy land!" exclaimed a London tourist in 1904, "the use of this instrument instantly transports the sufferer to the seventh heaven of delight." "It's action!" said the head of Field's maintenance division, "it makes you want to go up. Escalators bring circulation to upper stories, like blood to the veins."[11] Escalators also permitted merchants to distribute the "quick sellers" even more widely throughout their stores. The Bamberger management claimed in 1912 that its five escalators increased profits by allowing the store to "place the staple, year-round 'sellers' on the second and third floors, relieving the congestion of departments on the main floor."[12]

Along with the moving stairways and the other circulatory equipment was the glass environment, which expanded inside as rapidly as it did outside. Indeed, selling through glass, skillfully applied in this country, influenced all forms of merchandising. There were curved or straight glass doors and shelves, glass counters and containers, and, by 1905, forty-one different kinds of glass showcases.[13]

Harry Morrison, an engineer with a utopian streak, was convinced that the introduction of glass into interior display would "revolutionize" consumption. A spokesman for automatic selling through glass, he made his reputation in Chicago, where he built several cafeterias for the Wieboldt chain of department stores. In such new cafeterias and Automats, glass display cases speeded up turnover and encouraged impulsive eating. Cafeterias succeeded, according to one advocate, because "they sold more food by appealing to the sense of sight and smell . . . much more than the lifeless menu card ever could. When we started to eat in cafeterias, we always ordered more food than we could consume and it is only by training that you eat in a cafeteria without overbuying."[14]

In 1911 John Wanamaker hired Morrison to reconceive the glass interior of the new Philadelphia store. Wanamaker, in fact, was a nearly lifelong convert to the selling power of glass, outside and inside his stores. In the mid-1880s he was in Paris to inspect the interiors of such famous firms as the Bon Marché, Printemps, and the Louvre. Wanamaker swore by the greatness of Paris, "the best storekeeping city in the world," he told his son Rodman, who was living there. "Each day will offer new approaches to you that can be *coined into money* at our stores when you come back."[15] Among the things he noted in his diary on his 1886 visit were the "glass floors" in Printemps, "the linoleum plain with blue borders," and a "plate glass vestibule. Bridge glass floor, Spacious stairs. Plate glass elevator cage. . . . Plate glass room for electric lights. Goods displayed—*Great* point."[16] At home again, he bought many interior glass fixtures; he had, for example, glass cases illuminated by concealed light, many backed with mirrors. Morrison further persuaded Wanamaker to "place everything he could" under or behind glass. "In John Wanamaker's stores," Morrison wrote, "the system of showing goods under glass was developed to the utmost. Even women's apparel was taken out of the stock rooms and put in glass cases."[17]

Mirrored glass proliferated in stores (as well as in hotels and restaurants), embedded on sliding elevator doors, inserted into showcases and shelving, and suspended on walls and columns. The impact of mirrors was almost wholly illusory, as merchants themselves were the first to admit. Mirrors "seemed to increase the apparent floor space"; they "concealed" the unattractive parts of the stores; and they amplified the "allure" of goods by "showing them from every angle" in glass showcases. Mirrors "rejuvenated" and suggested "depth."[18] They had the power to draw customers into a narcissistic maze of self-reflection, creating an environment in which they might interact with the goods in the most intimate and personal way. At Wanamaker's in Philadelphia, in 1897, every pillar on the ground floor was encased in mirrors "from floor to ceiling." At Siegel-Cooper's on Sixth Avenue in 1904, the corset department was "covered with mirrors."[19]

"The Stage upon Which the Play Is Enacted"

Merchants of all kinds also began redecorating their once-serviceable interiors into attractive spaces for the display and sale of goods. By 1900 department store retailers tried to conceal from customers the bleaker parts of the stores, not only with mirrors but also by segregating the bookkeeping floors (or the manufacturing floors, if any remained) clearly from the merchandising ones. As late as World War I, Macy's in New York was still struggling to complete the isolation of its "nonselling employees" on the undecorated high floors, with the aim of getting rid of every indication that the store was really a business enterprise where people sweated and worked. The point was to give shopping space its own unique identity as a place for consumption and for nothing else. "The selling departments," said one retailer in 1902, "is the stage upon which the play is enacted."[20]

Bronze embellishments and mahogany woodwork displaced the old iron and plain wooden decorations; wooden floors were "ripped" out to make way, for instance, for "Tennessee marble" (at Field's) or travertine gray volcanic stone (at Lord & Taylor).[21] Carpets were laid and mirrors glittered on columns and walls. There was improved ventilation in the big commercial palaces, and better heating and cooling, although none sufficient—until much later—to overcome completely the summer heat or winter cold that afflicted stores in what merchants called the "dull seasons."[22] New forms of light began to appear in consumer interiors, although here we can only mark the beginning of a phase, not its completion, which would not come until the 1920s. Wanamaker was at the forefront, turning to Paris again for guidance and inspiration. "Spaces everywhere spent prodigally for light," he wrote of the Louvre. "Superb light" at the Bon Marché, "light wells everywhere, plethora of light."[23] The light for shopping or for merely walking about was enhanced at Wanamaker's and at other stores, too, as merchants installed indirect and semidirect lighting systems, which concealed light sources in translucent bowls or hid them in inverted saucers that projected the light against the ceiling, illuminating with a diffuse and "soft radiance." "I would compare the light to nothing but the light of bright spring morning," said a customer who had just walked through such a lighted interior. "The impression," said another, "is that of natural daylight."[24] (See plate 10.)

In the late 1880s architects such as John Root and Louis Sullivan were promoting, with limited success, the use of color in commercial spaces. Their goal was to bring the "outdoors indoors," achieved, Sullivan believed, in his Transportation Building, with its polychrome decoration and golden doorway, at the 1893 World's Columbian Exposition in Chicago, and in his Auditorium Theater in downtown Chicago, the first theatrical space to integrate color and light successfully into interior design. By the early 1900s the theatrical impresarios Mark Klaw and Abraham Erlanger and the Shubert brothers were building flagship theaters in New York and elsewhere with colored and illuminated interiors and luxurious lobbies, prefiguring the decorative excesses of the 1920s.[25]

One of the earliest recruits to this aesthetic project was Louis Tiffany, an ardent colorist, famed for his lamps and jewelry, who collaborated with

Maxfield Parrish in the creation of the "Dream Garden" mural at the Curtis Publishing Building in Philadelphia. In 1902 Tiffany designed for Marshall Field a blue, green, and gold opalescent glass dome, the largest single piece of iridescent glass mosaic in the world. Tiffany considered it the "acme of my most artistic work." He chose his colors carefully, conscious of an artistic tradition that linked them to "distance and boundlessness." Where yellows and reds suggested the "near and the full-blooded," these were "essentially atmospheric." The dome's shape, consisting of three concentric circles, contributed to the illusion of open-ended space or of a heavenly domain without limits. Similar to the dome Tiffany had over his own bed in his Long Island mansion, it borrowed its inspiration from Blakean mysticism. It conveyed the impression of an "infinity of needs," of longing and desire— a perfect aesthetic symbol for this consumer setting.[26] (See plate 11.)

Color schemes were increasingly obligatory in big consumer spaces by the turn of the century. The 1915 Panama-Pacific International Exposition in San Francisco, held to celebrate the building of the Panama Canal, was entirely color-integrated by colorist Jules Guerin, who was among a new group of painters to urge Americans to make more commercial use of color. The exposition was, Guerin said, "my color creation" and the "City of my dreams." "On every hand . . . color!—that is the magic quality our public buildings have missed so long. For color, like music, is the language of emotion."[27] In 1903, every floor of the Hotel del Coronado near San Diego, California—where L. Frank Baum vacationed and where he wrote, as he said, "the bulk of my Oz books"—had its own color scheme, and every room its own color-coordinated wallpaper, china, and hand towels.[28] Across the country, in the midteens, in New York's Greenwich Village, tearooms were being built, each with its own color theme or scheme, among them The Purple Pup, the Blue Horse, and the Aladdin Ship, where coffee and oriental sweets were served in a space that was a "riot of strange and beautiful colour—vivid and Eastern and utterly intoxicating."[29] In department stores, special rooms, individual floors, even entire stores were designed around a single color scheme. Green in all its tints and shades prevailed from basement to roof at Filene's in Boston in 1901. Green was everywhere in 1907 in Greenhut's, one of the last large middle-class stores to serve downtown Manhattan trade: Carpets, sidewalls, stool seats, and desk blotters were in various shades of green; there were green stock boxes and wrapping paper, green stationery, green string, even green ink and ribbon for the green store typewriters. One "progressive" southern store owner, "a staunch upholder of color schemes," painted his own store, inside and out, a bright lemon yellow.[30]

Seductions for the Masses
and the Classes

Along with the enhancement of goods through decoration and display and the reliance on such devices as glass cases, mirrors, elevators, and escalators, merchants endowed interiors with social meaning, some of it meant to reflect middle-class tastes, some to meet working-class needs, and whatever was left over to address both "class" and "mass" together.

The bargain basements were literally and figuratively the bottom spaces, growing out of the main-floor "bargain counters" of the economically depressed 1870s. Spartan, with little artifice, they sold marked-down goods and cheaper versions of the more expensive items upstairs, freed the main floor from congestion, and separated different classes of shoppers. The Chicago stores, it seems, were the first to have bargain basements, in the late 1890s. "It was a Chicago idea," said Louis Stern of Stern's department store in Manhattan, in an interview. In Chicago, unlike in New York, Stern claimed, "the classes" intermingle and "shop under the same roof." "And, this, for ought I know, may have led to the adoption of the Bargain Mart, as an experiment for separating the masses from the classes."[31] In 1900, Filene's in Boston created its "automatic" bargain basement, perhaps the most famous of all such basements. A few years later, John Wanamaker followed suit with his "Bargain Mart" and "Underprice Basement." The basement "idea" had come to stay, although merchants like Louis Stern wrestled with its social implications. "I do not admit there is a necessity" for the "basement," he said. "Such distinctions" [as it fosters] "are undemocratic and un-American—certainly alien to the New World ideas of equality." But "be that as it may, I see no reason why Bargain Basements should not be a success on their merits, apart entirely from such considerations."[32]

Other store spaces were of a different social character, "unstorelike" special spaces, "salon rooms," and small "arcade shops" built to meet what merchants believed to be middle-class desires and expectations. In the fall of 1902 the decorators at Simpson-Crawford, a downtown Manhattan department store, assembled three bright pavilions in the grocery department to display bottled goods, meats, fish, and crackers, each pavilion roofed over by a lighted opalescent glass dome and edged by oval glass display cases. Gimbels in New York set a precedent in 1912 when it arranged its linoleum artistically in the rug department; the rugs were assembled in big rolls to accent line, shape, and color, and the department itself had the look of an "oriental mosque."[33] In Chicago, Marshall Field's boasted a most enticing interior display in its fur department on the fourth floor. As in millinery, cloaks, and lingerie, the Field's management accommodated in its displays the pocketbooks of many customers: Thus, on one side of the department were tables, counters, and glass cases selling a cheaper line of fur and fur accessories; on the other side were the truly extravagant items, sometimes worth tens of thousands of dollars. Down the department center (and throughout the floor as well) were an array of large illuminated glass cases carrying a luxurious mix of fur garments.[34]

The whole interior of Field's fur display, keyed to class distinctions, was calculated to stir up feelings of social inadequacy and envy and meant to inspire impulsive buying. It worked, but not always in the best interest of Field's. By 1910, furs were so seductively on view that outbreaks of shoplifting were endangering the department's well-being. "Few" of the "shoplifters," however, "were professionals," as a Field's manager noted; rather, they were often adolescent girls (like Fannie Schmertzler) or, even more often, well-off, well-educated, genteel women who frequently took away fur accessories. They belonged to a larger group of thieves who, from at least the 1850s, were popularly called "kleptomaniacs," a pseudoscientific term meant to identify women who pilfered all sorts of goods on impulse and not out of necessity. Such women, often never prosecuted ("I never like to have cases against such women," John Wanamaker wrote a friend in 1883) and sometimes relatives of the very merchants they stole from, were the bane and often the joke of retailers.[35] They absconded with virtually anything portable—cheap gewgaws, jewelry, stockings, and underwear— and stashed it away in parasols and dress folds. But in furs, at Field's, kleptomaniacs or shoplifters of any kind were no joke. "Furs is the most dangerous spot in the store at Christmas," said a Field's wholesale sales manager in an interview, and to meet the threat of these thieves, they had "a detective right in the middle of the department." "He always looked at everybody, looked into the eyes of all."[36]

In addition to these enticing displays in the fur department and other such places, merchants introduced the model showrooms, the most visual of merchandising pictures. As Wanamaker's engineer Harry Morrison said about furniture, it was better to organize it into "pictures than to let it stand about without any meaning whatever." The management at Marshall Field's endorsed this same strategy. "When you enter Marshall Field's," it announced in a 1912 advertisement in the Chicago dailies, "you see not only exhibition but interpretation. There, displays go far beyond simple attraction and interest. Merchandise must be shown in arrangement and environment which brings out points of utility, demonstrates beauty and novelty, furnishes fresh suggestions and reveals wider possibilities."[37]

The origins of model showrooms may be found, perhaps, in the contemporary image-making in the nineteenth-century American commercial theater, a process that yielded high profits for theaterowners. Pantomine, *tableaux vivants*, and scenic spectacles were popular theatrical entertainments, cresting in the 1880s and 1890s, when such influential American theatrical producers as Henry Irving, David Belasco, and Steele Mackaye were in their prime. All three played down dialogue and narrative and played up "living stage pictures." Irving's Shakespearean shows were less noted for dialogue and characterization than for their "archaeological correctness" and "magnificent pictures," as one theater historian has explained it. Belasco, one of America's first masters of electrical light and color, boasted that "the characters present on the stage are really secondary to the light effects." Steele Mackaye made lasting contributions to modern theater techniques by integrating scenery, spectacular action, *tableaux*, electrical visions, and mass movements onstage. He masterminded the most realistic architectural pictures ever seen up to that time in the American commerical theater.[38]

American merchants applied this pictorial strategy to the interior display of goods, organizing model showrooms on a very limited scale as early as the 1880s. By the 1910s, the rooms sometimes consumed entire floors: three acres in Gimbel Brothers in New York; and a suite of rooms in Washington's Woodward and Lothrop, "a feature," the store's advertiser said, "that has met with abundant approval and is visited constantly by Washington housewives who are seeking something that can be adapted to their homes." In 1908 John Wanamaker's in New York opened the "House Palatial," the largest permanent exhibition of furniture and accessories yet seen, a "real" two-story, twenty-four-room dwelling right in the heart of the store's rotunda and extending from the sixth to the eighth floors. The

"House Palatial" cost a fortune to heat, ventilate, and maintain and stayed a feature of Wanamaker's merchandising until the next decade, when Rodman Wanamaker had it torn down to make way for more elevators and more efficient display space. "Authentic in almost every way," it could have been lifted right off a Belasco or Mackaye stage. It held—among other features—staircases, a butler's pantry, a servant's dining quarters, an Elizabethan library decorated with tiger skins, a Jacobean dining room, a Louis XIV salon, and even a large Italian garden off the dining room. Mannequins staffed its rooms and guarded the foyer. The set was decoratively lighted and looked lived in, with books tossed about and golf clubs propped against the walls. Complete assemblings of furniture, drapery, and art taken from departments throughout the store were set up in every room to give the public the most up-to-date standards of decorative "taste and beauty." Wanamaker built this "model showroom," he claimed, with the "mass market" in mind. But it was really a desire space empowered by a tension between mass and class and not by the homogeneous "mass." Indeed, if the House Palatial had really been for everybody, who would have wanted any of the expensive goods it contained? According to store reports, over 1 million people a year were visiting it after 1912.[39]

The "Eliminating" Power
of the Central Idea

Merchants and commercial impresarios of all kinds worked "central ideas" through their interiors, "core ideas" that associated their businesses or activities with some specific desirable feature. The purpose, as one displayman put it, was to "eliminate" the literal character of merchandising space, to sever its bond with commerce and business.[40] Once again, as in the case of the model showroom, the conception of the "central idea" may have originated in America's theatrical districts in the late nineteenth century; spectacle stage productions owed much of their appeal to the way directors and designers carried a single theme throughout a show. Dependence on central themes may also have come from the world's fairs, the success of which depended in part on the articulation of core themes. From the 1876 Centennial Exposition in Philadelphia commemorating the American Revolution to the World's Columbian Exposition of 1893 in Chicago and the

1904 Louisiana Purchase Exposition in St. Louis, themes bound the fairs together. As Herbert Croly, future intellectual leader of the Progressive movement, wrote of the 1901 Pan-American Exposition in Buffalo, "Gayety is the dominant note, transporting visitors into surroundings as different as possible to those to which they were ordinarily accustomed." "Everything is festive and entertaining" and proves that "seemly surroundings may be an element of happiness."[41]

The American pageant movement, so popular in middle America after 1900, may have also been a source for the "central idea" strategy, linking or tying parades, performances, and music into unified ensembles. For a scenario to succeed, wrote Bernard Sobel, expert pageant manager and later an important theatrical agent on Broadway, "it must have a unifying idea, capable of dominating the entire pageant." The design and color must be coordinated to make "a permanent and unified impression."[42]

Whatever the origins of the central idea as a basis for interior decoration, by 1915 it was *de rigueur* for theaterowners, restaurateurs, and department store retailers to design adult fantasy environments. In the late 1890s, the impresario Oscar Hammerstein transformed several of his roof-garden restaurants into hideaways where New Yorkers could escape the urban grind and grime. His Olympia Theater Roof Garden on Broadway and Forty-fifth Street became a pastoral grotto, with arbors, ponds, rocks, and a small bridge. "Here," wrote a visitor, "the wearied eye of the summer sufferer in Gotham can rest with a refreshing sensation upon the cooling spectacle of several swans in one pool of real water." Other roof gardens were converted into "a grand promenade at Monte Carlo," into a "Dutch farm" complete with a "cow-shed," and a duck pond with a "pretty rustic bridge."[43]

Elsewhere in New York City, tearooms and cabarets were opened with similar interiors, including such eating places in Greenwich Village as Romany Marie's Rumanian Tavern, with its decidedly "foreign decor"; the Mad Hatter on West Fourth Street, with its Dickensian ambiance; and the Pirate's Den on Christopher Street, fully rigged and fitted out in buccaneer style. One entered the Pirate's Den through a "small but heavily bolted oaken door," thence to finesse "a narrow hallway dimly lighted by flickering candles in ships' lanterns." As painter Newell Wyeth would later describe it, patrons were compelled to "grope [their] way up twisting stairways, along ships' balconys [sic], captains' walks, and such-like paths" until they "reached a large room stacked with guns, racks of cutlasses and hundreds of pistols. Ropes, tackle of all description, boarding irons, culverines, brass cannon, cages of parrots and monkeys—all lighted with ships' lanterns!"[44]

Retail merchants pursued similar strategies. "Eliminate the store by weaving through it some central ideas," advised Austrian émigré decorator Jerome Koerber in 1912; he headed display at Strawbridge and Clothier in Philadelphia and greatly influenced other decorators.[45] Let one "central idea" unify the goods, wrote a Wanamaker decorator in an essay, "Power of Store Decoration." "Every occasion for the emphatic treatment of certain goods should be treated in like manner, for I have seen, through years of practical experience, the truth substantiated, viz., 'People do not buy the thing, they buy the effect.' " "Subordinate the details to one central idea." "Make the whole store a brilliant showplace."[46]

Exploiting this concept in every way, merchants decorated their establishments to look like French salons, rose or apple-blossom festivals, cornucopias, "the streets of Paris," Japanese gardens, semitropical refuges in the middle of winter, or southern plantations.[47] "An indolent oriental atmosphere"—shieks, tents, exotically dressed women—"pervaded every nook and corner" of Sanger Brothers' Department store in Dallas in March 1900.[48] The Easter fertility theme ruled at Siegel-Cooper's in April 1900, with cages of live canaries suspended from ceilings and huge stuffed rabbits distributed throughout the store. Jerome Koerber (and his twenty-four assistants) played out the "opera theme" at Strawbridge and Clothier in January 1911. He decorated the rotunda and aisles in a "buff and gold color scheme," carefully arranged wax figures in furs and opera attire on the main floor, and hung portraits of famous opera performers on the walls. Louis XIV furniture was placed at entrance, exits, and in salon areas.[49]

John Wanamaker so excelled in these strategies that he was called the "Kiralfy of merchandising" by some of his admirers, a description he loathed because of the reputation of Imre Kiralfy as an often shameless architect of some of America's most notorious stage spectacles. Yet, from the 1880s until he died, there was little Wanamaker or his staff did not do to play up the decorative power of the central idea. In December 1895, for instance, figures of angels were used to dress the rotunda of the Philadelphia store. "They are all flying upward," Robert Ogden reported in a letter to Wanamaker of the core display of "Angels" (he called the whole display the "Flight of Angels"), which Wanamaker could not see himself because he was in Europe. Ogden made clear, however—and photographs he sent helped to verify—what the decorators had done. "The leading angel," he wrote, is "at a greater elevation than any of those that follow, each succeeding figure, or row of figures, being lower than the one in front. The descent from the first one to the last is probably fourteen or fifteen feet, although the differences do not appear so great when viewed from the floor." Ogden urged Wanamaker to hold the photographs above his head to get a better idea of what he meant. He also pointed out what Wanamaker could not see—the numerous "Brownies" interspersed with the angels (the negatives, he wrote, made these difficult to discern), the "color and light," and the full visual character of the display that had taken a "great deal of imagination to put . . . before you." It has been, he boasted, a "great success and has created a great interest."[50]

Much of this Christmas spectacle at Wanamaker's foreshadowed what would become in the 1920s garish use of religious iconography for merchandising purposes, as Wanamaker's decorators inserted "perfect replicas" of medieval church rose windows—and even entire facades of the Cathedrals of Rheims and Chartres—into the store rotundas.[51] But the precedent had been set earlier. For the 1898 Christmas season, Wanamaker erected a "huge model of a church" in the rotunda of the New York store, with an organ and choir standing ready at intervals to entertain customers.[52] (See plate 12.)

Secular themes were even more intricately interwoven into store life, binding together interiors and goods. In the winter of 1908 for two weeks, Wanamaker devoted all of the interior of his Philadelphia store to the central theme of the "Bride's Jubilee." The "whole store was surcharged with wedding vibrations." Pink and white colors appeared throughout on nearly every floor. Demonstrators, who worked in the furnishings department in the basement, conducted a "cooking school for brides," showing them how to operate new "gadgets" and kitchen equipment. High up on the eighth floor, a "bride's totally furnished house, rich in suggestion," was on display. Situated on nearly every floor—around every corner, near every elevator— were *tableaux*: a prenuptial scene with a bride and two bridesmaids "exquisitely gowned," "the bride at breakfast," two scenes showing the bride in French lingerielike gowns for receptions, dinners, and balls, the bride "receiving friends in her new home," the "bride's afternoon on the porch," the "bride in the kitchen," and so on. "Every bride's home is a palace," one card read, "is it not?—whether one room or a mansion." An organist in the grand court played wedding marches at intervals. In the store auditorium theater, a pianist demonstrated a domestic name-brand piano, "the Knabe ideal," as the "proper upright piano for a bride."[53]

A New Child World and
"Paradise in the Toy Department"

Merchants thought up special themes and special colors for children's merchandising as well. By 1910, American retailers were forming a significant "publicity structure," as they called it, for children, a shift that reflected the production of a whole new variety of children's goods. Before 1890, most American children wore, ate, and played with what their parents made or prepared for them. There were almost no domestically manufactured goods for children. But in the next twenty years, the sale of ready-wear clothing, sportswear, and candies for children ballooned, as did baby clothing. In 1915 the baby clothing industry alone was one of the largest national industries, with seventy-five factories operating in lower Manhattan.[54]

The growth of the American toy business was nothing short of phenomenal, output increasing by 1,300 percent between 1905 and 1920. "It is a marvelous industry today," John Wanamaker told his toy buyers in 1916, "and the people who manufacture toys get large salaries."[55] Before 1900, such stores as Macy's in New York and Wanamaker's in Philadelphia, both of which had reputations as toy dealers, displayed what toys they had en masse only on a seasonal basis, breaking up the toy sections once holiday festivities had run their course.[56] Siegel-Cooper's in Chicago opened its "Toytown" in 1908 on the sixth floor, laid out in graded streets and avenues and covering nearly an entire block, an expansion that broke through the limits of the older toy "section." Then, a few years later, Namm's in Brooklyn and The Fair in Chicago were among the many stores to embrace year-round toy departments, to "create a desire for ownership at all seasons of the year."[57] In 1912 Marshall Field's adopted the same policy and, in addition, systematized its toy displays, segregating the toys according to children's ages and by outdoor and indoor categories.[58]

Among the reasons for this growth were better manufacturing, exceedingly generous protective tariffs, a swelling demand for children's toys, and crucially, the crushing of the German toy business during World War I. Between 1913 and 1917 (and after the war as well), U.S. factories exploited German belligerency, reviling the Germans as "butchers" and their toys as "blood toys." American business relied on whatever stereotypes it could to eliminate German competition.[59]

Between 1915 and 1917 the United States achieved its first huge international mass market toy "success" with the marketing of the racist "Alabama Coon Jigger," a laughing, prancing mechanical toy Negro male.[60] (A "killing" was made off of this toy by domestic dealers, including John Wanamaker, who continued to replenish his stock whenever the "coon jigger" sold out.)[61] An array of toys mimicking on a miniature scale those commodities sold to or used by adults came into existence after 1905. Toy firms manufactured bicycles, tricycles, express wagons, and scooters; mechanical playthings besides the "coon jigger" multiplied, including electric trains, power stations, and signal towers; and educational toys—blocks, Erector Sets, spelling boards, and painting kits—emerged as profitable investments. Americans invented "cuddle" toys, talking dolls, soft-bodied dolls, and rubber dolls complete with lifelike limbs, real hair, and eyelashes. The money spent to make doll carriages and houses alone nearly matched the $3 million invested annually to construct baby carriages for real babies.[62]

The character the new child's publicity structure took, however, had its source not simply in this production but in a much broader shift in the treatment, care, and education of children. For most of the nineteenth century, children were enclosed within the adult society and economy. Unless removed from their homes to serve as apprentices, they usually worked alongside their parents or with other adults, nurtured or exploited within the context of these relationships. But after 1880 or so, growing numbers of children were separated from adults. The appearance of new kinds of adult labor (professional, technical, and corporate) required extensive schooling, and compulsory-schooling laws pulled children out of the work force. The growth of wages and salaries, coupled with greater reliance on birth control and a consequent decline in the birth rate, made it possible for many parents to devote more time and money to individual children. Psychologists and philosophers started to write about children as a distinct group with special needs.

Through no effort of their own, children acquired rights and preferences equal in importance and scope to those of adults. Yet, through no fault of their own and at the same time that their parents were becoming intimately involved in their welfare, children found themselves cut off from adults in new ways. They also became vulnerable to the stresses and exhilarations of new needs and expectations that children of former times barely had the occasion to imagine, much less experience or express.

American retail merchants recognized and exploited this trend. In 1902 Marshall Field's inaugurated its "Children's Day," because, as Harry Selfridge, Field's manager, said to his staff, "children are the future customers of this store, and impressions made now will be lasting." Five years later the store converted its entire fourth floor into "the Children's Floor."[63] Then, in 1912, Field's advertisers announced in the Chicago dailies that

> the vast unfolding of the modern child-world is important to this mercantile institution. Not every person realizes that there is a children's demand for merchandise and service. Yet there is naturally. Little people's interests, their desires, their preferences, and rights to merchandise are as strong and as definite as those of any adult portion of the community. An ever-growing attention is being given children and their requirements at Marshall Field and Co.

Merchants were sensitive to new patterns of culture and, in particular, to the new "child-world." And like urban merchants everywhere, Field's was developing strategies of enticement for children, devising separate displays for children, separate interlocking departments for children similar to those created for adults, a distinct child world. "Every attention shown the child," said one expert, "binds the mother to the store." Get people "as kids," another child market advocate reasoned, and "you will have them as customers for a lifetime."[64]

The heart of the children's merchandising structure was the toy store. Today, toy sections in department stores have shriveled; but in the early part of the century, they emerged almost out of nowhere to become the golden goose of holiday merchandising. They were not simply selling spaces but fantasy places, juvenile dream worlds, as retailers liked to claim. Through them merchants started to achieve age segmentation of the market and, in so doing, to place the "child world" on a par with the adult in strategic marketing importance. Fed by what seemed to be, at the turn of the century, an adult appetite for fantasy and escape, the merchandising treatment of toy departments forged an alliance among children, stores, and consumer desire. It helped impose heavy market pressures on adults, creating another channel for the flow of commodities and money.

"It was Paradise in the toy department," remembered Hughston McBain, president of Field's in the 1940s, whose mother brought him as a boy from Grand Rapids, Michigan, to Chicago on shopping tours in the early 1900s.[65] "What a change there has been," said another merchant in 1912, the year of the Field's editorial, "in the method of making toy displays, and what a revelation to children. . . . Now we have a horde of attractions that were not even dreamed of ten years ago."[66] Merchants transformed the interiors of toy departments. They radiated display areas with diffused colored light, hung globes of color, and decorated with "incandescent starlight." Toy departments became among the most visually "pleasing" and "fantastical" parts of the stores, expressing "the real romance of the fairyland of toys." "Give your toy store a name," suggested one proponent of color, "preferably with color attached." How about "At the Sign of the Red Rabbit?," "Pink Pig?," or "Purple Cow?," the man suggested.[67]

Practical and literal-minded merchants who once ridiculed the use of theatrical devices in retailing were now thinking in colors and metaphors, turning their stores or parts of them into "carnivals," into "fairytales" and "pink elephants," and, most profitably of all, into homes for Santa Claus and his Christmas elves. Before the mid-1890s, Santa Claus seems to have been an icon unattached to any single institution except the private bourgeois home and hearth (but even there, he was a relatively new fixture). But when the large department stores first began to overshadow retail districts, Santa Claus's status also started to metamorphose. The big merchants laid claim to him and to the imagery of the Christmas holidays. Urban merchandising began to give substance and form to the Christmas rituals. "Live" Santa Clauses took up residence in children's toy departments and sections.[68]

The commercialization of Santa Claus would have its most impressive flowering in the 1920s, as we shall see in the last part of this book. But long before then, retailers were groping for ways to exploit Santa Claus for commercial purposes. In the 1890s, stores put him in small, out-of-the-way sections. Then other strategies were tried, such as bringing him from the North Pole to town on railroads, meeting him at train depots, and depositing him with fanfare at the central stores. In the big urban toy departments, Santa Claus sat on lavishly decorated thrones, often working busily away (in a typical scenario) promising children the presents they asked for, attended by elf-workers in green and red.[69]

There were children's Christmas spectacles, the most sophisticated at Wanamaker's New York and Philadelphia stores, where the interior holiday parades were so costly that few other retailers could come close to matching them, although several tried. When a local minister complained that the focus on Santa Claus seemed out of keeping with a Christian Christmas, Wanamaker reassured him that "Young people very early grow to understand that [Santa Claus] is a mere pleasantry and tradition. I do not believe that it detracts from the story of the coming of Christ."[70]

Wanamaker already had a large children's business in the 1890s, but his toy section then was small, plain, and "just a sort of holiday thing," as he put it, a mere "incident" in store business. In fifteen or so years, however, the department became "a permanent thing" and "one of the best floors in the house."[71] By November 1912, he had decided to "eliminate the business atmosphere" in his children's sections and to redesign the toy stores "in a manner really theatrical in its appeal." He dressed the walls with decorative murals, hung semicircles of varied colored lights from ceilings, and planted "terrifying" green dragons and huge plaster heads of comic figures across the floor, where mirrors reflected flashes of colored lights.[72]

From this point on, toy departments in the New York and Philadelphia stores grew more and more elaborate, literally year by year. Wanamaker struggled to "outtop" himself and all other merchants; in December 1914 he moved the New York toy department from the basement to the fourth floor, where it stayed for the next forty years, and at Christmastime he decorated it and the rotunda with "monster Jumping Jacks," giant clowns, circus shadow pictures, gold and silver cubicle stars suspended from the ceiling, and the "largest Rabbit Family in the World."

Two years later, Wanamaker presented a store parade organized by his display team of William Marston and Harry Bird, the latter trained in the theater and a friend of the theatrical impresario and playwright David Belasco.[73] From November 9 to Christmas Eve, every day at ten-thirty in the morning, the lights were turned off in Wanamaker's toy department and thousands of children watched a parade, heralded by trumpets and drums and led by a uniformed brass band of Wanamaker employees. A stream of storybook characters from Jack the Giant Killer to Chanticleer and the Funny Clown flowed by, and finally Santa Claus appeared, seated on a royal palanquin [a kind of raised platform] and carried regally by four Eskimos to his Royal Red Theater in Santa Town. New features were added to the 1919 parade—little girls dressed as snowflakes and little boys as silver stars and tinkling bells, and a fifteen-foot locomotive "seemingly self-pro-pelled" and drawing a flatcar with a big packing box marked "Handle with Care." Santa Claus occupied a rainbow-colored balcony behind a blue and gold railing, looking like an oriental deity surrounded by his elves and gnomes. He passed out little three-inch dolls to the children who sat on his lap and whispered their desires.[74]

Santa Claus, then—and the whole spectacle of Christmas itself—belonged to the new constellation of interior enticements that formed a crucial part of modern merchandising. He belonged to the mirrored glass, the escalators, and the model showrooms; to ventilation and the "angels flying upward"; and to the class tensions stirred up in the fur department, as they all expressed the determination of businessmen to merchandise virtually every moment in the human life cycle, from the cradle to the bride's prenuptials. But there was another feature to this unfolding enterprise that proved, in some markets, to be just as lucrative, a strategy also driven by class and social differences and, above all, by the desire for the new.

Chapter 4

FASHION AND THE
INDISPENSABLE THING

"Fashion!" wrote Jerome Koerber, decorator and display manager at Strawbridge and Clothier in Philadelphia, "there is not another word that means so much to the department store as *Fashion*."[1] Fashion merchandising built on and complemented the new pictorial and theatrical strategies of business. It employed many women as well, some in high positions, most in the lowest paying jobs, just as display and advertising employed many men. Hundreds of women like Faith Chipperfield and Anne Evans worked as fashion buyers, traveling and living in Europe, and rising to positions of considerable influence.

Unique to Western business practices, fashion merchandising was a theatrical strategy *par excellence* that embodied the quest for the new. Like window display and the toy store, it democratized desire; it carried exciting meanings and introduced the mass of consumers to everything from the aristocratic glamour of Paris to the exotic allure of orientalism. "Fashion," a 1908 retailer said, "imparts to merchandise a value over and above its intrinsic worth" and "imbues with special desirability goods which otherwise excite only languid interest."[2] Its intent was to make women (and to a lesser degree men) feel special, to give them opportunities for playacting, and to lift them into a world of luxury or pseudo-luxury, beyond work, drudgery, bills, and the humdrum everyday. Its effect was often to stir up restlessness and anxiety, especially in a society where class lines were blurred or denied, where men and women fought for the same status and wealth, and where people feared being left out or scorned because they could not keep up with others and could not afford the same things other people had.

At the same time, in the context of the American mass market, fashion demanded constant change, incessant newness, gravitating to this idea or that idea depending on the idea's marketing potential. Since the specialness of any single fashion tended to go stale or vanish quickly as many consumers struggled to buy it, merchants had to supply the market at a feverish rate to maintain the fiction of glamour or uniqueness. This, of course, tended to serve business well if finessed skillfully, producing regular turnover and even addictive purchasing.

In an 1894 essay on women's dress, Thorstein Veblen said that fashion was based on the view that "nothing can be worn which is out of date. A new wasteful trinket or garment must constantly supersede the old one." Veblen's observation was not so much a critique as a rendering of the way things were: what he said was what businessmen themselves said. "When the impression is forced on consumers of all classes," wrote a business editor in 1903,

> that the last season's coat, costume, or hat is irretrievably out of date, a demand is created that cannot but result most happily for those whose business is to cater thereto. And this is particularly true in the United States, where the wearing of last year's hat or coat or costume is an evidence of inability to buy—an inability which every American man or woman hesitates to admit. This is the fact that should be recognized by all connected with the trade, nor should any fail to make use of the powerful lever thus put into their hands.[3]

Fashion pressed people to buy, dispose of, and buy again. It dealt not with the utility or the enduring artistry of goods but with their fleeting appeal. Merchants promoted this volatility by ritualistic announcements of the coming spring and fall fashions, preparing people in advance for the artificially created shifts in fashion.

Fashion was the thing itself—the "new," the heart, supposedly, of what was desired. By the outbreak of World War I, it was taking several forms, including outrageous "royalty" promotions, the fashion show, and the fashion extravaganza. In 1913 Rodman and John Wanamaker presented what was perhaps the most impressive early fashion spectacle of them all: the Garden of Allah.

The Growth of Fashion and A Gigantic Garment Industry

By the mid-nineteenth century much of the structure of the American fashion market was in place. Fashion magazines, such as *Peterson's*, *Harper's Bazaar*, *Godey's Lady's Book*, and *The Home Journal* carried fashion news to urban women and sent emissaries to Paris to learn the latest trends. Specialized shops and fancy dry goods stores, like A.T. Stewart's of Manhattan, dispatched buyers to Paris to report home about the new styles. Still, throughout most of that century, fashion was confined, by and large, to a small population in a few large cities; fashion's pace, its changes in style and design, were slow, due largely to the limits of travel and communication. After the late 1880s, telephones, the wireless, a transatlantic cable, and the appearance of the first steamships and cruise liners made swifter transmission of ideas and designs possible, intensifying the tempo of fashion. Marketing fashion became more and more important to stores, driven by the production of ready-to-wear goods, which altered the face of retailing.

At the foundation of this growth was a gigantic textile and garment industry expanding at a rate in the biggest cities after 1885—and especially in New York City—two or three times as rapidly as in any other industry. By 1915 the clothing trade was America's third largest, ranked only by steel and oil. Cotton and woolen mills proliferated in New England and moved into the South and Pennsylvania, along with silk factories. In 1875 silk was a small, luxury-market, and localized industry and, although mechanization was clearly under way (as it was not in Europe), it was still dependent on artisanal skills and hand-loom methods. By 1910, American silk manufacturers in centers such as Paterson, New Jersey, had dropped hand looms for full mechanized production, with reliance on high-speed automatic machines tended by cheap, "speeded up," unskilled labor. Such machines, which the industry quickly and uniformly imposed on a work force accustomed to traditional handicraft methods, yielded abundant silk cheaply, in 1900 alone making use of nearly 10 million pounds of raw silk (up from the 680,000 pounds of 1870).[4] A process called "dynamiting," or the injection of metals into the fabric, simultaneously added a new gloss—"glorious colors," as labor radical William Haywood called them—and shortened the fabric's "life and durability."[5] The market was now a large one, fueled by perhaps the highest demand yet for silk garments. As Elizabeth Gurley Flynn, also a labor leader, observed, although "silk [used to be] a luxury, in 1913 . . . it was stylish. Every woman wanted a silk gown, and the more flimsy it was the more she wanted it."[6]

By World War I, American silk mills were each year using more raw fiber than all of Europe combined, according to textiles specialist Morris D'Camp Crawford. Annual output in the garment industry as a whole was well in excess of $1 billion; fifteen thousand establishments made women's clothes in New York alone, employing more than five hundred thousand, mostly unskilled immigrant women and children at dirt-low wages.[7] Manufacturers fought for such labor because it saved money, made them competitive, and greatly increased profitability.[8] They relied on subcontracting, a system whereby a manufacturer paid only two or three men directly to organize the work; these men, in turn, hired other cheaper workers who, in turn, hired sublaborers (women, children, and other men); the whole chain was forged around cheap labor, keeping wages low—and working conditions intolerable—for almost everyone. The evolution of the fashion world rested, in fact, on the most exploitive, the most backbreaking, and the most sweated industry in all American business (as it still does today).

As pressures to push ready-made and other manufactured goods mounted, growing numbers of merchants became convinced that fashion was an indispensable abracadabra. "The way out of overproduction," wrote one fashion expert, "must lie in finding out what the woman at the counter is going to want; *make it*; *then* promptly drop it and go on to something else to which fickle fashion is turning her attention." "Constant change," wrote another, "through the entire gamut of material, color, and design, is essential to the prosperity, alike of producers and distributors."[9] Fashion had become "the kingpin of the entire dry goods industry, producing and distributing."[10]

Urban retailers built branch offices in Paris, Berlin, London, and Vienna. They sent "fashion promoters" over to copy the models of Paris couturiers "down to the slightest detail such as a lace insertion," because, as one American promoter wrote, "the only type of model that our public would then buy had been thoroughly publicized in the various fashion journals." With no American domestic designers of any reputation, retailers were forced to reproduce the "latest mode" from Paris, but for a broader, less affluent clientele, "at exactly one-third the cost."[11] The upper-class French trade, in other words, became an American mass market.

Women Buyers and the "Queens" of Paris Couture

As another sign of its booming expansion, the fashion industry also employed many women at high salaries, even as it degraded many more at low wages. In the early 1890s most buyers in the U.S. fashion business, as in merchandising generally, were men, but by 1915 almost a third of the 10,849 retail buyers were women.[12] At the forefront of the industry as a whole were such women as Rebecca Ehrich, founder of fashion-conscious Ehrich Brothers in New York; Mollie Netcher Newberry, owner and head of the mass-market Boston Store in Chicago; and Lena Himmelstein, creator in 1904 of the Lane Bryant specialty stores for "the big beautiful woman." But a rising number of merchandising managers, personnel directors, and advertising managers were also women.[13] Women buyers in particular represented so many branches of the business before World War I that John Wanamaker included them in his New York Board of Trade, the highest executive advisory board of his firm.

The rise of women buyers (nonfashion as well as fashion buyers) did not come without some dissent or discomfort from men, many of whom insisted on and were given control over high-volume, hard-line departments—shoes, for instance, or furniture, house furnishings, glassware, and carpets and rugs. As one of Field's male buyers confessed, "I chose carpets and rugs because floor coverings was more a mannish style of business."[14]

Wanamaker himself seemed to be of two minds in regard to working women, as were many merchants and manufacturers who were increasingly depending on female labor. He was conventional, sometimes, in his praise of the homebound woman who sacrificed everything for her husband and children; and he promoted men first in his stores and paid them bigger salaries. Yet he was a champion of woman's suffrage over many decades, and he urged the employment of women in any and all fields of endeavor. He had, in fact, a vested interest in muting whatever reservations he may have had about hiring women (and there appears to be nothing, in his existing private and public writings, to show he was ever very concerned about the exploitation of women, say, in the garment trades). Like the other businessmen throughout the consumer industries, he saw the competitive economic advantages in cheaper female labor, even as he noted the intellectual benefits for women in pursuing fulfilling work beyond the home. "Where is a woman's proper place?" he asked in an advertising editorial that appeared in all the influential Philadelphia dailies. "Anywhere." Women should not be "limited to scrubbing, dusting, and cooking and 'minding babies'!," he said in 1914. "Women everywhere have been and are now, educating themselves for business . . . for the sciences, and for 100 professional and expert callings." "For intelligent and educated women there are a hundredfold more and greater things for her to do in the world than ever before."[15]

Wanamaker treated many of his female buyers as essential to the success of his business; he praised them, though he paid them less than he did men, and many (but not all) became devoted to him. Nancy McClelland, an enterprising Phi Beta Kappa graduate of Vassar College, created Au Quatrième at Wanamaker's in New York in 1912, the first decorating and antiques department in a department store. She was perhaps the most imaginative antiques buyer in the country. Both Wanamaker and his son Rodman "guarded her from overdoing things which break down her health." When she decided to leave Wanamaker's to create her own firm, Nancy McClelland, Inc., at 15 East 57th Street in Manhattan, Wanamaker was dumbfounded. "I never thought that you would leave us," he wrote McClelland, in behalf of himself and Rodman, "and both of us have wanted to do, and tried to, everything we could to add to your happiness and to the success of the undertakings which were under your care."[16]

Many of the buyers Wanamaker and other merchants hired spent their professional lifetimes going back and forth to Paris and elsewhere, scouring for style ideas. In 1902 Wanamaker wrote Rodman of a seasoned forty-nine-year-old female buyer he had just employed to market cloaks and suits, that she "went to Altman's at the age of twelve, served there for thirty-seven years, left in a huff because of changes made in her department while abroad," and *crossed the ocean seventy times.*" In 1900, Lena Robenau, who had worked as a clerk in Macy's glove department for the previous five years, was promoted to buyer by Isidor Straus, Macy owner at the time. She remained at Macy's for the next thirty-one years. She was the first buyer of French gloves in the United States to go abroad; she bought gloves also in England, Scotland, Germany, Switzerland, and Italy. And whatever she bought, she bought as an independent merchant and under her own authority. Macy's, she said, "left me a free hand" and "almost never criticized me. All questions were left to my own discretion."[17]

The female fashion buyer who bought in Paris was the "queen" among the "queens of retailing," as the trade press often called her. Her trips abroad were celebrated by store staffs. People lined up at piers to drink champagne in her honor and to wave good-bye. Sometimes her departure was filmed, as in 1915, when Anna Robertson, millinery buyer for Namm's on Fulton Street in Brooklyn, left on her twenty-sixth European trip. Cameras recorded her arrival in Paris, her meeting with the heads of the Paris office, and her excursions about through the headquarters of the Paris stores. "I spent the happiest days of my life," another buyer recalled, "working before the war in Paris for one of the finest department stores in the country."[18]

Many fashion buyers went to Europe and remained there for as long as they could. In the early 1900s Faith Chipperfield, one of Wanamaker's Paris buyers, took advantage of Wanamaker's generous "health and recovery" policy by going on vacations in Europe for long stretches of time. "She was to be absent for forty days at our expense," an irate Wanamaker complained to Rodman, "but was so shattered in her nerves that she begged for and was granted more time, but she has stayed on and on indefinitely. She should now be called home or resign her place. . . . I think it demoralises our forces to have any of our people batting around as if they could do just as they pleased."[19]

Chipperfield rejected Wanamaker's appeals and resigned, promptly disappearing from the Wanamaker record books. But she resurfaced—almost immediately—in the records of Filene's in Boston as one of the store's Paris fashion consultants. In 1912 she formed a partnership in Paris called "Fashion and Merchandise Representations" with another fashion buyer, Anne Evans. Both women were college graduates. Chipperfield had two degrees, a B.A. and a B.S. (as her stationery indicates, although it does not say from where), and would even acquire a reputation as a translator of minor French novels for the American market, including Pierre Mille's *The Monarch* and Ch. Chivas-Baron's *Three Women of Annam*. Living in New York City in the 1950s, she wrote a historically sound and widely reviewed biography of Margaret Fuller, *In Quest of Love*. The book is very readable if a bit breathless, emphasizing "the story of Margaret Fuller's heart." "Is it not time to remember [the woman] who lived and longed for love?"[20]

Chipperfield's partner, Anne Evans, enjoyed "doing Paris" and spending time with colleagues and friends at "drinking places near the Sacré Coeur." In 1919 she bumped into Woodrow Wilson at a formal Paris reception, right after the signing of the Versailles treaty. "I was standing near him when he was unoccupied," Evans wrote a business associate, "and [the ambassador] had told him what our work was when we were presented to him. He engaged me in talk, and kept me there. It was a unique opportunity to speak to him, as one never expects to do more than see, at such large affairs. I shall certainly never forget it."[21]

Chipperfield and Evans worked together in their business for the next seven years, participating in the formation of a greatly enlarged international circuit of American fashion merchandising. They wrote, edited, and published their own fashion magazine, Paris Vogue, for such department stores as Gimbels. "I noticed last night the little fashion sheet of the Gimbel people mailed from Paris," wrote an envious Rodman Wanamaker to his father, "it certainly ranks with the best we ever had."[22] The two women collaborated closely with a group of stores—Scruggs in St. Louis; Forman's in Rochester; Rike-Kummler in Dayton, Ohio; Bamberger's in Newark; Lazarus in Columbus, Ohio; and the biggest of all stores in sales of women's clothing, Filene's in Boston. Both women "spent years pouring precious information into the stores" on an almost daily basis—information on prices, on manufacturing processes, on the latest lines, and on the American competition. "Though prices are high in Paris," they wrote in a typical report to Filene's, "Gimbels, Field's, F. Simon, and Jordan's are placing orders for as far as a year ahead, and are cancelling nothing"; and, in the same letter, "The waist manufacturers are getting up some mighty pretty merchandise, and they expect a lot of American buyers over here." They conducted analyses in great detail of the buying operations of the French department stores, and, after 1918, operated a mail order shopping service for Filene's so American parents could send packages to their sons at the front. In 1919 they conducted a thorough "survey of foreign markets" that helped lay the groundwork for the first Paris office of the Retail Research Association (RRA).[23]

The RRA was to provide a common pool of merchandising data on both the domestic and foreign scenes for more than twenty participating stores. It marked new trends—the consolidation of merchandising at home and a greater extension of American fashion merchandising on an international scale.

Rodman Wanamaker and
the Queen's Slippers

Believing that the magical link to everything Parisian was a near guarantee of fashion-minded customers, the big retailers imported any and all promising French devices or ideas. Harry Selfridge of Field's visited Printemps and the Bon Marché in Paris for help in converting Field's into a major retail store. John and Rodman Wanamaker looked continually to Paris for fashion suggestions. They loaded their daily fashion advertising with French phrases such as *offres merveilleuses, vente de blanc, en vente ici, ce qu'on doit savoir,* or *choisissez maintenant.* [24]

Rodman learned far more about Paris merchandising than his father ever imagined or expected when he sent him abroad to become resident manager of the Paris house after his graduation from Princeton in 1888. Immersing himself in French life and culture, Rodman became an urban "cosmopolite" with interests and passions quite contrary to those of his still-rural, still-plebeian father, a man who failed to attend high school. Rodman played the piano; composed fashionable French salon music; and studied French painting, sculpture, jewelry, textiles, tapestries, furnishings, antiques, and French museums and palaces. He collected art books and art objects in staggering quantity, and in 1893 he organized the American Art Association in Paris, to become in twenty years among the most prestigious gathering places for American artists. Rodman lived part of the year with his three children and first wife, Fernanda, in a "sumptuous apartment . . . on the Avenue of the Elysian Fields." He acquired a taste for silk underwear, and he sent blue silk underclothes to his female relatives. "One morning, last winter," a female relation wrote Rodman in 1894, "I had a glimpse of a 'dream of love' in blue—it was you in your underclothes after bath at Meadowbrook—Tommy, as you may know, has brought me a lot of those 'things' and I am in seventh heaven. They are the most beautiful and delightful garments imaginable. Next summer I am going to wear nothing outside them! Come over and see me!" In the mid-1890s he gave lavish dinner parties, bestowing on each of his guests at one of these affairs an entire leg of mutton, a basket of peaches, a double magnum of champagne, a bottle of rare wine, and a piece of costly jewelry thrown in as the evening's souvenir.[25]

In 1898 Rodman and his family returned to Philadelphia to join his father at home in running the business, a dream John Wanamaker had long hoped to realize. In 1909 Rodman was made full partner with his father, then resident partner in 1911, when he took command of the New York store. Probably because of him, Wanamaker's created one of the first Paris salon rooms for the display of French lingerie, rooms actually prepared in Paris and shipped intact to New York. During his years in Paris, he had sent home fashion advertisements, catalogs, clothes labels, designs for de- livery wagons, style illustrations, and countless artifacts for sale and display. "We didn't know what to make of it," his father said later of his son's behavior; we "began to think Rodman had gone off his head. We didn't understand the things he was sending over."[26]

Fashion by now had begun to infiltrate every dimension of the clothing industry, and although it would take another twenty or so years before it affected such other goods as furniture, sporting equipment, kitchenware, and so on, it was already securely on the tip of the tongue of every de- partment store merchant. Because "fashion is to be the keystone of our regular business," recorded a Wanamaker executive in 1911, "it follows that our purchase of special lots should be dominated by the same policy which would mean the exclusion of everything *conspicuously* out of fashion."[27] New fashion journals—*Vogue, Cosmopolitan,* and *The Delin- eator*—appeared, joined by *Women's Wear Daily,* soon termed the "bible of retailing," whose daily reporting on fashion and American merchandising in general reflected both the rise of the ready-to-wear clothes business and the quickening pulse of fashion itself.

To promote consumption, merchandisers exploited the "regal doings" of elites at home and abroad, hoping they could trickle down to shape the fantasies of ordinary consumers. They linked their goods to high-class status, to royalty and upper-class glamour, and to luxury of all kinds, including the luxury of notorious French courtesans. DuBarry lingerie and Pompa- dour silks were marketed, Imperial Underwear, Regina Petticoats, Royal Waist and Skirt Supporters, and Princess Loop-Belts, as well as Royal Typewriters. Wanamaker's had its Marie Antoinette rooms, Marshall Field's its La Belle France rooms. Lingerie rooms—"special boudoirs"—enticed women into the stores, often by invitation and with the promise that no men, of course, would be admitted into these sanctuaries, "so that milady might admire to her heart's content without embarrassment." The rooms, merchants claimed, offered access to "a little bit of another world," "a world little known even to American women."[28] In the fall of 1908 a rumor was purposely broadcast throughout the trade that perfumes "made and named for nobility exclusively, are now being sold in this country under numbers instead of names."[29]

"The woman of today," wrote one trade spokesman, "desires magnificence—desires it more than ever before. And she is willing to pay for it. And the minds that best understand how woman is pleased, and who devise all kinds of ingenious things to separate the aforesaid woman from her money, have not been idle. They have searched far and near for just those beautiful ideas which will titillate the Vanity of 'Her Majesty,' the money-spender. And they have succeeded admirably."[30]

In 1906 Wanamaker's in Philadelphia put on an extravagant exhibit in honor of the French Revolution, not the first nor the last of merchandising's trivialization of the historical record. The exhibit was capped by a display under glass of "exact" replicas of the severed heads of Louis XVI and Marie Antoinette, as well as their "genuine" coronation crowns. So commonplace was this kind of practice that it gave rise to professional tricksters who peddled fake royal artifacts to urban retailers. "I see," wrote one such shark to Macy's, "that your competitors advertised yesterday that they have on show the Coronation Robe of the Czarina. Would you like to go them one better? I have a pair of Silk Stockings worn by Queen Victoria on the occasion of her marriage, also the White Slippers. These are marked V.R. with the Crown, I can prove to your satisfaction that they are authentic. Are they worth anything to you to have on show for one week or so? If so, how much?" There is no record of response from the Straus brothers to this offer. But modern merchandising took such sleight-of-hand seriously.[31]

Fête de Paris: The Fashion Show

The most sensational innovation in American fashion was the introduction of the exclusive and intimate Paris fashion show into the mass market. In New York City, Ehrich Brothers, founded by Rebecca Ehrich in 1857 as a fancy specialty house that catered to upper-middle-class women, probably put on the first show, in 1903, although the precise beginnings of such trends are almost impossible to nail down. In ten years the form of the fashion show was nearly fixed: Living models paraded down ramps in store theaters or departments, spotlighted by light engineers to a musical accompaniment, sometimes with "dramatic effect, as in the theater," one trade magazine noted, "when an extra hazardous feat is being performed while the spectators are breathless." Often organized around themes—Parisian themes, yes, but also Persian, Chinese, Russian, Mexican—many of these shows presented "the spectacular settings of a well-staged play."[32]

Gimbel's "Promenade des Toilettes," first given in 1910, went through twenty variations in five years. Thousands of women streamed into the store on Thirty-fourth Street and Seventh Avenue in Manhattan to watch the models parade daily up and down the ramps in their fashionable Parisian costumes. In 1911 the store's theme was "Monte Carlo," with casinos, roulette tables, and fake Mediterranean gardens built into the store theater. Thirty-four models strolled down a promenade reaching all the way from the theater to the store's dining room, lined with "thousands of seats [along the route] to accommodate the thousands of women from New York and surrounding suburbs." Gimbels' tearoom was converted to look like the "Monte Carlo de Paris."[33]

Wanamaker's fashion shows in Philadelphia and New York were probably the most cleverly prepared shows of all, inspired as they were by the insights of Rodman Wanamaker. The fall 1908 presentation was a pretentious "fashion Fête de Paris," got up in the Philadelphia store theater in a gold and red setting meant to suggest the court of Napoleon and Josephine. On either side of the theater, Mary Wall, the show's impresario, had arrayed enormous picture frames trimmed in black velvet, with live mannequins in the latest Paris gowns posed inside. At intervals spotlights were directed to two of these models in *tableaux vivants* as they stepped out of their frames. Escorted by a child dressed as one of Napoleon's pages, the models strutted down the walkway into the audience to the sounds of soft organ music and Mary Wall's script describing the virtues of each costume. The event concluded with a full-scale re-creation of the coronation of Napoleon and Josephine.[34]

Wanamaker invited one hundred "socially prominent women" to the first day of the show, an elite in Philadelphia to inspect the delectables of the elite in Paris. For the next two days, the rest of the women of Philadelphia were welcome to see the show and, so the store reported, hundreds of thousands did. "This Fête de Paris," wrote one impressed journalist for *The New York World*, "has stamped Wanamaker's as the authorized interpreter of Paris, and proclaimed beyond question that the Empire was to be the dominant mode of the season."[35] Rodman Wanamaker's "Paris Conference" of New York outdid his father's "Fête de Paris" of Philadelphia. Rodman, too, had manipulated class distinctions to propel the little engine of fashion. He immersed the "entire store"—not just the theater—in the "glamour of Paris." In the "fashionable" afternoons, only the swagger rich could gain admittance; in the "less fashionable mornings," the unfashionable majority were allowed to enter the store. Live models displayed gowns by Poiret, Worth, and Paquin, with spotlights punctuating their comings and goings.[36]

In the late teens New York Wanamaker's interpreted other international themes—for instance, the peasant Mayan theme, then a proven hit in the fashion world. In 1917 Rodman staged the first "sports fashion show" based on the prevailing Mayan "motifs." Tall glass cases throughout the theater displayed garments modeled after Indian designs—purses with Mayan embroidery; sports hats bound with Mayan scarfs; cushions made from Indian blankets; and parasols copied from Indian ponchos. At the extreme ends of the promenade stage were framed pictures enlarged from photographs taken by the store decorator to show the "treasures" of the lost Mayan civilization. "Authentic" Indian women were placed strategically near these pictures, along with a "line of Indian huts" depicting various aspects of Guatemalan culture, each serving as an "educational" backdrop to the living models in the Mayan-inspired clothing.[37]

By 1915, from Baltimore, Maryland, to Waco, Texas, the fashion show could be found in nearly every sizable city in the country. It became a semiannual event. There were children's fashion shows and cooperative fashion shows assembled and given by several stores at once. These shows drew thousands of people at a time. They were so potentially disruptive to the ordinary conduct of city life that police in New York and elsewhere ordered merchants to take out licenses for all shows that employed live models, and, in Manhattan, even threatened to terminate the shows altogether.[38] Merchants, too, worried about the "demoralizing" impact on other store business as customers packed into theaters, tearooms, and restaurants, or lined the promenades.

For some merchants the situation deteriorated so badly that they were forced to move the shows out of the stores into local theaters, which soon emerged as competitive centers for fashion show productions. Fancy restaurants with built-in circular stages also began to put on fashion shows. The popular Terrace Garden, a "veritable dream garden," one merchandiser wrote, on Madison Street in downtown Chicago, was constructed in the shape of a Roman circus, with tables arranged in tiers, "one behind and above another and each one looking down on the stage." At special times of the year, for weeks on end, "the smartest fashion shows" were conducted, fifty to seventy models at a time parading before an audience of regular customers, eager fashion buyers, and manufacturers of wearing apparel.[39] By the late 1910s fashion shows had even evolved into fantastic spectacle pageants held outdoors, multimedia affairs with orchestras, models, and special effects.[40]

The Garden of Allah

Perhaps the most popular of all merchandising themes in the years before World War I was the oriental theme, fashion from the bottom up, as it were, not, as with much of Paris couture, from the top down. If Paris fashion modes often suggested escape from the hoi polloi into the genteel elegance of class and status, then orientalism hinted at something else, something perhaps not so urbane and genteel, even at something slightly impermissible—luxurious, to be sure, but also with touches of life's underside. Depending on the fashion of the month or year, each particular subtheme might be Islamic, Indian, Japanese, or Chinese, with stores decorated as mosques, temples, or desert oases. (See plate 6.) Organizers of the world's fairs, from the early 1890s on, interpreted similar themes, but especially at the fairs held in San Francisco, Buffalo, and St. Louis. Movies and the commercial theater also turned to the Orient to drum up trade. Ironically, in the very years when the U.S. government was restricting the immigration of Chinese and Japanese people into this country, American cities were creating Japanese gardens in botanical parks, and merchants were reveling in the money value of Chinese culture and aesthetics.

Literary critic Edward Said links this orientalism to Western imperialism and argues that personification of non-Western peoples as impulsive, primitive, uncivilized, and prone to uncontrollable passions and desires merely served to inflate Western self-esteem. By insinuating that non-Westerners were children and thus incapable of caring for themselves, orientalism justified Western predominance and the occupation and appropriation of foreign property. The historian Robert Rydell has argued similarly in *All the World's a Fair,* writing that American and European fairs at the turn of the century showcased Western prowess at the expense of other cultures and societies.[41]

Yet even as European and American orientalism distorted and demeaned non-Western cultures, it also exposed an underlying sense in Westerners themselves that they lacked something vital that "Orientals" had. Orientalism was symptomatic of changes taking place within Western society—and especially in cities—that had little to do with imperialism or with the desire to appropriate somebody else's property, but that symbolized a feeling of something missing from Western culture itself, a longing for a "sensual" life more "satisfying" than traditional Christianity could endorse. This dissatisfaction had begun to form in the United States from at least the 1850s, when the first generation of affluent American "tourists" visited non-Western countries and wrote home about the colors and designs they saw there; some published highly romanticized books about oriental attractions.[42]

By 1915 the dream life of many well-off Americans bore the imprint of orientalist fantasies. Students and faculty at Harvard and Yale, rebelling, perhaps, against the dull conformities of their parents and churches, devoured the steamy orientalist fiction of Rider Haggard, Edgar Saltus, and J. K. Huysmans. The urban rich of New York and elsewhere, floating on a tide of huge industrial wealth in the early 1900s, attended private parties dressed as pashas and rajahs, harem dancers, and Persian princesses. Louis Tiffany lived most of his adult life engulfed in oriental luxury. When Alma Mahler, composer Gustav Mahler's wife, visited Tiffany's Manhattan apartment in the late 1890s, she thought she had entered a Persian retreat, a mysterious "Paradise . . . filled with palms, divans, panes of flowering light, lovely women in iridescent gowns." "It was," she wrote, "a dream! *Arabian Nights* in New York." In the winter of 1913 Tiffany, beturbaned and wearing Turkish pants and a brilliant blouse, took part in an oriental costume ball at Delmonico's (one of many such balls held that year), where everyone's dress was modeled "after the treasures of the ancient past discovered in excavation by archaeologists."[43]

By 1918 Americans had seen numerous film versions of Cleopatra's life. The Broadway and operatic stage also had its share of orientalist shows, from Straus's *Salome* and Puccini's *Madama Butterfly* to John Masefield's

The Faithful and Edward Sheldon's *Garden of Paradise*.[44] Through the medium of orientalism, influential stage designers like Lee Simonson, Norman Bel Geddes, and Joseph Urban delivered more and more lavish color to American theater audiences. "The quality of the Oriental is in his work," wrote *The New York Times* of Simonson's stage designs (the same could have been said about the work of Urban and Bel Geddes as well), "which comprises some of the boldest and most beautiful stage designing America has yet seen. . . . He burst forth upon the peace of the American art world five years ago . . . with a disturbing insistence on a more courageous use of color."[45]

Novels explored oriental themes, also, from *The Damnation of Theron Ware* by Harold Frederic at the beginning of this period to Inez Haynes Irwin's *Ladies of Kingdoms* at its closing in 1917. In both novels, the orientalist decor symbolizes a radical break from Christian culture. In the Frederic novel, a young minister, Theron Ware, is seduced from his ministry by an "emancipated" young Irishwoman, Celia Madden, whose "apartment" resembles an orientalist dream, with colorful "cushions and pillows," statues of nude men and women, rugs and matched woods in yellow and blue, and a huge "oriental couch" consuming "about three sides of the room." Celia Madden is, in fact, the embodiment of the space she lives in—"lustrous and creamy," "exquisitely soft like the curtains," "fiery," and "intense."[46] Inez Haynes Irwin, a leader of the feminist movement in the United States, twenty years later virtually reproduced the same decor for her lead character, Southward Drake, and endowed it with the same feminist meanings. As the novel begins, Southward is living in her grandparents' mansion in rural Connecticut, where she has fashioned for herself, high up in the house, a fantastic "garret" decorated in oriental motifs; the walls are covered with colorful crepe, turning the room into a rajah's quarters. "It makes me think of the *Arabian Nights*," observes one of her few visitors. Here Southward lolls about on divans and dons orientalist garb, "a tomato-colored prince's coat" and "a high Chinese head-dress" with "many coloured silk pompons," and hatches her plans for individual pleasure and adventure.[47]

The creator of the bejeweled Emerald City, L. Frank Baum, wrote exotic novels, among them *The Last Egyptian: A Romance of the Nile* (1908); and *Daughters of Destiny* (1906), a story of Balukistan, an "oriental" country "where color is everything" and people live "amid the luxuries of perfumed baths . . . and musk-scented cushions of the oriental divans."

In contrast to "stiff Americans" and "scheming" and "deceiving" Western merchants, Baum says, Balukistanis were "free and wild," "children of impulse" who "obey only the dictates of their hearts spontaneously and scorn the cold formality so much affected by Westerners."[48]

Orientalism, then, was an extremely popular trope, entering into every kind of cultural activity. But the main cause for its spread lay in the nearly overnight efflorescence of America's new consumer industries, with their high distributive and marketing demands. American business purveyed the orientalist message and, seeing an opportunity, began to praise the very things—luxury, impulse, desire, primitivism, immediate self-gratification—that only decades before they had been disparaging as dangerous to economic productivity. Not that merchants ceased to criticize these new values—they did not (nor did religious groups or ordinary men and women). But they spoke now in two voices, each at odds with the other. For work and production, business (as much of the culture at large) emphasized repression, rationality, self-denial, and discipline; but for selling and consumption, it opened the door to waste, indulgence, impulse, irresponsibility, dreaming, or qualities thought of as non-Western.

Whatever the complexity of the widespread interest in things oriental, then, American business furnished the principal means for their transmission and for the creation of a new national dream life for men and women. Other groups might have transmitted a less distorted, a less ahistorical orientalist message—the new anthropologists and archaeologists, for instance, the radical and alienated young bohemians from Harvard and Yale, who might have at least tried to understand Eastern cultures as they were instead of resorting to them for therapeutic release and excitement, and the immigrants themselves from "orientalist" cultures. But these countervoices, even if they existed, were not strong enough to take hold over public sentiment.

Businessmen did what they wished with this new mythology, especially through the medium of the "tie-in," a concept unique to twentieth-century business. The tie-in allowed merchants to occupy the visual-psychic space of adults and children with many different kinds of imaginative material, not just with orientalism. In one small-scale tie-in in 1914, Macy's management "linked up Macy dresses and fashion articles," a seventeen-year-old "popular actress" (provided to the store by "Kalem Agency"), and the "fashion pages of local dailies."[49] On a larger canvas, retailers joined their resources to project uniform ideas in cooperative fashion and style shows, in cooperative advertising campaigns, and in the "synchronizing" of their holiday decorations and displays. [50] On a March night in 1916, for instance, all the merchants in downtown Birmingham, Alabama, unveiled their windows at the same time, opening "Fashion Week" and "turning the city into a blaze of light."[51]

In the most highly charged form of linkage, superficially dissimilar commercial institutions—theaters, retail stores, restaurants, hotels, and movie houses—embraced similar themes. Unlike the more sophisticated concoctions of the 1920s, these prewar tie-ins were largely informal, even slightly naive, and based on a mutual recognition by merchants that certain themes had obvious marketing appeal.

Among the earliest and most successful of such promotions occurred just before the war, when many commercial institutions exploited an extremely popular novel, *The Garden of Allah*, by Robert Hichens, an Englishman and son of a liberal preacher. Early in his life, Hichens wanted to become a dancer but, lacking much paternal encouragement, he turned to journalism and then to novel writing. An admirer of Oscar Wilde and André Gide, both of whom were attracted to oriental themes, Hichens, in the late 1890s, visited Algeria, Egypt, and other Islamic countries; he fell in love with them and began to write books with oriental themes, among them *The Spell of Egypt* (1908), *The Holy Land* (1910), and *Bella Donna* (1908). Two were made into plays, then into movies, both silent and sound. [52]

The Garden of Allah was Hichens's own favorite. In the overwrought style of a typical sentimental novel, it expresses European disenchantment with rational civilization, with conventional order and behavior. It seems to make a plea for emancipation from repression and for what Hichens called "new life" in touch with "animal" passions. In one form or another, the book was written over and over in this period by both men and women. Hichens's contemporary Rider Haggard could have written a book like Hichens's (and done it better), and L. Frank Baum tried to—but failed.

The Garden of Allah opens with the heroine, Domini, a thirty-two-year-old unmarried Englishwoman on her way to North Africa and bored with the rational West, "aching" for something to connect her with the "elemental forces" in the oriental world. "She wanted the roar of the tom-toms," Hichens writes. "She wanted more than she could express, more than she knew. It was there, *want*, aching in her heart." She wanted the "abrupt unveiling of the raw. There had always lurked in her an audacity, a quick spirit of adventure more boyish than feminine. She had reached the age of thirty-two without ever gratifying it, or ever fully realizing how much she longed to gratify it. But now she began to understand it and to feel that it was imperious. . . . Her soul seemed to hear the footsteps of Freedom treading towards the south. And all her perplexities, all her bitterness of ennui . . . were swept away. She was free from the pettiness of civilized life."[53]

These passages were the soul of the book. As the plot thickens, Domini is drawn into the mystery of the desert (the Garden of Allah). "I have the barbarian in me," she says. She visits a "wild" Arabic eating place where women dance "fiendish" dances and where she meets another "beginner in the desert," Boris Androvsky, an English-Russian who is "full of sex and passion." They "surrender" to one another, ride into the desert together or "into solitude, into the terror of it." They rush into marriage and begin to set up their desert home.

At this point in the novel Hichens had second thoughts and shuts off the heated flow of his narrative; the book's sex turns out to be all in the foreplay. In a ritual pattern common to this type of potboiler and at the very moment his characters seem to be getting down to business in paradise, Hichens forces both of them to pay for their heedless desires. In a burst of guilt, Androvsky confesses to a shocked Domini that he is really an ex-monk gone astray, and he must return to his Russian monastery. Domini weeps and grieves but soon recovers. After all, she will always have the memory of her Garden of Allah.

The 1904 publication of *The Garden of Allah* made Hichens a rich man. Although the book was a commercial failure in England, it had a terrific sale in the United States, passing through forty-four editions over the next forty years. Three films were made of it, two silent, the third a 1936 technicolor sound film starring Marlene Dietrich and Charles Boyer.[54] In 1907 Hichens was invited by the American actress Mary Anderson Navarro to adapt the novel for the stage at the New Century Theater on Broadway, a theater with capacity for "gigantic spectacles." Although the "sandstorm went all over the people" on the opening night and "the animals" made several "messes" onstage, the performance was "truly magical." It began, Hichens remembered, with a scene that was

> gradually flooded with light, and lo! there was the desert stretching before me. A pause! Another shout, this time behind the scenes:

the light gradually faded, night seemed to fall on the desert. I looked upwards and saw the firmament, a deep fathomless, blue sky studded with stars that seemed to hang on it. . . . I have never before seen such a perfect representation of a cloudless African night sky on stage. While I looked another change. Night faded gradually into a perfect representation of the strangely cold and mysterious coming of dawn.

Although Hichens was distressed that the producer ignored the dialogue or even the narrative as it had been conceived, he was delighted with (and, given the take-home pay, very thankful for) the "spectacle."[55]

In Chicago the "attendance was enormous," and people were turned away "for lack of room every time it was given." In a 1912 revival in New York the play was an even greater success. In this year—and for at least the next ten years—hotels and restaurants were decorated to resemble scenes out of *The Garden of Allah*. Commercial artists like Maxfield Parrish accumulated a tiny fortune creating magazine covers, advertisements for candy companies, and commercial posters of scenes from *The Garden of Allah*. In Hollywood, Alla Nazimova, the first actress billed as a movie star, built a fantastic country estate on Sunset Boulevard called the Garden of Allah, with a swimming pool shaped like the Black Sea; later she shrewdly converted the estate—keeping the name—into one of Hollywood's most talked-about hotels, the temporary residence, at one time or another, of most of America's movie screen royalty. Several large department stores organized sensational fashion shows around the Garden of Allah theme. In Chicago in 1912, troups of Arabic men from the cast of the Chicago production of the play were borrowed by Marshall Field's, the Boston Store, and The Fair to parade in sham Islamic dress around the main floor and theater during the fashion shows.[56]

The most extensive *Garden of Allah* fashion show was conducted at the New York Wanamaker store in April 1912. The stage was a facsimile of the "cloudless African sky" with the "lustrous stars" that had so impressed Hichens on his play's opening night. Six "Arab men and two women" (the men brilliantly turbaned and firmly muscled) were recruited from the Broadway cast to "walk about" through the store's arcades or to stand silently in the theater. Various bronze and oriental figurines, borrowed from Wanamaker's own collection, adorned the theater stage and lined the promenade. A string orchestra played oriental music as more than thirty models sashayed down the ramp, in costumes modeled after Algerian designs. Sometimes a spotlight was thrown on a "particularly stunning costume, and there were times, when a specially favorable impression was made, that the audience burst forth in applause." An inspiration of Rodman Wanamaker to excite interest in the new fashions based on Arabic themes, this *Garden of Allah* show attracted thousands of women, some unable to see a thing or to find seats, many refused entrance altogether.[57] (See plate 13.)

Fashion, interior display and decoration, and facades of color, glass, and light, then, were among the key strategies of enticement of early-twentieth-century American consumer capitalism, forming the basis of what was to come. But something else was at work as well, something even more encompassing, that greatly extended the frontiers of consumer society and that carved into the older American culture a newer culture, a culture that seemed to offer everyone access to an unlimited supply of goods and that promised a lifetime of security, well-being, and happiness.

Chapter 5

ALI BABA'S LAMP:
SERVICE FOR PRIVATE AND
PUBLIC BENEFIT

"The chief profit a wise man makes on his sales," Wanamaker wrote in 1918, in one of his many entries on service in a memorandum book, "is not in dollars and cents but in serving his customers."[1] Service was a recognition by merchants that they had some obligation to care for and cater to the needs of customers as well as of workers. It marked something of a turning point in industrial capitalism, which in the minds of many had for so long invoked only dark, satanic mills and undying penury. Its hallmark was not "the public be damned" but "the public be served."

Service included new kinds of consumer credit (charge accounts and installment buying) to ease the pain of purchase; a new work force to fuss and fawn over patrons; and multiuse spaces for consumer pleasure. It institutionalized what German Americans called *gemütlichkeit*, or a way of living given over to "pure" comfort and relaxation. An American form, service integrated "high art" with "low art," popular with elite culture. It led to the creation in stores and hotels of art galleries, of musical concerts, and of entertainments that covered the spectrum from the very refined to the very vulgar. Between 1880 and 1910 the concept of service had an almost grandiose character, an ambition to address or reflect some of the most pressing social needs of the country. Businessmen created it in part to mollify their own employees and to give the impression of public benevolence and goodwill. But the *raison d'être* of service, as with the other strategies of enticement, was always to empty pocketbooks and wallets. Its guiding logic was to awaken *individual* desire. As the Catholic radical Peter Maurin wrote in 1932, the service that emerged in America after 1880 was "commercialized hospitality" or "service for profits."[2] Service showed off commercial institutions to their best advantage, working its way quickly throughout the consumer sector to include hotels, restaurants, theaters, retail stores, and urban public utilities, where volume turnover was of decisive importance to economic success.

Service as a "Profitless Ideal"

By 1910, American businessmen were introducing a network of services into their institutions. The idea was relatively new, and Wanamaker—"peer among merchants," as his colleagues called him—probably was its most vigorous advocate. "My customers have a right to exact from me," he said in 1886, "all the service that it is possible for me to command."[3] "Stores ought not to exist," he said ten years later in a widely published advertisement, "simply for the benefit of the men who keep them but for the greatest good of the greatest number. This is not a Wanamaker store in one sense— it is the people's store, owned and managed by Mr. Wanamaker, who benefits himself and partners through the benefits secured by the store for the people." And again, five years after that: "The store of the future will command audiences only by the imperial right of superior service. It will be the employ of the Public."[4]

Wanamaker compulsively came back to this theme, as if he needed to persuade others who might be dubious about his motives that he was no capitalist, no moneymonger, but a Christian person committed foremost to the people's welfare. Wanamaker claimed that his "New Kind of Store," as he put it, was built principally for profit but also in response to the needs of the people. "This New Kind of Store," he said in a 1906 speech commemorating the expansion of his Philadelphia store, "as it was soon termed and quoted everywhere, came to life at the cry of human need. It met customers with conveniences as their due, and not courtesies. It rehabilitated the people in their rights by the new deal we instituted."[5]

Gimbels, Wanamaker's archrival on Market Street, shamelessly picked up this strategy—to Wanamaker's undying disgust ("Gumballs," he wrote his son, "are audacious and unscrupulous as copyists").[6] "Gimbels is not written in the possessive case," Gimbels Brothers announced in the same newspapers Wanamaker used. "We do not call it 'our store.' It's your store. It is an institution for service. And the statement is without buncombe." New York's Siegel-Cooper's followed the pack: "This is a People's Store," announced a store paper in 1904, echoing the populist-consumer rhetoric used by H. Gordon Selfridge in 1902 to open the new Marshall Field's store at the end of the retail wars.[7]

Hotel merchants Ellsworth Statler and Lucius Boomer pushed the service angle aggressively, Statler resembling Wanamaker in the ardor of his commitment to service, preaching the gospel of service to all who would listen.[8] Born in 1863 in Pennsylvania, he was the son of a poor German Reformed minister who grew to detest preaching and abandoned it for merchandising. In the 1870s the family moved to Ohio, where Ellsworth worked first in the local glassworks (tending the furnace, or "glory hole," as it was called) and then as a bellhop in a small hotel. In 1900, in Buffalo, he tried the restaurant business but failed because many still preferred eating at home, but he triumphed a year later there and in St. Louis after that, with two giant hotels to serve each city's fair. The hotels were dismantled when the fairs were over.[9]

In both Buffalo and St. Louis, Statler practiced a new kind of "perfected service," rejecting the exclusive palatial style hotel. Service, he said, must be seen in capitalist terms as a "salable piece of merchandise" or an exchangeable good like any other.[10] By 1919 he owned hotels in New York, Buffalo, Detroit, St. Louis, and Cleveland, the first chain of standardized hotels for the mass market in the world. Each had rooms for all pockets, from $1.50 up, and a choice of services ranging from cheap to deluxe. "The Wizard of the Hotel World" crusaded for what he called the "profitless ideal." "A hotel has just one thing to sell," Statler said, "and that thing is service. The guest is always right."[11]

Statler's ablest rival was the always immaculately dressed chairman of the board of the Hotel Waldorf-Astoria Corporation, Lucius Boomer, whose reputation rested on the management of hotels for the rich or well-off. His vision of service came to influence the entire hotel industry. A dropout from the fledgling University of Chicago, he was drawn into the booming hotel business of the 1890s and managed hotels in Florida; in Canada; in Brighton Beach, New York; and finally in Manhattan. In 1912 he opened the twenty-five-story Hotel McAlpin, according to him "the largest hotel in the world," in the heart of the retail district on Thirty-fourth Street and Broadway. By 1918 he commanded the chain of hotels that held, among other fashionable hotels, the Waldorf-Astoria. Boomer would rebuild the Waldorf to its present proportions in 1929.[12] "Housekeeping," Boomer wrote, "is the essence of hotelkeeping. It is housekeeping on a quantity basis. I expect my guests to be served as they expect to be served in their own houses—only better. The only limits we place on service are those of the law and comforts of others."[13]

Restaurants and theaters followed this new service approach, as did those businesses also in the public eye—the railroads and public utilities. In 1910 the Baltimore & Ohio Railroad and the Pennsylvania Railroad, in a declining sellers' market, scuttled their old policy of taking the public for granted and announced that they would "serve" it instead. At almost the same time, American Telephone & Telegraph, the country's premier utility, "discovered," as the company's president asserted, its duty to "give its patrons the best possible service" or to conduct a telephone company noted for the "Voice with a Smile."[14] A little later, Samuel Insull, owner of Commonwealth Edison Company, Chicago's largest electric firm, initiated a program to convince the public that his company was service-oriented: "I care not how good may be the franchise under which you operate," he said to his manager, "unless you can so conduct your business as to get the goodwill of the community in which you are working, you might just as well shut up shop and move away."[15]

Holiness or Commercial Hospitality

Why did "service" find so many advocates after 1895, so many businesses presenting themselves as dedicated to the well-being of the "community"? The Dutch historian Johan Huizinga, who visited America twice in the early 1920s, believed he had the answer: in Christianity. Service originated in the medieval Christian past, Huizinga wrote, when people created traditions of hospitality and worked for the public benefit on religious grounds. But Americans had broken from this older religious heritage, although at their best they still retained the spirit of service. They espoused a "new service," a sort of secular Christianity. At many universities, in government, and even in business, "the old, deeply ethical idea of the Middle Ages . . . is awakened to a new life."[16]

Many Americans would have accepted much of what Huizinga had to say, although they would not have agreed that their "service" amounted merely to some form of displaced Christianity. For some who thought of themselves as devoutly religious, service was not a substitute for Christian activity but the thing itself. In the 1880s, Wanamaker and other merchants—such as John V. Farwell of Chicago, for instance—came under the influence of a new wave of evangelical Protestant revivalism that stressed "individual holiness" above all things. This holiness entailed a "profound personal experience of consecration, a filling with Spiritual power, and a dedication to arduous Christian service," as historian George Marsden writes. It reinforced the older idea that rich Christians had a duty to act as selfless "stewards" to the rest of society.[17] The revivalist Dwight Moody was a key figure in this movement, preaching holiness everywhere and organizing holiness conferences and institutes. The phrase "power for service" was a favorite of his and by 1890 seemed to have been "adopted by nearly all his lieutenants."[18] Moody, as we shall see in Chapter 6, very much influenced Wanamaker's religious views, and it can be said confidently that Moody's concept of holiness contributed to Wanamaker's own notion of service.

The rise of a service ideology may have been influenced also by liberal republicanism after the Civil War, with its accent on better government ("civil service") and on a renewed republican spirit. This tradition, defended largely by genteel urban elites, advocated the public over the private good and "government by the best men." Doubtless it informed the views of many merchants, among them, once again, John Wanamaker, who, in fact, served in the federal government between 1889 and 1893 as postmaster general under Benjamin Harrison. Wanamaker's strong sense of "civil service" and the "public good" blended with his Christian views and might have shaped the service in his department stores.

A far more important explanation, however, for the rise of this ideology of commercial service—not unrelated to liberal republicanism or to Christianity—lay in the "image problem" of business. Between 1895 and 1915, when merchant enthusiasm for service reached its highest point, many Americans were reacting against what they perceived to be the repressive, sometimes violent practices of the new corporations. Industrial workers, badly treated, revolted against industry, and farmers organized a populist uprising against the railroads, the banks, the land speculators, and the utility companies for price-gouging and for robbing the country blind of its lands and forests.[19] Large urban retailers were condemned by small merchants as "all-devouring monsters" and by unions as selfish institutions indifferent to the workers' welfare. From New York to Chicago, reformers berated retailers for their policies, and the National Consumers League, led by reformer Florence Kelley and others, attacked them for paying dismally low wages to clerks, for exploiting children, and—because of their wages— for forcing some women into prostitution.

Businessmen revamped their public image to try to prove that they were operating in the best interests of all. For many laborers and artisans, the question of the "people's interest" was a matter of principle, not of image, a matter of their independence and freedom from exploitation; but for merchants, the question was, increasingly, one of image. It was in their interest to give the impression that they, not their employees or other workers, were the true populists and that consumption, not production, was the new domain of democracy.

Many merchants sought to tailor their reputations so as to seem concerned, compassionate, and decent. Percy Straus, vice president of Macy's after the death of his father, Isidor Straus, on the *Titanic* in 1912, tried to erase the notion that department stores sometimes were breeding grounds for prostitution, a belief that the Chicago Vice Commission first propagated a few years earlier and that Macy's own location seemed—in the minds of many—to reinforce (the store operated in the neighborhood of what was once a notorious red-light district).[20]

In 1913, Straus invited Manhattan's Committee of Fourteen, a vigilante group collaborating with the police to end "vice" in the city's commercial districts, to inspect Macy's. His goal was to establish Macy's as "the most decent store in New York."[21] Straus, no dour puritan, had a personal interest in leading a campaign against vice. For one thing, as a German Jew and spokesman for the Jewish community, he had to disprove the charge— widely made—that immigrant Jewish women (and many of his own employees, therefore) were more likely than other women to become prostitutes.[22] Straus became chairman himself of the committee in order to demonstrate that department stores were wholesome institutions that did not exploit women; and, soon after his appointment in 1915, the committee published a report confirming that "conditions" at Macy's were, in fact, "normal." On the other hand, testimony in the "secret reports" told a different tale. Saleswomen, it revealed, passed around pornographic cards and poems among themselves, talked openly about "sex" and "sex desire," and gossiped about "fairies," as one investigator put it. Private accounts by other investigative reformers echoed this view, that things at Macy's and in other department stores were hardly "normal" or "decent." "The strongest temptation of girls in department stores," warned one reformer, "is not poverty but luxury" and "money." "It is the standard of living you are setting up," said another, "compared with the moral standards set for the girls in their [home] surroundings. They are not regarding the sex morality from the standards their mother did."[24]

Utilities, railroads, and hotels also designed employee welfare programs in an effort to dispel any negative ideas the public might hold about their employment practices. They did not go as far as union recognition or any significant increases in worker power; their welfare programs were intended, rather—at minimal cost to the firms—to give employees a sense of involvement in some larger corporate "family." The manager of Mandels department store in Chicago put it this way: "Our plan is to change a mere employee of a big store to a member of a big family in which there exists friendliness and cooperation."[25] From the 1880s—and especially after the Haymarket Square riot of 1886—businesses introduced profit-sharing plans meant, in lieu of higher wages, to allow workers to earn some money through ownership of company stock and "to make them feel like actual partners."[26] Ellsworth Statler attempted an employee stockholder scheme in 1916.[27] Other firms, such as Commonwealth Edison, created benefit programs (paid for mostly, however, by the workers themselves), baseball teams, company-owned vacation camps, and recreation spas.[28]

Because of their great public visibility, the mass retailers devised probably the most elaborate employee welfare programs in the country. By 1915 hardly a major merchant in the country had failed to dump "employees" for "store family."[29] Macy's had an almost "perfect welfare system as far as it goes" (so said the Committee of Fourteen), including a hospital; a compulsory mutual aid association; a "private school"; and a "welfare department" run by a "matron" to look after the "welfare" of the salespeople.[30] In other stores, one-week paid vacations after one year of service (two weeks after three years) were part of the deal, along with summer vacations at store retreats, in the mountains or at the beach.[31] In 1917 Jordan Marsh bought Helen Keller's former two-acre estate in Boston as a "rest home" for "worn out" employees.[32] Sears, Roebuck printed *The Skylight* in 1901, perhaps the first company magazine, edited and written by employees, in merchandising.[33] Soon Siegel-Cooper's had its *Thought and Work* (to foster the idea of "one big family"), Filene's its *Echo*, Saks its *Saksograms*, Bamberger's its *Counter-Currents*, and L. S. Plaut in Newark its *Honey-Comb Briefs*; there were more than sixty such papers in all by 1915.[34] (Not to be outdone, Statler and Lucius Boomer published employees' papers, too, respectively *Statler Salesmanship* and *Apropos*.)[35]

All these papers, however, were started by management, and Macy's even charged its employees a penny for each copy.[36] Much of the rest of the welfare was phony, many employees viewing even the more "sincere" aspects of it with skepticism or contempt. The "girls" scorned Macy's "welfare," wrote one of Macy's private investigators in another unpublished report, "as philanthropy." They hated the "matrons" for nosing around in their private affairs. "Anything provided by the store, classes of instruction, amusements, and the like," the investigator wrote, "are looked at askance."[37] On the other hand, workers "spoke very highly" of conditions in Wanamaker's of New York, considering it "a very good store to work in."[38]

Wanamaker worked hard to outshine all rivals. Although his biographer insisted that Wanamaker encouraged his "Store Family" to initiate their own welfare programs and that he was, in no way, a "paternalist," Wanamaker wrote a customer in 1902 that "I stand to [my employees] in the relation of father in a measure."[39] Wanamaker believed he had a "duty" not only to pay "legal wages" but also "to cover the welfare and education" of his people as well, and that included "all" his "people"—men and women, boys and girls, white and black.[40]

Wanamaker, animated by a sense of stewardship and even of "holiness," pursued his goals out of a heartfelt commitment to his employees. But he must also have been reacting to the era's great economic turbulence, the labor conflict, and the attacks on corporations and department stores, although he never yielded to labor unions or labor demands. He introduced his welfare policies on his own terms, to reshape his public image, no doubt remembering the warning of his trusted colleague Robert C. Ogden, who advised him in the early 1890s to respond in some way to labor or risk jeopardizing his "popularity." In May 1890 Ogden urged Wanamaker to revitalize a fading profit-sharing scheme with workers, begun in 1886, because not to do so "could be demoralizing and dangerous. Our great prominence in relation to this question makes it very important that we should make a forward movement." "The community has never been so wrought up," he wrote a year later of a new wave of labor agitation,

> as at present and we have never been so thoroughly under criticism as at this very hour. . . . We need to be popular but I have good reason to fear the public are not quite so well disposed toward us as they have been and if that is true we need to be *very* careful. . . . My remark to you on Saturday p.m. that this business is a very fine piece of machinery which must not be handled roughly is true at every angle—merchandise, employment, advertising. They all touch the vital question of *popularity* and with the cessation of this element either with our own people or the public decay will begin.[41]

A few months later, he again reminded Wanamaker that "how the people *feel* is the gauge of our success."[42]

In October 1897, Wanamaker, showing perhaps how much he had learned about taking the offensive, published a full-page advertisement in a number of newspapers promoting his store as "a people's store," not "a Wanamaker store." But at the same time he was also laying out for Terence Powderly, head of the Knights of Labor, the character of his welfare program, and explaining why—despite Ogden's argument—he had decided to cut back on his "profit-sharing plan." There was a better way to help his employees, he said. The better way was his way.[43]

At about this time Wanamaker began using music to weave a spirit of unity and family feeling in his stores. To be sure, other merchants were doing much the same thing, some even assembling store orchestras and musical societies.[44] But Wanamaker, an admirer of Richard Wagner and much German music, sneered at most of their efforts. "Strawbridge and Clothier's, Snellenberg's, and Gimbels' Singing and Musical Society," he wrote to Rodman of his nearby competition, "are too kindergartenish. We have done enough of it ourselves."[45] He had a bigger vision; by 1915 he had organized his workers (who now numbered in both stores about 12,000) into separate drum and bugle corps for girls and boys, a 650-member junior chorus, a 30-piece orchestra, a Scottish bagpipe band, a John Wanamaker Cadet Chorus of 150 mixed voices, and a yearly Choral Festival Competition to "fill the world with music," as he put it. More than 50 black employees belonged to the Robert C. Ogden Band, named for Wanamaker's close friend, testimony to Wanamaker's commitment to his black employees as members of the "family" (more than 200 ran the elevators and worked in the restaurants). The workday at Wanamaker's literally began with music, with the employees singing such "morning songs" as "Look for The Silver Lining" or "If Your Heart Keeps Right." Often the Boys' Cadet Corps and Marching Band, in scarlet uniforms with gilt buttons, marched in at eight o'clock, to present the store with a concert of band music and song. "I am very proud of the boys as they come with their drums," the Founder (as he was called) said. "They mean something. They are going to be heard of. Who isn't proud of these big boys for leading us to love music."[46]

The Wanamaker stores also had employee restaurants and medical clinics, branch public libraries, pension plans, and clubs for language instruction and debates on women's suffrage. The roof of the Philadelphia store held the largest open-air gymnasium in the world (so Wanamaker claimed), with running tracks and courts for basketball, soccer, handball, and tennis. Employee athletic clubs competed nationally in Madison Square Garden. Workers vacationed in store camps on the New Jersey seashore and in the Pennsylvania countryside. A fully state-accredited "American University of Trade and Commerce" was conducted in the Philadelphia store "at our own expense" to teach young men and women the most important, up-to-date business subjects.[47]

The pursuit of a better public image, therefore, along with appeals to Christian and liberal republican ideas, point to some of the sources of the new service ideology. But there was an even more substantial (and quite obvious) source for the new service ideology, a source implicit in the treatment of workers. As Ogden indicated, a benevolent policy toward labor was very important but not in its own right; it was important because it projected the right image of merchant benevolence, ensured "popularity," and fulfilled the larger purpose of meeting consumer needs. Service emerged, in other words, because merchants had to move goods; and because they needed to move goods, they ultimately focused not on workers but on consumers and on making consumers feel at home. "Service depends upon the satisfaction of consumers' needs and desires," as one merchandising expert later put it.[48]

It was in this context that merchants created a new form of service—

consumer service (although it would not be called "consumer" service for some time). Such service, in the eyes of a merchant like Wanamaker, was even more significant than merely producing a positive public image, and it was fundamentally remote from the earlier republican and Christian traditions. Consumer service invoked aristocratic ideas, not republican ones; it focused on the self, not on the community or on public duty or on holiness. Although it attempted to meet community needs, it was largely hedonistic, in pursuit of individual pleasure, comfort, happiness, and luxury.

It was in the spirit of this personal consumer service, existing in tension with all the other "services," that merchants showed concern for their employees—so that the employees would express concern for the customers. Wanamaker told his workers that "in whatever capacity they served," they "represented him" to the public and that his "most precious asset, goodwill, depended upon how they treated customers."[49] Every worker in his stores had to contribute to store service. In the fall of 1910, when his black employees seemed upset by some hostile customer treatment, Wanamaker met with them in a rare nighttime meeting to "see," he wrote his son Rodman, "whether we cannot lift them. We cannot leave a single stone unturned to get better service. The hurt of the business is the lack of satisfying customers by avoiding blunders and preventing complaints and by not making promises we cannot fulfill."[50]

It was in this spirit, then, that merchants like Wanamaker not only promoted employee welfare but also devised a wide range of services for customers. These included concrete commodity services—returned-goods privileges, free delivery, and easy credit—and also what could be called contextual services, that is, those services intended to provide the public with a sense of well-being and comfort. Such services aimed to get stores, hotels, and other consumer businesses into the "lifeblood" of communities; they catered to community needs by supporting charities, providing spaces for marriages, and encouraging community art and culture. Finally, the new services attempted to integrate *gemütlichkeit* into the entire consumer setting.

"Maximum Max" and
Paying the Price in Court

Before 1880, most people bought raw materials in bulk and carried the purchases home themselves; there were no packaged goods and relatively little ready-to-wear clothing. Customers and owners often got to know one another very well; and, if the contacts were good ones, it was not uncommon for merchants to offer services to customers over long periods of time. But with the small scale and intimacy of retailing, merchants followed no common or uniform pattern with all customers. Such relationships often had a special individual character. Since fixed prices were not the rule throughout the economy, people often argued over price and sometimes bartered.

Between 1880 and 1915, the new economic conditions undercut this face-to-face interaction. Merchants began to sell at fixed prices as manufactured, packaged, and ready-to-wear goods multiplied. So many ready-to-wear articles proved defective, so many items often crumbled or were soiled in transport and delivery, and the trade volume was so large, that the older grounds for trust between customers and merchants had been undermined and new grounds were required. Stores devised a standard returned-goods policy to assure customers that the merchandise was reliable. "Nothing," wrote Newark's Louis Bamberger on his decision to follow the returned-goods policy created by John Wanamaker's in the 1880s, "helped to build the store more than *this* policy." Dry goods houses and the early department stores gradually fell in line. In August 1918, Percy Straus of Macy's in a survey of New York stores found that none "refused to take back goods."[51]

A relatively reliable free delivery system also emerged between 1880 and 1915. By 1913, 73 percent of retailers in thirty states relied on motor trucks to deliver goods. Store delivery zones sometimes reached far beyond the limits of the old local store territories. Macy's wagons traveled all the way to southern Jersey and western Pennsylvania. Macy's management promised customers free mail delivery from the "Atlantic to the Pacific." The most zealous practitioner was, again, Wanamaker, who mailed free all "prepaid and charged purchases of $5 or over to all parts of the world—within the international postal limits."[52]

Most important of all, a system of easy credit was created to speed up consumption under these new circumstances. From the late eighteenth century, peddlers often sold goods on installment, as did a few furniture dealers in New York and Boston in the early nineteenth century. For small loans, people were forced to rely on peddlers, and on the ubiquitous pawn-brokers and the small-time notorious "loan sharks," who fleeced the poor at exorbitant rates. Since banks lent no money for consumer spending (indeed, a usury law was still on the books in Massachusetts in 1833), people looked to local merchants for credit; in the bigger cities, fancy dry goods houses such as Arnold Constable and A. T. Stewart in New York or Wanamaker's in Philadelphia offered "charge privileges" to their most well-off customers, sometimes allowing their wealthiest clients to pay back at their leisure. By the early 1880s, however, monthly payments were becoming standard practice.[53]

After 1880, easy credit opportunities rapidly grew in a climate less and less likely to brand the personal lender for profit a crook. Whatever remained of the stigma attached to usury was fast weakening (although even in 1910 lending for profit was still being attacked as "unspeakable"). Small loan businesses began to appear and had produced at least two chains with more than a hundred offices by the turn of the century. Illegal and limited to a few major cities, such firms nonetheless prefigured what was to emerge on a far bigger, legal scale in the 1920s. There was also a push to get more and more people—not just the rich and upper-middle class customers—to adopt charge accounts. Wanamaker's in New York opened twenty-five hundred charge accounts in October 1896 alone. Even more liberal credit policies were adopted by Siegel-Cooper's, and then throughout the trade.[54] By 1910, every large retailer in town, with the exception of Macy's (which stayed a cash house for many more years), jumped on the bandwagon. "Temptations," lamented one observer in 1914 of the rising number of credit accounts, "have been flung broadcast for anyone."[55] Merchants were finding that charge account customers were preferable to other kinds of customers, apt to buy impulsively and in larger amounts. They could be depended on to stay loyal to the same stores for a long time.

Personalized policies based on individual discretion were now either discarded or modified as merchants competed with one another for new credit customers. Credit managers sent letters to established clients inviting them to nominate friends and neighbors as charge account customers. "We are convinced," wrote Lit Brothers, a popular department store on Market Street in Philadelphia, in a 1904 form letter to all its charge customers, "that shopping is made much less tiresome . . . by having a charge account. . . . We desire therefore to request of you as one whose patronage we value, to be kind enough to provide us in the card we enclose, the names and addresses of *Not More Than Three* of your acquaintances, to whom we shall be pleased to extend the privilege of an account with us." Ten years later, Lit's was offering enticements to its customers in exchange for information on new accounts: "As an inducement to you to assist us in opening desirable Charge Accounts, we will give you *One Full Yellow Trading Stamp Book,* containing 1000 Yellow Trading Stamps, for every new account opened through your influence, as soon as the party you have recommended to us has purchased at least Ten Dollars worth of any class of merchandise."[56]

Competition for customers so intensified in Philadelphia that Wanamaker's—formerly a resource for credit information for competing businesses—stopped sharing data. "With new concerns constantly starting in business," a Wanamaker credit manager explained to a disgruntled businessman who had been refused information, "we found that we were being used to a tremendous extent in creating [other people's] credit departments."[57]

To speed up charge transactions, merchants issued round metal identification "coins" to customers as early as the turn of the century and, by the teens, stores throughout the country were using them. "It is numbered," wrote Gimbels in Philadelphia to a client about their coin, "and that number becomes a feature of your account on our books." But the coins were often mislaid, lost, or left at home by shoppers. Sometimes, too, these tiny "charge plates" (as they were also called) proved "tempting bait" to "dishonest servants" and to "outsiders who found them and used them without authority."[58]

Along with the growth in the charge business, retailers tailored installment buying to fit the needs of their less affluent customers. From the early 1880s onward, the sale of goods on time penetrated into southern black communities and into the immigrant ghettos of the Northeast, where bilingual peddlers worked out of wholesale dispensaries. In both regions, peddlers sold everything through installments—but usually with a hefty initial down payment—from rugs, clocks, and bedding to sets of dishes, kitchenware, sewing machines, and furniture.[59] Even Leon Trotsky, exiled in New York on the eve of the Russian Revolution, relied on such a peddler to furnish his rented apartment in a working-class district of Manhattan's

Lower East Side. "That apartment," wrote Trotsky in his autobiography, *My Life*, was also "equipped with all sorts of conveniences that we Europeans were quite unused to: electric lights, gas cooking-range, bath, telephone." Because of "these things," Trotsky's children were "completely won over to New York." In the same year, the youthful Dorothy Day, who was living in Greenwich Village long before she became a passionate advocate of Catholic working-class radicalism, bought a small phonograph "for a dollar down and a dollar a week." In retrospect, Day called the installment plan a "plague of the poor," "that dishonesty," she wrote, "by which the poor are robbed of their earnings."[60]

Installment peddling was backbreaking and often vicious work, as many peddlers preyed on the poor—on the black laborers of the southern cotton fields and on the non-English-speaking immigrants in the North and West, extracting every cent at usurious interest rates.[61] At the same time, many peddlers were admired and loved figures, eager to serve the communities they themselves came out of, willing to wait months for installment payments. From the first sale of baby clothing to the final burial suit and coffin, such men struck up lifetime friendships with their customers, visiting them in their homes, offering a ready ear, gossiping.[62] A few, such as Lazarus Straus and Louis Kirstein, Adam Gimbel and Morris Rich, matured into great merchants; still others were memorialized in fiction.[63]

In the novel *The Rise of David Levinsky*, Abraham Cahan described a bilingual installment peddler whom he called "Maximum Max Margolis," a seller of clothing, jewelry, and furniture to the "frequenters of dancehalls" on New York's Lower East Side. "Many a young wife," Cahan writes, "who had met her 'predestined one' in one of these halls had her marriage ring and her front room furnished with a 'parlor set' bought of Max Margolis." Margolis, a moneylender as well as a peddler, is a symbol for Cahan of the new commercial forces pervading not only the Jewish immigrant ghetto but also much of early-twentieth-century urban America. Mendacious and filthy-minded, he is always on the lookout for suckers. In the middle of the novel, Cahan's leading character, David Levinsky, himself on the make and seeking a loan from Margolis, falls in love with Max's intelligent young wife, Dora, and Dora with him. The love affair turns Margolis into a pathetic, even tragic character, victimizer and victim, a man eager to rob and at the same time robbed himself.[64]

Installment buying began to characterize middle-class buying habits as well, largely because of the production of more and more "hard goods" or durables, including farm machinery, pianos, furniture, sewing machines, and, during World War I, automobiles. In some of the newer commodity lines, such as cars, installment selling required a lot of backup capital and thus took off only haltingly among merchants.[65] In other fields, the trend emerged more quickly. In 1885 Wanamaker wrote a customer in Philadelphia, "I regret to say that our rule is not to do an instalment business." By 1900, in the midst of great growth of his piano business and the opening of huge piano salons in New York and Philadelphia, he was selling pianos on a "contract basis" that resembled the installment plan. We "tell customers," Wanamaker announced in a bold-face 1903 advertising editorial designed to *"EDUCATE DESIRE,"* "how easy it is to possess these things. . . . We tell how easy it is to possess a piano, despite its seeming large cost. At length desire ripens. And where desire is earnest, the means can always be found." Wanamaker customers were permitted to sign "contracts" that committed them to monthly payments. Down payments were apparently not demanded.[66] Ten years later, several New York City department stores introduced "instalment clubs" to "sell certain articles"—phonographs, pianos, sewing machines, and kitchen cabinets—"on the monthly payment plan instead of selling for cash or on credit."[67]

The effectiveness of such credit policies as charge accounts and installment buying, along with the generous returned-goods practice and the free delivery, can be attested to in any number of ways, not least in the mountain of returned goods that started to build up after 1900, to the chagrin and fury of many merchants. "These people," complained Percy Straus of Macy's of the worst offenders, "go similarly to several stores on the same day, make a personal selection of articles in each store, and have these articles sent to their homes from each store under the C.O.D. privileges. When they have an array of bundles at their home they may decide upon a choice, returning all the rest." "Some people return half their purchases," a peeved buyer told John Wanamaker in 1916, "they just come in to shop because they haven't anything else to do and return the goods." Wanamaker himself reported to his buyers of complete room ensembles being returned. "We have got evidence in New York where people got furniture, rugs, paintings, china, to furnish their parlors for some fête or wedding, and then returned all these things."[68] For some retailers, the situation got so bad, so chronic, as to prompt punitive action against the offenders, even to terminating the returned-goods principle altogether.[69]

The extent of response to easy credit was also reflected in the rising flow of money judgments—hundreds and then thousands in New York City alone—that poured out of city courts, charging consumers with delinquencies and forcing them to make payments or face criminal charges. People were hauled into court, among them young dandies like Frank H. Hebblethwaite, who opened a charge account at Wanamaker's in New York in 1898 for his girlfriend Jireme G. Shear. In one afternoon she carried away a carload of goods, corsets, gowns, waists, drawers, gloves, and so forth, resulting finally in Hebblethwaite's humiliation before a judge. He was required to pay $1,500 in arrears to the court. Rug dealer Haigazam H. Topakayan bought thirty-eight Indian rugs in Gimbels' rug department in 1913 for $4,000 and failed to pay a penny in installments. So, too, affluent women such as Emma Swift, second wife of impresario Oscar Hammerstein, who embarrassed her husband's credit accounts when she charged more than $5,000 worth of goods at Gimbels in 1914. Patrick Daly, James Bernard, Frances Elliot, John Brunnell, and Anna Glynn, who bought name-brand pianos at $1,200 apiece or more, repeatedly defaulted on payments.[70]

The court records also give a clear picture of the credit defaults of middle-class or upper-class women who, dependent on their husbands' income, entered the department stores only to leave with a debt that their husbands' credit could not bear. After 1900, so many wives were behaving in this way that a new kind of court case appeared that reflected legal confusion over what "necessaries" were, about who was obligated to pay, and whether such women should be prevented by their husbands from shopping at all in department stores. The resolution of these cases was eagerly awaited by all retailers.[71]

A "leading" or precedent case, *Wanamaker v. Weaver*, passed through three different court proceedings between 1901 and 1903.[72] In early 1901 Alice Weaver, wife of Simon Weaver, a businessman in Rochester, New York, went alone to Philadelphia to attend a wedding; while there, she opened a charge account at Wanamaker's under her own name without telling her husband. With a "metal coin" issued her, she bought toys, towels, shoes, and table linens. She returned to Rochester, then came back again to Philadelphia for hosiery and more towels and shoes. When her debts mounted, she failed to pay. Wanamaker informed Mr. Weaver and took him to court, since according to Wanamaker's understanding, in common law, which still governed the obligations of marriage despite the passage of the married women's property acts in New York, husbands had a duty to provide wives with "necessities."[73] The question in this case was whether Mrs. Weaver had really purchased necessities and had a legal right to bind her husband's credit, even though she had opened the account under her own name.

At the trial before a Rochester jury, Mrs. Weaver testified in support of Wanamaker's position; she said that even though she was "well supplied," the goods she purchased were "necessaries." She had bought "hosiery at Wanamaker's," she said, "because they did not have in Rochester the kind she wore"; despite the numerous towels she already owned, she bought more of those, too, at Wanamaker's "because she thought they were a bargain." The jury ruled against Wanamaker because Mrs. Weaver failed to notify her husband, could not bind her husband's credit simply because she had married him, and because she had bought goods that were not "necessaries."[74]

Wanamaker appealed the decision before the Appellate Division of the New York Supreme Court, convinced "the principle was of considerable importance"—merchants had to be legally assured that they could dependably extract payment for goods purchased on credit by married women.[75] This time he won, the court deciding on his behalf that merchants should not be forced to make "inquisitorial examinations" of wives about their husbands' credit. It affirmed that a wife had a legal right to buy "on her husband's credit articles which are intrinsically necessaries in view of her position in life, though in fact not necessaries because of being adequately supplied, unless the goods are sold after his express prohibition to extend credit to his wife."[76] Mr. Weaver, inflamed by this decision, appealed to the New York Court of Appeals and was victorious, the court ruling on the same grounds as in the Rochester trial—that his wife had not gotten his permission, that she did not "need" what she bought, and that Weaver had already supplied her with enough "ready cash." Besides, the court said, in a rejection of common law, the 1880 marriage laws of New York State had established that wives could be agents in their own right rather than through their husbands. Mrs. Weaver, therefore, was liable to pay for goods she bought from Wanamaker because she had done so under her own name.[77]

Wanamaker v. *Weaver* constituted an attempt to clarify and resolve a thicket of issues, but it seems to have done so, ultimately, to no one's satisfaction. "The decisions in the books relating to necessaries," James Schouler, the most respected legal authority on marriage, would write in

1920, "are somewhat confusing; the more so since the dividing line between law and fact is not marked with distinctness. Sometimes the jury decides whether articles are necessary, sometimes a judge."[78] But *Wanamaker v. Weaver* exposed more than a failure of resolution; it also brought to light the enormous strain placed on marriage by the new commercial economy, which set husbands against wives and cut away at social bonds. Like the other default cases, it testified to the new dangers posed for everyone by the merchants' "education of desire" and by their servicing of easy acquisition.

Over the years those same merchants would launch many counter-measures to stanch the flow of defaults and returns, from lobbying for state laws allowing them to place garnishments on workers' wages to creating a new credit apparatus to provide credit information on consumers.[79] They helped found the National Association of Retail Agencies (1906) and the Retail Credit Men's Association (1912) to monitor consumer activities and to establish reliable consumer ratings.[80] But whatever their efforts to contain or discipline, in the name of service to the people, the floodgates had been opened. " 'Charge It' is the slogan of the great American consumer," wrote a retail credit man in 1915. "It enables a man to spend next month's salary with ease and safety. 'Charge It' is the modern Ali Baba lamp. Armed with these precious words an American citizen can go downtown with an empty pocketbook and return home reeking with luxury. Later he may find it necessary to liquidate a large number of bills at 37 percent, plus attorney fees."[81]

Customer as Guest in "Self-Sufficient Citadels"

Ali Baba's lamp held a great deal more by way of "service" than easy credit, returned-goods privileges, and free delivery. It contained as well a form of service to meet community needs and to treat customers as guests in pleasing, comfortable settings. This kind of service, which many Americans associated with the very essence of the democratization of consumption, was practiced not only in stores but also in hotels, restaurants, and other such places. It raised the eyebrows of many European visitors. "They would hardly believe it in England," wrote an English journalist in 1904 of the scope of consumer services in the United States. "It is a question," wrote another Englishman, "if the service has not been carried too far." "The first reaction of a European customer" to American merchandising, wrote a German American, "is referring to the service." Even Americans were sometimes surprised by what one merchant called "an unreasonable degree of service, that many people, indeed, act as if a store were some sort of eleemosynary institution, founded and maintained for the purpose of serving the public without regard to profit."[82]

To make customers feel welcome, merchants trained workers to treat them as "special people" and as "guests." The numbers of service workers, including those entrusted with the care of customers, rose fivefold between 1870 and 1910, at two and a half times the rate of increase of industrial workers. Among them were the restaurant and hotel employees hired to wait on tables in exchange for wages and "tips," nearly all recent immigrants, mostly poor Germans and Austrians but also Italians, Greeks, and Swiss, who suffered nerve-wracking seven-day weeks, eleven-hour days, low wages, and the sometimes terrible heat of the kitchens. Neglected by major unions until just before World War I, they endured sweated conditions equal in their misery only to those of the garment and textile workers of the day.[83]

Tipping was supposed to encourage waiters and waitresses to tolerate these conditions in exchange for possible windfalls from customers. Tipping was an unusual practice in the United States before 1890 (although common in the luxurious and aristocratic European hotels), when the prevailing "American plan" entailed serving meals at fixed times, no frills, no tipping, and little or no follow-up service. After 1900 the European system of culinary service expanded very quickly in the United States, introduced first to the fancy establishments and then, year by year, to the more popularly priced places. By 1913 some European tourists were even expressing "outrage" at the extent of tipping in the United States.[84] Its effect on workers was extremely mixed. On the one hand, it helped keep wages low, increased the frenzy and tension of waiting, and lengthened the hours. "The tipping business is a great evil," wrote an old, retired waiter in the 1940s. "It gives the waiter an inferiority complex—makes him feel he is at the mercy of the customers all the time."[85] On the other hand, some waiters were stirred by the "speculative excitement" of tipping, the risk and chance.

For customers, however, tipping was intended to have only one effect—to make them feel at home and in the lap of luxury. On the backs of an ever-growing sweated workforce, it aristocratized consumption, integrating upper-class patterns of comfort into the middle-class lifestyle. Tips rewarded waiters and waitresses for making the customer "feel like 'somebody,' " as one restaurant owner put it. Such a "feeling," he wrote, "depends" on the "service of the waiter," who ushers us to "our table" and "anticipates our every want or whim." "Courteous service is a valuable asset to the restaurateur. There is a curious little twist to most of us: We enjoy the luxurious feeling of affluence, of being 'somebody,' of having our wishes catered to."[86]

The big hotels began to implement, in a systematic way, the same "customer as guest" idea. Lucius Boomer's Waldorf-Astoria provided liveried servants, bellhops, and electric room buttons to "call up" food or drinks at any time of day. "The bedroom equipment and service," wrote one pleased customer, "reminded me of stories in the *Arabian Nights*."[87] Boomer trained his staff to behave in "servile" ways before customers, instructing the "front desk" to call up the "guests" in their rooms on a "timely basis" to find out what they might need. Is the room fine? Would you like some champagne sent up? More flowers in your room? Breakfast in bed?

Ellsworth Statler, whose hotels reached a wider cross section of Americans than the Waldorf, despised Boomer's "liveried flunkies," preferring instead to leave his "guests" in their own "self-sufficient citadels," free from any kind of interruption. He was in 1907 the first hotel owner to install private bathrooms in *all* the hotel bedrooms. Water circulated in every room for the first time in hotel history, along with the first closets in every room, the first lights in every closet, and the first lock plungers for every door, with markers to inform the housemaid whether the "guest" was in or out. The Waldorf-Astoria may have improved room service by putting electric buttons in every room, but Statler added telephones, each linked to a switchboard operator who took requests for "wake-up calls," announced callers, and arranged room service. In December 1914, Statler, who never stopped experimenting, eliminated the service charge for Sunday breakfasts. "Inasmuch as hotel guests are like other people and prefer to lie abed or lounge about in negligee on Sunday morning," he explained, "the hotel will do what it can to add to their pleasure by making it as easy as possible for them to have breakfast in their rooms."[88]

Many merchants hired women especially because "women knew how to treat people like guests"—at least Boomer made this claim whenever he was asked why he employed women as managers in his hotels. Women were "wonderfully equipped to be hostesses in charge" and to apply "instinctively" the "homelike" conception. Oscar Hammerstein, Manhattan theater impresario, hired women in his commercial theaters as "lady ushers" because of "their powers of politeness." In department stores, too, women served not only as clerks but as "hostesses," guiding customers through the departments and across floors.[89]

The big stores excelled in interpreting the customer-as-guest idea, "regardless," said Herbert Tilly, general manager of Strawbridge and Clothier in Philadelphia, "of her color, race, or religion." "We want [all our] customers to know," he said, "that we recognize every customer as more than a casual guest in the store." "We regard all the people who come into our house as our guests," Wanamaker wrote a customer in 1901.[90] Salespeople were grilled everywhere in the formulas of proper decorum—to be "gracious" at all times and neat in appearance, unobtrusive but accessible, careful to "emphasize the value of the merchandise," and equipped with the right questions. A trained clerk at Marshall Field's, for instance, might ask, "How do you do?" "May I help you?" "Isn't this attractive?" (But never, according to store instructions, "What size do you wear?" "What do you want?," "Could or can I help you?" or "Anything else?").[91] Department store merchants sought workers who knew their "stocks" and how to match "stock with customer." Increasingly, it was argued, clerks had to know how to differentiate between real and fiber silk, good and bad design, excellent and poor china, cheap and beautiful leather. Not all clerks, perhaps, were able to master these distinctions; but by the 1910s, it was clear to many merchants that given the growing complexity of merchandise, profitable turnover would depend in part on skilled clerks. As a result, merchants held store classes to "teach salespeople merchandise" or turned to trade schools or universities to do the "educating" for them.[92]

As early as 1900 store switchboards, staffed by hundreds of phone operators, were available to take orders from customers day and night. By the teens Wanamaker's had twenty-four-hour "tel-call" phone order service, and Bamberger's in Newark was full of little red phones at the ends of counters so that customers might pick up the receivers and ask questions at any time "regarding anything pertaining to the store." To meet the demands of their immigrant customers, such stores as Abraham & Straus in Brooklyn stationed translators, with knowledge of twenty to twenty-five languages, throughout the store. At Macy's a male-customer buying service was set up for men who hated shopping or who simply had no way of visiting the store. One man who lived in Indochina asked Macy's to buy him an automobile, as well as an assortment of furnishings and furniture. "Macy's," the management responded, "would gladly render him this service."[93]

Stores such as Mandels in Chicago, Altman's in New York, and Wanamaker's in Philadelphia boasted full-time staffs to give advice to customers on how to decorate their apartments or their houses. When a Philadelphia woman complained to Wanamaker that his men had failed to match the colors properly in the course of papering her house, Wanamaker had it "repapered" immediately to confirm the reliability of his service. He called his interior decorators "assemblers" or "connoisseurs in furniture and almost everything else that goes into a house." The "connoisseur helps you with your decorative schemes and suggests the right furniture, rugs, hangings, and, indeed, everything that the room or house requires." The connoisseur "assembles all this in the studios on one of the floors, just about as they would look in your house, so that you know for a certainty what the effects are going to be."[94]

The Wanamaker assemblers performed on a grand scale and, in 1910, carpeted and furnished the Ritz Carlton Hotel in New York from top to bottom. They would travel anywhere to decorate the interior of a customer's home. In 1912, at the request of the wealthy Manhattan corporate lawyer John R. Dos Passos, they decorated and furnished a three-room suite at Matthews Hall in Harvard Yard for his son John Dos Passos, who was just starting his freshman year. This experience may have left a lasting impression on the younger Dos Passos; many years later, in 1932, in his novel 1919, he would memorialize the decorator in the character of Eveline Hutchins, a feckless, indifferent figure committed to nothing beyond herself.[95]

"Distributors of Happiness"

Customers had available new commercial spaces—rooms, halls, auditoriums, restaurants, and so on—to address their "special needs and desires." Consumer institutions were (and are) the quintessential multiuse institutions; they were abundant in the United States after 1885 and often functioned as community social centers, competing or overlapping with the churches for the same clientele, and often filling many needs that other institutions were not responding to or saw no reason to fill.

Hotels and restaurants had spaces in which people might meet, strike up or finalize deals, celebrate, get married—all, of course, at a price. Boomer's McAlpin Hotel on Thirty-fourth Street and Broadway was built from the start in 1912 to provide for the independent needs of professional and shopping women; it was the first hotel of its kind in New York with a floor entirely for women, run by women, including a separate women's restaurant and a separate entrance and front desk for women. An inspiration of Anne Morgan, investment banker J. P. Morgan's daughter, such separate quarters, Morgan said, were needed because "there was no first-class hotel in the city where a woman, unescorted, might register and have assigned to her a room, without being compelled to apply at the main desk, there to undergo a scrutiny which to most women is an offensive ordeal."[96] Ironically, as early as 1913, sometimes three marriage ceremonies a day were performed at the McAlpin. The poet e. e. cummings was married at the Hotel Copley Plaza in Boston, although he was ignorant about how the "service" worked and depended on his wife-to-be to make the arrangements.[97] Trade associations and professional bodies of all kinds had regular access to hotel and restaurant banquet facilities, to catering services and reception rooms, and to the elaborately decorated ballrooms; and hotel and restaurant merchants encouraged businessmen to display their wares in exhibit rooms.[98]

Urban retailers were very sensitive to the need to keep their businesses at the center of city life. These were the keys: Get involved, express interest, be concerned, educate, uplift, mirror the aspirations of customers. "Businesses," wrote one expert, "must be public service institutions and reflect the character of their regions." "We must be an integral part of life."[99]

Merchants sometimes turned their stores over to women's groups, as in the case of Fantle Brothers-Danforth Company in Sioux City Falls, South Dakota, which opened the store to five different women's groups to use the store for one full day.[100] At the seven-story Wolf and Dessauer store in Fort Wayne, Indiana, women could "entertain their friends at card parties or tea" in the store theater and auditorium. "There is no charge," Wolf and Dessauer announced, "for the use of the tables on the stage. Music is furnished free of charge and the hostess may, and of course frequently does, order luncheon for her party and be assured of special service."[101] Merchants also did local charity work and acted as "distributors of Happiness" to poor children, donating toys and dolls, overcoats and underwear. They even invited the poor to attend holiday benefits in honor of the poor themselves. [102]

The department stores doubled as "educational centers." Demonstrators explained the merits of vacuum cleaners and kitchen stoves, shoe polish and coffeepots. Store managers conducted their own "industrial expositions" to illuminate where certain goods came from and how they were manufactured. The public "should have an opportunity to learn something about how the goods are made," a publicity man for Siegel-Cooper's in Manhattan said in 1912, soon after that store had organized a substantial display of more than "150 miniature factories all over the store, each in the department in which goods of the class manufactured are sold."[103] These exhibits, to be sure, taught the public "something," but they were essentially sanitized industrial displays along the lines of those shown at state or world fairs, shaped by employers' standards and without any reference to the character of the work—the costs, the suffering—involved.

It was in the department stores, not in the museums, that modern art and American art found their first true patrons. The pastel paintings of John La Farge, one of America's most original colorists, appeared in the show windows and picture galleries of Marshall Field's in 1902. Field's conducted its "Hoosier Salon," a picture gallery for young artists from Indiana and Illinois.[104] In 1910 Theodore Dreiser, in walks about Philadelphia, saw in Wanamaker's a Fauve-style mural in four panels, depicting scenes from Parisian life, by the American Anne Estelle Rice. Hung above the first-floor elevator, it "suggested" to Dreiser "a sense of life and beauty." "The light," he raved, "the space, the daring, the force, the raw reds, greens, blues, mauves, whites, yellows!" (Rice, an artist trained in Paris at the Academy of Art, founded by Rodman Wanamaker, was to become one of Dreiser's many female lovers.)[105]

The Gimbel brothers, inspired by the Armory Show of 1913, became among the most ardent supporters of modern art, buying up Cézannes, Picassos, and Braques, and displaying them in the store galleries in Cincinnati, New York, Cleveland, and Philadelphia.[106] Five years later Carson, Pirie, Scott in Chicago exhibited the work of Americans Henri Bellows, William Glackens, and John Sloan in its new galleries on the fifth floor, as well as the paintings of the Taos Society of Artists of New Mexico.[107]

John Wanamaker, the man most apt to advertise his stores as "public institutions," was, not surprisingly, also the most innovative merchant of all in his display of art.[108] He deplored the way museums jumbled pictures together "on the walls, destroying the effect of the finest things," and month after month, to sustain customer interest, he rotated pieces in his personal collection from the store "studio" in Philadelphia—a Constable here, a Reynolds there, to say nothing of a Titian or a Turner, a Wanamaker favorite—to his New York store and back again.[109] (Of the "moderns," Wanamaker admired Manet the most.) He applied what he called the "new display principles," setting a standard later followed by museum curators. He wanted to make art "breathe" by giving it plenty of space on the walls, as if it were to be sold. "What is not for sale," he said, "is still for sale." "Everything that is lovely, everything that is worthwhile needs the eyes of the merchant . . . to show it off to best advantage."[110]

Other kinds of space also appeared in the retail stores and in the large urban hotels, too—branch public libraries and city post offices; banks and dental offices; and little hospitals to care for ailing shoppers or hotel guests. Some stores had "silence rooms" where women could relax, reflect on the day, and even meditate.[111] By 1915 women and children could visit hotel and store beauty salons or (for children) barbershops and "Happylands." Many of the hotels, including those managed by Boomer and Statler, offered swimming pools, Turkish baths, roof-garden restaurants, cocktail lounges, barrooms, and cafés. Boomer's McAlpin in New York claimed to have the largest underground restaurant (a "rathskeller" on the German model, beer and all) in the city.[112]

Field's in 1899 had Chicago's first large tearoom, seating five hundred for afternoon tea, from three to five in the afternoon on the fourth floor. It was "famous for its rose punch." It "drew the society elect," remembered Anna Nelson, original tearoom staffer and later "hostess," with "a hand-embroidered linen menu laundered everyday."[113] By 1914 Field's had a crop of tearooms for middle-class ladies plus restaurants—the Walnut Room, the English Room, the Colonial Tearoom, the Narcissus Room, and the Crystal Tearoom. In the same year Wanamaker's in Philadelphia was serving pâté de foie gras in its Grand Crystal Tea Room, and Macy's not only had a long lunch counter where a patron might eat oysters and clams (or a "Macy club" sandwich), but also a restaurant for twenty-five hundred people on the eighth floor (advertised as "one of the largest restaurants in the world"). Though often regarded as financial liabilities by owners, such restaurants were lures to attract customers.[114]

Children had their own services, spaces, and "hours" in stores and hotels, as well as in libraries and museums.[115] Hotels such as the McAlpin and the Commonwealth, both in New York, offered children's playgrounds, and nurseries, staffed by trained nurses.[116] In 1911, Field's said that it had the largest children's playground in the country, a "permanent" spot to care for and entertain three hundred to four hundred children at one time throughout the year. The Boston Store on State Street competed with Field's by decorating its playground to look like an "immense forest," with walls of branches and vines and the store columns covered with bark. Small boats sailed across an indoor lake stocked with fish.[117]

Many women frequently brought their children to the nurseries—really de facto day care centers—sometimes leaving them there for hours to go shopping, ignoring the two-hour limit. Other mothers who had no intention of shopping dropped their children off with the nurses. What effects such practices had on children is debatable, although one Arnold Constable buyer in New York City reported that "once the children play" in the store's playground (which was closely "tied in" with a nursery, a toyroom, a large dollhouse, and a children's shoe store), "they never forget it. In fact we always have a hard time getting the children out. They never want to go."[118]

For adults as well as children there were free concerts and performances in the theaters, recital halls, and auditoriums built into department stores and hotels after 1900, spaces often equal in quality of acoustics and size to professional concert halls. Famous musicians like Arthur Rubinstein, Mischa Elman, and Anton Rubinstein played in store recital halls; choruses made up of store employees performed cantatas, oratorios, and other choral works for customers.[119] "Spectacular extravaganzas" were put on in the auditoriums, as, for example, in New York, Siegel-Cooper's six-week-long "Carnival of Nations," which climaxed in August with "Oriental Week" and an exotic show, *Phantasma, the Enchanted Bower*. Embellished by "thrilling" light-and-color effects, the show delivered a "glimpse of the Orient—a Turkish harem, a parade of Turkish dancing girls, a 'genie of the lamp,' and 'Cleopatra of the Nile.' " A year later the store staged its *Amazma Show*, with "weird transformations," "startling and beautiful electrical displays," and "incandescent illusions."[120]

By 1910, then, department stores and similar institutions were serving as powerful anchors for downtown civic life; they were not only selling goods but also disseminating free entertainment, ideas, information, and uplift—sometimes of indispensable value to their communities.

Gemütlichkeit *and the Utopia of*
Joseph Urban

Another dimension to consumer service, and one that had nothing whatever to do with community benefit and everything to do with individual consumer enjoyment, appealed to fantasies of escape and luxury, and provided customers with "atmospheres" of pleasure and comfort. At the heart of it was the pursuit of the perfect ambiance, musical and otherwise, intended to instill in consumers feelings of well-being. In the decades after the Civil War, and especially in cities where merchants began to compete for a wide market, music became a common element of this form of consumer service. In the early 1900s large middle-class cafeterias, novel in their own right, began to hire musical ensembles to entertain businessmen at lunchtime, as Michael Gold recalled in his novel *Jews Without Money.* "My mother," he wrote, worked for "a large, high-priced cafeteria for businessmen on lower Broadway. . . . It was one of those super-cafeterias, with flowers on the tables, a string orchestra during the lunch hour, and other trimmings."[121] On a warm evening in October 1910 a gloomy Theodore Dreiser watched a courtyard restaurant from a window of his Park Avenue hotel, where he was staying to escape domestic troubles and to reflect on the meaning of a hopeless love affair. The sight of "little red lamps on each table glowing like fireflies" and the ingratiating, soft sound of an orchestra playing to customers made him "unutterably sad."[122]

It is hard to know exactly where the custom of performing music in restaurants, hotels, department stores, and similar consumer settings came from, but a very good guess would be German immigrants with their tradition of *gemütlichkeit,* a term meaning something like "pure comfort" and marked by the mixture of music, food, and drink. Henry Morgenthau, Sr., a German-Jewish-American financier and statesman, described this tradition warmly on the first page of his autobiography, *All in a Life-Time.* There was in Germany, he wrote, a way of life "best expressed by a word that was forever on [the people's] lips, *gemütlich,* that almost untranslatable word that implies contentment, ease, and satisfaction, all in one." This word, tradition, and manner of life Morgenthau and other Germans brought with them to America and domesticated.[123]

Gemütlichkeit did not function alone, however, as a cultural activity; it was part of an even broader tradition of festival culture that all Germans shared. German Americans were the largest immigrant group in America (upward to 9 million in number by 1910); and they were also the most diverse, including Catholics, Jews, Protestants, and secular nonbelievers; urban cosmopolitans and rural peasants; skilled and unskilled workers; merchants and plowmen.[124] What held them altogether, as historian Katherine Neils Conzen has shown, was a common public festival culture, which fostered community among themselves. Many hoped it would constitute an important part of the German contribution to American culture. Public festival culture had two aspects—not only a *gemütlich* aspect emphasizing sociability and enjoyment but also a humanistic aspect focusing on the mind and spirit rather than on business and practical things. Both aspects seemed to be missing in the United States, many Germans believed. For one thing, Americans had no real high culture—no great music or art; for another, they seemed unable to relax, to let their hair down and enjoy themselves, or to celebrate in public. "Doing business and praying are the highest moments of the modern republican," complained a German American in 1846. "The American cannot get enthusiastic about anything," said another. "He can't even enjoy himself."[125]

From the 1840s onward, Germans from many walks of life, as Conzen and others have indicated, developed new public festivals in city after city—festivals celebrating Schiller, Goethe, and Beethoven; Maytime festivals; and *Volksvests* and other holidays of all kinds, many marked by singing, political exhortations, and appeals for "heroism," with banners, costumes, torchlights, and colorful pageantry.[126] Wherever Germans immigrated they brought music with them, creating a flourishing piano industry and great symphony orchestras. Germans almost single-handedly formed the early musical cultures of Milwaukee, Cincinnati, Cleveland, and St. Louis; besides orchestras, they organized choral groups, singing societies, and festivals (*Sangerfests*), and patronized opera, concerts, and music halls.[127]

German Americans combined beer and music into a single blend of entertainment, eating, and drinking. From the 1840s onward, they took over the beer industry, wresting control from the British.[128] At the same time, and against prohibitionist protest, they hired musical ensembles of all kinds for their numerous *biergartens* to entertain individual customers or whole families, since it was a German custom for families to "eat out" together in the beer halls. Portraits of Beethoven, Mozart, and Schubert hung on walls.[129] In his 1929 autobiography, *Up to Now*, Al Smith, governor of New York, described one of the largest beer gardens in New York City, the Atlantic Garden on the Bowery, "patronized by the German population" in the late 1870s. "Professor Esher had a band of lady musicians. Light lunches were served at tables and the universal drink at Atlantic Garden was lager beer. My sister and I were given chocolate to drink, and huge slices of cake, while the elders drank their beer, gossiped and listened to the entertainment."[130]

These contributions to American culture did much to improve it by encouraging all Americans to love music, to relax a little more, and to take pleasure in sensual and beautiful things. Americans needed festivity. But German festival culture and the tradition of comfort and enjoyment embedded within it took public expression in another way as well—in the emerging large-scale consumer institutions of the times.[131] In a process of transformation characteristic of capitalist society, merchants incorporated these use-value traditions into orbits of profit-making, just as they were commodifying other areas of social life.[132] German-American merchants themselves, perhaps, may have done more than any other Americans to commercialize these traditions, thus cutting them off from their more democratic-communal roots. As we have already seen, many leading American retailers by 1900 were of German descent—from John Wanamaker, Adam Gimbel, and Frank Cooper and Henry Siegel to the Straus brothers, Edward and Lincoln Filene, David May of May Department Stores in St. Louis, and Frederick L. Lazarus of F. and R. Lazarus in Columbus, Ohio.[133] Wanamaker even presented a commercialized version of the German *Volksvest* (but without the beer) in his store. In 1902, and for many years thereafter, as part of his policy of opening up the Philadelphia store to the ethnic groups in the city, he gave special treatment to the Germans. On March 22, 1907, for instance, the entire arcade of the store was decorated by photographs of the Kaiser; and twice daily a local German singing group, the Junger Maennerchor, entertained customers in the concert hall on the third floor.[134]

It would be a mistake, of course, to focus too much on German Americans; many other Americans, whose ancestors came from other countries (from the British Isles, in particular, as the backgrounds of such men as Marshall Field and John T. Pirie of Carson, Pirie, Scott in Chicago, Samuel Woodward of Woodward and Lothrop in Washington, D.C., and Joseph Lowthian Hudson of J. L. Hudson's in Detroit amply testify), also integrated comfort and enjoyment into consumer institutions. Nevertheless, it can be safely claimed that this tradition—German or some non-German variant—constituted a primary source for modern consumer service.

Large American vacation hotels, creatures of the 1880s and 1890s, helped institutionalize this tradition by entertaining guests with music during dinnertime and on special occasions. By the 1910s music and dancing were standard features of urban hotel life (to say nothing, of course, of the new nightclubs). "The hotel is surely marvelous," wrote Emily Frankenstein, a Chicago teenage daughter of a well-off Jewish physician, in a diary entry about the newly built Edgewater Beach Hotel. "We were given a table in the beautiful dining room just in front of the door out of which we could look and see Lake Michigan. Inside the scene was festive with many brightly colored lights—softened yet gay—and the orchestra playing beautiful selections." In the wintertime, Emily Frankenstein went dancing at the Cooper-Carleton Hotel in downtown Chicago. [135]

In 1913 Ellsworth Statler (also a German American) added musical entertainment to his hotel business. In the same year, Lucius Boomer installed the "keene-a-phone" at the McAlpin, a form of "canned music" (as he himself called it) mechanically piped in from a central location to several hotel rooms at once. Many of the "guests" were said to be so pleased with the experiment that they urged Boomer to "retain the machine permanently in his hotel."[136] String orchestras played "soft music during lunch hour" at Wanamaker's for years.[137] Other big department stores planted small musical ensembles on various floors to coax customers deeper into the stores and to relax and soothe them and to put them in a shopping mood. Siegel-Cooper's in New York hired an all-women orchestra—similar to Professor Esher's ensemble in the Atlantic Garden—to perform for shoppers in the store's grocery and wine department. In the Simpson-Crawford store farther downtown, "musicians were hidden behind vine-hung lattices" to give the impression that the music was somehow invisibly mixed in with the store's atmosphere.[138] After 1895 every major department store had an organist at the keyboard at all hours. Wanamaker's in Philadelphia installed the "biggest organ in the world," one Wanamaker himself had snapped up from among the leftovers of the 1904 Louisiana Purchase Exposition in St. Louis. Even at the Woolworth stores, famed for keeping their overhead costs under control, pipe organists played for customers "whenever required." By the beginning of the twentieth century, people "expected to do their shopping to the accompaniment of music."[139]

Other spatial pleasures to make people feel relaxed and comfortable were incorporated as well. At about the turn of the century, merchants not only displayed art in galleries but also commissioned prominent artists to create environments better suited to the new consumer businesses. These artists, some of whom treated their work in almost utopian terms, supplied a commercial aesthetic intended to delight customers and put them at ease. "We wanted to produce the necessary illusions," the stage designer Lee Simonson said, "and to exchange grey dullness for wonderful colors." We wanted to "answer the cravings" of all men and women for "rituals of sumptuousness."[140]

In 1914 the Associated Dry Goods Corporation, whose owner thought the "color question" of "great importance," invited a noted portrait artist to help redecorate one of its stores, McCreery's department store at Thirty-fourth Street and Fifth Avenue. Joseph Cummings Chase had graduated from Brooklyn's Pratt Institute in 1898 and had then studied in Paris, where he "discovered all he could about color—at any prices, at any sacrifice," he said. A color fanatic, he wrote books about color and studied its "therapeutic" capability, how it affected the senses, states of mind, the power of concentration. "If the ceiling of your best room," he explained, noting his favorite color, "is painted a tint of lemon yellow it will be easier for you to read your Sunday morning newspaper. The ceiling will look softer and quieter, but it will give more light in the room." Although he did most of his important work in the 1920s, Chase had an immediate impact earlier on McCreery's, selecting each color used there with an eye toward comfort and "suggestive atmosphere."[141]

One of the most influential artists to work for consumer institutions was Austrian Joseph Urban, a skilled decorative craftsman.[142] Born in Vienna in 1872, the son of Catholic bourgeois parents, he was to transform *gemütlichkeit* into what Lee Simonson had called a "ritual of sumptuousness." For Urban, music, decoration, and color all might blend into an experience of total pleasure. He had studied architecture in Vienna and had risen to fame as a member of a radical group of Viennese artists known as "the Secession," from which he resigned to form the Hagenband, a splinter group devoted to modern art. Backed by a patron, the Austro-Hungarian emperor Franz Joseph, Urban catered to the rich and well-born, designing the Imperial Jubilee of his emperor, villas for the nobility, and hunting lodges for the *haute bourgeoisie*. Crises in the empire coupled with artistic conflicts and seductive offers from the United States led Urban to emigrate in 1911 at age thirty-nine. He readily shifted his loyalties from the fading Hapsburg ruling class to America's regnant commercial capitalists, who now became his primary patrons.[143]

Until his death in 1932, Urban was a crossover artist *par excellence* for hotels, department stores, opera houses, cocktail lounges, commercial theaters, universities, and castles. One of his admirers, Otto Teegan, wrote that Urban "looked at everything, including life, in terms of color," and sought to "build colorful structures" whose "atmospheres" would "charm in gloomy days" and help erase the "ugliness" and "pain" from human existence. Like his mind-cure contemporary Paul Scheerbart, who believed "coloured glass destroys hatred," Urban thought "beautiful" architecture alone could make people happy. His interest in color, which he shared with a growing army of other commercial artists, helped make him one of the key builders of the commercial aesthetic.[144]

Americans first came to know Urban in his pre-World War I days as the leading stage designer for the *Ziegfeld Follies* and the Metropolitan Opera House. His "spiritual" life was wrapped up in the musical theater. "In our future life," he wrote, "the stage must have the same influence that the Church had in the past." "Here was a world of magic," said the American architect Ralph Walker of Urban's sets for Debussy's *Peleas and Melisande*. "Here was something that made Belasco look trivial."[145] Urban designed twelve Follies, seven roof-garden shows, and eighteen musical comedies. His first Follies, in 1915, was called *Blue Follies* because everything on his stage was in some shade or tint of blue.[146] Urban was a master at creating orientalized *tableaux* in the manner of the day, such as the voluptuous "Harem Scene" or the tightly wrought modernist "Temple of Color" at the Ziegfeld Theater. "He proved," wrote the American composer and music critic Deems Taylor, "that scenery for an ordinary run-of-the-mill Broadway show should be beautiful, and that people should respond to that beauty." Many people went to the theater to see Urban's sets rather than the performances.[147]

Along with American stage designers Lee Simonson and Norman Bel Geddes, who both also designed consumer interiors, Urban reconceived the stage as an integrated three-dimensional space that "we could vicariously inhabit." He rejected the crowded stage "realism" of the late nineteenth century for a new streamlined "modernity," for a theatrical depth, "dramatic" sweep, and "the right stage atmospheres." To achieve these effects he dispensed with painted scenery and emphasized "colored light," spot-lighting, and "indirect lighting."[148] And what he learned about light and color, about the dramatization of spaces and objects and the forging of "atmospheres," he brought to the interior décor of other consumer insti-tutions. The high-water mark of his work in this field was reached in the 1920s (see Chapter 10), but he received important commissions earlier, in the 1910s, from hotels, restaurants, roof gardens, cabarets, and department stores. In 1915 he broke new ground at Gimbels in the conception of the fashion show, matching the colors of the imported gowns with the colors of the store decorations and displays, and splitting the promenade stage into two, one half going stage right, the other stage left.[149]

A year later, in 1916, Urban teamed up with the commercial muralist Raphael Kirchner to redecorate the Paradise Room of Reisenweber's Hotel Restaurant at Columbus Circle in Manhattan. "No expense was spared," wrote an observer, "to make 'Paradise' a place suggestive of its name."[150] In 1917 the two achieved their most important success together—the design and execution of the interior décor of New York's new Coconut Grove Restaurant, a décor "unlike anything ever before created in New York." Urban, as principal decorator, transformed a bare cement floor compart-ment into a tropical fantasy space, one customers "could vicariously in-habit." Gold leaf decorated the domed ceiling and archways of the central dining area; a blue, green, and gold color scheme unified the furniture, ceiling, walls, silk window curtains, and floor. There were matching tropical birds in the border decorations, and coconut mats and "real" Palm Beach coconut trees were woven into the golden carpets. "Indirect lighting" ra-diated across the room, the performance stage, and the dance floor, and "huge globes" hung from the gold overhead dome. "The atmosphere of a coconut grove is there created," a critic said, "by the warm tones of the blended colors and the expert manipulation of the furnishings."[151] On either side of the performance stage were Kirchner's primitivistic murals, one depicting seminude "maidens cavorting in a coconut grove," the other a "nymph" waving invitingly from a distant shore to sailors on a galley ship. The gold, blue, and green of Kirchner's picture flowed through the res-taurant interior, with Urban designing the room itself to emerge magically out of Kirchner's tropical landscapes. When mingled with the music of the dance orchestra, the interior decor created an atmosphere of "perfect" ease and comfort.

A New Commercial Cultural Order

Service had become a protean strategy by 1915, done best by reasonably large corporate institutions committed to high-volume turnover. Initiated in the 1880s in a still Christian environment stressing stewardship and moral obligation, it evolved rapidly into modern consumer service. It came to mean not only a charge plate or free delivery but also inviting interiors, art galleries, musical pleasures, tropical landscapes, nurseries for the children of busy shopping mothers, doting waiters at tables, room service, and breakfast in bed. Its pervasiveness was beginning to make many people feel that America was, indeed, a wonderful place where every one might get the same treatment, the same first-class service.

Almost from the start, service had seemed to work as a new language—visual, musical, verbal—and a new way to obscure the underlying abiding quest for profit. But service could never really hide such a quest. Nor did many merchants themselves—or perhaps most consumers, for that matter—ever believe that it should be masked. After all, American consumer service, from easy credit to sumptuous atmospheres, was a capitalist, not a socialist art. It was "not true hospitality," as Catholic radical Peter Maurin said of "service," for it had nothing in common with the Catholic hospices of the past, which freely opened their doors to anyone in need and without cost. Consumer service had no depth and was not to be taken seriously. Like much else in this culture, one could take it or leave it. It was "commercialized hospitality," Maurin said; when it ceased to make a profit or to move goods, it, too, ceased or was modified to suit new commercial needs. Like show window glass, it was a symbol of the power and dominance of merchants, foremost a market activity that could be withheld or dissolved at any time. In the end service truly served only those who could pay their way. [152]

Still, if one wishes to understand why America became a mass consumer society, one could do worse than to look for something of an explanation in the rise of service. At a time of economic inequity and labor conflict, many Americans linked service with the "promise of America." It had a mollifying, reassuring purpose that seemed to say that in the midst of economic distress most people had nothing to worry about; security and pleasure would always await them. Service expressed what many economists then (and now) preferred to call the "benevolent side" of capitalism, that is, the side of capitalism that gave to people—in exchange for a dependable flow of profits—a better, more comfortable way of life. In this view, capitalism did not merely "strive for profits" but also sought "the satisfaction of the needs of others, by performing service efficiently." "Capital," said one turn-of-the-century economist, "reigns because it serves."[153]

Service, then, along with other strategies of enticement, helped give to the sphere of consumption an independent character and, increasingly, a definite set of values, with emphasis on material well-being, luxury, comfort, pleasure, and happiness without "ugliness" or "pain." These values, to be sure, had long been part of what many people thought to be the "American promise"; but in this era, as production and consumption split asunder and as corporate business began to organize consumer activity, such values—or, more correctly, the things that many Americans seemed most to "value"—seemed to gravitate to only one side of life.

This was unprecedented. Before 1880, consumption and production were, for large numbers of people, bound together, with men, women, and children living and toiling closely with one another (and, often enough, exploiting one another as well) in local or regional economies, and sometimes self-sufficiently. Most Americans knew where the goods and wealth came from, because they themselves produced them, knew their value, and understood the costs and sufferings required to bring them into existence. Elaborate associational meanings, moreover, that purported to confer on consumption an autonomous identity, were not a part of social life.

After 1890 the institutions of production and consumption were, in effect, taken over by corporate businesses. Business, not ordinary men and women, did most to establish the value and the cultural character of the goods—in this case, of the new machine-made goods. At the same time, merchants, brokers, and manufacturers did everything they could, both ideologically and in reality, to *separate* the world of production from the world of consumption (and, in the process, the men, women, and children were also divided up). If, in 1875, Alexander Stewart in New York still conducted manufacturing and selling in the same place, in full gaze of the customers, then, by 1910, such economic integration had all but disappeared. At stores like Macy's, as we have seen, management worked systematically to remove all traces of hard work from the selling floor. "The selling departments," one merchant had said, "is the stage upon which the play is enacted." Color, glass, and light, along with "central ideas," were enlisted to give consumption a new independent identity.

The advent of these two worlds, once together but now widely divergent, had many disorienting consequences for men and women alike. Women faced special hardships in negotiating consumption, as the economist Wesley Clair Mitchell, a pioneering authority on business cycles, was among the first to note in his 1912 essay "The Backward Art of Spending Money." Where once they had participated fully in the production of goods at home and were able to read in an instant their value, most women were now the principal shoppers several steps removed from production and compelled to study the prices and the enticements contrived by others. But, as Mitchell argued, how could any woman have the knowledge to evaluate the "prices of milk and shoes, furniture and meat, magazines and fuel, hats and underwear, bedding and disinfectants, medical services and toys, rugs and candy"? Did price really measure value or not? Did it reveal economic value and utility, or mere extravagance and social status?[154]

Was it possible anymore in this new money economy and culture to locate any "true" value at all, the meaning or worth of any commodity now that one's own labor played no real role in the making of goods? Was it possible, indeed, to control rationally consumer desire, even for oneself?

Women had to learn how to read through enticements and to assess the "authenticity" of claims by "interested advertisers and shopkeepers" who endowed goods with every kind of association.[155] Women—especially mothers—had to discover how to distinguish their individual desires from the needs and desires of their families. For men it was different and easier (at least Mitchell so argued); for men, "making money" was confined to their workplace, not to their homes. Most women enjoyed no such distance; the demands of "spending money" and providing love were inextricably intermingled in one place. Yet women needed to maintain distance to see clearly, in the interest of their families' well-being, the "true" worth to them of the goods on sale.

Some women easily adjusted to the new separateness of the consumer world by simply "accepting uncritically the scale of conventional values which their day and generation provided ready-made." Others, Mitchell argued, worried about the new "scheme of [pecuniary] values embodied in every housewife's work."[156] Still other women (as well as men) failed to make adjustments, fell prey to impulse, or went into debt; some even lost complete control and stole the goods they desired.

The separateness of the consumer world had other significant results. It helped to transform consumption somehow into the "true realm" of freedom and self-expression, the only refuge of comfort and pleasure, and as a place where all wishes were granted and anything was possible. If work and production offered less in the way of fulfillment for most people, then consumption—especially in this detached and floating context—surely seemed likely to fill the bill. Recently, the poet and essayist Lewis Hyde has observed that consumer society—or, more accurately, the huge numbers of machine-made commodities that mark that society—is exciting because it suggests a radical break from the past, a sense of rootlessness and a "floating away," a promise of newness and adventure. Pioneer American advertisers such as Artemas Ward noted these signs of consumer capitalism as they were taking shape when he said in 1892, "To each a world opens; to everyone possibilities are present."[157] American merchants and brokers, from John Wanamaker to Joseph Urban, recognized these features too, and they strengthened them with a complex system of services, with easy credit plans and with environments of luxury, desire, and exoticism.

All of this served to give to consumption its independent character, communicating a sense that, in the world of goods at least, men and women could find transformation, liberation, a paradise free from pain and suffering, a new eternity in time. They could find what historian of religion Joseph Haroutunian has called "being" through "having," "the good" through "goods." The separate world of consumer fantasy, in other words, began to foster the idea that men and women might become fulfilled human beings not through spiritual good or through pursuit of the "eternal" (to use Haroutunian's terms again) but through acquisition of "goods" and through the pursuit of "infinity," which Haroutunian associates with capitalism's tendency to produce new goods and new meanings "all the time."[158]

But this idea was illusory. It was illusory because the world of consumption, however seemingly severed from the world of production, was always dependent on and always vulnerable to the capitalist forces that created it. It was illusory as well because being and having could never have been reconciled under these new conditions. Being is finite, Haroutunian argues, confined by the fact that we "exist in our lifetimes" and must face the inevitability of dying. Having in the new consumer context, on the other hand, invites the belief that death can be overcome or that people can find the "eternal" in an "infinity of accumulation." In "our day, the goods a man might accumulate are virtually infinite, but the time in which he accumulates them is finite. Finite men are potentially infinite in the world of machines. Being remains circumscribed according to nature, but having has burst the bonds and is racing toward infinity. Men who

carry the mark of death are confronted with opportunity for infinite having."
But this was the greatest illusion of all, because it denied men and women
their humanity, their very being within time. "The passion generated by
the ideal infinite enters into their accumulation of the finite and turns their
whole existence into nonsense."[159]

The separateness of the consumer world carried with it other related
consequences: its presence tended to blot out the *human* contributions and
sufferings involved in its creation. The distance between consumers and
producers, critic Edmund Wilson wrote in the early 1930s, is part of "the
vast system of abstraction which dominates the [modern] world," whose
effects have "contributed to the deadening of feeling, the social insulation,
which impoverishes life in industrial communities." Those who "receive
dividends" care little or nothing about those "whose labor makes dividends
possible." "The capitalist system makes it very much easier for people not
to realize what they are doing, not to know about the danger and hardship,
the despair and humiliation, that their way of life implies for others."[160]

By 1910 more and more people were less and less aware about how
things were made and who made them. Besides, who would want to know
these things in a culture already disposed to encourage self-indulgence,
self-gratification, and self-pleasure? To acknowledge suffering caused by
capitalism under these new conditions would be to arouse one's own guilt
and to cause one's own distress. But the separateness of consumption made
it easy to deny the suffering: The outcome was a greater tendency toward
selfishness and a corrosive moral indifference.

This separate commercial culture was, then, an awesome creation. But
its separateness was not merely the product of corporate businessmen and
merchants; if that had been the case, the culture that finally did emerge
after 1900 would not have been quite so far-reaching, nor quite so awesome.
Nor might it have taken over so quickly. No; other groups, too, were
implicated in those changes, groups whose influence did much to establish
the extent and endurance of the new commercial culture.

II

Circuits of Power

Chapter **6**

"BUSINESS RUNS THE WORLD":
INSTITUTIONAL COALITIONS
BEHIND THE NEW ORDER

In the fall of 1989 Abraham & Straus opened a shopping mall on West Thirty-third Street and Broadway, the biggest ever to appear in Manhattan. Institutional forces of considerable magnitude, both public and private, joined together to get it built. Real estate developers drew on large reserves of borrowed capital for financing. The New York Transit Authority spent $50 million of public money to "modernize" subway stops in the area. Neighborhood associations and hotel owners worked to clear the homeless off the streets and out of alleys, and the city's Department of Parks renovated shabby Greeley Square across the street. Opening night was videotaped for later broadcast on national television; big name performers like Tony Bennett entertained hundreds of invited guests that September night in a glittery overheated setting of strobe lights and neon colors.[1]

In our time, of course, such coalitions have become a predictable feature of the development and redevelopment of American cities, as much symptomatic of a weakening domestic commercial culture—of its ever more noninnovative and even tiresome use of color, light, and glass—as a testimony to its still potent carnival appeal. Expensive projects from Baltimore to Minneapolis, each meant to revitalize the consumer sector and only slightly modified to capture local flavor and custom, have taken shape as public and private groups have come together in pursuit of a common objective. We know little about their history or about how central they have been to the formation of America's commercial life and culture. But any culture that endures rests on a similar base of relationships, a similar alliance among economic and noneconomic groups, and a similar circuit of power.

Before the outbreak of World War I, the new network of corporate business institutions that invented the modern strategies of enticement was already altering the cultural landscape. But such institutions were not enough in themselves to make anybody think or behave differently or to guarantee any lasting changes in American culture. Businessmen needed other institutions as well to ensure this kind of change; they needed other friendly partners (and, as we will see at the end of this chapter, even unfriendly partners) to help in the creation of the new commercial order of things.

In the next three chapters I want to explore the character of these institutions and how each, in their very different ways, helped give life to the mass culture of consumer capitalism. In the first chapter I describe four areas of institutional support. The first is educational and consists of commercial art schools, colleges, and universities (most notably the University of Pennsylvania and Harvard), which opened their doors to serve the educational needs of business. The second institutional area is cultural and focuses on the great urban museums and on their "new curators," on men like Morris D'Camp Crawford, Stewart Culin, John Cotton Dana, and Richard Bach, who were among the most ardent (even dreamy) converts in the United States to the goals of the new mass consumer industries. Federal and municipal governments form a third area of assistance and cooperation. Government involvement in the new economy was complex, fraught with tensions and contradictions, but it nevertheless did more to support than to impede the evolution of the new commercial culture. Finally, in the chapter's conclusion, I discuss an entirely unlikely participant in the new circuit of power—the Industrial Workers of the World, America's most radical labor union. No group in the country matched the IWW in its hatred of capitalism, yet it sometimes pursued tactics that mirrored and confirmed the power of that very capitalism—with tragic results.

The concluding chapters in Part Two examine another fundamental dimension of American institutional life: religion. They survey the landscape of institutional religion, dealing especially with John Wanamaker and evangelical Protestantism but also with other religious groups as they responded to the challenge of the new culture. The chapters describe a new mentality—mind cure—that suited ideally the hopes and expectations of many Americans. They also depart, in some degree, from the institutional aspect of the book, dealing with a shift in values and a change in spiritual life.

"Searching Out" and Satisfying "Human Wants"

Before 1898 or thereabouts no colleges or universities in the United States taught commercial business on a formal or professional basis with the sole exception of the Wharton School of Economics at the University of Pennsylvania in Philadelphia. "Commercial colleges" operated in the 1880s, but they gave only three-month instruction in arithmetic, penmanship, elementary bookkeeping, and "business" broadly conceived. Before the turn of the century, young people in the United States who wanted to study economic subjects in depth could choose agriculture, metallurgy, mining, engineering, and disciplines related to production. They studied, that is, how to "make things," not how to market and sell goods or how "to make money," as one business educator said. The educational system paid almost no attention to what a later observer called the "pecuniary aspects of business." Cost accounting was not only not taught, but it was also barely practiced by American firms. No two businessmen kept records the same way. And without uniform practices, it was almost impossible to keep track of the general flow of money and goods or to predict future flows.[2] Even the Wharton School, which aspired to advance the cause of professional business education, failed to get very far with this agenda in the early years; it offered only one-year instruction and focused primarily (and even here, not very well) on accounting and on business law and practice.[3]

No systematic examination of the economic institutions then emerging was undertaken, no study of the large mass retailers, of the credit system, of the investment bankers and their banks, or of the ever growing commodity markets that were penetrating hitherto insuperable economic frontiers. Nor did Americans devote much professional study, except within private, guild-like arrangements and in the secondary schools of some states, to art in relation to commerce. In England by the mid-1800s, as well as in France and Germany, large museums—from the English Kensington Gardens to the French Musée d'Arts Industriels—were cooperating with manufacturers in the teaching of industrial design. But in the United States, commercial and industrial art, display and decoration, advertising, style, and fashion were either just beginning to make strides or they were nonexistent fields of inquiry.[4]

After 1895, all this began to change, in response to the demands of industry and growth of corporate enterprise, until the United States by the late 1920s had the largest educational apparatus anywhere in the world for the study of such subjects. Art education in primary and secondary schools was championed by a whole new group of educators, an underlying aim of which, as art historian Diana Korzenik has written, was to get Americans to shift their interests and desires away from handcrafted goods to the new mass-manufactured consumer goods.[5] New materials, like colored chalk, colored crayons, and colored paper, were added to the stock of instructional materials. Philosophers like John Dewey spoke at conventions on the necessary relationship between "art and industry" and on why art education should be taught in the high schools.[6]

The new arts-in-industry movement or good-design movement rooted itself in the commercial art schools and museums of the pre-1920 period. Among the schools initially engaged in the nineteenth century in handicraft production or in the fine arts were Pratt Institute and the New York School of Fine and Applied Arts (later the Parsons School), both in New York City. After 1900 they switched to teaching commercial art. Pratt was hotly criticized by handicraft groups for catering to the "trade element," but year after year it absorbed new commercial subjects into the curricula—interior decoration, costume design, commercial illustration, and applied design. The commercial illustration class was so crowded in 1913 that it had to be divided into four sections, "there being 117 students in all." Two years later, Pratt students were beginning to find regular employment at such places as Bonwit Teller, Abraham & Straus, Gimbels, Best's, and Altman's.[7]

By the late 1910s, the New York School of Fine and Applied Arts, directed by Frank Alvah Parsons, had become a servant of mass market merchandising. Parsons, hired in 1906 to "promote a Department of Design and the teaching of it," in the next decade formed close ties with New York's clothing industry and stores. His curriculum consisted of such commercial subjects as display advertising and product design; his own personal specialty was interior decoration. Simplicity was his motto. "Anything irrelevant," he said, "is a waste of material, space, money, and mental consciousness." Influenced by psychologist Walter Dill Scott, he lectured his students to target the "imagination," "the instincts," "psychology," and "suggestion" ("rational" appeals, he said, usually failed). Create "associations" in the consumer's mind; exploit the "sex appeal of objects"; manipulate the "language of color." Color, he said, "makes a direct appeal to the emotions."[8] He was among the hundreds of new educators who wanted to break down the distinction between "beauty" and "commerce," high and low art, popular and elite, a distinction already dissolving in department stores, hotels, and world's fairs. "Art is not for the few," he said, "for the talented, for the genius, for the rich." When it comes to marketing goods, art is "for everyone." Parsons' lifelong aim was to "make the connection between art and trade easier."[9]

Beyond these art schools were the colleges and universities, upward to 125 by 1920, specializing in commercial subjects. Among them were three graduate programs in retailing, at Simmons College in Boston, Carnegie Institute of Technology in Pittsburgh, and New York University in Greenwich Village. The Prince School of Salesmanship at Simmons, founded in 1915, was headed by the inexhaustible Lucinda Prince, who, fourteen years earlier, had managed her own retailing school in Boston. Boston stores—Filene's, R. H. White, and Jordan Marsh—hired her graduates as an experiment, liked what they saw, and decided to throw their financial weight behind her. In 1915 they had her appointed educational director of the National Retail Dry Goods Association and financed the merger of her school with Simmons College. Two years later, Pittsburgh merchants united with the local public school system and Carnegie Institute of Technology to form the Research Bureau for Retail Training. Seven Pittsburgh department store merchants—Edgar Kaufmann of Kaufmann's leading the way—underwrote the Bureau with an annual donation of $32,000 over a five-year period, their goal to improve store service by training and hiring new personnel and by instilling a commitment to service.[10]

Better service was also the stated aim of the New York University School of Retailing, a pooled effort of merchants, the New York City Board of Education, and New York University. The idea here came from Anne Morgan, a rich chain-smoking feminist and daughter of J. P. Morgan, America's most notorious investment banker. As willful as her father and as contemptuous of his anti-Semitism as of his wealth, Anne Morgan combined a love of easy luxury with an advocacy of many social causes. It was Morgan who in 1912 had persuaded the management of Lucius Boomer's McAlpin Hotel in New York to create an entire floor run for and by women.[11] In 1915 she co-led the Department Store Association, a group of reform-minded society women who urged Elmer Brown, chancellor of New York University, to establish a retail training program for young women in department stores. "The Department Store Association," she said, "wishes to advance the all-round development and technical education of the girl in the department store. We feel that this is a problem of vital importance throughout the country and that here, as in many fields, the great task is the teacher's who gives the necessary training."[12]

At Morgan's behest Brown set up classes in retailing at the university's School of Pedagogy. Then Macy's vice-president Percy Straus stepped in, eager to get the program off the ground. Straus belonged to a new generation of merchants who wanted to keep some measure of family control while building up an efficient hierarchical managerial machine. In 1912 he and his two other brothers, Jesse and Herbert, had risen to power at Macy's when their father, Isidor, was killed in the sinking of the *Titanic*. Percy, a scholarly appearing Harvard graduate with pince-nez glasses, was determined to hold the reins of the business. He opposed his father's brother, Nathan, and his cousins, all of whom had as much right to the business as he did. Through a series of clever maneuvers, he, Jesse, and Herbert managed to get Nathan and his sons to sell out and, although Nathan hardly lost everything (he kept ownership of the Abraham & Straus stock), the outcome so alienated him that he never forgave Percy. "Since his father's death (my lamented brother Isadore)," Nathan wrote Chancellor Brown of NYU, after learning of his nephew's role as chair of an executive committee of the new retail school, "I have not been in the firm of R.H. Macy and Co., as this man, together with his older brother, made it impossible for me or my sons to remain, and I would not care to meet him. For your further information I would like you to know that if he got the office on the strength of his being a Jew, or representative of our people, he does not deserve it."[13]

The younger Straus wanted to bring Macy's into the "modern age," to free it from the stigma of being a cheap, unfashionable place known for nothing but bargains. He was a fanatic about rationalized merchandising and was convinced that the system of distribution and marketing demanded overhauling to ensure stable turnover of goods and money. Appalled by a long history of incompetence in keeping the books at Macy's, he instituted new cost accounting measures and more systematic personnel policies, as well as a Tayloresque time-study analysis. He hired the first controllers at

Macy's and filled the store with electric adding machines, Addressographs, calculating typewriters, stenciling machines, electrically driven devices for folding and unfolding envelopes, and better cash registers.[14]

Straus was fully aware of the efforts elsewhere to upgrade retailing, and he longed for his own educational fief where he could train salespeople. But apparently unable to finance and organize it himself, he joined other merchants to press New York University to give them their own retailing school. The first start-up executive meetings were held at Straus's private offices at Macy's and in the Mandarin Room at Lord & Taylor's on Thirty-seventh Street and Fifth Avenue. More than twenty merchants from stores in Newark, Manhattan, and Brooklyn attended these meetings, along with people from the New York City Board of Education and New York University. They hammered out structure and management and clarified lines of authority, with the university getting full control over hiring and curriculum. Straus chaired the executive committee, and Samuel Reyburn, head of Lord & Taylor and of the Associated Dry Goods Corporation, controlled the finance committee.

In May 1919 the university's School of Retailing opened its doors to train professionals to teach retailing in the city stores and high schools, with the overall intention of upgrading saleswork into "skilled labor." Its curriculum included distribution and management, textiles, color and design, store organization, and business ethics. The first formal philosophical statement of the school's agenda gave training in service high profile. "In an age of impersonal sources of power and an ever-increasing dependence on the personal resources of man himself," we must get "the human touch back into selling. . . . Much of the failure in modern retail selling arises from the lack of appreciation of the fundamental fact that the human equation is at the heart of the whole affair." The NYU School of Retailing "attempted to improve retail selling by raising to a higher level the development of the human factors upon which rest the task of distributing the world's goods."[15] Thirty students were accepted for the school's first year of courses, small peanuts perhaps but in retrospect very promising. Over the next ten years, New York University would emerge as the premier school in retail training in the country.[16]

Other universities boldly moved into the arena of business education as well, occupying an even bigger terrain than Straus's NYU and exercising a far more substantial influence. Between 1895 and 1915, the Wharton School, weak on the startup, fulfilled the mission mandated to it by its founder, industrialist Joseph Wharton: to advance the cause of professional business education. Under its new, consumption-minded director, Simon Patten, the school acquired international fame, and for the first time it became a four-year school; enrollments rose from 150 (in 1900) to 950 (in 1914), and the curriculum shifted to the study of such new fields as marketing, finance, and corporate management.[17] Among the leading faculty was economics professor Edward S. Mead, father of anthropologist Margaret Mead and husband of Emily Fogg Mead who was also an economist and a specialist in advertising. Edward Mead created the prestigious Evening School of Accounts and Finance at Wharton (in 1904) and the influential Extension School (in 1914). He led in the teaching of his favorite field—corporate finance (investment banking and corporate expansion through the marketing of securities). He believed that large corporations were the most efficient economic units and that their "centralized" structures offered the best means to control the flow of goods and money. To illustrate his point in class, he often singled out large department stores, detailing the way they used internal accounting procedures to control and manage their organizations. His books *The Story of Gold* and *The Ebb and Flow of Investment* were pioneering contributions.[18]

His wife, Emily, a feminist Progressive and mother of three, is herself a fascinating figure worthy of more scrutiny. She studied sociology and economics at Wharton (no doubt with Patten) between 1899 and 1900; later she published an analysis of the "possibilities" of American agriculture that won the Hart, Schaffner, and Marx prize (a newly minted prize awarded by this Chicago men's clothing business to scholars studying questions of distribution). She wrote a landmark piece on advertising—"The Place of Advertising in Modern Business"—that owed a great deal to Patten's views on consumption and that appeared in Thorstein Veblen's *Journal of Political Economy*; the piece was later cited by Veblen in his *Theory of Business Enterprise* and was reprinted in other journals, including *Fame*, a fleeting but influential advertising magazine edited by Artemas Ward. In this piece, Fogg Mead urged businessmen to penetrate the home, break down the resistance of ordinary housewives, and "forget the past" in their pursuit of profits. "Hence the necessity to apply new stimuli to convert the individual to the use of goods," she said, to "break up fixed habits, to allow new wants to develop, and to offer innumerable possibilities for their satisfaction."[19]

Even more groundbreaking in business education than Wharton, however, was Harvard University; in 1908 it created its Harvard School of

Business, the first independent professional school with a full-time faculty anywhere to offer masters degrees in business administration (M.B.A.s). "We take men without regard to what they have studied in college," wrote Dean A. Lawrence Lowell, "and we must teach them business, not political economy."[20]

The decision to teach business as a professional subject rested on the pragmatic insight that Harvard students were going into business in droves. "More than half of our senior class," President Charles Eliot said in 1908, "graduating last June went into business and for a good many years a large proportion have attained high place, particularly in corporation industries and the financial institutions of the country." If Harvard graduates were entering business, Eliot figured, then Harvard itself had better wake up and teach it. Harvard was also convinced that a new "expertise" was required to run the new corporate firms of the day. "The one-man ownership stage" in capitalism was dying, wrote one of the original Business School faculty. What was needed was training in management, "administrative organiza-tion," "large investment banking," and "large sales organizations"—in short, all those institutions and activities that formed the bedrock of the new corporate industrial order.[21]

The Harvard Business School's dedication to teaching these new sub-jects was its *raison d'être;* although underfunded in its first years, it did much to build a firm pedagogical foundation for such study. The school's first dean, forty-two-year-old economist Edwin Gay, knew a great deal in a scholarly way about patterns of distribution and consumption but next to nothing about practical business; but he saw clearly the drift of the age. Appointed in 1908, he helped channel economic thought away from pro-duction toward "the plastic elements of the economy," as he called them. "Concentrate," he said, "not so much on the way production is organized but on the methods of distribution and the widening market area."[22]

Under Gay, the Harvard Business School curriculum offered new sub-jects, among them advertising, investment finance, cost accounting, mod-ern banking, merchandising, retailing, and economic price movements. In 1914 one of the three required courses, "Economic Resources in the United States," was retitled "Marketing"—a shift of some note. Melvin Copeland, who first taught the course and published the first college text-book on it (a Harvard professor, Paul Cherington, also authored in 1914 the first textbook on advertising), wrote that marketing had been a term commonly used in schools of commerce before 1914 but meant only the study of "trade in raw commodities." The course at Harvard and soon at many other universities and colleges went well beyond this definition to "comprehend the whole process of physical distribution, demand activation, merchandising, pricing, and other activities involved in the exchange of products and services."[23]

Even more consequential than these changes was the opening in 1911 of the Harvard Bureau of Business Research, set up by Gay as part of the business school. It was the first such institution to study marketing, merchandising, and—Gay's personal province—distribution. Gay insisted that the "quantitative measurement for the marketing side of distribution" was central; and here he was guided by Archie Shaw, a millionare manufacturer of office equipment, editor of two influential business magazines—*System* and *Factory*—and an author himself of a widely circulated article on "the problem in market distribution."[24] At his suggestion Gay decided to organize the bureau. Other businessmen also expressed interest in the fledgling school, including national shoe retailers and manufacturers eager to overcome the disparities in their cost accounting methods.

Shaw believed that all energy should be spent on grappling with distribution. He persuaded the bureau to study middlemen—in particular, the new bankers and insurance companies that pooled the money many businesses needed to expand their marketing facilities. He argued that marketing should be examined in the broad sense described by Melvin Copeland. "Why has not systematic study been given to the problems of distribution?" Shaw asked. Industry had for too long been concerned with production; but "the problem of production" had been solved, Shaw argued—indeed, to such a degree that "our producing capacity" was "tremendous," "outstripping available markets" and threatening the United States with "overproduction," excessively low prices (too low for profits), and inefficiency. Factories had gone well beyond supplying the "staple needs" of the people; they were now "flooding markets" with novelties, luxuries, goods of all kinds, many attempting to meet needs "not even clearly formulated." Distribution was in a "chaotic condition" and a cause of "tremendous social waste."[25] "If our producing possibilities are to be fully utilized," Shaw said, "the problems of distribution" or of getting goods swiftly and profitably out of factories to consumers must be solved. A market must be found for the goods potentially made available. This means, in the main, a more intensive cultivation of existing markets. The unformulated wants of the individual must be ascertained and the possibility of gratifying them brought to his attention." How to identify and satisfy the "new desires," not to revile or repress them, was the business at hand. "There are some to be sure who deplore the increasing complexity of human wants," Shaw said. But "that is a problem for the philosopher, not the businessman." "The businessman finds his practical task in searching out human wants and providing the means of satisfaction."[26]

Marketing and distribution soon surfaced as top subjects for the bureau's analysis. At the request and with the help of shoe retailers and manufacturers, the bureau in its first year devised the first standard classification of accounts, which introduced a new uniformity into the shoe business. The shoe people had asked for a study of the industry's distribution methods, especially of the gap between factory costs and retail prices—a gap so big, one industry representative said, that "it is distribution that is being sold, not a manufactured product. The product itself and the cost of producing it bear a small percentage of the total amount of the labor, thought, and sacrifice that have gone into the transaction by the time the consumer gets the article."[27] The bureau's first study of shoe distribution, although done on a shoestring budget, was exemplary. Its "table of percentages," according to Copeland, was "the most valuable single research item ever published by Harvard." The shoe people praised it, printed its figures in the trade press, and gave their blessing to other similar investigations.

More distribution studies followed, each a collaboration between the bureau and merchants, who cofunded the research and willingly gave the bureau whatever operation statistics it desired. The bureau investigated the retail grocery business in 1914, wholesale shoe firms in 1915, the wholesale grocery business in 1916, retail general stores in 1917, retail hardware dealers in 1918, and retail jewelers in 1919. The National Association of Wholesale Grocers, like the others, was gratified by the fruits. "We feel," a spokesman said, "that this department of the university should be given all the encouragement possible. Not only is the information received valuable, but it has a great tendency to improve the accounting methods in the wholesale grocery business."[28]

In the late 1910s, the bureau was no longer a shoestring operation but big business. A 1920 study of department stores, the last in an unbroken sequence of yearly distribution studies, scrutinized more than five hundred department stores whose total sales volume exceeded $800 million. By Copeland's account, these investigations in retail and wholesale operating expenses were "the first studies of that type anywhere in the world."[29]

The Great Museums and the
New Curators

Side by side with these educational institutions, the great urban museums were also on the march to place their expertise and collections in the hands of mass market manufacturers and retailers. Today we have come to accept the alliance between museums and business as a commonplace and as a reflection of the intimate relationship between art and market forces. This relationship began, for all intents and purposes, in this earlier period, with four museums in particular—the American Museum of Natural History, the Brooklyn Museum, the Newark Museum, and the Metropolitan Museum of Art, all but one endowed by businessmen with extraordinary gifts to their collections, the most lavish of which were the donations to the Metropolitan from investment banker J. P. Morgan and by department store merchants George Hearn and Benjamin Altman.

A leader in this movement was Morris D'Camp Crawford, curator at the American Museum of Natural History and editor at *Women's Wear Daily*, who spent years promoting industrial design. He refused to follow in the footsteps of his father, a respected New York lawyer or those of his grandfather, a well-known Methodist minister who attracted public notice in 1857 when, as an abolitionist, he led the northern church in expelling southern slaveholders from the Methodist Conference. The young Crawford did follow in the footsteps of his Uncle Hanford, a member of that new generation of "transitional" merchants who helped guide American retailing from its family-owned, small-scale beginnings into mass market corporate merchandising. In 1899, Hanford Crawford was invited to take over the management of Scruggs, Vandervoort, and Barney in St. Louis, whose last surviving owner, Mr. Scruggs, was too feeble to keep control. Working around the clock, Hanford revamped the business into a full-fledged department store and imposed strict discipline on the work force. He opened buying offices in Paris and New York; in five years was president; and, with the aid of investment bankers, reorganized the store again, merging it with two large specialized retailing chains, one in carpets and furniture, the other in hardware. Hanford paid a price for this frantic pace; the "strain and worry" he felt as manager of a huge store—"a world in itself," he wrote, "in its discipline, its machinery, its relations"—undermined his health. He had a nervous collapse, breaking down in tears at the least cause both in public and private, and was not cured until he took up the piano (as a preventive measure, he even took a piano with him on business trips). At the same time, Scruggs, Vandervoort, and Barney became one of the commanding business organizations west of the Mississippi. By 1907, with Hanford still at the helm, a seventeen-story French Renaissance structure was built, noted for its huge show windows and its interior pillars covered with plate-glass mirrors.[30]

Morris D'Camp Crawford, then in his early twenties, was slightly repelled by his Uncle Hanford but mesmerized by what his uncle was accomplishing. As a young man, he worked for Horace B. Claflin, the ill-fated wholesale firm that collapsed in 1913, whereupon he turned to retailing, securing two posts he held nearly all his mature adult life—research editor of *Women's Wear Daily* and research associate in textiles for New York's American Museum of Natural History. The museum job was created expressly for Crawford by the museum's president, Henry Fairfield Osborn, in 1915, "in recognition of the work [Crawford] has been doing for us with Peruvian textiles."[31]

Crawford lectured at the museum to professional designers and factory managers on Peruvian fabrics (he was a national authority), on weaving and cotton, and on how to relate "primitive decorative art" to "machine processes."[32] Although the museum had a longstanding principle of supporting commercial design, Crawford, assisted by the head of the anthropology department, Clark Wissler, got the museum actively to open its collections to business on a regular basis.[33] He spoke publicly to industrialists on the wonders of the museum. In a 1916 speech before a National Silk Manufacturers Convention in New York, he urged his audience to come and see "the carving on a Maya tomb, the etched birchbark cradle of Labrador, the superb ponchos of archaic Peru, the rough raffia embroidery of Africa—all offer splendid, vital suggestions."[34] He put together exhibitions of contemporary costumes in the great North American Indian Hall, the design of every item "drawn from the aboriginal subjects" of the museum's collections.[35] President Osborn was delighted, giving Crawford and his associates "his every consideration and endorsement." Crawford was introducing everybody—not just the rich and upper class—to "art and beauty." ("My motto has always been," Osborn observed, "We must stoop to conquer.") As an excellent side effect, a new phase began in the evolution of women's dress in this country. At last, Osborn wrote, "our women" will wear American designs and "not have to express in their clothing the decadence which is so widespread in the countries of Europe."[36]

Sometimes Crawford imitated Fifth Avenue display strategies in his exhibits, however, that were a little too risqué, a little too European, for Osborn's tastes. In a 1919 show Crawford put lifelike "wax models" in silk garments in the "second alcove of the entrance" to the exhibition and several "living models" in the "silk loom exhibits." Osborn blanched and, through his director, Frederic A. Lucas, complained to Crawford that "these are Parisian rather than American."[37] He demanded that they be removed, and they were, although probably without much protest from Crawford who had, after all, achieved his larger goal of expanding his design movement. As an editor of *Women's Wear*, he took every chance to praise the American Museum of Natural History for being "the most progressive force in the development of the designer" and in "aiding the movement of industrial arts in this country."[38] He founded and managed the Textile Design Contests, sponsored for the first time in 1917 by *Women's Wear*. Through the pages of his magazine he arranged design activities on a national basis, spurring on museum curators everywhere, entreating them to take part in what he called his "Designed-in-America Campaign."[39]

Among the curators who followed Crawford's lead were Stewart Culin of the Brooklyn Museum and John Cotton Dana of the Newark Museum. Both, although a full generation older than Crawford, held positions of public prominence at the same time he did and both shaped their careers on behalf of industrial design. Culin—whom Crawford admired for his "flawless, inspired taste"—was born in Philadelphia in 1858 to German Lutheran parents. He became one of the foremost folklorists and anthropologists of his time. He traveled around the world collecting primitive artifacts and living with primitive peoples (his accounts of primitive games for adults and children are still drawn on today, including his groundbreaking *Games of North American Indians*, in 1907). In the early 1900s, under the sponsorship of John Wanamaker, Culin conducted three expeditions to study North American Indian cultures. He was named curator of the ethnological collection at the Brooklyn Museum in 1903, and through tireless collecting, built the Brooklyn Museum into a world-class institution.[40]

Less orderly in his evolution than either Culin or Crawford, John Cotton Dana was all over the map in his youth, looking for a life and an occupation that would free him from an intensely religious, guilt-ridden childhood in Woodstock, Vermont. Born in 1856 to strict Congregationalists who traced their origins straight back to John Cotton, "John knew the regimen of the inflexible moral law and of the old New England Sabbath," as a biographer put it.[41] After graduating from college in 1874, he worked in Colorado as a land surveyor, then came East to study law. Unsatisfied, he returned to Colorado to live on a ranch and marry the sister of a close Colorado friend. This marriage, coupled with the death of his parents (both events, in their very different ways, helping to end his dependence on his parents' world-view), plunged him into an agonizing religious crisis. The idea that "sin was a manifestation of wilful human depravity" became abhorrent to him. He adopted Unitarianism, but, as he himself said, "I was working a very different lead from Unitarianism." Restless and distraught, he went from job to job—construction work, journalism, bank-building. By 1890 all institutional religion was dead in him, the very thought provoking him to rage. Holger Cahill, the artist who worked with Dana at the Newark Museum, described Dana as "very vehement about religion." "He was opposed to it . . . vehemently opposed."[42]

Dana was becoming a "new man," rejecting anything that restricted his own personal freedom of choice and action and that cut him off from the "new" and "modern." As Cahill said, he became a true "Vermonter," a "libertarian who would let you do what he thought you really believed in." In the late 1880s he became a pioneering librarian in Newark, New Jersey, creating the first library for business materials and introducing "open stacks" to American libraries. In 1909 he founded the Newark Museum, not only as a place to exhibit "fine art" but also as an institution to serve business.[43]

Dana and Culin shared with Crawford a commitment to commerce, a commitment strengthened in part by the absence of any strong counter religious or moral conviction. Culin, from his many travels and a lifetime of ethnological reflection, had concluded that "everywhere from Nijni to Bucharest, from the Kirile Islands to Jahore, whatever is the nominal excuse, commerce is the center of life." For Culin, department stores epitomized "the social and commercial life of Americans." The stores, not churches, are "the greatest influences for culture and taste that exist today. They make it possible for us all to participate in the creative thought of a new and revolutionary era."[44]

Both Culin and Dana detested traditional museums; Dana saw them as "remote palaces and temples" inaccessible to ordinary people, gloomy and intimidating, and devoted only to the display of ancient artifacts and "fine art." It would be far better if all museums were like department stores. The stores were at the "center" of city life, "honest . . . steel and concrete" structures "filled with objects closely associated with the life of the people." They were "open at all hours"; they displayed "objects" alluringly; they provided "resting places" so that people could relax as they shopped. Department stores foregrounded "objects" and put them on sale for everybody, thus "increasing the zest of life."[45] For Dana, everything "new" (and thus everything "good") was related to business. "Business runs the world, or, the world gets civilized just as fast as men learn to run things on plain business principles. A public institution does its best work when it is useful to men of business." Like Walt Whitman but without the critical edge Whitman often showed, Dana celebrated the city's industrial life. He habitually walked the Newark streets, observing the "tenements and factories beside the railway and canal." "The streets were alive with men, women, and children," he told the Newark Board of Trade. "Smoke poured out of tall chimneys, and they and their factories loomed up in the mist, monstrous, picturesque, and imposing. Here was industrial America. Here was the machine age, and the fellow citizens-to-be of you and me, growing up to wait upon it."[46] It helped, of course, that businessmen themselves— above all Louis Bamberger of Bamberger's department store, who financed the expansion of the Newark Museum in the 1920s—gave freely of their money to Dana's experimental design enterprise.

Culin and Dana had no doubts or qualms about the strategic role that design played in increasing the profits of the mass-production companies. Nor did they believe that machine-made goods were in any way inferior to those goods produced by hands. "The handicraft of the day," wrote Culin to Morris D'Camp Crawford, "is not eminently distinguished in point of taste from the machine product," though machine-made goods could be often, but were not inevitably, weaker in pattern, line, shape, and color. Dana agreed, and he was aggressively critical of those "snobs" who, he said, worshiped at the altar of "the hand-crafted." Taking a page, he thought, from Veblen, he wrote that "the rich have usually been ready to adopt the older methods in art productions if for any reason they were inaccessible to the poor." "Today admiration for the hand-made is largely born of a desire to have something which, being unique in its kind, will impart a little of the old leisure-class exclusiveness to its owner."[47]

Animated by the same kind of consumer populism that typified Wanamaker and other merchants, Dana and Culin offered their museum facilities to designers from all walks of business. Dana organized design spaces in Newark and conducted large expositions of industrially made goods.

Probably the first U.S. museum director to dare such expositions, he believed that "the function of museums was to show the meaning of the arts in relation to industrial society." In 1912 he exhibited the work of Deutcheswerkbund, a German industrial design group and a major precursor of the Bauhaus, followed thereafter by "a great many shows of industrial art" from American firms. He was "prouder of the neglected art of the machine age than of the old masters."[48] Oil painting, which constituted the core content of the traditional museum, came close to boring him, because such art, in his view, had almost no relationship to the life or thinking of "ordinary people." Industrial art or machine art, on the other hand, was the art "the people" understood, because they could buy it themselves and bring it home. That the "people" did not conceive or "make" these goods hardly mattered. It was enough for him to assert merely that mass marketed machine goods were destined to reflect popular taste, whereas handcrafted goods—which *were* made by men and women themselves—were "removed" from the people, and inherently elitist, an argument more pro-business than pro-people.

Culin, for his part, made the Brooklyn Museum "a center for artistic industries"; his aim was to inspire industrial designers to integrate peasant and primitive designs and colors into machine-made goods. He viewed preindustrial cultures as "sensuously" and "vitally" superior to industrial cultures, which, he said, so often disparaged the primitive as "weak," effeminate, childish, and irrational. "I have refreshed myself," he said of his many visits with North American Indians, and "feel myself younger and more vital. I have realized my dreams among savages in whose lives and thoughts I have had glimpses of the dawn of the world." Getting the "primitive" into goods, Culin argued, would allow people to regain healthy contact with the "vital elements" while at the same time paying back to business a sure profit on a relatively cheap investment. Like so many others in the new commercial fields, he thought Americans had deprived themselves for too long of "bright" colors, falsely believing such colors childish. Besides, there is much to learn from childhood, just as from the "primitives." Why, I myself, he said, "had the child's eagerness and color desire" and "I still sympathize with this craving in children."[49]

In 1917 Culin opened a design studio in the Brooklyn Museum, and filled it with thousands of the primitive and peasant artifacts he had gathered on trips in Africa, Eastern Europe, India, Persia, and North America. A year later both the "studio" and Culin had "become very well known to some of our most successful designers," as Morris Crawford reported in *Women's Wear*. Culin, proud of "his laboratory of taste," boasted to his friend at the Museum of Natural History, the anthropologist Franz Boas, of the "intimate relations" that "have grown up between" his "department of the museum and a large number of professional artists."[50]

Furniture designers and designers of wrapping papers, combs, labels, and packaging visited the Brooklyn Museum. But, as a result of a lot of promotion by Crawford in *Women's Wear*, it was manufacturers and department store buyers of "fashion" clothing who flocked there. Fashion designers picked up ideas—primitive, exotic ideas—from peasant fabrics, and put them into American fashion. Museum space was at a premium because demand was so great. "I have set up my Indian materials on a stairway," he wrote a manufacturer in 1919, "employing the wood work I bought at Ahmadabad [in India]. Designers of women's clothes have turned to India for materials this winter and my Indian textiles and costumes have been in demand. The designers of women's clothes have been making much use of it."[51] At a moment's notice and on demand, moreover, Culin delivered folk artifacts to be used for display or as models for design virtually anywhere in the country to satisfy a current fashion trend.

Although the Newark Museum, the Brooklyn Museum, and the American Museum of Natural History contributed much to the new industrial design movement, none equaled in influence the Metropolitan Museum of Art in Manhattan. Shy in early years of taking part in the still inchoate industrial design movement (although the museum's charter mandated that the museum do something to help train artisans and artistic craftspeople), the Metropolitan found itself by 1915 enamored of the new frontier. Museum officials were immensely proud of recent acquisitions that, as the museum's *Bulletin* said, "enabled them to place at the disposal of the designer and manufacturer *an illimitable power of suggestion*."[52] In 1914, a new position was created there—associate in industrial arts—and Richard Bach was appointed to fill it. Bach commanded even greater resources than Culin, Dana, and Crawford. He supervised the museum's close collaboration with business and shared the others' same unequivocal romance with machines and industrial design. "It may be a startling assertion to make," he wrote, "but the machine is undoubtedly the greatest single advantage and aid that has ever been offered to civilization so far as the industrial arts are concerned. . . . If there is anything wrong with machine manufacture, it is not the fault of the machine." The prospects were exciting: "We have the possibility of disseminating a good design in 20,000 places, while under ordinary conditions of purely manual craftsmanship, there might have been no more than a dozen chairs of that kind."[53]

Bach recognized, perhaps even better than the others did, how strategic "design" was to the success of mass production. The surfaces and shapes of many kinds of objects, not their underlying structure or function, so Bach understood, offered the greatest potential for business profits. Indeed, "design alone" might yield "the entire profit." "Those who make and sell but never design," he wrote, "or those others whose last year's designs are still good enough, are only 'marking time' in dread of industrial cataclysms."[54] Under Bach's regime at the Metropolitan close ties were established between the museum and manufacturers and designers. The museum welcomed the organization of special exhibitions that showcased the design industries. In 1915 a touring exhibit, displaying and explaining the relationship between the laws of color and harmony and "actual textiles, wallpapers, and woods" was presented under the auspices of the Art and Trades Club. One of the club's members, William Sloan Coffin—furniture maker and future president of the Metropolitan—supervised the exhibit. A year later, the Metropolitan cooperated with *Women's Wear Daily* in the presentation of that magazine's first Textile Design Contest, including thirty-one participating states and with Henry Kent, the museum's secretary, serving as one of the judges.[55]

Regular lectures and seminars, arranged in consultation with merchants, were conducted in museum rooms. In 1916, the design "expert" Florence Levy delivered a lecture series on design for industry representatives, salespeople, and department store buyers; the course became standard at the museum, dealing with line, mass, harmony, and color. In the late 1910s, Percy Straus of Macy's induced Bach to create a seminar on color and design for Macy's salespeople and executive managers; it was led by Grace Cornell of Columbia University's Teachers College. Display man at Altman's, Herman Frankenthal taught courses in the "art of draping," and Louis Weinberg gave classes on color based on a "study of the museum's originals." (The Weinberg lectures were later published in book form as *Color in Everyday Life, A Manual for Lay Students, Artisans, and Artists.*)[56]

In all of these activities, museum design experts appealed for new commercial aesthetics wherein color would be used as "a more deliberately planned factor" in consumer goods. Weinberg believed that the American businessman—unlike other American men, who still, he said, viewed color as "effeminate"—was at last beginning to recognize color's commercial value. "In the field of business, which is engaging the expert thought of men today, there are few lines in which a knowledge of color is not essential. The business man uses color, and pays dearly for its use." "Color is a business asset" and "not to be underestimated in a business career."[57]

The Metropolitan's most popular industrial design service could be found in the museum's "laboratories" and workrooms, where designers thought up ideas for apartment house lighting fixtures, cheap jewelry, soap wrappers, toothpaste containers, cretonne, and lampshades. It was here, mainly in the design workrooms, that the museum made contact with mass production. Established in 1909 on a small scale, these rooms quickly grew into large operations, staffed by men and women expert in furnishings, advertising, jewelry, clothing, package design, and the "host of other decorative arts for which the public expends $1 billion a year." These experts advised visiting manufacturers and designers and were especially "acquainted," Bach said, "with the devious [sic] requirements of the enormous and intricate selling machinery of the country." The leading associate— Bach himself—visited factories and shops to keep "abreast of the market" and to "visualize trade values in museum facilities and thus help manufacturers toward their own objectives." He supplied thousands of photographs at cost to students and designers.[58]

In 1917 Bach launched his first big industrial arts exhibition at the museum to show off the manufactured goods designed in these museum studios. Each commodity was exhibited next to the artifact from which its design was derived—reproductions of Colonial furniture next to eighteenth-century "originals," affordable jewelry against "Byzantine ivories," "embroidered crests" against American "sport skirts." At the 1919 show, Bach wrote in the museum's *Bulletin*, visitors were "astonished" as they passed by "commercial containers" looking like "Athenian vases" or by wallpapers with the look of "ecclesiastical vestments." On display the following year were Cha-ming talc cans next to Ming vases "dating from the period 1644– 1662," La France Rose soap boxes in the company of Louis XIV jewel boxes, and Colgate toothpaste containers next to a variety of museum "art objects."[59]

Bach's exhibitions expressed the commitment of America's best museums to the emerging prerogatives of consumer capitalism. Bach, Culin, Dana, and Crawford, among others, all thought that ideas and images of the past were marketable goods, like any other goods, and that they should be enlisted in the cause of spreading the idea of "beauty" to the masses. They imagined a better world taking shape out of their collaborations with business. Still, they were opportunists who suspended judgment about businessmen and climbed on the bandwagon of catering to business needs. All argued that the large museums, if they wanted influence, status, and patronage, had no choice but to take this route, since commerce, they were all convinced, had overtaken religion as the center of life. Everything revolved around commerce—human aspiration, dreams, the imagination. Like numerous other men and women of their times—Frank Alvah Parsons, Joseph Urban, Faith Chipperfield, Nancy McClellan, Maxfield Parrish, and L. Frank Baum, among others—they were certain that commerce held the lion's share of power and that any institution or individual who failed to acknowledge that obvious fact would go under.

City Pageants and Hobnobbing with Mayors

Big merchants boasted of their closeness to city mayors and politicians. "We are intimate friends of Mayor Hylan," wrote John Wanamaker to an acquaintance about the mayor of New York. Mayor John Hylan "knows that none of us would do anything or permit anything to be done by others to hurt his splendid standing." "The mayor was our friend," remembered David Yates, Marshall Field's executive of Democrat Carter Harrison, and so also was "Bath House" John Coughlin, infamous and wily alderman of Chicago's First Ward at the turn of the century. "I'd see [Bath House] and he'd say: 'Don't worry what I'm going to say. I'm with you hook, line, and sinker, no matter what you do.' " And Bath House was, without question, smoothing the way for the store to buy up whatever real estate it needed to consolidate its place on State Street and Washington.[60]

After 1905, and as an outcome of many inside deals and appeals, many merchants managed to influence fundamentally the shape of urban space, acquiring new real estate to round out their properties and obtaining rights to destroy old structures to make way for new construction and better traffic conditions. Special subway stations were erected for the big department stores and hotels. Bus and train routes were created or rerouted to satisfy the business requirements of these and similar institutions. In New York, merchants like Abraham Abraham of Brooklyn's Abraham and Straus (who sat on the borough president's Traffic Committee in 1907) so influenced the planning of the subway lines that the lines converged in downtown Brooklyn, where several major department stores—including his own—did business. [61]

Sometimes the stores didn't even bother to petition the city, so confident were they in the public value of their actions. In 1913, without getting authority from the Board of Estimate, Gimbels on Thirty-fourth Street in New York built a covered footbridge from the elevated railway directly into the store. The city protested, and Isaac Gimbel responded with a letter explaining that the bridge removed congestion by encouraging the "free circulation of traveling to the avenue and streets surrounding the station and said store." It will, he averred, be "beneficial to the travelling public and the people of the City." No apologies, no admission of anything wrong. The references to "service" and "circulation" probably had their good effect, as intended. After another exchange of letters and a promise from Gimbels to "fireproof" the structure, the store was granted the right to do what it had already done. [62]

Mayors and other elected officials often made it their business to attend any important events having to do with the big stores. Occasionally they had to coax merchants fearful of making the wrong public impressions to accept the city's help. In the spring of 1901, a city alderman in New York wrote the Straus brothers at Macy's advising them to send representatives to a City Council meeting regarding a "resolution prohibiting push cart peddlers from certain parts of your district." "I have introduced" the resolution myself, the alderman said, so please "be present to give voice to it." The Straus brothers refused to go; advocating the removal of peddlers might upset some softhearted people. Didn't the Straus family come, after all, from a long pedigree of peddlers? Privately, however, the brothers were "in favor of the resolution" and they said so to city officials. [63]

The most important instruments for collaboration between city governments and merchants were the trade associations, groups that arose to shape the city in their own image and to counter the power of what they perceived to be irresponsible bosses and unsympathetic working-class Americans. New York City's Fifth Avenue Association, led by merchants, spawned imitators in cities throughout the country; it shaped—more than any other group—the entire evolution of the Fifth Avenue district. Between

1913 and 1920, the city implemented many of its demands. Streets were widened, trees planted, public space freed—to the "extent that it was possible"—of "riff-raff," as the association's reports noted. "Isles of safety" for pedestrians were created on the streets, and garish billboards were demolished. At the urging of the association, the city adopted new subway stations and rerouted bus service to serve the retail district better. As a result of intense lobbying "by a small group of our members" came new zoning and occupancy laws, meant to remove manufacturing from above Twenty-third Street and to prevent the "crowding caused by swarms of garment workers who loiter in the streets at mid-day and make it impossible for people to enter the stores, banks, and offices." These laws started the process by which much of Fifth Avenue became by 1929 a fully legally protected "Retail Zone" decisively set off like a jewel from the rest of the city and from all industrial development.[64]

Collaboration between city trade associations and city governments interjected a new consumer dimension into civic culture. In the summer of 1912 two prominent trade groups in New York City joined the Department of Parks and the Police Department in organizing a municipal pageant for children, "Around the World in Search of Fairyland," held on the Sheep Meadow of Central Park and adapted from a 1912 Hippodrome production of the same name. An allegory of consumer abundance in five parts, the pageant was designed, according to the city, to "promote real democracy" by "making for more 'inclusiveness' and by eliminating 'exclusiveness.' " It began by depicting "the search for fairyland," where children in Old World costumes "hunt and hunt but cannot find that wonderful land." It ended with dancing, colors, and electrical lights, and a "Feast" of "cakes, mineral water, ice cream, and candy."[65]

A fleet of automobiles, donated by many of the city's big merchants (including Gimbels, Macy's, and Greenhut-Siegel-Cooper), carried more than five thousand participating poor children from "the enormous mixed population" of the city's neighborhoods to Central Park. Edison Electric supplied red, blue, and white lights, decorations, and a "giant electrical 'Maypole,' " which contrived the "wonderful electrical 'Fairyland' scene." The Hotel and Business Men's League of Greater New York volunteered the sweets and refreshments for the concluding climactic "Feast."[66]

Similar large-scale pageants, collaboratively produced by city governments and merchants, occurred elsewhere in the country. In 1917 the municipal authorities of St. Louis cooperated with local businessmen to present a "spectacle," "the Fall Festival and Fashion Pageant," in the city's Forest Park. With cofunding from the Advertising Club and the St. Louis Fashion Show (both new trade groups), the city rushed all summer to finish constructing a new outdoor municipal theater in time for the pageant. It allowed the merchants and manufacturers to use the theater "rent-free" as long as they kept ticket prices low, donated their profits for maintenance and improvements, and brought workers and their families from around the city to the pageant performances.[67]

The first Fashion Pageant was unlike anything ever seen in St. Louis, a kind of consumer *Gesamtkunstwerk* or total theatrical spectacle integrating "all the arts"—theater, visual effects, dancing, music, and singing as well as merchandising. First came a military ensemble featuring a female marching band and bugle corps of over two hundred women, all employees from Famous-Barr, one of the city's large department stores. Hundreds of "live mannequins" paraded up and down giant runways that reached far out into the audience, displaying the "latest fashions" in footgear, coats, millinery, and evening costumes—150 different kinds of garments in all. Interwoven throughout were "artistic *tableaux* and ballet dancing," including the "Dance of the Statues," where marble figures "came to life" and were "magically" transformed into mannequins dressed in "glamorous evening clothes." A completely choreographed dance number, "The Revels of Dionysius," rounded off the pageant production.[68]

This event was so popular that it was held again and again over the next ten years. It was a gaudy symbol of the city's commitment to "democratizing" commercial culture. And it was perhaps the first time a municipal government had ever attempted, in such an open way, to use consumer enticements to influence public opinion (in the name of cultural uplift) and to divert it away from the conflicts and tensions plaguing the city. Of the pageant, a trade periodical said, "This was the first recorded instance when municipal authorities officially recognized commerce as a catholicon for the ills of urban life."[69]

The Widening Sphere of Public Action

A political apparatus on the federal level also emerged to support the new consumer economy and culture, joining the new chorus of supporting municipalities, museums, commercial art schools, and universities. After 1890, the administrative arm of the federal government expanded, prefiguring a new era in American history. In this Progressive period, the antigovernment bias of the nineteenth century would be greatly weakened.[70] In 1903, for instance, the Department of Commerce and Labor was set up, with a range of divisions from the Bureau of Corporations to the Lighthouse Board and Bureau of Statistics. In 1913 this department was, in turn, replaced by the new Department of Commerce and new agencies, including the Bureau of Foreign and Domestic Commerce and the Children's Bureau. A Department of Labor also was organized in that year. The United States Postal Service incorporated the parcel post in 1912 and a vastly expanded RFD. Congress also created the Federal Reserve Board (1913), the Federal Trade Commission (1914), and the Tariff Commission (1916).[71]

The reasons for this expansion related directly to the rise of corporate capitalism and to the conflict and disorder, as well as to the opportunities, attending that rise.[72] The expansion, however, was not an easy one for Americans to accept or undertake (as it was for Europeans who went through similar changes but were accustomed to state intervention), given the traditional American fear of centralized power in any form. It was shaped, therefore, by tendencies often at odds with one another.

On the one hand, many progressives insisted that the federal government act as a vigilant arbiter of the well-being of all the people, as a mediator, according to historians Barry Supple and Mary Furner, for "civic purposes larger than the ambitions of any particular interest."[73] In pursuit of this aim, new agencies were created to carry out public investigations and to monitor injustices inflicted by one group on another; their efforts also produced new laws to protect the public interest.[74] Thus the work of federal commissions and congressional committees from 1880s onward produced antitrust laws and a remarkable legacy of protective labor legislation.[75] In 1912, Congressman Arsene Pujo held hearings to investigate the banking system and uncovered what he called "the rapidly growing concentration of control of money and credit in the hands of a few [New York bankers]"; the result was the creation of the Federal Reserve Board, which introduced regulation into banking and attempted to eliminate New York banker control.[76]

From the 1890s onward, indignant citizens also turned to the U.S. government to protect the people from the dangers of contaminated food;

to prevent corporations from exploiting women and children in industry; and to regain, in some measure, the older consumer control over what was being produced and how. Recognizing the dangers inherent in the ever-yawning distance between the worlds of consumption and production, new consumer advocacy groups—especially the National Consumers' League under Florence Kelley—insisted that people be protected against rapacious, irresponsible businessmen. As historian David Thelen has shown, these reformers were disturbed that more and more consumers knew nothing about how goods were made, nothing about the human cost and suffering. To prevent this trend from continuing, Kelley and others called on the state; they testified before commissions and demanded new laws designed to force the government into vigilance and, they hoped, to "reunite consumption and production" on a more humane foundation. One result was the Pure Food and Drug Law of 1906.[77]

At the same time, the federal government was beginning to serve the cause of corporate business, forming the foundation that Herbert Hoover and others would build on in the 1920s. Washington had, of course, long helped business, giving land subsidies to railroads, tariff protection to many industries, and funds for the nation's world's fairs. But after 1895, the range of reinforcements and interventions increased, albeit unsystematically. The antitrust laws, strict on paper, were rarely applied in fact and never enforced at all for oligopoly (or market domination by a few firms); indeed, as recent business history has shown, due to legal conflicts with the states never clearly resolved, the federal laws actually legitimized the existence of these firms while at the same time giving Americans a sense—a "symbolical" sense—that something was being done when nothing was being done to "alter the nation's new brand of corporate capitalism."[78] Even more crucial, the corporations themselves and the concentration of economic power they signified would not have existed at all had it not been for the enabling powers of the state, which invested the corporations with the legal rights to exist. Journalist Walter Lippmann wrote in 1937 "that the concentration of control in modern industry is not caused by technical change but is a creation of the state through its laws."[79]

Many departments and agencies also acted to aid business by facilitating the movement of goods outward into foreign markets. The Federal Reserve Act not only sought to expedite a reliable flow of capital at home and abroad but also assured American companies that they could establish branch banks in foreign countries. The Tariff Commission supplied the president with (among other things) data on worldwide markets so he might decide how best to help business enter those markets. The Bureau of Foreign and Domestic Commerce sent trained drummers and commercial investigators abroad; it produced industrial films to promote the sale of American goods, published *Commerce Reports* (a daily paper on foreign trade possibilities), and placed commercial consular offices in foreign countries to monitor trade information and to help American business find new markets.[80]

The Federal Trade Commission (FTC), empowered by Congress to move against "unfair methods of competition in commerce," was, during these years, an exemplar of cooperation between business and government. It was headed in this period by men favorable to business who championed advertising practices, helped instruct companies in "exact cost accounting procedures," and assisted domestic exporters by gathering data on trade and tariffs.[81] The FTC (and its immediate precursor, the Bureau of Corporations) also responded to appeals from business to settle disputes among competing economic factions. Between 1911 and 1913, for instance, national manufacturers urged the Bureau (and then the FTC) to arbitrate a disagreement between mass retailers and manufacturers over which group had the right to control the resale price of goods. The large retailers wanted freedom to cut prices at will, while manufacturers sought assurances that they could retain control over the prices of their trademarked goods (the bureau ruled on behalf of the mass retailers).[82]

A few years later, the FTC and national manufacturers worked together—at the invitation of the manufacturers—on behalf of establishing uniform standards of "truth" in advertising (the industry was then being attacked for "lies" and "distortions") and to prevent wildcat advertisers from "invading the sanctity of trademarks and disparaging competing products." In addition, national advertisers successfully discouraged the FTC from making a critical assessment of advertising as an inherently biased activity. The effects of this victory are still felt to this day. "Every man," declared a trade representative before the commission in 1915, "should have the right to say about his product what he believes to be true. There are circumstances where exaltation brings the reader nearer to precise understanding than scientific statement of technical facts."[83]

The results of these collaborations were not always pro-corporate business, as the abiding hostility to concentrated power and the continued support for small businesses within the government showed. Nevertheless, these new institutional relationships between government and business, with the government acting as arbitrator, did help make the government a far more formidable ally of large-scale businesses, and of the whole evolution of corporate commerce.

Better Babies and Better Deliveries

Two other federal agencies—the U.S. Children's Bureau and the greatly expanded U.S. Postal Service—worked similarly in their relation to commerce. The U.S. Children's Bureau, that most soundly Progressive of all agencies, fought to promote the health and welfare of children. It also helped, both intentionally and unintentionally, to spread a new commodity ethic and culture.

Founded in 1912 under the able direction of Julia Lathrop, the bureau galvanized opposition to child labor and sought to lower American infant mortality rates (the highest in the West) and to raise nutrition levels (the lowest in the West). It also worked closely with the National Consumers' League, a group that had already paved the way, by establishing a children's agenda. From the 1890s on, the National Consumers' League had ferreted out the exploitation of children in department stores, in textile and garment factories, and in candy and glass manufacturing, where children worked long hours and at extremely low pay, especially during Christmastime. The goal again was to make Americans aware of the cost involved in the historic separation of production and consumption, and to make the government the agent for ending the suffering that, in many instances, could not be seen.

The Children's Bureau upheld and forwarded this mission. It collaborated with the league in urging strict compliance with the compulsory school attendance laws as the best way to prevent exploitive employment, and it supported a federal Child Labor Law (twice declared unconstitutional by the U.S. Supreme Court), which gave Congress the power to limit, regulate, and prohibit the labor of persons under eighteen. (This law finally was passed as part of the Fair Labor Standards Act of 1938.)[84] The Bureau created Baby Day in 1915, followed by Baby Week a year later, and Children's Year in 1918, all designed to publicize the need for better infant and maternal care.[85]

The achievements of the bureau and league were undeniable, bettering children's lot in this country. They were undertaken because they were in and of themselves good things. But these changes occurred as well because Julia Lathrop and her staff cooperated with American merchants to make certain a new and better child world emerged.

Here again, the National Consumers' League led the way for the bureau, by tireless work with department stores to abolish child labor. As Florence Kelley later put it, "we endeavored to redeem the holiday season for children." By 1911, in response to league protests, nearly all big stores in major cities had ended what Kelley called the "holiday cruelties"—the nighttime employment of children during the Christmas holiday season. In the process, both the department stores and the National Consumer League began to see eye to eye on common aims in regard to children's welfare. Kelley drew attention to this pattern when, in a speech at Gimbels in 1910 honoring the opening of the New York store on Broadway and Thirty-fourth Street, she praised "the cooperation in this movement extended by the heads of the great retail concerns in many centers."[86]

The U.S. Children's Bureau, too, recognized the importance of department stores, not only as exploiters but also as allies. To get its messages across, the bureau established a special liaison relationship with hundreds of stores, by now among the key institutional anchors of downtown city life.[87] It relied, for example, on department stores to publicize Baby Day, Baby Week, Children's Year, and the Back-to-School Movement, all of which the bureau had inaugurated. In Boston, stores held "baby-welfare exhibits and talks." Retailers of every description around the country sold "baby buttons" and displayed "baby clothes." "The little child at birth and for several years thereafter," wrote one baby-campaigner merchant, "has to have an entire world of its own, not only special clothes and special foods, but special furniture, special bathing arrangements, special articles of all kinds."[88] In one Missouri city, a large dry goods business built an auditorium especially designed for "baby-week lectures." In other cities, the bureau reported, the link between the retailers and the baby-week campaigners was so close that "the campaign was in danger of being considered a commercial advertising one."[89] (See plate 16).

Many merchants took up the children's campaign with a fervor equaled to that of public officials. "Backed by plenty of newspaper publicity and the government's sanction," wrote one retailing spokesman, "the baby welfare campaign has been proved a crowdbringer by many stores." Even before the "government's sanction" legitimized a wave of such promotions, some stores had begun "Baby Weeks," distributing baby literature and showing goods in the windows around Baby Week themes. Stores held inexpensive classes on nutrition and diet as well as baby-weighing contests, an important public service since a baby's weight indicated an infant's nutrition level and its capacity to survive.[90]

This collaboration between the bureau and urban merchants had two not necessarily compatible results. First, it supplied mothers with services they might not have been able to obtain elsewhere, as many women learned useful ideas and methods of child care. And second, it served the interests of the merchants. In 1912 the bureau, in effect, "owned" the days it had created—Baby Day and Children's Day; in a few short years, control over these days was passed to merchants, who exploited them to the hilt.

Although its own goal had nothing overtly to do with merchandising, the general impact of the U.S. Children's Bureau's joint effort with stores was to contribute, indirectly, to the expansion of the consumer economy. By relying on the stores, the bureau had, in fact, endorsed them as centers for "service" and implicitly justified the introduction and sale of more and more children's goods, the addition of children's departments, and the enlargement of older departments.

The impact of the reformed U. S. Postal Service on a consumer economy, on the other hand, was direct, immediate, and extremely wide-ranging. Before 1900, Americans living in the country and on farms had no mail delivery to the door. They had to go to town to pick up their mail. City dwellers, by contrast, had enjoyed direct mail delivery by the federal government since 1861. At the same time, everybody—urban and rural folk alike—was dependent on six large express companies to deliver packages, but at very high rates. The companies served adequately only a few areas of the country and delivered packages to the customer's door only in a few big cities. Between 1898 and 1920 the federal government took over parcel post and rural postal deliveries.[91]

The origins of this reform lay mainly in the hands of John Wanamaker. As writers on Wanamaker have noted, his dream as U.S. postmaster general from 1889 to 1893 was to increase the powers of the government so that all people would enjoy greater access to the goods and pleasures of modern life.[92] In 1889 he introduced fast mail-train service on a transcontinental basis. He had mailboxes built for city residences and raised the number of free city delivery offices from 401 to 610. He worked hard for the passage of rural free delivery and parcel post, achieving something of a victory in

1892 when he was given monies to experiment with rural free delivery in a few towns. But his success was limited, for despite considerable support from farmers (and the National Grange in particular), neither he nor they had the power to generate widespread congressional support. Nor were they able to mount a strong offensive against their fierce adversaries—the small-town merchants and the national express companies. Fearing (and, to some degree, rightly) that a bigger U. S. Postal Service would destroy them, these groups organized national campaigns against the new reforms.[93] In the Midwest, the heart of opposition, they focused on the proposed changes as "dangerous class legislation"; "the tendency of such legislation," wrote a typical critic, "is toward socialism, causing the government to enter the business competition with private enterprise."[94]

Throughout the 1890s and into the early 1900s, however, the tide began to turn against this coalition of forces. Increasingly, the public wearied of the price gouging of the express companies. A new political alliance began to take shape. The big mail-order houses—always the most powerful backers of an enlarged service—began to act aggressively for the first time, joining the small farmers and city people in urging passage of the new postal laws. Behind a new Washington lobbying group, the Postal Progress League, formed in 1902, stood Sears, Roebuck and Co. and Montgomery Ward, plus all the large urban retailers with significant mail-order divisions—Macy's, Wanamaker's, Altman's, Siegel-Cooper's. "The Postal Progress League," wrote a national importer to Jesse Straus of Macy's, "has the support of such firms as Montgomery Ward, National Cash Register, ourselves, etc. . . . That a Parcels Post and an efficient rural service would be a benefit to all mail-order dealers is obvious, and for that reason we beg you to do as much as you can to hasten its coming." Straus joined the cause. "The Parcels' Post Campaign," he said, "is bound ultimately to be crowned with success."[95]

Congressional advocates began to multiply, especially in the wake of the economic troubles that swept over rural America in the 1890s. In 1892, the House Committee on the Postal Service claimed that a bigger RFD would "aid materially in stopping much of the growing discontent that now seems to exist among the farming population." A similar argument was made by Progressives in defense of postal reform. Parcel post and RFD, they said, would save the nation; unite it; bring together conflicting elements; and, above all, stimulate the flow of goods throughout the country. The nation would be transformed overnight into "one transportation system." "Men became enchanted," one historian of the Postal Service has written, "with the possibilities of a new and revolutionary way of marketing goods."[96] Wanamaker testified repeatedly before Congress between 1895 and 1912 that postal reform would "compel construction of roads for mail deliveries," "encourage people to go to sparsely settled regions," and lead to the "vaster circulation of goods" needed to forestall economic stagnation and to eliminate depression.[97]

As a result of this lobbying, the federal government assumed the burden of the Postal Service, introducing both rural free delivery and parcel post. In 1897 there were only eighty-two routes in the country, but by 1905, the year Congress made it relatively easy for citizen groups to get their own mail routes simply by asking their congressmen for them, more than thirty-two thousand routes had been opened. In 1912 Congress created the national parcel post system, followed a year later by the adoption of government-owned motor vehicles to deliver packages cheaply and efficiently. It was fitting that the first parcel post packages mailed in any city were sent by John Wanamaker himself in Philadelphia and by his son Rodman in New York, both on January 1, 1913.[98] The original act mapped out eight postal zones and set a limit of eleven pounds per package, which was shortly afterward increased to fifty, then to seventy.[99]

Federally run parcel post and RFD quickly outstripped all rivals in speed and efficiency, adding thousands of workers to government payrolls and incorporating into government many functions hitherto carried out by private business. The U.S. parcel post and RFD led to the extension of the road system, which, in turn, required full-time involvement of the government in the upkeep and repair of roads and highways, reforms that contributed greatly to the institutional muscle that anchored and fueled the new corporate consumer economy and culture.

In the nineteenth century, the goal of the U.S. Postal Service was to make "knowledge and truth" available to more and more people. By the end of World War I, this goal had been altered; the greatest user of the mails was now American business. By 1920, government postal workers were carrying hundreds of millions of packages yearly to American doorsteps, as well as considerable amounts of commercial advertising and correspondence. If the express companies suffered at first, as did rural merchants and wholesalers, the mail-order houses—Sears, Roebuck and Montgomery Ward, along with the mail-order divisions of some department stores—reaped colossal dividends. Obstacles to their growth were virtually removed overnight, and their profits swelled from $40 million in 1908 to $250 million in 1920. Over the next decade, Sears, Roebuck in particular, would owe its great profits and its "golden age" as a mail-order house to the federal government, or to what one historian has called "the greatest distributing system on earth."[100]

The Paterson Pageant

Historian Caroline Ware long ago argued, in her book *Greenwich Village*, that American culture had undergone a major transformation by 1915. For most of the nineteenth century, Ware wrote, American culture was "essentially agrarian and mercantile, individualistic, mobile, and dominated by Protestant ethical values." Over time, that culture began to "wear thin," as new groups emerged to challenge it—business groups, immigrant and religious groups, and new industries. But still the culture "did not assimilate any important institutions." In the course of events, "industrialization greatly accelerated" and traditional American culture began to splinter; by World War I it had even begun to "disintegrate," not disappearing, but, in adjusting to the new institutions, becoming "disrupted." In the big cities especially, people were now "faced by fragments of conflicting culture patterns and conflicting principles of social organization." They were forced to adjust "in terms of themselves as isolated individuals rather than as parts of coherent social wholes." "The result was a great weakening of social controls and an almost complete absence of community integration."[101]

Ware's analysis drew on distinctions already widely held by European and American sociologists, and she applied them in an original and probing way to the history of Greenwich Village. But she failed to take seriously or even to note the newer culture—mass commercial culture—beginning to compete with and overtake the declining nineteenth-century one. Everything Ware described, in some degree or another, happened: Older social controls were weakened by industrial expansion and community integration in cities was disrupted (although, contrary to Ware, it had hardly disappeared "completely"). At the same time, a new capitalist culture—perhaps far more homogeneous than anything that ever appeared before—was beginning to fill the void created by the disappearance of this older coherence.

One measure of the power of this new cultural homogeneity was the degree to which it enlisted—as we have seen—the assistance of major institutions in the United States. The educational system did its part, as did the urban museums and the local and federal governments. Assistance also emanated from another institutional source as well: the labor movement and even from the most radical wing of the labor movement—the Industrial Workers of the World (IWW). The IWW damned the capitalist system lock, stock, and barrel as the most exploitive of all economic systems. Yet, the union leadership pursued tactical maneuvers and embraced an ideological agenda that could be seen as an institutional reinforcement to the very thing the union hated and attacked.

In June 1913 the IWW conducted a pageant at the newly rebuilt Madison Square Garden that showed the imprint of the new commercial culture. The pageant was part of a strategy to win a protracted painful strike against the silk manufacturers of Paterson, New Jersey. The union also hoped to capitalize on an already impressive string of strike achievements. In early 1912 it had been victorious over the woolen manufacturers in Lawrence, Massachusetts; months later in Manhattan it had led the first effective general strike against the hotel trade, an unheard of event in New York, hitting the august Waldorf, the Belmont, and Lucius Boomer's brand new McAlpin. Eighteen thousand workers walked off their jobs, asserting their existence before all New York and protesting the sweated misery of their labor. As Elizabeth Gurley Flynn, one of the strike's key organizers, later wrote, "mass picket lines encircled all the hotels and fashionable restaurants."[102] By and large, the strike was defeated, but a few gains were made—some hotels would pay slightly higher wages, the "pauperism of the tipping system" was exposed, as Gurley Flynn pointed out, and a basis for later organizing had been laid. The mere fact of the strike itself was exhilarating for many.

In the winter of 1912 the IWW had moved on to Paterson, New Jersey, to organize an even more daring strike of mostly unskilled silkworkers from many ethnic groups. The stakes were high. Wages had recently been slashed, hours were long, and many Paterson silk factories, where workers wove and dyed raw imported silk into fabrics, had just imposed technological innovations that greatly modified the character of the work. Before 1900 skilled weavers and dyers exercised much control over their work and no employee ran more than two looms at once; now, manufacturers were installing automatically driven looms, four per person. To replace skilled with unskilled labor, owners turned to the cheapest labor of all: immigrant women and children (over fourteen). By 1913 the silk market was immensely profitable, and Paterson businessmen struggled to meet the demand being generated by the New York fashion industry. When workers objected to the speedup and low pay, owners threatened to move altogether to Pennsylvania, where they had already built annexes, where the new looms were in full operation, and where the wives of local miners were willing to work for small wages to supplement their family income.[103]

In the winter of 1913 group after group of silkworkers walked off the job, until all the factories stopped running. At the forefront organizing were IWW leaders William Haywood and Gurley Flynn. The silkowners used every means available to crush the strike. "The whole city administration and the whole court system of the city," Ewald Koettgen, a member of the IWW General Executive Board, recorded, "were working overtime to suppress the IWW."[104] Workers began to starve, forcing Haywood and others into a campaign for more money and publicity; Haywood, furious at the dire turn of events and at New York newspapers for refusing to report on Paterson lest they arouse worker discontent in New York, made appeals for help in Greenwich Village (where he was living temporarily) from such wealthy intellectuals as Mabel Dodge, leader of a famous Village salon, and John Reed, a recent Harvard graduate enraptured by labor radicalism. At a meeting in Haywood's apartment, Dodge urged Haywood to "bring the strike to New York and *show* it to the workers. Why don't you hire a great hall and reenact the strike over here?" Haywood was impressed by Dodge's idea but wondered how to implement it, whereupon Reed, also present, volunteered that he would "do it!" "We'll make a pageant of the strike," he said, "the first in the world." The hope was to raise the spirits of the strikers and to get the attention of workers in New York. Whatever money came of it would be given to the union strike fund.[105]

The ensuing pageant was conceived by Reed and his Harvard classmate scenic designer Robert Edmund Jones, in six episodes to depict onstage the very strike then taking place at the Paterson silk factories. It was Jones, later well-known for his adroit use of light and color on the theatrical stage ("When I go to the theater," he wrote, "I want to get an eyeful"), who integrated the IWW color red throughout the show.[106] In Paterson, the waving of red cards and red handkerchiefs by factory operatives infuriated the owners; at public meetings where strikers, union officials, and owners met to discuss the strike, strikers who dressed in red were often thrown out or forbidden admittance.[107] But in Manhattan red played a different role, as Jones pinned red bows in the hair of the female program sellers and had male program sellers wear red ties. He hung red banners in the theater, put red costumes on the performing children, and gave everybody in the audience a red carnation. Atop the Madison Square Garden Tower, there were red lights in four ten-foot-high electric signs that read "IWW" and that could be seen for miles around. John Sloan, a noted Village artist, painted the scenery, with a backdrop depicting a huge silk factory set within an array of smaller mills.[108] (See plate 15.)

This pageant starred a thousand workers recruited from the actual strike. On the day of the pageant, after much rehearsing, the workers marched from Christopher Street to the Garden, holding red banners and accompanied by a marching band. Onstage they enacted, as the program described it, "a battle between the working class and the capitalist class conducted by the Industrial Workers of the World." A recent murder of a worker by an owner-employed detective was portrayed in the last scene, followed by speeches actually given at his funeral by Haywood and Gurley Flynn, who delivered them again in person onstage. (See plate 14.)

The show was a triumph of "realistic art," according to Reed. It was a triumph for him as well and, to celebrate and recover from what he thought to be a great success, he sailed off on a luxury liner with Mabel Dodge, her son, the son's nurse, and Robert Edmund Jones for a vacation in Italy in the Florentine sun.[109] Hutchins Hapgood, a liberal writer and frequenter of the Dodge salon, believed he'd seen "self-expression in industry and art among the masses . . . spreading a glow over the whole humanity." Mabel Dodge thought that one of the "gayest touches" was "teaching them to sing one of their lawless songs to 'Harvard, Old Harvard.' "[110] But in every way that mattered to the strikers, the pageant was a debacle. It provoked Gurley Flynn to a rage: "No money. Nothing." "This thing had been heralded as the salvation of the strike," but only "$150 came to Paterson, and all kinds of explanation!"[111] Far worse, the pageant marked the collapse of the strike and may have even precipitated the collapse. Days after the performance, factory after factory in Paterson settled independently with various groups of skilled workers (many of whom had joined the strike unwillingly); in a week or so, with starvation continuing to loom, all the workers were driven back to work, without a settlement.

Gurley Flynn blamed the strike's failure squarely on the pageant, even though she herself had participated in it. The workers who should have been picketing in Paterson, she observed in retrospect, were rehearsing their lines for New York. "The first scabs," in fact, "got into the Paterson mills, while the workers were training for the pageant, because the best ones, the most energetic [workers] . . . were the best pickets around the mills."[112] Flynn berated the "dilettante element" (Reed, Dodge, etc.) "who figured so prominently" behind the event, and she lamented, above all, the pageant's obvious "theatricality." "Diverting the workers' minds from the actual struggle to the pictured struggle," she said, "was fatal. Distraction from their real work was the first danger in Paterson. And how many times we had to counteract that and work against it!"[113]

As nothing else could have, the Paterson pageant exposed the extent to which the new commercial culture was beginning to penetrate the ideological center of American life, and to what degree it had established— even in the heart of labor radicalism—the character of what people longed for and fought for. Even here the widening distance between production and consumption was playing itself out, confusing the difference between the real and unreal, potentially making the most exploited workers insensitive to their own suffering. Were the workers in Paterson striking for the "eyeful" being dramatized in Madison Square Garden? Were the merchants and factory owners succeeding in the imagination, too, just as they were winning concrete battles on the shop floors of factories and department stores?

Like many IWW leaders, William Haywood lacked a well-thought-out vision of what workers should be striving for; many of his dreams were borrowed ones, taken, for instance, from utopian thinker Edward Bellamy, who put department stores and consumption at the heart of his conception of the good life. In a 1913 speech before the Paterson workers, Haywood described "the ideal society":

> It will be utopian. There will be a wonderful dining room where you will enjoy the best food that can be purchased; your digestion will be aided by sweet music which will be wafted to your ears by an unexcelled orchestra. There will be a gymnasium and a great swimming pool and private bathrooms of marble. One floor of this plant will be devoted to masterpieces of art and you will have a collection even superior to that displayed in the Metropolitan Museum of Art in New York. . . . Your work chairs will be morris chairs, so that when you become fatigued you may relax in comfort.[114]

Gurley Flynn, too, swore by the ideas of Edward Bellamy. Bellamy's *Looking Backward*, she later recalled, "made a profound impression on me, as it had on countless others, as a convincing explanation of how peaceful, prosperous, and happy America could be under a socialist system of society."[115] Yet, at the same time, in 1913, she insisted that there was something more compelling to fight for besides the comforts described by Bellamy and Haywood, or even besides the higher wages demanded by the strikers (although Gurley Flynn never denigrated these). "For workers to gain a few cents more a day, a few minutes less a day, and go back to work with the same psychology, the same attitude toward society is to have achieved a temporary gain and not a lasting victory," she said. "So a labor victory must be twofold, but if it can only be one it is better to gain *in spirit* than to gain economic advantage."[116]

By 1915 much of the United States was becoming a Land of Desire, formed by the corporate money economy, by the drive for profits, and by an ever-widening "distance between profit makers and operatives," as the Paterson situation shows.[118] The circumstance of material comfort and even of prosperity for most people throughout much of the nineteenth century was being superseded by the idea of possession, by being through having, by pageantry and show rather than by open confrontation with reality, by desire rather than by fulfillment.

In the early twentieth century, new economic institutions—department stores, national corporations, hotels, theaters, restaurants, and commercial and investment banks—were beginning to reshape American culture. Along with them were their brokers (men like L. Frank Baum, Maxfield Parrish, Joseph Urban, and O. J. Gude), who created new consumer enticements. At the same time, another circuit of noneconomic institutions and their brokers—museums, educational institutions, and governments—arose to meet the needs of commerce. And even the IWW, its leadership enticed and confused by the appeal of bourgeois strategies, had made its own unintentional contribution to the new circuit of power.

Chapter 7

WANAMAKER'S SIMPLE LIFE AND THE MORAL FAILURE OF ESTABLISHED RELIGION

When a preacher asked John Wanamaker in 1901 if he thought "modern commercialism" had had a negative "influence on church life," Wanamaker answered that he didn't think that anything negative had occurred. In fact, he said, "the last twenty years have been very favorable to a religious life."[1] But how could Wanamaker, a devout Presbyterian, have made this claim, given the character of the culture taking shape around him? What idea of the religious life led him to think this way? How could any religious person have looked at the fundamental changes going on in America—the rise of corporations, the new money economy, the spread of the culture of consumer desire—and not have wondered what impact they might have on spiritual life or what the future might be for religious vocations?

Something else besides department stores, government, museums, and universities was busy in behalf of this new culture: religion. And what is meant here by religion is not religion in only the institutional sense. What is meant is the "spiritual life"—or, more broadly, the principles people live by, their sense of right and wrong, their priorities and values. This chapter and the next explore the character of the religious response, examining not so much institutions per se but the ethical-spiritual resolutions of a relatively religious people as they considered or encountered the moral challenges of America's new commercial society.

For his part, Wanamaker believed that religion and commerce were both in a healthy condition in the United States, not the one declining, the other rising, because he himself had worked so hard to give life to both worlds. And he was hardly alone in this conviction. It was probably the majority view, shared by many affluent evangelical and liberal Protestants in established denominations, as well as by many middle-class Catholics and Jews. Although Wanamaker and others recognized the suffering inflicted by new economic conditions and tried to deal with it on Christian grounds, their perspective was affirmative, nearly unquestioning in its faith in the moral rightness of the new conditions. It embraced the view that culture and religion were not at loggerheads, but moving forward together hand in hand toward a kind of American millennium. The reaction of established religions was finally so sympathetic to America's new culture and economy as to form yet another pillar upon which the new order rested and was sustained.

To be sure, there were leaders in every religious community who understood and resisted what was happening. Religious culture at the turn of the century, unlike in our own time perhaps, was still vital enough to give voice to powerful dissent. Among the critics was Walter Rauschenbusch, a German Baptist pastor and famous social gospeler, who struggled to reawaken a prophetic strain in American Protestantism, to link religion closely to culture, and to look at it critically in relation to culture. "Competitive commerce," he said in 1907 in his most famous book, *Christianity and the Social Crisis*, "spreads things before us and beseeches and persuades us to buy what we do not want. Men try to break down the foresight and self-restraint which were the slow product of moral education, and reduce us to the moral habits of savages who gorge today and fast tomorrow." Economic abundance, he insisted, only begins to grapple with the needs of spiritual life, for modern men and women—even with untold comforts and goods—"may still be haunted by the horrible emptiness of [their lives] and feel that existence is a meaningless riddle and delusion."[2]

Catholics, too, produced a dedicated lifelong critic of consumer capitalism in Monsignor John Ryan, teacher of social ethics at Catholic University in Washington, D.C., and one of the earliest champions of minimum wage legislation. Ryan's critique had two sides. On the one hand, he recognized clearly that many Americans—perhaps one in eight in the early 1900s—were in poverty and needed to be brought up to an acceptable level of health, decency, and comfort. Ryan condemned those who defended "involuntary poverty" as a virtue, and he insisted that all "superfluous wealth" be shared with the poor. On the other hand, he warned Catholics and non-Catholics alike against the spiritual dangers of "consumption and material acquisitiveness." The standards he upheld were "frugal comfort," fulfilling work, and charity, not "diversified satisfaction of the senses" which "has produced an immense increase in self-love and selfishness, and a profound diminution of love of God and effective love of neighbor." There is an "unbridgeable gulf between the Catholic and capitalistic conceptions of life," Ryan asserted. Where Catholicism respects the "worth" of each individual, business "makes money values the supreme values" and resorts to "high-powered" selling to develop a "false sense of liberty."[3] Capitalism sees labor as "evil" to be endured "only because it leads to consumption and enjoyment." Catholicism honors labor as the essence of life—the "means of fulfilling one's faculties" and "attaining one's final end in compliance with the purpose of God." In 1908, Ryan wrote, critical of affluent Catholics in particular, the "standard of living is measured not so much by what (people) have as by what they desire and hope to have. Catholics are, to a deplorable extent, under the delusion that valuable life consists in the indefinite satisfaction of material wants."[4]

There were Methodist preachers, Unitarian ministers, and exponents of Ethical Culture who espoused a conception of the "whole personality" similar to Ryan's. Leaders like the Jewish liberal Felix Adler, founder of Ethical Culture in the late 1870s, feared that the human "personality" was threatened by "self-isolation" and "detachment." He warned that workers were being harmed by "the depersonalizing effect" of "machines." "Luxury," he wrote, "so far from maintaining personality, was undermining and hindering its development."[5]

In New York City, several Orthodox Jewish rabbis, recent immigrants from Eastern Europe, fought to hold back the impact of modern commodity forces as they threatened to subvert the rabbis' control over the religious practices of their people—especially over the dietary laws regulating the slaughter and marketing of meat *(kashruth)*. Control over *kashruth* was the central symbol of rabbinical authority and of a whole way of life.[6] In Europe, anyone involved in it, from the ritual slaughterer to the retailer, had to be Orthodox Jewish. In addition, the *kashruth* industry was run for public, not private benefit, with most of the functionaries employed by the local community and with the social welfare of the community as a whole supported by income from an excise tax on the meat. In America, by 1912, fraud, selfishness, theft, and sacrilege had invaded a hitherto protected communal domain. Commercial slaughterhouses were now hiring the majority of Orthodox functionaries (a forbidden practice, since it compromised those engaged in enforcing dietary laws), and private merchants (not the local communities) were reaping the profits, historian Arthur Goren writes, "from a product whose higher price derived from its religious value."[7]

The Orthodox clergy rebelled and joined with other Jews, equally fearful of the commercial dangers, in a short-lived experiment, the Kehillah experiment, whose aim was to create a new kind of unity among all New York Jews and to reactivate the fading rabbinical control over *kashruth*. It was a remarkable effort in a pluralist context and was headed by Judah Magnes, a Zionist reform rabbi. Secular Jews like Samuel Strauss, the publisher of the *New York Globe*, also joined the Kehillah. Magnes, eager to create an Orthodox center to his experiment around which lay Jews might come together, allowed the Orthodox rabbis full control over the *kashruth*, a concession that gave them a sense of renewed hope. Ultimately the effort failed, but for a brief moment before World War I it stopped the intrusion of secular market forces and reestablished some semblance of the older communal stability.[8]

These, then, were some of the resisting, critical voices raised against the new commercial trends. There were many other voices as well, from the members of the religious village of Amana, Iowa, who refused to let movies into their community, to many Protestant evangelicals in New York City and elsewhere who attacked the "wanton displays of luxury as marks of the end of the age," and "grasping after more" as "a menace to the peace and comfort of society."[9] Spiritual tension, conflict, and opposition existed then, as it still does, to some extent, today. But despite this dissent, some of it very penetrating, the movement in urban America was toward a new religious accommodation, a new ethical compromise that tried to integrate consumer pleasure and comfort and acquisition—the "American standard of living"—into what was left of the traditional Christian world-view.

Wanamaker as Liberal Evangelist and Institution Builder

To understand the evolution of established religion, one could do worse than begin with John Wanamaker, who contributed almost as much to

America's religious life as he did to its commercial expansion. From the 1850s onward, Wanamaker was very active in the development of urban American Protestantism; he helped build such major religious institutions as the Bethany Sunday Schools and the World Sunday School Movement, and he helped shape the cultural-religious ideas of America's urban middle classes. To see how he dealt with the new commercial order in religious terms is, I think, to get at the way most other middle-class Americans dealt with that order and still deal with it today. Wanamaker created two sets of institutions: one religious, the other commercial. He viewed the two as very interrelated and complementary, but each played quite a different role in his life, as in society. The commercial institutions satisfied Wanamaker's need for power, wealth, and well-being and helped produce a theatrical and secular culture subversive to traditional religious perspectives. The religious institutions fulfilled his need for personal salvation and protected him and others from facing the deepest implications of the new commercial culture. Such a split perspective reflected a division between public and personal goals and undercut the ability of religion to deal with the crucial public issues of the day.

Wanamaker's personal religious history was part of a significant change in American Protestantism, as it evolved from the strict Calvinism of the colonial period to the relatively nonsectarian evangelicalism of the 1850s. Calvinism had dwelled on the "evil" inherent in people, on human powerlessness before the sovereignty of God, and on the difficulties in achieving salvation; it viewed Christian life as a constant and demanding ordeal that involved every aspect of an individual's nature. Evangelical Protestantism, more upbeat and liberal, less dogmatic, unsure about divine sovereignty, and certain that everybody could be saved without too much strain or struggle, was more concerned with how people behaved than with how deeply they thought about God and sin. Ultimately it was a religious system far more compatible with a commercial economy than was Calvinism, which armed the self against the seductions of secular culture and alerted it to the dangers of spiritual decline and weakness.[10]

After the 1850s many mainstream groups—Presbyterians, Methodists, Congregationalists, and Episcopalians, among others—pooled their resources to build interdenominational evangelical institutions, especially Sunday schools, the YMCA, the YWCA, and later in the century, the Salvation Army, to help Americans cope with city life and to adjust religious experience to urban demands. By 1912 a far-flung institutional religious circuit was binding many groups across the country into a common cultural whole. Such new quasi-religious groups supplemented the work of common or public schools, which many believed had ceased to communicate religious beliefs to children. They were staffed and superintended by laymen and laywomen recruited from merchant and professional groups, those groups most concerned about inculcating proper values into children and young adults, a new tier of lay "experts" seen as having more religious authority than parents and almost as much as the clergy.

At Sunday school and in church papers and books, children and adults were taught the basic elements of a modern "Christian" ethos—self-control, temperance, a respect for the Sabbath, obedience, and devotion to simple scriptural teachings.[11]

At age twenty, in 1858, Wanamaker opened his own Bethany Mission Sunday School in Philadelphia, a few years before he launched his "other" career in the dry goods business. In the same year he was appointed the first paid secretary of the American YMCA; he organized countless prayer meetings, enrolled 2,000 members the first year, and inspired the nationwide growth of the organization. "I went out into the byways and hedges," he said of his YMCA work, "and compelled them to come in."[12] Bethany was (and remained) the greatest institutional interest in his life, with 50 children (and a few adults) the first year, in 1859; following the dedication of the new Bethany Chapel on South Street, there were 275 children and 17 teachers.[13]

Wanamaker could easily have become a revivalist of equal stature to his friend Dwight Moody, the most influential evangelical preacher of the post-Civil War period. Physically he was better equipped than Moody, who was short, beefy in middle age, and hardly handsome. Wanamaker, at forty, was almost six feet tall, with brown hair, aquiline nose and forehead, gray-blue eyes, a deep and resonating voice, and an ingratiating manner. As his biographer writes, "he had the habit of taking the arm of the one with whom he walked."[14] But in their religious and social terms, he and Moody were much alike. Only a year apart in age, both had fathers and grandfathers who were brickmasons; both shared the same evangelical beliefs and rose to prominence through the Sunday school movement and the YMCA (Moody was the first paid secretary of the Chicago YMCA).[15] As young men, both were enthusiastic about the retail business. In 1857 Moody moved from Northfield, Massachusetts, to Chicago, where he pursued a very profitable career as a shoe salesman; he also speculated in real estate and made personal loans at usurious interest rates (he was, in other words, a loan shark). Like so many other Americans at the time, he saw no contradiction between his business behavior and his religion. In a letter to his brother written in about 1858, he boasted of his moneymaking while at the same time exhorting his brother to "hold on to the promise of the Bible" and not permit "anything to keep you from the full enjoyment of God's love."[16]

A fundamental difference, however, divided these two men. In 1860 both underwent religious crises, with different outcomes. Moody, who was getting more worldly and prosperous day by day, decided to quit his business to become a preacher. According to his biographer, the choice was not altogether a risky one; though briefly impoverished by it, he knew that sometime in the future he might be able to depend on the rich Chicago merchant John Farwell, a devout Presbyterian, to foot the bills. For Moody, as for most other revivalists by this time, religion and business were too "deeply intertwined," making it hard for him (and other evangelicals) to criticize commercial ethics.[17] He also disliked complex ideas, too much thoughtful probing, and anything that led to doctrinal dispute. His message was the simple love of Jesus and individual salvation through Jesus; and he preached almost entirely against personal sins—especially theatergoing, violations of the Sabbath, drunkenness, and "worldly amusements."[18] Yet, for all this, Moody genuinely felt his ministry, believing, as historian James Findlay writes, that "only by committing himself utterly and completely to the demands of his religious faith could he truly find happiness." "I was driven to it," he later wrote.[19] To be sure, his decision never led to open criticism of business, but it did result in his "giving himself to God, in denouncing 'fashionable Christianity,' " and in "allowing the spiritual to engulf and control the secular aspects of life."[20] In 1871 he had a second conversion experience, in New York City, when he wept and "lost interest in everything except the preaching of Christ and working for souls." He joined a new "holiness" movement that stressed "dedication to an arduous Christian service and a filling with spiritual power." And he was even drawn to premillennialism, a pessimistic evangelical view of time, outside the optimistic evangelical mainstream, that saw in certain signs the collapse of civilization and believed everything was getting worse, not better.[21] Perhaps, given more encouragement from others (especially from those premillennialists who had little interest in capitalist enterprise), Moody might have become more critical of American life than he was.[22]

In 1860, John Wanamaker had a similar way open to him. In that year, he seriously wrestled over entering the ministry, but his dream of becoming another Alexander Turney Stewart, America's first great merchant prince, soon took stronger hold in his mind.[23] For a brief time, however, during the 1870s, the debate may have revived in him again, and he may even have contemplated following in Moody's footsteps. In 1875 he invited Moody to conduct a major revival in an old Philadelphia train depot, which he planned to convert, soon after the revival, into his Grand Depot dry goods store, a revival that not only thrilled him but also brought him into daily contact with Moody, now completely possessed of his "holiness" mission. Months after the revival, Moody wrote Wanamaker two letters from Chicago, urging him to leave his business. "I must set down and write you and make one more effort to get you out of your Business," he wrote. "Get out as soon as you can. It seems to me as if the Devil wanted to cheat you of your Crown." "I think you have done wrong to extend your business. I think it was a plan of the Devil to get you tied down hand and foot. I *beg* you do not let your heart freeze out a harvest."[24] Wanamaker may have been touched by these appeals. In 1878 he, along with a few close Moody friends, attended a conference in New York on premillennialism, a religious position as far removed from Wanamaker's conventional merchant's optimism as well as from his evangelical liberalism as any philosophy could have been.[25]

But once again Wanamaker retreated, too eager to go his own way and to embark on an even bolder mission than the one Moody chose. For Wanamaker intended not only to extend his business, he also believed that he did not need to give up one path to pursue the other. Rather than rejecting the profane route and rather than allowing the sacred to reshape his secular interests, as Moody had done, Wanamaker seemed to want it both ways. He shared with other evangelical liberals a desire—as historian of religion William Hutchinson has shown—to "renounce the long-standing [conflict] between sacred and secular."[26] He wanted it all, both kingdoms, both crowns. He wanted both being (the being that comes from the influx of spiritual grace) and having (the possession of more and more "things," commercial profit, comfort, material progress, power). Thus, in the religious field, he went about doing what Moody insisted all good Christians should do—but on a grand scale, and, throughout his maturity, Wanamaker abided by the spirit of Moody's simple evangelical piety. Wanamaker kept notebooks in which he jotted down religious thoughts and aphorisms that reflected his "simple" faith in what he called "the religion of Jesus Christ." "Jesus never laughed," he recorded in 1871. "Worldly choice is at great risk—we have something to do to be sacred."[27] On a trip to Europe in 1894, he noted that "Jesus had nowhere to lay his head. If He had had possessions He would have been isolated from His fellow men, whereas as it is He shares everything, gives away everything, keeps nothing for Himself."[28] "God is larger, fuller—impossible to exaggerate," he wrote in 1901, "all might of Infinite Love."[29]

Wanamaker also greatly expanded Bethany Mission Sunday School from its small beginnings in the late 1850s, until, by the 1890s, it was the biggest Sunday school in the world. The school was affiliated with Bethany Presbyterian Church, with its two pastors, diverse assistant pastors, supporting staff, many lay leaders, and thousands of congregants. Bethany Presbyterian Church was, in fact, one of America's prototypic institutional churches, a new kind of church found in many denominations that served religious goals and also satisfied social and cultural needs. As much as the later department stores did, these churches came to anchor community life; they had large budgets, facilities for singing, eating, and meeting, activities of all kinds. Many were "open every day and all day," as one pastor put it in 1891, and were concerned with urban poverty and conflict. They sought to relate religion in some measure to secular life, and they addressed "the entire life of man" from recreational and spiritual guidance to economic and humanitarian assistance. The most socially conscious of them were actually Christian settlement houses, running nurseries, employment bureaus, soup kitchens, and rescue missions. Others mixed social service with recreation. For instance, Oriana Atkinson, wife of theater critic Brooks Atkinson, grew up in Greenwich Village in New York City completely dependent, socially and religiously, on her neighborhood Methodist institutional church, the Metropolitan Temple on Fourteenth Street—"a magnet," she wrote, "drawing people for many blocks around." "Every day and night of the week there was something going on in the chapel and sometimes also in the church itself," she recalled in a memoir—including lectures, choir rehearsals, Bible classes, professional concerts, sewing circles, missionary meetings, and Sunday schools.[30] Atkinson's church, and others like it, often treated the church service as a "professional performance," and it showcased the power of the minister rather than the participation of the congregation. "Gradually," historian Herbert Schneider has written, such churches encouraged religious passivity, with people "coming to church service much as they would attend a concert or theater."[31]

Wanamaker's Bethany Presbyterian Church was not only among the first institutional churches, it also was as multifaceted as his department stores. As early as the 1880s, an orchestra played at the worship services; the stained-glass windows in the church mirrored the stained-glass windows in the stores; ushers acted with the same spirit of service as did Wanamaker's salespeople. (In the 1906 New York store, stained-glass windows enclosed the ninth-floor restaurant, the public comfort room, and the art galleries.)[32] At the same time, Bethany's two pastors, Arthur Pierson and J. Wilbur Chapman, both influenced by Moody's holiness preaching, labored to help the urban poor. In addition to Sunday school classes for children, Bethany sponsored evangelistic rallies in tents, a rescue mission, a seashore home, a daily vacation Bible school, evening classes on weekday nights, a day nursery, and domestic and foreign missions. Teachers operated the Bible Union, for adults on Sunday afternoon for Presbyterian and non-Presbyterian alike, and the Brotherhood, "for men only," in the morning.[33]

Wanamaker superintended Bethany for decades, teaching Sunday school there. "I never miss a Sunday," he wrote a friend in 1913, "unless I am ill or absent from the country because I know by personal experience that there is nothing that can take its place." By 1898 he was lecturing to nearly two thousand people at his Sunday Bible classes.[34] Dearest to his heart was conducting the "Brotherhood" in the morning, a group of men organized by Wanamaker in 1890 and renamed the "Roman Legion" ten years later, when Wanamaker was addressing the Book of Romans in the New Testament. Many of the Brotherhood were employees of his store, but others came from throughout Philadelphia and from neighboring towns. There were more than nine hundred members by 1900. Wanamaker loved teaching these men the simple stories and parables in the Bible. By the early 1900s he was spending a lot of time on his favorite biblical passages, Chapters 8 and 10 of Romans, demanding that the men memorize them. He sent letters of praise to women whose husbands had "recited" these verses before their families. "Those who live according to the flesh," the heart of Chapter 8 went, "set their minds on the things of the flesh, but those who live according to the Spirit set their minds on the things of the Spirit. To set the mind on the flesh is death, but to set the mind on the Spirit is life and peace. For the mind that is set on the flesh is hostile to God."[35]

Wanamaker's money funded what may have been the last important urban religious revival in America to follow in the wake of an economic crisis (the panic of 1873)—Moody's huge revival of 1876, a revival tailored more than any that preceded it to the needs of business and professional people who wanted to be freed from the guilt of doing what they were doing. It drew thousands of people, even President Grant and all of the members of the U.S. Supreme Court. Nearly forty years later, Wanamaker supported the revival work of the fundamentalist Billy Sunday with equal zeal, yearning to repeat the "glory" of the early time but failing in this, though not for want of trying. He placed his own personal services, his money, and the religious apparatus he had created at Billy Sunday's feet. "We will change his audience as many times as he will give us time to empty the house," he wrote Billy's wife. "I do hope that Mr. Sunday will live here for two or three months and help us to make a new Declaration of Independence." Whereas others—like Philadelphia liberal economist Scott Nearing—entreated Sunday to extend his message to include reform issues, Wanamaker, whose own pastors sometimes emphasized social service, pleaded that he spread the simple message of salvation through Jesus. [36]

Wanamaker was a senior elder in his Presbyterian church. He built four large churches in Philadelphia and continued to propose that more be built as newer ethnic and racial groups moved into the city after 1900, replacing people of older northern European stock who were moving elsewhere (Wanamaker was not one of those to bemoan demographic change). In the 1870s he breathed life back into *The Sunday School Times*, the pivotal American Sunday school paper, then fading rapidly for want of financing. He bought and printed it on his own presses (an unheard-of thing for a merchant to have done) until the subscription rate swelled well beyond five hundred thousand. He was president of the Philadelphia Sabbath Association for more than forty years, and he contributed to the rise and growth of the Salvation Army and of the YMCA. The YMCA was an excellent urban institution, Wanamaker thought; without it the moral life of young men would be much endangered. He gave nearly as much of his life to it as he did to Bethany. "I consider a well-organized YMCA," he wrote a friend in 1886, "indispensable to the best welfare of any City. . . . The reason for my large investment of money in it is because I do not know any other field which promises so good a return for the money. As a businessman, I believe the usefulness of the Association to be beyond value in offering safeguards and encouragement to the young men we employ."[37]

After 1895 the religious work of this Philadelphia merchant took on a global character, reflecting a popular trend in evangelical Protestantism at the time. His money built YMCA schools in Madras (1895), in Calcutta (1901), in Seoul (1901), and in Peking (1913). He created the Indian headquarters for the YMCA in 1900 and established the Mary Wanamaker School for Girls at Allahabad Christian College in India, an institution connected with Bethany Mission Sunday School. He was president of the World Sunday School Association in 1919.[38]

The Simple Life and Pastor Wagner

Surprising as it may seem, Wanamaker was also a founder of the "simple-life movement" in America, and that movement's busiest institutional sponsor outside of Theodore Roosevelt. Between 1901 and 1904 interest in the simple life had penetrated America's urban middle classes, its reach so far that, as historian David Shi writes, it "assumed the status of both a cult and a fad."[39] People in the "arts and crafts" movement embraced simplicity; so did a new group of interior decorators, among them Elsie De Wolfe and, for a while, Edith Wharton, whose first book, *Decoration of Houses*, in 1899, argued for an "aesthetic" of simplicity and a rejection of clutter and ornamentation. Country homes and rustic simplicity became popular pursuits of the well-to-do. Advocates of the new wilderness movement, supporters of conservation and "back to the land" ideas also favored a simple-life philosophy. John Muir, the great naturalist who founded the Sierra Club in 1894, believed that the simple life was the best and only alternative to the ethos of the "gobble gobble" school of modern capitalism. "Our mode of civilization engenders a multitude of wants," he said. "Yet few think of pure rest or the healing power of Nature."[40] The cult of the simple life affected the Boy Scouts of America, founded in 1910, and the new camping groups as well. Anthropology, which developed as a profession in the late 1890s, was inspired in part by simple-life ideology. Indeed, it could be argued that interest in simple life in anthropological circles—the need to find it expressed in other places and peoples—helped influence the romantic way anthropologists interpreted "primitive" peoples. Thus, as the ethnologist Walter Edmond Roth said of Guinean Indians: "They live under the most perfect equality. . . . Content with simple means, they evince no desire to emulate the habits or occupations of the colonists."[41]

But the primary audience for simple-life ideas was religious, especially middle-class urban Americans of liberal evangelical backgrounds. Many of these people, who felt morally uncertain or guilty about their increased wealth and comfort, found simple-life philosophy appealing. Once more, Wanamaker was at the forefront, the impresario of the simple life.

The best-known book in the movement was *The Simple Life* by the French cleric Charles Wagner, a middle-aged Lutheran minister with a nonsectarian liberal bent like Wanamaker's own. Wagner was concerned about the materialistic behavior of the Protestant French bourgeoisie; his book, published in 1901 and translated slightly later, gently scolded this class for its neglect of the spiritual life and enthusiasm for material goods.

The Simple Life, a failure in France, was a sensation in America. In it, Wagner discussed the impact on moral behavior of the new "complex materialism"—better housing, better food, more household goods, and a higher standard of living. He saw material advance as both good and as potentially hazardous because it lacked a secure moral center. People already well off desired more and more, producing a "general state of agitation . . . the more needs, the more desires we have, the more quarrelsome we become." "Fashion" and "luxury" were corrupting Europeans and Americans. People were caught up in the "wish to imitate the great and have forgotten how to be simple, authentic, self-sacrificing, and especially self-effacing." "One of the chief puerilities of our time is the love of advertisement. To emerge from obscurity,

> to be in the public eye, to make one's self talked of—some people are so consumed with this desire that we are justified in declaring them attacked with an itch for publicity. The abuse of showing everything, or rather, putting everything on exhibition; the growing incapacity to appreciate that which chooses to remain hidden. . . . One sometimes wonders if society will not end by transforming itself into a great fair, with each one beating his drum in front of his tent.[42]

There is no evidence, by the way, that Wagner thought these criticisms applied to *him*.

Wagner's biggest complaint was against "materialists" who had turned against the past to take up the "new" and "modern." No one cared anymore, Wagner said, for "family traditions," for the old "filial piety" and sacred beliefs, or for the old craftsmanship. "Instead of filling their houses with objects, which say: Remember!," married couples ("newly weds") "garnish them with quite new furnishings that as yet have no meaning" and are "symbols of a facile and superficial existence."[43]

Something had to be done. But what? Wagner made clear that we could not go back to the past. Like most "simple-lifers," it was not his plan to return to the "simple life" of the "old days" or to the simple life as once conceived, say, in traditional Christian terms, as a form of renunciation of the "things of this world." "I have nothing in common," Wagner said, "with those who lament constantly that they were not born in the times of their great-grandfathers. I am the son of *this* time. I find it everyday more fascinating."[44] Nor was the answer to be "socialistic" or anything of that sort. Large social programs, Wagner said, were wrong because they involved redistribution of wealth, and *that* was wrong; indeed, democracy and equality themselves were wrongheaded if carried too far. Rich and poor, workers and bourgeoisie—all were just fine in their place.

The solution he proposed was individual and personal. People should declare themselves openly for the simple life "in their own stations," everyone in their own way and in their "own mind." My book "merely says," Wagner later explained, "that if in mind we are simple, then we shall live the simple life no matter what our surroundings."[45] The point was to avoid everything that was ostentatious or too sophisticated. Don't think about "bad things" like "money," Wagner suggested. Avoid "pessimism" and "self-analysis"; be "confident" and "hopeful." Take up the older crafts again, Wagner said, and reinstitute the old family traditions. Try to "be yourself." "Simplicity is a state of mind. It dwells in the main intention of our lives. A man is simple when his chief care is the wish to be what he ought to be, that is, honestly and naturally human. Let a flower be a flower, a swallow a swallow, a rock a rock, and let man be a man, and not a fox, a hare, a hog, or a bird of prey: This is the sum of the whole matter."[46]

A Day at Bethany

Hundreds of thousands of copies of *The Simple Life* were sold in and around New York City alone.[47] By 1904, Wagner's name was "a household word," "his face so familiar to the American public" that people knew him instantly, his photograph seen throughout the country, just like the picture of one of his admirers, Elbert Hubbard.[48] Edward Bok, the publisher of America's leading women's magazine, *Ladies' Home Journal*, and Wanamaker's neighbor in Philadelphia, used the pages of his magazine to popularize Wagner's ideas to millions of Americans. President Theodore Roosevelt raved about Wagner's book, which Wanamaker himself probably put into his hands.[49] The demand for the book was so widespread that even the editors of *The Dry Goods Economist*, the trade's bastion of modern merchandising advice, found themselves promoting it. Its popularity, they said,

> furnishes some index to the reaction against the artificial and complex existence into which a great proportion of Americans are forced . . . ; and Pastor Wagner's honest, straightforward presentation of the old, unvarying straightforward alternative is a mighty wholesome thing for Americans to read.

It took only three months for a reaction to set in. In March 1905, the editors were arguing that "Luxury . . . is a relative term, Wagner and his *Simple Life* to the contrary, it is what all Americans are after in one degree or another."[50]

Wanamaker was Wagner's most ardent champion, though he had yet to meet him; Wanamaker was certain that the simple-life message would be the antidote for what he perceived to be the "decline of religion" in America. He attributed that decline, in his notebook, to "squabbles over articles of faith," the "higher [Biblical] criticism," and the "race for riches."[51] Wanamaker bought thousands of copies of *The Simple Life* to distribute to his employees, to Bethany people, and to friends.[52] He built a simple "bungalow" next to his palatial country home at Lindenhurst, Pennsylvania, so that whenever he felt the urge, "he could"—as his biographer says— "live *The Simple Life* of his friend Charles Wagner."[53]

One morning in Paris in the spring of 1903 Wanamaker visited Wagner's apartment to invite him to America "to study the conditions of religious life" and to go on a lecture tour.[54] Once at home again, Wanamaker wrote his friends of this "delightful man" and the "delightful interview" he had had. Wagner had even "sent me his picture."[55] In September 1904, Wagner was on his way. "America welcomes you!" said a telegram sent by the merchant midway through the voyage from Le Havre.[56] For the first two weeks, he was to stay with Wanamaker at Lindenhurst (but not in the simple bungalow), to get accustomed to America in congenial surroundings in preparation for a study of the country's "religious life."[57]

Wagner's first day at Lindenhurst began with the daily Wanamaker ritual—a reading from the Bible by the "head of the family" to the "assembled household, masters, and servants." Afterward, they toured the house, which struck Wagner as large and handsome but—he insisted—hardly "luxurious," although he did admit that Lindenhurst had some of the most costly paintings he had ever seen (including works by Gainsborough, Rembrandt, Titian, Turner, Hogarth, Constable, Velasquez, Rubens, Franz Hals, Reynolds, Corot, and Van Dyke) and that flowers, plants, medieval tapestries, statuary, and objects of art were everywhere. An organ with hundreds of pipes stood on the landing of the grand staircase. Wagner admired the greenhouses and the collection of orchids in the gardens, and he hiked through the countryside, returning exhausted to a "sort of rotunda" prepared for his return with "great clusters of purple grapes and golden pears on drooping boughs." He took a nap under this rotunda, only to be awakened by the giggles of little girls, who had set a table "heaped with fruit" before him. "I ate the delicious pears and the grapes with the flavour of muscatel."[58]

Wanamaker was overjoyed by Wagner's two-week visit, although he lost time from his business. He and Wagner became friends, both suitably impressed by each other's simplicity.[59] "I wish you could have been with me the last two weeks," Wanamaker wrote a Bethany friend, "when the incarnation of *The Simple Life* took lodgings with me." "Pastor Wagner is a noble spirit," he wrote another, "and I wish you and I might catch more of his simple nature. It is not only simple, but strong and sound."[60] "American laymen are a precious possession to their churches," Wagner said, "and among those of their number who know how to join perfect simplicity of heart to the weight conferred by an exceptional position, I would give a very special place to John Wanamaker. May coming generations give us men of his kind."[61]

Wagner lectured about the simple life up and down the East Coast, escorted for a good part of the time by Wanamaker. Wagner visited a "host

PLATE 1 In 1876 John Wanamaker converted an abandoned railroad depot into his "Grand Depot," perhaps the first department store in the United States. Photographed here in 1902, its turrets and filagree show the impact of orientalism on the commercial architecture of the day. (*Courtesy of John Wanamaker's, Philadelphia*)

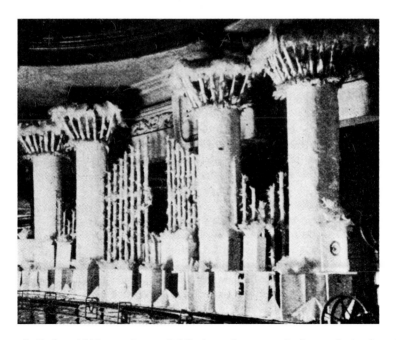

PLATE 2 Before 1900 merchants did little to focus on single goods in the windows. What they did do often was to mass them into architectual structures, as seen in this 1899 linen display in New York. (Dry Goods Economist, *c. 1899*)

PLATE 3 This picture, taken in 1923, shows the construction work on the second half of the north building of Wanamaker's store on Broadway and Astor Place. The first half was opened in 1906. The smaller five-story A. T. Stewart store, built in 1864, is on the far left side of the photo. (*Courtesy of the General Research Division, New York Public Library, Astor, Lenox, and Tilden Foundations*)

PLATE 4 These two covers for *The Fashions of the Hour*, an upscale fashion catalog published from 1912 on for the suburban customer, were done by first-class graphic artists in the richest colors. They were typical of Field's catalogs, as well as of such stores as Wanamaker's and Jordan Marsh. (*Courtesy of Marshall Field's*)

PLATE 5 Maxfield Parrish called this Mazda calendar, designed for Edison Electric in 1919, "The Spirit of the Night." The word "Mazda," meaning the "God of Light" in Persian, was itself intended by Edison Electric to impress customers with the mythic-magical power of light. (*Courtesy of the Dartmouth College Library*)

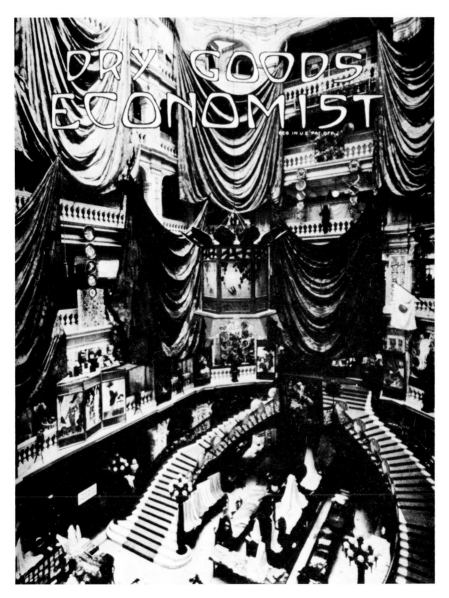

PLATE 6 The grand staircase and central rotunda of the old A. T. Stewart store (owned by John Wanamaker after 1896) decorated with Japanese-inspired drapes and screens. (Dry Goods Economist, 1913)

PLATE 7 This show window of Sibley, Lindsay, and Curr in Rochester, New York, one of twelve windows that appeared in the main front in the spring of 1912, indicates the improvements in display achieved by this time. Apart from the clearly focused goods arranged in pleasing geometrical ways, the window contained a dark-green velour background bordered at the top by a seven-inch golden cornice. (Dry Goods Economist, *March 23, 1912*)

PLATE 8 Nearly everything in this 1915 show window at Marshall Field's on State Street in Chicago was designed by Arthur Fraser. Fraser led displaymen in creating coherent pictures of luxury. The beautiful tapestry in the background was his signature. (*Courtesy of Marshall Field's*)

PLATE 9 A crowded, relatively unappealing store interior of the late 1890s. (Dry Goods Economist, *c. 1899*)

PLATE 10 By 1914 interiors of such major stores as Lord and Taylor's on 38th Street and Fifth Avenue in Manhattan had taken on an almost modern character. (Dry Goods Economist, *c. 1919*)

PLATE 11   The main galleried rotunda at Marshall Field's in Chicago, circa 1927, with its impressive Tiffany dome. The interior color of the dome's concentric circles is a deep marine blue, encircled by gold, blue, and green iridescent glass. (*Courtesy of Marshall Field's*)

PLATE 12 Wanamaker's Grand Court at Christmastime in 1928. The huge ornament at top center is bright red. By the late 1920s Wanamaker's decorating staff in Philadelphia was pulling out all the stops to create just the right cathedral-like atmosphere. (*Courtesy of the Historical Society of Pennsylvania*)

PLATE 13 Wanamaker's Garden of Allah fashion show of 1913 took place in Egyptian Hall, a huge store theater that for years put on free concerts and extravaganzas for customers. The starry background echoes the decor of the Broadway show. (*Courtesy of The Historical Society of Pennsylvania*)

PLATE 14 A scene from the Paterson Strike Pageant—Picketing the Mills—staged in the newly built Madison Square Garden on Twenty-sixth Street in Manhattan. (*Courtesy of the Tamiment Library, New York University*)

PLATE 15 Paterson pageant poster, designed by ashcan artist John Sloan, with a background in IWW red. (*Courtesy of the Tamiment Library, New York University*)

PLATE 16 In March 1916 *Dry Goods Economist*, the leading trade journal in mass merchandising, published this montage of typical Baby Week Ads, taken from the periodicals of twenty-seven stores. (*Courtesy of the General Research Division, New York Public Library, Astor, Lenox, and Tilden Foundations*)

PLATE 17 John Wanamaker (*top left*), L. Frank Baum (*top right*), Simon Patten (*bottom left*), Herbert Hoover (*bottom right*). (*Courtesy of John Wanamaker's, Philadelphia; Syracuse University Library; Pennsylvania University Archives; and United States Department of Commerce*)

of American institutional churches," marveling at their size, their "reading circles, sewing circles, and various entertainments." "In such ways the members," he wrote, "are brought together elsewhere than in religious meetings, and the church becomes a centre where the lonely may find a family, and youth have companionship."[62] The merchant presented Wagner to President Roosevelt in Washington. Wanamaker boasted to friends that he had "covered Wagner's expenses out of his own pocket," helped him prepare his lecture tour, and acted as a press agent to those newspapers and magazines interested in publishing Wagner's articles or excerpts from *The Simple Life*.[63] He collected money from his wealthy colleagues in Wagner's behalf, even though "Wagner doesn't in his simple way ever ask any one to give anything, but as he is a poor man and paying his own expenses to get acquainted with America, some of us feel that we want to help him to go home out of debt at least."[64]

Wagner visited all of Wanamaker's "religious institutions"—the YMCA, the various neighborhood "friendship" groups, and Bethany Mission Sunday School among them. At a reception for the Roman Legion, he passed out autographed copies of *The Simple Life* to the Brotherhood.[65] On his way to Bethany with Wanamaker, Wagner watched the merchant in awe as he sat in his car reading over the Bible passages he was to use that day and as he stopped, from time to time, to get out to distribute flowers to the sick.

Wagner's first experience at "Bethany Church, in Philadelphia," he later recorded in his *Impressions of America*, "introduced me to an expression of religious life in forms I had never hitherto encountered, though America was later to furnish me a great many examples of it, and I wish to consecrate, by a special recognition, the day, never to be forgotten by me, that passed there—September 25, 1904." The Brotherhood impressed him as "wonderful" in their "mutual encouragement in righteous living." He delivered a sermon before a thousand people in the big basement auditorium, and in the afternoon attended a meeting of the Bible class to hear Wanamaker and others expound on passages from St. Paul. These laypeople, Wagner said, had the right approach to the Bible; they didn't care about "dogmatic questions or scientific exegesis," only about "the vital and individual appropriations of the soul's treasure hidden in the Book." He found this congenial: nothing too deep, no "self-analysis," and certainly no "inhuman pessimism." In another auditorium, Wagner heard "thousands of children" and adults sing "very beautiful hymns" and listened to "a magnificent contralto, rich with an intensity of religious feeling that the finest art cannot simulate." The Sunday's general lesson followed as "a fountain with banks of flowers around it, played at the centre." "The picture of the younger generation receiving the teachings of evangelical tradition in this attractive place was altogether charming."[66]

But it was the evening communion service that made the most memorable impression on Wagner. As a crowd began to enter Bethany, he felt "a breath of adoration in the air" and "my soul full of a sense of the beyond." Wanamaker asked him to say something before the celebration of communion. "Tonight you are our guest at the Supper of the Lord," Wanamaker whispered to him, "talk to us like a brother." Wagner spoke, though he later didn't recall exactly what he said; he did remember that the assemblage was drawn together by a "golden cord that vibrated under the eternal emotions." "We were verily one soul," he remembered. And, as the head pastor pronounced "This is my body. . . . This is my blood," Wagner felt that "the secret sources of the higher life seemed to be unlocked, and currents of living water flowed over the fields of the spirit." "The centuries" were "bound up in that moment." Bethany had been transformed into the "garden of God." Why, it had become, Wagner wrote later, "none other than the house of God" and the "gate of heaven."[67]

All of this Wanamaker must have found extremely gratifying. In late November, just before Wagner sailed for Paris on December 2, 1904, he had McClure's publishing house arrange to have a *Pastor Wagner Year Book* issued in the next few months. Wanamaker went to New York to see Wagner off. On December 24, 1904, Wanamaker reported to a friend that "'we have had the most wonderful Christmas business in the history of the store." On New Year's Eve he wrote Wagner that he missed him at Lindenhurst. "You seem to belong to the house," he said, "and it is not quite the same when you are not here."[68]

Fairy Tales or Private Parables

Wanamaker's work on behalf of the simple life and his network of religious institutions were stunning. Even more remarkable was that, at the very same time, he was building a decidedly different set of commercial institutions that were transmitting what seemed to be a decidedly different set of values. Wanamaker may have praised simplicity, thrift, and traditions of filial piety. He admired Jesus because "He shares everything, gives away everything, keeps nothing for Himself"; and he may have insisted that the Brotherhood memorize biblical passages that argued that "to live by the flesh" is to live by death. He was, nevertheless, constructing a commercial culture that, on its face, contradicted everything these qualities and texts stood for.

More than any other merchant of the age, after all, it was Wanamaker who brought French fashion and merchandising to America. Though he seemed to admire Wagner for lamenting the modern quest after "the new," he himself embraced it. People often shopped in his stores merely to get "an education in what was new," as Wanamaker's own advertising claimed, to see the new machine-made goods (his whole business depended on the machine-made), and even to gawk at the "new machines" themselves. From the 1880s onward, in fact, Wanamaker himself conducted tours into the labyrinthine basements of his stores so his customers might observe the "power machines" that "ran" his business; he was proud of being the first big merchant to use electric lights in his stores, the first to sell automobiles and airplanes, the first to market the Marconi wireless.[69] He had the country's biggest furniture showrooms, yet he countenanced Wagner's assertion that "newly weds" were fools to give up their heirlooms. His stores were saturated with *gemütlichkeit*, his fashion shows—especially his *Garden of Allah* spectacle—the talk of the town. It pleased him that he could translate "luxuries into commodities or into necessities" (as he put it) with a speed unsurpassed by any other retailer. My stores, he wrote, "are beautiful fields of necessities."[70]

Although Wanamaker said he hated the "vileness of theatrical productions" and cringed when someone said he needed a license for his store auditorium because it was "a theatrical"—"We are not theatricals," he told his son Rodman—he was the greatest exponent of interior spectacle of his generation of merchants, "the Kiralfy of modern merchandising." He is "Barnumesque," said a contemporary. "The store is a great spectacular show."[71] Even Wanamaker himself thought of his stores in theatrical terms. And in the early 1900s, while he was studying the Gospels with the Brotherhood, he was also reading another kind of literature that was quite out of keeping with traditional Christianity but quite in harmony with his department stores and consumer activity. He was reading children's stories and fairy tales.

As late as the 1850s most American children were forbidden to read fairy tales, which were viewed as anti-Christian, anti-utilitarian, conducive to daydreaming, and subversive of the work ethic. Even into the twentieth century, people were still debating whether fairy tales were morally dangerous.[72] But Wanamaker was not only reading these "anti-Christian" tales, he was also writing them for his grandchildren. Unfortunately, none of these fairy tales survives. Some things do survive, however, that were akin to fairy tales: Wanamaker's advertising editorials.

From age seventy-two until his death at eighty-four in 1922, Wanamaker wrote hundreds of such editorials, most of them showing the imprint of fairy tales. They also reveal his inclination to see his department stores as other than what they were—that is, in theatrical terms. "There is a Garden of Merchandise in Philadelphia," he said,

> where orchids and hardy annuals of commerce bloom, ever, side by side. This Garden is for all people. . . .
>
> This Store is an Easter Egg.
>
> Our store is Five Miles of Golden Chain. . . . It is like a thick woods of Autumn colors and lovely things, interesting and beautiful to behold. . . .
>
> The Store floors are each one vast table groaning with the luxuries of the Season. . . .
>
> Is this Wishmakers' Town? asked a country man entering the front door. "Yes it is—though some people call it Wanamaker town."
>
> We have enough to get our huge crops into the Wanamaker Storehouse. . . .
>
> This immense building is not an illusion
> > It is easily found
> > It is on the road of the people's wants
> > It has an everyday fullness
> > Its fullness is that of freshness.
>
> This store is the Rainbow and the Pot of Gold. You remember Alice Ben Bolt, do you not, and how often we were told that there was a pot of gold at both the feet of the Rainbow? A splendid rainbow put me foot down on the corner on Market Street, where

this Store began, and its other foot was placed on the corner of
13th Street where the Store is now, and today there were some
huge golden pots at their feet! . . .[73]

These editorials painted capitalism's smiling face. But was that an honest,
sincere face? To "theatricalize" something was not in its own right a bad
thing to do, but if you hated "theatricals" the way Wanamaker said he did,
could you be believed? Wanamaker liked to compare his artificial goods to
flowers and vegetables, his stores to farms. But wasn't this another example
of a great showman's legerdemain?

How was it that Wanamaker was so capable of shifting from the language
of parables to the language of fairy tales and advertising? Why did religion matter to him anyway? One answer to this question can be found in Wanamaker's
sense of Christian stewardship; like other wealthy devout men, Wanamaker
felt morally obliged to commit much of his fortune to Christian institutions.
He also believed in Christian ideas and values. Another answer—and I
think this covers as much or more ground (at the same time, it is much
more difficult to prove empirically)—is that Wanamaker needed moral
authority. He had a *personal* investment in his religious institutions; he may
have needed them to sanctify what he was doing; he wanted to feel clean
and good on the same grand scale on which he was building retail stores.

Wanamaker was neither an intolerant man nor a strict evangelical
Protestant. According to his biographer Herbert Adams Gibbons, Wanamaker's distinguishing feature was his nonjudgmental approach to life.
"Two years of close study of the life and writings of Wanamaker," Gibbons
recorded, "have led [me] to think that possibly the epitaph that best fits
him would be, 'He sat in judgment on no man.' "[74] He was a teetotaler
who preferred the company of other teetotalers, but he was still understanding and even accepting of drinking by his employees within clear limits.
(He had trouble, for instance, with his store organist, a Mr. Browne, who
often got drunk and played the organ so erratically as to upset the customers.
Wanamaker became fed up; he "is *spreeing* again," he wrote Rodman, "as
he has been doing several times during your absence. I have only to say
that I do not believe we can, with any respect for ourselves, retain Browne
in our employ any longer, no matter how his music is and how fine a spirit
he is when *sober*. I believe he is disgracing the house by his frequent
sprees."[75]) Nor was Wanamaker inclined to impose his religious convictions
or his moral views on others. "There are two sides to every question," he

admitted to a minister friend in 1886. "I employ between 3 to 4000 persons and do not consider that I have any right to control them or dictate to them what they shall do in their own time outside of my business. Among them are Hebrews, Catholics, Enthusiasts of different sorts of all denominations, each of them entitled to their opinions and responsible for their own conduct."[76] "We never allow religion or nationality or color to enter into the matter of employment of men, women, or children," he wrote another customer in 1898.[77]

But when it came to his own life and his own place in the world—his own public image—Wanamaker turned to religious activity out of some need to sanctify his business. Money was always in his thoughts. The concept of "abundance," which he invoked again and again in his private notebooks, had as much to do in his mind with money as it did with grace and holiness. All the while he was in India in 1900 meeting with missionaries and expanding the YMCA, he was pondering the real estate transactions involved in building his new New York store. He abruptly cut short his world tour to return home to nail down these "deals." For the moment everything else fell to the wayside—religion, churches, the YMCA. He got what he wanted, not only a lease renewal for the old Stewart property but also a big new lease for the entire block in downtown Manhattan, the site for what would be the world's largest department store to that time. "Like a crystal rose scattered and swept out—as a dream when one awaketh," he wrote in his religious notebook soon after the completion of these deals, "so are the days that are past. O Lord remember not our shortcomings against us—We make haste to make our confession and beseech thee to cut the knots that bind us to evil. . . . ABOVE ALL to do ABUNDANTLY" . . . "do *exceeding abundantly above all.*[78]

It was a pattern Wanamaker repeated all his life, beginning with the Moody revival in his Grand Depot in 1876. It was almost as if he had to build big in one area to build big in another. At the very time Pastor Wagner was writing glowingly over the beauties of Bethany, Wanamaker was writing a friend that he was "employing every dollar that I can command in the erection of [my] two large buildings, the cost of which will enter into millions of dollars."[79]

In November 1904, the last full month of Wagner's visit, Wanamaker had broken off briefly to visit the Louisiana Purchase Exposition in St. Louis, where he paid tens of thousands of dollars for the entire collection of modern German furniture, including the *jugenstil* sculpture of a giant brass eagle he would later place in the rotunda of the new Philadelphia store. He also purchased at the exposition and put into his store the biggest concert organ in the world. Both the organ and the eagle became Philadelphia icons.[80]

What are we to make of these contradictions (if they really were contradictions)? What did Wanamaker make of them when people challenged him to think about the relationship between commerce and religion? When a preacher asked him in 1901 about "the influence of modern commercialism on church life," Wanamaker responded that he thought no "business properly conducted, unless it be a brewery, or a liquor saloon or a gambling den, or something akin to the three of these things, [could] possibly interfere with a Christian profession. So far as my observation goes I believe that the higher planes upon which mercantile business have set in the last twenty years have been very favorable to a religious life."[81] Didn't Santa Claus threaten the place of Christ in Christmas?, another minister asked. No, Wanamaker replied, not in the least; every child knew that Santa was a myth. A physician inquired if there was any potential danger in the "promiscuous bunching" of Wanamaker's young male and female employees. Wanamaker "had no knowledge" of any such activity, he said. Moreover, "it would be a slander, and possibly a libel" on his store to assume that his employees worked "under conditions that are detrimental to their highest interests."[82]

Commerce and religion, then, were not in conflict. "Being" and "having," grace and acquisition, the sacred and the secular were not at odds. And they were not at odds in part because Wanamaker believed they were the *same* thing. And he was right about this, although not in ways that reflected well on him or on liberal evangelical Protestantism. From at least the 1850s onward, many Protestant Americans, perhaps the majority, believed in the compatability of religion and commerce and that both were moving on a fast track toward progress.[83] Liberal Protestantism, in other words, with its strong nonjudgmental character, had made room for department stores, and Wanamaker exemplified this accommodation on a vast scale.

To be sure, he tried at times—at least he said he tried—to keep religion and commerce separate. He refused, for instance, to display paintings depicting Christ in his stores. "The fact that I have owned the two Munkácsy pictures of Christ before Pilate and Christ on Calvary," he wrote a customer in 1898 of the huge murals by Hungarian artist Mihály von Munkácsy that he bought in the late 1880s, "and that eight-tenths of the time they have been packed away in the dark, will prove to you that I am not willing to use a masterpiece of the Christ in connection with my business."[84] But Wanamaker did display "ecclesiastical pictures taken from the Chicago fair" in his stores, and he did install fake churches into his rotundas during the holidays. He could write that "I would like to use my store as a pulpit on week days, just as much as my desk at Bethany on Sundays, to lift people up that they may better lift themselves."[85] Mixing up religion and commerce never seemed blasphemous to him (as it does today, ironically, when religion to many people is probably far more irrelevant than it was in Wanamaker's time).

But it really didn't matter, anyway, whether Wanamaker felt ill at ease over what he had created. For him religion was not only nonjudgmental, it was extremely personal and private, as much unrelated to or removed from commerce as it was mixed up in it. Christianity's tenderheartedness and its pleas for sacrifice and service made Wanamaker feel good, virtuous, clean. He wasn't interested in religion as a body of critical ideas, as a prophetic light that might measure behavior by high standards of ethical probity and spiritual insight. This is not to say, of course, that he was indifferent to the social side of religion; all his missions and schools were intended to aid the poor as well as to promote a moral middle-class mentality, Christian paternalism, and orderly and polite behavior. But the piety, the personalism, stands out as the cardinal feature of his religious life. For him, as for countless others, religion brought him, as he put it, "closer" to "His strengthening touch" and "His love."[86] What Wagner said of Wanamaker and of the other Bethany people, then—that they cared nothing about dogma or about scientific exegesis of texts, and everything about mining "treasures" from the Gospels—was right on the mark.

Wanamaker's use of religion illustrates what was and still is a trend in mainstream American Protestantism—its failure to sustain a strong critical, intellectual tradition. Wanamaker's religious institutions were important; they organized and shaped social identity, contributed to the formation of the common cultural boundaries of a class, helped the outcast in some measure, and perhaps gave some people a sense of a Christian vocation, but as religious "thought" they had minimal depth. They were accommodationist. They promoted individual salvation, personal well-being, and harmony, not discontent, conflict, shame, or insight. Bethany Mission Sunday School and all the other institutions similar to it flourishing in

America were wholly incapable of reflecting critically on the "other" world that Wanamaker and others had done so much to bring into being.

Sin, Consensus, and Institution Building

A comfortable gentility, fearful of emotional extremes and of public embarrassment but capable of consumer extravagance, emerged as a feature of American middle-class urban and suburban life in these decades. For some people, going to church on Sundays, followed by shopping or going to the office on Mondays, took on the dimensions of a fixed middle-class ritual, complete with a whole range of accessory "downtown" activities, from meeting in "tearooms" on Tuesday to visiting the "clubs" on Wednesday. The ability to consume the new goods, moreover, as historian Herbert Schneider long ago pointed out, increasingly became a sign of sanctification rather than a symptom of moral failure. Poor people became the "objects of missions" not because of their faithlessness (many were very religious) but because of their inability to consume at levels rivaling those of the more affluent congregants. The more "depressed groups," Schneider has written, were "termed the 'domestic heathen,' and their heathendom [was] defined better in terms of their lack of privileges than in terms of their lack of faith. Though they [were] not hopeless, they became religiously an alien population."[87]

To the degree that such a cultural pattern led to any kind of moral indignation or fervor, it was of a shallow kind, intended partly to erase the appearance of sin and to assuage whatever guilt people felt about their own affluence. It was directed—as sociologist Edward Ross observed in 1907— at "vices," not "sins." Vice, Ross insisted, was an "individual" thing and might include drinking, visiting a prostitute, swearing, picking pockets, or causing a scene; vices related only to "individuals" and were "harmless" by and large, he said. Sin, on the other hand, was "social," and in its consequences to others "far more reprehensible" than vice. For Ross, it was those modern sins associated with commercial activities that most endangered the moral and social well-being of the country.

New kinds of sin had emerged, Ross said, the outcome of the new interlocking system of impersonal commercial institutions—corporations, large department stores, commercial and investment banks, and credit agencies—within which criminals might commit heinous crimes yet remain hidden from view. "Today," he wrote, in words as accurate now as they were eighty years ago, "the villain most in need of curbing is the respectable, exemplary, trusted personage who, strategically placed at the focus of a spider-web of fiduciary relations, is able from his office-chair to pick a thousand pockets, poison a thousand sick, pollute a thousand minds, or imperil a thousand lives. It is the great-scale, high-voltage sinner that needs the shackle."[88] Or, as one of Edith Wharton's characters says in her 1913 novel *The Custom of the Country*, "in America, the *real crime passionel* is a 'big steal.' "[89]

But it was precisely this kind of economically and socially sinful behavior that liberal evangelical Protestants tended to miss or ignore (or even secretly to admire), targeting instead those vices—what Ross referred to as the "small sins" of the flesh—least likely to threaten the economic order. There is reason to believe that Wanamaker, as founder and owner of his *own* business, was always on the lookout for institutional "sin." At the same time, it could be argued, he had an obvious vested interest in finding little fault with the world he had created or in suspending judgment in regard to it—in fact, a counterinterest. But Wanamaker swore with conviction by his faith; it was no pretense to him. Thousands of other Protestants swore with him; they joined his organizations and seemed to accept happily the justifying rationale they had fashioned together.

That pattern—loyalty to an "interior" Protestantism on the one hand, and to the consumer pleasures on the other—was characteristic of the American Protestant reaction generally, whether in its evangelical or liberal form, to the new economy and culture.[90] It was produced by several religious developments, not least of which was timidity or a refusal to rock the boat: "The Church senses the business obsession of our times," Ross said in 1912, "and shrinks from taking a stand that might bring her into clash with the profit mania."[91] The traditional American split between church and state played a decisive role here; so did the variety of religious institutions, leading to a fragmentation that made it very difficult for any one group to dictate (or try to dictate) or to shape the character of a culture or to establish the limits of what was sacrilegious. As U.S Supreme Court justice Felix Frankfurter was to declare in a 1952 Supreme Court decision, "in America" there is a "multiplicity of ideas of 'sacredness,' held with equal but conflicting fervor by the great number of religious groups," and thereby "making the term 'sacrilegious' too indefinite to satisfy constitutional demands based on reason and fairness."[92]

At the heart of the pattern in established Protestantism was the decline of what remained of a strong tradition of social criticism—a prophetic strain, a determination to judge social reality by religious standards. As Walter Rauschenbusch said, American Protestants had become "individualistic" and "private" in their religion. "While rich in piety and evangelistic fervor, [evangelicalism] has been singularly poor in the prophetic gift," he argued. "It lacks the vital interest in the total of human life which can create a united and harmonious and daring religious conception of the world."[93]

What was true of mainstream Protestantism, moreover, was—it seems to me—increasingly true of mainstream Catholicism and Judaism, as well, even though it took longer for these groups to align themselves so completely to the same trends and despite the existence—as I observed at the outset— of powerful critical voices. As Catholics and Jews struggled to assimilate, they, too, began to live in divided ways, on the one hand committed to the existing commercial society and, on the other, to an interior religion of separateness and piety that bolstered them as they adjusted to that society. In the process, whatever remained of a social gospel, of a prophetic tradition, or of a philosophy of charity and abstinence in either one of these faiths seems to have been undermined for many, many people.

Before 1900, Reform Jews were already mirroring mainstream Protestant YMCAs and "evangelical morality" by establishing Young Men's and Young Women's Hebrew Associations in cities throughout the country (later the Catholics would do the same thing).[94] From the late teens forward, moreover, middle-class Jews, who were moving in great numbers into New York suburbs, began to transform their most important religious institution—the synagogue—into a comfortable middle-class sanctuary.

Historian Deborah Dash Moore has illuminated this new Jewish institution building. Before 1910, she indicates, first-generation immigrant Jews in New York had already refashioned the synagogue into a *chevra* or into an "old-world Yiddish" institution "organized primarily for religious purposes" and dedicated to the social welfare of the communities. Second-generation middle-class Jews, on the other hand, as they migrated into the suburbs of Brooklyn and the Bronx, rejected this synagogue "model" in favor of the "Jewish community center," a new institution similar to the Protestant institutional church and made in their own middle-class image. These centers were inspired by educated Jewish Zionists who exchanged the *chevra*'s Old World customs for "a secular form of ethnic identification linked to American culture and the English language." At first they were supposed to integrate four activities: religious worship, study, social service, and recreation. But, over time, in center after center, the social service aspect was dropped, and cultural activities, sociability, and recreation took over. Religion stayed in focus, but "as each synagogue center grew, the primacy of religion receded," leading to "the secularization of the synagogue," according to one critic, Rabbi Israel Goldstein. Many of these structures, costing millions of dollars, combined synagogues, schools, pools, gymnasiums, and even "excellent kosher restaurants" (plus "genuine Jewish atmosphere") into single complexes; they resembled to a degree other American multiuse structures (e.g., hotels or Wanamaker's own Bethany). A contemporary compared them to "department stores with all merchandise under one roof to save the customer the expenditure of energy, and to provide the management greater economic efficiency."[95]

Institutional Catholicism made a comparable adjustment, its goal also to create a strong set of institutions designed simultaneously to integrate Catholics into American culture and to erect a hedge against that culture. By 1912, the American Catholic Church, established and extensive, was catering not only to a large working-class population but also to a prospering middle class. Parishes had multiplied, so had the numbers of bishops, priests, and nuns, and with this growth came involvement with the same matters that confronted Protestants and Jews—the need to build a base secure enough to meet the needs of large congregations and to influence public opinion.

To be sure, unlike most Protestants and like many Jews, Catholics were frequently forced to resolve religious disputes among different ethnic groups and to defend themselves against an often hostile Protestant culture.[96] But like the other religions, mainstream Catholicism, even in the pre-World War I period, began to assume an accommodationist approach to American culture. This is not to say that traditional ideas of charity and asceticism were abandoned. They were not. Indeed, in the early 1900s, the Catholic approach to charity (to voluntary giving rather than to "taking" or "having") was still so strong that, according to historian Aaron Abell, "some Catholics (were) unable to comprehend how a person could legitimately earn a money income from helping others" and "considered the professional social worker 'as a cold-blooded mercenary.' "[97] A whole new web of Catholic charities under the auspices of the various bishops was also coming into existence.

Moreover, members of such priestly orders as the Jesuits or Benedictines were required to take vows of poverty, so that they might go about their principal tasks without "becoming demoralized."[98] Even the parish priests and sisters of the day adhered to fixed patterns of behavior, all sharing something of a uniform moral discipline, a common dress, and a generally simple way of life.

At the same time the church started to let in the world around it. Gradually, many city parishes became social centers where men and women went to play cards or bingo and to attend bazaars, plays, minstrel shows, or picnics. (Although this shift was more characteristic of the 1920s—"the golden age" of the city parish—the outlines of it could be seen in this earlier period as well).[98] An earlier plain American Catholic style slowly gave way to a gaudier one in bigger and better churches, as historian Jay Dolan and others have shown. Like their American Protestant counterparts, flourishing Catholic parish churches were designed in expensive Romanesque or Gothic styles and filled with stained-glass windows and elaborate statuary and chapels. Many urban cardinals adopted what was called "Catholic Big" (and later "Babbitt Byzantine") in an effort to demonstrate that American Catholics, too, had the right to "go first class." In Chicago, the pioneer German-American cardinal George Mundelein indulged in a public ritual pageantry in the first decades of the century that would have been unheard of in the nineteenth century. He intended this display to express a newfound Catholic pride and to instill in ordinary Catholics an unquestioning loyalty to the church and respect for clerical authority. It was borrowed partly from older Catholic European traditions of religious performance (the German Catholics, in particular, showed a far greater enthusiasm for colorful pageantry than the Irish did), but was also reinforced by (and perhaps to some degree reflected) the new American fascination with show and display—with colors, lights, and spectacle. It could be argued, too, that Catholic pageantry and consumer spectacle were mutually supporting, each recognizing the effectiveness of grand spaces as a means of winning patronage.[99]

A new Catholic emphasis on a nonintellectual gospel rather than on a social gospel emerged alongside this new institution-building. Despite the social writings of thoughtful clerics such as Monsignor John Ryan of Catholic University in Washington, D.C., the church, by and large, sought to give Catholics "acculturation without ideas," as historian Mel Piehl has argued. "The American Church," Piehl writes, "generally refrained from making social teachings strong corollaries of religious commitment, as was done in Europe. . . . [That] undoubtedly eased the gradual acceptance of Catholics into American life," but "the cost was an effective abandonment of the essential Catholic tenet that religion should shape culture rather than culture shape religion."[100] The effect of this approach on Catholic university or college life must have been stultifying; indeed, it appears to have generated an interest in a bland form of Thomistic organicism quite unlike the critical Thomism of John Ryan and more like the "warm" approach of the future television evangelist Bishop Fulton Sheen. Sheen insisted on a vague "synthesis between religion and life" and on a feeling of spiritual "interdependence" among all Catholics. The climate he helped create did not foster philosophical depth or, for some, much hope. "The chief trouble with our teaching today," a depressed Catholic educator said in 1924, "is that we haven't anything to teach. . . . We haven't wisdom to teach. We don't know what to say about life as our fathers did."[101]

Many of the Catholic clergy embraced a devotional religion of piety also meant to promote cultural unity rather than spiritual reflection. They began to propagate a simple "evangelical code of morality" similar to that popular among Protestants. The Catholic clergy seemed even more determined than the Protestant to focus on the "small vices" of the flesh—sexual sins, in particular. Indeed, the Catholic hierarchy had for many years gone even further in insisting that sexual vices committed "in the mind" were as "wrong" as those committed in deed. (At the same time, the confessional allowed Catholics to rid themselves of the burden of sin far more readily than Protestants.)[102]

Like the mainstream Protestant groups and the Jewish ones as well, the Catholic hierarchy generally turned away from any duty to confront critically the new pecuniary culture and economy. Cultural unity and community were the priorities. While the new conditions day by day seemed to overtake inherited Christian ideas of self-sacrifice, "brotherly love," spiritual perfection, and renunciation of the world, the Catholic clergy was—despite strong, resisting traditions—drawn away by other matters. The tremendous intellectual and ethical challenge of modern capitalist culture, the way it called into question the whole legacy of the Church fathers, was left largely unmet. Philosophical and ethical issues of any magnitude were shunted aside, given the nature of mainstream Catholic evangelicalism, the obsession of most of the cardinals and bishops with expanding their institutions, the interest in learning business methods for success, and the commitment to "going first class."[103]

Down the Slippery Slope

On the whole, then, the mainstream religious response appears to have done little to give Americans deeper insight into the character of the new culture of consumer capitalism or into the nature of the moral challenge posed by that culture. Many evangelical groups, Catholic and Protestant, as well as middle-class Jews, turned inward and did not develop, it seems, a satisfying critical perspective. But the moral consequences of this failure for individuals were often debilitating, as the Wanamaker case illustrates. Religion for Wanamaker was largely a personal affair that had no immediate bearing on the conduct of his business, and it had little effect on the way he brought up his own children. He seemed unable to pass on his religious feelings or beliefs, especially to the dearest of his children, Rodman, who was earmarked to inherit the business.

Wanamaker's attachment to Rodman was almost primal. In letter after letter to his son he expressed his love with great tenderness and wholly without inhibition. "I can only heap up in this my love," he wrote in February 1903, "—it towers above the Rockies and Himalayas—you have made it larger. . . . You must let me build for you a summer bungalow as an annex to Lindenhurst." And, just a day later: "Your good night word is my Valentine, it is love all over and through and through." "A wee-bit of a love letter to you, dear son of mine," he wrote later, signing himself "Jonathan Loveman." "I have thought of you dear precious patient man forty eleven times and more today and loved you all over the lawn and the house." "This is your father who dreamed of you last night," he wrote playfully while on a trip to Florida in 1918, "and woke up, rolled over in bed, made room for you and actually reached out his arms to pull you in—why didn't you like my little bed well enough to stop with me and have the breakfast which calls at 8 to be ate?"[104]

Often the letters approached poetry, as did this one, which I give here as Wanamaker wrote in its entirety:

7:30 AM
before Breakfast
alone in the little
Library 26 June 13

Coming to you I am
    dear son dearest
first of all to say Good morning and
to take a bite of your cheek to
kiss you at the days starting point.
                Father[105]

In none of these letters to his son was there any mention of his religious views, nothing about the YMCA, not a word about Bethany, not even a passing reference to the Brotherhood.

Why did Wanamaker communicate so little of his religious convictions to Rodman, whom he loved so much? There were several reasons for this, I think, all of them interrelated. First, Wanamaker's love for his son far surpassed in expressiveness all other bonds or loyalties, even the religious ones. "I am your old father who loves you better than his life."[106] Next, Wanamaker was more concerned with passing on his business through Rodman than with imparting his own Protestant values to him. Wanamaker's religious personalism, with its strong nonjudgmental strain, may have played a role here as well. His institution building appeared to have satisfied something in him; it was *his*, and it kept him loyal, to some degree, to Moody's mission: to build institutions to spread the simple word of Christ and to help shape the moral character of his country. But his institutions did not apply to his son, especially as it seemed clear anyway that Rodman preferred a more urbane, secular, cosmopolitan life. Rodman was his own steward, and his religious convictions were his own business. It could be said as well that, when viewed in the context of the richness of earlier religious visions, Wanamaker actually had nothing of any power to transmit.

The moral consequences for his son—and for Wanamaker's grandson, his own namesake, John Wanamaker, Jr.—were considerable. Rodman cared nothing at all for the simple life, for Sunday schools, for the gospels, for Christian temperance and self-denial; if these things constituted what it meant to be Christian, then Rodman was no Christian. Unlike his father, he had no reservations about displaying the Munkácsy pictures depicting the crucifixion of Christ in the rotundas of the Wanamaker stores. (See plate

18). (They were shown, to be sure, after John Wanamaker had died. But really, would the old man have minded anyway?) Rodman lived in a world of nearly majesterial luxury. He had many houses, including, in Biarritz in France, the huge Villa Duchatel, once the property of Britain's Edward VII and where Rodman entertained the richest of Europe's crowned nobility.[107] His measure of success was whether a governor, a prince, or a princess had recently dined at his house. He threw lavish parties in Paris and New York, serving expensive wines and passing out diamond souvenirs to his guests. He had yachts (one called *Nirvana*) and countless servants. As a hobby, he wrote French piano music (including a "valse pour piano dedicated to my friend the Prince Mohamet").[108]

At the same time, Rodman remained a devoted and dutiful son. He condemned all public violations of a moral code he shared with his father and with his father's class. Nothing was to be allowed to besmirch the family name (although it must be said that his second wife divorced him in 1923 on the charge of desertion).[109] Above all, he built on the "uppermost wish of the Founder of our business." "I feel," he wrote in 1924 to his sister Minnie, of his father, "that the great spirit is very near to us, and it all means that we should accomplish what we were sent here for and what we were to do—to follow on with all our might and power those different accomplishments that would show to the world the great pioneering efforts that no one else has ever conceived."[110] He worked hard for the business, and under him the stores flourished.

Rodman's son John Wanamaker, Jr., was not so lucky. To him, the yachts and castles—and the beautiful women who were everywhere around him—had all the charm, while the churches and Sunday schools were nothing short of repellent. As a young man, he got lost in the moral labyrinth of the commercial culture of his father and grandfather. He drank heavily, and by the early 1920s was an alcoholic; he took drugs as well—"habit-forming powders, pills, compounds, and liquids."[111] To the "disgust" of his father, who eventually disowned him, his wife, and his children, John, Jr., was an irresponsible father who time and again abandoned his two children, a philanderer and whoremonger (to use words his grandfather would have understood). His own self-pleasure far exceeded in importance anybody else's well-being. In the midtwenties he was caught hiring a young woman in the Philadelphia store—a "kept" woman—for his own enjoyment.[112] By employing his family's institutional power to exploit women, he had crossed the line from "vice" into "sin." John, Jr. appeared to lack all the evangelical virtues that John, Sr., swore by. His entire attitude seemed to mock the old man's religious "achievement" and to jeer at its hypocrisy. There was nothing in all of his grandfather's institution building that seemed to offer him a clue about how to behave. What was weak in his father (the moral legacy, that is), disintegrated in him.

In the swiftness of its moral decline, the Wanamaker family cannot be seen as typical of the experience of most or even more than a few Americans. But it does mark a trend that was emerging more slowly in the lives of many less wealthy Americans, and it does illustrate the inadequacy of evangelical religion—and of mainstream institutional religion generally in this period—in dealing with the moral challenge of the new corporate industrial order. The Wanamaker case illustrates something else as well: It shows that if ordinary standards of religion are too weak as moral guides, then other guides will surely rush in and take their place.

On one level, the Wanamaker solution was a success story. After all, it gave structure to spiritual life for many people and it recognized—on a limited scale—the centrality of the interior Christian life. One can also say in Wanamaker's favor that by supporting the simple-life movement and by building his institutions, he was at least acknowledging that major changes had taken place in America and that they carried with them a moral challenge. He was recognizing as well that some kind of moral legitimacy, even some element of the sacred, was needed to justify and shape continued commercial development.

But the Wanamaker solution and the institutional religious response generally, by their refusal or inability to address in any systematic philosophical or ethical way America's new culture, dissatisfied many people. Some of these—John Ryan and Walter Rauschenbusch, for instance—rejected these compromises because they went too far in retreating behind hedges. Others rejected Wanamaker's pieties and his compromises because they did not go far enough in making way for and embracing the new order of things. These people showed none of Wanamaker's denials or equivocations. They took the culture for what it was and celebrated it. Their religious outlook was mind cure or positive thinking.

Chapter 8

MIND CURE AND
THE HAPPINESS MACHINE

For most people, the Wanamaker religious pattern—simple piety and in-stitution building on the one hand, accommodation on the other—was probably standard, providing a measure of comfort and stability. It may have blurred the lines between religion and commerce, but it did not erase them altogether. There was another response, similar to yet more radical than the Wanamaker approach, that did erase the lines. This was mind-cure, a spiritual outlook with roots deep in America and a general philo-sophical bias characteristic of the thinking of many Americans.

Mind cure produced new religious ideas and groups—for example, New Thought, Unity, Christian Science, and theosophy. As a general spiritual mentality, it was wish-oriented, optimistic, sunny, the epitome of cheer and self-confidence, and completely lacking in anything resembling a tragic view of life. In mind cure there was no darkness, no Melville or Hawthorne, no secrets, no sin or evil, nothing grim or untidy, only the safe shore and "the sunlight of health," in one mind-curer's words.[1] Mind cure suffused much of the culture, entering into the heart of American liberal political economy and influencing such major figures as Simon Patten, whose ideas on economics came to inform American business think-ing and political policy (other economists like Thorstein Veblen reviled mind cure). It was expressed in liberal popular culture in the writings of people such as Eleanor Porter, author of *Pollyanna*, and L. Frank Baum, the pioneer window trimmer and author of *The Wonderful Wizard of Oz*, perhaps the best-known mind-cure text ever written.

"The New Healers"

Psychologist William James first called attention to the mind-cure movement in a notable way in his 1902 book *The Varieties of Religious Experience*. The term had already been in vogue before, but James secured its place in history. Mind-cure groups, he observed, consisted of several religious sects that maintained that men and women could, merely by acts of will and conviction, cure their own diseases and create heaven on earth. Mind curers were also described as "new healers" or, later, as positive thinkers; they were more in touch than traditional religions with what was going on in America; and they proved more creative in taking advantage of new spiritual opportunities. Even Wanamaker might have called himself a mind curer, as might have his spiritual companion Pastor Wagner; both rejected "inhuman pessimism" and always took the confident and hopeful view. Yet these men stayed within established religion.[2] The mind curers, by and large, bolted to create new religions and a new outlook more in tune with the dominant business culture. In about 1915 they were competing for the loyalty of thousands of American women and men.

The mind-cure groups grew out of the great religious turmoil of the 1870s and 1880s, a turning point in American religious history that not only saw the advent of many homegrown religious sects (from Ethical Culture to the Jehovah's Witnesses) but that marked the decline of the preeminence of Protestantism, its earliest splintering into modernist and fundamentalist camps, and the rise of other religious communities and ideas. Historians have described this period as one of spiritual crisis, which resolved itself for most Protestants, Catholics, and Jews into inwardly directed institution building; for many Protestant evangelicals by 1915 into fundamentalism (a term coined about this time) or into retreat from what seemed dangerously "modern"; and for others into confusion, doubt, and even despair.[3] Still others—the mind curers—found a new certainty and seemed to have the right answers at the right time. Though often at odds with one another, taken together they constituted America's "only original contribution to the systematic philosophy of life," as William James said.

By the end of the century, their own literature, according to a recent historian, had reached "staggering proportions."[4]

A landmark event was the meeting of the Parliament of Religions at the World's Columbian Exposition in Chicago in 1893, when the spiritual leaders of three of the leading "healing" groups—two women and one man—seized the public eye. Chicagoans such as young Lucy Sprague from Chicago (later the wife of influential economist Wesley Clair Mitchell) was one of many to view their meeting—and the novelty of the whole ecumenical experience—as "a great event in my life."[5] Annie Besant from England, who had inherited the leadership of the Theosophical Society from Helene Blavatsky (who founded it in New York City in 1875), spoke about theosophy. Mary Baker Eddy, founder of Christian Science, explained the philosophy of Christian Science, making every effort to distinguish it from Besant's more "oriental" and "pagan" ideas. Swami Vivekenanda from India declaimed before the assembled throng in a turban of white silk and a long, soft, scarlet robe belted by a crimson girdle. He electrified his listeners with lectures on Vedanta, the basic philosophy of Hinduism, which had a strong influence on both theosophy and New Thought. After the Parliament, he toured the country, stirring up interest in Vedanta and in the entire mind-cure project.[6]

Mind curers often shared common roots with both liberal and evangelical Protestantism and carried to an extreme many of the most liberal tendencies in these faiths. The position they occupied—especially the more secular variants such as theosophy and New Thought—was pragmatic, reflecting in the most committed way the American conviction that people could shape their own destinies and find total happiness. These faiths wanted to make religion work in the modern era, to integrate it with secular and scientific aspirations, and to accommodate it to ever-expanding material desires.[7] Protestants like Wanamaker had maintained some loyalty to the inward life and to the distinction between commerce and religion, but mind curers looked outward, opening "the self" completely to what they perceived to be the "full abundance of the universe."

By and large, as historian Donald Meyer points out in his history of mind cure, *The Positive Thinkers*, the mind curers had no special politics to speak of and were, indeed, apolitical. But they did possess their own unique theological attitudes, their own psychology, and their own economics, which departed from earlier, nineteenth-century views and were consistent with the new commercial priorities.

On the surface, these sects appeared to be adversaries, theologically speaking. The more "traditional" Christian Scientists often pointed to the Bible as the primary source of revelation and spiritual insight; the theosophists and New Thought types looked *anywhere* for guidance, but very rarely to the Bible. Theosophists were especially daring (or even odd) in this regard, believing that "spirits" of dead people hover over the earth and can be reached readily at séances and through mediums. The American founder herself, Helene Blavatsky, arranged some very spectacular séances and was not above using her mesmerizing blue eyes (and other devices) with unashamed trickery. Many theosophists were also occultists, convinced that living things never die but metamorphose into new entities—animals, birds, or whatever. Karma and reincarnation were basic tenets of theosophy. [8]

At the same time, Blavatsky and other theosophists opposed any form of personal deity and were belligerently anti-Christian—and thus anathema to Christian Scientists (who, in their own right, were extremely cavalier in their biblical interpretations). Followers of theosophy and New Thought rejected belief in a traditional notion of afterlife: There was only the eternal "here and now." New Thought mind curers and theosophists both studied pagan beliefs and world religions like Buddhism and Hinduism in search of the "meta-spirit" behind all religions, first expressed, so they thought, in secret pagan mysteries of the ancient world.

Despite religious differences, all mind curers believed in "salvation *in this life*" and "fullness within time," not after death. [9] "Live and let live" was a cardinal tenet of all these sects. They rejected older concepts of evil, guilt, damnation, and depravity. Drawing on Hinduism, theosophists were the boldest of all in their opposition to sin and guilt. In place of a judgmental God, they put a beneficent being—"not a person at all," really, Blavatsky said, but a "divine force," an all-"healing and invigorating power" dwelling inside and outside the believer. God was a "whole" being, a happy fusion of Father/Mother, a complete abundance accessible to everybody, operating benevolently through all people and at all times. "The Universe itself," Blavatsky wrote, "is unfolding out of its own essence," and so we, too, are "ever-Becoming" into "pure spirit." [10] God was the embodiment, in effect, of a *child's* wish—the wish for love, protection, and sustenance at any moment. [11]

A new upbeat positive psychology, "affirming success even amidst failure," underpinned mind-cure theology. [12] As William James was among the first to observe at the turn of the century, mind curers were "healthy-minded." Every individual was "infinite possibility through the creative power of constructive thinking and obedience, which is the source of Inspiration, Power, Health, and Prosperity."[13] "We are really gods," Swami Vivekenanda told his followers, "not sinners. We must not beg for salvation but demand it as our spiritual birthright. Whatever we think, we shall become. So if we think we are sinners, we will indeed become sinners, but if we think we are divine, we shall really become divine."[14] Mind curers renounced all negative thinking—especially fear, worry, and anxiety. Fear is a "self-imposed or self-permitted suggestion of inferiority," wrote one believer, that "really belongs in the category of harmful" and "unnecessary things." It made people ill, keeping them from reaching the true plenitude in the universe. Think "success," and you will "have success." The only "God," Blavatsky said, "is latent in all" individuals.[15] "There is a latent power," wrote Orison Swett Marden, a movement spokesman, "a force of indestructible life, an immortal principle of health, in every individual, which if developed would heal all our wounds." "Wake up and stretch yourself. . . . The only thing that keeps us from taking plenty of either money or air is fear"; "All you desire is YOURS NOW. . . . You are born to dominion and plenty," other leaders said.[16]

Eugene Del Mar, popular exponent of New Thought, wrote in his "The Joy of Service" that Americans should banish forever the "idea of duty or self-denial." "To the emancipated soul there is nothing common or unclean. There is no necessary postponement of happiness."[17] "We all know the disastrous effects of wrong thinking—don't worry," Marden wrote. "If you want to get the most out of life, just make up your mind that you were made to be happy, that you are a happiness-machine, as well as a work-machine. Cut off the past, and do not touch the morrow until it comes, but extract every possibility from the present. Think positive, creative, happy thoughts, and your harvest of good things will be abundant."[18]

A positive approach to economics accompanied this psychology and theology of abundant energy, departing from earlier laissez-faire ideas of scarcity and self-denial in favor of the more appealing notions of supply and prosperity. In every way, the world was a very nice place to mind curers: No misery at all really existed. Poverty, injustice, inequities of all kinds were only in the mind. There was "plenty for all."[19]

This mind-cure ideology could be found in many areas of urban culture. "Crusades" for "cheerfulness," as they were called, and for a "no-worry" approach to life were "launched," often by prewar businessmen and advertisers who had picked up mind-cure ideas.[20] Business trade periodicals like *Success* magazine and Siegel-Cooper's employee magazine *Thought and Work* carried the latest releases from the mind-cure gurus. "Don't postpone your happiness," urged *Thought and Work* in 1904, "there is no doubt that man was intended to be happy and contented."[21] Advertising zealot Elbert Hubbard, who dabbled in New Thought, distributed business "preachments" around the country, reminding his readers that "fear is the great disturber. It causes all physical ills" and "positive thinking is essential for health and wisdom."[22] "I believe," he said, "we are now living in eternity as much as ever we shall."[23]

Mind-cure icons were marketed, such as the "no worry" Billikens doll designed by a young woman from Kansas City, Missouri, a squat, smiling doll, a kind of fat Buddha figure, sometimes male, sometimes female, representing "the God of things as they ought to be." The doll was "a hit without parallel in the toy trade," according to one dealer; it was on display in hotels, in restaurants and department stores, and in homes throughout America.[24] It helped incite the "doll craze" of the early 1900s, when, for the first time, Americans began to spend millions on toys and playthings. Variations—such as the "teddy-billiken doll" and the "Billycan and Billycant" dolls ("a pair of jokers," it was said, intended to "drive away difficulties, petty annoyances, and dull care")—were soon sold from New York to Seattle. It was a perfect mind-cure symbol for a new middle-class, consuming public. "An atmosphere of gorged content pervades Billikens," said a contemporary. "No one can look at him [or her] and worry."[25]

Thousands of Americans took seriously the "new healing." As early as the late 1890s, in the wake of Swami Vivekenanda's public success, a cult of swamis began to attract hundreds of disaffected, affluent women and overworked businessmen, culminating in the popularity of the Indian guru Krishnamurti in the late teens and early twenties (and much later as well). Businessmen took classes in meditation and yoga to develop the power of positive thinking. Mabel Dodge, rich Greenwich Village matron and co-inspirer of the 1913 Paterson Pageant, practiced many mind-cure therapies, seeking to become a "super-self," as one of her lovers, Hutchins Hapgood, said of her, "strongly connected with 'It'—the infinite."[26] People as diverse as Thorstein Veblen's first wife, Ellen, and the novelist Theodore Dreiser were drawn to theosophy, Christian Science, and New Thought. For Dreiser especially, this new "religious" perspective fit in neatly with the world of money, ambition, greed, and desire.[27]

Simon Patten's Political Economy of Mind Cure

The mind-cure outlook in American economic inquiry shaped the thought of some leading political economists. Economics itself—and sociology, its ally for many years until both parted company as separate disciplines— were relatively new fields in the United States.[28] In the 1880s, in the United States, where creativity in this field was especially strong, economics was marked by battles over theory and turf and the appearance of the first associations; by 1900 it was "fast becoming a permanent feature of the intellectual life of the country." College students were taking economics classes in droves, and "the profession was enjoying a tropical growth," as Joseph Schumpeter put it.[29] "So popular has economic thinking become," wrote Simon Patten in 1908, "that it seems a natural state of affairs that must always have existed. . . . Today economics is in every one's thoughts and on every one's tongue."[30]

The new interest in what for years had been called the "dismal science" signified efforts to come to grips with the new world of money, with the often frightening cycles of boom and bust, with the corporations and in- vestment bankers, and with the new consumer businesses. Some economic thinkers sought to assess the larger "meaning" of these changes, their effects on the welfare of the people, their spiritual-cultural and economic promise. There were many other economists (though fewer then than now), who steered clear of such questions, making no effort to examine the effect of market activity, which they conceived of as static and outside time, on the larger culture or society.[31] Many other economists—indeed, perhaps the majority in the early 1900s, as historian Mary Furner has argued—still reflected the earlier political economy of John Stuart Mill, Adam Smith, and others, who dealt with market questions in the context of politics and culture.[32] These economists included a "newer" group of thinkers who were interested in the whole shape and direction of the new consumer economy (although they did not call that economy "consumer"). They argued, too, that economists should consider many kinds of institutions—economic, political, and cultural—as they formed a society or civilization. Some were critical of American business and opposed the mind-cure outlook; others— such as Patten—embraced both.[33]

The critical voices in economics did not dominate, but we need to consider them, because the intensity of their criticism reveals the sig-

nificance of the historical changes then under way. An arch-critic was
Thorstein Veblen, America's most original economist, who was as far
from the mind-cure outlook as anyone could have been (despite the theosophy of his first wife, Ellen). He did agree with the mind curers that,
as he put it, "the ancient Christian principles of humility, renunciation,
abnegation, or nonresistance had been virtually eliminated from the
moral scene."[34] But he did not agree that the new capitalist world was
ensuring abundance for all; indeed, it was shrinking the possibilities of the
universe, not expanding them, as business focused desire toward consumption of goods and away from productive labor and the ownership of
land.[35]

Veblen scorned the idea that the new commercial world was in
any way an embodiment of a child's wish. True, capitalist abundance
seemed to respond to every child's dream by promising everything to
everybody, lifetime protection from pain and fear, but it was fostering a
society shaped by brokers—investment bankers, real estate agents and loan
sharks, dealers in fictitious goods, advertisers, merchandisers—who did no
productive labor and who merely merchandised the wishes of others to
"make money" and "to get something for nothing." Veblen despised this
class for shifting the economy away from making useful goods to making
money or profit. These new brokers, he argued, knew nothing about workmanship but everything about profit, volume turnover, and the chemistry
of wishes.[36]

This class was imposing on Americans a new "apparatus of salesmanship," as Veblen called it. Selling had been around for ages, but salesmanship was new, a function of the mass production of goods and a direct
outcome of the new reliance on credit, of the need to support overhead
charges, and of the system of prices. "Salesmanship is the end and animating
purpose of all business that is done for a price," Veblen said.[37] "The end
of salesmanship," he also said, "is to get something for nothing at the cost
of the consumer in a closed market"; it is "synonymous with business
enterprise."[38] He disparaged the new commercial schools, as well as the
universities and colleges, for teaching "financiering and salesmanship"—
or what he called "the art of putting it over."[39] In 1922, in his last significant
book, *Absentee Ownership*, he portrayed the strategies of enticement as
transforming an older work culture into a culture of "make-believe." Merchants, he argued, promised "personal prestige and status," a high level of
"personal well-being," "keeping in touch with times"—all "irrespective of

any inherent merit in the goods." They operated in the realm of "intangible" reality and of the "magical arts."[40]

Veblen saw nothing of value in the new commercial culture, since its "driving force was not an imperative bent of workmanship and human service, but an indefinitely extensible cupidity."[41] "The prevalence of salesmanship, that is to say, of business enterprise," he wrote in 1914, "is perhaps the most serious obstacle which pecuniary culture opposes to the advance of workmanship. It contaminates the sense of workmanship in its initial move and sets both the proclivity to efficient work and the penchant to serviceability at cross purposes with the common good."[42] On plain moral grounds, the new business culture was wanting, for, in its quest for the "new" and "the turnover," it undermined whatever of value remained of the older traditions of "brotherly love," the "parental bent," "mutual service," and "solicitude for incoming generations and the common good."[43]

Simon Patten had no such misgivings. For him, all was mind cure. He was America's most influential economist of capitalist abundance and consumption; his theories justified constantly rising levels of wishing and consumption and the creation of business strategies to drive the engine of consumption. Yet, in his personal life, Patten was "among the lonely souls of earth," as Rexford Tugwell, Patten's first and most perceptive biographer, said of him in 1922. When he was four, his mother died, leaving him without a steady source of affection. As an adult, he had few friends and no sustaining relationships with relatives. His only marriage, in middle age, was childless and disastrous, his wife leaving him for another man. Ironically, given his economic concerns with consumption and with what he repeatedly called, in his last writings, "the Wish," he lived a near "monk's existence," according to Tugwell. He had "no appreciation of the beauty of life." He "never knew what he ate or wore or looked at." He had no interest in "a home, a garden, books, clothes, paintings." "There was no thing, no instrument of existence that meant anything at all, really, to him."[44] At the same time, he could be extremely generous with others, though he cared almost nothing personally about money. In his later years, as an established teacher, he gave money away to students, and when students tried to pay him back, he pushed them off. "My interest is in your welfare," he said to one, "not in your income."[45] He seems to have denied himself nearly every pleasure of life, yet he believed he found in the market itself an ethos that flung open the doors to pleasure and happiness for the masses of men and women.

Patten was born in Cossumyuna, New York, in 1852, the son of migrating New Englanders and strict Presbyterians who traced their roots back to the Pilgrims. His family moved to Sandwich, Illinois, to a barely inhabited swampy prairie that Patten's father, William, transformed almost single-handedly into flourishing farmland. Simon, however, showed no interest in farming, and at twenty-four, with his father's help, he went to Germany for an education and took up economics. But on his return home, he could find no job. He tried law (at his father's insistence) and literally went blind—whether from emotional or physical causes it is hard to know—until he was able to leave the law altogether. Next, he took refuge in plowing and in pitching hay on his father's farm, then served as superintendent of schools in Iowa, all the while thinking and writing about economics. In 1886 he published his first book, *The Premise of Political Economy*, which led to an appointment at the Wharton School of Economics in Philadelphia. He was soon to make Wharton world-famous. He embraced Philadelphia, Wanamaker's hometown, and abandoned whatever was left of his family (he never saw them again), his father's farm, his rural town, and his family's religion. "My world," he later wrote, "was as different from that in which I was reared as the England of Darwin was from the tropics."[46] Yet he was proud of his father's economic success, which fired his beliefs in an ongoing American abundance. Between 1886 and 1922 he developed a theory of consumption that fused his rejection of the past with a dream of a better future. (See plate 17.)

Patten's political economy built squarely on the economic thinking of at least two generations of American economists who believed utterly that the United States was destined to escape what had historically been humanity's inevitable burden: scarcity.[47] Although he still clung to the traditional economic hedonism of Jeremy Bentham and others, he rejected the older, rigid laws of classical political economy—the iron law of wages, the fixed-wage-fund theory, the law of diminishing returns. He insisted that poverty could be ended, and he acclaimed the "rightness" of the new business civilization. Most of Patten's writings dealt with economic subjects, but his reach was extensive, touching religion and culture, the whole history of the West. He wrote bad poetry and in the last year of his life (1922) wrote a bad novel, *Mud Hollow*, a book about a young man looking for the perfect mate, which combined Patten's personal longings with futuristic economic thinking. The picture we get from all his writings is an economist's version of Orison Swett Marden's "happiness machine" or of L.

Frank Baum's *The Wonderful Wizard of Oz*. The factory-made goods, the department stores, the new corporate monopolies, the installment buying, the nickelodeons, the amusement parks—he saw all as examples of the new social surplus and of a new and improved humanity.

Patten argued that a new structure of values was necessary to support this growing business civilization. He believed there should be a perfect fit between a society's culture and its economic and political character. If an economy changed radically, so, too, should the related culture; every vestige of the older culture that did not "fit" rationally with the new material conditions should be discarded. Economists could play the big role here, Patten thought, since the United States was, by and large, a "business society." Economists—not priests or ministers—were best able to decide what "values" were most suited to new economic conditions. It was within their power, in fact, to establish "the origin or binding core of the moral standard" or the "morality of industrial society." Patten was claiming that people like himself should be on the front lines. For far too long, he wrote, ethics had been the "province of religion and philosophy." Business-minded people should now take over. [48]

Patten had a mind-cure mission. He attacked those "pessimists," critics, and utopians such as Henry George, Henry Demarest Lloyd, and others, who argued that the United States was following the Roman pattern of decline in retreating from the old moral certainties of the past. [49] To the contrary, he believed that rational moral progress, not irrational decline and conflict, was inherent to all history, including American history. The United States was in trouble not because it was leaving the past behind, but because it was not leaving it fast enough. The continuing grip of traditional Christian morality was frustrating progress. "The habits, instincts, and feelings we have inherited from our forefathers," he wrote in 1901 in *The Consumption of Wealth*, "are no longer safe guides for us to follow."[50] "Restraint, denial, and negation" are currently irrelevant. "The principle of sacrifice continues to be exalted by moralists at the very time when the social structure is being changed by the slow submergence of the primeval world, and the appearance of a land of unmeasured resources with a hoard of mobilized wealth." The old system of values that "inculcated a spirit of resignation and asceticism" and "emphasized the repression of wants must be removed before social ideas can stand out in contrast to primitive societies."[51]

The idea that "consumption of luxuries and the indulgence in them" is "sinful or immoral" was at an earlier time perfectly reasonable; it had helped "adjust a people to an environment and became the necessary means of making them content with a bad situation." But Americans were no longer living in primitive times. A new morality must be acquired to eliminate "all checks to full enjoyment" and to allow people to make rational choices.[52]

Where would the new moral perspective come from if not from older religious or philosophical sources? The answer was a simple one: It would come out of business, out of commodities, out of the modern market itself. In a 1902 address in Freiburg, Germany's greatest sociologist, Max Weber—fearful of growing capitalist domination and of the consequences involved in the apparent collapse of older belief systems—had insisted that it "was impossible to derive *independent* ideals from the subject matter of political economy."[53] But Patten thought otherwise, and he did so, in part, because he opposed socialism and hated labor battles. For him, the market was salvation, and it was his answer to the radicals.

Patten, more than any contemporary American economist or sociologist, updated in the new corporate context the older eighteenth-century conception of the market—the conception held by Adam Smith and later attacked by Marx and Veblen—that the steady pursuit of private wealth and the expansion of market relations led inexorably to peace, human betterment, stability, "gentleness," and civility (in the sense that it was in everybody's self-interest to be honest, dependable, and kindly).[54] Modern corporate capitalism was moral, Pattern concluded, because it "has increased the stability of industry and reduced the suffering coming from famine, contagious diseases and the lack of employment." No other economic system had ever achieved this, he claimed. Corporate business was moral because it had evolved economic patterns—cooperative, group-oriented, and altruistic patterns—worthy of emulation. In the past, businessmen cared nothing for the common good; they were "isolated" individuals governed only by selfish ambition. But new conditions had forced them to pool their resources and to take the "large view." "During the last sixty years," Patten explained in 1912, "the individual has been lost; the group is now everything. No one can succeed today who does not attach himself to some well-defined industrial group. The growth of large-scale capitalism has resulted in the elimination of the unsocial capitalists and the increasing control of each industry by a socialized group."[55]

He admired capitalist monopolies because they were "profit-making" institutions that "kept" and "balanced their budgets." In the old days, "primitive traders" who did not know capitalist methods were "notoriously unscrupulous." "They preyed on one another as well as on the community. It is from their cut-throat methods that the theory of competition arose." Not so the modern capitalist, who cooperated closely with other capitalists and kept accounts so that profits and costs became distinct. Measuring every act by the way it affected his profits, today's businessman thought only of the general condition of the society and the economy. "High social morality and high average profits," said Patten, "have the same roots because they are the results of the socializing influence of budget-making. Budget-making is the force uniting men into groups and blending smaller groups into larger ones."[56]

Patten was so taken with the moral outcome of budget-making that he singled out international bankers—Veblen's masters of the art of "getting something for nothing"—as the model of modern morality. Bankers "cooperate, avoid competition, serve the public. Banking morality is the highest morality because it lacks the limits that national, local, or creed morality possesses." "The long view has become the banker's view."[57] But he had much more to say about the ethical potential of corporate capitalism, contending that the consumer abundance produced by business, as well as by the economic "laws" supporting that abundance and variety, too, were moral and rational. Here his traditional classical hedonism came to the fore. Like Smith, Bentham, and other classical economists, Patten believed that people naturally hated work (pain) and longed for consumption (pleasure), but he modified this notion, adding a new ethical angle, by reversing the older American notions about the corrupting impact of luxury. Pleasure and spending did not mean more immorality; no, more pleasure and spending meant more morality. The more goods and services people had, the more they were allowed to desire and own, the less urgently or obsessively they would desire.

This was Patten's open sesame, the theoretical heart of his notion that a business-generated abundance society was far more ethical than old-fashioned "agrarian scarcity." A higher standard of living meant a higher threshold of desire; less intense desiring meant less corruption and immorality. Only primitive people, whose standard of living was low and who had only a few commodities in their diets, were the true greedy sensualists who, day after day, fought over and thought of nothing but the next meal. "Where the food supply is irregular," Patten wrote, "the imagination is usually the most active faculty. . . . Primitive men have powerful appetites" that they "have no idea how to use in moderation." They are "gluttons."[58]

Patten showed how the constant addition of new goods into people's budgets made them more ethical individuals. Careful attention to the laws of consumption, he wrote, which "philosophy and religion have avoided, may assist in laying the foundation of true ethical science." He dwelled on the law of marginal utility as the fundamental moral law, more lasting in its effect than any "golden" or biblical "rule."[59] According to this law, as each individual consumes more and more of a commodity, each increment becomes less and less desirable, inducing the consumer to buy other goods that are more pleasurable. Over time, as more and more goods are purchased, this response occurs again and again, each time shortening the desire span. Quickly satiated with the next incoming commodity, consumers pursue the next good, and then the next, a process that modifies individual behavior along new moral lines. The desire level is kept low, because it is always quickly satisfied. As consumers get more and more and spend more and more, they become less desiring, less like "animals," less and less given to "excesses."[60] "To have a high standard of life means to enjoy a pleasure intensely and to tire of it quickly. Any pleasure soon becomes stale unless it can be dropped to make place for something new."[61]

What was important here was the influx of "something new" at a consistent rate into one's standard of living. No economist of his times—indeed, no American thinker of the times, it seems to me—ever went as far as Patten did in bidding farewell to the past as a moral and intellectual guide. Patten radically translated an already clear American tendency (of seeing everything "new" as inarguably good and everything "old" as insufferable) into a theoretical law of civilization. He never looked back. "We think of culture," he wrote in 1912,

> as the final product of civilization and not as one of its elements. Yet if we look at the facts, we find that culture is an index of activity, not of ancestral tradition and opinion. Social tradition has been broken more in the field of culture than elsewhere. It is no longer the admiration of the old or of the foreign but an intenser form of enjoyment than that yielded by traditional pleasures. . . . Culture is the result of more satisfying combinations of consumption. Every new product modifies the direction which culture takes.[62]

And it modifies always for the good. Increased spending creates new men and women. It forces people to budget, thus endowing them with the altruistic virtues of "international bankers." As consumers take in more and more, and as their desire-levels reach an equilibrium, they channel their "surplus" energies into helping other people, and turn to creating public goods over private goods—public libraries, good roads, concert halls, and art galleries.[63] "The non-saver is now the higher type of man than the saver, just as the saver was an elevation of type above the extravagance of more primitive man."[64] A steady purchase of "new" goods transforms people into "better human beings" by removing the differences among them and by forming the grounds for a new unity and harmony in American society.

If the older source of social harmony had been stripped away by immigration and by the fragmentation of the old order, Patten claimed, then a newer one was preparing the way for a new "center" to American culture. Consumption patterns were "standardizing" people, Patten said, by making them think about and desire the same things. "The standardized succeed," Patten said, "the unstandardized leave town or drop into unmarked graves." The new consumers were generalists who saw the world whole. Primitive people, on the other hand, "lacked the power of generalization which would free them from the tyranny of local conditions." "It is only the newer impulses and ideals which all have in common that serve as a basis of unity. . . . There is nothing but disruption in the premises of isolating desires or in the local traditions of the incorporated factions."[65]

Patten was so certain about the redemptive power of this new ethic that he urged that people be exposed to every institution that fostered it. People must be in daily contact with the "objects of desire" and with "conditions" in which they will feel "desire for goods." "All traditional restraints on consumption, all taboos against luxury," he said, should be "eliminated." "The present situation is unsatisfactory because we compromise opposing schemes of morality instead of rigidly excluding the old and giving firm adhesion to the new."[66] His aim was mind cure: "There should be no personification of virtues and vices. The angels of Newman [a famous Catholic cardinal] must go along with Luther's devils. There must be no act of penance; forgiveness is free."[67]

The school and the state must help create this new order of things. "Too heavy a stress is laid on the duties of parents to children," Patten said. "We overestimate the power of the home to mould its members, and in consequence neglect to utilize the institutions of city life. We rely on restraint to shape the character of boys when we should be thinking of their recreations." Educators should teach children the law of marginal utility—of all things—because that was a basic moral law. "The moral education should begin with lessons from the economic world," he wrote, "because the mechanism of morality is the same as that of the standard of life. Economic activity exercises the faculties which, at a later period, become moral."[68] The state had a duty to assure to "lower classes" the same chance to consume as everybody else; "without some aid from society, the lower classes of today will be pushed to the wall." The state must educate these people; it must protect and institutionalize the "new rights," including the right to comfort, the right to security, and the right to live without fear. If Patten did not believe that the state should break up monopolies or redistribute wealth, or that landed property could be the basis of a citizen's independence and wealth, he did believe in wise allocation of resources. "The road to prosperity is not through class conflict, with its mulcting of the minority—it is rather in social improvements that take men from the margin of production and place them in contact with better resources and in more favorable situations." The state, finally, had the obligation to provide a "living income," a minimum wage, to all its citizens so that they might have regular access to goods and entertainment.[69]

Whatever the solution, the means were identical: to put people in touch with commercial institutions that, in turn, would convert them all into standardized consumers with low intensities of desire. Show people "the commercialized street itself"—along with the "amusements and recreations of parks, theaters, 'Coney Islands,' and department stores"—for "it contains the primary elements of climax . . . the climax of the new." Immigrants, especially, should forget their old institutions and proclaim the modern ones, the commercial ones that are so "wonderful" in "exciting presentation of the life processes." For immigrants who kept to the old customs, the result was continued degradation, for which they had only themselves to blame. Limited "primitive" appetites, Patten said, only invited exploitation by others with bigger and more balanced appetites. Indeed, Patten believed that such immigrants actually caused their own misery by helping the stronger class to take over. By remaining primitive and by failing to take advantage of a new environment "to its full enjoyment," they became the "ready means of fastening upon a nation a dominant class which consumes the extra produced and rejected by the moral code of the subject class. The real source of exploitation lies not in political causes nor in competition, but in old traditions, habits, and prejudices."[70]

In a bizarre little 1909 book, *Product and Climax*, Patten compared two sets of institutions, one, traditional (churches, libraries, and schools) and the other, "new" and "urban" (retail stores, theaters, nickelodeons, ice-cream parlors, penny arcades, etc.). His description makes plain which side of the street is better; in a radical switch, he put the new institutions on the "right side" (his term) and the older ones on the "wrong side." The older ones are literally in darkness and bolted shut, indicating their connection to the "barren" world of "prohibitory moral agencies" and to the "artificial morality with its manifold prohibitions." The new institutions on the commercial street, on the other hand, are "festooned with lights and cheap decorations," and "the doors of shops" are "wide open."[71]

There was something personal in this vision, which, at the same time, linked Patten with other Americans cut loose from the past, without moorings, longing for a new home. Desire, sexual desire, was in this vision, as Patten's title *Product and Climax* shows and which he probably intended to show, given his own peculiar reading and acceptance of the sexual theories of Freud.[72] Confusion and longing, augmented and fed by desire, were in this vision, and wishing was at its core. In his later books, especially in *Mud Hollow*, he even argued that the power of the "Wish" animated the entire evolutionary process. "Wish pulses and wish structure," he said, form "the key which unlocks the mysteries of organic evolution."[73]

Unlike Freud, who saw irrational instincts and insatiable drives lurking behind the face of wishing, Patten glimpsed only its seemingly "rational" character or the way it seemed to move everything forward in a "progressive way." Whereas other people might have viewed wishing as a childlike or childish activity or as a symptom of impotence and vulnerability, he took the opposite position. Wishing was positive, even biological; it caused action, it created "wants," which, in turn, automatically led to fulfillment and the obtainment of more goods and pleasure, which, in turn, spawned more wishes. "Wish directs energy toward fulfillment," he wrote, "and forces energy to move toward its goal. . . . Want wishes press for fulfillment." Patten wanted to free the power of "wishing" in everyone, not to curtail it; he wanted "millions of people" wishing, a whole culture "spending" and "groping toward fulfillment," individuals striving to imitate one another in acquisition and possession. Wish, fulfillment, wish, fulfillment, wishes piled on wishes—this was Patten's fantasy of America.[74]

In his mind, America was not only the Land of Desire (as Wanamaker would have had it) but also the Land of Wish. Like so many people of his time, from John Cotton Dana, Stewart Culin, and Joseph Urban to Maxfield Parrish, Orison Swett Marden, and L. Frank Baum, Patten wanted dearly to seize the day. He wanted to free himself from whatever inward emotional tyrannies haunted him. He wanted to open up, even as he feared it, and even as he argued that a new opening up would beget a new closing up, a raising of desire's threshold. At the same time, his thoughts reflected the new business drift of the times and seemed to satisfy the ideological demands of the new business order.

Patten had a decisive impact on the intellectual and political currents of his times. He was, for example, one of the guiding intellectual lights in the emergence of the new social work movement in this country after 1900. Social workers in New York City and other cities picked up his ideas on urban recreation, arguing that this form of organized play offered one of the best ways to integrate children safely into city life. He influenced generations of economists through the Wharton School of Economics and the American Economic Association, which he helped establish in 1885. His view that the American economy was moving ever forward into "complete abundance" added spine and shape to the thrust of liberal thought after 1900; in time it was an idea that swept the field.

Rexford Tugwell, a Patten student at the Wharton School and later a pivotal member of Franklin Roosevelt's administration, was a passionate Patten apostle. Throughout his life, even in old age, Tugwell would come back in his writings to Patten. "I believe his to have been the most profound mind of his generation," Tugwell wrote in 1982. He exercised "a greater influence than was ever exerted by any other teacher, with the possible exception of John Dewey, I believe, or William James, in American academic history. And, of course, it has not been repeated since."[75]

Sociologists like Franklin Giddings of Columbia University and political journalists like Walter Weyl, an ambitious intellectual spokesman for the progressive movement, were clearly affected by Patten's ideas. Although he often disagreed with him, Giddings conceded that Patten was "the one personal influence shaping my thought." Both Giddings and Weyl believed in the moral rightness of the new commercial world and in the idea that America's new complex and fragmented society could be structured through an ever-expanding "standard of living." In his books, Giddings spread the concept that standardization was the key to integrating America's diverse population into a "whole." If only Americans would desire the same goods and dream the same dreams, we would have nothing to fear from anarchists. "Chief among the assimilative forces" in modern life is "standardized consumption. We have only to call to mind such articles of universal use as the carpet or rug, wall-paper, table linen, piano or phonograph, expensive clothing and jewelry . . . by classes that were supposed to be unable to afford them, to realize how tremendous and marvelous has become the standardizing influence. . . . As consumers of wealth we exhibit mental and moral solidarity. We want the same things. We have the same tastes. So far as this part at least of our life is concerned we have the basis and the fact of a highly general consciousness of kind."[76]

Weyl, one of Patten's students at the Wharton School, was, according to the journalist Walter Lippmann, the most informed and respected economist among the Progressives. Weyl popularized Patten's idea of the "surplus" economy in his 1912 book *The New Democracy*. Among the most crucial "presidential texts" ever written, it influenced Theodore Roosevelt, among others.[77] In it Weyl was eloquent about America's economic promise; the scarcity mentality of the past was slowly being shunted aside by expanding abundance. "The surplus of society," he said, "overrides all our traditions and shapes all our philosophies"; it has the potential of eliminating all poverty and injustice in America. Patten's imprint was throughout, from Weyl's discussion of the new goods to his conviction that the state must intervene to "socialize consumption" and to ensure the progressive social movement. He insisted that a new and better morality, "a new ethics" of pleasure, a new mind cure would be derived from the economic order in conjunction with political democracy. "Democracy," he said, "means material goods and the moral goods based thereon." Like Giddings and Patten, he saw a new kind of unity emerging from within society based on a common quest for and common sense of entitlement to the social surplus.[78]

There were differences between Patten and Weyl, perhaps most clear in the way Weyl understood the new character of desire. The new goods were creating a new kind of desire based not on real but imagined poverty. "We are," he said, drawing here on Thorstein Veblen, "developing new types of destitutes—the automobileless, the yachtless, the Newportcottageless. The subtlest luxuries become necessities, and their loss is bitterly resented. The discontent of today reaches very high in the social scale. . . . The end of it all is vexation of spirit."[79]

This difference aside, Weyl and Giddings shared many of Patten's weaknesses, as did the other thinkers who followed him. Like him, they offered no critique of any principal structural feature of the modern economic system. They saw modern corporations as moral institutions. They had nothing negative to say (and almost nothing at all to say) about money and the role it was beginning to play in forming and distorting the character of desire. They argued that real "happiness" could be had largely through money incomes and consumption, not through satisfying labor or a stake in the community. Like other Americans who feared the social results of the industrial revolution, they believed Americans should forget about work and turn instead to leisure, entertainment, play, and consumption.

Patten helped create one of the ideological pillars of consumer liberalism (or of "progressive liberalism"; the terms, I think, are generally interchangeable), as important to the emergence of that liberalism as investment banks, show windows, electricity, museums, the Harvard Business School, Wanamaker's piety, and religious mind cure itself. He (and his students) supplied business with the perfect ethical rationale for the constant production of new goods or for what later came to be called a "full growth economic system."

Pollyanna and the Popular Culture of Mind Cure

Mind cure found its way also into popular culture, into films and Broadway musicals, and into children's stories and fairy tales. Eleanor Porter, author of *Pollyanna*, and L. Frank Baum, creator of *The Wonderful Wizard of Oz*, stand out among the writers for children who wrote from a mind-cure perspective.

Porter, born in New Hampshire in 1868 and descendant of Plymouth Colony's William Bradford, lived much of her life with sickness but wrote books about health and happiness. Her mother was an invalid for many years, she herself was a sickly adolescent, and she married a very rich and successful businessman—John Lyman Porter, president of National Separator and Machine Company—whose mother was chronically ill and required constant care. In the late 1890s, after overcoming her own bad health and ending what appears to have been a dead-end career in music, she simultaneously took up mind cure (probably of the New Thought variety, the ideas of Orison Swett Marden and Ralph Trine) and a new career in story writing. Among her many books was *Oh, Money! Money!*, a story of three cousins who each unexpectedly inherit $100,000 from an unknown relative and who deal in different ways with the money—an inspiration, perhaps, for a popular television series in the 1950s, *The Millionaire*. The moral is resoundingly "American": "It isn't the money that does things; it's the individual behind the money" (but isn't it wonderful to have money).[80]

Porter's triumph, *Pollyanna*, written in 1912, was every inch mind cure. The heroine is an eleven-year-old girl, Pollyanna Whittier, who, in the face of the most daunting misery, never stops smiling, feeling "glad" about life, or bringing "color and light" and health to everyone. "I wish I could prescribe her," says an admiring physician. After meeting Pollyanna, decrepit old men and women throw off their "greys and drabs" for "red and blue and yellow worsteds." Dour scrooges, accustomed to scrimping and stashing away their savings, learn to "live and let live" and "enjoy life." "I love rainbows," she says, along with "ice-cream" and "carpets in every room." She inspires worn-out ministers exhausted by preaching about evil and damnation to reject the gloomy biblical texts for the "800 rejoicing ones" in both testaments.[81] Her signature is her "glad game" or "just finding something to be glad about—no matter what." She is always "*glad*, glad, GLAD."

In the heart of *Pollyanna*, Porter presents a mind-cure message that governs her heroine's destiny and the book:

> What men and women need is encouragement. Their natural resisting powers should be strengthened, not weakened. Instead of always harping on a man's faults, tell him of his virtues. Try to pull him out of his rut of bad habits. Hold up to him his better self, his *real* self, that can dare to do and win out! . . . The influence of a beautiful, hopeful character is contagious, and may revolutionize a whole town. . . . People radiate what is in their minds and in their hearts. If a man feels kindly and obliging, his neighbors will feel the same way, too, before long. But if he scolds and scowls and criticizes—his neighbors will scowl for scowl, and add interest! . . . When you look for the bad, expecting it, you will get it. When you know you will find the good—you will get that.[82]

Even after Pollyanna's legs are paralyzed in an automobile accident, she is still "glad"—indeed, more glad than ever before. (She is rewarded, of course, with complete recovery.) By the end of the book "half the town are putting on blue ribbons, or stopping family quarrels, or learning to like something they never liked before, and all because of Pollyanna." Factory workers, once depressed about work and hating their employers, now are "glad for Monday mornings."[83]

Pollyanna made Porter nearly world-famous. Commercial products were named for Pollyanna, along with a popular parlor game. The book was translated into eight languages in almost that many years, adapted for the Broadway stage, and made into two successful films—one with Mary Pickford in 1920 and the other with Hayley Mills in 1960. It would be difficult to find out if factory workers liked or did not like the book (if they read it at all), but there is no question that John Wanamaker loved it. He gave it to his family, friends, and employees. *Pollyanna* offered the same moral recipes as *The Simple Life*—don't think too much, enjoy life, be temperate and good, and always look on the bright side.[84]

L. Frank Baum and Theosophy

L. Frank Baum's *The Wonderful Wizard of Oz* exceeded *Pollyanna* in popularity and shows as well the earmarks of mind cure. Baum was not only a businessman and window trimmer, he was also America's most successful fairy tale writer, and he also practiced theosophy, which he probably discovered through his mother-in-law, Matilda Joslyn Gage, a leader of the women's rights movement in the United States and coauthor of *The History of Woman Suffrage*. Gage hated established religion, partly because it opposed the emancipation of women. Theosophy was preferable to her, as it was to many other "progressive" people who were alienated from Christianity but who wanted to fuse some kind of religion with scientific knowledge and with a high regard for women. Gage greatly admired Blavatsky's book *Isis Unveiled*, a voluminous tribute to the great queen of Egypt. Isis, Gage said, quoting Blavatsky in *The History of Woman Suffrage*, "contained germs within herself for the reproduction of all living things."[85]

Baum, too, apparently admired Blavatsky. He conducted séances in his home and was a member of the Theosophical Society.[86] Theosophy's proscience, anti-Christian side appealed to him. "The age of faith," he wrote in 1890, "is sinking slowly into the past." Instead, we have a "new unfaith" and "an eager longing to penetrate the secrets of Nature—an aspiration for knowledge we have been taught is forbidden." "As our country progresses, as our population increases, the number of churchgoers is gradually growing less. The people are beginning to think [that] studying science . . . is the enemy of the church. Science we know to be true."[87]

Theosophy was a permissive form of mind cure, nonjudgmental and tolerant, and Baum found that congenial. Influenced by the Hinduistic belief that people do not sin and should not feel guilt, he said, in an article in his *Aberdeen Saturday Pioneer* in 1890, that "the good things of life are given to be used and that the 'rainy day' theory of saving is a good one in itself if it does not serve as an excuse for denying yourself comforts. Don't feel embarrassed, he insisted, about "having oranges" (then an expensive fruit) on the "breakfast table every morning," even if your salaries are too small to pay for them. So what if sometimes men might "be forced to borrow a few dollars." In any case, "who will be the gainer when Death calls him to the last account—the man who can say 'I have lived!' or the man who can say 'I have saved'?" "To gain all the meat from the nut of life is the essence of wisdom. Therefore, 'eat, drink, and be merry— *tomorrow* you die.' "[88]

Baum decorated his own home with mind-cure symbols, including a "no worry" Billikens doll, which sat on his piano.[89] He hated Prohibition and Sunday blue laws, and, after he became successful, he followed his own advice and went on shopping sprees, staying in the best hotels, taking long and luxurious vacations, and going into debt.[90]

Above all, of course, Baum wrote children's stories, stories for adolescents and adults, and fairy tales expressing a proconsumer outlook—permissive, *gemütlich*, nonjudgmental, and mind cure. Many of his books are crowded with goods, mechanical inventions, and artificial "things," with multicourse dinners and banquets, with edible landscapes of ripe fruit, delicious cakes, cream puffs, caramels, popcorn snow, jelly-bean pebbles, and with people made from chocolate, frosted bread, gingerbread, and raisins. These descriptions were meant partly to assure children that the world was a perfectly good and kind place, with abundant things for everybody. In traditional fairy tales—Hansel and Gretel, for instance—children are often threatened with starvation or death for desiring and eating forbidden foods. In Baum's "prosperity" kingdom, abundance is permanent and starvation unthinkable.[91]

An Affirmative American Fairy Tale

The best-known Baum book, *The Wonderful Wizard of Oz*, was among the most significant cultural documents to come out of the religious turmoil and economic changes of the late nineteenth century. As much as Patten's political economy and Orison Swett Marden's happiness machine, Baum's tale became ingrained in the landscape of American liberalism, the most widely read children's book of its day, and was translated into several languages in his lifetime (he died in 1919).[92] In the late 1910s a lively Oz industry sprang up, generating Oz toys, games, coloring books, puppets, and posters.[92] *The Wizard of Oz* became part of American advertising campaigns. In 1913, for instance, New York's Siegel-Cooper's erected reproductions of the same huge signboard all over New York, created by advertiser O. J. Gude and depicting famous figures marching to Siegel-Cooper's under the banner of "Everybody's Going to the Big Store." At the end of the parade was the scarecrow from *The Wizard of Oz*.[93]

No book, no text of any kind in the twentieth century, has proven a more prolific source of ideas than this fairy tale. Recently, its themes and characters have formed the basis for everything from shopping malls (the "Emerald City Shopping Mall" in Waltham, Massachusetts) to modern choreography (the "Oz" ballet by New Yorker Paul Taylor). Again and again, it has been adapted for other media, and no adaptation was more profitable than Baum's own, a 1902 musical extravaganza for the Chicago stage. The show was the longest-running musical production up to that time in American history. (As late as 1911 it was still playing at Boston's Castle Square Theater.) Victor Herbert's *Babes in Toyland* and other such shows were modeled after *The Wizard*. "*The Wizard*," Baum said in a 1910 interview, "is an extraordinary thing. It is the only musical comedy that has lived for eight years."[94]

Why was *The Wizard of Oz* so popular with Americans? The answers to this question lie partly in Baum's mastery of the fairy-tale form. Although it has no princes or princesses nor fairies, it nevertheless contains many of the classic features found in fairy tales—the journey motif, the tension between good and evil, the isolated hero/heroine in quest of a goal in a strange land, the magical helpers and nonhuman characters, the enchanted forests, and the countless other obstacles thrown in the hero/heroine's path. *The Wizard* has magical interventions and transformations, and much description of jewels, flowers, and good things to eat. These features had repeatedly proven their value as crowd-pleasers; children expected to find them in fairy tales, and Baum skillfully met their expectations.[95]

But he did something new with the fairy tale in *The Wizard of Oz*: He Americanized it. Arguably, he was the first American writer ever to combine effectively American materials with the fairy-tale form. Other Americans, from Washington Irving to Mark Twain, had succeeded in introducing native elements into other genres of children's literature, but Baum was the first to carry this intermingling through in a fairy tale, an achievement that, more than anything else, explains the lasting popularity of *The Wizard of Oz*.[96]

To say that Baum "Americanized" the fairy tale means that he wrote about matters and places that he himself had known and that most Americans of the time could have related to and recognized—axle grease, tin and chinaware, Kansas farmland and farmers, scarecrows and circus barkers, and a simple country girl uprooted from her home. In the book there is a lot of joking, which Americans—young and old alike—no doubt loved. America's peculiar obsession with mechanical technology is time and again invoked satirically in the person and behavior of the Wizard. Baum's book was also resonant with other journeys besides the classic fairy-tale one— the westward journey of Americans, their journey from the country to the city, and the religious journeys depicted in much of the uplift literature of the era.

In a lighthearted way, *The Wizard of Oz* shows the impact of John Bunyan's *The Pilgrim's Progress*, which middle-class Protestant Americans read in the first half of the nineteenth century. Bunyan's book was standard reading fare for children, many of whom memorized passages from it, as Baum probably did under the wing of his devoutly Christian mother. These books share the same archetypal journey motif and same symbol—the silver slippers (changed to ruby slippers in the 1939 film version). In *The Pilgrim's Progress*, Christian flees the City of Destruction, suffers terrible nightmares and seductions, and finally reaches the bejeweled Celestial City, whose streets are paved in gold. Lifted out of gray and dismal Kansas, Dorothy is dropped into Oz, overcomes many adversities, and eventually enters the bejeweled Emerald City, with its streets covered with gold and jewels. On his journey, Christian meets "By-ends," who lacks interest in religion except as it helps him become wealthy and respectable. "We are always most zealous," he says to Christian, "when religion goes in silver slippers." And Christian responds: "You must also own religion in his rags as well as when in silver slippers." In *The Wizard of Oz*, Dorothy's deliverance and salvation "go" only in "silver slippers."[97]

The Wizard of Oz, however, contained more than the leftovers of a major Protestant text or of the more everyday features of American life. Baum introduced into his fairy tale a mind-cure vision of America quite at home with commercial development of the country. Baum could have criticized American society. He could have used his fairy tale as a means of drawing attention to economic suffering and racial injustice, to the alienating new forms of industrial labor, to the extravagance and greed of many affluent Americans, and to the pooling of wealth and power that was becoming a distinguishing, abiding feature of American capitalist society. Evidence for these things had been all around him in the 1890s in cities where he lived—in the unrest of farmers in Aberdeen, South Dakota, and in the labor conflict in Chicago. Writers of fairy tales in other countries, where conditions were just as troubling, wrote about such matters. Kenneth Grahame, Charles Kingsley, George MacDonald, and John Ruskin turned to the fairy tale as a medium for debunking and even damning the new industrial order in England. Many Americans read these tales, but Baum did not choose to follow such writers.[98]

Many analysts have argued that Baum presented a veiled critique of American industrial society in *The Wizard of Oz*. Some have even called the book a populist parable that shows deep sympathy for downtrodden farmers (an interpretation still very much alive today).[99] In none of his writings, however, did Baum express much concern for poor farmers or for any mistreated Americans. All the evidence appears to point the other way—that he preferred to identify with the "best people," with the winners in American society, not with the losers. Of "American Indians" he wrote: "Why not annihilation? Their glory has fled, their spirit broken, their manhood effaced; better that they should die than live the miserable wretches they are. The Whites, by law of conquest, by justice of civilization are masters of the American continent."[100] More to the point, there is no trace of a critique of capitalism in *The Wizard of Oz*. The book is a totally upbeat American fairy tale that, far from challenging the new industrial society, endorsed its values and direction.

Mind cure pervades *The Wonderful Wizard of Oz*. On the most literal level, it appears as the spiritualist elements of theosophy, sometimes in satirical form. The good witches of Oz, for instance, resemble the powerful mother-goddesses studied and revered by Blavatsky. The meetings between the Wizard of Oz and Dorothy and her companions are very much like spiritualist séances where strange voices and weird phenomena are invoked. "Where are you?" Dorothy asks Oz in her second meeting with him, approaching him as if he were some disembodied presence. " 'I am every-where,' answered the Voice, 'but to the eyes of common mortals I am invisible. I will now seat myself upon my throne, that you may converse with me,' " whereupon the "séance" proceeds (p. 93). [101] The Wizard's many incarnations echo Hinduistic notions of metamorphosis, with the Wizard acting as the principal medium, speaking in many voices and taking many shapes. The kingdoms of Oz are also similar to those theosophical "planets" or "globes" described by Helene Blavatsky in her books and through which everyone must pass on the road to complete spiritual health and wholeness. [102]

On a broader ideological level, Baum expressed mind cure by taking the heartache and fear out of fairy tales. In the Emerald City and most of the Land of Oz, everyone is taken care of. There is little real distress; no significant struggle or conflict; no work to speak of; not much to feel guilty about; and, above all, nothing to fear (even, as it turns out, the wicked witch). *The Wizard of Oz* is what William James would have called a "no worry" text of "concrete therapeutics." As Baum himself said quite clearly in his introduction to the original edition:

> The time has come for a series of newer "wonder tales" in which the stereotyped genie, dwarf and fairy are eliminated, together with all the horrible and blood-curdling incidents devised by their authors to point a fearsome moral to each tale. . . . *The Wonderful Wizard of Oz* was written solely to please children of today. It aspires to being a modernized fairy tale, in which the wonderment and joy are retained and the heartaches and nightmares are left out [p. 36].

In the new consumerist American way, Baum broke the connection between wonderment and heartache. People could have what historically (and humanly) they had never had: joy without sorrow, abundance without poverty, happiness without pain. Like the other mind curers, Baum rejected that side of life—the suffering side, the growing-up side—that made the other side worthy of respect and affirmation.

This is not to say that there is no violence and nothing at all to be afraid of in the book. In Chapter 12, Dorothy's companions, in their quest to kill the wicked Witch of the West, are dashed to the ground or ripped apart; and the Witch herself, of course, is extremely scary. In other chapters, monsters such as the Kalidahs and the giant spider appear; and many of Dorothy's predators are violently destroyed, often beheaded. But despite these episodes, Baum's book is essentially what he intended it to be, a story with few "heartaches and nightmares."

But how did Baum banish "real" fear and violence from *The Wizard of Oz*? First, he distributed pleasing colors throughout the fairy tale to accentuate the material and natural abundance of Oz and the Emerald City. The book is virtually a hymn to color as well as to abundance (symbolized by the Emerald City itself). Baum had used color skillfully as a merchant; his theosophy encouraged it.[103] Thus, in *The Wizard of Oz*, gray is linked with hard work, scarcity, poverty, and death, while yellows, reds and blues are associated with a world overflowing with commodities, with plenty of food, and with jewels and precious metals. These color associations were historically commonplace, but Baum (and his illustrator William Denslow) developed them in a way no American writer had. In the original edition of *The Wizard of Oz*, Denslow adroitly added color to nearly every page to reflect the various colors Baum assigned to his people and places. "Denslow has made profuse illustrations for it," Baum wrote his brother in April 1900, soon before the book came out, "and it will glow with bright colors." The pages of Kansas were gray, followed by aqua blue for the Munchkin Country, rust red for the poppy fields and the Quadling Country, brown for the Dainty China Country (a land where all the "little people" are made out of colorful china—Baum's homage to his years as a glass and crockery salesman), and for Dorothy's homecoming on the last page, a rose red. On each page, Denslow's delicately tinted line drawings, placed beneath or around the printed words, amplified the book's pictorial density. He created colored plate inserts, which grew ever richer as the story unfolded, each depicting—in the most visually pleasing way—some character or incident. Today, anyone who looks at this original edition is impressed by Denslow's work, especially by the drawings in the chapters dealing with the Emerald City, where the pages seem to drip and glisten with tiny emeralds. The original edition of *The Wizard of Oz* was the most "colorful" children's book published to this time. It was a narrative and a visual work of art.[104] (See plate 19.)

Baum took the fear and heartache out of Oz in his treatment of his leading character, the trickster Wizard himself. "That was one of my tricks," the Wizard says. "Step this way, please, and I will tell you all about it" (p. 121). In the person of the Wizard, Baum focused on the trickster's trades—on advertising, acting, selling, mesmerism, transactions in fictitious goods—on activities that succeeded through illusion and deception. Historically, many Americans feared and suspected tricksterism, consigning its practitioners to the margins of culture. At least until the eighteenth century, the archtrickster was Satan, the being of many shapes and identities, the polymorphous demon.[105] To some extent, Baum himself still echoed this tradition, as some of his books and newspaper articles indicate. But in *The Wizard of Oz* (and in many other stories), he pursued a different line by affirming the trickster, the mediator, the broker of other people's dreams.

The Wizard appears in the very center of the book (and at the center of the country) because he *is* the center of the book, in both narrative and existential terms. Seeking to have their wishes granted, Dorothy and her friends each have a separate audience with the Wizard, who takes a different form with each of them: an "enormous Head" before Dorothy; a "lovely lady" with colorful fluttery wings before the Scarecrow; a great "Ball of Fire" before the Lion; and, before the Tin Woodman a "most terrible Beast" with five eyes, a head like that of a rhinoceros, five long arms, and five slim legs. The Wizard demands of all his supplicants that in exchange for having their wishes granted, they must kill the wicked Witch of the West. In effect he makes a deal with them: Kill her and I'll give you what you want.

After Dorothy carries out the deed, however, we learn that the Wizard is a liar, a fraud, and "a humbug," as he himself confesses, devoid of any "real" power to grant wishes. He is unmasked as a "little old man" who plays the part of Satan (the Devil, who himself plays many roles and takes many shapes) but who is quite harmless (p. 120). He is a confidence man, a cheat, a deceptive swami, a conniving display illusionist. But what is the response to his behavior? Outrage? Fury? No—surprisingly, no one really cares, which was an outcome Baum clearly intended. Baum himself looked favorably on the Wizard. The very density and liveliness of his characterization, coupled with the fact that he calls the Wizard "a very good man" though "a very bad Wizard" (p. 96) indicates how warmly Baum considered his character. Everybody in Oz, in fact, seems to like him and Dorothy "forgives" him, even though she has every right to condemn him as unethical, since he lied to her about his "powers."

As a trickster himself—merchant, showman, actor—Baum identified with the Wizard. "My father *was* the Wizard of Oz," his son Harry Baum writes.[106] Baum was himself a "promoter," interested in carrying new "schemes" to conclusion and in pushing goods. In 1904 he started work on a musical extravaganza that he planned to call either *The Title Trust* or *The Octopus*, in which he may have intentionally ridiculed a novel of the same name written in 1901 by a fellow Chicagoan, Frank Norris. Norris's *Octopus*, which portrays the pernicious impact promoters were having on the railroad industry, was one of the grimmest pieces of "realistic" fiction ever published by an American. Baum put a "grand pageant and a dress ball with a ballet" in the second act of this "opera." His collaborator, Paul Tietjens, thought "it was one of the funniest things I have ever come across." Of all the songs Baum wrote for the show, he was proudest of "I Am a Promoter," which "he sang" for others "several times."[107]

Baum's portrait of the Wizard and the tale itself can be interpreted as a tribute to the modern ability to create magic, illusions, and theater, to do in effect what God and the Devil had done: to make people believe, in spite of themselves. For even though the Wizard is exposed as a charlatan or as a "common man" without any magical powers in the true fairy-tale sense, nevertheless he is very powerful. He is powerful in the modern American capitalist sense, powerful because he is able to manipulate others to do his bidding, to make them believe what is unbelievable, to do what they might not want to do (or to buy what they might not want to buy), and to do it without realizing they are doing it. A superb confidence man, Oz excites a completely misplaced trust, but "the people" adore him anyway. When he first came to Oz—as he tells Dorothy—he "ordered . . . [the good people] to build this City, and my palace" (p. 96). Yet he is remembered with great affection, after escaping from Oz in a balloon, as the man who "built for us this beautiful Emerald City" (p. 104). This conviction is self-deception on a massive scale. And what do the Tin Woodman, the Lion, and the Scarecrow think of Oz long after he has flown off in his balloon?

By this time the depth of their self-deception is such that they actually believe it was *he* (not Dorothy and certainly not themselves) who saved them from the cornfield, from isolation in the forest, and from permanent paralysis "rusting in the woods."

Baum created a benign trickster, a man resembling Satan but with no sinister power, a character to admire and love, not to fear. Baum was telling his readers, through the Wizard, that there is nothing at all to be afraid of; there may be a fraud—a joke—at the heart of the universe, but there is certainly no "real" evil.

Baum took the heartache and fear out of Oz in an even more profound way: He made Dorothy's journey as pleasant and as free of anxiety and distress as any journey could possibly have been. Baum's Land of Oz lacks almost completely the strict judgments, repressions, laws, and punishments that one ordinarily finds in fairy tales. Oz is governed, for the most part, by a coalition of nurturing parental figures, in male form by the Wizard (who seems at first to be conventionally patriarchal—"Great and Terrible"— but turns out to be kindly and nonjudgmental), and in female form by the good witches of the North and South, who are very generous, sweet, and forgiving. It is a child's wish come true.

In this therapeutic context, Dorothy finds nearly invincible protection. As a kind of model mind-cure personality, she is neither frightened for very long nor worried very much. Unlike Alice in *Alice in Wonderland*, who always seems uncertain about who she is and where she is going, Dorothy forges ahead with unflagging confidence. She never feels threatened, in large part because she is thoroughly shielded from harm by the good Witch's "magic arts" and by the Witch's kiss mark on her forehead, by the silver shoes, by her devoted companions, and by the whole benign ambiance of Oz. Dorothy, of course, does not know to what degree she is protected, but we know—children know—and that's all that really matters.

Dorothy herself never intentionally commits any violent act. She does kill the bad witches, but the violence is robbed of its intensity by its accidental nature. (And, in the second instance, by the amusing provocation for the "murder": The Witch takes Dorothy's "pretty shoe," throwing Dorothy into a rage. "Give me back my shoe!" Dorothy exclaims, which is followed by Dorothy hurling water at the Witch, melting her.) As she says to the Wizard about the demise of the wicked Witch of the East, "That just happened. . . . I could not help it" (p. 72).

But Dorothy is fearless for another (but related) reason as well: Her character and her journey do not fit the classic oedipal pattern of most traditional fairy tales. In his book *The Uses of Enchantment: The Meaning and Importance of Fairy Tales*, Bruno Bettelheim argues that most traditional tales begin with betrayal or mistreatment by parents, followed by a journey in which the heroes/heroines feel profoundly isolated and threatened. The heroes/heroines often hate the people who have betrayed them. They are forced to confront extraordinary and often savage forces; and, along the way, they experience new insight into themselves and the world. Finally, they successfully achieve their own independence and fulfillment, usually by marriage or by some deeply realized relationship with other people. Bettelheim further claims—and this is the heart of his discussion—that these fairy tales with their traditional oedipal situations serve the emotional needs of children by depicting for them in safe, far-off places the *real* nature of their own experiences as children struggling to gain independence from their parents. For Bettelheim these tales reassure children that their strong (even violent) feelings toward their parents are not bad in themselves, and that, just like the princes and princesses in fairyland, the children too, will one day defeat obstacles, develop, and ultimately leave home and achieve autonomy. [108]

In *The Wizard of Oz*, this oedipal situation does not exist, which greatly diminishes the intensity of Dorothy's struggle and the dangers of her journey. Dorothy has no parents; her relationship to her aunt and uncle lacks any kind of intensity or depth; she is an "eternal" child, protected from the burdens of having to grow up. "Most fairy tales end with a wedding," writes critic Brian Atterbery, "but no one is paired off at the end of *The Wizard of Oz*."[109] More important, Dorothy is never really threatened in the way the characters in traditional fairy tales are threatened; she never feels—in the deep way Bettelheim says heroes and heroines must feel in fairy tales—the awful consequences of being "deserted" or "left all alone."[110] Baum, in fact, knew what he was doing when he refused to place Dorothy within the traditional family structure. As he claimed, his purpose was to get rid of the negative, anxiety-provoking things in fairy tales. He "was not interested in love and marriage or any terrible thing that might frighten a child," his niece said of him.[111]

The result for Dorothy is that she undergoes no change. She stays the same person (with the same goal) in the end as in the beginning. Her relationship with her aunt and uncle remains insubstantial and vague. She is essentially an abstraction; but, then, so are her companions—the Scarecrow, the Tin Woodman, and the Lion. They, too, undergo no fundamental changes, although each has a wish for something each thinks he is lacking—the Scarecrow for a brain, the Lion for courage, and the Tin Woodman for a heart. Yet, as the reader sees immediately and as is demonstrated again and again along the journey to Oz, these characters possess these things already. Under pressure and in crisis, the Scarecrow shows how smart he is. Twice he saves his companions by thinking up methods to escape disaster. "That is a first-rate idea," the Lion says of the Scarecrow's idea to traverse a "gulf across the road" by throwing a log over it so that everybody might "walk across it easily." (p. 53). The Lion, too, has in great measure what he thinks is missing. "Stand close behind me," he says to Dorothy in the middle of an attack from the fierce Kalidahs, "and I will fight them as long as I am alive." (p. 53). The Tin Woodman, in spite of his conviction that he has no heart, displays an exquisite tenderheartedness in the face of the smallest calamity. Even stepping on a beetle in the road makes him weep "several tears of sorrow and regret." (p. 49).

What Dorothy's companions lack is confidence in themselves, the belief that they are endowed with the very things they long for. They are burdened by what mind-curers called "poverty thoughts." The Wizard's role is, of course, to give them confidence and to encourage them to overcome their "misery habits." "You have plenty of courage, I am sure," says the Wizard to the Lion. "All you need is confidence in yourself." (p. 97). The Wizard doesn't really grant Dorothy's friends their wishes. What he does, in effect, is to connect the three with what they already are, with their true fullness, or—to use a mind-cure term—with their "latent powers." The result is truly empowering, for all of them go on to become monarchs over their respective kingdoms: the Lion over the Forest, the Scarecrow over the Emerald City, and the Tin Woodman over the Land of the Winkies.

The message here is mind cure: As long as one has confidence and realizes that the world is really a very plentiful place full of an overflowing divine energy, one need not worry about the future or that one will ever lack for anything. One need not struggle or suffer or go through the agonies of growing up or of developing. All one needs, really, is to think positively, to get in touch with one's own "latent powers" or intrinsic "royalty," and to overcome fear and worry, in order to inherit a kingdom. (*Every Man a Monarch*, as one mind-cure book title put it.)

Clearly, then, the Land of Oz and the Emerald City are rather nice places for a child to visit. But what do we make, then, of the fact that

Dorothy seems stubbornly immune to the attractions of the Emerald City? Again and again she indicates very plainly that she does not like Oz and that her sole goal is to get back to Kansas. "I don't like your country," she says rather decisively, "although it is so beautiful." (p. 72). "I don't want to live here, I want to go to Kansas, and live with Aunt Em and Uncle Henry" (p. 105). Should we take these statements seriously, as a sign that Dorothy (and, by implication, Baum) does indeed march to a different drummer? No. After all, no one else in the Land of Oz seriously believes that Dorothy would want to leave. In an amusing exchange with the Scarecrow, Dorothy insists that "there is no place like home" and that "all the people of flesh and blood" long to get home, no matter how "dreary and gray" their homes may be (p. 39). The Scarecrow is perplexed by this idea and, for once, almost rejoices in the fact that he has no brain (or, more correctly, it is Baum who is doing the rejoicing, because this is a joke only adults might get). "If your heads were stuffed with straw, like mine," he says, "you would probably all live in the beautiful places, and then Kansas would have no people at all. It is fortunate for Kansas that you have brains" (p. 39).

Several reasons might be proposed for why Baum made Dorothy so resistant to the Emerald City. One reason might have been literary or artistic: By keeping her focused on Kansas, Baum was heightening the narrative tension, making the story far more engrossing than it otherwise would have been. Another possible reason was that Baum was trying to reflect (and to empathize with) the reader's own guilt and anxiety over the attractions of the Emerald City. Dorothy's reservations, in other words, were intended to echo those of the reader, permitting readers to identify with Dorothy while vicariously enjoying the riches of Oz. But the most likely reason that Baum created Dorothy in the way he did (and this reason relates to the others) was his desire to increase the appeal of the Land of Oz. Through the power of mind cure, he invited the reader—as he did the Scarecrow— to ask the most obvious question. Why should anyone want to go home to Kansas, where everything is so grim and gray?

Baum's other Oz books confirm this argument. In *The Emerald City of Oz*, one of the last in the Oz series, the moral atmosphere is completely remissive. The book is also Baum's most thoroughly consumption-oriented sequel. In it Dorothy shows no shred of guilt about leaving Kansas, for she has whisked her uncle and aunt to Oz itself, never to return home. In Oz, Henry and Em are given a magnificent dwelling, and Dorothy has "everything her heart could desire"—"four lovely rooms in the palace," a "big marble bathroom," and closets hung with dresses cut exactly to fit her. "Here everything that was dear to the little girl's heart was supplied," Baum writes, "and nothing so rich and beautiful could have been found in the biggest department store in America. . . . Of course, Dorothy enjoyed all these luxuries." "Better a princess in Oz," Dorothy says, "than a housewife in Kansas." Or, as she reminds a "rabbit" friend of hers who wants to abandon city living for country solitude, "you'd be a reg'lar lunatic to want to leave the city for the forest, and I'm sure that any rabbit outside the city would be glad to take your place."[112]

Baum's mind-cure ideology—its color, its tricksterism, its "no worry" therapeutics—gave to The Wizard of Oz its very modern character. In a way that seemed to be uniquely American and that marked a new ideological stage in American industrial development, he was saying that abundance is everywhere and that everyone—even the strangest of creatures—can have access to it. Such a message must have been reassuring to all those children (and adults, too) who felt like misfits or outsiders. In the Land of Oz (America), Baum said, outsiders will be insiders; everyone will have a share in the good things of life. All one need do is wish for them.

The Wonderful Wizard of Oz was a product of the rise of a new consumer mentality. Along with Porter's Pollyanna and Patten's political economy, it was an expression of a new general mind-cure outlook. This philosophy was, in turn, strengthened by the mind-cure religions themselves, as well as by the religious compromises and spiritual concessions of many established religious denominations. Altogether, a new spiritual-ethical climate had grown up, working in relation to a new institutional life in America, with the government, the universities and colleges, the museums, and the art schools, as they collaborated with business in the creation of America's new culture. It allowed for new myths and dreams, all promising a life of ever-increasing abundance, comfort, and bodily pleasure, "a new heaven and a new earth," as one mind curer put it.[113]

Most disturbingly, the new "spiritual" perspective reinforced the indifference to pain and suffering fostered by the modern segregation of consumption from production. Mind cure especially, a ready-made consumer mentality, denied that pain and suffering existed at all.

Although several strong voices emerged to contest it, this capitalist ideology of abundance was helping to create a new cultural space being filled by commercial iconography, by visions of goods and of consumer activities in show windows and in advertisements, by fashion shows and interior displays, and by the huge electrical billboards that towered over city streets. As early as 1902, William James, in *The Varieties of Religious Experience*, noted its appearance: "We have lost the power even of imagining what the ancient idealization of poverty could have meant: the liberation from material attachments, the unbribed soul."[114]

III

Managing a Dream Culture:
1922 – 1932

Chapter 9

"AN AGE OF CONSOLIDATION":

GOODS, MONEY, AND

MERGERMANIA

In mid-November 1922, while still firmly in command of his Philadelphia store, the eighty-four-year old John Wanamaker came down with a ferocious cold. By mid-December he was very weak but still able to send a message to Evangeline Booth, commander of the Salvation Army. "Conditions continue that seem to tangle up the world and business, but God lives and loves his people, and better days are coming. I feel confident that the Salvation Army . . . will not be defeated by the stormy winds that may sweep our sky. . . . I will come the first day I am able to travel to New York."[1] This letter was the last one he wrote. On December 12, he died. Two days later, his body lay in state at Bethany Presbyterian Church to allow thousands of Philadelphians to pay their respects. The City Council closed on the day of the funeral; so did the public schools and the Philadelphia Stock Exchange. The private part of the service, ending with burial in the cemetery of St. James the Less, was a ponderous affair in the rain. Thomas Edison and Chief Justice William Howard Taft came. So did members of the Straus family (although not Percy and Jesse, leaders of the newer generation, both hostile to their uncle Nathan, who attended); John Shed, the president of Marshall Field's; U.S. senators and governors from Pennsylvania and New York; Howard Heinz, the millionaire soup king; and William Jennings Bryan. Rodman was too ill, down with a bad cold, to attend, but his family—including John Wanamaker, Jr., not yet disowned by his father—were all there.[2]

Soon after the funeral, an enormous sum of capital was set vibrating as financiers fell over themselves trying to persuade the store's new management to enter into a merger or some similar kind of arrangement. Twice during the next decade Marshall Field III tried to buy Wanamaker's out. "We are in an age of consolidation," wrote one banker to William Nevin, Wanamaker's head executive,

> and it is for the benefit of the individual owners of your business as well as for your company's benefit that we are approaching you with a proposition of financing.
>
> We are working with New York bankers, well known for what they have accomplished throughout the United States whose securities have constantly increased in value because of such banking contacts.
>
> A combination of good stores, well located in various cities, is what we are working for at this time, and should like to include *your* company in our calculations.[3]

Nevin repulsed this invitation, as he did many other letters and phone calls from lawyers and brokers offering to finance the business outright. For the time being Wanamaker's remained a privately owned, independent entity.[4]

Wanamaker died at a time when it seemed to many people that America was entering a new phase of production and consolidation. World War I, of course, had a great deal to do with this impression, for the country had mobilized and centralized its resources to an unheard-of degree, greatly accelerating economic productivity and the concentration of economic power. But more significant than the war was the inclination of many groups—cultural, economic, political, and religious—to open up America to further economic growth, to give business a freer hand, and to increase the tempo of change.

Postwar America, to be sure, did not begin in an upbeat way; in 1921 a painful depression hit, caused by overproduction and by the backing up of inventories. Prices plummeted and great unemployment resulted, throwing the economy for a loop and frightening officials in the federal government. Soon, though, the country was back to "normalcy," witnessing a greater growth in the corporate economy than at any other time.

Such growth was aided by the demise of labor radicalism and by a general context hostile to independent union activity. Unions had made many gains during the war—victorious strikes, shorter hours, better working conditions, and higher wages. But what followed was a disaster for labor, as historian David Montgomery has shown. Labor was virtually "decapitated," wrote one economist.[5] The resources of the state were marshaled against labor radicalism; the IWW was crushed and unions such as the AFL purged themselves of radicals. Union membership fell between 1920 and 1923, in textile unions by 75 percent, in the machinists' unions by 70 percent.[6] Corporate executives, taking the baton from labor, formed company unions; they dictated the character of existing labor unions, or banned labor unions altogether from the major industries of mass production— electrical, automobile, trucking, and chemical. Unions were forced to defend their gains; workers—especially in a time of chronic unemployment that afflicted many firms throughout the twenties—worried about keeping or losing their jobs.[7] It was bad enough that much of the labor movement had failed to develop a clear, independent position on consumer capitalism (as the IWW case illustrates), but it was far worse now that labor as a whole seemed to be silenced, leaving the economy and culture even more in the hands of corporate businesses and their institutional partners.

This chapter and those that follow deal with those corporate businesses and with a new managerialism that refashioned every strategy of enticement and that affected all areas of institutional life (including, as we will see in the last chapter, the federal government). This chapter in particular describes the consumer mentality—the "Consumptionism," one critic, Samuel Strauss called it—that emerged stridently, testifying to the completion of previous changes and to the beginning of new ones. It looks at a new wave of mergers, at the spread of chain stores, and at the power and character of investment bankers. The flow of goods and money in the twenties was extraordinary, aided more than ever by such institutions as Harvard and released by new methods of corporate organization and by the bankers, the masters of mergers and consolidations. Even the department stores, long resistant to the need to centralize resources, began to move toward merger and national store organization. By the decade's end the country was spinning with creations such as Federated Department Stores, perhaps the most notorious chain of all. America's urban landscape of consumer desire was fully operational.

"Consumptionism"

"A new society has come to life in America," wrote Frenchman André Siegfried in 1928, "the very basis of the American civilization is no longer the same." Siegfried had visited America four times, and each time the change appeared greater. It was not "clear to me in 1901 or 1904; it was noticeable in 1914, and patent in 1919 and 1925." In the earlier visits, he felt at home; the country still seemed linked to Europe and "the West." Now it seemed strange and foreign, a change he attributed to the rise of mass production and mass civilization and to a remarkable shift in what Americans considered "morally valuable." "From a *moral point of view*," he wrote, "it is obvious that Americans have come to consider their standard of living as a somewhat sacred acquisition, which they will defend at any price. This means that they would be ready to make many an intellectual or even moral concession in order to maintain that standard."[8]

Many Americans saw the changes; some were deeply disturbed by them. Samuel Strauss, a journalist and political philosopher, was obsessed to such a degree that—until the mid-1930s, when he seemed to have made "peace" with corporate capitalism—nearly everything he wrote dealt in some measure with "things" or with what he called "Consumptionism." In 1924, in *The Atlantic Monthly*, he argued that "something new has come to confront American democracy" that "the Founding Fathers did not foresee" and that would have "seemed abnormal to them." That something new was "Consumptionism," a process and a philosophy that had introduced "prodigious" and "astonishing" changes in the United States. First, Americans had stopped attacking "rich men" who, only twenty-five years before, had been berated as "the malefactors of great wealth." Second, Americans were beginning to focus on "luxury and security and comfort" as the essential elements of the "good life."[9]

Strauss was born in Des Moines, Iowa, in 1870, the son of German-Jewish immigrants. His father was Moses Strauss, a dry goods merchant whose millinery business (established in 1873 and still in existence in the 1920s) was not only the oldest one in Des Moines but also, by 1900, the most extensive millinery operation in the West. In 1872 he was elected (and later reelected) president of Des Moines' First National Bank; in 1907 he cobuilt the Majestic Theater of Des Moines, billed as "one of the finest amusement houses west of Chicago."[10] His son Samuel spurned millinery for newspapers. After graduating from the University of Notre Dame and with family capital, he became co-owner of a daily paper, *The Des Moines Leader* (later *The Des Moines Register*), and in 1902 he went to New York as publisher of *The New York Globe*. He raised the *Globe*'s circulation from 17,000 to 175,000.[11] Strauss was a secular Jew with a commitment to the humanist tradition and to what he called "life" values, and in about 1910 he became anxious over the cultural fate of America. He took part in the failed Kehillah experiment of Rabbi Judah Magnes, an experiment that attempted to unify all New York Jews around common humane values and designed, in part, to fend off the impact of commercialism on Jewish life (see Chapter 7).[12] In 1917 he left Manhattan (and *The Globe*) with his wife and daughter to live in Katonah, New York, a northern suburban village along the rail route to Manhattan. There, until 1925, he edited and published his own weekly periodical, *The Villager*. *The Atlantic Monthly* described it, ten years after the first issue appeared, as a "journal of personal philosophy extraordinary in the freshness of its observation."[13]

Strauss had created *The Villager* expressly as an organ of cultural reflection, and among his first extended essays was "Epicurus and America." In it he attacked the mind-cure movement—and American society generally—for going down the same road as Epicurus in shelving "belief in pain, fear, anger, conflict, and above all, death." The "removal" of "pain in the body" and "trouble in the soul," Strauss wrote, "was the task of Epicureanism" and it is an "outstanding" feature of "recent America." "The past half century has seen a battle waged against human suffering the like of which has never been known, and the results in serums and anaesthetics, in hospitals and dispensaries, in prisons, reformatories, social settlements, model tenements and all the host of easing philanthropy, are astounding when compared with conditions even as recent as our fathers' day. Someone has called this the age of the ambulance."[14]

Shortly before *The Villager* folded in 1925, Strauss wrote his eassy on "Consumptionism," which pursued further much of what he had already been writing in his paper. Consumptionism, he argued, was a philosophy of life that committed human beings to the production of more and more things—"more this year than last year, more next year than this"—and that emphasized the "standard of living" above all other values. "No minister in any pulpit offers any cure which requires that . . . the nation's 'standard of living' sags back." "The Capitalists and Socialists are at each other's throats, but the issue between them is, Which can ensure the distribution of the most goods to the people?"[15]

Consumptionism included another feature: compulsion to buy what was not wanted, the inescapable presence of business pressure, business manipulation of public life, and invasion of market values into every aspect of culture. "Formerly the task was to supply the things men wanted; the new necessity is to make men want the things which machinery must turn out if this civilization is not to perish. . . . the problem before us today is not how to produce the goods, but how to produce the customers. Consumptionism is the science of compelling men to use more and more things. Consumptionism is bringing it about that the American citizen's first importance to his country is no longer that of citizen but that of consumer."[16] Under the banner of making more things, Strauss saw the whole society being remade according to the priorities of Consumptionism. In his 1924 *Atlantic Monthly* article and in similar pieces, he observed that Consumptionism was encouraging Americans to shed respect for "wisdom" and "the continuity of life" and to exalt instead the "new and improved" and the young. One of the most "striking" features of the new age "is the common belief that the world is for the young and that the old are merely clogs on the chariot wheels of triumphant Progress."[17] Americans were also pursuing "luxury and security," and abandoning values and traditions that had historically enriched life and limited the power over individuals of consumer goods. In "normal times," he wrote in "Out of the Grip of Things" for *The Villager*,

there are spiritual goods in the market which compete with the merchant's wares automatically setting limitations on the number of material goods that can be forced upon the community. Ours, however, have been abnormal times; for more than a century things have little by little been filling the stream of existence, little by little absorbing the place normally held by the imponderables, by religion, by art and culture. The fact is that capital's appetite for profits, meeting with no restraint, has been literally eating its way into our right existence and throwing it all out of proportion.[18]

Strauss asserted that "today when the young man thinks of getting as rich as he would like to be, it is no dream; it is a program; and it can be a program because it reaches only so far as security and luxury and does not take in any of the intangibles, no magnificence, prestige, position, power, nor any such."[19]

Strauss believed that all forms of "particularism" were yielding before the requirements of a new class of men—the "key men," Strauss called them in 1927—in "manufacturing, in the engineering fields, in the new forms of retail trade"—men concerned only for "standardization, mass production, and mass distribution." They saw people not as people but as "units in mass" or as "mass consumers." "No more damnable philosophy was ever offered mankind," he wrote.[20]

Strauss was convinced that this process would go on unabated as long as ordinary Americans had reason to accept the trade-off—"luxury and security" on the one hand; the decline of democratic culture, the "extinction of the political state," and acceptance of managerial control on the other. He was certain that capitalism and socialism were both moving in the same direction, despite their basic differences over the ownership of property. All things considered, however, "industrialism is the greater danger." "Socialism would require a revolution of some sort for its institution, and that would imply plenty of consciousness. We should all know it for what it is and call it by its name. Industrialism involves nothing more than that we go farther in the direction we are now going, do more of what we are now doing."[21]

Goods and Money
"Flooding the Country"

Samuel Strauss in the United States and André Siegfried in France were, almost simultaneously, reacting to another tremendous surge in American capitalist development. A mark of that surge was the flow of goods—goods "flooding the country," said Raymond Loewy in the autobiography he wrote on his experiences as a French immigrant in the 1920s and as a leading industrial designer in the 1930s.[22] For example, perfumes and cosmetics, already big business before the war, had matured into the nation's tenth-largest industry—a $1 billion one by the late twenties. Tons of cheap perfume and mountains of facial creams, with new artificial smells and colors, found their way into the "beauty salons" and into the proliferating bedrooms of the new suburbs. From 1914 to 1926, annual sales of toilet goods at Filene's rose from $84,000 to $552,000. The yearly output of clocks and watches increased from 34 million to 82 million in ten years, making America the leading timekeeper. Electrical appliances and machines—refrigerators, vacuum cleaners, toasters, fans, stoves, and dishwashers—were the decade's gold mine commodities. By 1930, as historians have time and again noted, one of every six Americans owned an automobile; and people from all walks of life were buying phonographs, player pianos, and radios. When Monsignor Francis Spellman of Boston (later one of America's leading cardinals committed to "going first class") was named America's first presidential emissary to the Vatican in 1926, he helped ensure his popularity in Rome by having Filene's send the latest RCA model radios to several Vatican prelates.[23] A big building boom supplied the new "spaces"—the single-family dwellings, schools, hotels, restaurants and theaters, office skyscrapers—destined to contain these products.

The commercial circuit carried perishable "living" things as well as manufactured products. Steamship lines, equipped with refrigeration, brought rare flowers in bulk to American shores, a supply swollen by the domestic production of flowers in heated greenhouses near the largest cities. In the 1910s the pet business, too, began to prosper; by the 1920s, rare fishes and animals of all kinds, imported by large wholesaling companies, were common displays in American stores. Owners of pet stores bragged of the "millions of German canaries" and the "rare birds" they had in stock—the hyacinth macaws, parrot finches, bloodstained cockatoos, green shell lovebirds, and shama thrushes. Although the label "rare" was sometimes hype, more often than not the stock was unusual, even unique. By 1927 in the New York Wanamaker's, once a small dealer in pets and birds and now with one of the country's biggest pet store businesses, hardly a week passed without ads for new species, such as the "four very rare green parrots from the Seychelles Islands" off the eastern coast of Africa. Rothschild's in Chicago had one of the largest fish aquariums in the country and the largest collection of "rare" tropical and oriental fish. One can only guess at the waste and insensitivity of this traffic in living things.[24]

Along with the increased production and sale of commodities came an infusion of more money into the hands of consumers. By mid-decade

American wages and salaries were higher in many industries—transportation, mining, and automotive—than in those of any other country. To be sure, the scale was uneven from industry to industry, unemployment was chronic in some industries, and wage increases were dissipated by the rising cost of living. And certainly the distribution of wealth was more inequitable than ever in American history: Only 2 percent of the people owned 60 percent of the wealth, the bottom half only 5 percent. Still, wages were higher, due in part to previous labor militancy, and due also to the insight of industrialists such as Henry Ford in Detroit, who recognized the connections among high wages, high consumption, and high production. Ford saw that automobile workers would not continue to work under his driven regime of mass production without higher wages, and in the late teens he raised wages. His aim was also to prevent unionization. And he gave no benefits—no health insurance, no workmen's compensation, no pensions, no protection whatever, and in the case of the southern blacks whom he was the first to lure North by high wages, no allocation for housing. (Detroit soon had the worst ghetto in the country.)[25]

As wages rose, albeit always unevenly, so did the income of corporations and banks, but at a much higher rate. After the war, the United States was "cash-rich," enjoyed a large trade surplus, and investment bankers exuded excitement and confidence about the state of the money markets. "This country is now seeing an extraordinary importation of gold," one investment banker wrote to a client in 1921. "Capital tied up in merchandise is being freed and the real increase in American wealth which took place as a result of the war will manifest itself continually. Investment banking will receive a tremendous impetus. With the strain over, corporations and individuals will have surpluses in cash not required in their businesses, seeking investment."[26]

The means of distribution increased along with the quantity of goods and money. "Changes in distribution have occurred with bewildering rapidity," reported the U.S. Chamber of Commerce in 1927. "Goods flow in an ever-increasing stream to consumers, but it is a broad, swirling, tortuous current."[27] The infrastructure for moving goods, money, and consumers expanded: trucks and automobiles to transport goods; new bridges, tunnels, roads, and highways to carry the cars and trucks. The U.S. parcel post proved its economic worth by tripling its operations into cities and towns hitherto unreached by its services. In 1927 Gimbels customers in New York City could ride twenty-seven escalators, the most ever installed,

Gimbels claimed, in a retail store to that time. "In one hour," the management said, "Gimbel escalators will transport a city." A year later, Bamberger's in Newark bested Gimbels, with thirty-four escalators, moving through sixteen new stories above the ground and another four stories below it.[28]

Banks were now building branches at a quickening pace to cope with and to exploit the money supply, and the Federal Reserve System boasted that it could "move available credit to places where it is needed" in record time.[29] Movies and radio not only entertained but also transmitted information about the new goods widely and fast. The modern service economy also more clearly materialized, employing almost half of the labor force in the retail and wholesale business, in hotels and restaurants by 1929. "For the first time," wrote President Hoover's Committee on Economic Trends in 1928, we have " 'mass services' which have saved our country from a critical unemployment problem."[30]

Chains Across the Country

The outpouring of goods and money were some of the signs of new "Consumptionism" in the United States. But behind these signs were even more significant trends that explained the volatility and excitement and that fed "Consumptionism." After recovery from the sharp 1921 recession, merchants and manufacturers were busier than ever in organizing and financing the economy along mass production and mass consumption lines. The consolidation of mass merchandising, in particular, marked decisively the advent of what we think of today when we use the phrase "modern consumer society."

Intrinsic to this economic expansion was the spread of chain store methods and the consolidation of competing as well as noncompeting firms. Chains honeycombed the country, in groceries, drugs, meats, hardware, dry goods, and so on, doing more than any other institutions after 1920 to create a genuinely national market. Chains were centrally managed and depended on pooled buying and standardized advertising. Greater economies of scale were possible with chains. Their spread after 1920 followed a trend throughout the economy and signified a "tremendous concentration" of economic power (as one observer put it) in fewer and fewer hands. From all directions the small, independent retailer was competing with large firms and beleaguered. Distribution of some lines—men's apparel, for instance—was seriously threatened by the chains. In 1886 only 2 chains in all businesses operated 5 stores; in 1912 a total of 177 companies operated 2,235 stores; but by 1929 nearly 1,500 companies were doing business in nearly 70,000 outlets.[31]

The chain "idea" found favor throughout the food business. Grocery chains such as A & P and Kroeger's multiplied stores into the tens of thousands.[32] Restaurant chains expanded or were built from coast to coast, including Horn & Hardart, Schrafft's, Savarin, and Child's.[33] In 1923, Fanny Farmer (not the cookbook author) was running 61 candy stores; by 1927 she owned more than 100, with the promise of many others to come. All her 125 lines of candy were factory-made, though Farmer claimed that "artists" crafted the candy in her "studios." She wanted to "emphasize," she said, that "the production of really high-class candy is an art, not a commercial process." By 1927 she had competition from Loft's, Mary Lee Candy Shops, and Happiness Candy Stores.[34]

In 1919 Ellsworth Statler triggered an upsurge in the growth of hotel chains by building in New York the 2,300-room Pennsylvania Hotel (later the New York Statler). It remained the biggest in the world until Chicago's Sherman Hotel was erected in 1927. Also in 1927, in Waco, Texas, Conrad Hilton opened the fourth Hilton hotel in his new Texas chain; it followed the Statler model by offering "a minimum charge for maximum service" (Hilton called it "minimax").[35] By 1931, his son Conrad Hilton, Jr., was operating a chain of 19 hotels in cities and towns of Texas, New Mexico, and Alabama or in markets untouched by his father.[36]

Real estate companies and speculative builders fueled the growth of hotel chains, participating in "vast and wasteful overproduction," as Statler himself complained in 1928. Until the 1980s, this decade exceeded all others in hotel construction, generating more than 500,000 rooms (compare this to the 89,000 added between 1947 and 1955). In New York City alone, 84 large hotels went up between 1927 and 1933, increasing hotel space by 66 percent and yielding enough capacity to accommodate the city for another twenty years. "The country is witnessing the building of scores of hotels in cities where no actual proof can be offered that the need for new hotels exists. They are a menace," Statler said.[37] The growth had produced a supply far in excess of demand, spawning price wars, and conditions ripe for economic disaster.[38] When the Depression hit, the hotel industry was devastated.

By the mid-1920s eight big film companies controlled film distribution in theater chains throughout the country, each company commanding 500 to 1,000 theaters. The major cheap standardized retail chains, mostly redundant in character, doubled in size between 1923 and 1927: W.T. Grant's from 45 to 109, Penney's from 371 to more than 1,000, and Kresge's from 212 to 435. Woolworth's towered over them all in 1927 with 1,581 stores, well above the 600 mark set in 1912.[39] Fancy specialty chains of women's ready-to-wear clothes, such as Bedell's, Lane Bryant, and Peck & Peck, also dotted the country. There was a big Butler Furniture chain, a Walden Book Shop chain, a World Radio Corporation chain, and chain stores for Liggett's, Rexall's and Walgreen's "drugs" ("reorganized" in the twenties by investment bankers). The drug chains numbered 3,000 stores by 1927 (there were only 25 such stores in 1900), and they were decked out in ways that impressed some Europeans, who viewed drugstores in their own countries as suffocating and full of addictive drugs, sickening smells, and poisonous chemicals. "Instead of a dark, stuffy little pharmacy reeking of carbolic acid and wintergreen," the French emigrant Raymond Loewy wrote of his first encounter in the United States with one of these businesses, "here was a flashy, dazzling store crammed full to the ceiling with everything in the world from aspirin to roller skates, a garish phono blaring 'Dardanella,' and the smell of fresh coffee and Pinaud's Lilac trying to drown out iodine and cheese sandwich."[40]

By 1929, in the center of Marion, Ohio, the town where both President Warren G. Harding and socialist leader Norman Thomas grew up and where the houses all had front lawns, there were two Kresge's, two Kroeger grocery stores, three chain clothing stores, two chain shoestores, one Woolworth's, one Montgomery Ward, and one Penney's. So deeply had chain businesses intruded into the economy and culture of the country by this time, so totally had they completed the transformation of merchandising that had begun in earnest with the "retail wars" of the 1890s, that some people feared the influence of absentee managers (the chain owners) who cared little or nothing about local communities and a great deal about national "systems" and large-volume turnover. As Senator Hugo Black of Alabama (later a U.S. Supreme Court justice) said in 1930: "The local man and merchant is passing and his community loses his contribution to local affairs as an independent thinker and executive."[41]

Many chains were new; older ones grew by adding branches or by merging with other firms. These chains, in fact, belonged to a veritable "mergermania" in merchandising, as one expert put it, following the earlier mergers in heavy industry and manufacturing (and, to a limited degree, in merchandising as well). By the late 1920s, merger was the preferred method of expansion, with nearly 50 percent of the chains turning to it to dominate and control competition. "Tremendous concentration is taking place in all lines of business," wrote a contemporary analyst. "The tendency is over-whelmingly toward fewer and larger companies." The tendency surprised some economists, such as the classically trained and highly respected John Bates Clark, who, in about 1900, believed that Americans (as well as market forces) would not permit such pervasive concentration.[42] "The machine, quantity production because of the machine, great consolidation of capital because of both," Clark wrote in 1928, "are the factors in a transformation that has set at naught the forecast of the earlier economists. . . . Today the problem in America appears to be whether any business will long keep clear of the corporate form notwithstanding the fact that, in 'big business,' the owners of most of the capital are wholly divorced from management."[43]

Investment Bankers and Mergermania

At the helm of this merger activity were investment bankers, who knew better than anyone how to organize new merchandising circuits of money and goods and to score huge profits for the benefits of their clients and themselves. In return for large fees, investment bankers provided many services to corporations: floating corporate securities on stock exchanges to give business ready access to funds for expansion; promoting merger activity; and finding the capital for businesses to buy out their competitors.[44] In 1912 there were only 277 members of the Investment Banking Association (including main offices and branch offices); by 1928 the number had risen to 1,072, and by 1929 to 1,902.[45]

The growth of investment banking and of mass consumption industries were (and still are) closely related developments.[46] Capital brokers paved the way for the success of the bigger firms. "The large organization that is adequately financed," wrote one merchandising expert, "can take advantage of many opportunities that the small businessman cannot even consider."[47] Bankers assisted in undermining the competitive ethos by directing business interest toward concentration and easy economic fixes. They helped local monopolies become major national "players" almost instantaneously. Banker-inspired mergermania reinforced an already clear pattern in the economy away from "making goods" to "making money."

The crown firms were Lehman Brothers and Goldman, Sachs, who collaborated closely until the 1930s. Both started out in the nineteenth century as commodity brokerage houses, and by the turn of the century had carved out strategic places in the public financing of America's mass market retailers. World War I pushed them even farther into large under-takings. One partner, Herbert Lehman, later Democratic governor of New York, was especially eager to increase the "merger" business. Lehman had developed a taste for big coordinated deals during the war, when, in the War Department Division, he oversaw the disposition of supplies to military personnel. "I hope my firm and I can take an active part in the venture such as I believe we both have in mind," he typically wrote a merchant in 1923, of a possible merger deal. "I want you to know . . . that I am not only enthusiastically favorable to the plan but that I am entirely at your disposal in working it out in its various details."[48]

Waddill Catchings, merger specialist in the consumer sector and pres-ident of Goldman, Sachs, was one of the first American economic thinkers to write books on money, among them *Money* and *The Road to Plenty*. He also concocted some notorious financial schemes, the most grandiose and unseemly of which was Goldman, Sachs Trading Corporation, an umbrella company of several merged investment trusts whose aim was to hoodwink people into buying securities whose market value was far in excess of the value of a corporation's assets.[49] (The company collapsed in 1930, wiping out the investments of many innocent people.) "The mainspring of business is *Profits*," Catchings wrote in one of the many books he coauthored with economist William Trufant Foster. "The hope of profits drives the life-sustaining blood to every part of the economic body. The blood is money."[50]

Catchings and other bankers saw in the expansion of what the banker Paul Mazur called "the machine of desire" one of the keys to continual economic growth and profits. As brokers they believed it was not the business of business to judge other people's desires. Quite the opposite: Business succeeded (and people got jobs) only when business responded to desire, manipulated it, and extended its frontiers. The proof, Catchings said, was already obvious, in all the "cigarettes and cars" that corporations were making in "response to orders from consumers." The American economy had "to stimulate new and underdeveloped desires" to keep the money and goods flowing through the system. "The function of our economic organization," Catchings explained, "is not to determine what the people *ought* to want, but to make the machinery as productive as possible of what they *do* want."[51]

Quality products and craftsmanship, of course, remained important to many businessmen, but the economy overall became even more single-mindedly capitalistic. If, as Thorstein Veblen wrote, investment bankers knew little or nothing about goods, they knew a great deal about volume turnover, money, and profits. They helped to guarantee that market or pecuniary value would continue to be the value that most mattered in American culture.

In the food business, investment bankers managed the consolidation of firms and chain growth through mergers. For years the food industry was the country's largest but it was also the most individualized—its products sold in more places and in smaller amounts than those of other industries. In the twenties, investment bankers helped transform this pattern. Colgate-Palmolive Peet and General Mills were created, as was Borden's, the fresh-milk company that bought fifty-two businesses in cheese and ice cream. Standard Brands, Inc., controlled by J. P. Morgan's, consolidated four companies dominant in their fields—Royal Baking Powder, Chase and Sanborn, E. W. Gillette, and Fleischmann's Yeast Company. The addition of Fleischmann's was an especially adept maneuver, for that firm was creating the best food distribution system anywhere for perishable goods. It blanketed the nation with its nine hundred company-owned distribution centers, its thousands of motor trucks, and its seventeen hundred delivery routes to supply numerous hotels, bakeries, restaurants, and retail outlets. "These veins of distribution," reported *Business Week Magazine* in 1929, "are kept filled with fresh goods by special refrigerated expresses from fourteen factories scattered at strategic points in the country." The acquisition of Fleischmann's allowed Standard Brands to adapt a proven distribution system for its other products, to lower prices, and to generate far greater profits.[52]

Most of the food mergers of the 1920s were done almost overnight, but Postum's metamorphosis took four years. In 1923 Postum owned five companies; by 1929 General Foods (as Postum's was now called) operated fourteen companies, including Bran Flakes and Jell-O. The combination was the work of Wall Street financier Edward Hutton of Lehman Brothers and of Postum general manager Colby Chester, both of whom had studied the food industry for its inefficiencies and waste, discovering that Postum's salesmen were squandering their labor by selling only "one" product on the road. "Why not whole lines?" Chester asked. So "we acquired other products not by buying patents or starting new factories, but by buying factories and corporations which owned products." The point, they insisted, was "to serve the consumer." "On his behalf we bought not a package like a retailer or carloads like a jobber, but entire businesses. All were well-known products which we wanted easily to sell. Now we will utilize to the full our salesmen."[53]

By the end of the decade, Lehman Brothers and Goldman, Sachs had also financed several limited-price variety chains; many grocery-food chains; various corporations, such as Studebaker, Phoenix Hosiery, General Cigar, and Welch's Grape Juice; and the biggest "amusement organization" ever created in the United States—RKO (Radio-Victor-Keith Orpheum). RKO merged theaters, booking organizations, and RCA into a single corporation, "centering under one control almost everything available in the line of amusement."[54]

Catchings envisioned a great future in the chain movie theater business and did much to promote it. He was sure of the soundness of "sound films" long before many people in the film industry were, and in 1925 he agreed to finance Warner's if they would give him complete financial control over long-term business growth, and they did. Drawing on the combined capital of six banks, Catchings supplied Warner Brothers with a multimillion-dollar revolving credit line (a long-term loan that could be drawn on at will as long as regular payments were made), allowing them to achieve corporate solvency and to buy out Vitagraph, one of the country's founding film companies. As a result of this buyout and with little sweat on their part, Warner's acquired a nationwide distribution system *tout de suite*. Catchings extended it still more by purchasing ten new theaters in crucial markets (including Times Square). In 1928 he bought out First National, a major film company. He floated Warner's stocks, making Warner's and himself instantly even more rich. From 1925 to 1930 the value of Warner's assets rose from $5 million to $230 million. [55]

"*The Power Is All in Business*": *Chains of Department Stores*

Mergermania was so ubiquitous that it produced a glut in the number of chain units, periodic layoffs, waste, economic volatility, excessive competition, "irresponsibility, and over-issue of securities," as financial historian George Edwards has written. [56] But movement toward greater cooperation and concentration continued, even among department stores, which had been relatively immune to these pressures. Ever since the 1890s, when they first pushed aside their small retail rivals, department stores had been formidable local corporations. In the face of far more daunting competition from chain stores in the 1920s, department store owners greatly expanded their physical plants, developed new strategies of cooperation, enlarged older ones, and groped toward federated national systems of their own.

As far as the public was concerned, the clearest indication of the changes taking place was the building and rebuilding of the stores themselves. In the 1920s, large-scale merchandising experienced a building "frenzy" equal in intensity only to that of the period from 1896 to 1912. By 1930 Marshall Field's wholesale division occupied the Merchandise Mart in Chicago, a twenty-four-story-high indoor market equipped for the display and purchase of store stocks, and the world's largest commercial structure until the 1960s. [57] Field's was also among the many large stores to develop branch units in the suburbs, with three five-story branches in Evanston, Lake Forest, and Oak Park. In New York City, James A. Hearn's on Sixth Avenue opened a branch store in Stamford, Connecticut, Altman's on Fifth Avenue had a branch in White Plains, New York, and Saks Fifth Avenue had a branch in Chicago in 1930. Four of Philadelphia's most prestigious stores, including Strawbridge and Clothier, all had branch extensions by 1930; and Cleveland's Halle Brothers was booming, with five successful branches in Ohio and western Pennsylvania. [58] New York's Wanamaker's, long timid about yielding to any pressure to expand, could not escape the logic of the chain idea. "The rapid increase and success of chain stores," Joseph Appel, new president of the store after Rodman's death in 1928, wrote in a store memorandum that year, "suggest a plan I advocated years ago—to open new Wanamaker stores in various centralized localities in New York. To go where the people are in greatest numbers into their home neighborhoods, instead of attempting to force them to come to us."[59]

The stores were growing vertically as well as horizontally, using whatever means necessary to control available real estate. In Newark, Bamberger's added another fifty departments in 1922. Four years later, Gimbels opened its twelve-story-high store on Market Street in Philadelphia, with two subway stores and double the number of show windows. In 1927 J. L. Hudson's, the largest department store in Detroit, unveiled an even larger store, the tallest in the world, twenty-one stories high with floor space double that in the previous building.[60] In 1927 F. and R. Lazarus management of Columbus, Ohio, worked night and day to get possession of the full block of real estate that fronted their downtown store, so they could build a new store for storage and administration. To secure the property, Fred Lazarus, the president, had to "buy out" a big bordello that occupied it, the last remnant of what once had been the heart of the city's red-light district. The bordello's owner (a "very wise madam," Lazarus later recalled) joked that "you know this property is very valuable because the entire building has been put together by screws." Lazarus had a harder fight gaining permission from the city to erect a connecting bridge between the new store and the old. "We threatened the City Council that if they would not give us permission to expand into the block by connecting to the front store then we would direct our efforts not to expansion in Columbus but to expansion elsewhere." The City Council and the mayor backed down "unanimously." The outcome was a department store that filled two full blocks, the biggest Columbus had seen.[61]

Macy's in New York underwent the greatest metamorphosis of all. If Wanamaker had been the preeminent figure before the war, the Strauses emerged as the most powerful after it. Macy's had hardly been an insignificant competitor in 1901, the year Isidor Straus took it to Thirty-fourth Street; but in the 1920s it was selling each day what it took original owner Roland Macy a full year to sell in 1880. In 1922, caught up in a wave of expansionist fervor, the Straus brothers put the business on the public securities market, gaining access to bigger capital so they might build a bigger store. They added several stories to the eastern side of the building, doubling Macy's to about 1.5 million square feet. Continuing to expand, they created new space and 16 more escalators in 1928 and increased the staff to 12,500 people. Over the next three years, the Strauses acquired control of the entire block bounded by Seventh Avenue, Broadway, and Thirty-fourth and Thirty-fifth streets—except for a little parcel of real estate whose owner adamantly refused to sell to Macy's. Another multistory structure, built in 1931, completed the physical shape of the store we know today. Without question, the Strauses operated the "largest department store" with "the biggest volume in the world."[62]

Macy's was so big and successful that it was beginning to function not only as a mythical symbol of American mass consumption but also as the epitome of economic force. Even Dwight Macdonald—a recent graduate of Yale University and later a critic of American mass culture—was dazzled by the "power" of Macy's "tremendous organization," as he put it. Although he had a strong streak of anti-Semitism in him as a young man and could be a snob, Macdonald seemed to have suspended all bias when it came to the Straus brothers and their business. In 1928 he had a chance to work in the store and "anticipated" it "with more pleasure than dread." "The slight glimpse I had of the business machine in my contacts with the men I talked to," he wrote a friend, "at first terrified me, depressed me, and yet fascinated me. These men were so cold, so keen, so absolutely sure of themselves, and so utterly wrapt up in business that I felt like a child before them. They were so sure of their values that I began to doubt mine. Then my courage began to return, and it occurred to me that the sort of power those men had was the dominant power in America today and that it was what I wanted for myself." Like so many intellectuals (and many other Americans, too), Macdonald was envious. If only men of "art and letters" could have such influence, he thought. "The power is all in business," he concluded. "These men I saw were all of them keener, more efficient, more sure of their power than any college prof I ever knew."[63]

The physical growth of the stores caught the public eye, but there were other activities going on among department stores that were much less visible and far more important in terms of the movement toward consolidation and expansion. By the early 1920s, it was a common thing in cities, for instance, for all the big merchants to unveil their Christmas windows and to turn on the Christmas lights at exactly the same time. Consortia of stores in such places as Philadelphia, Cleveland, Boston, New York, and Chicago held huge cooperative fashion shows in local theaters. They organized common delivery systems. They published "cooperative shopping news," each store buying a proportional allotment of space for the year, and through local chambers of commerce and trade groups, organized cooperative publicity and advertising campaigns.[64]

To meet the challenge of "centralized chain store buying," department stores entered into "combines" of "noncompetitive" units, which allowed them to share vital sales statistics; exchange information on new styles and new selling tactics; and practice "group buying," pooling their orders in a single contract while retaining control over the character of the merchandise. (Central buying concentrated buying decisions entirely in the hands of a single buyer.) The first such cooperative "combination" was the Retail Research Association, brainchild of Louis Kirstein of Filene's, a strategic figure in the decade's retail merger activities and later a force in the Federated Department Stores chain. Kirstein attracted the enterprising zeal of fashion experts such as Faith Chipperfield and Anne Evans, who helped bring the RRA to life in 1917. He joined together such noncompeting stores (noncompeting in the sense that they operated in different cities) as Joseph Horne in Pittsburgh, Strawbridge and Clothier in Philadelphia, and B. Forman in Rochester. In 1921 the American Merchandising Corporation (AMC) was added to the RRA; it served sixteen of the nation's most prestigious stores, from Bullock's in Los Angeles to Bamberger's in Newark (it is still an extremely influential merchandising group). By 1926 both groups had evolved into "the largest of [their] kind in the world," according to Kirstein, their most ardent proponent. They circulated among the members valuable selling data showing "various costs," and they had "monthly contact with one another" to foster "statistical standardization" throughout the combine, thus making the movement of goods and money more rapid and efficient. The AMC bought large quantities of women's wear at excellent discounts in buying offices in Berlin, Paris, and London, and marketed its own trade-name $40 dress line called "Barbara Lee," which all the stores sold. In the midtwenties the AMC established a central New York office where—as one of its founders, Fred Lazarus, Jr., said—members were "advised on "markets, goods resources, and fashion trends.""[65]

There were imitators in many cities: a combine led by Mandels department store in Chicago; a cooperative group buying arrangement in 1929 between Macy's and Bamberger's; and the buying chain of medium-size department stores on the East Coast, led by P. J. Young's in New Brunswick and Steinback's in Asbury Park. Kirstein swore by the indispensability of the AMC. "The only way" the "competition of the large combinations can be met," he wrote to the group's members about chain stores, "is by the development of our purchasing power which is very much greater than any of these combinations and this is the paramount reason why we should develop group buying in every possible way. It is absolutely necessary for our own protection."[66]

Above all, there were the mergers, here as elsewhere carried out with the aid of investment bankers and against the grain of a strong tradition of independence and family ownership (there were exceptions, of course, such as May Department Stores and Associated Dry Goods, both chains since the 1910s). The efforts of bankers, lawyers, and retailers to persuade the Wanamaker management to sell out after Wanamaker's death in 1922 failed; the store remained independent. But the merger fever struck elsewhere, and some merchants—especially aggressive and suspicious ones such as Louis Kirstein of Filene's—saw competitors lurking everywhere eager to destroy them by buying up their stocks. "Is it true," Kirstein asked a banker friend in 1921, "that a gigantic corporation has been formed to monopolize the department store business?" "Is it in the whole country or only in certain places?"[67] To some degree Kirstein's paranoia was not off the mark, for mergers or outright purchases were increasingly a common feature of the decade.

In about 1920 the Straus brothers of Macy's tried to acquire a number of other stores, small and medium-size, around the country, successfully picking up LaSalle and Koch Company, the largest department store in Toledo, Ohio (1923); Davison-Paxon in Atlanta, Georgia (1925); and— most impressive of all—Bamberger's of Newark (1929). Store records reflect failed efforts to get Rothschild's on State Street in Chicago in 1921 (Field's got it in 1924), as well as stores in Pennyslvania and Maryland. Large store chains such as Hahn Department Stores, Allied Stores, and National Department Stores appeared in the twenties. Gimbel Brothers had a six-store chain by 1929: four Gimbels stores, Saks Fifth Avenue in New York City, and Kaufman and Baer in Pittsburgh. In that same year, just before the crash, Marshall Field's bought out Frederick and Nelson, the largest store in Portland, Oregon, and tried repeatedly to purchase Wanamaker's.[68]

Among the biggest "merger" events of the decade was the creation of Federated Department Stores in 1929, the most important chain of department stores in American history. Two merchants, in particular, guided by the advice of investment bankers, pushed for the merger: Louis Kirstein of Filene's and Fred Lazarus, Jr., of F. and R. Lazarus in Columbus, Ohio.

Louis Kirstein was born in Rochester, New York, in 1867 to well-off Jewish parents, and had run away from home at sixteen. He made money for a while playing and managing baseball in the bush leagues. In St. Louis he lived and worked briefly as a janitor in a bordello, befriended the local madam, and peddled a patent medicine consisting mostly of Mississippi water and silt (he would have been jailed for this had not the kindhearted madam paid his fine). By the early 1900s he was in Boston, working for the Filene brothers, Edward and A. Lincoln. In 1911 he was made junior partner, then the head of merchandising and publicity, and by 1920 he was the most powerful person at Filene's.[69]

Kirstein was tall, and towered over his fellow merchant Fred Lazarus, his Columbus-born collaborator in Federated Department Stores and son of a Jewish peddler from Germany. Lazarus grew up in Ohio, the state that gave birth to the Standard Oil trust, a fact Lazarus was well aware of, so aware that he wanted as an adult to create a department store empire just as big.[70] He was a showman and wanted his business to be like a "big circus" to attract customers.[71] Both he and Kirstein were agnostic and, like John Wanamaker, nonjudgmental in temperament. As an old man, Lazarus explained, "I don't like any of the control authority that goes into the whole religious picture. The idea that after life is much better than what you have here I believe is ridiculous and causes perhaps an altogether wrong concept of what living on earth really means."[72] Both men were preoccupied with absorbing their competitors. "We never saw Father when we were children," recalls one of Kirstein's three children, Lincoln Kirstein, resentfully. What Lazarus said of Kirstein could have been said of him as well—that he "wanted to expand continually."[73] In 1928 each man purchased outright a big department store, Lazarus taking over Shillito's in Cincinnati, and Kirstein R. H. White's in Boston.[74]

Kirstein seemed more frantic than Lazarus, and whenever and wherever he could, Kirstein bought out the stock of other companies: Lane Bryant; McCurdy's department store in Rochester; C. Cooper and Company, a large importing firm in Brooklyn; and others.[75] He (along with A. Lincoln Filene) conceived of the Retail Research Association and probably was the first to set the course toward the creation of Federated Department Stores. As early as 1920 or 1921 Kirstein was writing his banking friend Paul Mazur (who was soon to be partner at Lehman Brothers) about the desirability of organizing a huge chain to counter the power of the "gigantic department store corporation" he had imagined bestriding the economy. Mazur wrote back to Kirstein: "I accept your allusion to the chain project in the way you meant it tho I am not sure about it. I would like very much to talk to you about this chain store affair."[76]

Paul Mazur and Harvard's Helping Hand

Paul Mazur, like Lazarus the son of immigrant German Jews, played a primary role in the formation of America's mass consumer sector. He had graduated from Harvard in 1914, at twenty-two, with support from his wealthy father, then worked at Filene's. There Kirstein became a second father figure to him. Mazur joined the Army in 1918 and, like other businessmen, was excited by the magnitude of the forces marshaled to fight the war. Stationed for a few months in Europe, he wrote to Kirstein, "You just know America is the land of the future, the leader by right of progress and example. It is our heritage." The war, he predicted in a postscript, would have "two effects on the men's clothing business. The first is closer, tighter lines of the military uniform. The second is a bit more color in the neckties as a reaction against the sameness of O.D. [olive drab]. When young men come back there will be a tremendous demand."[77]

Back home again in New York City in 1920, Mazur sought to "get into the big operations," and went to Oklahoma to work in the oil business and "help reorganize a company."[78] According to his wife, Adolphina, his vocational predilection was not for buying and selling stocks and bonds; his dream was to own a large sheep farm in the country where he could live in the landed-gentry style favored by bankers of his day, far removed from the sharp deals and unrefined competitive frenzy of the market. But his personal tastes aside (and he did eventually get his farm), he plunged into the world of business.

For several months after his shortlived flirtation with oil, he tried unsuccessfully to create a regional chain-store system, the "Belmont Stores," in women's ready-to-wear clothes, a venture that briefly befuddled Kirstein, who thought Mazur might be staging a competition with him. Belmont Stores failed, but Mazur was sure—as he said in a report—that "the retail business of the United States is tending toward an era of consolidation, and there is a splendid opportunity for an organization, which is built around some central unit of well-established merit . . . to build the entire unit into the most outstanding retail establishment in the United States."[79] Mazur found his real niche at Lehman Brothers, working with Waddill Catchings and Goldman, Sachs to usher in the merger movement in mass merchandising.

He was the key merger person at Lehman's, just as Catchings was at Goldman, Sachs, making "the firm noted for its specialized knowledge of the distribution of consumer goods."[80] He did far more in the twenties, however, than make private merger arrangements or advise clients about which stocks were good or bad; like Waddill Catchings, he was a public advocate of mass centralized merchandising, and to ensure that others would listen to his voice, he relied for assistance again and again on his old alma mater, Harvard.

Harvard—or more precisely, Harvard Business School—was willing to help. By the midtwenties, when Paul Mazur turned to it, the school had greatly deepened its relationship with corporate business, partly because of the efforts of Mazur's old boss Louis Kirstein, chair of its school's fund-raising committee, who believed that "no agency was doing more to help business become a worthy profession than the Harvard Graduate School of Business."[81]

Harvard, of course, was not the only school to so extend a helping hand. Stanford established in 1925 what would soon become one of the most prestigious graduate schools of business in the world, its intent to teach the "essentials of management"—accounting, marketing, finance, and transport.[82] And by mid-decade Northwestern University, along with Michigan, Wisconsin, California, and Oregon, had adopted "bureaus of business research" similar to and modeled after Harvard's own Bureau of Business Research. UCLA had a new school of merchandising in 1929.[83]

In 1922 the American Hotel Association negotiated with Cornell University to teach hotel administration there, and the School of Retailing at New York University merged with the university proper and shifted its pedagogy from training salespeople to educating retail executives. Cornell's Hotel School, a privately endowed pioneering venture, concentrated squarely on training managers to supply the rapidly growing needs of the industry. Open to both sexes, it "was pretty well established" by 1930, "with the enviable distinction"—according to Howard Meek, its first dean—"that at no time did we have unemployment among our graduates."[84] Also open to women as well as men, NYU's student body studying retailing grew from

30 in 1920 to 750 in 1928, many taking classes in the Night Division on everything from store and window display to the psychology of salesmanship and chain store merchandising. Its Day Division was a graduate school devoted to training "retail executives" to feed the city's large stores with merchandising managers, buyers, and personnel directors.[85] Both Cornell and NYU were financially dependent on merchants and closely associated with individual patrons in the consumer service field—Cornell, with Ellsworth Statler, who, even after his death in 1928, continued to finance the school; and NYU, with Percy Straus, who treated the school almost as if it were his own educational fiefdom. The school's executive committee continued to meet in his store in the twenties, he chaired its board of trustees, and he donated large sums of money to the school and to the university, on whose executive council he served. In 1929 Straus gave NYU the biggest sum it had ever received from an individual—"an unrestricted gift" of $1 million.[86]

Still, no university could beat Harvard—then or in the future—in the bonds it built with business. Harvard Business School grew in leaps and bounds, driven in part by a 1922 mandate prepared by the school's evaluating committee to create "a strong profession" to "teach the protection of property and the management of property."[87] By 1927 the school had its own library, administration building, and dormitories, paid for by a $5 million gift from George F. Baker, president of New York City's First National Bank and a "side-whiskered chum" of J. P. Morgan.[88] The school revamped its pedagogy to reflect the concrete needs of business. Its case system of instruction posed problems that firms and corporations actually encountered in their daily operations, or, as one of the system's founders put it, those problems "faced for administrative decision by actual business executives." Four hundred cases were "collected and collated" by the end of the decade, published in book form for use by hundreds of colleges and universities throughout the country.[89]

Harvard courted—explicitly—the corporate marketing and merchandising sectors of the economy. Its evolution was intertwined in the 1920s with the development of America's new mass commercial economy. Harvard began to publish a new journal in 1922, *The Harvard Business Review*, soon the leading academic voice on merchandising and marketing.[90] "A great deal is being done for the retail trade by the Business School," wrote Louis Kirstein to a fellow merchant in 1925.[91]

In 1921 Melvin Copeland, director of Harvard's Bureau of Business

Research, wrote Lew Hahn, managing director of the National Retail Dry Goods Association (NRDGA), that Harvard was "an unbiased agency" "with only a scientific interest in" the "management problems" of business.[92] Donald K. David, assistant dean (and later dean) of the school, in a letter to Percy Straus in 1921, similarly explained Harvard's involvement with the NRDGA on the grounds that it helped the school develop "the best courses for the preparation in retailing."[93] All this was doubtless true, but it hardly meant—as Copeland implied—that Harvard was interested in merchants on intellectual grounds alone. For years the NRDGA, along with many individual merchants, had underwritten (and would continue to underwrite) the finances of Harvard's Bureau of Business Research to the tune of hundreds of thousands of dollars.[94] Merchants and managers from Filene's, Procter & Gamble, Jordan Marsh, and the movie industry lectured at the school; and Joseph P. Kennedy, banker and owner of the Film Booking Offices of America, conducted a course on the film industry in 1927.[95] Merchants "subscribed" (funded) courses and made numerous generous gifts to the school's endowment. Harvard faculty and merchants mixed socially as well (Kirstein liked to "golf" with the dean).[96]

No educational institution in the world came close to Harvard in the way it served the practical requirements of corporate business and helped build the new mass consumer economy. No university better symbolized the expansion of the American commitment to studying marketing, advertising, retailing, finance, real estate, management, and consumer psychology as an interrelated whole. Indeed, only in the United States did any such liaison develop. Even the German educational system, which most closely rivaled the American in size, refused to pay any mind to practical needs of business, specializing instead in research and theory, developing expertise in theoretical accounting, but ignoring advertising and marketing. The Germans thought that business, not universities, should train people to "do business."[97] In Germany, England, and other European countries, there were no M.B.A.s—except American-educated ones—at all until the 1970s. In 1930 a total of 1,070 M.B.A.s were enrolled in Harvard Business School, almost triple the figure in 1920.[98]

Harvard was quite ready to respond to the special needs of Paul Mazur. In 1924 *The Harvard Business Review* published his article "Future Developments in Retailing," about the competitive advantages of consolidation and merger. Mergers bring growth, he said, by making "available continuous market knowledge of an intensive character. Retail mergers must continue because they offer management efficiency, overhead reduction, and the economy of purchasing large volumes. Large-scale operations will be most effective not through the building of an unlimited number of new retail units, but through the consolidation of existing stores and chains." Such consolidation would act as a bulwark against the instability caused by inevitable shifts in fashions and styles.[99] In 1925 Mazur again wrote for the *Review,* this time on the strategies of consumer enticement. "The machinery which has developed consumer demands has become so completely accepted that we forget our *duty* to it. We are apt to forget the benefits of the system and find fault with apparent burdens. And yet the safety of the industrial superstructure depends upon the strengths of the marketing foundations, just as the foundation would have no value without the industrial structure." "A staggering machine has been built," he said a few years later, developing on these ideas, "to satisfy consumer demand and even the consumer's whispered interest. The machine is here. It now has an appetite of its own which must be satisfied."[100]

Mazur's analyses attracted much attention and were widely excerpted. The National Retail Dry Goods Association reprinted his 1924 piece in its *Confidential Bulletin,* circulated to retailers around the nation.[101] The essay ignited debate and led to a major collaboration among the NRDGA, Lehman Brothers, and Harvard Business School in 1924, when the NRDGA commissioned Lehman's (Mazur in particular) to join with the school in a study of new organizational trends in merchandising. It was the first time a banking firm had been involved in a study of mass merchandising.[102] Harvard's faculty were eager to join in. "I shall be *very* glad to do whatever I can to help," Professor Donald David wrote to Lew Hahn of the NRDGA in June 1925, soon after the study was begun, "I really think that a good bit can come from such an investigation, and naturally I shall be most interested to be connected with it."[103] David directed the fieldwork in all the participating fourteen stores; he chose the three fieldworkers and was especially proud of his third choice, a 1924 Harvard graduate named Myron Silbert, who became Mazur's favorite. "He is a Jew," David wrote Mazur, in language that may have rankled Mazur, "which fact will probably not be a hindrance in the type of work he will do this summer."[104]

Together, David, Silbert, and Mazur, after eighteen months of research, produced a classic study, *Principles of Organization Applied to Modern Retailing.* Mazur wrote it. It was the standard study of the subject for the next fifty years. Its argument dealt with a current focus in corporate business—that scrutiny must be given to "the whole field of distribution" and "merchandise methods" rather than to "mass production." "All manufacturers," Mazur wrote, "can learn a great deal from the progressive retailer concerning the anticipation of sales possibilities and planning and control of inventories." The study showed Mazur's excitement over the consolidating changes under way in retailing. "There have been external developments of significant interest pregnant with unusual possibilities," he asserted. "The growth in numbers of and importance of resident buyers, centralized merchandising agencies, centrally operated lease departments, associations of stores using consolidated buying, and financial consolidation has been startling."[105]

Mazur abstracted from these reforms in retailing what he believed to be the best hierarchical structure for large-scale merchandising, singling out specialized function and management rather than ownership. At the top of the chart were the general manager and the board of managers, followed by the four major store components (controller, merchandise manager, publicity manager, and store manager), and so on down to the lowest rung of stock- and salespeople. It was a structure that characterized the most "progressive" stores in which consolidating tendencies were clearly manifest. Mazur recommended it to businessmen who wished big success in retailing.[106]

By 1927, the year the retailing study was published, Mazur had achieved a national reputation. He was operating at the center of a new circuitry of institutions and was positioned to argue his case to a wider audience. The next year his book *American Prosperity* was published, bringing him brief national fame. In it he described a new American mentality, accustomed to change and to the "satisfaction of desires." America, he wrote confidently, had shifted from a "needs" to a "desires" culture. People were now "trained to desire change, to want new things even before the old have been entirely consumed." "Man's desires can [now] be developed so that they will greatly overshadow his needs." Mazur saw nothing whatever wrong with this; indeed, just as economists such as Simon Patten had done for years (and just as Mazur's colleague Waddill Catchings was doing, too), Mazur urged skeptical businessmen to accept it as a fact of life. "Of course there exists theoretically that danger point when consumption has reached its limit," he admitted, but such a breaking point is probably nonexistent. Human desires seem to have no limits. Food products may reach a point where people's appetites are satiated or oversatiated—a day, however, far distant or at least hardly imminent. But when that day comes, there will be other wants and desires that are just as real—the satisfaction of which will still provide new sales opportunities. Give the world and his wife the funds with which to satisfy every need, desire, and whim, educate the world and his wife to want, and the production capacity of the country will actually groan under the burden of enormous demand. There may be limits to the consumption of particular products. There is no theoretical limit to general consumption possibilities. [107]

This was core capitalist ideology. For Mazur, modern capitalism was positively liberating; by its very nature, it rejected all traditions and embraced desire. All businessmen needed to do to ensure capitalist success was to "educate" men and women to these ideas, to suggest, impose, shape a new mentality.

In his new position of power, Mazur also continued to advise his clients (and the public at large) on what he believed to be the advantages of centralization. He helped do the financing for Macy's, Gimbels, Allied Stores, Interstate, and May. His most important merger deal—Federated Department Stores—was arranged with Louis Kirstein and Fred Lazarus, Jr. By 1925 it was clear the organizations Kirstein and Lazarus had set up to serve as instruments for group buying and the transmission of basic data among core stores—the Retail Research Association (RRA) and the American Merchandise Corporation (AMC)—could form the basis for the new holding company. That year Mazur defended mergers before the "strategic members" of the RRA, although at least one member—A. Lincoln Filene—objected on the grounds that if a merger had to occur, then momentum should come from within the RRA itself, not from some investment banker. Mazur went ahead anyway, presenting his case for consolidation as an "impartial spokesman." "It is my conviction," he said, "that a great deal of progress has been made and that there is a possibility of creating a partial consolidation within a reasonable length of time. I feel that if some outstanding figure in the RRA will champion the cause, we can make progress."[108] It took another four years, until mid-1929, for the pieces to fall into place, and even then there was much suspense and some acrimony over how things should be done.

In the summer, Kirstein was sweating over the outbreak of what seemed to be another wave of mergermania. "I was in New York for two or three days," he wrote to Filene in July 1929, "where rumors are rife that everyone is buying out everybody else."[109] Everyone, it seemed—May Department Stores, the Hahn chain, the Straus brothers of Macy's—wanted to take over Bloomingdale's at East Fifty-ninth Street and Lexington Avenue in Manhattan. The Strauses were also on the prowl after other prey and surprised everyone by purchasing the highly profitable Bamberger's, whose owner, Louis Bamberger, decided to quit the business and spend the rest of his life giving away his money (to Princeton, for example, for the Institute for Advanced Study).

As Kirstein saw it, Bamberger, a trusted member of the American Merchandising Corporation, should have contributed some of his stock to the creation of Federated. It should not have gone over to the archenemy— Macy's![110] He was livid. "I think it is the worst, low-down trick anyone could play on a crowd of his associates. . . . It is the most inexplicable thing I have ever come in contact with and in all my business experience, I have never felt I was let down like this." Mazur was busily completing the Federated arrangements (and seducing Bloomingdale's to join the merger; it did, but two months after the others).

In the late summer of 1929, Mazur, with Filene, Kirstein, and Lazarus, sailed to the Caribbean on a yacht owned by Walter Rothschild, president of Abraham & Straus. In this secluded floating luxury they put the last touches on the creation of Federated Department Stores. "At the time," Mazur later said, "I was the common denominator."[111]

The Urban Landscape of Desire

The impact of this new age of consolidation on America was considerable. It helped produce a new urban geography. New York City, perhaps, revealed the impact best, in not only being actually restructured by the economy but also by creating districts of such magnitude that Americans thought of them as spatial metaphors for changes taking place in other cities as well. In New York, the interrelated districts each served a particular dimension of commodity production and exchange. Before 1900 Wall Street, lying in a half-mile-square patch between Fulton Street and Bowling Green in lower Manhattan, had no tall buildings. Trinity Church was still the dominant architectural structure. By 1929 the district was a "canyon" of twenty-story skyscrapers, the headquarters for banks, insurance companies, and brokerage businesses. A mark of its transformation was the shift in venue of the "curb," an open-air securities exchange on Broad Street for the sale of newer and cheaper securities not offered elsewhere; for years on the "outside" (and literally held on the street curb), it went inside in 1921, housed in a monumental building at 86 Trinity Place (it was also formally called the Curb Exchange, and then, in 1953, the American Stock Exchange). Wall Street was now disgorging securities and wheeling and dealing in mergers on a huge scale and in every kind of business, synonymous with the capital behind capitalism. [112]

Fifth Avenue had been largely a residential street, even into the late 1890s; now, much of it—or at least the district between Thirty-fourth and Fifty-ninth Streets—had come to represent to the nation the very idea of "retailing and shopping," a change retailers themselves facilitated by lobbying successfully for passage of important zoning legislation from 1913 on. By 1929 the district was fixed when the New York State Court of Appeals upheld the validity of the "new Retail Use District" just established by the city's Board of Estimate. One block east of Fifth Avenue on Madison Avenue, buildings numbered from 200 to 650, had become the home of America's most powerful advertisers, a veritable trope for the rise of this national industry. [113]

Another specialized district was created, in part, by the same zoning laws. The bare outlines of development on Seventh Avenue were just beginning to form before World War I, the result of the 1916 zoning law designed to keep factories downtown and to rid Fifth Avenue of a flood of factory workers during lunchtime. But "the great change" writes a historian of fashion, "began after the war, and, like everything else in this fantastic industry, immediately went into superlatives." [114] After much consultation among retailers, manufacturers, and real estate developers, it was agreed that the women's ready-to-wear garment industry would be concentrated principally in one crucial area in Manhattan: on Seventh Avenue between Fortieth Street and the lower thirties. Between 1921 and 1929 three tall fireproof buildings between West Thirty-sixth and West Thirty-eighth Streets anchored the district, each containing numerous garment factories (fifty-eight in 1921 alone), showrooms, studios for designers in the fashion industry, and cooperative buying agencies (eight hundred by 1928). These structures were at the heart of "the garment center capital."[115]

Today only fashion designers and showrooms remain on Seventh Avenue (although several factories and sweatshops have returned, farther downtown). But by the end of the 1920s the entire region had come to represent or embody "fashion," or more precisely, the concrete historical expression of the women's ready-to-wear industry.[116] Here a large population of mostly immigrant workers, male and female, labored day and night to supply the needs of this "fantastic industry." Seventh Avenue was symbolical of New York City's hold over the fashion world, the center of the country's women's wear business, and also a "defining" term—as one expert put it— to describe and capture "an industry rather than a geographical location."[117]

And blocks away was Times Square, hardly a place at all of any consequence before 1912, but in this decade the very essence of mass entertainment, of nightlife, and of consumer titillation.

Along with the districts came a new vocabulary of mass consumption, disseminated by people such as Paul Mazur, Waddill Catchings, and Melvin Copeland of the Harvard Business School. "Consumer"—a term not in regular currency before the war—began to compete for prominence with "citizen" and "worker" as well as with an earlier meaning of consumer developed by "consumers' leagues," which implied activism and not the passivity of the newer term. Related phrases or terms became popular, among them "consumer desires and wishes," "consumer appeal," "consumer sovereignty," "commodity flow," "the flow of satisfactions," and "sales resistance." This language expressed what had actually happened and, at the same time, ideologically explained it and gave it credence. The most inclusive governmental study of the economic character of the decade—*Recent Economic Changes*, produced by the Hoover Committee of 1928—was replete with such phrases and, indeed, was probably an important medium for their transmission.

At the same time, old terms such as "desire," "luxury," "necessity," and "standard of living" were redefined, rounding out an evolution in language that began as far back as the eighteenth century during the English and French Enlightenment but only clearly perceivable in the United States after 1880, in the work of such people as Simon Patten. Desire was domesticated and endowed with an enabling power, as Mazur's own usage shows.[118] So, too, the concept of luxury. In the 1860s and 1870s, luxury was seen by many Americans as morally corrupting, able to make men and women "effeminate, weak, and dependent." In the 1910s, confusion over the difference between luxuries and necessaries (and their relative moral stature) still existed, as the many marital court cases of the times dealing with defaulted credit payments testify. By the 1920s, luxury seems to have lost for many people much of its negative meaning. "The modern definition of luxury," wrote Edwin R. Seligman, influential economist at Columbia University, in 1927, "is neutral so far as the ethical connotation is concerned. If we consult the dictionary, we find that a luxury is nowadays defined as anything that pleases the senses and is also costly or difficult to procure."[119] Samuel Strauss said that Americans now saw luxury as healthy and "empowering": "Luxury's connection with the millions" has led to "luxury's complete redefinition." Today it is seen as "a source of strength" and as an entitlement "pledged" by America to the "masses of people."[120]

The economic meaning of luxury had also changed. It had become, in Seligman's words, a "necessity" for America's new mass market economy. "Professor Patten," he wrote, "was one of the earliest of modern economists to formulate what is now a commonplace, namely that 'the primary law of social progress is that society progresses from a simple . . . to a varied consumption.' Progress may be the process of converting superfluities into conveniences, and conveniences into necessities. The diversification of consumption lies at the root of human development."[121]

Standard of living, a related and significant concept, was also modified in the twenties. The original concept, or something like it, was rather old, invented in Europe and England in about the early 1800s but popular in the United States only at the end of the century. Almost entirely economic in character, it measured income spent on material (rather than on nonmaterial) well-being, and it had two emphases. The first emphasis was on family expenditures—housing, food, clothing, and health—which were inelastic and, according to some investigators, interchangeable with reasonable levels of subsistence and the "living wage."[122] The second emphasis was on nonfamily and elastic expenses—consumer goods, education outside the home, commercial pleasures, and luxuries rather than necessities. Simon Patten dwelled much on this aspect of the standard of living, viewing its expansion as potentially unlimited and as the primary unifier of American culture.[123]

In the 1920s, the Patten side of the older equation came to the fore, as the concept was changed to incorporate more and more "fields of desire" (as one writer called them) into the realm of "satisfactions"—adventure, sports, travel, "hunger for sex," and "self-assertiveness" (a "fundamental desire so powerful that it probably dominates the choice of the consumer in most lines of goods") as well as more provisions for individual physical space—"a standard of one room per person exclusive of bath."[124]

Behind these increments was a theory of "advancement expenditures" informed by two assumptions. One assumption was that the standard of living was not static but always getting better, and that income would always grow so that American "children could expect, if not to start where their parents left off, at least to finish ahead of them."[125] A related idea was that the standard was desire-oriented, reflecting not the way people actually lived but how they wanted or hoped to live, a "sort of inkling of what might be," a sense of entitlement to the better life, an expectation of more and more.[126] This view, some critics said, was conditioned largely by the "profit motive in business and manufacturing." Thus, "advertising attempts to habituate people, if not to the commodity, at least to the expectancy thereof—to persuade people that silk lingerie, for example, is among the things they should take for granted and insist upon, and give up other things, such as books and babies, in order to secure." The theory also assumed that "extra-family life is better for the masses than home life" and implied that "individualism should develop more and more and that this will build up the morals of the people."[127]

Other attempts were made to redefine the standard of living along more noneconomic lines compatible with family rather than individual income. Harvard University sociologist Carle Zimmerman worried over the "very one-sided" bias toward individualist consumption, proposing instead the insertion into the standard of living of something that he claimed had never been there before—a "nonmaterial dimension," an emphasis on "absolute values" (religious, family, and community). He wanted the standard to be an "integrated whole," not "a series of separate mechanical acts," that included "income-making as well as income-spending, sacrifice as well as reward, security as well as stimulus, or long-time as well as short-time factors."[128] Zimmerman believed that what he called the "individualist" drift of the American standard, fostered by business, was undermining ordinary community and making it hard for people to establish strong relationships. He wanted desire shaped by "absolute values found not only in goods but also in the order and discipline arising out of strong forms of social organization."[129] Rejecting Patten and Wanamaker, he argued that "all values imply scarcity and sacrifice." At the same time, he was pessimistic that the standard of living could be changed along these lines unless, he wrote, the "business classes" could be persuaded to share control over the character of desire.[130]

The age of consolidation also led to further changes in social structure, just as modified concepts, new vocabularies, and new districts came into being. The number and power of brokers in the United States was greatly augmented, clustering heavily in such cities as New York and Chicago. Investment bankers were among them; so were securities dealers (250 just before the war, 6,500 by 1929, an awesome 250,000 by 1990).[131] New advertising agencies (Young and Rubicam) or merging older ones (Batten, Barton, Durstine, and Osborne) attracted thousands of new advertising specialists. In 1917 only 17 people were enrolled in the National Credit Men's Association; by 1923, there were 650; and by 1928, the total was 18,000.[132] Finance agencies expanded, too. So did the numbers of display people, sales personnel, hotel clerks, waiters and waitresses, and promotional and fashion experts. As Herbert Hoover announced in a 1928 campaign speech: "Due to increased efficiency, hundreds of thousands of men and women have been transferred from the factories to our filling stations, our garages, our hotels, and our restaurants."[133] The "art" of public relations, hardly a field at all before the war, attracted a legion of practitioners in Manhattan. Commercial artists found a comfortable, lucrative place in this new world in which they had never dominated before.

The goal of these groups was to probe the domestic market up and down from every angle, to squeeze out every last dollar, and to create such a resilient consumer mentality as to outlast any economic crisis. This goal demanded fresh methods, and the age supplied them. After 1920 a new phase opened in the exploitation of the market. A new managerialism emerged and soon became a cardinal feature of American mass merchandising. In the years after World War I, trained experts and technicians started to dictate the character of consumer enticements, from the organization of fashion modeling to the presentation of commercial parades. At the same time, the U.S. government intervened further on behalf of consumer industries and businesses. Under the leadership of Herbert Hoover, as secretary of commerce and as president, the federal government created a great variety of bureaus and agencies to assist business in the management of the Land of Desire.

Chapter 10

"SELL THEM THEIR DREAMS"

"Sell them their dreams," a woman radio announcer urged a convention of display men in 1923. "Sell them what they longed for and hoped for and almost despaired of having. Sell them hats by splashing sunlight across them. Sell them dreams—dreams of country clubs and proms and visions of what might happen if only. After all, people don't buy things to have things. They buy things to work for them. They buy hope—hope of what your merchandise will do for them. Sell them this hope and you won't have to worry about selling them goods."[1]

Although this message was not a new one for business, the confidence and sophistication expressed in it set it apart from similar prewar messages; for behind the sale of dreams was a new managerial angle to enticement not clearly present before, an angle demanded by the corporations, by the mergers, by bigger capital investment. Greater investment in mass production required greater skill in mass seduction, less reliance on amateurism and serendipity, and more sure-fire professional methods to guarantee turnover. In the realm of consumer credit, retailers expanded opportunities, especially by the end of the decade, when it became clearer that money income alone, for most people, would not be enough to keep the economic motors going. (The result, of course, was a level of consumer debt almost as high as the debt being generated to carry out the fancy mergers.) Devices such as commercial air conditioning, the commercial mural, and color coordination appeared to attract the consumer; and such artists as Norman Bel Geddes, Georgia O'Keeffe, and even the socialist illustrator Boardman Robinson made money working for business.

In all areas of selling, the managerial emphasis took over, and a new breed of specialist emerged to create the first modernist show windows, the first fashion modeling agencies, and the first style agencies and consultancies. These groups pushed standardized messages and strategies in a way and to a degree never seen in the United States. Huge style expositions, reminiscent of those held at museums to display machine-made goods before and during the war, were organized. The expositions, now in department stores, were bolder, more glittery and go-getting, were put together by skilled showpeople such as Dorothy Shaver at Lord & Taylor, and were the envy of curators such as John Cotton Dana and Richard Bach (who were, in fact, often called on to advise the stores). Model showrooms were done with the touch of the expert decorator in both museums and in department stores. And sales promotion took a big step in a managerial direction with the work of Edward L. Bernays, an entrepreneurial genius of American public relations. Bernays was among the legion of people and groups who gave to the period between 1922 and 1932 its special tone, its sense of urgency, its aggressive hard sell.

The Consumer Credit Apparatus

Consumers were engulfed in a sea of easy credit after 1922, with installment buying, charge accounts, and a range of small loans adding up to a multibillion-dollar business.[2] The most liberal credit policies "tended to become the rule" to make up for the relative inequity in incomes, with merchants "hesitating to press desirable customers for prompt payment for fear of driving them to more lenient competitors."[3] Much of the pressure to liberalize credit came from the corporations that had bought out many independent department store retailers and established chains. Personal finance companies furnished much of the capital to facilitate the growth of installment credit and made it possible for stores to add more and more charge customers.[4]

By the end of the twenties, Marshall Field's charge business had risen to 180,000 accounts—almost double the 1920 figure.[5] In such New York stores as Lord & Taylor, Best's, Abraham & Straus, and Arnold Constable, charge operations made up 45 to 70 percent of their total business.[6] Personal consumer loan departments in city banks opened for the first time, and between 1913 and 1929, the number of regulated small-loan offices increased from 600 to 3,500, with loan balances up sixfold, due in part to the reinvestment of profits and in part to house-to-house sale of securities. In 1928 Household Finance Corporation, a large chain, floated preferred stock on Wall Street with the aid of investment bankers. "Thereafter," as one analyst wrote, "investment markets were opened to small loan company securities and bank credit became available on more liberal terms."[7]

Expanded credit completed the shift from "class-based" to "mass-based" buying under way before the war. Many middle-class people in 1915 still disdained installment buying; by 1925 their reservations were fast withering. Consumers of all classes bought automobiles "on time"—and then, with the ice broken, washing machines, refrigerators, and dishwashers.[8] After 1920 a new banking system for consumers, similar to the one functioning in the world of production, fed the growth of consumer credit. "Just as credit and its availability [underlay] the entire *productive* machinery of the nation," an observer wrote of the new "structure of banking for the masses," "so it is now being recognized" that "credit sustains the whole system of distribution" as well.[9]

Dangers lurked behind the walls of these banking and quasi-banking institutions. In the past, consumers who wanted easy credit had to rely on loan sharks and pawnbrokers, who often gouged their customers but could be bargained with face-to-face. Now these sources of cash were being displaced to some extent by more impersonal finance companies and banks, who joined the creditmen's associations and retail store detectives in shadowing, monitoring, and disciplining consumer behavior. Consumers had much to dread from the credit agencies and merchants, which, on the one hand, encouraged impulsive spending and heavy reliance on credit, even in the face of growing inequities in income, and, on the other hand, extracted payments, imposed liens on wages, and took laggards to court.

So, too, the businesses had much to fear from consumers. As credit policies were liberalized, the rate of customer default on payments and the pile of returned goods grew. Customers carried a huge volume of merchandise back to the stores, irritating and sometimes infuriating merchants. Never had consumers shown such disregard for goods or more contempt for contractual obligations to merchants. In Boston, Chicago, and New

York, 15 percent of gross sales, amounting to hundreds of millions of dollars, were returned.[10] Most consumers delayed a day to one week to return merchandise; others took weeks and sometimes months. A study of nine Boston stores showed that customers often brought back luxurious coats months after purchase. They returned nightgowns they had worn for weeks. And one woman, with a taste for expensive dinnerware, returned first one dinner set and then another and another, complaining that the patterns were all wrong.[11] Business schools conducted studies to get at the root causes for the "returned-goods evil." City trade groups organized similar studies. Even the federal government was drawn into the inquiry, carrying out citywide investigations of "major causes for return of goods."[12]

What these studies discovered was that credit customers returning large quantities of ready-made clothing and furniture said generally that the goods did not fit or contained "imperfections" or were the "wrong color" or aroused "family objections." Many merchants narrowed the list of goods that could be returned. Some lashed out at consumers as immoral and "unreasonable," but couldn't think of how to stem the tide. The matter is "of deep concern," said one manager before the National Retail Dry Goods Association in 1929, "for it represents a complete indifference on the part of the buying public to their responsibility in being fair to those from whom they buy. It represents a recklessness as to the results of such unfairness."[13] The fiercest assault came from the least likely of places—from the management of John Wanamaker's, the store that began the practice in the first place. In 1931, Grover Whalen, then general manager of the New York store, told a convention of the Controllers' Congress of the National Retail Dry Goods Association that "returning goods" was a "malignant practice." It was "chronic and steadily increasing" and had developed into "a grave combination of serious economic waste and burdensome expense. Considering the psychology of the customer, the return of merchandise is a negative transaction. In attempting to capitalize on such liberality, the purchaser becomes a liability to the store."[14]

Some placed the blame squarely on banks and merchants. "The amounts returned," observed the Bureau of Business Research of Ohio State University in a 1928 study of Ohio department stores, "follow closely the liberality of the selling plan. Although charge sales constitute but little over half of total sales, charge returns were found to constitute four-fifths of the value of the total returns."[15] Another academic expert, asked by the U.S. Commerce Department in 1929 about the feasibility of convening a "national conference on returned goods," responded with blunt skepticism: "I believe that a national conference on the returned goods problem would be fruitless. As you know, the abuse of the return privilege can be traced directly to the doors of the merchants. It has been encouraged by them, and now it is getting out of control."[16]

Both groups—the merchants and the consumers—had become victims of the new world of mass-produced consumer goods (and of the new ethics related to it). On the one hand, merchants fostered constant turnover, desire for more and more, and the purchase of goods that ordinary people had done little or nothing to create (and thus had little reason to be loyal to). Many customers responded in kind, immune to attacks that they owed something to merchants. The older entrepreneurial economy, formed around a shared sense of contractual obligation and of common moral premises, was on the defensive. On the offensive was the lively economy of desire, with its support of the cult of the new and its indifference to past loyalties.

Air-Conditioned Murals and "One White Fur"

The managed world of consumer enticement also gave birth to innovations in the layout and activities of department stores, restaurants, hotels, and theaters. Ellsworth Statler introduced jazz orchestras in his hotel ballrooms and radio receivers in every room by mid-decade, transmitting the "best programs" on two radio frequencies "from 10 A.M. to 12 midnight each day."[17] In 1927 the Paramount Theater opened on Broadway, with seating for four thousand people and with a nursery, broadcasting station, a fully furnished toyland, tearooms, restrooms, a reserved-seat section served by private elevators, and a promenade surrounding the upper part of the interior of the theater.[18]

One of the newest amenities was air conditioning, the summer analogue to central heating, which had helped to banish nasty drafts from hotel lobbies and to make shopping more comfortable in cold weather. Air conditioning had come into vogue first in the commercial field, preceding by many years its residential use. (As late as 1937, the "market for air conditioning" was still "by a wide margin in the commercial field").[19] Movie

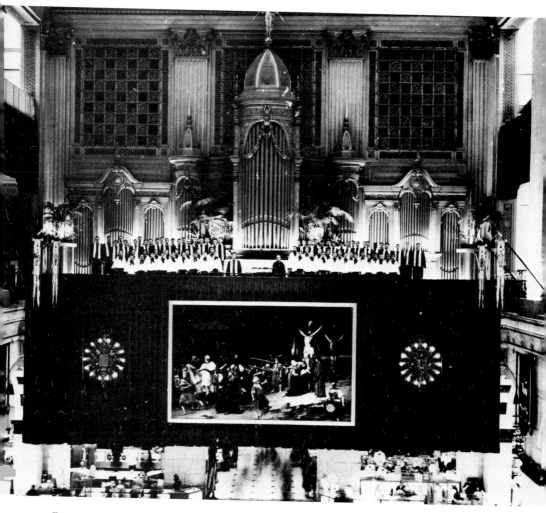

PLATE 18 Sometime in the mid-1920s Rodman Wanamaker, ignoring his father's wishes, allowed the Munkacsy mural, "Christ on Calvalry," to be exhibited at Eastertime in the rotunda of the Philadelphia store. In such a setting one might shop without guilt. This photo was taken in the late 1930s. (*Courtesy of The Historical Society of Pennsylvania*)

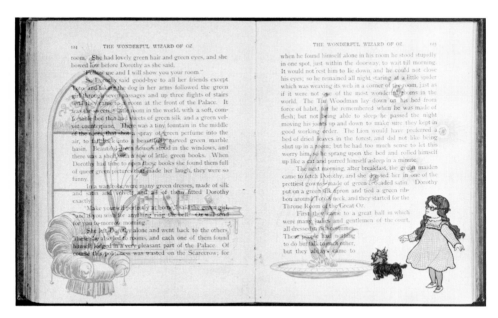

PLATE 19 William Denslow, a dashing cartoonist with a walrus moustache, designed the images that bedecked L. Frank Baum's *The Wonderful Wizard of Oz*. The illustrations are in green, including the glistening emeralds. (*Courtesy of Rare Books and Manuscripts, Butler Library, Columbia University*)

PLATE 20 Arthur Fraser designed this 1922 toy window, not untypical for the big stores and indicative of the enormity of toy departments of the time. (*Courtesy of Marshall Field's*)

PLATE 21 The image on the right is a close-up from the huge mural shown below at the now defunct Ziegfeld Theater, on Sixth Avenue and Fifty-fourth Street in New York, designed by Joseph Urban. Urban wrote that the "scheme of decoration consists of a single mural painting which covers the entire [auditorium of the theater]. The carpets and seats are in tones of gold which continue up the walls to form the base of mural decoration where heroes of old romance form the detail in flowering masses of color interspersed with gold." (*Courtesy of Rare Books and Manuscripts, Butler Library, Columbia University*)

PLATE 22A This mural was one of ten done by Boardman Robinson for Kaufmann Department Store in Pittsburgh. Seven of these murals portrayed commerce at different moments in the history of Western civilization. This mural depicts the Carthaginians in the Mediterranean at the "dawn of the Christian era." (*Courtesy of Nelson Atkins Museum*)

PLATE 22B In another Boardman Robinson mural the English are shown creating the British India Company in China or, as the original catalog indicated, "forming a firm foundation for the future domination of trade." (*Courtesy of Nelson Atkins Museum*)

PLATE 23A-B Windows created by Arthur Fraser at the height of his pictorial style. (*Courtesy of Marshall Field's*)

PLATE 24 The Rainbow House, photographed in 1930, indicates how carefully Stewart Culin lighted his ethnological space. He also separated the display cases along lines set by department stores, to foster relaxed and comfortable viewing. What we cannot see here is the distinguishing feature of the exhibition—the color. (*Courtesy of the Brooklyn Museum*)

PLATE 25 Macy's unveiled its first helium-inflated balloons in 1928 at the Thanksgiving Day Parade. (*Courtesy of the General Research Division, New York Public Library, Astor, Lenox, and Tilden Foundations*)

PLATE 26 The Cliquot Ginger Ale sign in 1924, one of the most famous signs—an O. J. Gude sign, too—ever to appear in Times Square. Note the advertisement for movie theater air conditioning. (*Courtesy of The New York Historical Society*)

PLATE 27 The United States Commerce Building soon after its opening in 1932. (*Courtesy of the United States Department of Commerce*)

theaters had cool air on hot summer days by 1925, hotels and restaurants soon thereafter. "With the coming of summer," wrote one retailing magazine, "the importance of indoor weather should not be minimized."[20] In 1929 Macy's installed the largest air-refrigeration system of any retail store, cooling its first floor and basement store, succeeding in fulfilling the longtime merchant dream of extending the shopping season into the summer months. By the early thirties, stores around the country—from Shillito's in Cincinnati to Miller and Rhoads in Richmond—had picked up this lucrative idea.[21]

New art in interiors and show windows accompanied the air conditioning. So many artists worked for business in the twenties that Herbert Hoover, then U.S. secretary of commerce, could say in 1925 that no "artist in America need live in an attic or in a patron's hall bedroom." "The Midas of advertising has given artists freedom and independence."[22] Sherwood Anderson wrote ad copy for Long-Critchfield, a Chicago agency, and John P. Marquand performed similarly for J. Walter Thompson in New York. F. Scott Fitzgerald thought up "We keep clean in Muscatine" for the Barron Collier Agency in New York.[23] Charles Scheeler did fashion photography for Vogue, and Georgia O'Keeffe reaped a small fortune as a commercial artist, painting, for instance, five pictures in 1927 for the Cheney silk firm, each picture in a different color promoted by Cheney's that season.[24] Her pictures were shown in the windows of Altman's and Field's and "set the keynote for stores throughout the country."[25]

Artists painted numerous commercial murals throughout this era. Newell Convers Wyeth, father of Andrew Wyeth, was already accustomed to commercial commissions and did what his biographer called a "great mural" in 1924 for the Hotel Roosevelt in Manhattan, three panels depicting the *Half Moon*, a Dutch ship, sailing up the Hudson in 1609 against the majesterial Palisades as a background. A year later he decorated the east wall of the Franklin Savings Bank on Forty-second Street with "An Apotheosis of Franklin."[26]

Joseph Urban, already famous, was in great demand, his name synonymous with luxury (he died in 1932).[27] By the midtwenties he was floating "Venuses in soap bubbles" on the Broadway stage, plus "mermaids bathed in blue lights." His interiors were sought after by rich homeowners, hotels, restaurants, and theaters.[28] The mural was at the center of much of his work, an art form he had begun to experiment with before the war. Urban designed a room's entire interior around the mural, which he made as cheerful and fantastic as possible.[29] In 1926 he conceived an immense oil painting with floriated patterns and harlequins, a carnivalesque panorama for the Ziegfeld Theater at Forty-fifth Street and Sixth Avenue in Manhattan. It violated conventional architectural boundaries, reaching beyond the interior walls of the auditorium to cover the ceiling. Urban called it "The Joy of Life." "The Painting has no tale to tell," he said, "no continuous action as its basis. Under a roof of flowers and foliage, among castles and hamlets, music-making, singing, kissing, loving—human beings in mad, happy medley—no deep meaning, no serious thoughts or feelings—only joy, happiness, and a veritable trance of color."[30] (See plate 21.)

Urban's influence may have helped inspire other artists into painting commercial murals. Perhaps the most remarkable were those painted by Boardman Robinson for Kaufmann's department store in Pittsburgh. In 1929 Edgar Kaufmann, a champion of modernism and friend of Martha Graham, commissioned Robinson, an unlikely choice. Robinson had been a socialist for years and a follower of John Reed before the war and had illustrated for the radical papers *The Masses* and *The Liberator*. When Reed died and was buried in Moscow, Robinson wrote a tribute to him for *The Liberator*. Kaufmann obviously admired Robinson's talent, but why Robinson accepted his offer is something of a mystery. Perhaps he needed the money, or admired Kaufmann, or had lost his political convictions. Robinson spent months at the Brooklyn Museum researching his subject, which was—of all things—the evolution of capitalism. His artistic aim was to depart from the "idealized" and "merely decorative" mural painting of the past, to get away from "imaginary" subjects, and to confront the "real world." In a panorama of ten panels, he traced the history of capitalism, from the primitive bartering of the Persians and Arabs before the Christian era to the "welter of structural, industrial, and commercial activities of the present day."[31] The murals, his biographer said, were the "first of any significance to appear in the United States." But according to one critic, their "realism" failed to capture the suffering that had come in the wake of capitalist development.[32] (See plates 22A-B.)

Other artists created new kinds of modernist show windows, exploiting the availability of great amounts of glass. By 1925 consumption of polished plate glass in this country was almost 120 million square feet annually, nearly double the amount consumed ten years before, when Americans were already using half of the world's supply. It must have seemed to outsiders as if Americans were literally eating glass. In the early twenties, glass manufacturers increased output (and devalued skilled labor) by converting their factories from the discontinuous to the continuous production of plate glass, a technological feat that more than accommodated demand.[33] The appetite for glass reflected the quest for an effective, high-density visual environment to encourage consumers to replace old styles rapidly with new ones. As one retailer said of "back to school" promotions of luggage, "the cumulative value of having *thousands of store windows* show trunks and luggage with a 'back to school' theme should be the most logical means of carrying across a message of the need of replacing the old-fashioned trunks and luggage with new and modernized merchandise at values heretofore unknown."[34]

New show window shapes were also in demand—small island windows for jewelry and hats; deep windows for furniture, shallow, curved vestibules for lingerie; and variegated shapes for "zigzag entranceways" designed to exert a "suctionlike effect on the passerby."[35] As windows diversified, so did the mannequins behind them. There were unmeltable papier-mâché and metal mannequins; modernist mannequins in bizarre and fantastic shapes in all sizes; and mannequins with illuminated heads, arms, or legs.[36] Storefronts were constructed with spotlights in the "tops of columns," some operated by automatic dimmers (the front of Bloomingdale's was rebuilt this way in 1925, as was the front of Herpolsheimer department store in Grand Rapids, Michigan, in 1927). In the late twenties, merchants often concealed the lighting altogether to create an "aura" around windows— "aura-frames," as the Austrian émigré designer and architect Frederick Kiesler called them, that could provide "attractive rhythms of light along the whole building front."[37]

The new display men were now moving the "art" of window display toward greater simplicity and sharper targeting of goods. Not all display people followed this trend—not Arthur Fraser of Field's, for instance, whose windows remained "pictorial." Fraser was still at the top of the profession in the 1920s. But no longer dependent on flat scenic backgrounds, he was now making "superwindows"—complex pictorial images, wish windows of goods and three-dimensional backgrounds, as one critic said, forming integrated "color pictures that made wonderful effects that one never tired looking at."[38] Cecily Staples, an admirer of Fraser's, later wrote of his approach: "Display managers [like Fraser] realized that nothing was impossible, that people expected display windows to reflect in some measure their own experiences, their own daydreams, and childhood fantasies."[39] (See plates 23A-B.)

The Fraser style continued to influence display (it still does), but there was also a sharp reaction against it, and by the end of the twenties, a new modernist display aesthetic was in the ascendency, one hostile to Frazer's "window pictorialism" and that emphasized the goods over the artistic impression. This modernism was an aesthetic phenomenon, coming out of both Europe and America and exhorting artists to simplify their materials, zero in on their messages, and cut out filigree. Modernist artists included the French emigrant and admirer of American drugstores Raymond Loewy, whose earliest work in America was as display director at Macy's. In 1919 the Strauses had hired him to improve the Macy display, but his maiden effort disappointed them—it was a single mannequin in a black evening gown with a fur and a few accessories "scattered" about, as he put it, on the floor. "I left the window in semidarkness. The only illumination came from three powerful spotlights focused on the figure. The result was a contrast of violent shadows. It was dramatic, simple, and potent. It sang." The Strauses were unpersuaded, even offended. They "misunderstood me," Loewy recalled, and "before I could be fired, I quit."[40]

In time modernism caught fire, and modernist artists had much success in the late twenties.[41] Frederick Kiesler, employed by Saks Fifth Avenue, was well known for his simplified, "spotlighted" windows. Accent one chair, he urged, "one white fur." "One sees only a chair," he said of one Saks window, "over which a coat and a pair of gloves have been thrown, displayed against a vast background. The background is of a neutral uniform gray, the coat is black velvet with a white fur collar, the gloves are also white, the cushion chair red, the wood of the chair gray."[42] Lee Simonson, leading stage designer in the twenties and consultant to department stores, helped to convert Macy's to the modernist display approach. If we are to control our "immense accumulations of objects," he said in a 1927 article on an exposition of merchandise at Macy's, "we must break up vistas, isolate objects, use every constructional means to focus vision instead of dissipating it."[43]

Norman Bel Geddes, perhaps the most ambitious of the new generation of displaymen, reshaped practically every major commercial visual activity in America, not store windows alone. Bel Geddes hated the Fraser style because it failed to direct one's full gaze to the goods.

Bel Geddes had grown up in poverty in Adrian, Michigan, after the death of his father, a successful farmer and horse-breeder. As a child, he escaped into fantasy by reading dime novels or rereading his favorite fairy tale, *The Wonderful Wizard of Oz*. In the ninth grade, he discovered chalks, marveling at their different colors, and was expelled for drawing a chalk caricature of the principal on the blackboard.[44] As a result of periodic visits to the Chicago morgue, he learned how to sketch human figures. In the 1910s he attended the Chicago Art Institute, then began to illustrate for fashion magazines, painted posters, wrote a play called *An Arabian Night*, and worked for a time as a theatrical stage designer. Light was his specialty. In 1914, Bel Geddes (according to him) devised a "new way to light the stage" by directing light from lamps attached to the auditorium balcony. Two years later, he and architect Frank Lloyd Wright designed what quickly became standard theatrical lighting—a system of high-intensity lights that could produce any color, with the degree of lighting controlled by a dimmer mechanism and pointed at any location on the stage.[45]

Between 1926 and 1927, or shortly before he settled down into his most famous activity (industrial design), Bel Geddes left the stage to become display manager for Franklin Simon department store on Fifth Avenue. Simon knew, Bel Geddes said, that "we were exploring regions of the window which were all unknown."[46] Bel Geddes himself dismissed anything that obstructed the presentation of the goods in store windows. One of his 1928 windows for Franklin Simon contained only three articles: one scarf on an aluminum bust, a second scarf of vermilion and chartreuse green, and a handbag in matching colors on a circular glass platform supported by a bust. Large "triangular shapes" formed a muted background, directing all eyes at the goods themselves; hidden spotlights cast shadows against the background. "It was simple and unexpected," Bel Geddes wrote, describing the impact of his handiwork. "Shoppers looked and stopped. Observers from the other side of the avenue crossed over, only to discover that the center of attraction was an almost empty window."[47]

The theater was Bel Geddes's model: "The store window is a stage on which the merchandise is presented as the actors."[48] He embraced the picture but loathed what he called the "showcasey" windows of "half-baked artists." He rid the windows at Franklin Simon of anything "stationary"— the stationary backs, the stationary lighting—and of all visual clutter. His key word was *flexibility*: interchangeable and variable backs of glass, wood, metal, and textiles that could be moved in any direction; a palette of colors (he used thirty-seven tints and shades) that could be "strategically" put near the goods to rivet the gaze; and an "attention-compelling spotlight." He sought to "kindle an emotional excitement in viewers" or, as Baum would have said, to arouse a "cupidity and longing to possess the goods."[49]

European merchants visiting the United States in the twenties were impressed with such stripped-down selling. They liked Fraser's "fantasy" displays, too, but Bel Geddes and his imitators were "uniquely American." As one German displayman said after touring Fifth Avenue department stores, Americans had learned "how to transform goods into roses"; they knew how "to allure the imagination" and how "to stir up insatiable appetites." He had a low opinion of his own "selling windows" in Germany (as other observers recorded, German and French retailers still "barricaded" their storefronts with "bargain goods"), but he heaped praise on the Americans: "The leaven of artistic selection, arrangement, and decoration permeates the entire system of American department stores." "The motto of the American window dresser is rapidly coming to be 'I'll make it beautiful if it kills me.' "[50]

In 1926, on a journey through several American cities, the Dutch historian Johan Huizinga came away with a very different sense of American show windows, modernist or nonmodernist. "Extravagant waste" seemed to him to mark American merchandising. "Anyone who walks home at night along Fifth Avenue past the store windows illuminated at the late hour," he wrote, "would grow elegiac over all the light that burns without giving joy to anyone, all the words which are never read, all the shoes which will never be worn, all the silk which will never cover a shoulder, all the flowers which wither away behind show windows."[51]

"Brokers in Beauty"

Managers of fashion and style also began to populate the field of merchandising, and by 1930, hardly an item was left untouched by them. "There is not a commodity today," wrote one fashion merchandiser, "that escapes fashion; there is fashion in furniture, cars, washing machines, tires, and so forth." "Fashion makes things live and people buy!" The design or style factor that had affected the making of expensive jewelry, hats and dresses, inexpensive china and glassware was transforming other machine-made goods. Style features such as color, line, and shape (or what was broadly called "the look") rose to a central place in the manufacture of a vast range of merchandise.[52]

Brokering agencies and consulting firms mushroomed to supply merchants with "fashion resources" and "counsel" and to showcase the idea of fashion and style. John Powers founded what was apparently the first successful model agency in 1923, at Fifty-second Street and Seventh Avenue in Manhattan. He had wanted to be an actor and even toured for a few years with a Shakespearean company. Then, one day, he spotted a newspaper ad by a commercial photographer for models. "Why not set up an agency," Powers told his wife, "there must be lots of commercial photographers looking for models." He saw real promise in this business, not only because of a rising demand for models but also because of the many improvements in fashion photography. "When I started the first model agency," he wrote, "the camera was just beginning to come into use in advertising. Believing that an attractive picture could be more effective in selling than the written word, I hammered away at the idea."[53]

Ever since the early 1900s, merchants could recruit fashion models from the theater and the circus, from factories, and even from among their own employees. The models in Wanamaker's 1912 Garden of Allah show, for instance, were probably taken from the store's own employees or may have been obtained through ads in the theatrical trade press. Powers now helped to convert modeling into a "profession" and a lucrative one at that. In 1923, the average model made about $35 weekly; by 1930, a Powers model drew $100 weekly, and exceptional models often commanded that sum or more for a single show or photographic session.[54] Powers treated models "as commodities which must meet certain requirements," he said. A "broker in beauty," as he called himself, he supplied big retailers, wholesale showrooms, and commercial photographers with a regular reserve of women who "sold practically everything" and who appeared in what seemed to be a non-stop stream of fashion "parades" and fashion shows. His models—and he boasted more than four hundred active models in high demand "on my list" by 1930—were adept at stimulating desire. The skills of Betty Maar, for instance, raised the profits of a New York furrier because, according to one professional photographer, she knew "how to droop her lids just to the right hundredth of an inch" and how "to let her hand play" lovingly over the fur coats she wore. By placing her "right thumb just so on a wrap," she "simply told observing eyes that she cherished" it, that "she tugged at its luxury and would not part with it."[55]

With help from the new field of fashion photography, Powers created a standardized conception of female beauty that may have greatly exceeded, in psychological tyranny over women, the stilted one-dimensional standards of nineteenth-century fashion drawing. He also freed (or he tried to free) modeling from its unsavory associations with loose, off-color theatrical living; in a slight-of-hand maneuver so typical of a broker's methods, he tried to make modeling acceptable to women (and to men) by connecting it with "naturalness" and the "all-American way." His "girls," he said, came from the best homes and the best finishing schools; none walked in the "mincing artificial manner" of the ordinary actress-model; and none wore "excessive makeup." His "girls" were "typical American girls, pretty, healthy, vivacious, and self-reliant."[56]

Other fashion agencies and consulting businesses offered "indispensable" services to merchants around the country seeking fast turnover and high profits. One group, The Standard Corporation of New York, kept merchants posted on style trends, recommended potential market winners, and financed in 1924 a fashion magazine, *Modes and Manners*, for eight major department stores, in Toledo, Cincinnati, Boston, St. Louis, Pittsburgh, San Francisco, Philadelphia, and Los Angeles (only the advertising varied from store to store). Like its principal rivals (Marshall Field's *Fashions of the Hour* and Bamberger's *Charm*, which appeared, respectively, in 1914 and 1924, as well as the independent *House and Garden*), the sleek and glossy *Modes and Manners* served the suburban market and dealt largely with fashion—"fashion, that is, not alone in dress but also in furniture, furnishings, sport, etc."[57] Its many photographs and drawings—as those of its competitors—aimed to foster vicarious daydreaming, fantasies of fulfillment and escape through the acquisition of goods. Mixing feminism with luxury (again, in the manner of *Charm* and *Fashions of the Hour*), it printed articles on successful women and on women in politics; at the same time, it tried to lead readers to believe that if they only bought the right bathroom accessories or the most up-to-date dining-room china, they would be carried off to "glamorous worlds" and achieve the social "status" of a Consuelo Vanderbilt or of a Dorothy Parker (not rich, perhaps, but "very smart"), whose lives and "manners" its articles so lovingly described.

"*Modes and Manners*," wrote the editor in chief, Margaret Macy, "is a mirror of the necessary luxuries of life," which "not only reflects authentically what is new and most desirable in the mode, but assures you of the opportunity of securing the things most of you fancy here in this store." An "aristocratic" magazine, it invites "you to be a hostess," not a "housewife." It is a "magic carpet of your mind" that "leads only to amusement." "It's there, the magic, even in one carved chest, a hanging against a plaster wall, or a wrought iron candelabrum. This carpet helps you visualize the activities of the Junior League. But always the magic carpet returns to *you*—*your* clothes, *your* surroundings, *your* amusements."[58]

Other influential consulting firms in the twenties were Amos Parrish, Inc., and Tobe Collier Davis's "fashion advisory service." Parrish, "one of the big promotion guys of the twenties," as fashion designer Elizabeth Hawes put it, helped build a selling machine equal, he thought, to the demands of commodity markets. He published a popular journal, *Amos Parrish Magazine,* and his magazine *Breath of the Avenue* for retailers presented the most "advanced" instruction on "scientific buying." He invited storeowners, merchandising managers, advertising managers, display managers, and buyers—in short, the royalty of merchandising—to attend "Amos Parrish Fashion Clinics," held twice a year because "fashion is on everyone's tongue . . . in everyone's home . . . in everything everyone wants or hopes to own."[59] For a fee, the "students" heard him (or his surrogates) lecture on "how to make everything new through fashion," for without "newness" there is no turnover. "Nothing is going to stop fashion. It wears things out. And industry wants things worn out in order to make more things to build bigger businesses, to pay larger dividends. Things must grow. Fashion is the one thing in the world that will do it. And without fashion it won't be done. But it will be done." Hundreds of representatives from more than one hundred stores countrywide regularly packed into Parrish's own spring and fall classes on the Upper East Side in New York City.[60]

Tobe Collier Davis created in the late twenties a fashion advisory service and, in 1931, the Fashion Group, headquartered at Rockefeller Center, which brought together the most skilled, successful women in fashion merchandising (in the first years, 75 women belonged to it; by 1972, 5,000) to build alliances and to share inside data on fashion trends.[61] Behind Davis stood many women in managerial positions—merchandising managers, restaurant and branch store managers, personnel directors, advertising managers, and shopkeepers.[62] "In the Gimbel organization," Ellis Gimbel said in 1926, in a not unusual statement by this time from a leading merchant, "women not only have equal rights but have equal pay with men, some receiving salaries equal to congressmen and judges."[63]

The first women display directors were doing windows and interiors in the late twenties and early thirties, notably Rose Van Sant at Gimbels in New York and Polly Pettit at Black, Starr, and Frost-Gorham, a fashionable Fifth Avenue jewelry company (she was also the first woman to hold executive positions in New York's Metropolitan Display Men's Club, in 1929).[64] By 1924, 41 percent of the total 17,493 buyers in the United States were women, up 10 percent from 1914. In New York City women buyers now formed a "distinct caste," "the Brahmins of the ready-to-wear store world," hardworking, highly paid women who kept to themselves and, to the degree it was possible, traveled together in the now common buying trips to Europe and the Far East. They also provoked constant ridicule from both men and women unaccustomed to such independence and power in women. "She laughs too much," wrote one woman critic of the "perfumed movie queen buyer." "She argues too readily. She is used to getting her way. She is Success. What of it if, around Christmastime, she gets a little lonesome at the prospect of an expensive Christmas dinner at the best hotel with another lady buyer?"[65]

Tobe Collier Davis knew this prejudice firsthand but must have taken it in her stride. Backed by her real estate broker husband, Herbert Davis, and by a retailing father who urged her forward, she helped transform a relatively devalued area of work (relative to male-dominated banking and industrial production, that is) into a lucrative field for women. In New York City her advisory service delivered daily news on fashion trends and on how to make profitable use of them; it was the most sought-after service of its kind in the business. "The heads of Federated, as well as Macy's and Gimbels—all of them counted on her advice and business know-how. . . . She made big money for them, and for herself," remembered Julia Coburn, who in 1938 helped Davis found the Tobe-Coburn School of Fashion, which still exists.[66]

In 1927 Davis also became what was said to be the first professional "fashion stylist," focusing on the surface, shape, design—and, above all, the color—of machine-made goods.[67] Merchants and manufacturers had long depended on commodity styling and design to enhance the visual appeal of goods; but as banker Paul Mazur wrote in the year Davis became a stylist, "whereas ten years ago style was the label only of women's clothes, today, everything from automobiles to washing machines reeks of instability in style."[68]

There were other specialists in color as well, including Margaret Hayden Rorke, a prewar suffragist who, in 1918–19, became the first managing director of the Textile Color Card Association of America, which declared independence from French color standards. In time, hundreds of fabric manufacturers and retailers joined the association "to educate the public to a color sense" and to standardize in America and Europe the names of colors announced each fall and spring season "expected to be fashionable." The organization worked to ensure that everyone operated in the same world of color. "I address you as magicians," said museum curator Stewart Culin in a speech before this association in 1925, for "you have taken charge of the color consciousness of the American people. Whether or not you so intended you have assumed a grave responsibility, a place involving serious duties, an office once filled by a board of high officials in an Imperial Court." What you do, Culin told them, has a "decisive influence on man's happiness and determines the value of most of the material things he prizes."[69]

In Style with Dorothy Shaver

Margaret Rorke and other color specialists worked arm in arm with the stylists whose job it was to alter the appearance of goods so that people would be persuaded to buy them. Together they participated in the style expositions of the 1920s, held not in museums but in department stores, now the major vehicles for the transmission of the new style ideas. Begun at Field's in 1922 and cresting at the end of the decade with shows at Macy's (there were many later shows as well), these style expositions introduced the shopping public to a great variety of "everyday" machine-made goods "transformed" by changes in color, line, and design.[70] The first Macy's Exposition, held for a week in May 1927, typically showed the impact of modernism on American-designed lamps, rugs, glass, pottery, and furniture. It was a collaborative event, pooling the resources of Macy's and the Metropolitan Museum of Art.[71] Richard Bach, industrial arts associate at the Metropolitan, was constantly on hand giving advice, so much so that *The New Yorker* joked that "Mr. Bach has taken his soul down to Macy's."

"The cooperation of Macy's and the Metropolitan Museum of Art was arresting," it observed, "demonstrating that the Lorenzo de Medici attitude is now adopted as a commercial asset by manufacturers and retailers, and is no longer the privileged function of a single individual."[72]

European diplomats, international artists, U.S. government officials, and museum people attended the opening of the 1928 exposition, with its 16 show windows, 18 modernistic showcases, and 15 exhibition rooms. Three hundred exhibits were presented, and, according to Macy's, close to 250,000 people visited during the two-week exposition.[73] Numerous modernist objects were displayed, designed by such established artists as the Austrian Josef Hoffman; the German Bruno Paul; and Kem Weber, an American from Los Angeles.[74]

The 1928 show inspired imitators nationwide, from Jordan Marsh in Boston to Bullock's in Los Angeles, to say nothing of all the leading New York City stores.[75] The big urban museums got into the act as well, and Richard Bach toured the country in the late 1920s, consulting with big-city retailers and manufacturing firms on style and design. "It has been my desire," he wrote in 1927 in one of his reports to the secretary of the Metropolitan Museum, "to spread our influence."[76] Bach greatly enlarged the display arena for styled goods in the museum itself. By 1929 a total of 160 firms were exhibiting in the museum's industrial arts show (up from the 26 firms of 1917), with more than 1,600 objects (also up from the 73 pieces of 1917). Public attendance, too, rose impressively—in 1920, a total of 7,943 people visited the museum show, and more than 185,000 people visited in 1929. "Manufacturers, merchants, and the Museum of Art," Bach boasted, "together seem to form a new magic circle of industry, a continuous and certain means of bringing art into the furnishings and clothing and other homely factors of daily life."[77]

Many other reputations were made on the basis of the production of such shows, and among the most lasting was Dorothy Shaver's, the first woman ever appointed, on the grounds of ability alone, to head a major department store (Lord & Taylor). Her impact on the evolution of urban merchandising was "simply enormous," as an admiring contemporary recently remarked.[78]

Shaver, born in 1897, grew up comfortably in Mena, Arkansas, in a large plantation mansion. Her father was a judge and both her grandfathers were local "legends": One was an ex-Confederate general; the other, the last man alleged to have fought a legal duel in Arkansas. In the early 1920s,

Shaver went to Chicago to study at the University of Chicago and lived there with her sister, Elsie, a dollmaker and artist who specialized in painting children with big, black, sorrowful eyes. In 1923 the sisters moved to New York, where they set up a little retail store at 3 West 47th Street in Manhattan. There they sold the "Little Shaver" dolls Elsie had invented. The Lord & Taylor management spotted this store and, after seeing Dorothy Shaver at work, hired her as a comparison shopper. Luckily for her, Samuel Reyburn, a fellow Arkansas native and president of Associated Dry Goods (owner of Lord & Taylor), believed that women—single, married, with children—could do in merchandising whatever men did. "To the objection urged," he wrote in 1924 of working mothers, "that children will not get proper attention, I answer that a mother with a well-organized business mind may give them even better attention."[79]

A year after she was hired, Shaver established an interior decorating service, the Bureau of Fashion and Decoration at Lord & Taylor, and soon became a member of the board of directors of Associated Dry Goods Corporation, and, in 1931, the store's vice president of advertising and promotion. In 1946 she was appointed president of Lord & Taylor, a post she held until her death in 1962.[80] "You blazed the trail for us," Mildred Custin, later president of Bonwit Teller's, wrote Shaver in 1958. Shaver was convinced that women (and she obviously meant white, educated women) could go far in merchandising—as far as they wanted to go, in fact. "There is only one thing that keeps women from going ahead in department stores," she said in a 1931 interview, "and that's themselves. The opportunities are vast. . . . There is no reason why women can't take a major part in organization and control."[81]

Throughout the 1920s, Shaver belonged to what she called "an army of people who were delicately attuned to new trends and to how to 'put them over.' " Through her Bureau of Fashion and Decoration she executed the "first room in the modernistic style" at Lord & Taylor (in 1925) and labored to "get the glamor and excitement of New York life into clothes—the color which is the American scene," as well as style. In 1928, after visiting Paris, she organized a show of French modernist decorative art at Lord & Taylor, the first of its kind in the United States. It was intended not only to sell the pieces but also to inspire a "closer alignment," as she put it, "of the artists and manufacturer in the production of beautiful objects for general consumption." She organized it as if it were an opening of a new play or movie. The lighting of the objects—appearing from invisible sources or glowing through flat slabs of opaque glass—especially struck visitors. "It is certainly a stunning exposition," wrote Stanley McCandless, assistant professor of lighting in the theater department at Yale University, to Shaver, and "I was particularly impressed by the lighting of the large room, because it caught the idea that it is light distribution and not the fixture that's important."[82] The exposition was an immense public success for Shaver. As one awed critic said, "this show—full of Picassos, Braques, and Utrillos—was presented with a flourish of a Theater Guild premiere— red carpets on the sidewalk, blazing floodlights, and Miss Shaver floating about in a white evening dress—it was a sensation."[83]

Shaver sold images, impressions, and surfaces; she was master of a marketing language of pseudosophistication that now pervades American public culture. In the early 1930s Shaver proselytized for what she called "the American Look." She knew how to transmute a serious respect for the past or a loyalty to a tradition into a "fashion trend." Her own radio advertising in 1937 pushed the latest styles:

> Last spring we were casual, given to poses and worries, restless, unhappy—and our clothes accurately reflected our state of mind. This spring we are more natural, more poised, more correct, more serene, happier. We treat with more sentiment the simple and real things of life. We are more romantic about our personal relation- ships—more interested in family life. Without being fully aware of it we are swinging back into the more formal gracious manners of the prewar period.

Shaver's angle was the one that French writer Albert Camus described in *The Rebel*, in which "nothing was any longer good or bad, but only either premature or out of date."[84]

A store was not a store to Shaver, nor a dress a dress, a table a table. "Sell them their dreams" could have been her motto. "Really, you are a wonder," one of her friends wrote her in 1928, soon after the Lord & Taylor French decorative art show opened, "and it's a good thing Mr. Barnum died some time ago. How his publicity ability would have paled before yours. And I mean that in all seriousness. Underneath the obvious qualities of personality, ability in merchandising, good taste, etc., is your dramatic instinct. Just because you happen to exercise yours in more cultural spheres doesn't separate you and Mr. Barnum a great deal. . . . But unlike the old days, I believe you have educated them all in this business of 'retail drama' to such an extent, that they don't begin counting pennies the first few months. And, that is why you're such a great publicity person. You work it inside as well as outside your organization. My hat's off to you."[85]

Accessorizing on the Grand Scale

Another pictorial or visual method of grabbing attention was the ensembling of merchandise or "making pictures" with goods. Ensembling, as noted earlier, was part of merchandising well before 1920; but again, in this decade, it took fresh managed forms. There was "color coordination" in store departments and hotel suites, and merchants taught their staffs how to color-coordinate goods. Experts such as Hazel Adler traveled about the country, from store to store, telling women how "great is the need for color expression. A few years ago, [women] were confined in their color, now they can, with a little advice, match their hair, their complexions, and their clothes in one color ensemble." Filene's salespeople in Boston, using a "colorscope" evolved from a Munsell color atlas, offered customers "color readings" so they might "match" their "complexions" with the clothing on sale. As a service to retailers, the National Retail Dry Goods Association created a special color-coordination committee in 1930.[86]

The accessorizing of goods became standard practice in nearly all department stores and similar institutions. "To better serve our patrons," Washington's Woodward and Lothrop announced in 1921 in a full-page ad, "we have systematically arranged kindred merchandise into groups to facilitate convenient and satisfactory shopping." "Unit formations and the use of related lines as accessories" as merchandising practice "have come to stay," another retailer said a few years later.[87] "I had the idea to bunch associated articles," boasted Clara Wilson of Marshall Field's of her work in the late twenties. She claimed also to have "introduced match colors so a customer could have an ensemble of color." Against the wishes of Field's imperious Arthur Fraser she distributed the first spotlighted mannequins around Field's fashion departments. As she said, spotlighting made it possible to create really "dramatic" ensembled goods.[88]

Display people and stylists "accessorized" nearly everything (not only clothing) into little "unit formations," at the core of which was a primary commodity accompanied by secondary or related goods. "See what tie-ups can be made with shoes," suggested a Gimbels buyer in Manhattan. "And why not an inexpensive evening bag with every evening dress, if you have an assortment on hand. Gimbels highlights a different bag every few days by calling it 'The Bag of the Hour.' " The point here was to promote impulsive ensemble buying. As one retailer put it in 1923: "When accessories are displayed with the apparel with which they are intended to be used they take on and present to the customers an entirely different meaning—an appeal."[89]

Merchants accessorized departments as well as goods, "consistently grouping allied merchandise throughout the store." Thus children might shop with their parents in the toy department, then move directly into an adjacent children's shoe department, or women might visit the handbag and hosiery departments, which adjoined the women's shoe section, "so that matching these items with a purchase of shoes is at once convenient and tempting."[90] Now, the model room—that most pretentious of accessorized spaces—could be found in nearly every major store, a pattern reflected and driven by the opening of the American Wing of the Metropolitan Museum of Art in 1924, with its sixteen period rooms to display American antiques in authentic colonial settings. These rooms, themselves inspired by commercial prototypes, in turn ignited copying by merchants."[91] As part of its "new display policies," Macy's executive council decided to "show furniture and home furnishings in the atmosphere in which they should be used in the properly appointed home." And Bamberger's actually built two free-standing homes—one the "Nottingham House," the other the "Ideal Home"—both with a complete suite in the basement "ready for entertaining." They attracted thousands of visitors from around New Jersey.[92]

The first modernist model rooms appeared in the twenties, most spectacularly in the major department stores. Here Americans saw chromium-plated kitchens and sunken glass-lined living rooms; carpeted dens and playrooms; and, most seductive of all, mirrored boudoirs and bedrooms. At the 1928 Macy's style exposition, two rooms by the American designer Kem Weber were hits—especially his bathroom with its recessed jade green bathtub, its shower room in the wall with a glass door, and its dressing table flanked by glass shelves. At the same exposition, the "all-glass" boudoir "for the modern woman" by Austrian Josef Hoffman aroused so much interest as virtually to disrupt the store. The room was covered with mirrors on the floor, walls, and ceilings, and so situated as to allow a visitor to see herself or himself in ten separate images. The only accessories were a table and a brass stool to reflect the light concealed in the room. "Yesterday afternoon," *The New York Times* reported, "the crowds in front of this room had to be held back."[93]

Merchants enlisted experts to implement the promotional tie-ups to transmit a single merchandising message, tie-ups that in the days of the *Garden of Allah* had been achieved more informally. After assembling its first interior decorating staff in 1924, Macy's hired a "manager of interior display" in 1927 "to coordinate the interior display of the store with our store windows and store advertising and with general store style and sales efforts." The object was to activate at one time as many of the components of the store's "publicity structure" as possible. Specialists from outside the store were called in to make certain that strategies reinforced one another. "Coincident with each issue of *Modes and Manners*," wrote the managers of Standard Corporation, which owned the magazine, "there will be close connections with the advertising, window dressing, and store display department of each store."[94]

The Pseudoevents of Edward L. Bernays

The most impressive of all promotions, however, took place *across institutions*, tying department stores, theaters, hotels, and other consumer institutions into one collaborative ensemble. Here again, merchants turned to managers for help. Among the most skilled at such promotions was Edward L. Bernays, perhaps the most important public relations man of the 1920s. Farseeing in his methods, he, like the Wizard of Oz, spent his life behind the scenes, working pulleys and levers that manipulated other people. Bernays was (he still was in 1992, at age 102) a shrewd promoter who knew how to transform the profane into an imitation of the sacred, to give goods and corporations new meaning and what he called "truth."

Bernays was the son of Jewish immigrants from Vienna and a nephew of Sigmund Freud. His career began in the theater when, in 1913, at age 23, he was employed as press agent for Klaw and Erlanger, a theatrical syndicate on Broadway that monopolized bookings and "encouraged the production of only surefire attractions," as Bernays put it. He redesigned the job in a new way, shifting it from mere "space grabbing" in the newspapers to producing "public events" to excite interest. "My role," he remembered in his 1962 autobiography, "was not to 'chisel' space in the newspapers" but "to compete with other news, to make my plays or actors so newsworthy that papers would give them attention in their columns."[95]

The job at Klaw and Erlanger lasted only a year but made a big impact on Bernays "entirely out of proportion to its duration." He loved Broadway. "I hobnobbed with actors and actresses whose names shone on marquees," he later said. "I went backstage whenever I wanted to, had free run of most theaters to catch a glimpse of an act. . . . Life was one thrill after another."[96] Later he was publicity man for traveling artists and shows, and helped almost single-handedly—according to him—to assemble a multiclass audience for classical music and opera in this country.[97]

As early as 1917, Bernays had learned well how to tie things together and to make imaginative connections. He worked for the U.S. Committee on Public Information under George Creel during World War I, later noting that the committee "excelled" in developing collaborative strategies and "opened the eyes of the intelligent few in all departments of life to the possibilities of regimenting the public mind." It was during the war that the full "value of associative processes" in forming taste and determining choice dawned on Bernays.[98]

After the war Bernays got a firm professional foothold near the heart of Times Square, at 19 East Forty-eighth Street—the "center of the universe," as he later put it. Like such prewar reformers as Florence Kelley, Bernays perceived a new void opening between consumers and producers although, unlike Kelley, he viewed the void as an opportunity for managed selling, not as something to regret and redress. Something, he thought, had to be done to explain to consumers why they should buy the new manufactured goods. Trained "intermediaries" like himself had to intervene to interpret reality for the public. They had to provide "truthful" information and to connect the various "publics" back together again into a "cohesive" whole. In Bernays, the push, push promotional zeal of Elbert Hubbard flowered into a carefully contrived system of manipulation.[99]

Bernays conceived public relations as a nonjudgmental technique similar to psychoanalysis, to be applied to any institution, person, or commodity that needed its "image" (ego) refurbished in the public arena. He began by studying his client, although, like many psychoanalysts, he refused to "treat" pathologically "antisocial" groups or people. Next he observed the "mental equipment" of his patron's targeted public, hoping to find their "stereotypes" that might be "tapped" and exploited. Then he interpreted the client's product, devising "associations" between the product and ideas, and drawing on his knowledge of the "stereotypes." Finally he "crystallized" these associations for the public through a coordinated mobilization of largely visual media.[100]

In the spring of 1924 Bernays mounted a "saturation campaign" for "transparent velvet" to "titillate the spending emotions of 3½ million women, all potential consumers." The commodity seemed alluring enough, but Bernays thought it was not being pushed with sufficient conviction by its manufacturer, Sidney Blumenthal. So Bernays persuaded Blumenthal to "change his approach to the public." Researching the market, he discovered that many women carried a "stereotype" of "style and beauty" around in their "heads," and he set out to establish connections between the stereotype and the product. He "tied up" velvet with the "sex and glamor" and the "sophistication" of New York and Paris. He brought several media together to project a coordinated cluster of images. He dispatched letters to theatrical agents and movie producers, offering dresses of transparent velvet to female stars, who took them and, at Bernays' invitation, wore them in public and onstage and on screen. At the same time, he arranged for photographs of velvet gowns to be published in fashion magazines and in the rotogravure sections of newspapers. Bernays and Blumenthal "worked out a deal" with several chains of movie theaters "in twenty-four key cities" to present "a tabloid musical comedy" as an "adjunct to movie bills," and in this advertising "short" all the female performers were dressed, of course, in transparent velvet.[101]

Bernays sought simplicity, reducing "public relations" to "continuous interpretation and dramatization by high-spotting," terms he picked up from the Broadway stage. "Continuous interpretation," he explained, "is achieved by trying to control every approach to the public mind in such a manner that the public receives the desired impression, often without being conscious of it. High-spotting, on the other hand, vividly seizes the attention of the public and fixes it upon some detail or aspect that is typical of the entire enterprise." He was the first noted architect of what Daniel Boorstin has called "pseudoevents." A finagler of the truth, Bernays staged happenings carrying packaged information for immediate public consumption. His events relied for effectiveness on the marshaling of many different kinds of institutions and media, from department stores to movie theaters, and had the effect of overshadowing the more significant and "real" events of the times. His business belonged to that new array of institutions and groups— the professional consultancies and agencies—that sold dreams and worked behind the scenes to support the agenda of America's now flourishing consumer society. [102]

Chapter 11

THE SPECTACLES

In a short story, "Absolution," written in 1924, F. Scott Fitzgerald described an encounter between a lonely eleven-year-old boy, Rudolph Miller, and a tormented, half-mad Catholic priest, Reverend Adolphus Schwartz. The setting is a Dakota town in the hot, dry summer. Rudolph has committed several sins, most of them small, but one big—stark rebellion against his father. To get absolution, he confesses his sins to Father Schwartz on three separate occasions. In their final meeting, the priest acts very strangely, even crazily; he has, in fact, lost his faith and longs for a new life. Indifferent to Rudolph's sins, he blurts out that "When a lot of people get together in the best places things go glimmering." The boy is confused, but the priest only repeats himself: "The thing is to have a lot of people in the center of the world, wherever that happens to be. Then things go glimmering." "Why, they have lights now as big as stars—do you realize that? I heard of one light they had in Paris or somewhere that was as big as a star. A lot of people had it—a lot of gay people. They have all sorts of things now that you never dreamed of." Rudolph is frightened, although the priest's behavior is also a revelation, awakening in him the same desire for something beyond the town and beyond his religion. Rudolph "sat there, half terrified, his beautiful eyes open wide and staring at Father Schwartz. But underneath his terror he felt that his own inner convictions were confirmed. There was something ineffably gorgeous somewhere that had nothing to with God."[1]

Much glimmered in the twenties. Fashion spectacles glimmered in such cities as Philadelphia and Chicago. There were color and light spectacles, too, and big spectacle parades for adults and children, including extensive pre-Christmas parades. America's mecca of color and light, Times Square, emerged as the nation's most famous glimmering district. And behind these spectacles, as rationally managed in their way as the contemporary promotional strategies, was what Fitzgerald said, in *The Great Gatsby*, could be heard in the voice of beautiful Daisy Buchanan: "Her voice was full of money."[2]

The Rainbow House and the Palace of Fashion

In 1925, curator Stewart Culin took the unusual step of bringing the dream life of capitalism into the Brooklyn Museum; he created a new gallery called the "Rainbow House," in the heart of the museum's new wing. The Rainbow House evoked the fairy-tale world of L. Frank Baum, and Culin himself much resembled Baum. The Rainbow House allocated space for the exhibition of primitive objects and costumes, echoing Culin's version of the Zuni myth of the Creation (Culin's favorite myth, for he had lived in the early 1900s among these pueblo-dwelling Indians of western New Mexico) as a "timeless place" where all good things happen and where summertime "lasts forever." The Zuni, in a yellow setting, stood at the center of Culin's gallery, which he divided (as Baum might have done) into sections painted in vivid colors, each assigned to a people or tribe whose artifacts and costumes were being shown. The African section was a soft green, India was pink, and a deeper red signified the South Sea islands.[3]

Culin tried to give life to his objects: "Once dead and inert, these things have now come to life and blossomed under the glowing color of their immediate surroundings. To bring them to life, to coordinate them with living things, had always been my object, but never before had that object been so nearly achieved." His gallery, wrote a *New York Times* reporter, "marked a radical departure in the manner in which ethnological collections are exhibited. . . . The 'house' is as gay and as brightly decorated as an Easter egg."[4] (See plate 24.)

In 1925, at work on this "house," Culin also acted as art consultant to the "Palace of Fashion" exhibit in Philadelphia, which was part of the impending Sesquicentennial Exposition to commemorate the 150th year of American independence. The first exposition in the country financed largely by business corporations, it had a "gladway," named in honor of Eleanor Porter's Pollyanna; a two-hundred-feet-high "Tower of Light"; and a reproduction of a portion of the Taj Mahal.[5] The "Palace of Fashion," an octagonal structure taller than the other buildings, displayed textiles and wearing apparel donated by well-known merchants and manufacturers. Many groups, from trade school educators and theater people to government officials and ethnologists, banned together to design and construct the large arena.

Oriental themes, now predictable to American merchandising, were visible in the palace and in the exposition itself. The architectual style was "Assyrian and Babylonian," and every floor was color-coordinated. As one promoter gushed,

> Wherever the eye alights, as the enchanted visitor enters, the portals are in color, there is light, there is life. The dominant note is color—the harmonious blending and melting into one another of all the brilliant shades and hues of the rainbow.[6]

Plate-glass windows covered the full frontage of the palace; inside was an amphitheater seating ten thousand spectators, as well as a circular stage for daily fashion shows. Culin's role at the palace was to help "glorify the American ready-wear industry." By the midtwenties he had reached the zenith of his influence to become—as *Women's Wear Daily* claimed— "the ultimate fashion dictator of America, the czar of the fashion designers."[8] He leaped at the chance to work on the fair, partly because, as he wrote a friend, "this was the first exposition at which the industries were themselves responsible for the exhibits and had its outcome in their hands."[9] But it was appealing also because the promoters chose "color" as the main theme of the fair. He pressed for more and more color and even proposed that the name of the "Palace of Fashion" be changed to "Rainbow House." "Palace of Fashion," he argued, was "deadly and predictable," but "Rainbow House" suggested something "living," "summery," and "full of brilliant plumage."

Culin's advice was ignored, although it showed what little difference there was, in his own mind, between the Rainbow House of the Brooklyn

Museum and the ready-made world of the Palace of Fashion.[10] Both were accessorized spaces and both played out some of Culin's favorite themes—his desire to expose Americans to the "vitality" of the "primitive" and the "childlike," and to find refuge from the "deadly grind" in preindustrial dreams and fantasies. Both spaces revealed the cultural power of the commercial world: In the Rainbow House commercial methods were enlisted to exhibit the primitive; in the Palace of Fashion the primitive was exhibited to enhance the appeal of the commercial.

The Commercial Parade

The Rainbow House and the Palace of Fashion belonged to a new pattern of spectacle activity that was spreading throughout the country. Businessmen organized color and light spectacles in various cities to publicize the introduction of street lighting into the retail districts and—a more important point—to invite people to do their shopping at night as well as by day. Such events were managed by groups of merchants in collaboration with city officials and police. At the Chicago State Street Illumination Festival of October 1926 many firms, including the Edison Company, the Commonwealth Edison Company, the Chicago Rapid Transit Lines, the Orpheum Circuit (a theater booking agency), several local theaters and hotels, chain stores such as Walgreen's, Bedell's, Kresge's, and Schulte Optical Company, and, above all, the department stores in the neighborhood combined to celebrate the new General Electric lighting standards on State Street.[11]

Paid for by the merchants, tall lightposts or standards lit up the street with light two and a half times brighter than any other streetlights in the world, according to their principal promoter, Roy Schaeffer, the aggressive advertising manager at Field's who headed the whole operation. The light, Schaeffer said, was not blinding or dazzling, but diffused and soft, a light to "please and invite and as close to artificial daylight as possible." State Street was closed to traffic for three "nights of festivity," the biggest public merchandising "party" ever given in Chicago, Schaeffer said. The merchants radiated the streets and buildings with colored searchlights; they built arches and towers speckled with "crystal jewels"; and they hired jazz bands and gaudily dressed women to participate in a big nighttime parade depicting the history of artificial light. The parade began the minute President Calvin Coolidge in Washington, D.C., flipped a switch to turn on the lights. On the first night the crush was so great police had to stop the parade; and show windows had to be protected from breakage.[12]

Commercial parading on this scale was by no means unusual for this decade. Indeed, such spectacles formed something of a new genre of American parade. The decade itself had begun with spectacle parading—the "welcoming home of troops" from Europe—that had all the earmarks of commercial, consumer-oriented promotions. In New York City in May 1919 the biggest welcome home parade of all was organized by two department store merchants who chaired the official "Committee of Welcome"—Rodman Wanamaker and Grover Whalen, the former, of course, the president of the New York store and the latter soon to be appointed its general manager. Whalen, who was to serve as New York's first "official greeter" from the midtwenties into the 1960s, was well disposed to transform the city into a consumer's dream. Although, as Wanamaker manager, he was to condemn customers for returning goods, he himself was "a vicious spender." "Oh, he spent money like water!" recalled New York City politician George McAnery.[13] Recklessly Whalen and Wanamaker gave the troops free passes to plays, sporting events, movies, and subways, as well as free hotel accommodations and free food and drink at restaurants and nightclubs. On Fifth Avenue they built a giant grandstand flanked on both sides by amber-tinted lights, along with two triumphal arches encrusted with artificial jewels and floodlighted in color, and through which the troops marched. "Never before had there been such splendor in the great city," wrote F. Scott Fitzgerald in his 1919 short story "May Day," a fictional tribute to this homecoming celebration. The city was "transformed into an orgy of luscious feasts" and "vanished entertainments. So gaily and noisily were the peace and prosperity impending . . . that more and more spenders had gathered from the provinces to drink the wine of excitement."[14]

Later in the twenties, as chairman of the permanent committee to welcome guests to New York, Whalen helped organize other spectacular parades. He is said to have introduced ticker tape to New York, and he conducted his parades in a way that reflected his own lavish personal tastes. The parades showcased American athletic prowess, technological advances, the visits of European royalty, and patriotism, the most impressive the 1927 parade for Charles Lindbergh. "The crowds were tremendous," remembered a police officer. "Never in my life have I seen such a cheering throng as when the motorcade went up Broadway! The air was alive with clippings, ticker tape, and all sorts of paper flying through the air."[15]

Toys, Spectacles, and the Child Experts

Of all the parades, however, none left a greater mark on urban life than the holiday spectacles for children. Before the war the attention given to children as a special group with special needs was already a noticeable trend. In the twenties, spokespeople for children abounded, from advocates such as Stewart Culin, who thought everybody should seek therapeutic pleasure in childlike activities (Culin also collected children's games and was an expert on puppets), to social reformers of all kinds, who formed a vocal chorus of support for the advancement of the health and happiness of children. "Does he need exercise toys to develop his muscles?" went a typical question in the child welfare literature. "Or is he too active, and does he need quiet occupational games to quiet his nerves? Has he a longing for a certain toy that interests him especially and should be supplied?" "It is tragic," said Emma Kidd Hulburt in her essay "Every Child Needs a Playroom," "when children do not have a place to keep all their strange treasures, and where they can feel quite free to paint, hammer and saw, put on private theatricals, wash doll clothes or do any other delightful thing their lively imaginations dictate."[16]

Businessmen plunged into this widening swirl of opportunity. Indeed, by the midtwenties practically every object having to do with children was being manufactured. If in Europe most clothing and toys were still made at home, in America they were bought. By 1926 the United States was the greatest producer of toys and playthings in the world—toys for the backyard, toys for the beach, toys for camping, toys for the "little private room, which every child desperately needs to fulfill his or her individuality." "Play is the child's business; toys the material with which he works."[17] Merchants' overtures to children now constituted the core of many store promotions. "Usually the parents decide upon purchases," a report from the federal government said in 1924, "but in America a growing influence of children is noted. This has led to any appeal to the children in an attempt, through them, to direct purchasing power."[18] (See plate 20.)

In 1928, Jesse and Percy Straus at Macy's, alert to trends, organized an extensive "toy exposition"—really a little spectacle in its own right—to display thousands of different toys and to show parents the advantages of more playtime for children. To illustrate the educational value of their toys the Strauses invited child experts, some very well known and highly regarded, to lecture at the exposition on "why children should have toys." These experts, in the service they performed for Macy's (and for other stores as well), epitomized the collaboration among social workers, child-welfare advocates, and mass consumer institutions that had begun to form before the war and whose overall effect was to "educate" middle-class parents and children into consumer values and perspectives.[19]

Among the speakers at Macy's in 1928 were Joseph Jastrow, eminent lecturer in psychology at the New School for Social Research in New York, and Sidonie Gruenberg, president of the Child Study Association. Jastrow had written *Character and Temperament* in 1915, a book on progressive psychology that established his reputation. In the 1920s he turned his hand to the popularization of psychological ideas, writing one of the first mass market books on "everyday psychology," *Keeping Fit Mentally,* published the year of Macy's exposition. The book opens with mind-cure advice on how to "keep happy" and ends with chapters on "the cult of beauty" and "the psychology of everyday sports." Chapter 2 deals with children and displays an upbeat, reasonably balanced, and generally permissive orientation to childrearing. Jastrow borrowed from this chapter in his Macy's talk. He praised the Strauses for their system of "graded toys." "Failure," he said, "is one of the most serious distractions" for children; "hence it is excellent that you have that graded series of toys. You give a child a tricycle before you give it a bicycle, and so on." Jastrow also maintained that play and its tutelary servant the toy nourished the imaginative life of the child, thus making a "crucial" contribution to the child's development.[20]

In relation to Macy's goals, Sidonie Gruenberg was a more ideal figure than Jastrow. She had long been recognized as an authority on flexible, permissive care of children. Her stamp carried more weight than Jastrow's did. A Jewish immigrant from Austria whose psychology mixed the ideas of such famous educators as G. Stanley Hall, Edward Thorndike, John

Dewey, and Sigmund Freud, Gruenberg had been appointed head in 1904 of the Society for the Study of Child Nature, an organization renamed the American Child Study Association in 1924 with her at the helm and with funding from the Rockefeller Foundation. Like Jastrow, she was a popularizer, but unlike him she began her writing career with a mass audience in mind.[21]

In *Your Child Today and Tomorrow,* written in 1912 and the first book of its kind—according to Gruenberg—intended for mass consumption, she expounded ideas widely held by other psychologists compatible with and supportive of an emerging culture of consumer capitalism. The ideas clearly explain her presence at Macy's. Gruenberg discoursed on the separateness of the child world. Unlike adults, she said in this book and in her Macy's talk, children do nothing of "moral significance"; neither good nor bad, they are governed by instincts that must be channeled and rationalized. Children have a special right to imaginative play and "individual expression," Gruenberg claimed, and should not suffer from "repressive penalties imposed by an arbitrary puritanism which suggests every desire and impulse of being Satanic." Moreover, they should have regular access to money in the form of an "allowance" so that they might better understand it by "spending it."[22]

Besides these collaborations with reformers, merchants like the Strauses published magazines for children, operated their own radio shows for children, and conducted elaborate shows in stores. Throughout the twenties, stores coast to coast put on little fairy-tale playlets for children in makeshift theaters in toy departments or in store auditoriums. The most popular show was the department store version of Baum's *The Wonderful Wizard of Oz.* Children seemed to find this playlet particularly irresistible—but a little Barnum trickery helped. At Field's, where the city's Junior League was perhaps the first to present the Baum tale, children wore green-tinted eyeglasses to see the performance, and Field's own Emerald City.[23] By the midtwenties, at Christmastime, nearly every city in America, according to one report, had its own department store "radio Santa Claus." As early as November 1925, Gimbels in New York was getting thousands of letters from children weekly, all reportedly answered by the staff who signed "Santa" and who indexed the names for future use. Wanamaker's, Bloomingdale's, and other stores produced costly motion pictures of these holiday activities that were shown as advertising shorts in city theaters.[24]

Ragamuffins and
Macy's Thanksgiving Day Parade

The most anticipated events in the year-round children's promotions were the pre-Christmas parades. Businessmen had been conducting holiday parades on a small scale for some twenty years, but after the war the parades began to displace an even older form of Thanksgiving parading linked with scarcity and poverty. Often called "ragamuffin parades" and probably rooted in European traditions of carnival, these parades had been popular from at least the midnineteenth century—especially in New York City, where they brought both children and adults dressed in homemade colorful costumes, blowing horns, and carrying bells and banners, into the streets. As the novelist William Dean Howells wrote in 1907 of the New York tradition, "the poor recognize [Thanksgiving] as a sort of carnival. They go about in masquerade on the eastern avenues, and the children of the foreign races who populate the quarter penetrate the better streets, blowing horns, and begging of the passers." "Memory discloses a troop of mounted men clattering up Avenue A on Thanksgiving Day in grotesque costume," recounted one German New Yorker in 1947; "it seemed a weak reflection of the carnival spirit," with "little groups of children wandering about . . . begging for pennies."[25]

Ragamuffin parading sometimes developed complex community forms. Al Smith, the Irish Catholic governor of New York in the 1920s, had participated in this carnival activity as a child growing up on Manhattan's Lower East Side. "Thanksgiving Day in the Lower East and West sides," he recalled in his 1929 autobiography, "provided amusement for the people by a parade of what are still called ragamuffins." In those days, he said

> the children dressed up and the men paraded under the name of the Rangers. We had the James Slip Rangers, who usually formed the line of parade in James Slip. The Rutgers Rangers had their headquarters on Madison Street; and the Hudson Rangers came from Hudson Street on the West Side. They were arrayed in all kinds of fancy costumes. One man would be dressed up as Uncle Sam, another in the costume of a prince, and there one could see all the various costumes that might be expected at a masquerade ball.

In another account, women were described as taking equal part in the Thanksgiving masquerade activity, along with the masquerading children, who got "up early" to beg for pennies or for whatever else they could get. Into the 1890s the "spirit was strongest and the color strangest and most evident" under the elevated trains on Manhattan's East and West sides. [26]

By the mid-1920s ragamuffin parading had nearly vanished from Manhattan, although traces could still be found at the end of the subway lines in the Bronx, or in the Flatbush and Greenpoint sections of Brooklyn. "The old ragamuffin tradition," recalled a senior policeman in an interview with *The New York Times*, "is indeed a dead racket." In its place was a new and far more professional "racket"—the department store pre-Christmas circus parade, with floats, clowns, marching bands, reindeer, and Santa Claus, and exemplified best by the Macy's parade down Broadway from 145th Street to West 34th Street. The Straus brothers at Macy's did not originate the spectacle Thanksgiving Day Parade; Gimbels in Philadelphia had been moving in this direction for many years, as had Eaton's Department Store in Toronto, the largest store in Canada. Nor did the Strauses invent the standardized carnival grotesques that quickly became the climactic feature of the parade. From at least the turn of the century, American manufacturers and showmen had been turning out these figures on almost an assembly-line basis for use in the major urban fairs and in merchandising. The most unusual was showman Frederic Thompson, who designed giant ninety-feet high toys—including "the biggest suffragette in the world"— for a display he called "Toyland Grownup" at the Panama-Pacific International Exposition in 1915 in San Francisco. [27]

But if the Strauses did not pioneer the spectacle parade tradition, they were surely making the most of it by the midtwenties. By 1924, the year of their first parade, they had just completed a massive rebuilding, doubling the size of their store. They had made a controlling purchase of LaSalle and Koch, Toledo's largest department store, and were eagerly seeking other acquisitions. And, as the collaboration with child-welfare reformers in 1928 demonstrates, they were avid toy merchants; Macy's probably had the largest toy store in the world. "It was the toy department," in fact—as one Macy's buyer said in 1930—that " 'made Macy's.' "[28]

In the 1920s Macy's was what Dwight Macdonald had called it: a "tremendous organization" run by men obsessed with business profits and volume turnover. Under the Straus brothers—Jesse Straus, president, and Percy Straus, vice president—Macy's had become a full-fledged corporate business, with systematic control wielded from above, operating according to the most "advanced" cost accounting principles, committed to scientific management, and nonunionized.[29] "The big bosses were all men and they took advantage of you," recalls Marjorie Pleshette, a retired Macy's buyer.[30] The object was "training," training for management and training in "specialized selling."[31] Aiming for "excellence," the Strauses ignored their own employees and sent representatives around the nation to recruit potential executives from the best colleges and universities. "There were really top people at Macy's," remembers another retired buyer, Smith College graduate Dora Sanders.[32]

In 1925 Macy's was the nation's first store to inaugurate intelligence tests for its employees; and two years later it hired a full-time psychiatrist and social workers to give psychological tests and to staff a psychiatric clinic inside the store. Dora Sanders briefly administered the tests in the early thirties, finding the whole experience—as the Depression deepened—"both wonderful and sad at the same time." Young people, she remembered, were accustomed to taking such tests and often did very well on them, but the older applicants—lawyers and engineers thrown out of work—"often failed." "But we often hired them anyway," she recalls, "realizing the hardships they were suffering." Until the midthirties, when money ran out to conduct them, the tests were given to all employees, even to executives, so that no "out of step" individuals (as the firm called them) got hired or promoted and no emotional snags or "personality traits" obstructed the smooth running of their business. Social workers walked the floors, watching workers and managers; by the fall of 1927, according to the employment manager, Dr. V. V. Anderson, "their work had shown that the most outstanding cause of work failure, of disciplinary problems, of layoff and resignation is the mental attitude of the individual worker himself." At first, Anderson reported in 1930, some executives up for promotion "showed considerable reluctance and fear" about such oversight; "but now all the intelligent ones desire it."[33]

In 1924, the Straus brothers' investment in their business led to a decision—taken haltingly before the war but rapidly after it—to enlarge the company's promotional equipment. A new electrical sign, "visible to our customers in outlying districts," was erected with the largest letters of any sign in New York.[34] Macy's extended "shopping time," highlighted store "comfort," added air conditioning, and then, in about 1930, led all New York stores in staying open until nine o'clock on Thursday night and on

Saturday night as well. (This reform, unmodified until the 1960s, occurred at the same time in Chicago in response to the rise of suburban shopping.)[35] Like the store's art-in-industry shows, the new Thanksgiving Day parade was part of this new policy. It testified to the Strauses' passion for display and theatrical spectacle as well as to their commitment to what they called "institutional publicity"—for there was nothing like this parade to get the store inside the imaginative center of New York's community life.[36]

By 1924 Jesse and Percy Straus had converted fully to children's merchandising and to Christmas parading. They kept the carnival aspect of the older ragamuffin tradition but took complete managerial control over who or what marched, thereby preventing the parade from becoming spontaneous or democratic. This parade was to stand for what journalist Samuel Strauss called in 1924 "Consumptionism," not for traditions invoking poverty or ethnic heritage. To be sure, the store's immigrant employees marched in the parade, and, in the first year, many of them appeared to have worn the colorful costumes they might have used in a ragamuffin parade; but despite the claims by today's Macy management, the idea of the parade did not come from employees but from store executives, as the "minutes" to executive council meetings in 1924 make clear.

In June of that year the store's secretary was explicitly "directed to put on the calendar the matter of a Christmas parade." Two months later, the store consulted with Eaton's Department Store in Toronto regarding that "store's method of conducting the Christmas parade" and hoped that Eaton's "might be able to cooperate in the preparation of suitable floats." In September the plans with Eaton's fell through, but the Strauses persisted. Between September 25 and November 16, the management decided the time for the parade (9:30 A.M. to 12 noon) and worked out its route, determining that "the Christmas parade will be conducted without special features such as a reviewing stand, prize essays, and so forth." Macy's got "special permission from city authorities" to hold the parade on Thanksgiving Day and made arrangements with the city police to be out in force on that day.[37]

To guarantee the parade's success, the Straus brothers hired Tony Sarg, a designer of colorful murals for hotel bars and nightclubs, and—above all—a famous puppeteer and proponent of the marionette theater. German-born and -educated, Sarg had grown up with a "passion for the object in miniature—toys, small dolls, and many boats."[38] In pursuit of a theater career, he immigrated to England and then to America, in 1915.[39] The

Strauses put him to work in the summer of 1924 "sketching the proposed floats" for the parade. He was assigned the extra job of filling the giant 34th Street windows with a "marionette spectacle" depicting several fairy tales in a series of complex mechanical *tableaux*. In the wake of the success of these windows, he took over the design and construction of the floats for the new parade, prepared the visual advertising, especially the large multicolored posters, and had them put up all over the city on the subways and suburban commuter trains long before the parade began. By 1926 Sarg was replaced—but only temporarily for the year—by the stage designer Norman Bel Geddes, who conceived everything from the carnival theme to the costumes.[40]

In none of these decisions were any rank-and-file employees consulted. There is no reference whatever to employees in the minutes of the executive council meetings. It appears that, probably from the very first year, Macy's actually paid its workers to march, thus considerably undercutting the basis for volunteer participation. "Employees who are looking for an extra day's salary," announced *Sparks*, the store employee magazine, in 1928, "and a great deal of fun, should see one of the captains at once about getting into the parade."[41]

Thousands watched the first Macy's parade as it moved from 145th Street and Convent Avenue down to West 34th Street and Broadway guided by "a large force of policemen that had its hands full maintaining the police lines." One account reported that the parade "surpassed in glamor and splendor the familiar circus parades of former days."[42] Five bands marched the entire route—a seventy-five-piece military band, a fife and drum corps, a bugle corps, a jazz band of Macy's Negro employees, and a clown band, also of Macy's personnel. Other workers paraded as sheiks, acrobats, men on stilts, and "red star" (Macy's label) princes and princesses. Hundreds of children of employees ran freely through the parade dressed as the comic-strip characters Mutt and Jeff. There was a profusion of professional entertainers, too, with clowns and bareback riders. There were wild animals in cages—lions, elephants, and bears—and five Sarg floats depicting scenes from familiar fairy tales. But the most "impressive" sight in the parade was Santa Claus himself, sitting on a huge "pile of ice," snapping his whip at his "deer" in the direction of Macy's. When the parade reached its destination at West 34th Street and Broadway, about twenty thousand adults and children watched as Santa Claus climbed onto the store's marquee, and Tony Sarg's mechanical fairy tale window scenes, full of hundreds of marionettes, were set into motion on a continuously moving stage.[43] In November and December 1926 an average of five thousand children a day, attracted by the notoriety of the parade and by the other Christmas promotions, visited Macy's Christmas grotto; because of the crowds, Santa Claus was moved out of the fourth-floor toy department to a "safer" place on another floor.[44]

The initial response to the first parade (and to the next) was extremely favorable, so much so that the Strauses decided to make it a permanent feature of their "holiday activities."[45] But there were also protests from some patriotic groups who—as a Macy's man said—believed that the parade, because it was held on Thanksgiving Day morning, was "an offense against a national and essentially religious holiday." The Strauses hired William H. Baldwin, a public relations man, to finesse these objections and to find some way to "root the parade into New York's traditions," as Baldwin put it. Baldwin urged that the parade time be changed to the afternoon, which, although it was a time in "competition with football games," was at least after "church services." Percy Straus balked at this, so Baldwin appealed to Straus's friend the police commissioner, who concurred with the public relations expert. "This time," as Baldwin remembered it, "I reported more formally to 'Mr. Jesse,' and he assented. The change in time was publicized and the parade was held without further protest."[46]

In November 1927 the parade took on, to some extent, the character of what we think of today when we think of the Macy's parade. Sarg's giant grotesque "animals and humans" first appeared in 1927, although they were not yet helium-inflated and thus did not float lumberingly over the parade line. Four hundred Macy's employees led the way, each wearing one of "the unusually large masks" designed by Sarg. Behind them marched a sixty-foot "smoke-breathing dinosaur" attended by several "prehistoric cavemen." A twenty-five-foot dachshund went by, so did a giant float depicting Robinson Crusoe's desert island, preceded by "a forest of walking trees." Heading a "Funny Face Brigade" was a "Human Behemoth" twenty-one feet tall. Towering tigers, lions, monkeys, and giraffes paraded—all, like the other parading beasts, in papier-mâché—along with hundreds of fairy-tale figures, a flotilla of bands, and many professional clowns. At the end of the parade came Santa Claus in the cockpit of an airplane. In what had by now become a "city ritual," Santa ascended a flight of red-carpeted steps to his throne on the store's marquee and signaled the unveiling of Sarg's panoramic marionette spectacle windows.[47]

By the late 1920s the cult of Santa Claus had reached almost absurd proportions everywhere, and there was a glut of parades throughout the country. Supply businesses, such as Messmore and Damon in Manhattan, appeared to provide big department stores with a steady stream of giant standardized carnivalesque figures, all based on the same fairy-tale and cartoon characters, and all available only to mass market merchants wealthy enough to pay for or rent them. So many department store Santa Clauses had their own radio shows that some merchants feared that "Santa was being radioed out." Anxious adults began to oppose what they considered the excessive "commercialization" of Santa Claus, his image on every street corner and in every store. "Can you tell me," wrote a reform-minded woman from Texas to the U.S. Children's Bureau, "what is being done about the widespread use of Santa Claus as advertising medium at stores and on street corners? Some of the women's organizations in Houston concerned with this practice have come to me for information, and I am, in turn, coming to you." "I do not know of any groups interested in doing away with the commercialism of Santa Claus" was the answer she got from the assistant to the chief of the bureau. "I am afraid I have no suggestions to make."[48]

Criticism of this kind seems to have fallen on deaf ears, and the business cult of Santa Claus grew. In Los Angeles in 1929, merchants and property owners pledged that downtown Los Angeles would stage "the 1929 Wonder Christmas of all joyous, radiant Christmases that have gone or are yet to be." They assembled a "series of dramatic events" on a "magnificent scale" to "reawaken the Christmas spirit" and to set a standard for all "community celebrations for children." In October they distributed a "proclamation by Santa Claus," illustrated with four-color photos. On November 2 the merchants borrowed hundreds of "dwarfs" from Hollywood studios and dispatched them to downtown stores to open all the Christmas departments simultaneously. Five days later all of the city's show windows were unveiled at the same time, followed by the synchronized appearance of "snow castles" on top of lightposts, with festoons of greenery and tinsel and arches of colored lights spacing the avenue and leading to the stores. On November 28 came the parade itself, with giant fairy-tale "grotesques," bands, and a "glittering" Santa Claus and reindeer.[49]

Not to be outclassed, Philadelphia's Wanamaker's constructed an entire amusement park—the Enchanted Forest—in its toy store in 1927 that remained a city attraction for years. Wanamaker's also ended 1929 with a cheap trick. At the New York store, Santa Claus, enthroned in an "enormous igloo," amazed every child who visited him with knowledge of the child's "exact desires." Santa got his data from one of his "helpers," who, seated at the bottom of a ramp the children used to reach Santa, found out the children's wishes and then communicated them to Santa through an invisible Dictaphone.[50]

In 1928, the year Sidonie Gruenberg defended playthings and play at Macy's, Sarg achieved a sensational dimension in the store's parade with the first helium-inflated floating balloons. (See plate 25.) Two years later, even as the Depression began to deepen, Macy's gained the highest-volume turnover in its history, its parade, now in the national limelight. Ten bands marched in the 1930 parade on a cold, wintry day that was threatened by a heavy snowfall. Santa Claus traveled on a Zeppelin dirigible held down to the ground by men dressed as elves. There were fifteen enormous floating balloons of comic figures, including a Katzenjammer Kid that was to have a strange destiny that day. All the figures were to be released in the air when the parade ended at 34th Street, with the promise of a $25 reward for every balloon retrieved. When Santa Claus reached the store and climbed out of his Zeppelin onto the store marquee, thousands of smaller colorful balloons rose in the air around the store. A crowd of more than twenty-five thousand lined up before the Sarg windows, guarded by ten mounted police, fifty policemen, and two motorcycle officers. Then, with the ritual trumpet flourish, the giant parade figures were released into the air. One caught the crowd's attention. The Katzenjammer Kid had not floated directly up but, according to a reporter for *The New York Times*, had "made straight for the new Empire State Building, backing into what appeared to have been the seventieth story." The Kid then "leaned over as if looking down at the crowds! . . . Then [it] moved to the corner, slowly seemed to peer around it, and, when it was caught in the teeth of the strong wind, went dancing and whirling out over the East River, indistinct in the snow."[51]

America's Mecca of Light and Color

Times Square was not an ephemeral spectacle. It was not, to be sure, Macy's Thanksgiving Day parade, Culin's Rainbow House, Philadelphia's

Palace of Fashion, or Chicago's color and light show. Times Square was all these things combined, on a permanent spectacle site, in a place that stood still but was in perpetual motion. It was the country's most spectacular expression of the commercial aesthetic, a pictorial environment packed with giant images and signs designed to move goods, money, and people on a massive scale. It had become the gravitational center of the commercial "universe," as Edward Bernays put it, drawing people in by the pull of its lights and colors.

Before the war, Times Square was beginning to achieve economic prominence, although it had yet to win a secure place in the popular imagination. Real estate investors were still uncertain about how profitably to invest in its properties.[52] After 1918, the district's emergence as an entertainment center quickened with more and more people streaming into it. By the early twenties, "hundreds of thousands of people," one guidebook writer observed, "are now thinking of New York in terms of the 'whiter light' district . . . centering around Times Square. To them this is the spirit of New York." By decade's end, according to police reports, nearly five hundred thousand people were passing nightly in and out, creating the "greatest night street traffic that moves anywhere in the world." Traffic jams hobbled the district until traffic lights and one-way streets were finally added in 1929.[53]

Why this transformation? Why were so many people visiting Times Square? People went because the new transportation system made it easy to get there, picking up and moving crowds readily and efficiently both above and beneath the ground. The district was alluring because so many movie palaces, theaters, restaurants, hotels, and retail stores clustered there. And the capital investments of national corporations, bankers, and real estate developers who by now had "great confidence in the real estate values of the midtown section" transformed the square into an attractive, titillating place—into a pecuniary space where everything was possible and where few limits were placed on what could be bought or sold.[54] By 1925, money had erected an invisible wall around Times Square, protecting it from "moral crusaders" and ensuring its continued existence as a desired site in the national circuit of consumer markets.

At the heart of this pecuniary excitement were the huge electrical and illuminated signs, facilitated by the passage of a 1916 zoning law permitting full-scale building of giant billboards. Signboard advertising after 1920 prospered everywhere in the United States, due largely to the advent of automobiles, which encouraged advertisers to plaster even more signs on every barn, along every new road and highway, and at as many intersections as possible. In the midtwenties, Bullock's department store in Los Angeles built a series of notorious signs at strategic locations in the city, each sign with a giant word—"Happiness," "Imagination," or "Hospitality"—written beneath a pretty picture and meant to stand for the things one might find at Bullock's. Between 1920 and 1930, the money spent on such outdoor advertising rose from $25 million to $85 million.[55]

Much of this money was invested in signs in Times Square, giving the place its carnival identity. Outdoor advertising was booming by 1922; expenditures had increased sixfold over the previous three years.[56] On any one day or night in February of that year, passersby could see electrical signs advertising actress Marion Davies in *Buried Treasure*, Macy's department store, the Fisk Tire Company, the Paramount Theater, Chalmers Underwear, or Ivory Soap ("It Floats"). National corporations in particular—above all, automobile companies, movie theater chains, gasoline firms, and cigarette and soda businesses—swamped the area, grabbing so many advertising leases that smaller businesses could not compete. Outdoor advertising companies—now monopolies themselves, reflecting the corporate consolidation of the businesses they served—aided in excluding small dealers by charging exorbitant prices. Times Square had become the most dense and costly advertising space in the world.[57] In such a commercial combat zone, only the most opportunistic, the most unscrupulous, and the best banker-financed survived. "Advertising magnates battle like Vikings for strategic locations," said a commentator in 1923, "sometimes paying for a location and not using it simply to keep others out."[58]

Two significant features of the signs in Times Square were their "spectacular character" (spectacular was an industry term) and their growing reliance on colored light. Signs jumped and wiggled and flashed and seemed to shake the buildings or the airspace above them. By mid-decade, customers looked forward to these sensational signs as part of the whole experience of "going to the movies." In February 1925, the Criterion Theater, at Broadway and 44th Street, advertised Cecil B. DeMille's *The Ten Commandments* in a forty-feet-high display that covered the entire facade of the building. It depicted 600 chariots headed by the pharaoh in a "tumultuous scene" of black horses that seemed to leap "madly toward the spectators." A giant Moses, holding God's tablet of the Ten Commandments, glared grimly down on the busy street. Every few minutes, 100,000 volts of energy flashed across the sky in a bluish flame as a "streak of lightning"—one observer reported—struck the tablet in a "crack" of light. At night the ad was floodlighted in a different color.[59]

The Wrigley Spearmint Gum sign, erected in 1917 and lasting for nearly seven years, was billed as the biggest electric sign "in the world." Eighty feet high and 200 feet long, with 17,500 lamps, it took over a space at the heart of the square and cost $9,000 a month to rent. An animated army of elves jabbed the night with spears in off and on flashes of light, pointing to the words "Wrigley Spearmint Gum." In 1923 the O. J. Gude Company built at 54th Street and 8th Avenue, on the outer fringe of the square, a flashing sign to advertise the gas and oil products of Purol and Tilene. A flash revealed a huge bull's-eye pierced by a streak of lightning, followed by a flashing on of the title "Twins of Power," followed by "Purol," "Gasoline," and "Pure Oil Company," successively, and then again and again.[60] A three-story bottle of Cliquot Ginger Ale towered over the square in the summer of 1924. The bottle stood in a giant sleigh driven by a smiling Eskimo boy in white furs. In flashing sequences he snapped a six-foot whip to prod three other Eskimo boys to pull the sleigh. Another whip crack set the name "Cliquot" lighting up the sky, then "Ginger Ale," as the boys "ran bravely in the night to bring that precious bottle of Ginger Ale into camp." (See plate 26). The next spring 5,000 lamps radiated from a 100-foot-wide General Motors sign 82 feet above the General Motors Building at 57th Street, facing Times Square. "General Motors" and the motto "A car for every purse and purpose" burned constantly throughout the night. Flashing alternately on and off were the names of GM products—Chevrolet, Oldsmobile, Buick, Cadillac, Oakland, and GM trucks—along with the reassurance that each car had a "body by Fisher."[61]

"What a magnificent spectacle," wrote the English critic G. K. Chesterton after he first saw the signs on Broadway, " . . . for a man who cannot read."[62]

Year by year the signs occupied more space. In 1928 the automobile manufacturer Dodge Brothers hoisted onto the top of the Strand Theater at 48th Street "the largest electrical sign in structural dimensions on Broadway," or so Edward Bernays, public relations man for Dodge, described it. At the top was the Dodge Brothers name, at the bottom a moving sign or electrical ribbon motograph announcing the "Variety Six and other Dodge cars." This "moving sign," said Bernays, who could monitor it from his top-floor office window at 19 East 48th Street, "was half a city block in length." It could be seen "by a million people passing through Times Square in a day."[63] A year later, Warner Brothers, now heavily financed by the investment firm of Goldman, Sachs, erected the "biggest sign in the world" at Broadway and 52nd Street, just north of Times Square, 80 feet high and weighing 115 tons.[64]

Color reinforced the ballyhoo. In the early twenties most of the signs were in white light, although some ads used floodlights of colors to attract crowds (as in *The Ten Commandments*) or tried color-coated incandescent lights (generally unreliable). The invention of neon light by the Frenchman Georges Claude in about 1915 changed all this; and by the end of the next decade, *The New York Times* reported, "the white lights celebrated in song and legend [were] almost obliterated by the reds, greens, and orange-yellows" (the *Times* should have included blues also) "made possible by the luminous gas arrangements."[65] Contemporary accounts observed that neon light was the greatest advance in advertising since the invention of Edison's incandescent filaments. A cheap, cold light, neon wasted little energy and required minimal electrical current. Yet it was a powerful light and, given the peculiar properties of its rays, could not be absorbed by sunlight. It seemed to glow brighter at a distance and—most important of all—could be seen by day, by night, through fog, and through rain. It permitted selling "in light all the time."[66]

Luminous signs, which came in many gas forms besides neon, lit up Times Square by mid-decade, soon after an electrical sign factory, financed by real estate developers and city wholesalers to supply Times Square, was built uptown, at Amsterdam Avenue and West 132nd Street. In a few years, the *Times* reported, luminous colors were visible at the square from every point on the compass. "Looking to the east," the *Times* said,

deep red is easily the favorite. At the northern end is the most prominent advertising spot in the Gay White Way, which alone illustrates the color riot that Broadway's outdoor decorators have concocted. At the very top is an electric sign in deep yellow advertising a brand of coffee. Below this is a white sign on a blue background dotted with yellow lights, calling attention to a brand of automobile. Further down, one's eyes are assailed by a large square sign advertising a toothpaste, which first flashes a message in orange-yellow, switching to red and finally to green. Underneath this is a cigarette advertised in white letters on a large red background.[67]

Nowhere else in the world, by the end of the 1920s, was so much commercial color and light to be found concentrated in one place.

Paris and Berlin also, to be sure, were known as "cities of light" at the time, and earlier. As far back as the seventeenth century Louis XIV installed lanterns lit by tallow dips along many of the streets of Paris. At the turn of the century, the Champs-Élysées and surrounding boulevards were the most completely illuminated arteries in the world, flanked by thousands of gas and electrical lights that burned night and day. By 1912 the French had begun to floodlight their public buildings and monuments, to the chagrin of the novelist Edith Wharton, who was convinced that Paris was now imitating the worst commercial excesses of America. By the mid-1920s nearly six thousand neon advertising signs crowded the Parisian night horizon. These "alluring advertisements written in the dark by thousand-candle power," one German visitor wrote in 1929, "reach to the high, retreating sky. A big green drop drips into a gigantic champagne goblet. Immense glass tubes glow with red fire, or gleam with condensed sunshine." In Berlin, too, commercial neon lights appeared. When Christopher Isherwood arrived in the midtwenties, "the first thing I saw there were two enormous cinemas, the Ufa Palast and Gloria Palast with neon lights." In Berlin "glimmering reflections of advertising gave the boulevard an intimate feel."[68]

The German and French governments, however, both restricted the spread of such "spectacular" advertising, and Paris laws were especially severe. In June 1929, the prefect of the Seine ordered removal of "all electric signs that did not advertise goods actually sold on the premises." In other words, advertising by national businesses was forbidden. The law sent shock waves across the Atlantic to cigarette and automobile companies in the United States, though it delighted French citizens, one of whom said, "Paris is proud to be known as the City of Light, but she wants it to be intellectual rather than electric."[69]

In New York, there was also some attempt to control electrical advertising—indeed, the commercial aesthetic as a whole—but not in the sweeping French manner. Americans confined such activity to a limited space, yet at the same time liberated it. Through the decade, rival trade associations quarreled over the restrictions, the Broadway Association wanting no controls whatever placed on signs, the Fifth Avenue Association insisting that all "projecting and illuminated signs" be banned on Fifth Avenue from Washington Square at Eighth Street to One hundred tenth Street. In 1922 the Fifth Avenue group persuaded the city's Board of Aldermen to pass a sign ordinance to legalize the ban and extend it to include parts of Madison Avenue and Thirty-fourth Street as well. The Broadway and Forty-second Street associations launched a counter assault but actually had little to fear, for the Fifth Avenue Association had no plans to advocate a ban on signs in Times Square. The prominent sign advertising business the O. J. Gude Company—to say nothing of Macy's and Gimbels, both Times Square advertisers—was, in fact, a member of that association. The merchants on Fifth Avenue wanted the patronage of tourists attracted to New York by the lights of Times Square and had nothing against commercial light and color itself, as their hundreds of show windows demonstrated. What they did not want was a "carnival spectacle" that might bring the "wrong kind of people" onto the avenue, jeopardizing real estate values and undermining the control these merchants had over their property.[70]

The ordinance stuck, richly rewarding both business groups. Signs may have been forbidden on Fifth and Madison Avenues and Thirty-fourth Street, but the carnival won out in Times Square itself. The ordinance, in fact, stimulated growth in a more concentrated space, where businessmen, by and large, did what they pleased.

"All the Colours of the Rainbow Belong to Mr. Bilge"

The overall visual outcome was a provocative, startling, brilliant, and sometimes suffocating blend of color, glass, and light, never subtle, always carnivalesque, employing a prescribed palette of colors and aiming to circulate money and goods in the biggest conceivable volumes. Many people saw promise in New York's nighttime sky, the promise of a "new art" and of a new abundance for all. Ezra Pound, during a visit to New York, asked, "Is not New York the most beautiful city in the world? It is not far from it. . . . Electricity has made for the seeing of visions superfluous. . . . Squares upon squares of flames, set and cut into one another. Here is our poetry, for we have pulled down the stars to our will." Stewart Culin viewed the sky-signs in Times Square as "a great achievement in the newest and most amazing medium for artistic expression." On invitation from Edward Bernays as part of a 1928 publicity campaign, Culin wrote of the Dodge Brothers' sign on Forty-eighth Street that it "is prophetic, not only of man's uninterrupted activities through all the hours driving night away, but of the coming of masters who will create with light as the painters of old did with pigment."[71]

Other Americans were not so sure, nor so sanguine. Thorstein Veblen, who lived in New York in the 1920s, was repelled by the spectacle. In his *Absentee Ownership*, written in 1923, he blasted America's "sales publicity" for enlisting all the devices and strategies of religion—the old Catholic "propaganda of the faith" in particular—in behalf of the marketing of goods. He cared nothing about religion, but he did despise the desecration of the classic Christian strategy—the promise of "the Kingdom of Heaven" that could not be delivered. "Spectacular displays," he wrote, have been assembled in a "dim religious light" to make fraudulent promises to Americans. With their signs and symbols, colors and lights and "gestures," sign advertisers have invested their goods with "sacred" meanings that ultimately mean nothing and go nowhere. "The wriggly gestures with which certain spear-headed manikins [sic] stab the nightly firmament over Times Square," Veblen said in regard to the Wrigley Spearmint Gum sign, "may be eloquent and graceful but they are not the goods listed in the doctrinal pronouncements." They do not deliver chewing gum. "Bona-fide delivery . . . would have to be a tangible performance of quite another complexion, inasmuch as the specifications call for Hell fire and the Kingdom of Heaven."[72]

The German film director Fritz Lang was inspired to "make a film" about "the sensations" he felt when he first saw Times Square in 1923: a place "lit as if in full daylight by neon lights and topping them oversized luminous advertisements moving, turning, flashing on and off . . . something completely new and nearly fairy-tale-like for a European . . . a luxurious cloth hung from a dark sky to dazzle, distract, and hypnotize." The film Lang made turned out to be *The Metropolis*, an unremittingly dark vision of the modern industrial city.[73]

Lewis Mumford, in a more ambivalent 1923 analysis, wrote that the district was indispensable to Americans oppressed by the industrial grind and looking for "outlets" for "their repressions." "Broadway is . . . the great compensatory device of the American city," Mumford wrote. "The dazzle of white lights, the colour of electric signs, the alabaster architecture of the moving-picture palaces, the aesthetic appeals of the show windows—these stand for elements that are left out of the drab perspectives of the industrial city. People who do not know how to spend their time must take what satisfaction they can in spending their money." At the same time, Mumford viewed Times Square and Broadway as symptoms of "spiritual failure." "The principal institutions of the American city," Mumford concluded, "are merely distractions that take our eyes off the environment, instead of instruments which would help us to mould it . . . a little nearer to humane hopes and desires."[74]

The English writer G. K. Chesterton visited Broadway and Times Square in 1922, or about the same time as Veblen, Mumford, and Lang. A year later Chesterton published "A Meditation in Broadway" in a volume called *What I Saw in America*, a more penetrating and complex assessment of Times Square than any written by his contemporaries. Chesterton was a devout Roman Catholic convert and a firm democrat; he brought to his analysis a respect for religious traditions and an awareness of the role color, glass, and light had played in Western history. Times Square delighted him on artistic grounds. "I disagree with the aesthetic condemnation of the modern city," he said,

> with its skyscrapers and sky-signs. I mean that which laments the loss of beauty and its sacrifice to utility. It seems to me the very reverse of the truth. As a matter of art for art's sake, they seem to me rather artistic. If a child saw these coloured lights, he would dance with as much delight as at any other coloured toys; and it is the duty of every poet, and even of every critic, to dance in respectful imitation of the child. Indeed I am in a mood of so much sympathy with fairy nights of this pantomime city, that I should be almost sorry to see social sanity and a sense of proportion return to extinguish them.

Besides, no educated person—whether Oxford professor or literate peasant—is socially influenced by advertising signs, Chesterton argued. Independent, sensible, and thoughtful people "are not impressed by" signs selling "Paradise Tooth Paste or the Seventh Heaven Cigar." "Almost any other men in almost any other age would [see] the joke." "It is only among people whose minds have been weakened by a sort of mesmerism that so transparent a trick as that of advertisement could ever have been tried at all."[75]

But Chesterton objected to the "colours and fire" in the square—on "social and scientific grounds" because they represented what he later called the "vulgarisation of the symbolic." In the past, color and light had been closely linked to the "sacred" as well as to nationalism and to popular resistance movements (Chesterton singled out the "bonfires of Guy Fawkes Day" as an illustration here); now they "were being . . . made stale by the commercial connections of our time." Powerful meanings had once been attached to them; but today, "the significance of such colours and such lights has been entirely killed." Moreover, the "new illumination has made people weary of proclaiming great things, by perpetually using it to proclaim small things."[76]

The colors and lights of Times Square meant something even more than the loss of religion or of heroic commitments; they also signified the rise of what Chesterton believed were antidemocratic business corporations. Chesterton greatly admired America for its traditions of equality and citizenship, which made the country unique in the world. "Citzenship is still an ideal in America," he said; and "equality is an absolute of morals by which all men have value invariable and indestructible and a dignity as intangible as death."[77] But industrial capitalism was threatening these ideals, he argued. "Industrial capitalism and ideal democracy are everywhere in controversy; but perhaps only [in America] are they in conflict." Only in America had democracy advanced so far; but only in America was "industrial progress . . . the most undemocratic." "The reality of modern capitalism," Chesterton claimed, "is menacing the [democratic] ideal with terrors and even splendors that might well stagger the wavering and impressionable modern spirit. Upon the issue of that struggle depends the question of whether this great civilization continues to exist, or even whether any one cares if it exists or not."[78]

To Chesterton, the color, glass, and light in Manhattan's nighttime sky visually expressed the power of capitalism; they formed the aesthetic of capitalism and of the "new inequalities" emerging under it. They were ascendant over all other competing aesthetics. Any literate peasant accustomed to thinking about colors and lights in religious terms would "have to conclude"—upon seeing Times Square for the first time—"that all the colours of the rainbow belong to Mr. Bilge." "This is the real case against that modern society that is symbolised by such art and architecture. It is not that it is vulgar, but rather that it is not popular." No one fought for the colors and lights on Broadway, as English republicans would have fought against "Popery," Chesterton said. No one saw the glory of God in the commercial colors and lights. No one voted for them. "These modern and mercantile legends are imposed upon us by a mercantile minority and we are merely passive to the suggestion. The hypnotist of high finance or big business merely writes his commands in heaven with a finger of fire. We are only the victims of his pyrotechnic violence; and it is he who hits us in the eye."[79]

Chapter 12

HERBERT HOOVER'S
EMERALD CITY
AND MANAGERIAL
GOVERNMENT

From the air over Washington, D.C., the building looked like a colossal white Mediterranean hacienda with a red tile roof that glowed even redder in the sunlight. It occupied three full city blocks, extending from the Washington Mall to Pennsylvania Avenue and Fourteenth Street, in the shadow of the Washington Monument. But it was no hacienda: It was the new Commerce Building, and nothing like it had ever appeared in the nation's capital. "It takes one's breath away by its very size," wrote the journalist R. L. Duffus in 1932, the year the building opened, an "imposing landmark to the economic development of the United States." President Herbert Hoover had laid the cornerstone for it in the spring of 1929, digging with the same trowel and gavel George Washington had used to lay the cornerstone for the Capitol Building in 1793. "Hamilton, gazing at it, would realize that his theories of government had triumphed," Duffus wrote. "No half nation, no nation in which the central government was weak or ineffective would [have needed] such a milestone as this."[1] (See plate 27.)

The building, which still serves the nation in much the same way, is a rectangular monolith; it stood on what had been a swamp shunned by early city residents because of the mosquitoes and wolves that lurked there. "Where the wolves are killed off," said Melville in *The Confidence Man*, "the foxes increase," and many Washingtonians, in 1932, mired in the deepest trough of the Depression, might have felt the same way, whether they knew the history of this building or not.[2] It belonged to a new complex of government structures modeled after an imperial neoclassical style befitting the nation's presumed new status on the world scene. "Enter and stand at the end of one of its magnificent corridors," Duffus marveled, "and human figures at the other end dwindle to the size of dolls." The building's three independent rectangular units were attached together by accordion-type expansion joints that stabilized the building (since, after all, it rested on swampy ground) and permitted it to expand three inches in the summer and contract in the winter, thereby protecting it from structural damage. Spacious courtyards separated the units; glass partitions divided the offices, inviting communication and contact.[3] In the building all the components of the U.S. Department of Commerce long dispersed around the city, were now amalgamated—the Bureau of Foreign and Domestic Commerce, the Patent Office, the Census Bureau, Lighthouses, Mines, Fisheries, Coast and Geodetic Surveys, Steamboat Inspection, Aeronautics, and so forth. Only the Bureau of Standards remained housed in other quarters, due to the delicate scientific work done there and the potential for explosions.[4]

The Commerce Building was the biggest office structure in the world, bigger even than the Empire State Building in New York or the Merchandise Mart in Chicago (both built at about the same time). The Woolworth Building, the Equitable Building, and Madison Square Garden could have been comfortably reassembled altogether to fit in the Commerce Building cellar, as Duffus pointed out in his article. "The first impression," he said, "is one of opulent immensity, of a solidity and immovableness comparable with that of the earth itself. One feels that no wind, no force of nature could shake it or disturb its equanimity." It would not be surpassed in size until the Pentagon appeared a decade later.[5]

Duffus—who had been a student of Thorstein Veblen at Stanford before World War I (and had even lived with him for a time, with other students in a small cottage in Cedro, just outside Palo Alto)—would later write the most moving remembrance of Veblen ever published. And Duffus was right in seeing the Commerce Building as emblematic; it stood not only for the government's new might but also for the new circuitry of institutions that had been forming since before the war to serve the interests of "big business." The urban museums and universities belonged to this circuitry, but by the twenties the government operated at its very center, and the U.S. Commerce Department under Herbert Hoover was its crown jewel.

The presence of the federal government in the lives of ordinary Americans was already manifest between 1895 and 1920; after 1920, it became still more impressive. The federal government, alongside the large financial intermediaries and corporations, was acting as a decisive agent in the making of the new American mass consumer economy and culture. It reacted to change (as did the museums and schools), but it was an economic catalyst, too. It guided and intervened.

Today it is widely held that the federal government has grown (and only grows) in response to military needs or to the needs of the poor, sick, elderly, and unemployed. But this is only part of the truth; the fact is that after 1920 and long before there were entitlement programs, every area of the federal bureaucracy became stronger, including the law enforcement agencies—the FBI, the Narcotics Division, and the Bureau of Prohibition. But "the change of greatest apparent significance," said one highly regarded report in 1934 of the period after World War I, "was the tremendous expansion of activities designed to control or promote commerce and industry and transport on sea and land." Government grew, in other words, in response to business demands. It increased its subsidization of American shipping and air transport through the U.S. Postal Service. It paid for the first federal highways to help streamline the movement of goods, and it created specialized bureaus and agencies to provide market services. "Outstanding developments in this field," the 1934 report continued, "included the unprecedented expansion of services to commerce performed by the Bureau of Foreign and Domestic Commerce, to agriculture by the Bureau of Agricultural Economics, and to shipping through the Shipping Board." Such "aids to business" (and there were others) illustrated "what may well be regarded as the most significant trend of the period: the *shift from control to service,* an apt exemplification of the philosophy of government prevalent during these years."[6]

Herbert Hoover's
Pursuit of Knowledge

But why such a pronounced increase in government "service" to business? Herbert Hoover was a major architect of the change. Hoover served as the secretary of commerce for seven years, from 1921 to 1928, and as president for one term, from 1929 to 1933; Franklin Roosevelt defeated him in his bid for reelection in 1932.[7] Hoover was born in 1874 in West Branch, Iowa, a small midwestern agricultural town (population, about seven hundred) made prosperous by pioneering farmers and by the railroad, which first reached the town in the late seventies. He was the third child of a local town politician, an inventor who tinkered away in his own blacksmith shop, and of a devout Quaker mother whose principles of simplicity and sobriety left a lasting impression on him. For the rest of his life, in fact, even while helping to bring into being a new consumer world, Hoover followed the ideas of the "simple life" advocated by Pastor Wagner and John Wanamaker. And, to some degree like them, he turned regularly to the Bible for its simple truths, "the Book of Books," he wrote, "a postgraduate course in the richest library of human experience."[8]

Orphaned by the age of ten, Hoover was an intensely independent youth who prided himself on his individualism. In 1891, he enrolled as an undergraduate at Stanford University, majoring in geology and mining. Over the next twenty years, he built a career as a mining engineer and businessman that carried him around the world, from Melbourne to Petrograd to Johannesburg. He took part in the first big surge toward global capitalism, wherein frontiers were opened and boundaries toppled everywhere by new industries and markets (in 1900, only two countries—Russia and Turkey—required passports). In the late 1890s he became chief operating engineer over several Australian gold mines, achieving a reputation as an efficient manager of men, minerals, and money. In China he directed a giant coal mining company and, back again in Australia, created the Zinc Corporation, destined to become one of the world's leading multinational minerals companies. In 1908 he left engineering to become a mining "financier" or promoter using his immense knowledge of mines to instruct businessmen when to buy or sell mines or what enterprises required venture or development capital; in exchange, he received either free stocks or part of the profits. Hoover called himself a "Professional Speculator." He lived in London for sixteen years, at the hub of financial capital, often acting as an underwriter for many stock flotations and helping to organize and re-organize some "giant corporations," a colossal irony given what would befall him and the United States in 1929. By 1912 he was a multimillionaire, able to tell a friend that a man "who has not made a million dollars by the time he is forty is not worth much."[9]

In 1913 Hoover, tired of "making money," left the mining field alto-gether for wider public service. In 1915 he worked briefly as American promoter in London of the Panama-Pacific International Exposition in San Francisco (as a publicity stunt he tried to get King George V of England to visit).[10] When the war got worse, he became one of the chief admin-istrators of Belgium relief, a job that fit him like a glove because of his experiences as a manager of the movement and distribution of many com-modities. On the basis of this service, President Woodrow Wilson in 1917 made him director of the Food Administration, to supervise the distribution of food at home and abroad; after the war he became director general of the American Relief Administration. Both jobs imparted luster to his public image, and for many Americans it was the only image they had of Hoover before his presidency. It confirmed his rising public reputation as a man capable of managing and organizing anything, given enough authority.

In 1920 and in 1921, the year President Warren G. Harding appointed him secretary of commerce, Hoover was faced with an enormous challenge to his managerial skills. (See plate 17.) The economy had gone into an ugly postwar tailspin. Between 1921 and 1922, America experienced its worst depression in thirty years. Prices fell to their lowest level in the shortest period of time in American history; businesses were unable to free them-selves of huge inventories accumulated during the war years, and unem-ployment rose to nearly 12 percent of the work force. The productive apparatus that had been buzzing at a feverish pitch for four years now seemed to have ground to a halt, threatening the country with disaster. There was talk of revolution along Bolshevik lines.[11]

As the situation darkened, Hoover and his advisers saw what they believed to be an alarming divergence between production and consump-tion. Hoover thought there was something especially wrong with the system of marketing and distribution. He agreed with Julius Klein, one of his key directors in the Commerce Department, that mass production methods, fed by demand during the war, were yielding "an appalling expansion of industrial capacity" and an oversupply of goods that was not getting to consumers, either because prices were too high, income too low, or markets too glutted. A new complicated transportation system, intended to expedite the "flow" of goods, was blocking the flow. The rapid shift of population from urban to suburban centers was upsetting an already unclear market picture. So swift were these changes, Hoover believed, that businessmen often had to sell in "blind markets" or had trouble planning for the future. Where were the markets? Hoover asked. How did merchandise get from one place to the other? Surprisingly, no one new exactly. No one had tried to trace properly the movement of a single commodity from manufacturer to consumer. "We are almost wholly lacking in the basic data of distribution," Hoover later told Klein.[12]

It was in the context of this "crisis" that Hoover began to consider new ways of using the power and expertise of government to assist business. To be sure, he was already thinking in this direction; the vast mobilization of governmental power during the war, coupled with his performance as food administrator, gave him a taste of what was possible. He was already inclined to view government in a positive light and not as an automatic threat to individual enterprise.

Hoover has been described by historians as a "corporate liberal," which meant that he accepted the existence of the big corporations as a permanent fact of life. He also believed that the laissez-faire competitive world of the nineteenth century was dead, and he argued that economic and social structuring should be left largely to cooperative arrangements among businessmen in the private sphere (the government or the state, in other words, should stay out of it). At the same time, he departed from this position to embrace a "mild" version of managerial statism, asserting that the government should do whatever it could—short of coercion and upfront regulation of private business—to keep capitalism on the right track.[13]

That Hoover was a managerial statist who believed that market forces had to be watched and guided in order to work efficiently is not the current view of him; rather, many historians see him as antistatist, as very reticent about intervening into the economy, and as inclined to allow corporate business to call the shots in a still largely laissez-faire context. But this conception is misconceived and does little to recognize how innovative Hoover was as both commerce secretary and president.

Many streams of influence converged to form Hoover's position, not the least his belief that corporate capitalism was too indispensable to human welfare and progress to be left to its own devices. Capitalism was not, Hoover wrote in 1920, a system based on "taking advantage of other persons" or on "selfish snatching" but one based on the expansion of the "total variety of production and [securing] its diffusion into consumption." In accord with Simon Patten, he thought capitalism was potentially the most moral system in the world and the international capitalist—the man with the widest grasp of things who always "cooperated" with others and who thought in "social harmonies"—the most moral individual of all.[14] It was in the government's interest, therefore, to assist business endeavors because they would lead to the creation of a better humanity.

Another source for Hoover's managerial approach lay in his conviction—one he picked up from the "new economics"—that the fluctuations in the business cycles could be controlled and corrected through technical means and that economic misery could be ended.[15] Hoover was also persuaded by another principle of the new economics: He was convinced that Americans were destined to have what would be later called a "full-growth economy" (no more poverty, no more scarcity) and that government should play a role in creating "permanent prosperity." As a corollary, he maintained that just as the economy was constantly growing, so, too, were human desires; the one, in fact, invoked and required the other. As his most famous report, *Recent Economic Changes*, written by academic economists, would later say, the U.S. economy had "proved conclusively what had long been held theoretically true, that wants are almost insatiable: that one want satisfied makes way for another. The conclusion is that economically we have a boundless field before us, that there are new wants which will make way endlessly for newer wants, as fast as they can be satisfied." The only hitch, so Hoover and his economists argued, was to learn how to balance desire with production. "Economists have long declared," the above report claimed, "that consumption, the satisfaction of wants, would expand with little evidence of satiation if we could *so adjust* our economic processes as to make dormant demands effective." Establishing the character of this adjustment, Hoover contended, was partly the aim and function of government.

Hoover held an even more "modern" economic view by this time, implicit in the foregoing—he was as consumer-oriented as he was producer-oriented. Although some historians have argued that Hoover was mostly interested in production and cared more about factory outputs than department store sales—his mining career and his own statements were along these lines, as was his invocation of an older individualist tradition—he was also the most consumption-minded person up to this time ever to hold the highest position in the U.S. government. For one thing, he did not take consumption for granted, as traditional economists did; he realized that consumption, like production, had to be created and managed in the new corporate economy. He started his career at Commerce on the same note on which he began his presidency—proud of the nation's capacity to transform a "luxury" into a "commonplace."[16] "America's high standard of living" was the nation's most precious gift to "civilization." "Our ancestors," one of his many reports would later say, "came to these shores with few tools and little organization to fight nature for a livelihood. Their descendants have developed a new and peculiarly American type of civilization," one in which mass services and mass consumption "have come to rank with other forms of production as a major economic factor."[17] Everything, Hoover said, should be done to "eliminate the barriers between goods and people."[18]

The "crisis" of 1921–22 intensified Hoover's commitment to these ideas and—as I have said—induced him to reflect on his options.[19] As a corporate liberal, he rejected government ownership of property and any direct economic intervention as well; any attempt to control overtly the process of capital accumulation (the pursuit of profits) or to force business to adopt policies would be inimical to individual initiative and freedom. And yet market forces, the whole business cycle, needed to be managed, as if behind a veil, lest the society be time and again thrown into panic and chaos. The economic system was too interdependent, Hoover thought, to be left altogether to the play of market forces. Hoover finally resolved his two opposing positions—corporate capitalism and managerial statism—into a hybrid mixture, combining an emphasis on control and management with noncoercive cooperation between business and government. His solution entailed some degree of regulation in utilities and in areas of child health and welfare; he also backed protective tariffs for certain industries, and he believed that immigration should be limited by the state, to prevent further declines in the wages of native-born Americans. But, far more crucial, his solution consisted of a twofold focus: establishment of close alliance between government and business, and delivery to business by government of huge quantities of "objective knowledge."

Hoover's conception required the government to create a system of regular contacts with business elites—and with similar elites in universities and foundations committed to improvements in economic management. The purpose was to make business more rational and less wasteful. He hoped that these contacts would encourage the business community voluntarily "to cure its own abuses" and to convert its leaders into cooperative public servants.[20] He chose trade associations—the elites of America's organized corporate businesses and professions—as his principal collaborators in this new cooperative venture. Rather than dealing directly with small businesses, which he often praised but knew were weakening in strength, he concentrated on those "associations who represented the managers of a given industry" and that would, he hoped, put him in contact with the cream of America's corporate managers.[21]

Many businesspeople rejoiced at this policy, seeing in it opportunities for greater profits and institutional legitimacy. When Hoover addressed a meeting of the U.S. Chamber of Commerce in Atlantic City in 1921, A. Lincoln Filene wrote home to Louis Kirstein of Filene's: "Hoover seems to be turning towards the business men, as represented in this organization, for real help. . . . I believe we are really going to make good progress in the way of having the business men tied up with the government through Hoover's department."[22]

Others objected, however, on the grounds that trade groups could not be trusted to act in the "public's interest" because they shared data in a collusive manner and contributed to greater concentration of economic power. Both the U.S. Department of Justice and the Federal Trade Commission, in fact, ruled to this effect but Hoover—shocked by the opposition, arrogant and determined—refused to relent. In 1925 he was confirmed in his position by a conservative U.S. Supreme Court, which overruled the Department of Justice by permitting interindustry trade groups to exchange data. This, Hoover said, "opened the door to reasonable cooperation in matters of public interest." "We brought the trade groups effectively into our programs," Hoover boasted. "We defended their rights to representation before public bodies."[23]

In fashioning this cooperative plan, Hoover crystallized several tendencies and thereby made a lasting—if disturbing—contribution to American government. For one thing, he was perhaps the first major American leader to consult closely with America's new managers—not with those, in other words, who founded or owned factories and businesses, but with their managers—as the group with which government had to negotiate and bargain. Hoover believed that "the directors and managers of large concerns," as he called them in *American Individualism*, offered real promise, because, unlike the robber baron types who only lusted after wealth, these men were altruists who sought only what was best for the society as a whole.[24]

Hoover also transformed an informal institutional circuitry—the one operating loosely among businesses, universities, and governments before the war—into a permanent, established network. In so doing, he reinforced the antidemocratic trend of American political and economic life. Like Simon Patten, Walter Weyl, and others before him, Hoover believed that it was in the interest of business to democratize consumption by raising wages and salaries, because to do so would ensure higher levels of production and of profits. But the way he chose to reach this goal was antidemocratic—working closely with managerial elites, insisting that all "solutions" to problems be technical and administrative rather than political, and claiming that experts—or those people who understood how the economy "really" worked and what should be done about it—should exercise the real power.

But Hoover's compromise went even farther than this, to include a major government service to business: the provision of technical data of all kinds and in unprecedented quantity to the business community. If, as some historians claim, the growth of the modern state has occurred as an outcome of the state's ability to supply private interests with objective knowledge, then Herbert Hoover was among the most successful state-builders of the twentieth century; for his aim was not only to cooperate with business and to create an enabling environment for economic development, his goal was also to create a central database to inform business and to supply it with "reliable" information on every aspect of the economy. Knowledge—"facts, facts, facts," as one of Hoover's aides put it—was the key. Access to "facts," according to Hoover, would lead to rational change, persuading businessmen to manage their factories and stores in the interest of the "whole system" and not merely in the interest of profits.[25]

Commerce as Database and Julius Klein, Master Broker

Hoover reorganized the Commerce Department in the twenties to serve business on a regular, even daily, basis. With the advice, principally, of Edwin Gay, first dean of the Harvard Business School, and of Wesley Clair Mitchell, who taught at the New School of Social Research and at Columbia and was America's greatest authority on business cycles, Hoover changed the Commerce Department into a brokering agency to feed American businesses an ongoing flow of data so they might achieve "better control of economic forces" and "equilibrate" and "rationalize" consumption and production.[26] Both Mitchell and Gay longed to create a centralized apparatus that would coordinate all existing statistical agencies in government and establish the government as an ideal source of "objective" knowledge.[27] Hoover adopted this agenda. In 1921–22, his first year as commerce secretary, he absorbed into the department numerous agencies that had for years been scattered about in other departments. He created new divisions, including the Division of Simplified Practice, whose instructions to business on how to end waste through the standardization of production were ridiculed throughout the decade as institutional Babbitry promoting homogeneity of product lines. But Hoover, ever the engineer, praised its work highly.

Hoover emphasized three bureaus as the structural core of the department's work: the Bureau of Standards, the Census Bureau, and the Bureau of Foreign and Domestic Commerce. Under Hoover, the Bureau of Standards, originally intended to test materials used by the government, was assigned to help business solve its most difficult scientific problems. By the end of the twenties it contained the world's largest research laboratory. Under Hoover as well, the Bureau of the Census began in 1921 to publish *Surveys of Current Business*, which listed current levels of production and inventories. It continues to this day as a firm business ally.[28]

By far the most significant of the three structural pillars of the Commerce Department, however, was the Bureau of Foreign and Domestic Commerce (BFDC), which underwent the most comprehensive reform of any component of the federal government. Between 1921 and 1930, congressional appropriations for it rose from $100,000 to more than $8 million, an increase of nearly 8,000 percent, while the size of the staff climbed from one hundred to twenty-five hundred. No other government agency enjoyed such generous treatment. The Labor Department as a whole got a pittance; divisions such as the Children's Bureau, the Bureau of Labor Statistics, and the Women's Bureau hobbled along on slender budgets. Not so the BFDC. Its expansion belied Hoover's claim that he was opposed to any kind of government bureaucracy as well as to the least intimation of centralized control. For here was bureaucracy of indisputable power and scope; more than any other, it fed the growth of the federal government.

The BFDC was reconstructed over a seven-year period, from 1921 to 1928, when Hoover resigned to run for president. In the first phase, 1921–22, the foreign side of the bureau was greatly widened to help business locate and exploit foreign markets. Seventeen new commodity divisions were created, each headed by an experienced business manager representing the automotive industry, iron and steel, electrical equipment, fuel, shoes and leather, and textiles. While running for president, Hoover repeatedly boasted in speeches around the country that "we had reorganized the Department of Commerce for the promotion of American trade abroad on a greater scale than had ever been achieved or ever attempted by any government anywhere in the world."[29] In the next phase, beginning in 1923, Hoover aggressively expanded the domestic focus of the bureau, seeking to target and deepen markets in the United States. He hired a staff of agents to "investigate domestic, commercial, and industrial problems with particular emphasis on marketing." He instructed them to deal with "consumer wishes and desires" and with "how to discover what the consumer really wants."[30] He created a Merchandising Research Division, a Domestic Regional Division, and a Marketing Service Division to "give businessmen expert guidance in meeting such problems as have been caused by the chain store movement, the large number of mergers, the pressure of mass production for new outlets, and the trend toward installment selling." He published a weekly journal, *Domestic Commerce*, issued solely—as the bureau's director told an inquisitive Edward Bernays—to "inform its readers of significant developments in distribution."[31] By decade's end a new Commerce Department "section" had as its sole mandate to "study consumer habits and preferences for all types of commodities."[32]

At the helm of the BFDC Hoover placed the Harvard-trained economist and historian Julius Klein, one of the many academic authorities Hoover called on to help develop and administer his programs. Other academics he turned to included the economist Wesley Clair Mitchell, who helped found the National Bureau of Economic Research in 1921. In the early years of this century, just emerging as an important figure in economics, Mitchell was critical of American economic life and feared that business standards—pecuniary valuation—were beginning to overwhelm all other standards of value. The upswings and downswings of the business cycle, and all its related miseries, were not normal occurrences, as classical economists would have argued, but the results of economic activity organized under capitalism. Business, he knew, was responsible—and had to be held accountable—for whatever hardships struck the economy. In his landmark 1913 *Business Cycles*, Mitchell also wrote that "money standardizes [men's] wants, deeply colors their vision of the good. . . . Upon human activity and human ideals it has stamped its own pattern." A little later, in a paper on price economics, he wrote with concern that "the technical exigencies [of money] help cause the dreadful recurring depressions. Its standards of success have much to do with laying waste our days."[33]

By 1927, however, when Mitchell came to write an updated edition of *Business Cycles*, much of this early tone of misgiving or reservation was gone. Mitchell, in fact, had been pondering a more important agenda— to gain new legitimacy for his profession (economics) and for his particular specialty (statistics). One way of achieving this was to put his skills at the service of Hoover, who greatly admired him and continued to seek him out for advice and to head his many investigatory committees. The cost of Mitchell's reorientation must have been considerable, not only to him personally and professionally but also to the culture. As he became more technically engaged, Mitchell ceased to view the culture and economy with the same open critical depth, and this at a time when the spread of pecuniary valuation seemed to confirm his earlier fears. His "compromise" (as historian Guy Alchon has called it) muted his critical insights, an evolution that affected other "experts" in their pursuit of respectability and power.

Julius Klein seems to have had few conflicts about his own work for Hoover and was never coopted. More conservative and probusiness than Mitchell, he was also far more the broker, far more the amoral bureaucratic functionary. Klein was an intermediary par excellence, a go-between who repressed his own convictions and feelings in behalf of promoting profitable relationships among groups and people. He belonged to that new generation of brokers who were beginning to have an enormous impact on American life. He was a governmental analogue to the advertising man, the window display manager, the new public relations expert, the securities dealer, and the investment banker, with each of whom he personally identified. He created the connections among the collaborating groups. He was also constantly preoccupied with consumers and consumption, thus confirming Hoover's own interest in these subjects.

Born in 1886 in San Jose, California, Klein grew up near San Francisco Bay and never forgot the teeming life there, the loading and unloading of exotic cargoes in the harbor. In 1915 he and his wife drove by car across the country from Boston to Berkeley, a "trip that was a joy to remember," he said. All means of transport—railroads, the Panama Canal, the Pan American Highway—stirred his imagination. He spent much of his professional life untangling or trying to untangle the problems of movement and commodity circulation, and like the man who hired him, he dreamed of creating a seamless economic system without frontier or boundary and without conflict, a system of perfect liquidity that would allow for the "efficient movement of ideas, capital, and commodities."[34]

Klein thought of becoming an artist in his youth, but his university teachers persuaded him to study economic history instead. At Harvard in the midteens, he worked with Edwin Gay, the dean of the Business School, who led in moving economic study away from production toward distribution and consumption.[35] Klein assisted Gay in his classes and strove to emulate his outlook on the "processes of distribution," which Gay stressed as of greater importance than production. In 1915, to prepare for a course he was to teach the following year, Klein traveled to Latin America on a Harvard fellowship, armed with letters of introduction from Gay. Traversing mountains and sailing up and down rivers, this intrepid traveler saw firsthand Costa Rican banana plantations, sugar processing in Havana, port works in Chile, and coffee plantations in Brazil. "I seem to have come at just the right time," he wrote Gay, "to see the greatest number of economic processes."[36]

Klein completed a dissertation under Gay on the Mesta, a powerful Spanish sheep-grazing and marketing organization that contributed to the economic and political unification of Spain in the late medieval period, and in this study, the fruit of research in Spanish archives and later published by Harvard University Press as The Mesta, he showed how this fifteenth-century organization served as the major circuit for movement and distribution of goods throughout Spain, paving the way for the brief emergence of a Spanish national market. The book displayed the clear impact of Gay's ideas.[37]

A solid career of scholarship and teaching awaited him, but instead Klein entered the Commerce Department, his own real-life Mesta, where advancement was fast and satisfying. He was ambitious and worked very hard. "I stand constantly amazed," wrote an admirer, "at the enormous amount of work you do personally."[38] Recognizing the new "knowledge as a strategically important factor in competition," Klein turned the Bureau of Foreign and Domestic Commerce into a bulging databank for businessmen. Access to "sound statistical and economic data," Hoover believed, "was the first step in controlling economic cycles and in bringing consumption in balance with production."[39] As Klein himself wrote, "in these days of highly sensitive commercial organisms, of closely knit, almost magical systems of communications, of instantaneous economic repercussions around the world, precision of information is of paramount importance for every merchant, manufacturer, banker, and shipper."[40]

Klein's primary mandate as director of the BFDC was to promote foreign trade. His bureau made industrial motion pictures—"the story of a watch," "the story of an automobile"—to drum up interest in American goods abroad.[41] He relied on "experts" from the commodity divisions and on commercial agents in the bureau's different regional divisions (Latin America, Europe, and the Far East) to locate investment opportunities for businessmen. Each division published its findings in "confidential circulars," in trade information bulletins, or in *Commerce Reports*, a weekly journal circulated to firms throughout the country. The agents stayed in touch with the national trade associations and responded dutifully to the thousands of inquiries from business regarding world markets; they delivered data on the quality and quantity of shipments, average prices, lists of dealers and importers, rating of firms, and global business conditions. Among the many early concrete results of the bureau's foreign work were the discovery of oil deposits in Argentina, leading to the entrance of American companies in that field; the first successful shipment of fruit from Argentina to the United States; and the passage of a bill reducing import duties on Peruvian commodities.[42]

On the domestic front, by the end of the decade, the work of the BFDC probably surpassed in volume the output of the foreign divisions. Under Klein's orders and at the request of trade groups that cofunded them, the first citywide surveys of markets were begun. Soon the reach of the bureau moved out to "cover the distribution facilities and methods, the population and purchasing power, and the economic backgrounds of a number of major distributive regions in the United States." "Never before," Klein boasted, "had there been such an arrangement of statistical measures of consumer demand."[43] In the late twenties, the bureau surveyed the returned-goods "evil" and the "delivery question." At the behest of the National Retail Credit Men's Association and reflecting the rising uneasiness over the excessive reliance on credit, it organized a massive study of retail credit conditions covering installment selling, open book credit, and commodities sold on cash.[44]

Many American businesses, from candy to toys, welcomed the bureau's work on distribution and marketing. "It has made a hit here," wrote Victor Cutter, president of United Fruit Company and a member of the New England Council, a major retail trade group, to Klein, of the domestic market survey of New England; "now I certainly hope this matter of a foreign trade survey of New England will have your personal interest."[45] In 1927 the Association of National Advertisers, at its national convention, took time out to "recommend the extension" of the bureau's work, urging it to "furnish American business with basic information about logical trading areas."[46] "The establishment of your office," wrote an executive of J. L. Hudson's, a twenty-one-story Detroit department store, to a chief of the Commerce Department's Domestic Division, "offers a *great opportunity* to those engaged in domestic commerce to articulate to the people of the United States through an accredited and responsible channel."[47]

At every point in the evolution of his domestic policy, Hoover urged Klein to make certain that the bureau responded only to business overtures and never initiated anything on its own. When businessmen failed to originate such requests in regard to matters that Hoover deemed crucial, he resorted to arm pulling to give the impression they had done so. Hoover did everything, in other words, to make it seem that his department was only "reactive," not activist, even when it was quite clear that the overture was his.

In 1924, for instance, Hoover and his staff decided that a large-scale Census of Distribution, along the lines of the national population census, had now become a necessity for American business. But no trade group had stepped forward to request it, so in late spring Hoover invited a "small group" of men to his office—including A. Lincoln Filene—to discuss the census and to drum up support for a trade initiative. Still, no result. A year later, on the advice of Edwin Gay and Frederick Feiker, he tried again, at a Washington Conference on Distribution, organized by the U.S. Chamber of Commerce. A plan was hatched by Gay, longtime advocate of such a census, and by Feiker, an engineer and a key adviser, for Hoover to give the opening address at this conference and, during the session, to form a "committee" of businessmen that would represent the chamber and thus have the power to request a census. "Gay and I," Feiker explained to Hoover, "were conscious of your desire not to set up a committee of the Department of Commerce which would have for its function a propaganda program directing the attention to the department, and Mr. Gay and I felt that the movement should come from an expressed desire on the part of businessmen in accordance with your wishes." If Hoover addressed the chamber's general meeting on distribution problems, Gay and Feiker decided, "it might be possible to place the broad facts of such an inquiry as has been proposed before them, and to anticipate as a result a request from the Conference on Distribution which would be widely representative of businessmen that you would appoint a committee."[48] When the time came, Hoover chose his committee—with Edward Filene and Herbert Tilly of Strawbridge and Clothier among the members; they were empowered to prepare a resolution for the chamber calling for a census of distribution.

This census, supervised by the BFDC and the Bureau of the Census, turned out to be historic. In 1926 and 1928, Klein's staff conducted sample censuses in eleven cities, with cofunding from the U.S. Chamber of Commerce. In 1929, Congress approved the Census of Distribution, to be carried out every ten years with the regular decennial census. The "Census of Consumption," as it was sometimes called, was widely hailed in Europe as a noteworthy step in business-government cooperation (Britain would not conduct such a census until 1950, and European countries only thereafter), and it was one of the most rewarding boons to business ever proposed by any government. Sales personnel and public relations people greatly valued it, since, as its promoters explained, it indicated "what kind of goods offered the least resistance to sales promotion." It reported on the local passage of goods through each stage of distribution and marketing and made clear where goods were "overdeveloped" and what kinds of goods should be handled by different kinds of stores. It pointed out, according to a bureau summary, "where the consumers were" and "what quantity of goods they would consume." A "master analysis of our distribution system," as Robert P. Lamont, new secretary of commerce under Hoover, said in 1929, it was the fullest, most authoritative piece of market research yet undertaken by a country or an institution.[49]

Under Klein, the BFDC did more than disgorge to businessmen vast amounts of useful statistical data. Again and again, it considered ways of breaking down "all barriers between the consumers and commodities."[50] BFDC studies, without judging the people who bought or their buying practices, propagandized and endorsed national retail advertising, cooperative advertising, service devices, fashion, style, and display methods of all kinds. Information flowed from the bureau on how best to deliver goods, widen streets, construct parking lots and underground transportation, employ colored lights, foster store circulation, and present merchandise in "tempting ways."[51]

Klein, as director of the bureau and, later, between 1927 and 1932, as assistant secretary of commerce, went before Congress and the American people, exploring every available medium to praise and plead the cause of corporate business. He commended Hollywood—the land of "miraculous dream-shadows"—for "starting a regular prairie-fire of enthusiasm for American specialities."[52] He published articles explaining the reasons for "American prosperity." America is "prosperous," he wrote in 1929 in *The New York Times Magazine*, because it "is tending toward the realization of desire." The "large corporations," labor output and absence of labor dissent, the colossal domestic market with its "exceptional consuming capacity," and the "spirit of cooperation between government and business" all worked to promote "prosperity." People know "tomorrow will be better than today—better not simply materially but culturally; yes, and even spiritually."[53]

Klein brokered knowledge to corporations, but went beyond that to become a booster of those same corporations. And he was merely fulfilling the mandate Hoover had laid out for him—to forge the closest "bonds" between the state and business. "Cooperation," Klein said in one of his radio talks, "erects a protective bulwark for our business. It creates a staunch 'wall of will.'" Some ex-Commerce Department officials balked at his style. "He gets my goat," one wrote, "he's a man unwaveringly committed to booming expansion. . . . He's very smart but he is a crusader, which I find detestable." Hoover himself thought Klein a "perfect public servant."[54]

Like Hoover, who was the first president to have a telephone in the Oval Office and to talk on radio to Americans, Klein was a communications man, perhaps the first official in Washington to have a regular radio show. From 1928 into the early thirties, he ballyhooed American business and its methods in a nationwide weekly broadcast from the capital. (The source for the funding, public or private, is unclear.) In one show he praised "the independent merchant," at the same time invoking the "large and financially powerful corporations" that really formed the new economic bedrock of America and that—as he said later—were "mounting increasingly to the planes of diversion, entertainment, spiritual enrichment."[55]

In radio show after radio show, as Hoover's front man, Klein talked glowingly about American advertising, merchandising, industrial design, and all the other strategies of enticement calculated to feed consumer desire.

"Advertising is the key to world prosperity," he said on the air in October 1929, after returning home from Berlin stimulated by an advertising convention. In March 1930, speaking about show windows on Fifth Avenue in Manhattan, he argued that "American business is proving that an essentially mechanized civilization can nevertheless be majestic—vivid—satisfying—luminous." A year later he was gushing over the "advances" in industrial design and style that had permeated mass production methods. "Art as business," he said, "has yielded a profit of 700 percent." Business was (and these are his words) "liberating" Americans from the "utilitarian" and "Puritan" past. Because of business, Americans "live in an everyday world of beauty"; they have "bathroom symphonies," "chromatic plumbing," shoes in "color harmonies," pretty dishpans, and self-service turnstiles. "Who of us," he asked, "will say that the effect of this new Persian luxury is not delightful?"[56]

"It is imperative," he asserted on another broadcast, "for each enterprise to convey to its prospective patrons the most *vivid conception* of the distinctive qualities and merits of the product." "Lure the glance," he told Americans on the air, "fire the imagination by means of brilliant primary colors, unusual composition and mastery of line."[57]

Klein, a wholly loyal government evangelist of business at home and abroad, ended up on October 21, 1929, to no one's surprise, in Times Square to help honor Thomas Alva Edison as part of a national commemoration celebrating the inventor of electrical light. An even grander tribute was taking place simultaneously in Dearborn, Michigan, where Hoover and Henry Ford (with Edward Bernays providing the public relations) heaped praise on the aged Edison. Klein addressed the Broadway Association on the importance of effective commercial lighting. "Light," he explained to the already converted, "increases the advertising value" of interiors and exteriors. The district, of course, excelled in the use of light. Its electrical signs with their "infinitely complex and dazzling gyrations" were truly "magnificent" to behold, showing how far advertising had come from its "simple beginnings in Roman times." Klein spoke almost reverentially of "Broadway with its miles of light and its sunburst center at Times Square."[58]

Light had enriched many Americans by the twenties; it was the god of the commercial aesthetic, the radiant core of the consumer revolution. What would business have been without the spotlights in the windows and floodlights on facades, without the new frosted, recessed, and diffused lights in the interiors, without the colored light on the retail thoroughfares, without the lights in American homes and the holiday lights? Light had created a multibillion-dollar utility industry run by titans like Samuel Insull, who, in the early 1900s in Chicago, first produced electrical light cheaply, thereby disproving the widely held claim that such light would remain a luxury, and who, in the early 1930s, would be humiliated and destroyed for violating the public's trust. There was money in light.[59]

''Home, Sweet Home''

Less the transparent booster than Klein, Hoover had his own methods of getting across the same messages. He filtered them through an ornate system of public conferences that brought together leaders in business, the professions, and government. Hoover, as secretary of commerce and then as president, convened hundreds of such conferences between 1921 and 1932, nearly all intended to remake the nation, from end to end, into an efficient economic machine. Each conference collected data on specific issues and generated standards and guidelines. A few stand out as both strategically and ideologically significant.

One of the most interesting was the first, the Unemployment Conference of 1921–22. Opening in the crisis atmosphere of a depression, with Hoover as secretary of commerce, it was chaired by Owen Young of General Electric Company, funded by the Carnegie Foundation, and conducted jointly by the Commerce Department and the National Bureau of Economic Research. Its goal was to find strategies for ending the poverty, joblessness, and suffering caused by the turbulence of the business cycle. As the 1921 recession waned, the conference moved more probingly into its subject, seeking ways to manage the ups and downs of economic change. Its report advised voluntary "countercyclical measures on the part of business." Cut back on inventories, the report said; raise wages; institute some kind of unemployment insurance for workers. The report suggested that the federal government itself might also act countercyclically by funding public works programs for workers laid off in seasonally controlled industries.[60]

A 1925 Conference on Street and Highway Safety urged cities and businesses to adopt "model municipal traffic ordinances" to free up and streamline the movement of goods and people in American cities and suburbs. Other conferences showcased the advantages of home ownership in the suburbs. It was Hoover's cherished dream that all Americans own their own homes in quiet and stable communities. He disliked cities and considered multifamily dwellings (e.g., apartment houses) "abnormal" and deadly for adults and especially so for children. And yet he was drawn to the "new," or thought he understood its hold over people. Hadn't he, after all, campaigned for the presidency in 1928 under the banner of the "new day" and the "new era"? Like Simon Patten, he wanted people to consume all the "new" goods and to do so on an endlessly rising curve. He wanted Americans to be both stable and unstable, standing in one place yet always moving as "happiness machines." Give families "traditional" settings nearby shopping centers where they can buy "electrical appliances, radios, swings for the backyard, carpets, books and bookcases, or whatever." Hoover wrote later in his memoirs, "a primary right of every American family is the right to build a new house of its heart's desire at least once. Moreover, there is the instinct to own one's own house with one's own arrangement of gadgets, rooms, and surroundings."[61]

In 1922, as secretary of commerce, Hoover had created the department's Division of Building and Housing as a liaison to builders, real estate developers, social workers, and homemakers. The division did economic research and published materials on zoning laws and on methods of home purchase and financing. It helped the building trades extend their seasonal period, recommended "reasonable credits for homes," and promoted home ownership. A master at making public policy through private means, Hoover vigorously publicized the division through an arrangement with a private group, the Better Homes Movement. In 1923 he helped reorganize that association, had himself appointed president, and worked, as he put it, to make Better Homes a "sort of collateral arm to the Housing Division of the Department of Commerce."[62] In 1925–26, aided by a $250,000 grant from the Laura Spelman Foundation, he coordinated a public relations drive that blanketed the country with "homebuying ideas" mediated through more than eighteen hundred Better Homes local committees. The committees distributed posters, lectures, fliers, and pamphlets (including Own Your Own Home from the Commerce Department); they produced a film, Home, Sweet Home, in the national office for general circulation; and they constructed "demonstration model homes" in city after city.[63] The "homes" added yet another layer of enticement to the model rooms, model homes, and "period rooms" already on display in the urban department stores and museums.

The president's 1931 Conference on Home Building and Home Ownership addressed, according to its final report, "the whole problem of housing" and was, all in all, a remarkable conference, its agenda greatly modified to reflect the imperatives of the ever-deepening Depression. In consultation with the building industry, architects, engineers, and city planners, its many committees assessed everything from "slums and decentralization" and "Negro housing" to "home finance and taxation." But many of its proposed guidelines, published as *Housing Objectives and Programs*, simply rehashed the ideas and standards of the previous decade. Crucial among these ideas were the advocacy of single-family "private houses" over "multiple dwellings"; suburban over urban housing; and provision of several rooms in every house, each with a separate function, including a fully electrified kitchen, and a bedroom for each family member. "It is undesirable," the report said, "to have two children occupy the same bed—whatever their age." The report advised that shopping centers should be "accessible to residences within a radius of a quarter to a half mile and concentrated on the boundary streets of a residential area."[64]

Another conference of personal importance to Hoover was an earlier 1929 Conference on Child Health and Protection, which mirrored almost exactly his work as secretary of commerce on home building and home ownership and his longtime interest in the health of children. In the early 1920s he had been elected president of the American Child Health Association and in the midtwenties he led this private association in publicity campaigns, renaming May Day as "Child Health Day." "The Communists," he said later, "had previously appropriated the ancient festival of May Day for their demonstrations; and I took special satisfaction in giving them this particular competition." Later he got Congress to establish May Day as a special national day, and just for the occasion wrote a widely circulated "Child's Bill of Rights." In 1924, the year that Macy's department store launched its first Thanksgiving Day parade, he had parades of his own, May Day parades for children. "They carried banners," he said, "demanding the protection for their health."[65] In 1929, several months into his administration, Hoover opened the White House Conference on Child Health and Protection. The conference reiterated many of the reformist ideas of the child welfare movement: abolition of child labor, enrollment of more children in schools, and reduction of the comparatively high mortality rates of children. The guidelines and standards that emanated from the conference foreshadowed those outlined in the later housing conference. Children should live in "primarily residential neighborhoods" and "homes should not be located within an industrial district." "The preferable location for a home is on a minor street so planned that it does not invite traffic," "within relatively easy access of churches and schools, and civic, cultural, and shopping centers." "Neighborhoods should, insofar as possible, have charm and distinction and be free from ugliness and monotony and conditions which tend to depress or to humiliate the family." "The neighborhood should be free from 'moral nuisances' such as disorderly houses, centers of liquor traffic, and gambling houses."[66]

The conference report, *The Home and the Child*, contributed to a redefinition of "the child world" that had been under way in the United States for almost thirty years. Children, it said, were independent "individuals" with the same desires as adults for their own commodities and their own spaces. "The child—beloved as he is," began the report's chapter on "Furnishings and Equipment,"

> is often an alien in his home when it comes to any consideration
> of his special needs in the furnishings and equipment of the home.
> He belongs nowhere. He must accommodate himself to an adult
> environment—chairs and tables are too big and too high for him;
> there is no suitable place for his books and his toys. He moves in
> a misfit world with nothing apportioned to his needs. Often this
> results in retarding his physical, mental, and social development.

The report proposed several panaceas. Give children their own "furniture and eating equipment" suitable to each child's age and size; provide playrooms inside the house, and stock the backyard with "toys, velocipedes, sawhorses, wagons, wheelbarrows, slides, and places to keep pets." "Generally a sleeping room for each person is desirable." As the child grows "older and becomes more social he wants games and toys that he can share with his friends." When the family is deciding on "the purchase of a piece of furniture or a musical instrument" of common interest, be sure to consult the children. Take them shopping for their own "things" and let them pick them out by themselves. "Through such experiences personality develops." Such "experiences have the advantage also of creating in the child a sense of personal as well as family pride in ownership, and eventually teaching him that his personality can be expressed through things."[67]

Two attitudes—one reformist, the other commercial or consumerist—seemed to be at war in Hoover, as they also seemed to be in other child welfare reformers and progressives, such as Julia Lathrop and Florence Kelly. I say "seemed to be" because these perspectives were inextricably mixed. Hoover was doubtless a sincere advocate of child welfare, and he admired the work of the U.S. Children's Bureau, still a busy if underfunded agency in the 1920s, and supported its program of better housing, nurture, and medical care. But like the reformers themselves, Hoover incorporated into his vision—into his entire concept of the "standard of living"—an emphasis on the consumption of goods and children's special role in that consumption. And, in the end, the commercial side was the predominant side of his vision. In the White House conference as in all the other conferences he had convened as secretary of commerce and as president, his intent was to "raise" the standard of living and to advance and "equilibrate" the levels of production and consumption. Whatever he did—whatever most of the government did—was compatible with the goals of the mass consumer order and of the "new day."

Dissent and the "Torments of Desire"

Hoover helped to create a new institutional bureaucratic language of consumption. As president he legitimated this language; terms like "mass leisure," "mass consumption," and "mass services," invented at colleges and universities by social scientists and economists, now entered both popular vernacular and theoretical discussions as ways of understanding American society. They shaped the way Americans thought about consumption, just as the colors of Times Square helped them visualize it. On Hoover's watch, government took on a new burden: Not only would it protect the political rights and interests of individuals, but it would further the fulfillment of their "needs" and "desires" as well. To Hoover's mind, as to the minds of increasing numbers of Americans, rights, desires, and needs were equivalent.

Hoover's institutional structure became the envy of other European countries. "Within the last decade," wrote the editor of a European economic journal in 1933, "the Department of Commerce of the United States, largely under the inspiration of President Hoover, has worked in collaboration with businessmen and business organizations to a degree unparalleled by any government of the world." A Commerce Department official echoed the same view. "The Bureau of Foreign and Domestic Commerce," he reported to a friend of his within the bureau, "should be recognized by businessmen of all kinds as the outstanding arm of government that has done and is doing more to aid them than any bureau of the government has thought capable of achieving."[68]

While many businessmen welcomed help from the federal government on their behalf, others objected to what seemed a bias toward consumer goods. "It strikes me," wrote a spokesman of the machine tool industry to the bureau in 1928, "that you are focusing too much attention on consumer goods and wants. Does anybody really know the relative importance of producer goods and consumer goods in total volume?"[69] And others criticized the bureaucratic bloatage of the Commerce Department. Almost from its founding, the department's divisions and subdivisions (especially the BFDC) met "a barrage of criticism," with one politician attacking the BFDC as the "best example of paternalism that we can lay our hands on," and a few merchants and manufacturers objecting to it as an extravagant expense "calculated to weaken" and "interfere with individual initiative." Stung by these attacks, Klein instructed his staff to tell the "critics" that "we have made sincere efforts not to undertake work which businessmen either individually or through their organizations can do for themselves" and that "no private agency can secure business information in the same manner in which the government can."[70]

Some ex-Commerce Department officials came away from their government jobs with feelings of bitterness and hostility, expressing a view similar to the one held by the earlier populists about railroads, department stores, and corporations. "I always thought," wrote Donald Breed, a former bureau official from the Midwest who became a journalist, "that the growth of commodity divisions and of the regionals was noxious." Hoover, he said, had made an "octopus" with its "arms" stretching through a "vast agglomeration of subbureaus."[71]

Conflicts of a different order percolated through the government itself, as they had for years, over the limits and character of the relationship between the federal government and corporate business. Many progressive reformers in the Children's Bureau and individuals like Klein disputed how far commercial themes should be allowed to shape children's issues. Some reformers tried, seemingly in vain, to play down "commercial" themes. Klein, for his part, apparently saw no problem in them. Conflicts erupted between the Federal Trade Commission and the Justice Department, on the one hand, and the Commerce Department, on the other, over regulating versus serving business interests. Many in both the FTC and in the Justice Department argued for regulation of some kind, fearing the power of the corporations and the vigilant trade associations and their threat to competition. The Commerce Department, however, believed that whatever dangers existed (and there were few, according to Hoover) would be outweighed by the economic benefits of government cooperation with business.

Confusions about other matters existed between federal law enforcement agencies and the Commerce Department. In the 1920s the Bureau of Prohibition had swelled into a fat, arrogant agency, staffed by zealous puritans and self-interested bureaucrats and supported by a police force of unusual size. It labored day and night to try to control alcohol consumption. The Commerce Department, staffed by zealots of its own, urged people to buy new goods and to move into neighborhoods that made consumption of such goods a necessity. Discipline, control, and repression, on one hand; desire and indulgence, on the other.

In the late 1920s a dispute arose between the prostyle and procommercial color contingent in the Commerce Department and the antistyle, anticolor, antiwaste group in the Division of Simplified Practice. Perhaps influenced by Veblenian "production for use" reformers, the simplifiers wanted to get rid of "overdiversification." "If simplified practice means anything," one such engineer said, "it means the reduction of variety in sizes, dimensions, and *immaterial* differences, as a means of eliminating waste, decreasing costs, and increasing profits and values in production, distribution, and consumption." "Can not simplification be invoked," the same engineer inquired, "to curb or at least curtail the tendency to apply color to everything?" "Utilitarian things . . . in a simplified range of colors perform their destined functions just as well." Klein considered such a position hopelessly misconceived. But he, too, was guided by a certain form of rationality—planned obsolescence—that put irrational desires at the service of the "rational" market. An economist, not an engineer, he welcomed color, especially if it furthered the rapid turnover of goods.[72]

Tensions also existed within Herbert Hoover, an engineer and Quaker.

In the summer of 1925 in Houston, Texas, to deliver an address, "Advertising Is a Vital Force in Our National Life," before the Associated Advertising Clubs of the World, he returned again and again to the theme of "desire"—its relation to advertising, its role in economic theory, and its place in culture. He began by congratulating advertisers for their contributions to "our standard of living" and for "expanding our upper levels of desire." Advertising was fueling the competitive process by "spreading a restless pillow which drives others to further and faster exertions to keep apace." "You have devised," he said, "an artful ingenuity in forms and mediums of advertising. The landscape has become your vehicle as well as the press. In the past, wish, want, and desire were the motive forces in economic progress. Now you have taken over the job of creating desire. In economics the torments of desire in turn creates demand, and from demand we create production, and thence around the cycle we land with increased standards of living."[73] It was a sunny picture, painted with the brush of Simon Patten.

Yet even his phrases, though taken probably for the most part out of textbooks on neoclassical economics—"restless pillow," "the Midas of advertising," "fearful ingenuity," "the torments of desire"—appeared to betray a half-hidden anxiety about advertisers. In this Houston address, moreover, he lectured his audience about the dangers of playing around with human desire. Advertisers should not "unhitch desire," he said, but they should "make certain that the desire they create is satisfied by the article they present." Advertising, he was arguing, must act rationally and efficiently, presenting goods in such a way that does not distort their meaning or raise false hopes about what they can do. To arouse desire and then fail to satisfy it, Hoover may have been saying, was wasteful and immoral.

A similar sense of unease surfaced again during the 1928 presidential campaign, when Hoover revisited his birthplace in West Branch, Iowa. In a speech, he described how much had changed in West Branch since his childhood. The old Quaker meeting house was now a movie house. He remembered how his devout Aunt Hannah had denounced the "rise of modern ways"; she had predicted that churches and meeting houses would one day be "transformed into places of abomination." In the 1880s everyone shared communal pleasures, and the town was independent and self-sufficient. "We ground our wheat and corn on toll at the mill," he said.

We slaughtered our hogs for meat; we wove at least part of our own clothing; we repaired our own machinery; we got our own fuel from the woods; we erected our own buildings; we made our own soap; we preserved our own fruit and grew our own vegetables. Only a small part of the family living came by purchases from the outside. Perhaps 20 percent of the products were sold in the markets to purchase the small margin of necessities which we could not ourselves produce and to pay interest on the mortgage.

In his childhood there was no poverty in West Branch and little suffering from the downswings in the Chicago market. Now, in 1928, the market could affect the town's whole economy and wipe out from "25 to 50 percent of the family net income and make the difference between comfort and freedom from anxiety or, on the other hand, debts and discouragements."[74]

Hoover was quick to remind his audience of the progress the United States had made, and of the many "benefits" of economic change. "I do not suggest return to the great security which agriculture enjoyed in its earlier days," he insisted, "because with that security were lower standards of living, greater toil, less opportunity for leisure and recreation, less of the comforts of home, less of the joy of living." Yet, with this said, he came back again to his bittersweet theme, emphasizing "sentimental regret" over what had disappeared. He acknowledged that one could not really go back home and that change was "inevitable." "I have sometimes been homesick for the ways of those self-contained farms of forty years ago as I have for the kindly folk who lived in them. But I know it is no more possible to revive those old conditions than it is to summon back the relations and friends in the cemetery yonder. . . . We must accept what is inevitable in the changes that have taken place. It is fortunate indeed that the principles upon which our government was founded require no alteration to meet these changes."[75]

For all of the tensions and contradictions and ambivalences in Hoover's political world, what stands out—it seems to me—is the degree of the institutional consensus. Hoover's West Branch speech was poignant in its way, but it was also nostalgia, ending in self-serving optimism; at its heart was a fervent belief in "progress" and a total confidence in the rightness (the inexorable rightness) of America's evolution. Hoover had little sympathy, it appears, with those writers of the decade who also believed that America's cultural life was embodied in the West Branches of America—

small towns, face-to-face intimacies, shared loyalties, and a common sense of destiny—but who feared the pace and character of progress. Northern writers like Joseph Wood Krutch, Harold Stearn, and Stuart Chase, and southern ones like John Crowe Ransom and the young Robert Penn Warren were increasingly convinced that the America they admired was the doomed America, being crushed by "civilization," by industrial growth, by excessive reliance on technology as a cure-all for all ills, by an endless quest for novelty, and by "progress" reckoned only in quantities of goods and money. [76]

For Hoover the choice seemed clear: civilization over culture, international and national markets over local and regional ones, an ever-expanding standard of living over the relatively unchanging but sufficient simple life, mass production and mass consumption over West Branch. What is lost, alas, is lost.

In this decade, the federal government placed the capstone on the institutional coalition grouped behind the Land of Desire. Prestigious universities built even stronger alliances with the new economy and culture; so did museums, along with a great ensemble of other institutions, from art schools to investment banking groups. Together they galvanized the economic circuits of chain stores, department stores, hotels, restaurants, and movie houses, of public relations firms, model agencies, fashion groups, and advertising businesses, to say nothing of the huge industrial corporate infrastructure that undergirded it all.

The age was a time of the Rainbow Houses, from Stewart Culin at the Brooklyn Museum to Hoover's dreams for the suburbs. The amenable cultural climate shaped earlier by the religious compromises of John Wanamaker and by others and by the emergence of a mind-cure mentality at home with acquisition and consumption, had apparently won the day. Although groups of people were locked out from it and some resisted it, the new American culture seemed to others (and we will never know how many) in harmony with L. Frank Baum's vision of a society in which "wonder" had no "heartache" and every child and adult might find the road to the Emerald City.

A new commercial aesthetic had flowered, a formidable group of cultural and economic intermediaries had emerged, and an elaborate institutional circuitry had evolved, together creating the first culture of its kind that answered entirely to the purposes of the capitalist system and that seemed to establish and legitimate business dominance. Corporate business now orchestrated the myths of America, and it was through business, with the blessings in many ways of the federal government and other agencies, that the American dream had found its most dependable ally. "To each a world opens," said advertiser Artemas Ward in 1892, "to everyone possibilities are present." By 1929, after almost fifty years of growth and struggle, the modern American capitalist culture of consumption had finally taken root.

LEGACIES

When the great crash of 1929 came, the writer Edmund Wilson almost welcomed it with a sigh of relief. It seemed, he thought, to be breaking the grip corporate capitalism had over the economy and culture. "To the writers and artists of my generation," he wrote, "who had grown up in the Big Business era and had always resented its barbarism, its crowding out of everything they cared about, these years were not depressing but stimulating. One couldn't help being exhilarated at the sudden unexpected collapse of that stupid gigantic fraud."[1]

Wilson went so far as to locate the origins of the "fraud" in the very beginnings of the republic, when the defender of individual liberty Thomas Jefferson joined hands with the defender of "centralization" Alexander Hamilton to "establish the protection of the propertied classes."[2] Throughout the 1800s, Wilson argued, the cultural implications of this compromise did not fully reveal themselves; the country was immersed in the "exhilaration of the wildness and size of the continent—the breaking it in to the harness of the railroads, the stumbling upon sudden riches." "During these last years" (or since World War I), however, "hope and our faith have all been put behind the speed of mass production, behind stupendous campaigns of advertising, behind cyclones of salesmanship." "Money-making and the kind of advantages which a money-making society provides," Wilson insisted, "are not enough to satisfy humanity—neither is a social system like our own where everyone is out for himself and the devil take the hindmost and [there is] little common culture to give life stability and sense." With this unlinear view, it is no wonder Wilson rejoiced when the stock market shattered, promising to bring with it the toppling of corporate business from its throne of the 1920s.

Other intellectuals and reformers were so disturbed by the onslaught of the Depression as to abandon or greatly modify deeply held convictions. Child-welfare advocate Sidonie Gruenberg altered her earlier sentiment that children benefited from the new permissive consumer world. Gruenberg had lectured everywhere in the twenties—even at department stores such as Macy's—on the need to give children "lots of play time," lots of toys, and even an entirely separate world of their own so that their "personalities" might develop spontaneously and freely. But in a book written with her husband, Benjamin, in 1933, *Parents, Children, and Money,* she retreated from this emphasis. The earlier attitude, she now admitted, had not done much to prepare children to cope with the demands of "work" and of the "real world." She even went so far as to question the goals of the child-welfare legislation she had once so strongly defended. "One of the consequences of thus shielding childhood against serious injury in commercial employment," she wrote, "was to discredit work in general." We have "glorified all work-avoiding individuals. . . . Almost everybody has by now learned that 'only saps work.' " By so doing, we made it seem as if consumption and spending were more crucial to life then fulfilling work. But "young people want to accomplish something, something of which they can be proud: Being a parasite is nothing to brag about." Moreover, by shutting children off in their own little communities, we isolated them "from daily contact with . . . adults—contacts that are necessary in the process of growing up."[3]

Critics like Lewis Mumford, John Dewey, James Rorty, and Stuart Chase expressed degrees of outrage and sadness over a business culture that had divorced individuals so much from the community fabric, transforming them—in Mumford's words—into "their own separate personalities [without] all sense of social responsibility or contact with the surrounding environment."[4] At the same time, these critics believed that out of the maelstrom might emerge something more than just another stage in commercialism and the pursuit of what Rorty called "comfortable survival" or what Mumford called "money, size, and efficiency."[5] Mumford urged the rejection of the myth of infinite progress and constant growth (more next year than this), and the acceptance of a sense of limits. He, along with the others, saw possibilities for the appearance of stable communities in which individuals might prosper as "whole human beings." As Dewey wrote in a 1930 book on individualism, "originality and uniqueness" could only flourish in communities that were emotionally and economically secure, not in contexts driven by competition and continually destabilized by unregulated corporate growth and by ever-expanding consumer markets.[6]

None of these men demanded, it must be said, that Americans "give up" consuming (an absurd idea in any case), retreat into a kind of voluntary Spartan poverty, repudiate drinking and the pleasures of dress, stop entertaining, or turn away from enjoying life. What they rejected, and what frightened and upset them, was the way corporate business had shaped the economy, the way it had organized the "new," the way it had influenced the character of luxury and necessity, and the way it had infiltrated into the tastes and desires of everybody. Most of these critics hoped that Americans could regain their "better past," a shared democratic past that existed before the full advent of corporate capitalism.[7] They opened up debate on important cultural and political questions as well, on who was accountable for the depth of the misery.

For all of the criticism and desite hope for renewal, the profound cultural changes introduced between 1880 and 1930 were too entrenched to be overturned or reversed easily. To be sure, the Depression as well as World War II and, to some degree even the beginnings of the Cold War, may have delayed the expansion of the culture of consumer capitalism by calling Americans to better standards. The fighting of World War II, especially, drew on the strengths and sacrifices of all the people, inspiring heroism and sometimes even nobility. But such episodes in our history obviously neither stopped nor reversed the course of events.

Even in the 1930s, and especially as the New Deal took hold, corporate capitalism was in no great danger, as many critics were quick to observe. To Samuel Strauss, "the managing and directing kind of men" and "the pliers of appetites and desires" seemed more in control than ever before.[8] Both *The Nation* and *The New Republic*, which at first championed Roosevelt's New Deal as a step away from past mistakes, were by the mid-thirties reviling it as an "indirect subsidy to bankers and manufacturers" and as helping to "accelerate the trend toward monopoly" and to "stimulate demand for privately produced goods." And, indeed, after 1935 the government increased its aid to business by, among other things, providing funds for vocational education in "distributive occupations," or by supplying millions of dollars worth of loans under the 1936 Federal Housing Act, which promoted business "modernization" as well as home ownership and led, for instance, to the installation of much more air conditioning in department stores, hotels, and theaters.[9]

Journalist James Rorty took a trip across America in the midthirties and encountered little to show that the Depression had dampened the power of what he called the "dream culture." If anything, he wrote, both economic misery and the profit motive had "augmented the demand for dreams." A "valueless process" still held sway, "in which money begets machines, machines beget money, money begets money." From one coast to the other, what Rorty saw was a fully realized consumer landscape with separate regions carved out, catering to different parts of the consumer paradise: Detroit to the "manufacture of mobility for the continent"; Hollywood to the "manufacture of the soothing, narcotic dreams of love, of riches, of powerful untamed egos"; and New York to "the manufacture of cheerio radio optimism . . . and commodity fetishism intoned by unctuous announcers." The United States had plenty of "Protestant and Catholic Churches as culture-makers and culture-bearers," Rorty admitted, but they were "without effect." What was having effect, what was dominating, whether the people wanted it or not, Rorty claimed, was "the specialized, heavily capitalized, highly speculative and technologically advanced system of dream-manufacture." No "counterapparatus" seemed waiting in the wings to challenge the new culture. "The mass production of a mass culture" was stronger than ever. Indeed, there were "no other unifying bonds" in America.[10] The distinguishing feature of the period after 1930, then, was not discontinuity, not the making of a new kind of community but continuity, the ongoing surge of consumer capitalism.

An immense legacy was passed on, an institutional legacy of corporations, investment and commercial banks, business schools, commercial art schools, museums, universities, and the federal government. These institutions and the services they performed for business grew dramatically, especially after 1950. In our own time, business schools exceed in number and scope of services anything imaginable in 1925, graduating yearly thousands of one-, two-, and three-year M.B.A.s. The U.S. government, too, serves business in a way Herbert Hoover could never have conceived of. "Remove the regime of capital," observes political economist Robert Heilbroner of the current scene, "and the state would remain, although it might change dramatically; remove the state and the regime of capital would not last a day."[11]

The state and business are profoundly intermingled with one another, with business dependent on government guarantees of bank deposits and farm loans to protect it and bail it out from its recklessness and corruption. Wall Street analyst Michael Grant writes that in the 1980s the "government intervened more actively than it had ever done before to absorb the losses" caused by the gross lending practices of commercial banks.[12] Business relies on the Postal Service to move commercial materials (the bulk of what is mailed); on government-built and government-repaired roads, highways, and air terminals to move goods; and on federal monies to educate workers for employment. The government (especially since the Reagan years) acts through a revised immigration policy as a primary provider of cheap labor (both skilled and unskilled) to small businesses and corporations. Government agencies generate tons of data every day, informing businesspeople about the economy's shape, its potential path, and the character of the international economic scene. Data flow uninterruptedly from an array of government serials, available both free and at cost, such as the *Federal Reserve Bulletin* (est. 1915), *Survey of Current Business* (est. 1921), *Business Statistics: A Supplement to the Surveys of Current Business* (est. 1931), *Economic Indicators* (est. 1948), *Business Conditions Digest* (est. 1961), *U.S. Industrial Outlook* (est. 1960), *Commerce News* and *Recent Commerce* (est. 1979), and *Commerce Publications Update* (est. 1980).[13]

Today, the Commerce Department is only one among many government agencies serving the business community. Still, it single-handedly conducts economic censuses every five years on U.S. manufacturers, the retail and wholesale trades, the service industries, transportation, and the mineral industries. It does analyses of business trends (which includes constructing econometric models and elaborating a system of business cycles indicators) and presents regular reports on national and international accounts, with up-to-date detailed pictures of consumers, producers, investors, governments, and foreign customers. The Technology Administration, created in 1990, exists inside the Commerce Department to promote a favorable climate for private sector innovation, improvements in the use of technology, and constantly expanding productivity. The Commerce Department has the International Trade Administration to develop the export potential of U.S. firms; it generates nonstop assessments of the competitiveness of U.S. companies and delivers marketing services directly to and through the Foreign Commerce Service. This service helps U.S. business expand their exports, locates long-range trade, ferrets out investment opportunities, and develops "remedial strategies."[14] After the Gulf War, the Commerce Department emerged as a ready source of free information regarding investment opportunities in Kuwait; all a businessperson had to do was pick up a phone and dial the Commerce Department "hot line" for tips on Persian Gulf investments.[15]

As for the commercial aesthetic (commercial color, glass, and light), the money spent on such means of visual enticement reaches well into the billions of dollars. The strategies have intensified through new media—above all, through television satellites, which can beam consumer desire into every hamlet and village around the world. Businesspeople and advertisers boast of their ability, through telecommunications, to "homogenize" tastes throughout the world and to encourage everybody to desire the same goods and services.[16] At home, visual enticements continue to flourish but, as Michael Schudson has claimed in regard to advertising, more as an expression of corporate power than because of their effect on consumer purchasing. To be sure, the strategies of enticement appear to shape tastes in certain new immigrant communities, in many sectors of the youth and children's market, in communities of impoverished and uneducated consumers, and even in those more upscale markets of educated consumers who boast that they are unaffected by seductions. But in all of these markets, as Schudson has shown (although he focuses largely on educated professionals), there are people who are indifferent to and contemptuous of advertising and who depend largely on their families, friends, and consumer groups for information about goods. Growing investment in advertising is not (and has not) been grounded solely on its immediate or obvious impact on consumer choice; rather, it is based on the need of business to have unopposed cultural influence.[17]

The average adult American—who is today plied day and night by banks and corporations, on the phone, through the mail, and in mass media—has three or four credit cards. Americans (including adolescents and children) use more than 1 billion credit cards (the Germans and the French, with a total population about half that of the United States, use only 24 million cards, although Germany in particular has a reputation as being an intensely consumer-oriented society); Americans carry more consumer debt than all other peoples in the world combined.[18] The American fashion industry bestrides the globe, competing fiercely with the Japanese and the Europeans and still feeding off the designs and colors of traditional peasant and folk cultures. An example of its parasitism is the activity of the National Institute of Fashion Technology in New Delhi, India, a recently created branch of New York City's Fashion Institute of Technology (which has similar progeny in Mexico, Israel, Barbados, and Japan), staffed by young designers constantly on the prowl for fashion ideas in rural parts of India and in impoverished urban ghettos. Hilda Z. Friedman, a visiting professor from the institute, explained to the *New York Times* that, "We want them to have this Indian heritage, this Indian feeling. But we want the clothes to be international."[19]

Another corporate legacy passed on from the pre-1930 years is the concept of the human being as an insatiable, desiring machine or as an animal governed by an infinity of desires. This concept of humanity argues that what is most "human" about people is their quest after the new, their willingness to violate boundaries, their hatred of the old and the habitual (unless enlisted in behalf of the new, as in fashion and style, or used in some way to promote consumption, as in encouraging brand loyalty or selling old-fashioned Quaker Oats, etc.), and their need to incorporate "more and more"—goods, money, experience, everything. There seems to be much truth in this concept, as such great writers as Emerson, Whitman, and William James long ago explained. It appears that many human beings not only seek but also *need* to seek new goods, new adventures and experiences, and new insights to feel alive and fulfilled. There may be no inherent limit to what people can or might desire or to what they can or might be invited and tempted to do—economically, sexually, politically, morally. Human beings are infinitely flexible and endowed with considerable imaginative powers. Art historian Anne Hollander has recently argued that the desire for "fluidity" and "permutations," the enthusiasm for putting on and taking off masks and for experimentation "is ingrained in our civilization."[20]

At the same time, the conception of the desiring self, as expressed in capitalist terms and exploited by capitalism, offers a one-sided and flawed notion of what it means to be human. It rejects what is also "human" about human beings: their ability to commit themselves, to establish binding relationships, to sink permanent roots, to maintain continuity with previous generations, to remember, to make ethical judgments, to seek pleasure in work, to remain steadfast on behalf of principle and loyal to community or country (to the degree that community or country strives to be just and fair), to seek spiritual transcendence beyond the self, and to fight a cause through to the end.

But however flawed, the capitalist concept of self, the consumer concept of the self, is the reigning American concept. It is a broker's view of people (e.g., that people have no basic commitment to anything except what is coming next and can be encouraged and seduced—without much ado— to change their minds and habits). It is also youth-oriented, resting on the idea that it is unfortunate, and somehow antihuman, to grow old. It is child-oriented, too, because the very vision of the self it presents is that of a demanding child, susceptible to outbursts of both primal rage and primal yearning. It is also a permissive mind-cure notion that people prefer to be open completely to the "abundance" of the universe and to have no boundaries separating the self from the outside world.

Two other legacies, both related to the idea of the desiring self, have been transmitted to us from the earlier period: one, the myth of the separate world of consumption as the domain of freedom, self-expression, and self-fulfillment; the other, the conception of the market as always expanding and as always without boundaries. Today the myth of consumption as the ideal world of freedom has grown, fostered by commercial media that depict every consumer moment as a liberating one and every purchase as a sexual thrill or as a ticket to happiness. The cultural outcome has been to intensify the old dangers; for despite progressive laws to protect adult and child workers and to expose consumers to the nature of workplace exploitation, the trend toward abstraction, indifference, and narcissism has increased, not decreased. The distance between consumers and workers (in fact but especially in the imagination) has gotten wider, a trend the government and media have conspired to create by denying the true nature of work. Today, the factory goods "made by unknown hands," as Wesley Clair Mitchell wrote in 1912, are even more unknown, produced, as most of them are, by faceless individuals in Third World countries (or—perhaps in the future— in America's own Third World cities). Thus Nike, the sneaker company with a $3 billion profit in 1991, whose media promotions have been acclaimed as "the high-water mark of American advertising," pays its factory workers in Indonesia, who are "mostly women, poor, and malnourished,"

$1.03 a day, not enough for food and shelter.[21] But these workers are so far away and have so few advocates that there is little reason for people to care how they are treated, about what their wages are, or about who is responsible for such treatment.

Before 1930, the conception of the market without boundaries and as open to all forms of selling was at the center of much business practice. In 1923 the New York journalist Samuel Strauss, disturbed by the rise of what he called "Consumptionism," noted to what degree capitalist forces had penetrated through national boundaries. American business had already created the largest domestic market in history; but now, he observed, the movement was reaching into other countries. Strauss was worried about this trend and warned that deeper market intrusions would lead to the destruction of local communities and of local cultures, or of what he called "particularism." "Make no mistake about it," he wrote, "[industrialists] believe that boundary lines no longer exist . . . only people exist . . . the world is all alike; the world is one." Strauss feared that the world was being reduced, inch by inch, to the standardized pattern that Simon Patten had believed was the precondition for ethical progress. World War I "had not been fought for democracy or for nationalism," Strauss wrote, but for "industrialism." It was waged to ensure that "the power of production would never again be endangered" and that the production of "more next year than this year" would go on unimpeded.[22]

And he was right, by and large, despite disastrous slumps. Today the world without boundaries—a truly "global" world—is with us, in part in reality but, more important, in ideology, as corporate businesses and business-minded governments remind us daily that national boundaries are disappearing, mere old-fashioned obstacles to achieving market share, and that Americans—if they wish to survive—must turn away from the narrow particularism of a special culture, of a special belief, or of a special tradition. The global market conception is the outlook of such orthodox Republican think tanks as the American Enterprise Institute and the Heritage Foundation, both advisers to Presidents Bush and Reagan and both champions of a world without boundaries, of global capitalism, and of mind-cure consumer culture. Global American popular culture—especially the heart of that culture, the consumer entertainments, goods, and services—is "one of the great democratic instruments in history," according to Ben Wattenberg, a passionate promoter of this view, "good for America and good for the world."[23]

American corporate businesses—AT&T, ITT, Nabisco, Coca-Cola, General Motors, and McDonald's, among many others—are the most ardent supporters of the expanded market vision or of the "new" global competitive order (I say "new" because it is really an old idea, expounded by people such as Herbert Hoover in about 1910). The first loyalties of these firms, increasingly, are not to America but to building factories and "outlets" in other countries and to marketing Frosted Flakes in China, jeeps in Jerusalem, hamburgers in Moscow, and cigarettes anywhere. In 1989 the conglomerate Philip Morris Companies mounted a commemoration of the Bill of Rights—one of the sleaziest promotions in recent memory— while, at the same time, saturating the world with its principal products— beer, synthetic cheeses, and cigarettes. Ten years earlier, in an equally sleazy venture in Guatemala, the company marketed a new cigarette called "Commander" at a time when the Guatemala military was seeking to destroy the trade unions, a crucial source of resistance in the country. Philip Morris (or its local factory "Tabacalera Centro America s.a.," 91 percent owned by Philip Morris) created the cigarette to attract patronage from army men. The unions opposed it because it glorified the military, and by most accounts, succeeded in stopping the company from introducing its new brand.[24] As liberal political economist Robert Reich, Secretary of Labor under President Bill Clinton, has written with praise in the *Harvard Business Review*, "successful global competitors like IBM, Shell, Procter & Gamble, and McDonald's have willingly shed their national identities and become loyal corporate citizens wherever they do business around the world."[25]

It appears, then, that the consumer capitalism of pre-1930 America has achieved a new level of strength and influence. It seems to be making advances everywhere, especially in the wake of the collapse of communism. It also appears to have a nearly unchallenged hold over every aspect of American life, from politics to culture, so much so that the United States looks like a fabulous bazaar to much of the rest of the world. For some Americans the continued power of consumerism has led to further degradation of what it means to be an American or of what America is all about. For others, this evolution has only enhanced the country's appeal, making it appear more than ever like an Emerald City, a feast, a department store to which everyone is invited and entitled. Just as cities in the United States once operated as generators of consumer desire for internal markets, today America functions similarly on a global scale.

Yet, at the same time, in the midst of this apparent victory, consumer capitalism seems in jeopardy in the very country that did the most to create it—in America, the Land of Desire. Today, as in the period following the 1929 crash, the economy and the culture are once again under siege. Thus huge overbuilding and overspeculation have propelled countless corporations to lay off thousands of workers and to consolidate their managements—all necessary for economic "health" but also caused by the managers themselves in their reckless quest for profits and disregard for others.[26] Today, moreover, disparities of wealth are greater than they have ever been in American history. A profound sense of insecurity has swept through every sector of American society. America's standard of living, which Herbert Hoover and others called the country's most precious gift to the world and identified as the heart of America, is declining. The fundamental American conviction that the next generation will be better off than the one prior to it is on the brink of being dashed.[27]

But there are opportunities here for those who demand change and want and seek new directions. The new dilemmas facing Americans may lead to the revitalization of an older insurgent politics, one articulated by such progressives as Frank Walsh of the Committee on Industrial Relations in 1912, the man who exposed the rapacity of John D. Rockefeller II, or by the reformer Florence Kelley, who demanded that consumers take responsibility for the world they lived in, that they look capitalism squarely in the face, and that they acknowledge the working people who make the goods and under what conditions. The new circumstances may activate a sense of outrage and a demand that corporate business, and the institutions that collaborate with corporate business, must take responsibility for what has been wrought. As Wesley Clair Mitchell insisted, business must be held accountable for the miseries—and chaos—that strike the economy, "laying waste our days." One would hope, given all the assistance business has received from the government over the years, that it could be persuaded (at the very least) to pay its due.

The challenges may encourage Americans to return to other voices as well, to those voices of the early thirties, for instance—to critics like James Rorty, Edmund Wilson, and Peter Maurin, or, even farther back, to such thinkers as Thorstein Veblen, Charles Cooley, Walter Rauschenbush, John Ryan, William James, and Elizabeth Gurley Flynn. These thinkers rejected business values, the cult of the new, the constant pursuit of mere comfort, the culture of desire. Instead they argued for a larger vision of what it meant to be human, a fuller sense of being, and a refusal to accept having and taking as the key to being or the equivalent of being. As historian of religion Joseph Harountunian said, "The good is not in 'goods.' The good is in justice, mercy, and peace. It is in consistency and integrity, in living according to truth and right. It inheres in men and not in things. It is other than the goodness of goods and without it goods are not good."

NOTES

Abbreviations for Notes

AMNH   American Museum of Natural History
BFDC   Bureau of Foreign and Domestic Commerce
CW   *Credit World*
CUOHP   Columbia University Oral History Project
DC   *Domestic Commerce*
DGE   *Dry Goods Economist*
DW   *Display World*
HBR   *Harvard Business Review*
HBS   Harvard Business School
HH   Herbert Hoover
JK   Julius Klein
JW   John Wanamaker
JWA   John Wanamaker Archives
LFB   L. Frank Baum
LC   Library of Congress
LK   Louis Kirstein
LKP   Louis Kirstein Papers
MA   Macy Archives
MFA   Marshall Field Archives
MRSW   *Merchants' Record and Show Window*
NA   National Archives
NRDGA   National Retail Dry Goods Association
NYHR   *New York Hotel Review*
NYHS   New York Historical Society
NYPL   New York Public Library
NYT   *New York Times*

NYUA   New York University Archives
PM   Paul Mazur
PRL   *Philadelphia Retail Ledger*
PT   *Playthings*
PS   Percy Straus
RW   Rodman Wanamaker
SC   Stewart Culin
SCP   Stewart Culin Papers
ST   *Signs of the Times*
TN   *Toys and Novelties*
WWD   *Women's Wear Daily*

Notes

Introduction

1.   Herbert Duce, *Poster Advertising* (New York, 1912), p. 96; for the Wanamaker quote, see Wanamaker's advertising editorial, *North American* (April 5, 1906), clipping in advertising scrapbook, WA, Philadelphia, Pennsylvania (the Wanamaker collection is now housed in the Pennsylvania Historical Society, Philadelphia).

2.   On these beliefs, see Charles L. Sanford, *The Quest for Paradise: Europe and the American Moral Imagination* (Urbana, Ill., 1961, pp. 10–11, 74–93. See also David Potter, *People of Plenty: Economic Abundance and the American Character* (Chicago, 1954) and Henry Nash Smith, *Virgin Land: The American Myth as Symbol and Myth* (New York, 1950).

3.   Artemas Ward, "Stray Shots," *Fame* 1 (December 1892): 323; Lewis Hyde, *The Gift: Imagination and the Erotic Life of Property* (New York, 1983), pp. 67–68.

4.   Twain, quoted in Sanford, *The Quest for Paradise*, p. 113; Channing, quoted in Rush Welter, *The Mind of America, 1820–1860* (New York, 1975), pp. 7–8.

5.   These phrases from Emerson are quoted by Christopher Lasch in *The True and Only Heaven* (New York, 1990), pp. 261–79.

6.   For this early-nineteenth-century phrase, see Joyce Appleby, *Capitalism and the New Social Order* (New York, 1984), p. 44.

7.   On Clark and Croly, see Dorothy Ross, *The Origins of American Social Science* (Cambridge, Eng., 1991), pp. 121, 152.

8.   Quoted in Ross, *Origins of American Social Science*, pp. 100–101. On the populist movement, see Lawrence Goodwyn, *The Populist Moment* (New York, 1978) and Christopher Lasch, *The True and Only Heaven*, esp. Chap. 5; and on the perspective of one facet of the labor movement, see Nick Salvatore, *Eugene V. Debs: Citizen and Socialist* (Urbana, Ill., 1982), pp. 23–177.

9.   Quoted in Thomas Cochran, *200 Years of American Business* (New York, 1977), p. 8.

10.   Wesley Clair Mitchell, *Business Cycles* (Berkeley, Calif., 1913), p. 21.

11.   Ibid., p. 599.

12.   Charles Cooley, *Social Process* (Carbondale, Ill., 1966), pp. 301, 303, 332–33. See also Cooley, "The Sphere of Pecuniary Valuation," *American Journal of Sociology* 19 (September 1913): 188–89; "The Institutional Character of Pecuniary Valuation," *American Journal of Sociology* 18 (January 1913): 549; and "The Progress of Pecuniary Valuation," *The Quarterly Journal of Economics* 30 (November 1915): 1–21. See also Hugh Duncan, *Culture and Democracy* (New York, 1965), esp. Chap. 13, "The Glamorization of Money in Art," pp. 142–52.

13.   Robert Heilbroner, *The Nature and Logic of Capitalism* (New York, 1985), p. 156.

14.   This prejudice is currently being overturned in the field of business history, with the publication of such books as Susan Strasser's *Satisfaction Guaranteed: The Making of the American Mass Market* (New York, 1989), and Richard Tedlow's *New and Improved: The Story of Mass Marketing in America* (New York, 1990), two very different books offering nearly opposing arguments about the character and benefits of the marketing revolution. Strasser is critical and sometimes biting, Tedlow upbeat and almost always glib.

15.   See, on this historical pattern, Michael Schudson, *Advertising, the Uneasy Persuasion: Its Dubious Impact on American Society* (New York, 1984), pp. 222–33. Schudson, in turn, draws on the anthropological work of Clifford Geertz.

16.   Paul Scheerbart, *Glass Architecture*, ed. Dennis Sharp and trans. James Palmes (New York, 1972; orig. pub. 1914), pp. 8–9. For the American "utopian" approach to color, glass, and light that supported commercial aims and emerged simultaneously with commercial developments, see Faber Birren, *Color and Human Response* (New York, 1978) and Edwin D. Babbitt, *The Principles of Light and Color: The Classic Study of the Healing Power of Color*, ed. and annot. Faber Birren (New York, 1967; orig. pub. 1878). A pencil and pen manufacturer and father of Irving Babbitt, Babbitt embraced spiritualism and color therapy in the 1870s in New York City and became the guiding light of colorists for many years thereafter.

17.   Quoted in *MRSW* 69 (August 1931): 40.

18.   Samuel Strauss, "Rich Men and Key Men," *The Atlantic Monthly* (December 1927): 726.

19.   For a recent discussion of this evolution, see Ann Fabian, *Card Sharps, Dream Books, and Bucket Shops: Gambling in 19th Century America* (Ithaca, N.Y., 1990).

20.   Emily Fogg Mead, "The Place of Advertising in Modern Business," *Fame* 10 (April 1901): 165 (repr. *The Journal of Political Economy* [March 1901] and ed. Thorstein Veblen). On Emily Fogg Mead, see Margaret Mead, *Blackberry Winter: My Early Years* (New York, 1975), pp. 1–72; and obituary, *The New York Times* (February 23, 1950), p. 27.

Chapter 1

1.   Edward Sherwood Mead, *Corporation Finance*, 6th ed. (New York, 1931; orig. pub. 1910), pp. 361–62. On the rise and evolution of the corporation, see Morton Horwitz, *The Transformation of American Law* (Cambridge, Mass., 1977); William E. Nelson, *The Americanization of the Common Law* (Cambridge, Mass., 1985); Harold Underwood Faulkner, *American Economic History* (New York, 1958), esp. chap. 21, "Consolidation of Business," pp. 420–48; and R. Jeffrey Lustig, *Corporate Liberalism: The Origins of Modern American Political Theory, 1890–1920* (Berkeley, Calif., 1982).

2.   On rugs and carpets, see *DGE* (June 18, 1904); on glassware and crockery, see *The Crockery and Glass Journal* (July 28, 1904); on jewelry, see *DGE* (August 1, 1903); and on food, see *The American Grocer* (November 29, 1905): 7. All these journals drew directly from the reports of the U.S. Census. See also U.S. Department of Commerce, Bureau of the Census, *Historical Statistics of the United States: Colonial Times to 1957* (Washington, D.C., 1960).

3.   Emily Fogg Mead, "The Place of Advertising in Modern Business," *Fame* 10 (April 1901): 165 (repr. *The Journal of Political Economy* [March 1901] and ed. Thorstein Veblen).

4.   Cyril Ehrlich, *The Piano: A History* (London, 1976), pp. 132, 139. See also on the growth of the American piano business, Arthur Loesser, *Men, Women, and Pianos* (New York, 1954), pp. 569–73; Craig H. Roell, *The Piano in America, 1890–1940* (Chapel Hill, N.C., 1989), pp. 69–107.

5.   Fogg Mead, "The Place of Advertising" 10:165; on the new energies and technologies, see Douglas C. North, *Structure and Change in Economic History* (New York, 1981), pp. 162–71; Alfred D. Chandler, Jr., *The Visible Hand: The Managerial Revolution in American Business* (Cambridge, Mass., 1977), pp. 224–83; David Hounshell, *From American System to Mass Production, 1800–1932* (Baltimore, 1984).

6.   Thomas Cochran, *200 Years of American Business* (New York, 1977), pp. 70–90; George W. Edwards, *The Evolution of Finance Capitalism* (London, 1938), p. 154.

7.   On capital pooling, see Marshall Sahlins, *Stone Age Economics* (Chicago, 1972); Douglas North, "Capital Accumulation in Life Insurance Between the Civil War and the Investigation of 1905," in *Men in Business: Essays on the Historical Role of the Entrepreneur* (New York, 1962), pp. 238–54; and Marquis James, *The Metropolitan Life: A Study in Business Growth* (New York, 1947), pp. 131–50.

8.   Edward Sherwood Mead, *Trust Finance: A Study of the Genesis, Organization, and Management of Industrial Combinations* (New York, 1903), pp. 65–66, 76–80. For an excellent study of the rise of corporations with an analysis similar to Mead's, see Naomi Lamoreaux, *The Great Merger Movement in American Business, 1895–1904* (Cambridge, Eng., 1985), pp. 1–45.

9.   Arthur Hadley, *Standards of Public Morality* (New York, 1907), pp. 69–70. On the corporation as an "organization to produce dividends for its owners," see

Mead, *Trust Finance*, pp. 153–54; and on mergers and industrial securities, see Ralph Nelson, *Merger Movements in American Industry, 1895–1956* (Princeton, 1959), and Thomas Nevin and Marion Sears, "The Rise in the Market in Securities," *The Business History Review* 29 (June 1955): 105–39.

10.   Veblen, quoted in Joseph Dorfman, *Thorstein Veblen and His America* (New York, 1934), pp. 160, 326; and Thorstein Veblen, *The Theory of Business Enterprise* (New York, 1904), pp. 45–85.

11.   Mead, *Corporation Finance*, pp. 218, 362; and Robert Heilbroner, *The Nature and Logic of Capitalism* (New York, 1985), pp. 36–38.

12.   Heilbroner, ibid., p. 36.

13.   Veblen, quoted in George W. Edwards, *The Evolution of Finance Capitalism* (London, 1938), p. 162.

14.   Philip Scranton, *Proprietary Capitalism: The Textile Manufacturers at Philadelphia, 1800–1885* (Cambridge, Eng., 1983).

15.   Alfred D. Chandler, Jr., "The Beginnings of 'Big Business' in American Industry," in *Managing Big Business*, ed. Richard S. Tedlow and Richard R. John, Jr. (Boston, 1990), pp. 2–31; and Faulkner, *American Economic History*, pp. 420–48.

16.   Matthew Josephson, *The History of the Hotel and Restaurant Employees and Bartenders International Union, AFL-CIO* (New York, 1955), pp. 4–9, 84–86; Russell Lynes, *The Tastemakers* (New York, 1954); Rufus Jarman, *A Bed for the Night, the Story of the Wheeling Bellboy, E.M. Statler and His Remarkable Hotel* (New York, 1952), pp. 3–16, 99–105; and Neil Harris, "Urban Tourism and the Commercial City," in *Inventing Times Square, Commerce and Culture at the Crossroads of the World*, ed. William R. Taylor (New York: 1991), pp. 66–82.

17.   On Chandler's argument, see Chandler, *The Visible Hand*, pp. 237–38.

18.   For a good general history, see H. Pasdermadjian, *The Department Store, Its Origins, Evolution, and Economics* (London, 1954). See also James B. Jefferys and Derek Knee, *Retailing in Europe, Present Structure and Future Trends* (London, 1962), pp. 1–64, which contains some useful historical material.

19.   On these stores, see "Paris Big Stores Seek Popular Trade," *DGE* (May 13, 1911), p. 37; and "New Features in Big Paris Stores," *DGE* (December 14, 1912), pp. 31–33. For histories of French merchandising and consumer culture, see Michael Miller, *The Bon Marché* (Princeton, N.J., 1982); Rosalind Williams, *Dream Worlds: Mass Consumption in Late-Nineteenth-Century France* (Berkeley, Calif., 1982); Richard Sennett, *The Fall of Public Man* (New York, 1978), pp. 140–49; Walter Benjamin, *Illuminations* (New York, 1967); and Emile Zola, *The Ladies' Paradise*, with introduction by Kristin Ross (Berkeley, Calif., 1992).

20.   On Japan, see "Japan's Big Department Store," *DGE* (October 31, 1908), pp., 38–39, p. 73; Edith Wells, "When Milady Shops in Tokyo," *World Outlook* 9 (May 1915); pp. 26–27; "Did Japan Start 'One Price' Policy?" *DGE* (September 23, 1922), p. 13; and Miriam Silverberg, "Problematizing Commodity Culture in

Inter-War Japan: The Reconstruction of Modernity," paper presented at "Global Americanization" workshop, Rutgers University (May 8–9, 1987).

21.   On Selfridges, see Jeanne Catherine Lawrence, "Steel Frame Architecture versus the London Building Regulations, the Ritz, and American Technology," *Construction History*, Vol. 6, 1990, pp. 23–45. On English merchandising generally, see Neil McKendrik and J. H. Plumb, *The Birth of Consumer Society: The Commercialization of Eighteenth-Century England* (Bloomington, Ind., 1982); Christina Fulop, *Competition for Consumers* (London, 1964), pp. 43–155; W. Hamish Fraser, *The Coming of the Mass Market, 1850-1914* (London, 1981), pp. 110–33; and Alison Adburgham, *Shopping in Style: London From the Restoration to Edwardian Elegance* (London, 1979), pp. 138–154.

22.   On the German stores, see Karl Gerstenberg, "Observations on American and German Department Stores," unpublished manuscript (May 1, 1941), Bobst Library, NYUA; "German Retail Methods," *DGE* (May 11, 1907), p. 29; and Jefferys and Knee, *Retailing in Europe*, p. 60.

23.   M. Auguste Guembe, "Les Grands Magasins des États-Unis," *DGE* (April 3, 1915), p. 191 (my translation).

24.   Theodore Delemos, of the firm Delemos and Cordes, architects for Siegel-Cooper's and Macy's, quoted in "Third Largest Retail Establishment in the World," *The Dry Goods Chronicle* (July 22, 1896), in the Delemos and Cordes scrapbook, "Newspaper Clippings," NYHS.

25.   Herbert Adams Gibbons, *John Wanamaker* (New York, 1926), vol. 2, p. 9.

26.   "A Scene at Stewart's," *U.S. Economist and Dry Goods Reporter* (June 22, 1869), p. 2; and Gail Hamilton, *Harper's Bazaar* (June 10, 1876). For descriptions of Stewart's and accounts of the development of his business, see "The Yankee Style," *The American Builder* (August 1872); William Leach, *True Love and Perfect Union* (Middletown, Conn., 1989), pp. 222–27; Harry E. Resseguie, "Alexander Turney Stewart and the Development of the Department Store, 1823–1876," *Business History Review* 39 (1965): 301–22; Resseguie, "A. T. Stewart's Marble Palace: The Cradle of the Department Store," *New-York Historical Society Quarterly* 48 (April 1964): 131–62; Roger A. Wines, "A. T. Stewart and Garden City," *The Nassau County Historical Journal* 19 (Winter 1958): 1–15; and Mary Ann Smith, "John Smook and the Design for A. T. Stewart's Store," *The New-York Historical Society Quarterly* 55 (January 1974): 18–33.

27.   Hattie Newal of Atlanta, Georgia, to A. T. Stewart (January 24, 1871), and L. Simms of Culpeper, Conn., to Stewart (October 17, 1871), A. T. Stewart Papers, NYPL. This collection consists of hundreds of letters, mostly requesting, many pleading for aid of all kinds.

28.   Eddie Comstock to Stewart (August 20, 1871); Lou Cameron, Brooklyn, to Stewart (September 28, 1871); A. Kappel of Washington County, Ohio, to Stewart (November 14, 1870); and J. E. Allen of Fernandina, Florida, to Stewart (May 8, 1871), Stewart Papers.

29.   Parker Pillsbury, "The Largest Store," *Revolution*, September 3, 1868.

30.   Gail Hamilton, "The Blameworthiness of Wealth," *Harper's Bazaar* (June 10, 1876). On Stewart's funeral, see *NYT* (April 11, 1876), p. 1; *NYT* (April 12, 1876), p. 8; and *NYT* (April 14, 1876), p. 10; "The Deceased Millionaire," *Frank Leslie's Illustrated Newspaper* 42 (April 22, 1876): 105, 111; and James Grant Wilson, "Alexander T. Stewart," *Harper's Weekly* 20 (April 29, 1876): 345–46.

31.   JW to Powell Day (February 8, 1908), Wanamaker Letterbook, "December 14, 1906 to February 20, 1908," p. 941, WA. Wanamaker wrote in the same letter that "R. H. Macy and Co. . . . in its early days was not a store that included a full assortment of goods. Such as were then sold in it was of a class much lower than any of the 6th Avenue stores [in New York] carry today." On the absence of window display and advertising, Gibbons, *John Wanamaker*, vol. I, pp. 124–25, and Bessie Louise Pierce, A *History of Chicago: The Rise of the Modern City, 1871–1893* (New York, 1957), vol. 3, pp. 177–78.

32.   "The Third Largest Retail Establishment in the World," Delemos and Cordes scrapbook, Manuscripts Collections, NYHS. On Siegel's deal with Goldman, Sachs, see *DGE* (May 11, 1895). And for more on the store, see Siegel-Cooper and Co., *New York—a Bird's-Eye View of Greater New York and Its Most Magnificent Store* (New York, 1898), p. 96, NYPL; *The Dry Goods Chronicle* 22 (September 26, 1896): 27; and *The American Grocer* 56 (September 16, 1896): 6. For biographical sketches of Siegel and of Cooper, see *DGE* (August 22, 1896); and on growth of the Chicago store, Harry Resseguie, "The Men Who Wrecked Sixth Avenue," unpublished manuscript in the possession of Baker Library, HBS, Cambridge, Mass., p. 15.

33.   JW, quoted in *PT* 13 (February 1915): 116.

34.   Interview with Fred Lazarus, 1965, Oral History Project, Records of the Federated Department Stores, Butler Library, Columbia University, pp. 30–39; Bessie Louise Pierce, *History of Chicago*, vol. 3, pp. 47–59, 268–88.

35.   On Wanamaker's, see interview with Charles Butler, treasurer of Brentano's (February 13, 1914), Resale Price Investigation (RPI), Record Group 122, file 7224-6-1, Records of the Bureau of Corporations, NA, p. 1; on Macy's, see interview with Macy's rug buyer (November 1914), file 7224-64-1, RPI, RG 101, NA, p. 1; and on Field's, see Emily Kimbrough, *Through Charley's Door* (New York, 1952), p. 51, and interview with Alfred Harcourt by Lloyd Lewis, transcript of "Lloyd Lewis Interviews" (1946), MFA.

36.   On Siegel-Cooper's, see *The American Grocer* 83 (March 2, 1910): 12; and on Simpson, Crawford, Simpson, see *The American Grocer* 74 (December 13, 1905): 19.

37.   Interview with Macy's food buyer, William Titon, by Arthur Johnson (September 30, 1965), Record Group 10, Harvard History Project, Box 4 of 4, "Harvard Interviews," MA.

38.   *Quarterly Catalog and Price List Winter 1914–15*, submitted as part of store interview (November 10, 1914), Resale Price Investigation, RG 122, pp. 25–30, NA. Macy's did not mail its alcoholic beverages indiscriminately: "As some towns and states have prohibition laws, and the delivery of wines and liquors C.O.D. has

recently been interpreted by the courts as a sale on the spot where the goods are paid for, we cannot in the future ship wines and liquors C.O.D. to any point outside of our wagon deliveries" (p. 68).

39.   JW to George V. Wendel (December 13, 1899), vol. 24, p. 154, WA. Wanamaker experimented with groceries sometime in 1895 but discontinued the business in 1896; see *The American Grocer* 55 (January 1, 1896): 7.

40.   On Macy's, see R. H. Macy and Co., "R. H. Macy and Co. Importers, Manufacturers, and Retailers" (New York, 1890), in the Bella Landauer Collection of Advertising Art, NYHS. On Field's, see "Department Stores Cash In," *Business Week* (May 12, 1934), p. 14; on Stewart's, see Harry Resseguie, "Alexander Turney Stewart and the Development of the Department Store"; and on Wanamaker's, interview by author with Richard Bond, president of Wanamaker's in the 1950s and 1960s (June 20, 1985), and John Wanamaker and Co., "Souvenir Guide Book of the Wanamaker Store in New York City" (New York, 1907). On vertical integration in department stores, see "Case Studies in Department Store Expansion," *HBR* 6 (October 1927), and Susan Benson Porter, "The Clerking Sisterhood," *Radical America* 12 (March–April 1978): 41–55.

41.   Interview with the Mandels management (December 5, 1913, and January 7, 12, and 15, 1914), Resale Price Investigation, RG 122, file 7224-26-1, NA, p. 3; and on Bloomingdale's, see Bloomingdale and Co., "Bloomingdale's Diary 1909 and Souvenir" (New York, 1909), Bella Landauer Collection of Advertising Art, NYHS.

42.   James C. Worthy, *Shaping an American Institution: Robert E. Wood and the Sears, Roebuck* (Chicago, 1984), p. 31. See also Boris Emmet and John E. Jeuck, *Catalogues and Counters: A History of Sears, Roebuck Co.* (Chicago, 1950), pp. 132–33, 170–72; and Tom Mahoney and Leonard Sloan, *The Great Merchants* (New York, 1966), pp. 221–43.

43.   Allan Nevins, *Herbert Lehman and His Era* (New York, 1963), p. 49.

44.   John Winkler, *Five and Ten: The Fabulous Life of F. W. Woolworth* (New York, 1940), pp. 175–76.

45.   T. J. Carlson, "A Corporate History of Associated Dry Goods Corporation" (New York, August 1977), Associated Dry Goods Corporation Archive, New York, pp. 3–24; "Costs of Doing Business" and "Memoranda—Miscellaneous Excerpts from Statements of Firms Having Experience with Price Maintenance," Resale Price Investigation (RPI), Bureau of Corporations, RG 122 (1913), file 1371-8, NA, pp. 4–8; and William Ingersoll, "Remedies Needed for Unfair Practices Leading in the Retail Market," pamphlet (December 12, 1913), file 7222-106-1, RPI, NA; and *DGE* (April 1 and 11, 1903). On the change of Claflin's into a corporation in 1890, see Thomas V. Nevin and Marian V. Sears, "The Rise of a Market for Industrial Securities, 1887–1902," *The Business History Review* 29 (June 1955): 123.

46.   "Miscellaneous Information . . . on the Famous and Barr Department Store," gathered for the RPI, Bureau of Corporations, RG 122, file 7224-36-1, NA.

47.   "Henry Siegel Has Chicago Store," *DGE* (January 11, 1902). "Siegel," this journal reported, "has purchased the interest of partner Frank H. Cooper."

48.   Siegel-Cooper and Co., *A Bird's-Eye View of Greater New York*; and *DGE* (August 22, 1896, October 19, 1901, January 6, 1903, May 2, 1903, April 30, 1904, and September 16, 1905). On Siegel's purchase of the old Macy's store, see "Another Big Store," *DGE* (January 31, 1903).

49.   Henry Morgenthau III, *Mostly Morgenthau: A Family History* (New York, 1991), pp. 109–209.

50.   Henry Morgenthau, Sr., *All in a Life-Time* (New York, 1902), pp. 34–38.

51.   Henry Morgenthau to Lincoln Filene, recorded in Lincoln Filene, "Notes on Meeting on Basis of Capitalization" (October 1909), accompanied by cover note to LK (November 1, 1909), folder "New Stores," no. 62, LKP, Baker Library, HBS. For Morgenthau's role at Siegel-Cooper's, see "Siegel-Cooper and Co. in Combine," *MRSW* (December 1910) (Morgenthau's name appears as the only banker vice president on the board of officers). Morgenthau does not mention either one of these clients in his autobiography.

52.   "Causes of the H. B. Claflin's Co.'s Failure," *DGE* (June 27, 1914), pp. 31–33; and Carlson, "A Corporate History of Associated Dry Goods Corporation," p. 14.

53.   *DGE* (January 10, 1914, February 7, 1914, March 28, 1914, November 14, 1914, November 28, 1914, June 26, 1915); and "Henry Siegel Dead at 78; One Time Merchant Prince," *New York World*, August 27, 1930, Delemos and Cordes, "Newspaper Clippings."

54.   Alan Trachtenberg, *The Incorporation of America* (New York, 1982).

55.   W. J. Lampton, "Department Stores and Advertising," *Fame* 1 (June 1897): 143.

56.   W. Hamish Fraser, *The Coming of the Mass Market, 1850–1914* (London, 1981), p. 101. On France, see Michael Miller, *The Bon Marché* (Princeton, 1982).

57.   Quoted in *DGE* (February 7, 1891), pp. 1–3.

58.   Quoted in *DGE* (November 17, 1894).

59.   "Fighting That Octopus," *DGE* (May 15, 1897). For California, see "Fighting That Octopus"; for Illinois and Minnesota, see "The Big Store War," *DGE* (April 3, 1897), p. 8; for Maryland, "Among the Trade," *DGE* (April 2, 1898); for New York and Massachusetts, see "Oppose Department Stores," *DGE* (April 16, 1897).

60.   For the volatile character of the political climate in Chicago during this time, see the mayor's record, 1897–1902, in Carter H. Harrison, *Stormy Years: The Autobiography of Carter Harrison, Five-Time Mayor of Chicago* (New York, 1935).

61.   Interview with John W. Hughes, retired head of delivery and operations, "Lloyd Lewis Interviews," transcript (1946), p. 12, MFA.

62.   Marshall Field's ledger books record even children—cash boys especially—

being fired "for being a "striker," for "getting mixed up with strikes," or for "striking." See Personnel Record, 1882–1901," p. 421, and "Records of Cash Boys, II, 1903–1906, Ledger," pp. 20, 29, 130, MFA. See also Robert Twyman, *History of Marshall Field and Company, 1852–1906* (Chicago, 1954), pp. 164–66; John Hughes, "Lloyd Lewis Interviews," pp. 14–18; and Herbert Harris (Field's buyer in early 1900s), "Marshall Field—A Great Mercantile Genius," unpublished manuscript, pp. 6–7, MFA. Field "ordered" out of his stores anyone associated with unions, Harris writes. See also, for descriptions of Field's antilabor policies, Pierce, *History of Chicago*, vol. 3, p. 252, and Ray Ginger, *Altgeld's America* (New York, 1958), pp. 41–42, 101–104.

63.   Marshall Field to Victor Lawson (December 22, 1903), Victor Lawson Papers, Newberry Library, Chicago, Ill.; and "Big Clash Pending," *Hearst's Chicago American* (June 1, 1903), clipping in Lawson collection.

64.   Joel A. Tarr, "The Chicago Anti-Department Store Crusade of 1897," *Journal of the Illinois State Historical Society* 64 (Summer 1971): 166; Twyman, *Marshall Field and Company*, p. 120; and Samuel P. Hays, "City Fathers and Reform: The Politics of Reform in Municipal Government," *The Pacific Northwest Quarterly* 55 (October 1964): 157–69.

65.   Hays, "City Fathers and Reform"; and Lewis interview with John W. Hughes, p. 11.

66.   Edward Bellamy, *Looking Backward* (New York, 1888), pp. 49–58; Tarr, "The Chicago Anti-Department Store Crusade of 1897."

67.   "Assailing Department Stores," editorial, DGE (March 6, 1897): "In Chicago, the women, or at least some of them, have taken up the fight and will endeavor to create a sentiment against patronizing the department stores."

68.   DGE (August 7, 1897).

69.   DGE (February 20, 1897); DGE (March 6, 1897), p. 2; and DGE (November 6, 1897), p. 2. On Mayor Harrison's attempt to compel the stores to abide by the new provisions, see DGE (October 30, 1897), p. 66. To meet the challenge of department stores, small Chicago merchants also organized a "cooperative experiment" similar to the ones being attempted throughout the United States at the time. This effort attempted to consolidate the strength of the merchants while at the same time allowing each merchant to retain his individual autonomy—his own business and market territory—"with exclusive right to sell his particular line of goods under the protection of the organization." The organization was called the "Merchants' Cooperative Mart" and was designed to "resemble a department store but to be run strictly on a cooperative basis." The deal was this: "Any trade the smaller merchant cannot handle he is to divert, so far as is in his power, to the central mart." "Inasmuch as one third of the profits of the mart are to be divided among such merchants as stockholders, every time one of them sends a dollars' worth of business to the mart he not only diverts trade from the department stores but increases his own profits."

I do not know the outcome of this experiment, but the position of the trade press suggests what happened. The scheme will fail, the *Dry Goods Economist* editor argued, because it "lacks the exceptionally able management which is so signal a cause of the financial success of the great department stores, and, secondly, the cohesion which can only be obtained by bringing the final management of a business into a very few hands." This plan does not call for a "president or board of directors" but will "let the merchants try to manage a common business by holding meetings and passing resolutions." "We hardly think that the department stores will lose much sleep over this new form of competition." See editorial, "New Form of Cooperation," *DGE* (April 9, 1898).

70.   Robert C. Ogden, "Ethics of Modern Retailing" (c. 1898), pp. 7–8, Box 22, the Papers of Robert C. Ogden, LC, Washington, D.C. On the Downtown Business Men's Association, see "Oppose Department Stores," *DGE* (January 16, 1897).

71.   "After the Department Stores," *DGE* (January 20, 1900).

72.   *DGE* (March 3, 1900), pp. 1–2; and *DGE* (July 20, 1901).

73.   *The Outlook* 65 (July 28, 1900): 711–12.

74.   "Department Store Indorsed [sic]," editorial, *DGE* (July 13, 1901); and *DGE*, "Big Stores Upheld" (February 8, 1902).

75.   Quoted in "Marshall Field and Company, Retail," *Chicago Dry Goods Reporter* (October 11, 1902), "Advertising III," p. 1, copy in MFA. The terms "fine silk" and "swagger rich" were popular terms to describe Chicago's upper class. See "Rogan" to Victor Lawson (April 1, 1903), Lawson Papers.

76.   Memorandum of Thomas Clement of Wanamaker's to the store management (April 23, 1903), in Wanamaker "Scrapbook, Business ephemera, store policy, 1880s to 1900s," WA. Clement does not identify his source by name except to say that she is "a very clever girl." See also, for description of this opening, "Marshall Field and Company, Retail," *Chicago Dry Goods Reporter*, and "Chicago's Giant Store," *DGE* (October 4, 1902).

77.   JW to H. Gordon Selfridge (October 18, 1902), "Mr. Wanamaker Personal— June 21, 1902 to November 22, 1902," p. 669, WA.

78.   Memorandum, Thomas Clement, p. 1. The Clement memo also mentions Harrison's invitation to Field's to remain open.

79.   JW speech, "At the Laying of the Corner Store of the New Building" (June 12, 1909), in "Miscellaneous Addresses, May 12, 1902–July 1, 1915," privately bound volume, p. 89, WA.

80.   Gibbons, *John Wanamaker;* vol. I, pp. 8, 57.

81.   JW, "The Evolution of Mercantile Business," *Annals of the American Academy of Political and Social Science*, vol. 15, supplement, "Corporations and the Public Welfare" (Philadelphia, 1900), pp. 123–35; *United States and Dry Goods Reporter* (November 18, 1876), p. 4; and *The American Builder* (November 1876), p. 13.

82.   JW to Dwight L. Moody (November 27, 1876), Wanamaker letters, WA; and Gibbons, *John Wanamaker*, vol. 1, pp. 137–39.

83.   See, in particular, Dwight Moody to JW (October 7 and November 5, 1877), WA. These letters were among the many I found in a file cabinet in the Wanamaker Archive in Philadelphia (they are now in the hands of the Pennsylvania Historical Society). Wanamaker's official biographer, Herbert Adams Gibbons, made no use of them; indeed, there was much Wanamaker material that Gibbons failed—or refused—to use.

84.   By 1895, Wanamaker's was furnishing and supplying many hospitals, homes, churches, schools, hotels, and restaurants in Philadelphia and its environs. See Thomas Clement (Wanamaker executive), "Comparison of Schedules and Collections for November and December 1894 and 1895"; and "Comparisons of Schedules and Collections for September and October 1896 and 1897," WA. In both documents, Clement lists such institutions as the Hotel Bellevue, the Stratford Hotel, the city of Philadelphia (Board of Education), the Brotherhood of St. Andrews Home, the Continental Hotel, the Episcopal Hospital, the Aldine Hotel, the Bourse Restaurant Co., Presbyterian Hospital, the Hotel Stenton, the University Club, the Custodians of the Church Home, the Bureau of Charities and Correction, Cottage State Hospital, Hahnemann Hospital, the Board of Health, the U.S. Marine Corps, Villa Nova College, Ursinus College, Temple College of Philadelphia, St. Elizabeth's Church, Hotel Walton, and so on.

85.   On Wanamaker's as a "sight," see the guidebook by Clara E. Laughlin, *So You're Visiting New York* (Boston, 1939), p. 21.

86.   JW to Alexander Orr (March 11, 1903), Letterbook (November 22, 1902–August 11, 1903), WA; and Gibbons, *John Wanamaker*, vol. 1, p. 145.

87.   Quoted in Gibbons, *John Wanamaker*, vol. 2, pp. 4–5.

88.   JW, speech, "At the Luncheon by the Merchants of the United States at Sherry's in New York" (November 16, 1911), in "Miscellaneous Addresses," p. 182, WA.

89.   Daniel Burnham, quoted in Thomas Hines, *Burnham of Chicago* (Chicago, 1982), p. 303; and Gibbons, *John Wanamaker*, vol. 2, pp. 199–201.

90.   JW diary entry (January and November 1907), quoted in Gibbons, *John Wanamaker*, vol. 1, pp. 126, 130.

91.   JW to Rev. Edwin Nobbs (October 7, 1901), Wanamaker letters (August 20, 1901, to June 21, 1902), WA, p. 194. The full citation is: "I beg to say I am not a capitalist; I am only a merchant." See also JW to Mr. Walker (January 5, 1900): "You are writing me as though I were a banker or a capitalist, whereas I am only a merchant." (Wanamaker letters, vol. 24, p. 333). Wanamaker incorporated his stores in 1906–7 to establish permanent continuity in ownership and formally end the status of Wanamaker's as a family-owned business and partnership; see "John Wanamaker, New York, Organization Records," Frederick Garvin, Solicitor (May 1907), WA. Both Gimbel Brothers and Marshall Field incorporated in 1903, creating stock companies and giving their executives the chance to buy stock. "The shares are to be held by the incorporators," declared Gimbels, and "none will be sold" (*DGE* [July 4, 1903], pp. 24–25). As retired Field's executive John Hughes observed in a 1946 interview, Field's "formed a company which bought the stock

and let you subscribe and pay out of salary and dividends. This was done to quiet the man and keep the machine together." ("Lloyd Lewis Interviews," p. 27, MFA). On the shift, generally, from partnerships to corporations after the 1880s, see Thomas A. Navin and Marian V. Sears, "The Rise in the Market for Industrial Securities," *The Business History Review* 29 (June 1955): 105–38.

92.   JW to General William Booth (January 23, 1907), Wanamaker letters (December 14, 1906, to February 20, 1908), pp. 867–69, WA.

93.   "Production and Consumption," *U.S. Economist and Dry Goods Reporter* (May 6, 1876), p. 7. See also "Causes of Depression," *DGE* (June 13, 1896), p. 18.

94.   Archie Shaw, "Some Problems in Market Distribution," *Quarterly Journal of Economics* (August 1912): 703–65; and Herbert Duce, *Poster Advertising* (New York, 1912), p. 5. On the debate over overproduction or underconsumption as a problem, see Paul Sweezy, *The Theory of Capitalist Development* (New York, 1964), pp. 214–39; and James O'Connor, *Accumulation Crisis* (London, 1986).

95.   Thomas Riggio mentions this essay in his edition of Dreiser's diaries, *Theodore Dreiser, American Diaries 1902–1926* (Philadelphia, 1982), footnote 43, p. 105.

96.   Dorothy Ross, *The Origins of Social Science* (Cambridge, Mass., 1991), pp. 113–22.

97.   Katherine Rolston Fisher, "Ad-Writing and Psychology," *Fame* 8 (September 1899); and Fogg Mead, "The Place of Advertising" 10:163, 166. Fisher also wrote that "the advertiser's problem . . . may be considered the controlling of other people's imaginations for his own advantage. It is a certain state of mind, and *not the real condition of things which is essential to the advertiser's success.*"

Chapter 2

1.   JW, "Editorials of John Wanamaker" (October 1, 1912 to December 31, 1917), editorials dated October 10, 1912 and November 9, 1916, bound collection in WA.

2.   Henry James, *The American Scene* (Bloomington, Ind., 1969), pp. 94–96.

3.   Edna Ferber, "Maymeys from Cuba," *The American Magazine* 72 (September 1911): 705–11; Willa Cather, quoted in Ellen Moers, *Two Dreisers* (New York, 1969), p. xiv.

4.   Theodore Dreiser, *Color of a Great City* (New York, 1923), p. 4.

5.   Milton Fuessle, "Elbert Hubbard, Master of Advertising and Retailing," *The Advertising World* 20 (August–September 1915): 139–44. For an excellent biography of Hubbard, see Freeman Champney, *Art and Glory: The Story of Elbert Hubbard* (New York, 1968).

6.   Fuessle, "Elbert Hubbard," pp. 139–41; and Hubbard, *The Advertising World* (July 1911).

7.   Hubbard, quoted in Champney, *Art and Glory*, p. 16.

8. Quoted in Champney, *Art and Glory*, p. 188.

9. *The Advertising World* (July 1911).

10. This material on advertising is taken from the following useful historical studies: Frank Presbrey, *The History and Development of Advertising* (New York, 1929); Otis Pease, *The Responsibilities of American Advertising, Private Control and Public Influence, 1920–1940* (New Haven, Conn., 1958); Stuart Ewen, *Captains of Consciousness: Advertising and the Social Roots of the Consumer Culture* (New York, 1976); Sarah Stage, *Female Complaints: Lydia Pinkham and the Business of Women's Medicine* (New York, 1979); Daniel Pope, *The Making of Modern Advertising* (New York, 1983); Stephen Fox, *The Mirror Makers: A History of American Advertising and Its Creators* (New York, 1984); Michael Schudson, *Advertising, the Uneasy Persuasion: Its Dubious Impact on American Society* (New York, 1984); Roland Marchand, *Advertising the American Dream, Making Way for Modernity, 1920–1940* (Berkeley, Calif., 1985); William Leiss, Stephen Kline, and Sut Jhally, *Social Communication in Advertising* (New York, 1986); and Susan Strasser, *Satisfaction Guaranteed: The Making of the American Mass Market* (New York, 1989).

11. On spread of advertising and percentage of national income, see Thomas Cochran, "Business in Veblen's America," in *Thorstein Veblen: The Carleton College Veblen Seminar Essays*, ed. Carlton C. Qualey (New York, 1968), pp. 47–71; Fox, *Mirror Makers*, pp. 1–40; Strasser, *Satisfaction Guaranteed*, pp. 89–123. On crucial early reliance on magazines, see Presbrey, *The History and Development of Advertising*, pp. 446–85.

12. JW, quoted in *The Advertising World* 22 (November 1917): 179; on the "everyday advertisement," see DGE (March 23, 1895); on "continuous advertising," *Printer's Ink, Fifty Years: 1888 to 1938* (New York, 1938), p. 131; and on "the newspaper of today," see DGE (July 16, 1904). See also, on Wanamaker's importance, DGE (July 16, 1904); Printer's Ink, *Fifty Years*, p. 131; and Presbrey, *The History and Development of Advertising*, pp. 324–39.

13. *Printers' Ink, Fifty Years*, p. 146. On the emergence of the powerful agencies, see Presbrey, *The History and Development of Advertising*, pp. 522–31; Fox, *The Mirror Makers*, pp. 35–77, and Pope, *The Making of Modern Advertising*, pp. 112–83.

14. Strasser, *Satisfaction Guaranteed*, pp. 9–11, 163–202.

15. Fox, *The Mirror Makers*, pp. 41–43.

16. Macy management, "A Typed Statement About Advertising, Pasted into the Advertising File for 2/12-3/14," Harvard History Project, 1934, Record Group 10 (13–14), MA; DGE (February 2, 1901); *The Advertising World* 21 (November 1916): 210; DGE (September 2, 1905 and September 9, 1905).

17. *The Poster* (April 1913); 13. See also DGE (December 5, 1896): "Display advertising . . . is the wave of the future"; DGE (January 27, 1900): "Our advice to advertisers is to use cuts. The picture in the ad is the chief 'eye-catcher' of all"; DGE (January 4, 1901), p. 7: "The adman so transposes and transfigures . . . the qualities of merchandise into the picture that will impress fully the man or woman

whom he addresses"; and *Fame* (September 1899): "The pretty picture makes a pleasant impression forever to be associated with the articles advertised." Similar quotations from this period (1895 to 1920) could be readily cited in the hundreds.

18.   JW to Charles Simonet (May 13, 1913), Wanamaker Letterbook, "April 5, 1913 to October 25, 1913," p. 346, WA; JW, personal memorandum book, "Things to Remember" (1911), pp. 1–2; and Manly Gillam, interview, *DGE* (September 17, 1904).

19.   David Anderson, "Washington Shopper, A.D. 1880," *The Washington Post*, POTOMAC (November 2, 1969), pp. 24–25, District of Columbia Historical Society; and, on advertising cards in general, see the rich collections in the Warshow Collection of Business Americana, Archive Center, NMAH, Smithsonian Institution, Washington, D.C.; and in the Bella Landauer Collection of Advertising Art, NYHS, New York City.

20.   My description of the early catalogs is based on a reading of the hundreds of catalogs in the Warshow Collection of Business Americana and the Bella Landauer Collection of Advertising Art, and in the John Wanamaker Archives in Philadelphia. Mail-order magazines were also popular in this period, especially *Comfort*, which advertised the mail-order catalog business to millions of readers after 1890. On the birth of the mail-order magazines (especially of *Comfort*), see Dorothy Steward Sayward, *"Comfort* Magazine, 1888–1942: A History and Critical Study," *University of Maine Bulletin* 62 (January 20, 1960): 1–108. *Comfort* magazine was the biggest mail-order magazine in history.

21.   Paul Nystrom, "Notes on The Mail Order Houses," testimony before the Bureau of Corporations, Resale Price Investigation (1913), 7222-108-1, Record Group 151, NA; and "Recent Trade Catalogues," *DGE* (November 2, 1902).

22.   On Siegel-Cooper's, see *The American Grocer* 83 (March 2, 1910): 12; on Simpson, Crawford, Simpson, see *The American Grocer* 74 (December 13, 1905): 19. For Wanamaker's, see *Baby Coaches* (Spring 1891) and *Bicycles* (1897), WA.

23.   *DGE* (April 6, 1907); *The Advertising World* 22 (May 1918): 12, 396.

24.   John Wanamaker and Co., *Fall and Winter Catalogue, 1899–1900*, no. 4, Warshow Collection of Business Americana; and H. O'Neill and Co., *Holiday Gifts Catalogue* (New York, 1898), Bella Landauer Collection of Advertising Art.

25.   Artemas Ward, copy of the contract with the Interborough Rapid Transit Company (December 27, 1913), p. 5; and Artemas Ward, "A Pictorial Presentation of Interborough Medium" (New York, 1925), pp. 5, 18–21. Both these documents are in the possession of the NYPL.

26.   On visual change generally, see Presbrey, *The History and Development of Advertising*, pp. 244–359; Fox, *Mirror Makers*, pp. 40–44; and C. J. Shearer, advertising manager at Bloomingdale's, for "great change" in advertising between 1889 and 1897, *MRSW* (June 1908).

27.   Strasser, *Satisfaction Guaranteed*, pp. 43–46.

28.   Rupert Brooke, "extracts from an article in the *Westminster Gazette*" (October

18, 1913), p. 2, WA. On poster art generally in this period, see Herbert Cecil Duce, *Poster Advertising* (Chicago, 1912), pp. 107–13; and Presbrey, *The History and Development of Advertising*, pp. 490–97.

29.   Joseph Huneker, *New Cosmopolis: A Book of Images* (New York, 1915), p. 149; *Fame* (December 1896); *The Poster* I (January 1896): 1; *The Poster* (February 1896): 14–17; Presbrey, *The History and Development of Advertising*, pp. 512–21.

30.   Quoted in Quentin J. Schultze, "Legislating Morality: The Progressive Response to American Outdoor Advertising, 1900–1917," *The Journal of Popular Culture* 17 (Spring 1983): 38.

31.   On the evangelical "premillennial" preaching in New York and elsewhere in about 1912, and on Isaac Haldeman's *Signs of the Times*, see George M. Marsden, *Fundamentalism and American Culture: The Shaping of Twentieth-Century Evangelicalism: 1870–1925* (New York, 1980), esp. subsection "This Age Condemned: The Premillennial Extreme," pp. 125–26.

32.   "Be It So, Electrical Advertising Has Only Begun," *ST* (December 1912).

33.   Presbrey, *The History and Development of Advertising*, pp. 507–11; *ST* (August 1912): 9; Leonard G. Shepard, "Sign Lighting," in *Illuminating Engineering Practice: Lectures on Illuminating Engineering*, ed. Charles Steinmetz (New York, 1917), pp. 535–46; and David E. Nye, *Electrifying America: Social Meanings of a New Technology, 1880–1940* (Cambridge, Eng., 1990), pp. 51–55.

34.   O. J. Gude, "Art and Advertising Joined by Electricity," *ST* (November 1912): 3; for short sketches of Gude and his business, see Robert Grau, *The Business Man in the Amusement World* (New York, 1910), pp. 247–48, and Presbrey, *The History and Development of Advertising*, pp. 505–6.

35.   Fogg Mead, "The Place of Advertising in Modern Business," *Fame* 10 (April 1901): 163.

36.   Gude, "10 Minutes' Talk on Outdoor Advertising," *ST* (June 1912).

37.   Gude, "Art and Advertising Joined by Electricity": 3; *ST* (August 1912): 9; *ST* (October 1912): 246–47.

38.   Fogg Mead, "The Place of Advertising," 10:168.

39.   Edward Ross, *Changing America: Studies in Contemporary Society* (New York, 1912), p. 100.

40.   See John J. Costanis, "Law and Aesthetics: A Critique and a Reformulation of the Dilemmas," *Michigan Law Review* 80, I (January 1982): 400–415.

41.   Philip Tocker, "Standardized Outdoor Advertising: History, Economics and Self-Regulation," in *Outdoor Advertising: History and Regulation*, ed. John W. Houck (Notre Dame, Ind., 1969), pp. 32–33.

42.   Faber Birren, *Color and Human Response* (New York, 1972), pp. 63–65; K. Venkataramen, *The Chemistry of Synthetic Dyes* (New York, 1952); David Paterson, *The Science of Color* (New York, 1900). On the Munsell standards, see Birren, p. 63.

43.   Reyner Baynam, *The Architecture of the Well-Tempered Environment* (Chicago, 1969), p. 70; Matthew Luckiesh, *Torch of Civilization* (New York, 1940) and *Artificial Light* (London, 1920).

44.   *DGE* (October 18, 1902), p. 13; Printers' Ink, *Fifty Years*, p. 118; Presbrey, *The History and Development of Advertising*, esp. chap. 41, "The Tremendous Effect of the Half-Tone," pp. 356–60; Estelle Jussim, *Visual Communication and the Graphic Arts: Photographic Technologies in the 19th Century* (New York, 1974), pp. 1–73, 111–19; Peter Marzio, *The Democratic Art: Chromolithography, 1840–1900: Pictures for a 19th-Century America* (Boston, 1979); Neil Harris, "Iconography and Intellectual History: The Half-Tone Effect," in *New Directions in American Intellectual History*, ed. John Higham and Paul Conkin (Baltimore, 1979), pp. 198–201; and "The Making of Cuts," *DGE* (May 19, 1906): "Any article can be photographed and made into a cut."

45.   Manly Gillam, *DGE* (September 17, 1904); *DGE* (Gillam) (November 11, 1897); and *DGE* (Gillam) (February 2, 1901).

46.   Robert Ogden to W. H. Baldwin (February 12, 1903), "Letters," Ogden Papers, Box 3, LC; and Philip W. Wilson, *An Unofficial Statesman—Robert Ogden* (New York, 1924).

47.   JW, speech at a "Meeting Held in the Board Room, regarding the death of Robert Curtin Ogden" (August 7, 1913) in unpublished "Miscellaneous Speeches," p. 274; and JW to RW (August 7, 1913), WA.

48.   Robert Ogden to H. P. Ford (August 9, 1893), Box 3, Ogden Papers.

49.   Robert Ogden, quoted by S. C. Mitchell in his unpublished biography of Ogden, pp. 60–61, Box 27, Ogden Papers; Wilson, *An Unofficial Statesman*, p. 6, and Diary of Robert Ogden (June 9, 1879), Box 1, Ogden Papers.

50.   Robert Ogden to JW (April 14, 1890, and February 9, 1891), Ogden Papers; Robert Ogden, "Ethics of Modern Retailing," undated speech, Box 22, Ogden Papers; Robert Ogden to RW (July 24, 1898), WA.

51.   Robert Ogden, "Advertising Art," *DGE* (May 15, 1898); for Ogden's own copy, see Ogden Papers (April 13, 1898).

52.   Coy Ludwig, *Maxfield Parrish* (Oswego, N.Y., 1973), pp. 106, 141–45.

53.   Adeline Adams, "The Art of Maxfield Parrish," *The Magazine of Art* 9 (January 1918): 85–101; and Ludwig, *Maxfield Parrish*, pp. 1–13.

54.   Ludwig, *Maxfield Parrish*, p. 143.

55.   Robert Koch, *Louis Tiffany: Rebel in Glass* (New York, 1964), pp. 84–85; and Alma Gilbert, *Maxfield Parrish: The Masterworks* (Berkeley, Calif., 1992), pp. 127–128.

56.   Samuel Strauss, editorial, *The Villager* 3 (March 20, 1920): 182–83.

57.   Ludwig, *Maxfield Parrish*, p. 134.

58.   G. Schonfarber, "What the Advertiser Wants," *The Advertising World* 21 (November 1916): 210.

59.   John Crawford Brown, "Early Days of Department Stores," in *Valentine's Manual of Old New York*, ed. Henry Collins (New York, 1921), pp. 134–35. On older practices, see *DGE* (October 12, 1889, December 2, 1889, July 21, 1892, and esp. "Piling Goods Outside," June 27, 1896).

60.   *DGE* (October 12, 1889).

61.   On the proliferation of merchandising manuals of this kind, see Leigh Eric Schmidt, "The Commercialization of the Calendar: American Holidays and the Culture of Consumption, 1870–1930," *The Journal of American History* (December 1991): 887–916.

62.   For description of Rose Lawn, see Frank Baum and Russell MacFall, *To Please a Child: A Biography of L. Frank Baum, Royal Historian of Oz* (Chicago, 1951), p. 150.

63.   Allan Nevins, *John D. Rockefeller*, vol. 1 (New York, 1940), chap. 8. Maud Baum, Baum's wife, claimed in her biographical notes for *The Cyclopedia of American Biography* (1922) that "John D. Rockefeller worked for him" (Benjamin Baum). See "Biographical Notes," Papers of Lyman Frank Baum, Arendts Library, Syracuse University.

64.   On Benjamin Baum's oil activity, see Russell MacFall to Dr. Justin Call (July 29, 1974), LFB Papers, Arendts Collection, Syracuse University; and MacFall and Baum, *To Please a Child*, p. 17.

65.   LFB, *The Aberdeen Saturday Pioneer* (hereafter *Pioneer*) (May 10, 1890); and quoted by Matilda Gage, "The Dakota Days of L. Frank Baum," pt. II, *The Baum Bugle* (Autumn 1966).

66.   *Pioneer* (February 1, 1890, February 8, 1890, February 15, 1890, and March 1, 1890).

67.   MacFall and Baum, *To Please a Child*, pp. 32–33; Robert Stanton Baum, "The Autobiography of Robert Stanton Baum," pt. I, *The Baum Bugle* (Christmas 1970); Alla T. Ford and Dick Martin, *The Musical Fantasies of L. Frank Baum* (Chicago, 1958), p. 14; and *The Syracuse Herald* (November 19, 1899), LFB Papers.

68.   MacFall and Baum, *To Please a Child*, pp. 60–61; Matilda J. Gage, "The Dakota Days of L. Frank Baum," *The Baum Bugle* (Spring 1966); *Pioneer* (April 19, 1889).

69.   *Pioneer* (December 22, 1890).

70.   *Pioneer* (May 17, 1890); *Pioneer* (February 8, 1890).

71.   *Pioneer* (March 8, 1890).

72.   *Pioneer* (June 28, 1890).

73.   Max Weber, quoted in Marianne Weber, *Max Weber: A Biography*, trans. and ed. Harry Zohn (New York, 1975, orig. pub. 1920), p. 286. See also, on the spectacular growth of Chicago in this era, Bessie Pierce, *A History of Chicago: The Rise of the Modern City, 1871–1893*, vol. 3 (New York, 1957), pp. 64–277; Christine Rosen, *The Limits of Power: Great Fires and the Process of City Growth*

(Cambridge, Mass., 1986), esp. chap. 6, "The Rebuilding of Chicago," pp. 92–176; Vincent Carosso, *Investment Banking in America* (Cambridge, Mass., 1970), pp. 105–9; U.S. Works Project Administration for the State of Illinois, *A Descriptive and Historical Guide* (Chicago, 1939), pp. 195–223; Cyril Ehrlich, *The Piano: A History* (London, 1976); and U.S. Works Project Administration for the State of Illinois, *Chicago's Candy Kettle* (Chicago, 1941), pp. 1–21.

74.   Harry Neal Baum, "Santa Claus at the Baums," *The Baum Bugle* (Christmas 1965).

75.   LFB, *The Art of Decorating Dry Goods Windows and Interiors* (Chicago, 1900), p. 7; and LFB, *The Show Window* (December 1899): 255–57.

76.   *MRSW* 21 (January 1908): 58.

77.   MacFall and Baum, *To Please a Child*, pp. 75–78, 93–95; "The Autobiography of Robert Neal Baum," *The Baum Bugle* (Christmas 1970), p. 2; and LFB to "My Darling Sister" (October 3, 1897), LFB Papers.

78.   LFB, *The Art of Decorating*, pp. 87, 109, 128.

79.   LFB, *The Art of Decorating*, p. 15.

80.   LFB, *The Art of Decorating*, pp. 7–8, 82–86.

81.   LFB, *The Show Window* (April 1899): 66; (May 1899): 243; (October 1900): 33; and LFB, *The Art of Decorating*, pp. 7–9, 14–15, 22, 82, 140, 213–44.

82.   *DGE* (November 23, 1907); and "The New Wanamaker Store," *Architects' and Builders' Magazine* 38 (June 1906): 365–72.

83.   On "all glass fronts" and "splintering maze," see *DGE* (January 29, 1910); and on the domestic production and consumption of plate glass, see U.S. Department of Labor, Bureau of Labor Statistics, "Productivity of Labor in the Glass Industry," no. 441 (Washington, D.C., 1927), p. 170.

84.   W. Hamish Frazer, *The Coming of the Mass Market, 1850–1914* (London, 1981), pp. 94–109.

85.   Frederick Kiesler, *Contemporary Art Applied to the Store and Its Display* (New York, 1930), p. 70; on Philadelphia in the 1850s, see Marion Bell, *Crusade in the City: Revivalism in Nineteenth-Century Philadelphia* (Lewisburg, Pa., 1977), p. 171.

86.   Lizabeth Cohen, *Making a New Deal: Industrial Workers, 1919–1939* (New York, 1990), pp. 114–15.

87.   Ralph Waldo Emerson, "Nature," in *Selected Writings of Ralph Waldo Emerson*, ed. William H. Gilman (New York, 1965), p. 189.

88.   On the earlier precapitalist tradition of interdependency that included the poor's entitlement to help from the rich, see Robert L. Heilbroner, *The Nature and Logic of Capitalism* (New York, 1985), pp. 38–42.

89.   Artemas Ward, Inc. *A Pictorial Presentation of Interborough Medium* (New York, 1925), pp. 5–12; "Illinois Tunnel Company . . . Chicago Subway System"

(Chicago, c. 1910), NYPL; Edward Eldredge to LK, superintendent of Filene's department stores (September 12, 1909), LKP, Baker Library, HBS; *MRSW* (April 1908, May 1908, July 1908, January 1908, and March 1908). On Philadelphia's Wanamaker's, see Herbert Adams Gibbons, *John Wanamaker*, vol. 2 (New York, 1926), p. 211.

90. "The Art of Paneling," *DGE* (August 28, 1897). This article notes that "quite a few stores" are beginning to "panel back and ceiling alike."

91. *DGE* (January 25, 1908), p. 81; *DGE* (July 7, 1917); *DGE* (July 21, 1921), pp. 59, 79; and Matthew Luckiesh, *Light and Color in Advertising and Merchandising* (New York, 1922), pp. 146–70, 207–17.

92. On grouped figures in anthropological exhibits, see Ira Jackins, "Franz Boas and Exhibits; On the Limitations of the Museum Method of Anthropology," in *Objects and Others: Essays on Museums and Material Culture*, ed. George W. Stocking (Chicago, 1985), pp. 75–111.

93. Interview with Field's displayman, Arthur Frazer, "Lloyd Lewis Interviews" (1946), MFA; *MRSW* 33 (November 1913): 20–21, 40–41; *MRSW* 34 (June 1914): 20–21, 36–39; and *MRSW* (April 1908): 16–19. On evolution of the mannequin industry, see "The Evolution of Expression," *Visual Merchandising* 5 (February 1978): 49–51 and "Mannequins from the Beginning" 4 (May 1980): 42; The *Department Store* 3 (April 1914): 61–63; *Show Window* 3 (January 1, 1899): 12; *DGE* (October 12, 1889), p. 15; *DGE* (December 10, 1898), p. 12.

94. Leonard Marcus, *American Store Window* (New York, 1978), pp. 34–35; *DGE* (August 18, 1908), p. 3; *DGE* (July 26, 1913), p. 8; *DGE* (February 21 and April 14, 1914), pp. 3, 17; *DGE* (October 27, 1917), p. 14; and *DGE* (July 12, 1919), p. 23.

95. Hundreds of "many small dealers," reported one trade journal, "work hard to imitate the big store displays," even if the costs "seem too high." See *The American Grocer* 74 (December 13, 1905): 19.

96. On the Altman window, see *DGE* (March 5, 1910); and on the Gimbels window, see *MRSW* (February 1916).

97. John Dos Passos, *1919* (New York, 1932), p. 99.

98. *The Dry Goods Reporter* (August 15, 1908).

99. *MRSW* 44 (June 1919): 12–13; *Fame* 7 (May 1899): 217; *The Department Store* 2 (August 1914): 3; *The Dry Goods Reporter* (August 15, 1908), p. 13; and Emily Kimbrough, *Through Charley's Door* (New York, 1952), pp. 101–3.

100. *MRSW* 47 (October 1920): 29–30.

101. *DGE* (April 3, 1920 and October 9, 1920).

102. On Macy's, see *The Department Store* 3 (April 1914): 61–63; *MRSW* 47 (October 1920). On Wanamaker's and Greenhut's, see, respectively, Wanamaker's show window photographs (1911), WA; and *Signs of the Times* 3 (December 1912):

4. See, on similar displays in windows, *DGE* (December 6, 1917), p. 10; and *MRSW* 47 (October 1920): 29–39.

103. "A Window Without Reflection," *PT* 11 (January 1914): 103. On Allert's interior displays, see "A Notable Series of Displays," *MRSW* (November 1913); and on his center-floor display fixtures, see Macy's Council Minutes (May 25, 1914), Record Group I, MA.

104. *DGE* (April 22, 1916); and quoted by Joseph Purdy, "Notes on New York," *MRSW* (April 1916 and May 1912).

105. On Allert's conversion to Christian Science, see *MRSW* (October 1916), 40; and on his resignation from Macy's, see *MRSW* (September 1916).

106. Herman Frankenthal, quoted in *MRSW* (December 1916, May 1912, September 1916, January 1917, and "Draping Deluxe," April 1908).

107. Selfridge, "Selfridge, Harry, Notes Concerning Subjects of Talks . . . to Department Heads," compiled by Waldo Warren (1901–4, April 14, 1902), MFA.

108. "Chicago's Rapid Growth," *DGE* (March 30, 1901), p. 3. Lloyd Lewis interviews with John W. Hughes and David Yates, "Lloyd Lewis Interviews" (1946), MFA.

109. *MRSW* 79 (November 1936): 4–5; *MRSW* 30 (November 1913): 20; interview with Fraser, "Lloyd Lewis Interviews"; S. H. Ditchett, *Marshall Field and Co.: The Life Story of a Great Concern* (New York, 1922), pp. 87–91; Robert Twyman, dissertation on Field's, University of Chicago, 1950, copy in MFA, p. 386; *MRSW* 61 (October 1927): 7; and Earl Dash, "Fraser Was the Greatest Displayman of Them All," *WWD* (July 8, 1947), p. 71.

110. Fraser, "Lloyd Lewis Interviews," MFA.

111. Frank Robertson, "Window Displays Deluxe," *MRSW* 30 (February 1913): 12.

112. *MRSW* 53 (October 1923): 4; interview with Fraser, "Lloyd Lewis Interviews"; Ditchett, *Marshall Field*, p. 88; and Robertson, "Window Displays Deluxe."

113. *MRSW* 56 (February 1925): 31; and Fraser interview, "Lloyd Lewis Interviews."

114. "Questionnaire for Guides," Training Division (June 21, 1933), "Employment Development Box," MFA.

115. Theodore Dreiser Diary (November 10 and 26, 1917), in *Theodore Dreiser: American Diaries, 1902–1926*, ed. Thomas Riggio (Philadelphia, 1982), pp. 204, 222.

Chapter 3

1. Sophie C. Hall Diary (February 1879 and January 31, 1879), Manuscript Division, NYPL.

2. Louis Ferkin, counselor at law, to PS (January 12, 1921), Shoplifting File, MA.

3.   For a description of such decorations, see, on Wanamaker's, *The Public Ledger* (December 19, 1887): 182: "The walls and pillars are gaily decorated with the goods in the store wrought into fanciful designs. . . . Hanging from the second floor of the transept dome are specimens of the upholsterer's work. A plush embroidered piano cover hangs from the railing, attracting the eye from below" (Wanamaker scrapbook, "Notices, Invoices," WA).

4.   *The Show Window* (June 1899): 297–98; and *DGE* (December 8, 1894), p. 3.

5.   "A Model Store Front," *DGE* (February 5, 1898), p. 9.

6.   "Revolving Doors," *DGE* (April 13, 1907); and "Revolving Doors Best," *DGE* (August 20, 1904).

7.   JW to A. I. English (December 20, 1899), Wanamaker Letterbook, vol. 24, p. 215, WA.

8.   Theodore Delemos, *The Dry Goods Chronicle* (July 23, 1895), Siegel-Cooper Scrapbook, NYHS.

9.   *DGE* (March 25, 1916), p. 25; and *MRSW* 32 (June 1913): 12–13.

10.   See JW to Thomas Wanamaker (February 22, 1898), WA, and "Escalator a Success," *DGE* (November 24, 1900), p. 37.

11.   R. F. Starr, "Lloyd Lewis Interviews," MFA; "Through English Eyes," *Store Life* (October 1904): 8–9; *DGE* (November 24, 1900), p. 14; *DGE* (January 25, 1908), p. 83; *DGE* (February 6, 1915), p. 60; *DGE* (May 22, 1915), p. 67; and *DGE* (January 25, 1913), p. 61.

12.   "How Escalators Contributed to the Development of a Great Store," *DGE* (January 25, 1913), p. 61.

13.   On the variety of display cases, see *DGE* (September 24, 1898), p. 9; *DGE* (April 14, 1900), p. 14; *DGE* (January 21, 1905), p. 55; Warren C. Scoville, *Revolution in Glassmaking: Entrepreneurship and Technological Change* (Cambridge, Mass., 1948), pp. 78–83, 103–4, 253–59; and Freda Diamond, *The Story of Glass* (New York, 1953), pp. 79–128.

14.   Harry Morrison, "Modern Store Designing," *MRSW* 1 (January 1922): 1; *DGE* (January 21, 1905), p. 55; *DGE* (April 14, 1900), p. 14; *DGE* (September 24, 1898), p. 9; and *The Advertising World* 22 (November 1917): 206–8.

15.   JW to RW (January 2, 1891, August 10, 1890, and October 24, 1890), WA.

16.   JW, "Memorandum Book: Trip Abroad, 1886," in metal tin box, WA.

17.   Morrison, "Modern Store Designing," *The Show Window* (June 1899); *MRSW* 30 (March 1913): 20; and *DGE* (August 7, 1897).

18.   "Mirrors in Stores," *DGE* (September 24, 1898), p. 9.

19.   *DGE* (February 20, 1904), p. 32; and "Mirrors in Stores," 9.

20. Macy's, "Minutes of the Board of Operations" (February 19, 1920), MA; *DGE* (August 23, 1902), 21.

21. Interview with Reynard F. Starr, head of maintenance and construction at Marshall Field's, 1923–40, "Lloyd Lewis Interviews" (1946), transcript, MFA.

22. W. J. McC., "Report" (July 24, 1902), beginning "I first visited Gimbels," WA. On the "dull season" blight, see JW to Reverend Eckels (December 6, 1895), JW Letterbook, vol. 15, p. 930; and JW to William Nesbitt (January 9, 1897), vol. 17, p. 987, WA.

23. JW, memorandum book, "1900" (September 7, 1900); and memorandum book, "1894," p. 10, WA.

24. *MRSW* (March 1913); *DGE* (May 20, 1905).

25. Mary C. Henderson, "Theater Architecture as Corporate Symbol: Syndicate and Shubert Theaters: (1988), unpublished manuscript in author's possession; Harriet Monroe, *John Wellborn Root: A Study of His Life and Work* (Park Forest, Ill., 1966; orig. pub. 1896), pp. 207–46; Robert Twombly, *Louis Sullivan: His Life and Work* (New York, 1986), pp. 163–96, 247–79, 337–47; Lauren S. Wingarden, "The Colors of Nature: Louis Sullivan's Polychromy and Nineteenth-Century Color Theory," *Winterthur Portfolio* 29 (Winter 1985): 243–60; and on Sullivan, William Gray Purcell, "Creating Background and Atmosphere Which Sell Merchandise," *MRSW* (January 1930).

26. Unsigned, "The Educational Value of a Great Shop, *House and Garden* 13 (May 1904): 21–25; and Samuel Howe, "One Source of Color Values," *House and Garden* 10 (September 1906): 105–13. The May 1904 *House and Garden* article gives the only evidence I know of that Tiffany himself designed the dome. For a discussion of the symbolic significance of green and blue, see Oswald Spengler, *The Decline of the West* (New York, 1991; orig. pub. 1932), pp. 128–29.

27. Jules Guerin, "The Magic City of the Pacific's Architects, Painters, and Sculptors Offer Their Best to the Panama-Pacific Exposition," *The Craftsman* 26 (August 1914): 465–80.

28. Ann Halpenny Kantor, "The Hotel Del Coronado and Tent City," in *Victorian Resorts and Hotels: Essays from a Victorian Society Autumn Symposium*, ed. Richard Guy Wilson (New York, 1982); and on L. Frank Baum's output of stories at the hotel, see Scott Olsen, "The Coronado Fairyland," *The Baum Bugle* (Winter 1976).

29. Anna Alice Chapin, *Greenwich Village* (New York, 1925; orig. pub. 1917), pp. 209–40; and Lewis Erenberg, "Village Nights: Episodes in the Nightlife of Greenwich Village, 1910–1950," unpublished manuscript in possession of author, pp. 1–3.

30. *DGE* (September 21, 1907), p. 36; *DGE* (February 2, 1904), p. 58; *DGE* (April 6, 1901), p. 12; *MRSW* 50 (December 1923): 6.

31. "Store's Bargain Mart," *DGE* (May 19, 1901). On the evolution of the bargain basement, see *DGE* (December 14, 1889, August 29, 1891, November 7, 1894,

November 17, 1900, May 18, 1901, October 18, 1902, and October 2, 1912).

32. Quoted in "Store's Bargain Mart," p. 11.

33. *DGE* (April 12, 1912); *DGE* (October 25, 1902).

34. On these interior display strategies, see "Marshall Field and Company, Retail," *Chicago Dry Goods Reporter* (October 11, 1902), an extensive article written soon after the opening of the new store, copy, MFA; and interview of Michael Cary, Field's sales manager in wholesale in the early 1920s and a cash boy in the 1890s, "Lloyd Lewis Interviews," MFA.

35. JW to G. Harry Davis (May 2, 1883), Wanamaker Letterbook, "J.W. Private, 1883–1884," p. 33; and JW to George Burgurn (February 24, 1886) in Wanamaker Letterbook, "J.W. Personal—December 22, 1885 to December 2, 1886," p. 154, WA. For a "lenient" judge, see Frederic Kernochan, chief justice of Special Sessions, to Jesse Straus (April 24, 1919), Shoplifting File, MA.

36. Michael Cary, interview, "Lloyd Lewis Interviews," MFA. For a recent book on kleptomania, see Elaine Abelson, *Ladies Go A-thieving* (New York, 1988). And for an analysis of the "syndrome" in France, see Michael Miller, *The Bon Marché* (Princeton, N.J., 1982).

37. Quoted in WWD (January 2, 1912), pp. 6–7.

38. A. Nicholas Vardac, *Stage to Screen: Theatrical Method from Garrick to Griffith* (New York, 1949), pp. 139–51, 89–135; Elizabeth Kendall, *Where She Danced* (New York, 1979); and Dolf Sternbeger, *Panorama of the 19th Century*. The Vardac book is especially useful in demonstrating the relationship between the theater and other forms of visual representation.

39. JW and Co., *New York: Metropolis of the World* (New York, 1916), p. 53; JW and Co., *The Guide Book and Information Concerning the Wanamaker's Mail Order Service* (New York, 1910), p. 32; *Betty Comes to Town* (New York, 1920), pp. 11–65; *The Wanamaker Originator* 2 (November 1908): 2, WA; *DGE* (October 17, 1908); and *The Dry Goods Reporter* (October 17, 1908).

40. Jerome Koerber, "Store Decoration," *MRSW* 23 (April 1912): 54.

41. Herbert Croly, "Some Novel Features of the Pan-American Exposition," *The Architectural Record* 11 (October 1901): 591–614.

42. Bernard Sobel, "Pageantry Possibilities," *Proceedings of the Mississippi Valley Historical Association* 9, I (Cedar Rapids, Ia., 1917): 301–6. For a recent discussion on the pageant movement but from a different perspective, see David Glassberg, "History and the Public: Legacies of the Progressive Era," *The Journal of American History* 73 (March 1987): 957–80.

43. Margaret Knapp, "A Historical Study of the Legitimate Playhouses on West Forty-second Street Between Seventh and Eighth Avenues in New York City," Ph.D. diss., City College of New York (1982), pp. 56, 80–81; and Stephen Burge Johnson, *The Roof Gardens of Broadway Theaters, 1883–1942* (Ann Arbor, Mich., 1985).

44.   Quoted in Erenberg, "Village Nights," p. 9; on the other Village places mentioned here, see Erenberg, pp. 3–4.

45.   "Store Decoration," MRSW 2 (April 1912): 54.

46.   DGE (December 5, 1895); DGE (July 8, 1905); "The Power of Store Decoration," Store Life (October 1904); MRSW (June 1918).

47.   On these various fantasy interiors, see DGE (March 20, 1897), p. 97; (October 6, 1900), p. 20; and (May 24, 1902), p. 73.

48.   "Oriental Display," DGE (March 17, 1900), p. 62.

49.   "Special Interior Displays," MRSW (January 1911); "Elaborate Easter Displays," DGE (April 21, 1900).

50.   Robert Ogden to JW (December 31, 1895), Box 5, "Letters to John Wanamaker," Robert C. Ogden Papers, Library of Congress.

51.   On these facades and rose windows, see the Christmas photographic display albums of Howard Kratz, display manager in Philadelphia (1921, 1924, and 1928), WA; on the New York store displays, see WWD (February 4, 1928), p. 3. To get the details of the facades "just right," the New York displayman, Kratz and William Larkin, relied on the handbook of the American Wing of the Metropolitan Museum of Art.

52.   DGE (December 3, 1898).

53.   MRSW 23 (February 1908; April 1908).

54.   "Wonderful Industry for American Baby Built Up in Last 60 Years," DGE (November 19, 1921), p. 225; and PT (March 19, 1920), p. 144.

55.   "To the Members of the Toy Section," in "Addresses to Store Chiefs," privately printed (October 30, 1916), p. 203, WA. On percentage of increase in the American toy business, see U.S. Department of Commerce, "International Trade in Toys," Trade Information Bulletin no. 445 (Washington, D.C., December 1926).

56.   DGE (September 21, 1893; November 25, 1893).

57.   On Siegel-Cooper's, see The Dry Goods Reporter (December 12, 1908) and DGE (December 19, 1908), p. 19; on Namm's and The Fair, see DGE (November 10, 1910).

58.   PT 10 (March 1912): 75.

59.   "Report on Value of Toy Manufacturers Based on Summary of Questionnaires Issued by War Industries Board," Toys—General—1918–25, file 205.6, Record Group 151, BFDC, NA; Fletcher Dodge, secretary of Toy Manufacturers of U.S.A., to the Bureau of Foreign and Domestic Commerce (March 5, 1921), 205.6, RG 151, BFDC, NA; DGE (August 29, 1896), p. 49; and DGE (February 9, 1918), p. 80.

60.   PT 15 (September 1917): 19; and Toy World 2 (March 1929): 48.

61.   JW to RW (November 30, 1915), Wanamaker Letterbook, p. 851, WA. In

this letter, Wanamaker asks his son in New York to send him some toy "jiggers" from the Manhattan store, since "you seem to have an abundance of them."

62.   U.S. Department of Commerce, "International Trade in Toys." See also, on cuddle toys, *DGE* (September 13, 1919); and on dolls, *DGE* (March 28, 1918).

63.   "Important Dates Marshall Field and Co., 6/25/1887–Sept. 7, 1933, Inclusive," compiled by F. L. Morgan, MFA; and Harry Selfridge, "Children's Day" (September 25, 1905), from "Notes Concerning Subjects of Talks Made by H.G.S. to Department Heads . . . as Compiled by Waldo Warren, 1901–1906," MFA; and *Toys and Novelties* 4 (April 1911): 10.

64.   *TN* 4 (April 1911): 10; and, for Marshall Field editorial, see *The Advertising World* (March 1912).

65.   Hughston McBain, "Lloyd Lewis Interviews" (1946), MFA.

66.   *PT* 10 (December 1912): 44.

67.   *PT* 15 (June 1917): 5; and *DGE* (November 11, 1922), p. 17.

68.   Siegel-Cooper and Co., *New York—a Bird's-Eye View of Greater New York and Its Most Magnificent Store* (New York, 1898), p. 136, NYPL; *The Show Window* (November 1899): 209; *Fame* 5 (January 1897): 419; *DGE* (December 22, 1894); *DGE* (October 30, 1920), p. 43; and *The Washington Star* (December 18, 1899), p. 13.

69.   *ST* (December 1912); *DGE* (December 4, 1913), p. 107; and *PT* 18 (December 1920): 174.

70.   JW to Reverend S. W. Steckel (December 11, 1907), in Wanamaker Letterbook, "Personal Letters of John Wanamaker, December 14, 1906 to February 20, 1908," p. 763, WA.

71.   JW, speech "To the Members of the Toy Section" (October 30, 1916), in "Addresses to the Store Chiefs," privately printed for store staff, p. 202, WA.

72.   *PT* 10 (December 1912): 34; *PT* 11 (December 1915): 52–54; *DGE* (December 22, 1894), p. 15; and John Wanamaker and Co., Wanamaker advertising card, "Visit Santa Claus and See the Toys in the Basement," c. 1900, Dry Goods Collection, Warshow Collection of Business Americana, Archive Center, NMAH, Smithsonian Institution.

73.   *PT* 12 (December 1914): 64. On the 1914 transfer of the toy department to the fourth floor, see JW to RW (August 10, 1914), Wanamaker Letterbook, WA.

74.   *PT* 12 (December 1914): 64.

Chapter 4

1.   Jerome Koerber, quoted in *MRSW* (February 1912).

2.   *DGE* (September 14, 1901); and *The Advertising World* 21 (October 1916): 172. "Style" affects the "value" of a commodity and is "highly changeable. A style value commands an extra cost to the purchaser. Just as soon as a style begins to pass, their value begins correspondingly to decrease."

3. *DGE* (August 15, 1903); and Veblen, quoted in Dorfman, *Thorstein Veblen* (New York, 1934), p. 113.

4. On the increased use of raw silk, see *DGE* (June 18, 1904).

5. William D. Haywood, "The Rip in the Silk Industry," the *International Socialist Review* (May 1913), repub. in Joyce L. Kornbluh, ed., with introductions, *Rebel Voices: An I.W.W. Anthology* (Ann Arbor, Mich., 1964), pp. 205–6. As Kornbluh points out, Haywood later used the material in this article, based on his own research, as data testimony before the U.S. Industrial Relations Commissions on employer use of "sabotage" in industry, to the great embarrassment of the Paterson silk manufacturers. On the evolution of silk production methods, see Philip Scranton, ed., *Silk City: Studies on the Paterson Silk Industry, 1860–1940* (Newark, N.J., 1985); Melvyn Dubovsky, *We Shall Be All: A History of the Industrial Workers of the World* (Chicago, 1969), pp. 229–69; and James D. Osborne, "Paterson: Immigrant Strikers and the War of 1913," in *At the Point of Production, The Local History of the I.W.W.*, ed. James R. Conlin (Westport, Conn., 1981), pp. 61–78.

6. Elizabeth Gurley Flynn, "The Truth About the Paterson Strike" (January 31, 1914), repub. in Kornbluh, ed., *Rebel Voices*, pp. 215–26.

7. On the garment industry, see Irving Howe, *World of Our Fathers* (New York, 1976), pp. 154–56; and Graham Adams, Jr., *Age of Industrial Violence, 1910–1915* (New York, 1966), pp. 103–12. For the Crawford citation, see Morris d'Camp Crawford "Address Delivered Before the National Silk Convention," November 23, 1916, Box 10, 1913–1916, Central Archives, AMNH, New York City.

8. Dubovsky, *We Shall Be All*, pp. 267–68.

9. *DGE* (August 15, 1903); and *DGE*, editorial (November 12, 1898).

10. *DGE* (August 15, 1909), p. 3.

11. M.D.C. Crawford, *The Ways of Fashion* (New York, 1941), p. 114; Alexander Deutsch, "The Trend in Fashion," *The Department Store* (April 1914): 7–11.

12. The figure on the buyers is from *Sheldon's Retail Trade in the United States* (New York, 1916). This directory furnished the retail business with a list of all buyers in the country and is still published today. I would like to thank Jerome Bompard for helping me count the buyers.

13. On Mollie Netcher, see "Boston Store to Build," *MRSW* (January 1910); on Rebecca Ehrich, see *DGE* (March 17, 1900); and on Lena Himmelstein, see Robert Hendrikson, *The Grand Emporiums: The Illustrated History of America's Great Department Stores* (New York, 1979), pp. 178–79, and Tom Mahoney and Leonard Sloane, *The Great Merchants* (New York, 1966), pp. 244–57.

14. Interview with Lloyd Lewis (1946), transcript, MFA.

15. JW advertising editorials (January 8, 1914, and January 26, 1916), in *Editorials of John Wanamaker*, vol. I (October 1, 1912–December 31, 1917), WA. On Wanamaker's almost lifetime support of suffrage, see JW to Naomi Pennock

(January 23, 1912), in letterbook (August 10, 1911 to March 22, 1912), p. 721. See also Wanamaker's speech "To the Members of the Toy Section" (October 30, 1916): "When this store began, women did not work in stores. All they were interested in then was in sewing and scrubbing, and housekeeping. Now it comes to pass that women are in competition with men. I could take you to the place where they are making as much as $10,000 a year. 'You say where are they?' Some of them are in architects' offices, where they are making plans. Women are great planners, and when a woman starts out and says, 'I am going to be an architect' and if she is a woman of the right sort, she will do it. There is no reason why she cannot do it as well as a man." "Addresses to Store Chiefs," privately printed, p. 204, WA.

16.   JW to Nancy McClellan (January 9, 1922), and JW to Elizabeth Kaufman (November 29, 1921), Wanamaker Letterbook, "August 24, 1921 to June 15, 1922," WA. For biographical material on McClellan, see her obituary, NYT (October 2, 1959), p. 29.

17.   Interview with Macy's buyer, Lena Robenau, Harvard History Project, Box 4 of 4, Record Group 10, MA.

18.   Mae De Mon Sutton, I Reminisce (Fort Lauderdale, Fla., 1942), pp. 29–39, 59–67; and "Style Show in Theater," DGE (September 4, 1915), p. 36.

19.   JW to RW, April 19, 1911, letters to RW, WA.

20.   Faith Chipperfield, In Quest of Love (New York, 1957), p. 19; and Faith Chipperfield, letter to The New York Times (July 7, 1957), for New York City reference.

21.   Anne Evans to LK (June 6, 1919), Box 22, LKP, "Business Methods"; and Lincoln Filene to LK (July 28, 1914), Box 22, LKP, Baker Library, HBS.

22.   RW to JW (March 8, 1912), Wanamaker Letterbook (August 10, 1911 to March 22, 1912), p. 894, WA.

23.   Evans and Chipperfield to LK (April 28, 1919, February 19, 1919, and June 6, 1919), Box 22; LK to Chipperfield and Evans (July 2, 1919), Box 22; A. Lincoln Filene to LK (February 11, 1919), Box 65, "Filene, A. Lincoln," LKP, Baker Library, HBS.

24.   Wanamaker advertisements, MRSW (February 1914).

25.   Obituary of RW, New York Telegram (March 9, 1928), p. 2, and Evening Journal (March 9, 1928), p. 1, "In Memoriam, Rodman Wanamaker, 1863–1928," scrapbook, WA; DGE (April 3, 1897); JW to Emily Sartrain (May 16, 1908), WA; Joseph Appel, The Business Biography of John Wanamaker (New York, 1930), p. 402; and "Sam" to Rodman Wanamaker (October 20, 1894), WA.

26.   DGE (January 16, 1897), pp. 42–43; DGE (November 20, 1897), p. 97; JW, quoted in Appel, The Business Biography of John Wanamaker, p. 402.

27.   R. H. Helmer to JW (c. 1911), Wanamaker Letterbook, vol. 48, p. 45, JW.

28.   Quoted from DGE (October 29, 1900); DGE (March 8, 1902), pp. 53, 77–86; MRSW (June 1913).

29. *DGE* (October 19, 1908).

30. *DGE* (March 8, 1902), pp. 53, 77–86.

31. W. H. Coade to Macy's (c. 1902), Harvard History Project, RG 10, pp. 1501–1700, MA; and John Wanamaker, Scrapbook, "The 30th Anniversary of a New Kind of Store" (Philadelphia, 1906), pp. 2–3, WA.

32. *MRSW* (February and April 1912). On Ehrich's, see *DGE* (October 10, 1903), p. 14. See also "Showing Gowns on Living Models," *MRSW* 25 (November 1909): 39; "Living Models," *MRSW* 22 (May 1908): 45; and *DGE* (August 19, 1911), p. 49; *DGE* (April 12, 1913), p. 55; *DGE* (October 3, 1914), pp. 45–46; Lillian Drain, "Many Artists in Fashion Show Poster Contest," *Poster* 3 (October 1912): 23–24; Albert Morenson, "Fashion Show Posters in Los Angeles," *Poster* 3 (October 1912): 43–44.

33. *MRSW* (September and November 1915); *DGE* (March 31, 1917); *MRSW* (November 1911).

34. *The Wanamaker Originator* 2 (November 1908): 1, copy in WA.

35. *The Wanamaker Originator* 1.

36. *DGE* (October 5, 1912), p. 117; *DGE* (October 2, 1909), p. 12; *DGE* (October 8, 1910), p. 23.

37. *MRSW* (March 1917).

38. *WWD* (April 26, 1912), p. 5.

39. Vernie Connelly, "The Oasis of Madison Street," *The American Restaurant* 3 (July 1920): 13–15, 48.

40. *DGE* (March 3, 1917), p. 15; *DGE* (August 25, 1917), pp. 77, 95; *DGE* (July 12, 1919), 24; *DGE* (August 27, 1921), pp. 16–17.

41. Edward Said, *Orientalism* (New York, 1982); Robert Rydell, *All the World's a Fair* (Chicago, 1984).

42. See, e.g., Bayard Taylor, *The Land of the Saracens* (New York, 1855), pp. 133–48; George Curtis, *Nile Notes* (New York, 1851), pp. 128–32; and Nathaniel Willis, *Health Trip to the Tropics* (New York, 1853), pp. 63, 88–89.

43. On this ball, see *Town and Country* 66 (September 6, 1913): 33; and for the Alma Mahler quote, see Robert Koch, *Rebel in Glass* (New York, 1967), p. 69. On Tiffany's orientalism, see Samuel Howe, "The Long Island Home of Mr. Tiffany," *Town and Country* 68 (September 6, 1913): 24–36; Howe, "One Source of Color Values," *House and Garden* 10 (September 1906): 105–13; and Koch, pp. 142–45. On college student and upper-class interest in orientalism, see Virginia Spencer Carr, *Dos Passos: A Life* (New York, 1981), p. 89, and Jackson Lears, *No Place of Grace* (New York, 1981), pp. 142–43, 175–77, 225–41.

44. *NYT* (October 10, 1919), p. 18; Loren Ruff, *Edward Sheldon* (Boston, 1982), pp. 101–3. On Cleopatra, Egypt, and commercial orientalism generally, see Terry Ramsaye, *A Million and One Nights: A History of the Motion Picture Through*

1925 (New York, 1926), pp. 700–704; Miriam Hansen, *Babel and Babylon* (Cambridge, Mass., 1991), pp. 172–87, 237–41; and Antonia Lant, "Egypt and the Cinema," project description, New York University, in possession of author, part 3, p. 4.

45.   *NYT* (October 10, 1919), p. 18; *Theater Arts Magazine* (hereafter *TAM*) 3 (April 1919): 90–92; *TAM* 3 (July 1919): 181; *TAM* 2 (December 1917): 8–9; and *TAM* 2 (December 1917): 12–17. See also Ramsaye, *A Million and One Nights*, pp. 702–6.

46.   Harold Frederic, *The Damnation of Theron Ware, or Illumination*, ed. Charlyne Dodge (Lincoln, Neb. 1989; orig. pub. 1899), pp. 191–203.

47.   Inez Haynes Irwin, *The Lady of Kingdoms* (New York, 1917), pp. 24, 99–103, 472, 475.

48.   LFB, *Daughters of Destiny* (Chicago, 1906), pp. 57–58, 173, 197, 202–3, 305.

49.   Kalem Agency to Jesse Straus (November 30, 1914), Harvard History Project (1934), RG 10, p. 1837, MA.

50.   "Store Decorations on Big Scale," *DGE* (July 20, 1907), p. 29.

51.   Jerome Sterne, "Merchants Cooperate in Holding a Fashion Week," *DGE* (April 1, 1916), p. 73.

52.   Robert Hichens, *Yesterday: The Autobiography of Robert Hichens* (London, 1947), pp. 67, 180–81, 244–45.

53.   Robert Hichens, *The Garden of Allah* (New York, 1904), pp. 6, 27, 106.

54.   Ethan Mordden, *The Hollywood Studios: House Style in the Golden Age of the Movies* (New York, 1988), p. 207.

55.   Hichens, *Yesterday*, pp. 140, 168–69, 244–45.

56.   On Nazimova, see Amy Porter, "Garden of Allah, I Love You," in *Hello, Hollywood!: A Book About Hollywood by the People Who Make Them*, ed. Allen Rivkin (New York, 1962), pp. 352–59. See also on the Garden of Allah hotel, Sheila Graham, *The Garden of Allah* (New York, 1970).

57.   *MRSW* (June 1912 and October 1912).

Chapter 5

1.   JW, 1918 memorandum book, pp. 3–4, tin box, WA.

2.   Peter Maurin, "To the Bishops of the U.S., a Plea for Houses of Hospitality," *Catholic Worker* (October 1933); repub. in Peter Maurin, *Catholic Radicalism: Phrased Essays for the Green Revolution* (New York, 1949), pp. 7–8; and "Communist Action in Schools: A Challenge to Catholics," p. 39.

3.   JW to William Mason (May 18, 1886) in Wanamaker Letterbook, "J.W. Personal—December 22, 1885–December 2, 1886," WA. For a description of

Wanamaker as "a peer among merchants," see Alfred B. Koch (himself owner of a department store), "The Stevens Bill and Manufacturing Monopolies," *Industrial Outlook: A Business Review* 12 (December 1915): 7: "Long before the manufacturers of branded articles announced to the world that they stood behind [their] articles, John Wanamaker proclaimed that he would give money back to any customer who was dissatisfied with any purchase made in his store, branded or unbranded."

4.   JW, quoted in *DGE* (October 4, 1902); and JW to Mrs. Jane Wright (January 18, 1897), Letterbook vol. 18, p. 719, WA.

5.   JW, speech "at the opening of the Market St. Section of the Philadelphia Store" (March 12, 1906), in "Miscellaneous Addresses," pp. 80–81, bound collection, WA.

6.   JW to RW (December 3, 1897 and July 25, 1902), "letters to Rodman Wanamaker," WA.

7.   *Thought and Work* (July 15, 1904); for Gimbels citation, see *MRSW* (May 1911).

8.   Edward L. Bernays, *Biography of an Idea* (New York, 1962), p. 236.

9.   Rufus Jarman, *A Bed for the Night: The Story of the Wheeling Bellboy, E. M. Statler and His Remarkable Hotel* (New York, 1952), pp. 3–16, 98–105; Statler obituary, *NYT* (April 17, 1928), p. 29.

10.   Jarman, *A Bed for the Night*, p. 99.

11.   Ellsworth Statler, *NYHR* 14 (March 24, 1919): 13; Jarman, *A Bed for the Night*, pp. 132–70; *The Hotel Gazette* 40 (April 22, 1916): 4; *NYHR* 8 (June 14, 1913): 25; *NYHR* 11 (December 23, 1916): 1.

12.   Bernays, *Biography*, p. 238; Horace Sutton, *Confessions of a Grand Hotel* (New York, 1951), p. 18; Lucius Boomer, "The Greatest Household," in Frank Crowinshield, *The Unofficial Palace of New York* (New York, 1939), p. 11; Henry Lent, *The Waldorf-Astoria: A Brief Chronicle of a Unique Institution Now Entering Its Fifth Decade* (New York, 1934), p. 32. On the Hotel McAlpin and Boomer, see *NYT* (December 30, 1912), p. 18; *The Hotel Gazette* 40 (October 23, 1915): 9 and *NYHR* 12 (January 20, 1917): 27–28.

13.   Lucius Boomer, quoted by Kurt Heppe, "Attracting Hotel Patrons with Your Cuisine," *The American Restaurant* 4 (January 1921): 1.

14.   On A.T. & T. and the railroads, see Alan R. Raucher, *Public Relations and Business, 1900–1929* (Baltimore, 1968), pp. 35–52.

15.   On Insull, see Forrest McDonald, *Insull* (Chicago, 1962), p. 114.

16.   Johan Huizinga, *America*, ed. and trans. Herbert Rowan (New York, 1972; orig. pub. 1926), pp. 310–11.

17.   George Marsden, *Fundamentalism and American Culture: The Shaping of Twentieth-Century Evangelicalism; 1870–1925* (New York, 1980), pp. 72–73. My argument here draws in part on Marsden's analysis of Moody.

18. Marsden, *Fundamentalism*, p. 79. On the Puritan-evangelical stewardship tradition after 1870, see James F. Findlay, Jr., *Dwight L. Moody, American Evangelist, 1837–1899* (Chicago, 1969), p. 85.

19. On the responses of farmers and industrial workers, see, e.g., Norman Ware, *The Labor Movement in the United States, 1860–1895: A Study in Democracy* (New York, 1929) and Lawrence Goodwyn, *The Populist Moment* (New York, 1978).

20. Straus started his "career" in investigating "vice" between 1908 and 1909, if not earlier. In February 1909, *The Dry Goods Economist* reports him as being a member—along with Samuel Bloomingdale—of a committee of the National Retail Dry Goods Association to investigate "certain picnic places, amusement resorts, dancing halls, etc." *DGE* (February 13, 1909), p. 4. On department stores as possible sources for prostitution, see Mark Connelly, *The Response to Prostitution in the Progressive Era* (Chapel Hill, N.C., 1980); and Rheta Childe Dorr, *What 8,000,000 Women Want* (New York, 1910), p. 196.

21. "Report of Miss Faith Habberton" (October 16–October 31, 1913), p. 17, "Special Investigation, Committee of 14," Folder 2, Box 39, Committee of Fourteen Records, Manuscripts Division, NYPL.

22. On this view of Jewish immigrant women see Arthur Goren, *New York Jews and the Quest for Community* (New York, 1970), pp. 134–58.

23. Natalie D. Sonnichen, written report, entries (November 27, 1913, and December 1, 1913), Folder 2, Box 39, "Special Investigation, Committee of 14"; "Report of M. Sidney," entries (October 7, 1913), pp. 11–12 (December 10–16, 1913), p. 2, NYPL; "New York Store Workers' Morality O.K'd," *DGE* (February 20, 1915), p. 49.

24. Katherine Bennett Davis, "Report of Meeting of April 18, 1913," investigation of the National Civic Association, "Department Stores—Wage Survey (4 of 6)," p. 13; same report, James Bronson Reynolds, p. 2, National Civic Association Papers, Manuscripts Division, NYPL.

25. "Commissary for Employees," *MRSW* (March 1913).

26. Robert C. Ogden to JW (May 1, 1890), "Letters," Box 5, Robert C. Ogden Papers, LC. On these profit-sharing schemes see Daniel T. Rodgers, *The Work Ethic in Industrial America, 1850 to 1920* (Chicago, 1978), pp. 45–62.

27. *NYHR* 11 (December 9, 1906): 36.

28. McDonald, *Insull*, pp. 114–25.

29. "Store Family," *DGE* (October 23, 1915).

30. Macy's, "Minutes of the Managers' Association, 1911–1916," Record Group 1 (May 18, 1916), MA; and "Interviews, R. H. Macy Department Store, Herald Square" (November 6–12, 1914), pp. 2–4, Resale Price Investigation, RG 122, Bureau of Corporations, File No. 7224-64-1, NA.

31. For a detailed discussion of this kind of "welfare work" in department stores, see unpublished survey of the National Civic Federation, "NCF—Welfare Department—Department Stores—Wage Survey (5 of 6)," pp. 6–30; Gertrude Beeks, "Survey of the Department Stores," Box 83, Papers of National Civic Federation, Manuscripts Division, NYPL.

32. "Wage Survey, 5 of 6," Survey of the Department Stores (April 29, 1913), National Civic Federation, Box 83, Manuscripts Division, NYPL; and "Estate for Employees' Use," DGE (June 23, 1917).

33. Boris Emmet and John E. Jeuck, Catalogues and Counters: A History of Sears, Roebuck and Co. (Chicago, 1950), pp. 137–49.

34. On Filene's, see PRL (May 7, 1924), p. 4; on Saks, DGE (May 22, 1915); on Bamberger's, DGE (October 23, 1915). On Plaut's, "Papers for Employees," MRSW (July 1913). On Siegel-Cooper's, see Thought and Work (hereafter TW) (June 15, 1904). On "personals," see TW (November 15, 1904); TW (December 15, 1904); and TW (September 15, 1905). By 1921 the number of employee magazines in all industries had reached 334 (Emmet and Jeuck, Catalogues and Counters, pp. 137–49, and fn. 8, p. 733).

35. On Statler, see NYHR 12 (January 20, 1917): 62; on Boomer, see NYHR 12 (January 29, 1917).

36. Interview with Macy's executive, A. S. Donaldson, Harvard History Project interviews (1934), RG 10, Box 1, MA.

37. Faith Habberton, private report (entry July 26, 1913), p. 14; Committee of Fourteen, "Department Store Investigation Report of the Sub-Committee" (1915), p. 12, Committee of Fourteen Records, Manuscripts Division, NYPL.

38. Wanamaker investigation notes, Committee of Fourteen Records, Folder 1, Box 39 (April 1913).

39. JW to Hannah Jones (October 31, 1902), in "Mr. Wanamaker Personal, June 21, 1902 to November 22, 1902," p. 755, WA; and Henry Adams Gibbons, John Wanamaker (New York, 1926), vol. 2, p. 262.

40. JW, address, "At the Laying of the Corner Stone of the New Building" (June 12, 1909), p. 95, in "Miscellaneous Addresses," WA.

41. Robert C. Ogden to JW (February 9, 1891 and May 1, 1890), Ogden Papers.

42. Ogden to JW (June 2, 1891), Ogden Papers.

43. JW to Powderly (August 6, 1896) in Wanamaker Letterbook, vol. 16, p. 717, JA.

44. Marshall Field's even assembled an employee choral society as good, apparently, as any professional group in the country, that performed such works with the Chicago Symphony as Rossini's Stabat Mater, Elgar's oratorio King Olaf, and Haydn's The Creation. See "Store's Choral Society," DGE (April 23, 1910), p. 5; and "A Treat for Lovers of Good Music" (November 15, 1904).

45. JW to RW (August 8, 1911), "letters to Rodman," WA.

46.   JW, address, "Upon the Occasion of Vacating the Chestnut Street End of the Store" (September 14, 1908), in "Miscellaneous Addresses, May 12, 1902–July 1, 1915," WA; and "Morning Songs" (John Wanamaker, N.Y., 1917), WA. On the JW Cadet Choir and other musical groups, see Wanamaker Guidebook, *New York City and the Wanamaker Store* (New York, 1924), p. 34, and JW and Co., "The John Wanamaker Store Army" (Philadelphia: John Wanamaker, 1918), p. 26, WA. On the number of employees in 1915, see Gibbons, *John Wanamaker*, vol. 2, pp. 199–201.

47.   See Gibbons, *John Wanamaker*, vol. 2, pp. 218–35, 259–303; Wanamaker Medical Department, "Safeguards and Aids to the Health and Well-Being of Employees" (Philadelphia and New York: Wanamaker's, April 1917), WA; Meadowbrook Club, *Yearbook 1929* (Philadelphia, 1929), p. 3, WA; JW to J. B. Learned (on "own expense") (February 15, 1908), Wanamaker Letterbook, "December 14, 1906 to February 20, 1908," p. 965; "Wanamaker 'Firsts,' " list compiled by the store, WA.

48.   Paul Mazur, *American Prosperity* (New York, 1928), p. 20.

49.   Gibbons, *John Wanamaker*, vol. 2, p. 259. These words are a Gibbons paraphrase of Wanamaker.

50.   JW to RW (November 13, 1910), "Letters 1910, JW to RW," WA.

51.   PS, "Minutes of Operations" (August 15, 1918), MA; and Louis Bamberger, quoted by Christine Bennett in "Do the Wise Thing if You Know What It Is. . . . but Anyway Do Something!," *The American Magazine* 95 (June 23, 1923): 73; and *DGE* (April 12, 1913), p. 31. Also, on decline of face-to-face relationships and rise of returned goods, see Susan Porter Benson, *Counter Cultures: Saleswomen, Managers, and Customers in American Department Stores, 1890–1940* (Chicago, 1986), pp. 97–100; and Susan Strasser, *Satisfaction Guaranteed: The Making of the American Mass Market* (New York, 1989), pp. 29–57.

52.   On JW, see *DGE* (February 5, 1910), p. 12, and *RSW* March 1910; on retailers in thirty states, see *DGE* (December 27, 1913), p. 61; and on Macy's, see "Advertising," 1906, store folder, in RG 10, Harvard History Project, p. 2606, MA. And, generally, on rise of this form of service, see Harold Berger, *Distribution's Place in the Economy Since 1869* (Princeton, N.J., 1955), pp. 35–36.

53.   On these early practices see Rolf Nugent, *Consumer Credit and Economic Stability* (New York, 1939), pp. 43–65; Edwin R. Seligman, *The Economics of Instalment Selling*, vol. 1 (New York, 1927), pp. 19–22; and James Grant, *Money of the Mind. Borrowing and Lending in America From the Civil War to Michael Milken* (New York, 1992), pp. 77–95.

54.   *DGE* (April 26, 1902), p. 18; and Grant, *Money of the Mind*, p. 83.

55.   *The Department Store* (May 1914); *DGE* (April 26, 1902); and *DGE* (February 2, 1901).

56.   Lit Brothers to Mrs. S. Oppenheimer (May 10, 1915); and Lit Brothers to its charge customers (April 1904) in JW Scrapbook, "Business ephemera, store credit policies, 1880s to 1910s: discounts, charges, etc.," WA.

57. Wanamaker credit manager to L. W. Ayer and Co., Indianapolis (April 8, 1908), JW, "Business ephemera, store credit policies, 1880s to 1910s: discounts, charges, etc.," WA.

58. CW 7 (July 6, 1919): 15.

59. Nugent, *Consumer Credit*, pp. 68–70.

60. Dorothy Day, *The Long Loneliness: An Autobiography of Dorothy Day* (New York, 1981), p. 57; Leon Trotsky, *My Life* (New York, 1970), p. 217.

61. Nugent, *Consumer Credit*, pp. 70–76.

62. Nugent, *Consumer Credit*, p. 8; Irving Howe, *World of Our Fathers: The Journey of East European Jews to America and the Life They Found and Made* (New York, 1976), pp. 76–87; Elizabeth Ewen, *Immigrant Women and the Land of the Dollars: Life and Culture on the Lower East Side, 1890–1925* (New York, 1985), pp. 168–71.

63. On the early peddling activities of these merchants, see Leon Harris, *Merchant Princes* (New York, 1979), pp. 18, 36–37, 71.

64. Abraham Cahan, *The Rise of David Levinsky* (New York, 1917), pp. 105, 116, 223–51.

65. Barger, *Distribution's Place*, pp. 33–36; Gordon Dakins, *Retail Credit Manual: A Handbook of Retail Credit* (New York, 1950), pp. 9–10.

66. JW editorial repr. in *DGE* (April 14, 1903); JW to customer (March 16, 1885), ibid.

67. *MRSW* (January 1913).

68. JW, "Conference in the Merchandise Room" (October 6, 1916), in "Addresses to Store Chiefs" (July 1, 1915 to December 31, 1921), privately printed, pp. 163–64, 172, WA; *DGE* (February 12, 1916), pp. 35–36; and "Interview with R. H. Macy and Co." (November 6–12, 1914), Resale Price Investigation, Bureau of Corporations, Record Group 122, File 7224-64-1, NA, Washington, D.C. Susan Porter Benson describes the emergence of the "returned goods evil" in *Counter Cultures: Saleswomen, Managers, and Customers in American Department Stores, 1890–1940* (Urbana, Ill., 1986), pp. 95–101.

69. "The exchange system is out of date, antiquated," a buyer told John Wanamaker to his face in 1916, at a general meeting in the "merchandise room" in the store. "When the store was started by you, the line of merchandise was not large." Wanamaker rejected his argument, however, arguing that "I have spent all of my life exploiting an idea, rather than making money, and the store expresses that idea as near as I can. We introduced this principle" and "it is very difficult to take away a privilege from people that they have had." "Conferences in the Merchandise Room" (October 6, 1916), pp. 162–63, 169, privately printed, WA.

70. Elliott, LJ (legal judgment) 1908 E 183 (April 7, 1908); Daly, LJ 1900 D 23 (December 6, 1900); Brunnell, LJ 1906 B 347 (June 8, 1906); Glynn, LJ 1907 G 157 (March 16, 1907); *Oscar Hammerstein* v. *Gimbels*, money judgment 26569-

1915 (January 28, 1921); Topakyan, money judgment 15747 (May 21, 1913); and Hebblethwaite, LJ 1903-H-76 (April 28, 1903); Municipal Archives, Manhattan, New York City. These legal judgments, very useful as a measure of consumer spending in this period, were among the hundreds I looked at in the Municipal Archives and Record Center of New York.

71.   For the attention given such cases, see *DGE* (July 12, 1902), p. 62; *DGE* (October 24, 1903), p. 49; and *DGE* (July 5, 1905), p. 61. Among the most important of these cases had to do with the "liability of the husband for the wife's necessaries when he has furnished her with money." According to the *Harvard Law Review* 43 (1930): 961–62, these cases appeared most frequently between 1902 and 1915.

72.   The *Wanamaker* v. *Weaver* case is described as "leading" in Albert Jacobs and Julius Goebel, Jr., *Cases and Other Materials on Domestic Relations*, 3d ed. (Brooklyn, N.Y., 1952), p. 752.

73.   For this background see "*Wanamaker* v. *Weaver*," Supreme Court, Appellate Division, Fourth Department (May 20, 1902), *New York Supplement*, vol. 76, pp. 392–94.

74.   *New York Supplement*, vol. 76, pp. 393–94.

75.   Judge Haight, "*Wanamaker* v. *Weaver*," *New York Reporter*, vol. 176, p. 78.

76.   *New York Supplement*, vol. 76, p. 392.

77.   "*Wanamaker* v. *Weaver*," *Northeastern Reporter*, vol. 68, pp. 135–38; "*Wanamaker* v. *Weaver*," *New York Reporter* (October 1903), vol. 176, pp. 75, 83.

78.   James Schouler, *A Treatise on the Law of Marriage, Divorce, and Separation and Domestic Relations*, 6th ed., vol. 1 (New York, 1921), p. 110. Still, *Wanamaker* v. *Weaver* remained on the books as a guide to later decisions in similar cases. The most notorious of such cases in the 1920s was *Saks* v. *Huddleston*, which hit the front page of *The New York Times* and involved the wife of Congressman George Huddleston of Alabama, later a leading New Dealer. In 1925 Mrs. Huddleston bought a broadtail fur coat and fox scarf from Saks Fur Company in Washington, D.C. Huddleston had forbidden her use of his credit, which resulted, of course, in her failure to pay. Saks phoned Huddleston repeatedly at his congressional office and finally forced him to testify against his wife before the Municipal Court. Citing *Wanamaker* v. *Weaver*, the judge supported Huddleston, adding that this decision will "tend to check extravagance and protect husbands." *Federal Reporter*, vol. 36 (January–March 1930), pp. 537–38; *Harvard Law Review*, vol. 43 (1930), p. 961; *Washington Star* (December 2, 1929), p. 1; *NYT* (December 3, 1929), p. 1.

79.   CW 6 (June 1915): 64; CW 7 (December 9, 1918): 12; CW 3 (March 1, 1918): 22.

80.   CW 5 (December 1914): 6–10; CW 5 (May 1915): 12; CW 6 (June 1915): 52; CW 7 (September 1918): 11; CW 7 (July 6, 1919): 8; *DGE* (May 15, 1920).

81.   George Fitch, "Charge It," CW 5 (April 1915): 30; CW 7 (August 30, 1919): 12; JW, interview, *DGE* (January 5, 1918).

82. "For Discussion of Delivery Problems," *DGE* (October 28, 1916); *DGE* (August 30, 1919, and April 3, 1915), p. 143; Karl Gerstenberg, "Observations on American and German Department Stores" (May 1, 1940), Manuscripts Division, NYUA, p. 3; and *Store Life* (October 1904), p. 9.

83. Matthew Josephson, *The History of the Hotel and Restaurant Employees and Bartenders International Union, AFL-CIO* (New York, 1955), pp. 4–5, 84–95.

84. Barger, *Distribution's Place*, pp. 4, 92–93. Also, on the earlier "American plan," see Josephson, pp. 4–5.

85. Quoted in Josephson, p. 90.

86. W. L. Dodd, "Service, Sanitation, and Quality," *The American Restaurant* (August 1920): 37.

87. *The American Restaurant* 4 (January 1921): 23.

88. *NYHR* 9 (December 12, 1914): 31; *NYHR* 8 (August 25, 1913): 35; Jarman, *A Bed for the Night*, pp. 2–4, 130–32.

89. Vincent Sheean, *Oscar Hammerstein: The Life and Exploits of an Impresario* (New York, 1956), p. 21; *The Hotel Gazette* 40 (September 25, 1915): 11; Horace Sutton, *Confessions of a Grand Hotel*, p. 30. Also, on theater ushers, see Lary May, *Screening Out the Past* (Berkeley, Calif., 1980), pp. 157–58; and on department store hostesses, see "Special Care of Customers," *DGE* (January 16, 1904), p. 21.

90. JW to Mrs. S. W. Anderson (October 18, 1901) in "Letters: August 20, 1901 to June 21, 1902," WA. For the Strawbridge and Clothier quote, see "Saleswomen and Salesmen," *MRSW* (July 1911).

91. These questions and phrases are taken from an employment training department statement of Marshall Field's, "Let Us Agree," in "Employment Development Box," MFA.

92. *DGE* (February 20, 1909); *DGE* (May 15, 1909).

93. Macy's, "Minutes of the Board of Operations" (July 22, 1920), MA; on Wanamaker's phone service, *DGE* (July 30, 1910), p. 101; and on translators, "Abraham & Straus Centennial Celebration, 1865–1965, Records, 1965, Brooklyn Historical Society, p. 15. See also on Wanamaker's "tel-call system," Macy's report, "Minutes of the Board of Operations" (April 27, 1917), and on Bamberger's "red phones," "Minutes of the Board of Operations" (September 14 and 21, 1917), MA.

94. JW and Co., *Betty Comes to Town: A Letter Home* (New York, 1909); and JW to Mrs. H. P. Hill (December 15, 1898), Wanamaker Letterbook, 428, WA.

95. John Dos Passos, *1919* (New York, 1969), pp. 123–45; Virginia Spencer Carr, *Dos Passos: A Life* (New York, 1984), p. 53. On decorating the Ritz Carlton, see JW to RW (December 12, 1910), "1910 Letters from JW to RW," WA.

96. Anne Morgan, quoted in *NYT* (June 7, 1912), p. 1; *NYT* (December 30, 1912), p. 18.

97.   *NYHR* 5 (July 5, 1913): 10; Richard S. Kennedy, *Dreams in the Mirror: A Biography of e. e. cummings* (New York, 1980), p. 249.

98.   On the relationship between an emergent tourism at about this time and the hotel industry, see Neil Harris, "Urban Tourism and the Commercial City," in *Inventing Times Square: Commerce and Culture at the Crossroads of the World*, ed. William R. Taylor (New York, 1991), pp. 66–98.

99.   *DGE* (January 20, 1900); *DGE* (December 26, 1910); *DGE* (June 11, 1919); *The American Restaurant* 40 (December 25, 1916): 11.

100.   *DGE* (July 8, 1922); *DGE* (November 12, 1904); *DGE* (December 16, 1911); *MRSW* 21 (December 1907): 23; *MRSW* 11 (January and February 1905): 1.

101.   Shirley Ware, "Lots of People Are Tired of Hearing 'Service,' but They Surely Appreciate Getting It," *DGE* (May 6, 1922). This article traces the history of Wolf and Dessauer from its rise in 1895 to its dominance in city retailing by 1910.

102.   *DGE* (November 12, 1904 and December 16, 1911); *MRSW* 21 (December 1907): 23; *MRSW* 11 (January and February 1905): 1.

103.   *DGE* (September 14, 1912); *DGE* (June 8, 1897); *DGE* (August 20, 1910), p. 11; *DGE* (February 8, 1908).

104.   On the Field gallery, see C. Balliet, *Apples and Oranges: Emotional Expression in Modern Art* (Chicago, 1927), p. 197; on the La Farge showings, see "Catalogue of an Exhibition of the Work of John La Farge" (December 1–21, 1902), in scrapbook, "Marshall Field and Co., Ads," Adv-XB1, MFA.

105.   See Theodore Dreiser, *Gallery of Women*, vol. 1 (New York, 1929), pp. 143–66; and Rodman Wanamaker's list of paintings, "Among the works of art in the 'Lindenhurst' collection and at the Store," WA. Anne Estelle Rice appears in the Dreiser work under the pseudonym Ellen Adams Wrynn. The Wanamaker list declares that "Anne Estelle Rice (now Mrs. Drey) was educated by Mr. Rodman Wanamaker. Large murals hanging above the Market Street Elevators, Main Floor, by A. E. Rice."

106.   On the Gimbels showings, see Martin Green, *New York 1913: The Armory Show and the Paterson Strike Pageant* (New York, 1988), pp. 186–87.

107.   Advertisement of Carson, Pirie, Scott in *Fine Arts Journal* (January 1918): 61.

108.   On the Wanamaker stores as "public institutions," see editors, "Wanamaker Advertising," *MRSW* (May 1911): 1: "His stores have been advertised, not only on account of the merchandise sold, but as public institutions. This has been done so cleverly and persistently that Wanamaker is one of the best-known names in America and most people know just what the name stands for."

109.   See folder, "Mr. Wanamaker's Private Collection of Paintings. General Inventory . . . Listed by P. Farine, 1908," WA. Included as well were works by Van

der Velde, Hogarth, Rubens, Watteau, Holbein, Tintoretto, Van Dyck, and Gains-borough (many Gainsboroughs).

110.   JW, quoted in Gibbons, *John Wanamaker*, vol. 2, p. 81; *MRSW* (May 1913). Art was also shown in picture galleries in major hotels. See, on the Waldorf-Astoria roof-garden art gallery, Kennedy, *Dreams in the Mirror*, p. 240.

111.   *DGE* (February 28, 1903), p. 68; *DGE* (January 16, 1904), p. 21; *DGE* (August 22, 1908); *DGE* (November 12, 1910); *PT* 17 (June 1919): 97; "A Branch of the New York Public Library to Be Opened Shortly in the Big Store," *Thought and Work* 1 (January 15, 1905); *DGE* (January 27, 1912); *DGE* (February 15, 1919); *DGE* (December 4, 1920), 73; and "The History of Growth of the Woodward and Lothrop Store," Folder 1, Manuscript 4, Woodward and Lothrop Archives, Washington, D.C. (1913), p. 2.

112.   *NYT* (December 30, 1912), p. 18; on the range of hotel facilities, see Kurt Heppe, "Attracting Hotel Patrons," *American Restaurant* (January 1921), pp. 19−23; *The Hotel Gazette* (*HG*) 40 (December 25, 1916): 11; *HG* 40 (March 18, 1916): 1; *HG* 8 (June 21, 1913): 28−29; *NYHR* 12 (February 3, 1917): 12.

113.   Interview of Anna Nelson by Lloyd Lewis, "Lloyd Lewis Interviews" (1948), MFA.

114.   Macy's, "À La Carte Menu" (c. 1914), presented as a document by Macy's to the U.S. Government, Bureau of Corporations, as part of the 1914 Resale Price Investigation (interview dated November 10, 1914), RG 122, file 7224-64-1, NA; and Wanamaker menu, "Afternoon Tea" (John Wanamaker, Phil., c. 1915), WA. On restaurants as liabilities but as necessary "services," see Ina Hamlin and Arthur Winakor, "Department Store Food Service," *Bulletin*, Illinois University Bureau of Business Research 46 (Urbana, Ill., 1933): 7. On Marshall Field's tearooms and restaurants, see employment training department, "Questions on the History of and Physical Facts about Marshall Field and Company" (1933), "Employment Development Box," MFA.

115.   *DGE* (November 12, 1904); *DGE* (December 16, 1911); *MRSW* 21 (December 1907): 23; *MRSW* 11 (January and February 1905): 1.

116.   *The Hotel Gazette* 40 (March 18, 1916): 1; Kurt Heppe, "Attracting Hotel Patrons with Your Cuisine"; *Bulletin of the Metropolitan Museum of Art* 12 (March 1917): 72.

117.   *TN* 4 (April 1911): 3; Wanamaker and Co., *The Guide Book and Information Concerning the Wanamaker Mail Order Service* (New York 1910), pp. 17−18.

118.   *The Advertising World* 24 (January 1914): 245; *DGE* (November 12, 1910); *MRSW* (March 19, 1913); *PT* 17 (June 1919): 97; *PT* 18 (May 1920): 85; *PRL* Second Issue (October 1924): 8.

119.   JW, "Sonata Recital," Wanamaker Program (April 15, 1914), WA; *DGE* (April 11, 1903); *Outlook* 64 (January 13, 1900): 94−95; "30th Anniversary of a New Kind of Store" (March 1906), Wanamaker Scrapbook, p. 19, WA.

120.   Leach, "Transformations in the Culture of Consumption," *Journal of American History* 71 (September 1984): 329−30.

121.   Michael Gold, *Jews Without Money* (New York, 1930), p. 247.

122.   Richard Lingeman, *Theodore Dreiser: An American Journey, 1908–1945* (New York, 1990), p. 30.

123.   Henry Morgenthau, *All in a Life-Time* (New York, 1922), p. 1.

124.   On the numbers and the diversity, see Frederick C. Leubke, *Germans in the New World: Essays in the History of Immigration* (Urbana, Ill., 1990), pp. 14–15, 163–69; and Kathleen Neils Conzen, "Ethnicity as Festive Culture: Nineteenth-Century German America on Parade," in *The Invention of Ethnicity*, ed. Werner Sollars (New York, 1989), p. 48.

125.   Quoted in Conzen, "Ethnicity as Festive Culture," pp. 51–52. The argument made here regarding *gemütlichkeit* and German festival culture is based partly on this essay.

126.   Conzen, "Ethnicity as Festive Culture," pp. 56–60.

127.   Joseph Wandel, *The German Dimension of American History* (Chicago, 1979), pp. 114–21, 126–29; Cyril Ehrlich, *The Piano: A History* (London, 1976); and Loren Baritz, *The Good Life* (New York, 1989), pp. 9–14.

128.   The industry was so German that the proceedings of the new national society—the U.S. Brewers' Association (1862)—were conducted in German for many years. By the 1890s, the biggest companies were all owned by German Americans. On German dominance in the beer industry, see Thomas C. Cochran, *The Pabst Brewing Company* (New York, 1948), pp. 72–74; and on rise and organization, see Stanley Baron, *Brewed in America: A History of Beer and Ale in the United States* (Boston, 1962), pp. 175–80, 214–16. On "German" cities generally, see Baron; on Milwaukee, see Cochran; and on Cincinnati, see William L. Downward, *The Cincinnati Brewing Industry* (Cincinnati, 1973), pp. 65–71.

129.   Baron, *Brewed in America*, pp. 180–81; Cochran, *The Pabst Brewing Company*, pp. 37–41; on eating out as families, see Downward, *The Cincinnati Brewing Industry*, p. 68.

130.   Al Smith, *Up to Now: An Autobiography* (New York, 1929), pp. 6–7.

131.   In her essay "Ethnicity as Festive Culture," Kathleen Conzen seems to argue that the historical trajectories of American commercial culture and German festival culture were developing, largely, on different tracks (see pp. 73–74). There is another (and quite obvious) argument to make, however, especially given the number of Germans in merchandising: The two traditions were interactive, but to the detriment of the German festival tradition.

132.   On this process of commodification as intrinsic to capitalism, see Robert Heilbroner, *The Nature and Logic of Capitalism* (New York, 1985), pp. 60–61.

133.   For a general biography of many of the leading American merchants, see Robert Hendrickson, *The Grand Emporiums: The Illustrated History of America's Great Department Stores* (New York, 1979); and Leon Harris, *Merchant Princes: An Intimate History of Jewish Families Who Built Great Department Stores* (New York, 1979).

134. "Annual Volksfest" (March 22, 1907), in Wanamaker scrapbook, "The Thirty-First Anniversary of the New Kind of Store," pp. 47–50; "The Fourth Annual Volksfest," *Anniversary Herald* (March 12, 1906), p. 4, WA.

135. Emily Frankenstein Diary (June 9, 1918, and December 24, 1918), The Chicago Historical Society, Chicago.

136. *NYHR* 8 (July 5, 1913): 10; *NYHR* 8 (June 7, 1913): 15; Jarman, *A Bed for the Night*, pp. 127–28.

137. *DGE* (June 20, 1914), p. 273.

138. Linda L. Tyler, " 'Commerce and Poetry Hand in Hand': Music in American Department Stores, 1880–1930," *Journal of the American Musicological Society* 45 (1992): 75–120.

139. *DGE* (November 17, 1900), p. 15; *DGE* (March 16, 1895), p. 32; *DGE* (July 16, 1898), p. 79; *DGE* (August 22, 1896), p. 16; *DGE* (March 27, 1897), pp. 39–41; *DGE* (April 21, 1906), p. 87; Strawbridge and Clothier, *Store Chat* (store magazine) 1 (April 1907): 1; John Winkler, *Five and Ten: The Fabulous Life of F. W. Woolworth* (New York, 1940), p. 128.

140. Lee Simonson, "The Painter and the Stage," *Theatre Arts Magazine* 1 (December 1917): 5–16.

141. *MRSW* 59 (August 1926): 29; *MRSW* (March 1, 1922): 28–29; Joseph Cummings Chase, *Face Value: Autobiography of the Portrait Painter* (New York, 1962), p. 57; and Joseph Cummings Chase, *An Artist Talks About Color* (London, 1933), pp. 12–13.

142. Otto Teegan, "Joseph Urban's Philosophy of Color," *Architecture* 69 (May 1934): 258.

143. On Urban's significant role in forming the modern commercial aesthetic, see Robert A. Stern, Gregory Gilmartin, and Thomas Mellins, ed., *New York 1930: Architecture and Urbanism Between the Two World Wars* (New York, 1987), esp. pp. 235–40 but throughout the volume; and William Leach, "Strategists of Display and the Production of Desire," in *Consuming Visions: Accumulation and Display of Goods in America, 1880–1920*, ed. Simon Bronner (New York, 1989), pp. 99–132.

144. Teegan, "Joseph Urban's Philosophy of Color" 69: 257–71.

145. Ralph Walker, *Architecture* 69 (May 1934): 271; Joseph Urban, "The Stage," *Theatre Arts Magazine* (1919), quoted in *Theatre Arts Anthology*, ed. Rosamund Gilde (New York, 1950), pp. 399–400.

146. Gregory Gilmartin, "Joseph Urban," in *Inventing Times Square*, ed. William R. Taylor (New York, 1991), p. 276.

147. Deems Taylor, "The Scenic Art of Joseph Urban," *Boston Advertiser* (May 23, 1920), pp. 286–90; *The Architectural Review* (July 1921), p. 31, clippings scrapbook, Urban portfolio, part 1, p. 38, Joseph Urban Papers, Butler Library, Columbia University.

148.   Taylor, "The Scenic Art of Joseph Urban," p. 35.

149.   *MRSW* (September and November 1915); *DGE* (March 31, 1917); *MRSW* (November 1911).

150.   *NYHR* 35 (February 3, 1917): 34; *NYHR* 11 (December 30, 1916): 40.

151.   *NYHR* 35 (February 3, 1917): 34.

152.   Maurin, *Catholic Radicalism*, p. 8.

153.   Quoted in Robert R. Locke, *The End of the Practical Man: Entrepreneurship and Higher Education in Germany, France, and Great Britain, 1880–1940* (London, 1984), p. 111.

154.   Wesley Clair Mitchell, "The Backward Art of Spending Money," *American Economic Review* 2 (June 1912): 269–81, repub. in Wesley Clair Mitchell, *The Backward Art of Spending Money* (New York, 1950), p. 4.

155.   Mitchell, *The Backward Art*, p. 4.

156.   Mitchell, *The Backward Art*, p. 19.

157.   Artemas Ward, "Stray Shots," *Fame* 1 (December 1892): 323; Lewis Hyde, *The Gift: Imagination and the Erotic Life of Property* (New York, 1983), pp. 67–68.

158.   Joseph Harountunian, *Lust for Power* (New York, 1949), pp. 55–60.

159.   Ibid., pp. 59–60.

160.   Edmund Wilson, "An Appeal to Progressives," orig. pub. in 1930 and repub. in Edmund Wilson, *The Shores of Light* (New York, 1961), p. 522; and Wilson, quoted in Richard Pells, *Radical Visions and American Dreams* (Middletown, Conn., 1984), p. 281.

Chapter 6

1.   *NYT* (September 5, 1989), p. D4.

2.   On early business education see L. C. Marshall, "The American Collegiate School of Business," in *The Collegiate School of Business: Its Status at the Close of the First Quarter of the Twentieth Century*, ed. L. C. Marshall (Chicago, 1928), pp. 4–44; Stephen A. Sass, *The Pragmatic Imagination: A History of the Wharton School, 1881–1981* (Philadelphia, 1982), pp. 19–20; Melvin Copeland, *And Mark an Era: The Story of the Harvard Business School* (Cambridge, Mass., 1958), p. 210; Edward Hurley, *Awakening of Business* (New York, 1917), pp. 4–5.

3.   Sass, *The Pragmatic Imagination*, p. 140.

4.   On the absence of industrial art schools in America, see Jacob Schoenhof, "The Example of French Industrial Art Schools," *The Forum* 33 (May 1902): 257–303; *DGE* (November 6, 1897); and Marshall, "The American Collegiate School," pp. 4–44. On American art education in the nineteenth century, see Diana Korzenik, *Drawn to Art* (Hanover, 1985) and "Why Government Cared," *Art Edu-*

cation Here (Massachusetts College of Art, 1987), pp.59–74. On the design movement here and abroad, see Adrian Rorty, *Objects of Desire* (New York, 1986); Russell Lynes, *The Tastemakers* (New York, 1954); Doreen Burke et al., eds., *In Pursuit of Beauty, Americans and the Aesthetic Movement*, the Metropolitan Museum of Art (New York, 1986).

5.   Diana Korzenik, "Why Government Cared," in *Art Education Here* (Boston, 1987), published by the Massachusetts College of Art, pp.61–73.

6.   "Proceedings of the Joint Convention of the Western Art Teachers' Association and the Eastern Manual Training Association" (New York and Brooklyn, June 1 and 2, 1906).

7.   "Reports of the Art School, 1916–21"; "Reports of the Art School, 1901–06," vol. 3, pp. 7–8; and "Reports of the Art School, 1911–16," vol. 5, p. 10, Pratt Institute Archives, Brooklyn, New York.

8.   Frank Parsons, *The Art Appeal in Display Advertising* (New York, 1921), pp. 6–13, 52–65; Parsons, "Art in Advertising," *Playthings* 13 (April 1915): 3, 92. There is no adequate history of the New York School of Fine and Applied Art (the Parsons School of Design), but see Marjorie F. Jones, "A History of the Parsons School of Design, 1896–1966," Ph.D. diss., School of Education, New York University (1968), pp. 6–61, 83–90.

9.   Parsons, *The Art Appeal in Display Advertising*, pp. 6–65.

10.   Carl Liebowitz, "An Historical Study of the School of Retailing, NYU, 1919–1963," Ph.D. diss. (School of Education, New York University, 1966), pp. 12–29. On the growth of business education, see Frank Presbrey, *The History and Development of Advertising* (New York, 1929), especially chapter 62; James A. Bowie, *Education for Business Management* (London, 1930), pp. 98–99; Paul Nystrom, *Economics of Consumption* (New York, 1929), pp. 21–50; and Joseph Dorfman, *The Economic Mind in American Civilization*, vol. 3, 1865–1918 (New York, 1949), pp. 238–9.

11.   On the Strand roof garden, see "Strand Roof Garden," *The Hotel Gazette* (October 16, 1915); on the McAlpin, see *NYT* (June 7, 1912), p. 1 and *NYT* (December 30, 1912), p. 18. See also Jane S. Smith, *Elsie de Wolfe* (New York, 1982), pp. 125–33; Ron Chernow, *The House of Morgan* (New York, 1990), pp. 140–1; and Charles Schwartz, *Cole Porter, A Biography* (New York, 1979), p. 42, 52.

12.   Anne Morgan to Elmer Brown (December 15, 1915), Elmer Brown Papers, Box 21, Folder 1, "Department Store Education Association, 1915–18," NYUA.

13.   Nathan Straus to Elmer Brown (May 26, 1924), Box 67, Folder 15, Brown Papers, NYUA; Margaret Case Harriman, *And the Price Is Right* (New York, 1958), pp. 53–87.

14.   Ralph Hower, *History of Macy's of New York, 1858–1919* (Cambridge, Mass., 1943, repr. 1967), pp. 312–334, 366–372.

15.   "Training School for Teachers of Retail Selling of NYU" (February 18, 1919), Brown Papers, NYUA.

16.   "Commerce School and Retailing," NYT (June 15, 1929), Box 18, Folder 6, Brown Papers, NYUA.

17.   Sass, *The Pragmatic Imagination*, pp. 131–158.

18.   Sass, *The Pragmatic Imagination*, pp. 140–151; and Margaret Mead, *Blackberry Winter* (New York, 1975), pp. 33–35.

19.   Emily Fogg Mead, "The Place of Advertising in Modern Business," *Fame* 10 (April 1901): 160–65; Fogg Mead, obituary, NYT (February 23, 1950) p. 27; and Mead, *Blackberry Winter*, pp. 1–72.

20.   Quoted in Copeland, *And Mark an Era*, p. 7.

21.   Copeland, *And Mark an Era*, pp. 16–18.

22.   Quoted in Herbert Heaton, *A Scholar in Action, Edwin P. Gay* (Cambridge, Mass., 1952), pp. 18, 39–40, 62–70, 80, 98–99.

23.   Copeland, *And Mark an Era*, pp. 205, 431. On the Cherington book on advertising, see Quentin J. Schultze, " 'An Honorable Place': The Quest for Professional Advertising Education, 1900–1907," *Business History Review* 56 (Spring 1982): 27.

24.   Harvard Business School, "Object and History of the Bureau in Brief, with Some Preliminary Figures on the Retailing of Shoes," *Bulletin of the Bureau of Business Research*, Harvard University, 1 (May 1913): 4.

25.   Archie Shaw, "Some Problems in Market Distribution," *Quarterly Journal of Economics* (August 1912): 703–65.

26.   Shaw, "Some Problems," 2.

27.   Quoted in Heaton, *A Scholar in Action*, 55; Harvard Business School "Object and History of the Bureau," p. 3; Copeland, *And Mark an Era*, p. 209; and Shelby D. Hunt and Jerry Goolsby, "The Rise and Fall of the Functional Approach to Marketing: A Paradigm Displacement Perspective," in *Historical Perspectives in Marketing, Essays in Honor of Stanley C. Hollander*, ed. Terrence Nevett and Ronald A. Fullerton (Toronto, 1988), pp. 36–51.

28.   Copeland, *And Mark an Era*, p. 220.

29.   Copeland, *And Mark An Era*, pp. 214–16.

30.   Frank Crawford, *Morris D'Camp Crawford and His Wife, Charlotte Holmes Crawford: Their Lives, Ancestors, and Descendants* (privately printed by Frank Crawford, Ithaca, N.Y. 1939), pp xi–xii, 52–83, 137–47; on the new 1907 store, see "St. Louis' New Store," DGE (November 23, 1907), p. 13; on Hanford's reflections, see Hanford Crawford, "Ethics of a Big Store," *The Independent*, August 12, 1909, p. 359.

31.   Henry Fairchild Osborn to Clark Wissler, October 21, 1915, Box 10, 1913–1916, Central Archives, AMNH; Morris D'Camp Crawford, *The Ways of Fashion* (New York, 1941), pp. 269–74; author's phone interview with Morris D'Camp Crawford III (December 19, 1989).

32.   Clark Wissler to Mr. Sherwood, April 15, 1916, Box 10, 1913–1916, Central Archives, AMNH; and "Exhibitions of Designs," December 1917, Box 130, Central Archives, AMNH.

33.   Morris D'Camp Crawford, "Address delivered before the National Silk Manufacturers' Convention," November 23, 1916, p. 8., Box 10, Central Archives, AMNH.

34.   Ibid, p. 7.

35.   Henry Fairfield Osborn to Mrs. John F. Hylan, November 14, 1910, Box 130, Central Archives, AMNH.

36.   Henry Fairfield Osborn, excerpt from letter, November 1919, Box 130, Central Archives, AMNH.

37.   Director Frederick A. Lucas to Herbert Spinden (and Morris D'Camp Crawford), November 13, 1919, Box 130, Central Archives, AMNH.

38.   Women's Wear Daily, August 4, 1919, Folder A/8, textiles collection, SCP, Brooklyn Museum, Brooklyn, New York.

39.   Morris D'Camp Crawford, "Address delivered before the National Silk Manufacturers' Convention," p. 10; and Crawford to Dr. Fred A. Lucas, August 9, 1916, Box 10, Central Archives, AMNH.

40.   William Leach, "Strategies of Display and the Production of Desire," in Consuming Visions, ed. Simon Bronner (New York, 1989); Ira Jackins, "Biographical Sketch of Stewart Culin," transcript, SCP, Brooklyn Museum; Crawford, The Ways of Fashion, p. 272.

41.   Frank Kingdon, John Cotton Dana: A Life (Newark, N.J., 1940), p. 12.

42.   Oral interview with Holger Cahill, 1966, Columbia Oral History Project, Butler Library, Columbia University, pp. 159–60, 167, 175–76; and Kingdon, John Cotton Dana, p. 38.

43.   Kingdon, John Cotton Dana, pp. 12–97; Charles Hadley, John Cotton Dana: A Sketch (Chicago, 1943), pp. 9–63.

44.   SC to Booth of A & S (January 27, 1928), SCP; TN (January 1927): 349.

45.   John Cotton Dana, The Gloom of the Museum (Woodstock, Vt., 1917), pp. 5–6, 14–23; Dana, "A Plan for New Museum, the Kind of Museum It Will Profit a City to Maintain" (Woodstock, Vt., 1920), Rare Book Room, NYPL.

46.   Quoted in Hadley, John Cotton Dana, pp. 56–57.

47.   Dana, The Gloom of the Museum, pp. 6–8.

48.   Oral interview with Holger Cahill, pp. 108, 166–68; oral interview with Dorothy Canning Miller (Dana coworker) (June 24, 1957), p. 595, CUOHP; The American Magazine of Art 9 (March 1918): 202–3. In the belief that machine-made goods were artistically sound, Dana even enjoyed duping museumgoers with his displays. Without telling anyone, he once exhibited cheap pottery in display cases and against satin draperies purchased from Bamberger's department store in

Newark. According to Dana, everybody thought the pottery was ancient and hand-crafted. This was enough proof for Dana; it reinforced his mission to improve "popular taste" through the medium of affordable machine-made goods. Hadley, *John Cotton Dana*, pp. 66–68.

49.   SC, *PT*, vol. 18 (May 1920) (5), pp. 105–6; SC, "The Magic of Color," *The Brooklyn Quarterly* (April 1925), SCP; Culin, "Precious Color," unpublished speech, SCP; SC, "The Magic of Color," *MRSW* 56 (March 1925): 9.

50.   Quoted in *The Brooklyn Citizen* (March 6, 1923), p. 2; SC to Franz Boas (January 28, 1919), SCP; *WWD* (January 3, 1919), Culin Scrapbook, textiles, SCP; *WWD* (October 8, 1919); Culin Scrapbook; and Charles R. Richards, *Art in Industry* (New York, 1922), pp. 5–45, 253–57.

51.   SC to Mr. Brown (March 19, 1919), Textile Collection, SCP; SC to Lockwood de Forest (January 12, 1919), Textile Collection, SCP.

52.   Unsigned, "Manufacturers, Designers, and Museums," *Bulletin of the Metropolitan Museum of Art* 13 (January 1918): 26.

53.   Richard Bach, "Mobilizing the Art Industries," *American Magazine of Art* 9 (August 1918): 412–18; Jay Cantor, "Art and Industry: Reflections on the Role of the American Museum in Encouraging Innovation in the Decorative Arts," in *Technological Innovation and the Decorative Arts*, ed. Ian M. G. Quinby and Polly Ann Earl, 1973 Winterthur Conference Report, pp. 332–54; Neil Harris, "Museums, Merchandising and Popular Taste: The Struggle For Influence," in *Material Culture and the Study of American Life*, ed. Ian M. G. Quinby (New York, 1978), pp. 140–74.

54.   Richard Bach, "Fifth Exhibition of Industrial Art," *The Bulletin of the Metropolitan Museum of Art* 15 (December 1920): 264.

55.   Crawford, *The Ways of Fashion*, p. 273; *DGE* (April 24, 1915), p. 21.

56.   Louis Weinberg, *Color in Everyday Life: A Manual for Lay Students, Artisans, and Artists* (New York, 1918), pp. xi–xii; *Bulletin of the Metropolitan Museum of Art* (hereafter *Bull.*) 11 (May 1916): 111; *Bull.* 12 (March 3, 1917): 72; *Bull.* 12 (April 1917): 98; *Bull.* 12 (October 1917): 87; *Bull.* 14 (February 1919): 41; *DGE* (February 21, 1920), pp. 275–76; *MRSW* 41 (May 1920): 42; interview with A. S. Donaldson, a Macy's executive and founder of Macy's "Executive Training Course," Harvard interview (1934), Box 1, p. 91, MA; and Cantor, "Art and Industry."

57.   Weinberg, *Color in Everyday Life*, pp. 16, 145–56.

58.   Richard Bach, "The Museum as a Laboratory," *Bull.* 14 (January 1919): 2–3; "Fifth Exhibition of Industrial Art," *Bull.* 15 (December 1920): 204; Bach, "Mobilizing the Art Industries," pp. 412–13; Bach, "Museums and Industrial Arts," *Industrial Arts Monographs*, no. 1, (Metropolitan Museum of Art, 1926), pp. 1–8; and Bach, "Museum Service to the Art Industries," *Museum Work* 4 (1921): 55.

59.   *Perfumery Art: A Monthly Trade Paper Devoted to the Industries of Essential*

Oils, Perfumery, and Perfumed Toilet Articles 3 (August 1920): 10; and Bach, "The Museum as a Laboratory": 2–3.

60.   Oral interview with David Yates (1946), "Lloyd Lewis Interviews," MFA; and JW to Mrs. Doty (November 21, 1921) in "November 10, 1916 to November 28, 1921," p. 341, WA. On "Bath House" John Coughlin, see Carter H. Harrison, *Stormy Years: The Autobiography of Carter H. Harrison* (New York, 1935), pp. 227–30; and Lloyd Wendt and Herman Kogan, *Bosses in Lusty Chicago: The Story of Bathhouse John and Hinky Dink* (Bloomington, Ind., 1967).

61.   "The first century of Abraham & Straus, February 14, 1865 to February 14, 1965," p. 12, Abraham & Straus Collection, "The Centennial Celebration, 1865–1965," Records, 1965, Brooklyn Historical Society, Brooklyn, N.Y.; on rerouting, see *Minutes of the Board of Estimate and Apportionment of the City of New York, Financial and Franchise Matters* (hereafter *Minutes*) (January 1–February 29, 1910): 118–19; *Minutes* (January 12, 1906): 259; *Minutes* 124 (June 22, 1911): 2656, 2670; *Minutes* 125 (July 27, 1911): 2824; *Minutes* 149 (January 1913): 385, 1049, 1347; *Minutes* 175 (July 27, 1910): 4771; *Merchants' Association Review* (San Francisco, April 1903): 27.

62.   *Minutes* 123 (June 8, 1911): 2261–63; *Minutes* 124 (June 22, 1911): 2656, 2670.

63.   Herbert Parson to Macy's (June 4, 1901) and PS to Alderman Parsons (June 7, 1901), Record Group 10, Harvard History Project, pp. 836–37, MA; *DGE* (October 12, 1918), p. 4; *DGE* (December 11, 1909), p. 13; *Nammson News* (June 1920), pp. 4–6, store paper, Namm's Department Store, Brooklyn Historical Society Archives.

64.   *Annual Report of the Fifth Avenue Association, 1912–13* (New York, 1913), pp. 5–8; *Annual Report for the Year 1914* (New York, 1915), pp. 5–6, 17–18; *Annual Report* (1917), pp. 14–15; *Minutes* 175 (July 27, 1916): 4772.

65.   *Annual Report of the Commissioner of Parks* (Borough of Manhattan, New York, 1912), pp. 46–48. I would like to thank Elizabeth Blackmar for directing me to this source.

66.   *Annual Report of the Commissioner of Parks*, pp. 49–52.

67.   Caroline Loughlin and Catherine Anderson, *Forest Park* (St. Louis, 1986), pp. 116–19; *DGE* (June 16, 1917), p. 69.

68.   *DGE* (August 25, 1917), p. 77; *DGE* (March 3, 1917), p. 15; *DGE* (January 13, 1917), p. 81; *DGE* (January 26, 1918), p. 60; *DGE* (August 25, 1917), p. 95; *DGE* (July 20, 1918), p. 31; *DGE* (August 16, 1919), p. 31.

69.   *DGE* (June 16, 1917), p. 69.

70.   Lloyd Short, *The Development of National Administrative Organization in the United States* (Baltimore, 1923), p. 26. "A fundamental change has taken place," wrote Short, "in the attitude of the American people toward their government, since the adoption of the Constitution. There has been a great increase in administration in recent years, while prior to the 20th century, the administrative organization and activities of the government were scarcely mentioned."

71.   Donald R. Whitlah, "Department of Commerce," in *Government Agencies: The Greenwood Encyclopedia of American Institutions*, ed. Donald R. Whitlah (Westport, Conn., 1983), pp. 91–97; Henry Barrett Learned, *The President's Cabinet* (New York, 1912), pp. 355–67; Short, *The Development of National Administrative Organization in the United States*, pp. 397–407; and Robert Higgs, *Crisis and Leviathan: Critical Episodes in the Growth of American Government* (New York, 1987), pp. 105–16.

72.   For this new shift in state policy, see Louis Galambos and Joseph Pratt, *The Rise of the Corporate Commonwealth: U.S. Business Policy in the Twentieth Century* (New York, 1988), pp. 39–40; Stephen Skowronek, *Building a New American State: The Expansion of National Administrative Capacities, 1877–1920* (Cambridge, Eng., 1982), pp. 1–30; and Mary O. Furner and Barry Supple, *The State and Economic Knowledge: The American and British Experiences* (Cambridge, Eng., 1990), pp. 3–39. For a discussion of the renewed interest in the state as a crucial factor in historical change, see Theda Skocpol, "Bringing the State Back in: Strategies of Analysis in Current Research," in *Bringing the State Back in*, ed. Peter Evans et al. (Cambridge, Eng., 1985), pp. 1–26.

73.   Furner and Supple, *The State and Economic Knowledge*, p. 10.

74.   Mary Furner, "Knowing Capitalism: Public Investigation and the Labor Question in the Long Progressive Era," in Furner and Supple, *The State and Economic Knowledge*, pp. 241–86.

75.   Furner, "Knowing Capitalism," pp. 274–282; and Graham Adams, *Age of Industrial Violence, 1910–1915. Activities and Findings of the United States Commission on Industrial Relations* (New York, 1966), pp. 64–69, 168, 171.

76.   Quoted in Galambos and Pratt, *The Rise of the Corporate Commonwealth*, p. 677; and Vincent P. Carosso, *Investment Banking in America: A History* (Cambridge, Mass., 1970), pp. 138–53.

77.   David P. Thelen, "Patterns of Consumer Consciousness in the Progressive Movement: Robert M. LaFollette, the Antitrust Persuasion, and Labor Legislation," in *Quest for Social Justice*, ed. Ralph M. Aderman (Madison, Wis., 1983), pp. 19–43.

78.   Galambos and Pratt, *The Rise of the Corporate Commonwealth*, pp. 60–65. See also, on the Federal government's failure to develop a clear pattern of regulatory law for corporate business, Naomi Lamoreaux, *The Great Merger Movement* (Cambridge, Eng., 1985), pp. 159–186.

79.   Walter Lippmann, *The Good Society* (New York, 1937), p. 14.

80.   On the BFDC, see Whitlah, "Department of Commerce," pp. 90–97; on the BFDC, the Tariff Commission, and the Federal Reserve, see Emily Rosenberg, *Spreading the American Dream: American Economic and Cultural Expansion, 1890–1945* (New York, 1982), pp. 40–68, 140–45); and James Livingston, *Origins of the Federal Reserve System* (Ithaca, N.Y., 1986), pp. 129–88.

81.   See, on FTC recommendations on cost accounting and market assistance, *PT* 17 (January 1919): 211–12; and *PT* 13 (December 1915): 67. On the FTC's

overall positive approach to the advertising business, see Daniel Pope, *The Making of Modern Advertising* (New York, 1984), pp. 207–8.

82. Pope, *The Making of Modern Advertising*, pp. 94–110.

83. Quoted in Richard Tedlow, "Competitor or Consumer," in *Managing Big Business*, ed. Richard Tedlow (Cambridge, Mass., 1990), p. 288. Both Tedlow and Pope provide good discussions of these relationships.

84. National Consumers League, "Fourth Annual Report, Year Ending March 4, 1903"; and "Highlights in the History of National Consumers League, 1938," film 113, Papers of the National Consumers League, LC.

85. U.S. Department of Labor, Children's Bureau, *First Annual Report of the Chief of the Children's Bureau to the Secretary of Labor for the Fiscal Year Ending June 30, 1913* (Washington, D.C., 1913), pp. 5–15; *Third Annual Report* (1915), pp. 11–12; *Fifth Annual Report* (1917), pp. 22–24; *Ninth Annual Report* (1921), pp. 5–6; U.S. Department of Labor, "Fair Labor Standards for Children," Folder 6 (1939), Papers of the National Consumers League, LC.

86. *DGE* (October 12, 1910), p. 49.

87. U.S. Department of Labor, Children's Bureau, *First Annual Report*, pp. 5–15; *Third Annual Report*, pp. 11–12; *Fifth Annual Report*, pp. 22–24; *Ninth Annual Report*, pp. 5–6; *Thirteenth Annual Report* (1925), pp. 1–6; U.S. Department of Labor, "Fair Labor Standards for Children."

88. *DGE* (June 14, 1919), p. 167.

89. U.S. Department of Labor, Children's Bureau, *Baby Week Campaigns*, miscellaneous series no. 5 (Washington, D.C., 1917), pp. 23, 63–64; "Pittsburgh Baby and Child Welfare," Record Group 102 (1914–20), file 8-1-4-2-1, Papers of the Children's Bureau, NA.

90. *DGE* (November 1, 1913), p. 47; *DGE* (June 28, 1919), p. 35; John Wanamaker and Co., "The Baby: His Care and Needs" (Philadelphia, 1913), WA; Mary Rontahn, director of the Pittsburgh Baby and Welfare Week, to Anne Louise Strong of the Children's Bureau (June 7, 1915), file 8-1-4-2-1, "Exhibits," RG 102, Children's Bureau Records, NA; and "Child Welfare Exhibit Number," *The Dallas Survey: A Journal of Social Work* 2 (May 1, 1918): 12, file 8-1-4-1, "Exhibits," Children's Bureau Papers, NA.

91. Gerald Cullinan, *The United States Postal Service* (New York, 1973), p. 187; Wayne E. Fuller, *RFD: The Changing Face of Rural America* (Bloomington, Ind., 1964), p. 203.

92. Herbert Adams Gibbons, *John Wanamaker*, vol. 1 (New York, 1926), pp. 303–5; Cullinan, *The United States Postal Service*, p. 108.

93. Cullinan, *The United States Postal Service*, pp. 108–9; Fuller, *RFD*, p. 24.

94. Quoted in "Chicago Rejects Parcels Post," *MRSW* 22 (January 1908): 29.

95. Jesse Straus to Frederick Ingram (May 24, 1910); George Twitmayer to Straus (October 1, 1906), Harvard History Project, RG 10, pp. 2618–19, 2635, MA. See

also Boris Emmet and John E. Jeuck, *Catalogues and Counters: A History of Sears, Roebuck and Co.* (Chicago, 1950), p. 22; and Fuller, *RFD*, pp. 211–17.

96.   Fuller, *RFD*, pp. 219–22; Clyde Kelly, *United States Postal Policy* (New York, 1931), p. 111.

97.   Quoted in Gibbons, *John Wanamaker*, vol. 1, pp. 282–83; Kelly, *United States Postal Policy*, p. 111; Fuller, *RFD*, pp. 219–20.

98.   "Wanamaker 'Firsts,' " p. 16, WA.

99.   Kelly, *United States Postal Policy*, pp. 182–87; Fuller, *RFD*, p. 230.

100.   Fuller, *RFD*, pp. 197–98; Emmet and Jeuck, *Catalogues and Counters*, pp. 898–90.

101.   Caroline F. Ware, *Greenwich Village, 1920–1930* (New York, 1977), pp. 4–7.

102.   Elizabeth Gurley Flynn, *The Rebel Girl* (New York, 1955), pp. 152–55; and Matthew Josephson, *The History of the Hotel and Restaurant Employees and Bartenders International Union, AFL-CIO* (New York, 1955), pp. 94–97.

103.   On the Paterson silk industry and conditions leading up to the strike, see Howard Levin, "The Paterson Silkworkers' Strike of 1913," *King's Crown Essays* IX (Winter 1961): 44–64; Melvyn Dubovsky, *We Shall Be All: A History of the Industrial Workers of the World* (Chicago, 1969), pp. 264–90; Joyce L. Kornbluh, ed., with introductions, *Rebel Voices: An IWW Anthology* (Ann Arbor, Mich., 1964), pp. 196–201; James D. Osborne, "Paterson: Immigrant Strikers and the War of 1913," in Joseph R. Conlin, ed., *At the Point of Production: The Local History of the IWW* (Westport, Conn., 1981), pp. 61–89); and Steve Golin, "The Unity and Strategy of the Paterson Silk Manufacturers During the 1913 Strike," in Philip B. Scranton, ed., *Silk City: Studies on the Paterson Silk Industry, 1860–1940* (Newark, N.J., 1985), pp. 73–97.

104.   Ewald Koettgen, letter to fellow workers in Industrial Workers of the World, "Stenographic Report of the Eighth Annual Convention of the Industrial Workers of the World, Chicago, Illinois, 9/15-9/29/1913" (Cleveland, 1913), pp. 38–39, Tamiment Institute Library, New York University.

105.   For accounts of this meeting and exchange and events leading up to them, see Adams, *Age of Industrial Violence*, pp. 77–100; Richard O'Connor and Dale L. Walker, *The Lost Revolutionary: A Biography of John Reed* (New York, 1967), pp. 74–75; Dubovsky, *We Shall Be All*, pp. 272–73; and Mabel Dodge Luhan, *Movers and Shakers* (Albuquerque, New Mexico, 1936, 1985), pp. 186–89.

106.   Robert Edmond Jones, *The Dramatic Imagination: Reflections and Speculations on the Art of the Theater* (New York, 1941), p. 24.

107.   Golin, "The Unity and Strategy of the Paterson Silk Manufacturers," pp. 88–89.

108.   Kornbluh, ed., *Rebel Voices*, p. 201; Dodge Luhan, *Movers and Shakers*, p. 203; and, for a recent discussion of the pageant, see Martin Green, *New York*

1913: The Armory Show and the Paterson Strike Pageant (New York, 1988), pp. 98–202.

109.   O'Connor and Walker, *The Lost Revolutionary*, p. 84.

110.   Mabel Dodge and Hutchins Hapgood, quoted in Kornbluh, ed., *Rebel Voices*, p. 202.

111.   Elizabeth Gurley Flynn, "The Truth About the Paterson Strike" (January 31, 1914), republished in Kornbluh, *Rebel Voices*, p. 221.

112.   Ibid.

113.   Ibid.; and quoted in Green, *New York 1913*, pp. 201–12.

114.   William Haywood, quoted in Kornbluh, ed., p. 197; on the ideological roots of the IWW in Edward Bellamy, see Dubovsky, *We Shall Be All*, p. 156.

115.   Elizabeth Gurley Flynn, *The Rebel Girl: An Autobiography, My First Life (1906–1926)* (New York, 1955), p. 48.

116.   Flynn, "The Truth About the Paterson Strike," pp. 215–16.

117.   Cochran, *Two Hundred Years of American Business*, p. 63.

Chapter 7

1.   JW to Rev. T. Harry Sprague (September 9, 1901), Wanamaker Letterbook, "August 20, 1901 to February 20, 1908," p. 109, WA.

2.   Walter Rauschenbusch, *Christianity and the Social Crisis* (New York, 1964; orig. pub. 1907), p. 338.

3.   Quoted in Patrick W. Gearty, *The Economic Thought of Monsignor John M. Ryan* (Washington, D.C., 1953), pp. 146–47, 166; and Ryan, "Ethics of Speculation," *The International Journal of Ethics* 12 (April 1902): 346. On Ryan's attack on the "diversified satisfaction of the senses," see "Charity and Charities," *The Catholic Encyclopedia*, vol. 15 (New York, 1912), p. 603. On the relative weakness of the Catholic social gospel as compared with the Protestant, see Mel Piehl, *Breaking Bread: The Catholic Worker and the Origins of Catholic Radicalism in America* (Philadelphia, 1982), pp. 38–39. On Ryan's importance, see Piehl, pp. 36–37; Gearty, p. 39; and Francis L. Broderick, *Right Reverend New Dealer* (New York, 1963), pp. 105–7.

4.   John Ryan, "The Cost of Christian Living," *The Catholic World* (December 1908): 576–88, and quoted in Broderick, *Right Reverend New Dealer*, p. 55; Ryan, "The Economic Philosophy of St. Thomas," in Robert E. Brenen, ed., *Essays in Thomism* (Freeport, N.Y., 1942, 1972), p. 248. See also Ryan, "The Fallacy of Bettering One's Position," *The Catholic World* (November 1907): 145–56; and "False and True Welfare," in *The Church and Socialism, and Other Essays* (Washington, 1919), pp. 197–202, 213–216.

5.   Felix Adler, *The Ethical Philosophy of Life Presented in Its Main Outlines* (New York, 1918), pp. 185, 192, 203, 275. On Unitarianism, see Daniel Howe,

The Unitarian Conscience (Cambridge, Mass., 1970), pp. 60–61; on "personality" as a spiritual concept, see Casey Nelson Blake, *Beloved Community* (Chapel Hill, 1990), pp. 6–7, 49–60.

6.   Arthur Goren, *New York Jews and the Quest for Community: The Kehillah Experiment, 1908–1922* (New York, 1970), pp. 74–85; Mordecai Kaplan, *Judaism as a Civilization* (New York, 1934), pp. 28–29. Goren's study provides a wonderful glimpse into a remarkable experiment.

7.   Goren, *New York Jews*, p. 79.

8.   Ibid., pp. 76–85. It is interesting that in the same year the Kehillah experiment was launched, the Protestant Federal Council of Churches attempted, also without success, to achieve greater all-Protestant unity by organizing a commission on the evangelism (or on the orthodox wing of Protestantism) to "counterbalance" its liberalism and "well-known social activism." George Marsden, *Fundamentalism and American Culture* (New York, 1980), p. 91. For a very different view of the Jewish response to American market culture, see Andrew Heinze, *Adapting to Abundance: Jewish Immigrants, Mass Consumption, and the Search for American Identity* (New York, 1990). Heinze argues that Jews adapted rather readily to the new culture with little conflict and tension. The experience, he says, was a positive and "liberating" one, as Jews became "Americanized," and as virtually all Jewish holidays were re-packaged to suit the needs of the consumption and "shopping."

9.   David Haldeman, quoted in George Marsden, *Fundamentalism and American Culture*, p. 84; on the Amana community, see Herbert Wallace Schneider, *Religion in Twentieth-Century America* (Cambridge, Mass., 1967, orig. pub. 1952), p. 4.

10.   For a discussion of the Calvinist world-view, see Ann Douglas, *The Feminization of American Culture* (New York, 1977).

11.   For a good recent history of these institutions, see Ann M. Boylan, *Sunday School: Formation of an American Institution, 1790–1880* (New Haven, Conn., 1988); and Sydney E. Ahlstrom, *A Religious History of the American People* (New Haven, Conn., 1972).

12.   Quoted in Gibbons, *John Wanamaker* (New York, 1926), vol. 1, p. 43.

13.   Gibbons, *John Wanamaker*, vol. 1, pp. 54–56.

14.   Ibid., p. 245.

15.   On Moody, see James F. Findlay, Jr., *Dwight L. Moody, American Evangelist, 1837–1899* (Chicago, 1965), pp. 32–58.

16.   Quoted in Findlay, *Dwight L. Moody*, p. 88.

17.   Findlay, *Dwight L. Moody*, p. 86.

18.   For a discussion of Moody's views, see Marsden, *Fundamentalism and American Culture*, pp. 32–39.

19.   Quoted in Findlay, *Dwight L. Moody*, p. 91.

20.   Findlay, *Dwight L. Moody*, pp. 132–33, 225–26; Aaron Abell, *The Urban Impact on American Protestantism* (London, 1962), p. 15.

21. Marsden, *Fundamentalism and American Culture*, pp. 73–75, 92; Findlay, *Dwight L. Moody*, p. 132; on the holiness movement, see also Ahlstrom, *A Religious History of the American People*, pp. 816–23.

22. Findlay, *Dwight L. Moody*, pp. 250–61. For slightly different views of Moody, see William McLoughlin, *Revivals, Awakenings, and Reform* (Chicago Press, 1978), pp. 141–45; and James Gilbert, *Perfect Utopias: Chicago's Utopias of 1893* (Chicago, 1991), pp. 169–207.

23. On Wanamaker's debate in 1860 over a ministerial career, see Gibbons, *John Wanamaker*, vol. 1, pp. 57–62.

24. Dwight Moody to JW (October 7, 1877 and November 5, 1877), WA.

25. Findlay, *Dwight L. Moody*, pp. 251–53.

26. William R. Hutchinson, *The Modernist Impulse in American Protestantism* (Cambridge, Mass., 1976), pp. 8–11.

27. JW, address book, under "E" and "Q" (1871), WA.

28. JW, notebook dated 1894 (May 13, 1894), p. 19, WA.

29. JW to George Bailey (June 26, 1913), in Wanamaker Letterbook, "April 5, 1913 to October 25, 1913," p. 413; JW journal (1901), black notebook, paper wrapper, dated 1901, WA.

30. Oriana Atkinson, *Manhattan and Me* (New York, 1954), pp. 63–65; Abell, *The Urban Impact on American Protestantism*, p. 156. On institutional churches generally, see Abell, pp. 135–65.

31. Schneider, *Religion in Twentieth-Century America*, pp. 10–11. See also on institutional churches Marsden, *Fundamentalism and American Culture*, pp. 82–83.

32. "The New Wanamaker Store," *Architects' and Builders' Magazine* 38 (June 1906): 365–72.

33. Gibbons, *John Wanamaker*, vol. 1, pp. 336–37; Marsden, *Fundamentalism*, pp. 83–85; and Abell, *The Urban Impact*, pp. 155–56.

34. JW to Harry T. Alumbaugh (June 21, 1913), in Wanamaker Letterbook, "April 5, 1913 to October 25, 1913," p. 382, WA.

35. "Book of the Romans," *The Holy Bible*, Revised Standard Version (New York, 1952), p. 147. For samples of the letters Wanamaker sent the wives of the "Brotherhood," see JW to Mrs. Reinert (September 24, 1904), "August 25, 1904 to January 13, 1905," p. 192; JW to Mrs. McCreery (September 23, 1904); and JW to Mrs. Allen (September 23, 1904), WA.

36. JW to Mrs. William Sunday (September 6, 1913, and March 5, 1914), "From October 24, 1913 to May 28, 1914," WA; and Marsden, *Fundamentalism and American Culture*, pp. 96–97.

37. Gibbons, *John Wanamaker*, vol. 2, pp. 322, 330, 347; and JW to J. C. Ensign

(September 24, 1886), Wanamaker Letterbook, "December 22, 1885 to December 2, 1886," WA.

38.   Gibbons, *John Wanamaker*, vol. 2, pp. 346, 354.

39.   David E. Shi, *The Simple Life, Plain Living, and High Thinking in American Culture* (New York, 1985), p. 176. This book traces the development and impact of simple-life ideas in America from the Colonial period to the present. It is a good and thoughtful book. Unfortunately, however, it fails to mention John Wanamaker, but Wanamaker's role in building the movement was crucial. Shi's discussion—especially in the best chapter, "Progressive Simplicity," and partly because of his failure to deal with Wanamaker—does little to show how this "movement" ended up or tended intrinsically to support the thing it resisted.

40.   John Muir, quoted in Shi, *The Simple Life*, p. 197; see also chap. 8, "Progressive Simplicity," pp. 174–214.

41.   Walter Edmond Roth, quoted in Michael Taussig, *Shamanism, Colonialism, and the Wild Man: A Study in Terror and Healing* (Chicago, 1987), p. 57, and published as "An Introductory Study in the Arts, Crafts, and Customs of the Guinean Indians," in *The Thirty-eighth Annual Report of the Bureau of American Ethnology: 1916–1917* (Washington, D.C., 1924), pp. 725–45. See also Shi, *The Simple Life*, pp. 208–14.

42.   Pastor Wagner, *The Simple Life* (New York, 1903), pp. ix–x, 111–12. On the book's rank as a bestseller, see Frank Luther Mott, *Golden Multitudes: The Story of Best Sellers in the United States* (New York, 1966), p. 324.

43.   Wagner, *The Simple Life*, p. 134.

44.   Quoted in Stickley, "M. Charles Wagner . . . ," *The Craftsman*, vol. VII, p. 131.

45.   Ibid, p. 138.

46.   Wagner, *The Simple Life*, p. 17.

47.   Editorial, *DGE* (December 3, 1904).

48.   George Wharton James, "Two Days with M. Wagner," *The Craftsman*, vol. VII, pp. 184–85.

49.   Gibbons, *John Wanamaker*, vol. 2, p. 149; and JW to Fred G. Finley (November 28, 1902), Wanamaker Letterbook, "November 22, 1902 to August 11, 1903," p. 30, WA.

50.   Editorial, *DGE* (December 3, 1904, and March 11, 1905).

51.   JW, Wanamaker notebook (1900), unpaginated, WA.

52.   JW to Charles Stock (January 16, 1903), Wanamaker Letterbook, "November 22, 1902 to August 11, 1903," pp. 386–87, WA.

53.   Gibbons, *John Wanamaker*, vol. 2, p. 143.

54. JW to Miss S. C. Glass, James C. Pond Lyceum Bureau (September 10, 1904), "August 25, 1904 to January 13, 1905," p. 113, WA.

55. JW to Pastor Miller (July 6, 1903), "November 22, 1902, to August 11, 1903," p. 804, WA.

56. Ibid., p. 13.

57. Charles Wagner, My Impressions of America (New York, 1906), p. 41.

58. Ibid., pp. 41–44, 51; for list of paintings in Wanamaker's home, see typescript record, "Among the Works of Art in the 'Lindenhurst' Collection and at the Store," WA.

59. Wagner, My Impressions, p. 12.

60. JW to John Brisbane Walker (September 27, 1904), "August 25, 1904 to January 13, 1905," p. 253; JW to Reverend John T. Beckley (October 4, 1904, p. 351); and JW to Professor F. H. Green (October 4, 1904), p. 345, WA.

61. Wagner, My Impressions, p. 84.

62. Wagner, My Impressions, p. 96.

63. JW to Ralph H. Graves (The New York Times), September 30, 1904, "August 25, 1904 to January 13, 1905," p. 271; and JW to F. W. Squire, editor (Booklover's Magazine), October 20, 1904, p. 502. On Wanamaker's presentation of Wagner to Roosevelt, see JW to Reverend Joseph Cochran, September 21, 1904, "August 25, 1904 to January 13, 1905," p. 182, WA. "On Monday next I am going with Reverend Charles Wagner to Washington to present him to the President."

64. JW to Mr. Griffiths, October 24, 1904, p. 540, WA.

65. See file card on Charles Wagner, arranged by Herbert Adams Gibbons, October 1, 1904, Gibbons file cabinet, WA.

66. Wagner, My Impressions, p. 85.

67. Wagner, My Impressions, pp. 87–89.

68. JW to Pastor Wagner, December 31, 1904, "August 25, 1904 to January 13, 1905," pp. 911–12; JW to Harry Peak, c/o John Wanamaker's in Paris, December 24, 1904, p. 885; JW to Robert McClure, November 26, 1904, "August 25, 1904 to January 13, 1905," p. 703; and JW to Reverend Fordyce Argo, December 2, 1904, p. 742, WA.

69. According to Wanamaker's own store history, Golden Book of the Wanamaker Stores, Wanamaker's was the "first store lighted by electricity" and, in November 1909, the "first store" to sell "flying machines" (Philadelphia, 1911), pp. 67, 125. On his "power plant" and other facilities and activities, see Golden Book, p. 281.

70. Gibbons, John Wanamaker, vol. 2, p. 369: "He alone created a French atmosphere."

71. DGE (April 6, 1901). On Wanamaker's opposition to "theatricals," see JW to Walter Crowder (March 24, 1900), Wanamaker Letterbook, vol. 24, p. 835. A

Sabbatarian, he also opposed in 1893 having the World's Columbian Exposition in Chicago open on Sunday. It would be a "disgrace," he wrote, to make Sunday a symbol of "recreation and pleasure." See JW to Fred Ingles (June 6, 1893), "May 17, 1893 to September 13, 1893," p. 209, WA.

72.   See Daniel T. Rodgers, *The Work Ethic in America, 1850–1920* (Chicago, 1978), pp. 125–52, and Brian Atterbury, *The Fantasy Tradition in American Literature: From Irving to Le Guin* (Bloomington, Ind., 1980), pp. 64–72. On the emergence of the Victorian fairy tale, see Humphrey Carpenter, *Secret Gardens: The Golden Age of Children's Literature* (Boston, 1985); Jack Zipes, ed. with introduction, *Victorian Fairy Tales: The Revolt of the Fairies and Elves* (New York, 1987); and Michael Patrick Hearn, ed. with introduction, *The Victorian Fairy Tale* (New York, 1988).

73.   JW (August 1, 1917, April 14, 1917, December 9, 1916, March 21, 1915, November 2, 1915, September 24, 1914, August 18, 1914, October 10, 1913, October 2, 1913, March 10, 1912) in the "Editorials of John Wanamaker, Volume I, October 1, 1912 to December 31, 1917," WA.

74.   Gibbons, *John Wanamaker*, vol. 2, p. 317.

75.   JW to RW (December 1, 1910), "1910, JW to RW," WA.

76.   JW to H. Laggart (March 9, 1886), "December 22, 1885 to December 2, 1886," p. 185; and JW to Thomas Stevenson (October 14, 1886), p. 544, WA.

77.   JW to A. S. Nickerson (October 10, 1898), Wanamaker Letterbooks, p. 23. However, Wanamaker did write in 1907 to one of his Bethany friends that "the Hebrews are growing in every city in the world. I am told that there are 1,150,000 Jews in New York, which is probably about the entire population of Philadelphia. It is very significant to see the hold that the Hebrews are getting upon the country." See JW to Thomas Marshall (November 16, 1907), "December 14, 1906 to February 16, 1908," pp. 227–28, WA.

78.   JW, 1901 journal, black notebook in paper wrapper dated 1901, WA; and Gibbons, *John Wanamaker*, vol. 2, pp. 66–67, 101–5.

79.   JW to John Oburn (September 12, 1904), "August 25, 1904 to January 13, 1905," p. 126, WA.

80.   JW to Ferdinand Widerholdt, Commercial Office of the Imperial German Commission, Palace of Varied Industries, Louisiana Purchase Exposition, St. Louis (November 18, 1904), p. 627; JW to Anthony Comstock (November 12, 1904), p. 579, WA; Gibbons, *John Wanamaker*, vol. 2, pp. 82–3, 188.

81.   JW to Rev. T. Harry Sprague (September 9, 1901) "August 20, 1901 to June 21, 1902," p. 109, WA.

82.   JW to J. B. Learned, M.D. (February 15, 1908), "December 14, 1906 to February 20, 1908," p. 965, WA.

83.   Findlay, *Dwight L. Moody*, p. 88; Hutchinson, *The Modernist Impulse in American Protestantism*, pp. 8–11.

84.   JW to Eugenia Bacon (November 23, 1898), "October 7, 1898 to March 18, 1899," p. 296, WA.

85.   JW to Rev. R. M. Luther (December 31, 1896), vol. 17, p. 875; JW to Robert Ogden (April 4, 1897, vol. 18, p. 68, WA.

86.   JW, 1901 journal, WA.

87.   Herbert Wallace Schneider, *Religion in Twentieth-Century America*, pp. 8–9. Schneider goes on, p. 8: The "depressed groups" were "equally conspicuous in urban and rural life, and equally unimportant from the point of view of their civilized neighbors. Fortunately, so far during this century they have been a relatively 'small class.' "

88.   Edward Ross, *Sin and Society: An Analysis of Latter-Day Iniquity* (New York, 1907), pp. 29, 88–91.

89.   Edith Wharton, *The Custom of the Country* (New York, 1913; reprint, 1981), p. 134.

90.   For a recent discussion of the liberal position and its accommodation to the new culture, see Richard Fox, "The Discipline of Amusement," in *Inventing Times Square: Commerce and Culture at the Crossroads of the World* (New York, 1991), pp. 66–82. See also, on this same accommodation, William McLoughlin, *The Meaning of Henry Ward Beecher: An Essay on the Shifting Values of Mid-Victorian America, 1840–1870* (New York, 1970); Douglas, *The Feminization of American Culture*; and Altina L. Waller, *Reverend Beecher and Mrs. Tilton: Sex and Class in Victorian America* (Amherst, Mass., 1982).

91.   Edward Ross, *Changing America: Studies in Contemporary Society* (New York, 1912), p. 103.

92.   Quoted in John J. Costanis, "Law and Aesthetics: A Critique and a Reformulation of the Dilemmas," *Michigan Law Review* 80 (January 1982) (1): 413.

93.   Walter Rauschenbusch, *Christianity and the Social Crisis* (New York, 1907, 1964), p. 338. See also Sydney Ahlstrom, *Religious History of the American People*, p. 847: "The message and teaching of this increasingly homogeneous religious tradition and the attitudes it inculcated were closely adapted to what Americans wanted to hear and highly conducive to complacency and self-righteousness. The prophetic note tended to get lost. The sins most universally condemned were the middle-class 'don'ts' applicable to any would-be self-made man."

94.   Benjamin Rabinowitz, *The Young Men's Hebrew Associations, 1854–1913* (New York, 1948).

95.   Deborah Dash Moore, *At Home in America: Second Generation New York Jews* (New York, 1981), esp. chap. 5, "From Chevra to Center," pp. 123–46.

96.   Jay Dolan, *The American Catholic Experience: A History from Colonial Times to the Present* (New York, 1985), pp. 197, 321–46.

97.   Quoted in Aaron Abell, *American Catholicism and Social Action* (New York, 1963), p. 183.

98.   Carle Zimmerman, *Consumption and Standards of Living* (New York, 1936), p. 304; *The American Catholic Experience,* pp. 195–220. On Catholic charities, see Marguerite T. Boylan, *Social Welfare in the Catholic Church* (New York, 1941), pp. 21–62; and John O'Grady, *Catholic Charities in the United States* (New York, 1971). These reflections are also based on a conversation with Professor Reverend Paul Robichaud of The Catholic University, Washington, D.C. (November 10, 1992). As in many other areas in the religious history of these times, there is much research to be done.

99.   Dolan, *The American Catholic Experience,* pp. 349–51; on Mundelein, see Edward R. Kantowicz, *Corporation Sole: Cardinal Mundelein and Chicago Catholicism* (Notre Dame, Ind., 1983), pp. 3, 47–48, 171. On the orders for the contemplative life that existed in America, which though very tiny in this period, nevertheless testified to the fact that America could support a "theology of asceticism," see John Tracy Ellis, *American Catholicism* (Chicago, 1969), pp. 133–36.

100.   Mel Piehl, *Breaking Bread: The Catholic Worker and the Origins of Catholic Radicalism in America* (Philadelphia, 1982), pp. 28–29, 53.

101.   Philip Gleason, "In Search of Unity: American Catholic Thought, 1920–1960," *The Catholic Historical Review* 65 (April 1979): 189–91, 194.

102.   Dolan, *The American Catholic Experience,* pp. 206–15, 231–33, 351. Dolan points out, on p. 227, that Catholicism's two "major sins" were "drunkenness" and "impurity." The urban cardinals also created their own youth organizations (the most famous being the CYO), which imitated in every way the YMCA of the Protestants. See Kantowicz, *Corporation Sole,* pp. 173–75.

103.   On "going first class," see Kantowicz, *Corporation Sole,* p. 3.

104.   JW to RW (February 11, 1918); and, for 1903 citations, see JW to RW (February 13 and 14, 1903), "letters to Rodman," WA. For other citations, see May 30, 1913 (telegram), August 8, 1913, March 5, 1917, and August 23, 1919), WA.

105.   JW to RW (June 26, 1913), WA.

106.   JW to RW (August 11, 1913), WA.

107.   Gibbons, *John Wanamaker,* vol. 2, pp. 69, 162–63.

108.   See RW, collection of sheet music by Rodman Wanamaker, WA.

109.   *Eve Journal* (March 9, 1928), 1, scrapbook, "In Memoriam, Rodman Wanamaker, 1863–1928," WA.

110.   RW to Minnie Warburton (July 28, 1924), in tin box, estate of JW, miscellaneous papers, WA.

111.   The evidence for John, Jr.'s, behavior were preserved in the Wanamaker archives in a closed tin box, which I had opened for inspection at the store. This particular citation comes from a formal oath signed on December 16, 1927, by

John Wanamaker, Jr., in which he promised not to drink or otherwise indulge himself. "Failing to live up to the agreement as stated above," he promised further, "I agree, with the consent of my father and at the instigation of two or more reputable physicians to place myself, or have my father place me in an institution selected by said physicians and my father, for a period of one year." ("Miscellaneous Correspondence, Capt. John Wanamaker, Jr.") A detailed discussion of John, Jr.'s, character also appears in a private dictation (also preserved in the closed tin box) by William Nevin, president of the Philadelphia store (dated March 24, 1928), WA.

112.   "John Wanamaker, Jr., Correspondence Between Rodman Wanamaker, Mr. Rebmann and Mr. Whitney, Years 1923–1928." See, in particular, Mr. Rebmann to A. M. Peeples (December 16, 1927), WA.

Chapter 8

1.   Charles Brodie Patterson, *In the Sunlight of Health* (New York, 1913).

2.   Herbert Adams Gibbons, *John Wanamaker* (New York, 1926), vol. 2, p. 462.

3.   See Arthur Meier Schlesinger, "The Critical Period in American Religion, 1875–1900," *Proceedings of the Massachusetts Historical Society* 64 (1932–33): 523–47; Paul Carter, *The Spiritual Crisis of the Gilded Age* (DeKalb, Ill., 1971); Sidney Ahlstrom, *A Religious History of the American People* (New Haven, Conn., 1972), pp. 731–857; and George M. Marsden, *Fundamentalism and American Culture: The Shaping of Twentieth-Century Evangelicalism, 1870–1925* (New York, 1980), esp. chap. 1, "Evangelical America at the Brink of Crisis," pp. 11–39. On the despair and doubt (and the "therapeutic" reaction) engendered by this religious "crisis," see T. Jackson Lears, *No Place of Grace* (New York, 1981).

4.   Stephen Gottschalk, *The Emergence of Christian Science in American Religious Life* (Berkeley, Calif., 1973), pp. 112–13; William James, *The Varieties of Religious Experience* (New York, 1958), pp. 137–39, 284. For brief histories of the mind-cure movement in the United States, see Johan Huizinga, *America* (New York, 1972; orig. pub. 1928), pp. 187–203; Harold Faulkner, *The Quest for Social Justice, 1898–1914* (New York, 1931), pp. 213–18; Ahlstrom, *A Religious History of the American People*, pp. 1020–38; and Warren Susman, *Culture as History: The Transformation of American Society in the Twentieth Century* (New York, 1984), pp. 270–85. For a greater-length treatment, see Donald Meyer, *The Positive Thinkers: Popular Religious Psychology from Mary Baker Eddy to Norman Vincent Peale and Ronald Reagan* (Middletown, Conn., 1989). For a discussion of the conflicts within the mind-cure movements as a whole, see Gottschalk; and see also Charles Braden, *Spirits in Rebellion: The Rise and Development of New Thought* (Dallas, 1963), pp. 14–25.

5.   Lucy Sprague Mitchell, *Two Lives: The Story of Wesley Clair Mitchell and Myself* (New York, 1953), pp. 70–71.

6.   Horace W. Dresser, *A History of the New Thought Movement* (New York, 1919), pp. 176–80; Wendell Thomas, *Hinduism Invades America* (New York, 1930), pp. 73–77; Gottschalk, *The Emergence of Christian Science in American*

Religious Life, pp. 150–57; Carter, *The Spiritual Crisis of the Gilded Age*, pp. 210–21.

7.   James, *The Varieties of Religious Experience*, pp. 88–89. For a discussion of trends in liberal Protestantism similar to those in the mind-cure movement, see Richard Fox, "The Discipline of Amusement," in *Inventing Times Square: Commerce and Culture at the Crossroads of the World*, ed. William R. Taylor (New York, 1991), pp.83–98.

8.   Bruce Campbell, *Ancient Wisdom Revealed: A History of the Theosophical Society* (Berkeley, Calif., 1980), pp. 23–29; Marion Meade, *Madame Blavatsky: The Woman Behind the Myth* (New York, 1980), pp. 101–35, 160–75, 180, 224, 232; and Helene Blavatsky, *The Key to Theosophy* (Corina, Calif., 1946; orig. pub. 1889), pp. 27, 33, 61–65, 75.

9.   J. H. Leuba, "Psychotherapic Cults: Christian Science; Mind Cure; New Thought," *The Monist* 22 (July 1912): 350–51.

10.   Blavatsky, *The Key to Theosophy*, pp. 27, 33, 61–65, 75; and Campbell, *Ancient Wisdom Revealed*, pp. 3–9.

11.   Meyer, *The Positive Thinkers*, pp. 73–82; James, *The Varieties of Religious Experience*, p. 96.

12.   Horace Dresser, *Handbook of the New Thought* (New York, 1917), p. iii.

13.   Dresser, *A History of the New Thought Movement*, p. 211.

14.   For Vivekenanda citation, see Wendell Thomas, *Hinduism Invades America*, pp. 107–08.

15.   Blavatsky, *The Key to Theosophy*, p. 26.

16.   Elizabeth Townes, *Practical Methods for Self-Development* (1904), quoted in Meyer, The Positive Thinkers, p. 199; Ralph Waldo Trine, *What the World Is Seeking* (New York, 1896), pp. 171–79. Other quoted material comes from James, *The Varieties of Religious Experience*, pp. 90, 97; and Orison Swett Marden, *Peace, Power, and Plenty* (New York, 1909), p. 12.

17.   "The Joy of Service," *The American Cooperator* (June 6, 1903): 20.

18.   *Success Magazine* (August 15, 1903, September 26, 1903).

19.   Meyer, *The Positive Thinkers*, pp. 198–99.

20.   "A Monograph on Worry," *The Poster* (November 1912); articles in *The Department Store* and *Advertising World*.

21.   "Don't Postpone Your Happiness," *Thought and Work* (May 15, 1904).

22.   Quoted in Freeman Champney, *Art and Glory: The Story of Elbert Hubbard* (New York, 1968), pp. 39–40, 144–46.

23.   "Elbert Hubbard's Creed," *The American Cooperator* (July 4, 1903): 24.

24.   *The Dry Goods Reporter* (August 7, 1909): 18.

25.   Quoted in *MRSW* (November 1908). For references to the Kansas City designer, see *Business Women's Magazine* (December 1914); and for popularity of Billikens, see *DGE* (February 27, 1909); *DGE* (May 29, 1909), p. 132; and *DGE* (March 6, 1909), p. 35.

26.   Mabel Dodge, quoted in Lois Palken Rudnick, *Mabel Dodge Luhan: New Women, New Worlds* (Albuquerque, 1984), pp. 132–37. See also, on the reception of New Thought, Nathan Hale, *Freud and the Americans: The Beginnings of Psychoanalysis in the United States, 1876–1917* (New York, 1971), pp. 245–49.

27.   On Ellen Veblen, see R. L. Duffus, *Innocents at Cedro* (New York, 1944), concluding chapter; on Dreiser, see Richard Lingeman, *Theodore Dreiser: An American Journey, 1908–1941* (New York, 1990), p. 48, 108–112, 123.

28.   On the unity of the social sciences up to the 1890s, see Daniel Fox, *The Discovery of Abundance: Simon N. Patten and the Transformation of Social Theory* (Ithaca, N.Y., 1968), pp. 156–58; on the conflicts among them, see Mary Furner, *Advocacy and Objectivity* (Louisville, 1975).

29.   Joseph Schumpeter, *Ten Great Economists from Marx to Keynes* (New York, 1951), p. 241. On the rise of economics as a field, see William Barber, "Political Economy and the Academic Setting Before 1900: An Introduction," in Barber, ed., *Breaking the Academic Mould: Economists and American Higher Learning in the Nineteenth Century* (Middletown, Conn., 1988, pp. 3–14); and Mary Furner, "Knowing Capitalism: Public Investigation and the Labor Question in the Long Progressive Era," in *The State and Economic Knowledge*, ed. Mary Furner and Barry Supple (Cambridge, Eng., 1990), pp. 242–45.

30.   Simon Patten, "The Conflict Theory of Distribution," in *Essays in Economic Theory*, ed. Rexford Tugwell (New York, 1924), p. 240, repr. from *The Yale Review* 17 (August 1908).

31.   On the continuing (and even more widespread) trend in modern economics to focus only on "abstract market forces," see Robert Heilbroner, "Reflections, Economic Predictions," *The New Yorker* (July 8, 1991), pp. 70–77.

32.   Mary Furner, "The Republican Tradition and the New Liberalism: Social Investigation, State Building, and Social Learning in the Gilded Age," manuscript in possession of author. On the squeezing out of history and the larger view from economics after 1915, see Richard Swedberg, introduction to *Joseph A. Schumpeter: The Economics and Sociology of Capitalism*, ed. R. Swedberg (Princeton, N.J., 1991), pp. 31–33.

33.   This overall perspective was (and is) known as "institutional economics," an interdisciplinary field that blended economics, sociology, history, and other subjects and that insisted on making ethical judgments about the nature of economic and social change. On institutional economics, see David Sechler, *Thorstein Veblen and the Institutionalists* (Boulder, Colo., 1975), pp. 1–17; Edward Jandy, *Charles Horton Cooley: His Life and His Social Theory* (New York, 1968; orig. pub. 1942), pp. 255–56; Allan Gruchey, *Contemporary Economic Thought: The Contribution of Neo-Institutional Economics* (Clifton, N.J., 1972), pp. 17–67; Joseph Dorfman, *The Economic Mind in American Civilization* (New York, 1959), vol. 4, pp. 352–

97; Wesley Clair Mitchell, *Lecture Notes on Types of Economic Theory* (New York, 1949), vol. 2, pp. 225–27; and Lev E. Dobriansky, *Veblenism: A New Critique* (Washington, D.C., 1957), pp. 217–21, and chap. 7, pp. 289–343.

34. Thorstein Veblen, "Christian Morals and the Competitive System," repr. in *Essays on Our Changing Order*, ed. Leon Andzrooni (New York, 1964), orig. pub. in *The International Journal of Ethics* 20 (January 1910): 216.

35. Joseph Dorfman, *Thorstein Veblen and His America* (New York, 1934), p. 327. Dorfman's is still the most complete biography of Veblen, although John P. Diggins's more recent, intellectually focused *The Bard of Savagery: Thorstein Veblen and Modern Social Theory* (New York, 1978), is also useful. In many ways, the best and most moving account of Veblen is R. L. Duffus, *The Innocents at Cedro: A Memoir of Thorstein Veblen and Some Others* (New York, 1944).

36. Veblen, quoted in Dobriansky, *Veblenism: A New Critique*, pp. 315–17; Dorfman, *Thorstein Veblen*, pp. 205, 252; and Thorstein Veblen, *The Theory of Business Enterprise* (New York, 1904), pp. 45–85.

37. Thorstein Veblen, *Absentee Ownership and Business Enterprise in Recent Times: The Case of America* (New York, 1923), pp. 97–98, 313. Veblen divided salesmanship into two categories: "newsprint" and "outdoor advertising"; the first included advertising by mail and in newspapers and magazines; the second included advertising through posters and bulletins, and the new signboards and "spectacular" electrical displays. Between these two categories were what Veblen described as the "formidable minor devices"—show windows, indoor display, packaging and labels, decorative interiors, trademarks, and decorative containers. On the validity of his views on the relations among credit, rising prices, and salesmanship, see Dobriansky, *Veblenism: A New Critique*, pp. 305–9, 330; Charles Friday, "Veblen and the Future of American Capitalism" and Thomas Cochran, "Business in Veblen's America," in *Thorstein Veblen: The Carleton College Veblen Seminar Essays* (Minneapolis, 1968), pp. 16–71; and Joel B. Dirlam, "The Place of Corporation Finance in Veblen's Economics," in *Thorstein Veblen: A Critical Reappraisal*, ed. Douglas F. Dowd (New York, 1958), pp. 212–29.

38. *Absentee Ownership* (New York, 1923), quoted in Dorfman, *Thorstein Veblen*, p. 98.

39. *The Higher Learning in America* (1911), quoted in Dorfman, *Thorstein Veblen*, p. 407.

40. Veblen, *Absentee Ownership*, pp. 309–11, 318–23.

41. Thorstein Veblen, *The Vested Interests and the Common Man* (New York, 1964; orig. pub. 1919), pp. 27–30, 71–76, 94–100; *Absentee Ownership*, quoted in Dorfman, *Thorstein Veblen*, p. 473; Veblen, *The Engineers and the Price System*, (New York, 1921, 1965), pp. 108–11.

42. Veblen, *The Instinct of Workmanship*, quoted in Dorfman, *Thorstein Veblen*, pp. 324–25.

43. Veblen, "Christian Morals and the Competitive System," p. 216; and *The Instinct of Workmanship*, quoted in Dorfman, *Thorstein Veblen*, p. 327.

44. Rexford Tugwell, "Notes on the Life and Work of Simon Nelson Patten," *The Journal of Political Economy* 31 (April 1923): pp. 182–83. Unless otherwise noted, most of the biographical material on Patten in this chapter is taken from Tugwell's article (still the best thing written on Patten) or from Daniel Fox, *The Discovery of Abundance: Simon N. Patten and the Transformation of Social Theory* (Ithaca, N.Y., 1968). For a very different analysis of both Patten and Veblen from the one I present here, see Daniel Horowitz, *The Morality of Spending, Attitudes Toward the Consumer Society in America, 1875–1940* (Baltimore and London, 1988), pp. 30–41.

45. Simon Patten, quoted in oral interview of Dr. William H. Allen, director of the Bureau of Municipal Research, and secretary, New York City Municipal Civil Service Commission, by Owen Bompard (December 1948–January 2, 1950), pp. 26–31, CUOHP.

46. Patten, *Mud Hollow* (New York, 1922), p. 229.

47. On earlier American views, see Paul K. Conkin, *Prophets of Prosperity: America's First Political Economists* (Bloomington, Ind., 1980); on Patten's debt to earlier thinkers, see David B. Schulter, "Economics and the Sociology of Consumption: Simon Patten and Early Academics in America, 1894–1904," *The Journal of the History of Sociology* 2 (Fall–Winter 1979–80): 132–62.

48. Patten, "The Economic Cause of Social Progress" (pub. 1912), repr. in Rexford Tugwell, ed., *Essays in Economic Theory* (New York, 1924), p. 167.

49. On the theme of decline reviled by Patten, see John L. Thomas, *Alternative America: Henry George, Edward Bellamy, Henry Demarest Lloyd, and the Adversary Tradition* (Cambridge, Mass., 1983), pp. 1–36.

50. Patten, *The Consumption of Wealth* (New York, 1901), p. vi.

51. On "inculcated . . ." and "emphasized . . ." see Patten, *The Theory of Prosperity* (New York, 1902), p. 162; on "the principle of sacrifice," see Patten, "The Economic Cause of Social Progress," in Tugwell, ed., *Essays in Economic Theory*, pp. 21, 316; and on "restraint, denial, and negation," see Patten, *The New Basis of Civilization* (New York, 1907), pp. 50, 129. On Patten's "new religion," see also Fox, *The Discovery of Abundance*, pp. 72–73, 108–9.

52. On "checks to full" and "adjust a people," see Patten, *The Theory of Prosperity*, p. 162.

53. Quoted in Marianne Weber, *Max Weber: A Biography*, trans. and ed. Harry Zohn (New York, 1975; orig. pub. 1920), p. 307.

54. On the early eighteenth-century position on commerce, see Albert O. Hirschman, *Rival Views of Market Society and Other Recent Essays* (New York, 1986), pp. 41–43, 105–9. Mistakenly, I think, Hirschman argues in his otherwise fine essay that there were no American economists in the nineteenth and early twentieth centuries who "kept alive" the earlier notion that "market societies forged all sorts of social ties of trust, friendliness, sociability, and thus helped to hold society together" (p. 122). Clearly, Patten and his followers did much to keep it alive, albeit in a new corporate market form.

55.   Patten, "Reconstruction of Economic Theory" (pub. 1912), repr. in Tugwell, ed., *Essays in Economic Theory*, pp. 310–12.

56.   Ibid.

57.   Tugwell, ed., *Essays in Economic Theory*, p. 22.

58.   Patten, *The Consumption of Wealth*, pp. 10, 168–69.

59.   Historian Dorothy Ross argues that Patten never placed much stock in the theory of marginal utility. He "never regarded marginalism," she writes, "as more than a minor analytical technique." Ross may be able to prove this claim, but here it is clear that Patten attributed much significance to marginal theory. See Dorothy Ross, *The Origins of American Social Science* (Cambridge, Eng., 1991), pp. 195–96.

60.   Patten, *The Consumption of Wealth*, pp. 10–13; Patten, "The Scope of Political Economy," p. 182, in Tugwell, ed., *Essays in Economic Theory*.

61.   Patten, *The Consumption of Wealth*, p. 51.

62.   Patten, "Reconstruction of Economic Theory," p. 337.

63.   Patten, *The Theory of Prosperity*, pp. 168–69; Patten, *New Basis*, p. 141.

64.   Tugwell, ed., *Essays in Economic Theory*, p. 22.

65.   Patten, *The Theory of Prosperity*, pp. 164–65, 208; Patten, *Mud Hollow*, pp. 239–40.

66.   Patten, *Product and Climax* (New York, 1909), p. 62; Patten, *The Theory of Prosperity*, p. 182.

67.   Simon N. Patten, "Hymn Writing," *The Survey Magazine* (December 20, 1913): 403–4.

68.   Tugwell, ed., *Essays in Economic Theory*, pp. 175–77.

69.   Ibid., p. 13.

70.   Patten, *The Theory of Prosperity*, p. 162; *Product and Climax*, p. 18–22, 55.

71.   Patten, *Product and Climax*, p. 62.

72.   Fox, *The Discovery of Abundance*, pp. 133–34.

73.   Quoted in Rexford Tugwell, *To the Lesser Heights of Morningside: A Memoir* (Philadelphia, 1982), p. 135. On Patten's wish theory, see also Fox, *The Discovery of Abundance*, pp. 134–35.

74.   Patten, *Mud Hollow*, pp. 297, 325, 350–51.

75.   Tugwell, *To the Lesser Heights of Morningside*, pp. 44, 154. On Patten's influence on social workers and on the economic profession, see Joseph Dorfman, *The Economic Mind in American Civilization* (New York, 1959), vol. 3, pp. 187–88, 209.

76.   Franklin Giddings, *Studies in the Theory of Human Society* (New York, 1922),

pp. 61–63, orig. pub. as "Quality of Civilization"; and Tugwell, "Notes on the Life and Work of Simon Nelson Patten," p. 191. Daniel Fox argues, in his biography of Patten, *The Discovery of Abundance*, p. 161, that Giddings and Patten were "poles apart." But as these statements indicate, they agreed on the role standardization played in the culture and economy.

77.   On Lippmann's views of Weyl, see Charles Forcey, introduction to Weyl, *New Democracy* (New York, 1965) p. xiv.

78.   Weyl, *New Democracy*, pp. 194, 251–52.

79.   Ibid., pp. 246–47.

80.   On *Oh, Money! Money!* see Grant M. Overton, *The Women Who Make Our Novels* (New York, 1922), pp. 119–20; for biographical materials on Porter, see Overton, pp. 108–18, and Stanley Kunitz and Howard Haycroft, ed., *Twentieth-Century Authors* (New York, 1942), pp. 1116–17.

81.   Eleanor H. Porter, *Pollyanna* (New York, 1912), pp. 24, 149, 186, 223–25, 276.

82.   Ibid., pp. 226–27.

83.   Ibid., p. 287.

84.   On the novel's reception, see "Eleanor Porter," in *Notable American Women*, ed. Edward T. James (Cambridge, Mass., 1971), pp. 85–86.

85.   Matilda Joslyn Gage, *Woman, Church, and State* (included in the first volume of *The History of Woman Suffrage* (New York, 1893), p. 31; and Campbell, *Ancient Wisdom Revealed*, p. 3.

86.   John Algeo, "A Notable Theosophist: L. Frank Baum," in *The American Theosophist* 74 (August–September 1986): 270–73; *The Aberdeen Saturday Pioneer* (a Baum-edited newspaper; hereafter *Pioneer*) (April 5, 1890); Matilda Joslyn Gage (grandniece of Mrs. Gage), "The Dakota Days of L. Frank Baum," Part III, *The Baum Bugle* (Christmas 1966).

87.   *Pioneer* (January 25, 1890, and February 22, 1890).

88.   *Pioneer* (May 10, 1890); and quoted in Matilda J. Gage, "The Dakota Days of L. Frank Baum," Part II, *The Baum Bugle* (Autumn 1966).

89.   "L. Frank Baum and His New Plays," newspaper article, p. 63, LFB Papers, Arendts Collection, Syracuse University.

90.   *Pioneer* (November 8, 1890, February 22, 1890, March 1, 1890, March 15, 1890, March 22, 1890, May 3, 1890, and February 8, 1891).

91.   For Baum's edible landscapes, see LFB, *The Emerald City of Oz* (Chicago, 1910), pp. 181–82, 299; LFB, *The Purple Dragon and Other Fantasies* (Lakemount, Ga., 1976), ed. with foreword by David L. Greene, pp. 18, 21; LFB, *Tot and Dot in Merryland* (Chicago, 1901), pp. 103–5; and Frank Baum and Russell MacFall, *To Please a Child: A Biography of L. Frank Baum, Royal Historian of Oz* (Chicago, 1951), pp. 21–32.

92.   On the Oz industry, merchandising, and advertising, see Baum and MacFall, *To Please a Child*, pp. 251–56; *The Baum Bugle* (Christmas 1964); and *The Baum Bugle* (December 1962). On the popularity of *The Wizard of Oz*, see Frank Luther Mott, *Golden Multitudes: The Story of Best Sellers in the United States* (New York, 1966).

93.   "Why 'Everybody's Going to the Big Store,' " *ST* (September 1, 1913).

94.   Quoted in a Baum newspaper interview, "L. Frank Baum and His New Plays" (1910), LFB Papers, Arendts Collection, Syracuse University Library. See also on the production, Baum and MacFall, *To Please a Child*, pp. 5–15, and *The Baum Bugle* (Spring 1969). On recent adaptations, see, on Emerald City Mall, *NYT*, September 24, 1989, p. 25 and, on "Oz," *NYT*, October 29, 1992, p. c19.

95.   On traditional elements in fairy tales, see Brian Atterbery, *The Fantasy Tradition in American Literature: From Irving to LeGuin* (Bloomington, Ind., 1980), pp. 91–92; Bruno Bettelheim, *The Uses of Enchantment: The Meaning and Importance of Fairy Tales* (New York, 1977), pp. 3–19; and Laura F. Kready, *A Study of Fairy Tales* (New York, 1916), pp. 13–22.

96.   On the uniqueness of Baum's achievement, see Atterbery, *The Fantasy Tradition in American Literature*, pp. 81–3; and Humphrey Carpenter, *Secret Gardens: The Golden Age of Children's Literature* (Boston, 1985), pp. x, 16–17.

97.   John Bunyan, *The Pilgrim's Progress: From This World to That Which Is to Come*, pt. I, ed. with introduction by James Thorpe (Boston, 1969), pp. 147–82, 194, 199. On the popularity of the Bunyan book, see Daniel T. Rodgers, *The Work Ethic in America, 1850–1920*, p. 128; and Paul Fussell, *The Great War in Modern Memory* (New York, 1977), pp. 137–44.

98.   On this critical tradition of fairy-tale writing, see Carpenter, *Secret Gardens*.

99.   The most well-known and wide-eyed of these analysts is Henry Littlefield, whose "The Wizard of Oz: Parable of Populism," *American Quarterly* (Spring 1964): 47–58 is still widely used. See also Fred Erisman, "L. Frank Baum and the Progressive Dilemma," *American Quarterly* (Fall 1968): 616–23; and Brian Atterbery, *The Fantasy Tradition in American Literature*, pp. 86–90.

100.   *Pioneer* (December 20, 1890). Baum was editor of this newspaper when he lived in Aberdeen, South Dakota, a region of intense farmer unrest and populist activity. Yet he devoted almost nothing in his paper to this unrest, which is surprising if one believes that Baum was greatly interested in populism. Baum was more interested in writing about costume parties given by the "best people," about theater and musical activities in Aberdeen, and about show windows and goods.

101.   The page references to *The Wizard of Oz*, which henceforth will appear in the narrative, come from *The Wonderful Wizard of Oz*, ed. William Leach (Belmont, Calif., 1991).

102.   On these kingdoms or "globes," see Bruce Campbell, *Ancient Wisdom Revealed*, pp. 61–74.

103.   The relationship between theosophy/spiritualism and color is briefly explored

in Faber Birren, *Color and Human Response* (New York, 1978). On a colorist who preceded Baum and may have influenced him, see Edwin Babbitt, *The Principles of Light and Color: The Classic Study of the Healing Power of Color*, ed. and annotated by Faber Birren (New York, 1967; orig. pub. in 1878). A Presbyterian like John Wanamaker, Babbitt "converted" to spiritualism in 1869 at age forty (p. vi). "Wonderful," he wrote on p. 93, "are the healing properties of light and color, so gentle, so penetrating, so enduring in their effects."

104.   On Baum's use of color, see Harry Neal Baum, "My Father Was the Wizard of Oz," manuscript, LFB Papers, Arendts Collection, Syracuse University, pp. 13–14; and Michael P. Hearn, introduction to *The Annotated Wizard of Oz* (New York, 1973), p. 114.

105.   On the historical significance of tricksterism in America and its gradual domestication by the 1870s and 1880s, see Neil Harris, *Humbug: The Art of P. T. Barnum* (Chicago, 1973), pp. 72–79; Karen Halttunen, *Confidence Men and Painted Women* (New Haven, Conn., 1982); and Ann Fabian, *Card Sharps, Dream Books, and Bucket Shops: Gambling in 19th Century America* (Ithaca, N.Y., 1990).

106.   Harry Neal Baum, "My Father Was the Wizard of Oz."

107.   Paul Tietjens, "Excerpts Pertaining to L. Frank Baum Taken from the Diary of Paul Tietjens, 1901 to 1904," LFB Papers, Syracuse University Library.

108.   Bettelheim, *The Uses of Enchantment*, pp. 61–66, 78–83, 143–50.

109.   Atterbery, *The Fantasy Tradition in American Literature*, p. 93.

110.   Bettelheim, *The Uses of Enchantment*, pp. 144–45.

111.   Matilda Gage Baum, "Great Men and Women: L. Frank Baum," *The Baum Bugle* (Winter, 1980–81).

112.   LFB, *The Emerald City of Oz* (Chicago, 1910), p. 31.

113.   Patterson, *In Sunlight and Health*, p. iii.

114.   James, *The Varieties of Religious Experience* (New York, 1958), pp. 137–39, 284.

Chapter 9

1.   Quoted in *NYT* (December 14, 1922), p. 21; on Wanamaker's death, see *NYT* (December 13, 1922), p. 1.

2.   *NYT* (December 15, 1922), p. 19.

3.   J. M. Giddings to William Nevins (August 2, 1918), folder "Correspondence Regarding Inquiries into Sale of Business," cabinet file JW, WA.

4.   For these proposals to Nevin and RW, see Louis Boissevain (February 2, 1925); phone memo from Mr. Mandel to William Nevin (December 11, 1925) (for Gimbel Brothers); Carl E. Whitney (of Wise, Whitney, and Parker) to William Nevin (September 12, 1928); Wilson Prichett (representative of Goldman, Sachs) to RW (December 12, 1924); M. L. Freeman (representative of banking group) to Nevin

(April 26, 1927); Russell Thayer (representative of banking interests) to Nevin (February 3, 1927); and Daniel Cohn to Nevin (October 15, 1924), in folder "Correspondence Regarding Inquiries," WA.

5.   Archie Shaw, quoted in Guy Alchon, *The Invisible Hand of Planning: Capitalism, Social Science, and the State* (Princeton, N.J., 1985), p. 147.

6.   David Montgomery, *The Fall of the House of Labor* (Cambridge, Eng., 1987), pp. 406, 432.

7.   Ibid., p. 464.

8.   André Siegfried, "The Gulf Between," *The Atlantic Monthly* (March 1928): 289–96.

9.   Samuel Strauss, "Rich Men and Key Men," *The Atlantic Monthly* (December 1927): 721–29, and " 'Things Are in the Saddle,' " *The Atlantic Monthly* (November 1924): 577–88. On Strauss's later abandonment of his critique, see his *American Opportunity* (Boston, 1935). The book constitutes, in fact, a *major* reversal in analysis and also lacks much of the rich cultural thinking of his earlier criticism. Strauss could write *uncritically*, for instance, "that the common man wishes always more things, always better things" (p. 124).

10.   "Moses Strauss," biographical sketch, *History of Des Moines and Polk County, Iowa* (Chicago, 1911), pp. 178–81; L. F. Andrews, "He Rounds Out a Half Century as a Businessman in Des Moines," *Des Moines Register and Leader* (December 1, 1907), p. 30, courtesy of the State Historical Society of Iowa, Iowa City, Ia.

11.   "Moses Strauss," p. 181.

12.   On Strauss's membership in the Kehillah, see Arthur Goren, *New York Jews and the Quest for Community: The Kehillah Experiment, 1908–1922* (New York, 1970), p. 175.

13.   "Contributors' Column," *The Atlantic Monthly* 140 (December 1927): 858; obituary, *NYT* (April 3, 1953), p. 27.

14.   Strauss, "Epicurus and America," *The Villager* 1 (May 19, 1917): 15–16.

15.   Strauss, " 'Things Are in the Saddle' ": 577–88.

16.   Ibid.

17.   "Progress," *The Villager* (April 9, 1921), review of J. B. Bury's *Progress; The Villager*, "Some Thoughts on the Time" (December 4, 1920): 111.

18.   "Out of the Grip of Things," *The Villager* 3 (July 5, 1919): 47–48.

19.   "Why Great Wealth Is No Longer Envied," *The Villager* 6 (June 30, 1923): 299.

20.   "Out of the Grip of Things"; "Rich Men and Key Men," pp. 727–29.

21.   "Buyers Instead of Citizens," *The Villager* 6 (July 28, 1923): 170–71.

22.   Raymond Loewy, *Never Leave Well Enough Alone* (New York, 1951), p. 73.

23.   Monsignor Francis Spellman to LK (May 6, 1930), LKP, HBS; Frederick Lewis Allen, *Only Yesterday: An Informal History of the 1920s* (New York, 1964; orig. pub. 1931), pp. 87–90; George Mowry, *The Urban Nation* (New York, 1964), pp. 6–15; U.S. Department of Commerce, "International Trade in Clocks and Watches," Trade Information Bulletin no. 585 (Washington, D.C., November 1928), p. 1; sales chart for "Toilet Goods Department" (1914–26), William Filene Department Store, Box 21, Elizabeth Arden File, LKP; *DC* 7 (February 20, 1931): 5; U.S. Department of Commerce, "World Trade in Toilet Preparations," Trade Information Bulletin no. 344 (Washington, D.C., May 1925).

The best contemporary account of goods production in this period can be found in the National Bureau of Economic Research, *Recent Economic Changes in the United States* (hereafter *REC*), Report of the Hoover Committee on Recent Economic Changes, of the President's Conference on Unemployment (New York, 1929), pp. ix–xxiii, 1–68.

24.   On Rothschild's, see *PRL* (May 2, 1923), p. 4; "The Wanamaker Pet Shop," *The Pet Shop* (hereafter *PS*) (July 1926); *PS* (September 1926); *PS* (December 1926); *PS* (January 1927); PS (November 1928); and *PS* (April 1929).

25.   Richard Fox, *Reinhold Niebuhr: A Biography* (New York, 1985), pp. 90–96; Stephen Meyer III, *The Five Dollar Day: Labor Movement and Social Control in the Ford Motor Company, 1908–1921* (Albany, N.Y., 1982); Montgomery, *Fall of the House of Labor*, p. 397.

26.   PM, "Memorandum for Mr. Kirstein, No. 1, Change in the Financial Status of the United States," May 12, 1921, Box 38, PM, LKP; Ron Chernow, *The House of Morgan* (New York, 1990), pp. 205–6; Ramsay Muir, *America the Golden: An Englishman's Notes and Comparisons* (London, 1927), pp. 65–87.

27.   Quoted in *MRSW* 61 (December 1927): 39; Harold Barger, *Distribution's Place in the American Economy Since 1869* (Princeton, N.J., 1955), pp. 4–16.

28.   On Gimbels' elevator, see WWD (November 12, 1927), p. 7; on Bamberger's, see *WWD* (May 5, 1928), p. 2.

29.   *REC*, p. xi.

30.   *REC*, pp. xvi–xvii.

31.   John Allen Murphy, *Merchandising Through Mergers* (New York, 1930), p. 15; on the character of chain methods, see Edith M. Stern, "Chain Department Stores," *American Mercury* 30 (October 1933): 152–59; for statistics regarding the number of chain stores from 1886 to 1929, see U.S. Federal Trade Commission, *Chain Store Investigation* (Washington, D.C., 1935), pt. 4, "Growth and Development of Chain Stores," pp. 6–7, and Muir, *America the Golden*, pp. 78–79.

32.   Murphy, *Merchandising Through Mergers*, pp. 43–44.

33.   On Child's, see *The American Restaurant* 3 (November 1920): 38; on Savarin's, see *The American Restaurant* 4 (January 1921): 19–23.

34.   *REC*, pp. 365–67; on Fanny Farmer, see *PRL* (April 4, 1923): 4; for 1927, *REC*, p. 363.

35.   Whitney Bolton, *The Silver Spade: The Conrad Hilton Story* (New York, 1954), pp. 41–67; Rufus Jarman, *A Bed for the Night: The Story of the Wheeling Bellboy, E. N. Statler and His Remarkable Hotels* (New York, 1952), p. 170; Murphy, *Merchandising Through Mergers*, p. 92.

36.   "Hilton Brothers Broaden Hotel Activities," *The American Greeter* 25 (November 1932): 32.

37.   Quoted in *NYT* (September 26, 1928), p. 20.

38.   These figures and analysis are taken from Morris A. Horowitz, *The New York Hotel Industry: A Labor Relations Study* (Cambridge, Mass., 1960), pp. 3–8, 17–25.

39.   *REC*, pp. 365–67; also on Penney's, see *MRSW* 63 (October 1928): 54.

40.   Loewy, *Never Leave Well Enough Alone*, p. 73; on Walden's, see *MRSW* 66 (March 1930): 26; on Bedell's, see *MRSW* 65 (May 1929): 19; on Peck & Peck, see *MRSW* 61 (December 1927): 51; on the World Radio Corporation chain, see Ernest Henderson, *The World of 'Mr. Sheraton'* (New York, 1960), pp. 57–72; on the number of drugstores in 1925, see Muir, *America the Golden*, p. 79; and on reorganization of the drug business, see Murphy, *Merchandising Through Mergers*, pp. 7, 114.

41.   Quoted in Leon Harris, *Merchant Princes: An Intimate History of Jewish Families Who Built Great Department Stores* (New York, 1979), p. 351. On Marion, Ohio, see Charles Wesley Wood, *The Passing of Normalcy* (New York, 1929), p. 2; and W. A. Swanberg, *Norman Thomas: The Last Idealist* (New York, 1976), pp. 1–11. Also on chain stores, see Robert and Helen Lynd, *Middletown* (New York, 1929), pp. 45–47.

42.   Murphy, *Merchandising Through Mergers*, p. 15.

43.   Clark, quoted in Joseph Dorfman, *The Economic Mind in American Civilization* (New York, 1949), vol. 4 (1918–33), pp. 254–55.

44.   Murphy, *Merchandising Through Mergers*, pp. 68–69, 76–77.

45.   On this membership, see George W. Edwards, *The Evolution of Finance Capitalism* (London, 1938), pp. 228–29.

46.   On the debate over the role financiers have played in shaping American economic life, see Douglas Gomery, "Rethinking U.S. Film History: The Depression Decade and Monopoly Capital," *Film and History* 10 (May 1980): 32–37.

47.   Murphy, *Merchandising Through Mergers*, p. 56.

48.   Herbert Lehman to LK (November 29, 1923), LKP; Allen Nevins, *Herbert H. Lehman* (New York, 1962), pp. 62–65. Due to the absence of archival materials, no historian has been able to study Lehman's early investment career in any depth or even at all. Nevins has nothing to say about it. This letter to Kirstein, then, is of some consequence, because it is one of the few (that I know of, at any rate) to show the extent of Lehman's interest and involvement.

49.   John Kenneth Galbraith, *The Great Crash of 1929* (Boston, 1961), pp. 48–

70. On Catchings, see Dorfman, *The Economic Mind in American Civilization,* vol. 4, pp. 339–41; and *NYT,* obituary (January 1, 1968), p. 15.

50.   Waddill Catchings and William Trufant Foster, *Progress and Plenty: Two-Minute Talks on the Economics of Prosperity* (New York, 1930), p. 45. This book is a compendium of articles Catchings and Foster wrote in the late twenties.

51.   Waddill Catchings and William Trufant Foster, *The Road to Plenty* (New York, 1928), p. 173, and *Progress and Plenty,* p. 18.

52.   *Business Week* (September 14, 1929), p. 29.

53.   Ibid.

54.   Murphy, *Merchandising Through Mergers,* pp. 19–20. On the merger work of these firms, see Carroso, *Investment Banking in America* (Cambridge, Mass., 1970), pp. 19–20, 82–85; Neal Gabler, *An Empire of Their Own: How the Jews Invented Hollywood* (New York, 1988), pp. 123–28; Boris Emmet and John E. Jeuck, *Catalogues and Counters: A History of Sears, Roebuck and Company* (Chicago, 1950), pp. 55–58; Anna Rochester, *Rulers in America: A Study in Finance Capital* (New York, 1936), pp. 81–82, 186, 246; and *Lehman Brothers: A Centennial, 1850–1950* (New York, 1950), pp. 31–46.

55.   J. Douglas Gomery, "Writing the History of the American Film Industry: Warner Bros and Sound," *Screen* 17 (Spring 1976): 4053; Gomery, "The Coming of Sound: Technological Change in the American Film Industry," in Tino Balio, ed., *The American Film Industry* (Madison, Wis., 1985), p. 248; "Waddill Catchings: 25th Anniversary Report, Harvard Class of 1901, Harvard University Alumni Records, pp. 124–26; Gabler, *An Empire of Their Own,* pp. 132–38.

56.   Edwards, *The Evolution of Financial Capitalism,* pp. 229–31.

57.   For description of this mart and on Field's expansion, see *The Shield,* employee magazine, vol. 1 (September 1931), pp. 5–6, MFA; and "The Cathedral of All Stores," *Fortune Magazine* (1936), pp. 78–87, 134–41, copy in MFA.

58.   On branch expansion, see *HBR* 6 (October 1927): 81–89; "Department Store Branches in Suburbs Succeed, Multiply," *Business Week* (October 1, 1930), p. 10; and on the Saks branch in Chicago, see *MRSW* 66 (February 1930): 18.

59.   Joseph Appel, "Analysis of the Situation," internal memorandum "written . . . in 1928, at the time of Rodman Wanamaker's death," p. 8, WA.

60.   On Gimbels, see *MRSW* 59 (December 1926): 22; on Hudson's, see *PRL* (Second November Issue, 1927): 10; and on Bamberger's, see *DGE* (August 5, 1922), p. 14; *DGE* (November 18, 1922), p. 108.

61.   Oral interview with Fred Lazarus, Jr., by Edward Edwin, CUOHP, Records of the Federated Department Store Company, pp. 118, 122, 147–48.

62.   On Macy's, see *WWD* (January 4, 1928), p. 8; *WWD* (April 18, 1928); Murphy, *Merchandising Through Mergers,* p. 106; *DGE* (February 18, 1922), p. 32. On volume of sales surpassing all others by the early thirties, see *Fortune Magazine* (October 1936) and *MRSW* (November 1936): 4. On the doubling of

Macy's store size in 1923, see *MRSW* (March 1923): 20. On the Straus acquisition of the entire block and store doubling again, see *NYT* (September 13, 1929), p. 31, and *NYT* (September 28, 1930), p. 16. On sales volume and comparison to the early store, see Ralph Hower, *History of Macy's in New York, 1858–1919* (Cambridge, Mass., 1967; orig. pub. 1943), pp. 398–400.

63.   Dwight MacDonald to Dinsmore Wheeler (April 12, 1928), quoted in Robert Cummings, "The Education of Dwight MacDonald, 1906–1928: A Biographical Study," Ph.D. diss., Stanford University (1988), pp. 238–39. On the intellectuals' envy of institutional power, see Christopher Lasch, *The New Radicalism in America [1889–63]: The Intellectual as Social Type* (New York, 1965).

64.   On cooperative shopping news in Boston, Cleveland, Chicago, and Phila-delphia, see *WWD* (May 24, 1928), p. 16; Alfred Lief, *Family Business: A Century in the Life and Times of Strawbridge and Clothier* (New York, 1968), p. 178; *PRL* (September issue, 1927): 1; and "How The *Chicago Shopping News* Was Started," interview with Field's advertising manager, G. R. Schaeffer, "Lloyd Lewis Inter-views," MFA. On cooperative advertising and fashion activities, see *MRSW* 55 (November 1924): 36; and on "mutual protection" groups, see *PRL* (March 7, 1923): 7. On common delivery, see PRL (December 1928): 8, and *PRL* (First October Issue, 1927): 1. On simultaneous window displays, see *MRSW* 61 (Sep-tember 1927): 24.

65.   On the founding of the AMC and the RRA, see Fred Lazarus, Jr., oral interview by Edwin Edwards, pp. 110–12.

66.   Memorandum from LK to "Merchandise Organization" (December 10, 1925), attached to letter from Paul Nystrom (director of the AMC) to LK (January 7, 1926), file Nystrom, Box 84, LKP. On medium-size combines, see *WWD* (May 6, 1928), p. 1; on Mandels' chain, see *MRSW* 64 (March 1929): 47; on Macy's and Bamberger's, see Macy's, "Executive Council Minutes" (October 2, 1929), MA; on history of RRA (and AMC), see Kenneth Dameron, "Cooperative Retail Buying of Apparel Goods," *HBR* 6 (July 1928): 443–56; David R. Falk, "Central Buying by Department Store Mergers," *HBR* 7 (January 1930): 265–71; and Paul Nystrom to LK (January 19, 1926), file Nystrom, Box 84, LKP. "We met the buying power of the chain stores by group buying," A. Lincoln Filene said in 1928. "We did not create group buying—it was created for us." Quoted in *WWD* (February 26, 1928), p. 5.

67.   LK to PM (June 3, 1921), Box 28, file AMC-Federated, LKP.

68.   On Field's, see *Toy World* 3 (July 1929): 54; *PRL* (January 2, 1924): 4; and William Nevin to Thomas A. Hayes of Field's (October 29, 1925), folder on JW, WA. On Gimbels, see *DGE* (July 1, 1922); *PRL* (Second December Issue, 1925): 4, and *PRL* (First March Issue, 1926): 4. On the national chains, see Murphy, *Merchandising Through Mergers*, pp. 40–41, and *PRL* (January 17, 1923): 12. On Macy's expansion, see "Correspondence, confidential reports, and other memo-randa on expansion into Reading and Easton, Pennsylvania; Cumberland, Mary-land; and other cities of similar size, 1921," RG 63, MA; D. F. Kelly (general manager of Mandel's; re Rothschild's) to Jesse I. Straus (July 7 and October 18, 1921), "Store Expansion Correspondence," RG 63, MA; Margaret Case Harriman,

And the Price Is Right (New York, 1957), p. 113; and on LaSalle and Koch, see *NYT* (January 1, 1924), p. 8.

69. For biographical materials on these men, see Harris, *Merchant Princes*, pp. 17–32, 338–39.

70. Ibid., p. 338.

71. Robert Hendrickson, *The Grand Emporiums: The Illustrated History of America's Great Department Stores* (New York, 1979), p. 75.

72. Fred Lazarus, Jr., quoted in oral interview by Edward Edwin (1965), CUOHP, pp. 44–45.

73. Ibid., p. 239.

74. For acquisitions of Shillito and R. H. White, see Lazarus oral interview, p. 40; *MRSW* 63 (December 1928): 68, and *PRL* (First December Issue 1928): 29. For Lincoln Kirstein on his father, see Harris, *Merchant Princes*, p. 32.

75. On stock purchases, see LK to C. O. Cooper and Co. (March 4, 1921), file "C. O. Cooper Store," no.75f.6, LKP; J. J. Kaplan to E. J. Frost (May 25, 1920), LKP; and Ruth Alley (secretary to PM; re Lane Bryant) to LK (March 25, 1925), PM file, Box 38, LKP.

76. PM to LK (June 9, 1921), Box 38, LKP.

77. PM to LK (October 14, 1918), LKP; LK to PM (November 5, 1918), LKP; author's interview with Mrs. Paul Mazur, New York City (June 5, 1988); *Who's Who in America*, vol. 29 (1956–57), pp. 1661–62.

78. PM to LK, undated (but probably 1920), letterhead "Oil Issues Company," LKP.

79. PM, "Report of the First Year's Operation of Belmont Stores Corporation" (August 24, 1922), file 588, PM, Herbert Lehman Papers, Columbia University Library, pp. 11–12.

80. Lehman Brothers, *A Centennial: Lehman Brothers, 1850–1950* (New York, 1950), p. 46.

81. LK to Fred Lazarus (March 11, 1925), LKP; and, on his chairmanship, see LK to Robert Armory (February 19, 1923), LKP.

82. James A. Bowie, *Education for Business Management* (Oxford, Eng., 1930), p. 103.

83. *The Journal of Retailing*, New York University (October 1929): 27; Bowie, *Education for Business Management*, pp. 107–11.

84. Transcript of interview with Howard B. Meek, Statler Hotel School, Cornell, by Sharon Carroll (September 1964), Cornell University Archives, pp. 24, 45, 55; Morris Bishop, *A History of Cornell* (Ithaca, N.Y., 1962), pp. 482–83.

85. On curriculum in day and night schools, see *NYU School for Retailing Bulletin* (1923–24), pp. 26–29; on enrollments, see *The School of Retailing Bulletin*

(October 1928), pp. 1–3; on creation of graduate school, see "Memorandum Re: School of Retailing" (October 18, 1922) and "Minutes of Luncheon Meeting of the Executive Committee of the New York University School of Retailing in the Executive Offices of R. H. Macy and Co., Inc. (January 18, 1922), p. 2, NYUA; and on employment placement in city stores, see *The Journal of Retailing* (hereafter *JR*) 1 (October 1925): 23; *JR* 2 (October 1926): 23; and *JR* 3 (October 1927): 29.

86.   On this gift, see *NYT* (June 5, 1929), Folder 6, NYUA; on his chairmanship, see *JR* 2 (April 1926): 2; and on the meetings of the executive committee at Macy's, see "Minutes of Luncheon Meeting of the Executive Committee of the New York University School of Retailing in the Executive Offices of R. H. Macy and Co., Inc." (November 29, 1921–October 14, 1932), NYUA.

87.   "Extract from Report of the Visiting Committee, Harvard Business School (Draft)" (1922), Box 25, "Harvard Business School, 1921–30," LKP. The report also read that "this is a so-called capitalistic country and not a socialistic country. If property—that is, capital—is protected and properly managed, we believe many other problems such as the so-called 'labor question' will gradually diminish in importance. . . . 'Big business' as at present conducted is one of the greatest factors in the nation for the development of citizenship and leadership, is a great Americanizing force and out of it will come many of the future leaders of the country."

88.   Samuel E. Morison, *Three Centuries of Harvard, 1636–1936* (Cambridge, Mass., 1936), pp. 471–72; on Baker's relationship to Morgan, see Ron Chernow, *The House of Morgan*, p. 143.

89.   Melvin Copeland, *And Mark an Era* (Cambridge, Mass., 1958), p. 255.

90.   For an indication of the school's relationship to commerce, see the changing curriculum in the Index to School Correspondence (1919–45), HBS.

91.   LK to R. C. Hudson of O'Neill and Co., Baltimore (March 12, 1925), LKP.

92.   Melvin Copeland to Lew Hahn (April 23, 1921), HBS.

93.   Donald David to Percy Straus (January 28, 1921), HBS.

94.   Lew Hahn to PM (August 6, 1924): "I should explain to you that our Association for some years now has supplied funds for the use of Harvard in making an entirely independent study each year of operating costs in department stores." (Mazur file, LKP). And Donald David (assistant dean) to PS (December 13, 1920): "It was exceedingly kind of you to make the suggestion that Macy's would be willing to join with others to underwrite the finances of the Bureau" (HBS).

95.   Joseph P. Kennedy, ed., *The Story of Films* (Chicago, 1927), p. xiii.

96.   LK to Dean Walter Donham (July 9, 1924), LKP.

97.   Robert R. Locke, "Business Education in Germany: Past Systems and Current Practice," *Business History Review* 59 (Summer 1985): 232–53; Locke, *The End of Practical Man: The End of the Practical Man, Entrepreneurship and Higher Education in Germany, France, and Great Britain, 1880–1942* (London, 1984), pp. 110–11.

98.   Copeland, *And Mark an Era*, p. 278; for recent MBA enrollment figures in Europe and the United States, see *NYT* (May 29, 1991), p. D1 and *NYT* (June 30, 1991), p. F5. Cambridge University in England had no M.B.A. program until October 1991.

99.   PM, "Future Development in Retailing," *HBR* 2 (July 1924): 434–46.

100.   PM, quoted in *PRL* (Second February Issue, 1927): 1; "Is the Cost of Distribution Too High?," *HBR* 4 (October 1925): 5–6.

101.   Lew Hahn to PM (August 6, 1924), Mazur file, LKP. On the debate aroused by the essay, see *DGE* (July 12, 1924).

102.   See newspaper clipping, *Fourth Estate*, a Wall Street paper, in PM to LK (October 26, 1926), LKP.

103.   Donald David to Lew Hahn (June 9, 1925), Mazur file, LKP.

104.   Donald David to PM (June 15, 1925), LKP.

105.   PM, *Principles of Organization Applied to Modern Retailing* (New York, 1927), pp. 2–3, 6–7, 31–33, 67.

106.   Ibid., pp. 8, 33.

107.   PM, *American Prosperity: Its Causes and Consequences* (New York, 1928), pp. 24–25, 224–25.

108.   PM, "Memorandum on Retail Research Consolidation" (May 1, 1925), LKP; PM to A. Lincoln Filene (March 26, 1924, and December 23, 1924), LKP.

109.   LK to A. Lincoln Filene (July 12, 1929), Box 65, "Correspondence with Lincoln Filene," LKP.

110.   Ibid.

111.   PM, oral interview by Edward Edwin (January 14, 1965), CUOHP, p. 57; Kirstein to Filene (July 12, 1929), LKP.

112.   On the growth of Wall Street, see Alexander Dana Noyes, *The Market Place: Reminiscences of a Financial Editor* (Boston, 1938), pp. 53–54; Matthew Josephson, *The Money Lords: The Great Finance Capitalists, 1925–1950* (New York, 1972), pp. 1–2, 53; Harold G. Moulton, *Financial Organization and the Economic System* (New York, 1938), pp. 212–14; and Robert Sobel, *The Great Bull Market: Wall Street in the 1920s* (New York, 1968), pp. 30–35.

113.   Martin Mayer, *Madison Avenue, U.S.A.* (New York, 1957), p. 6; the Fifth Avenue Association, *Bulletin* (September 1930): 1.

114.   M.D.C. Crawford, *The Ways of Fashion* (New York, 1943), p. 264.

115.   On the buying agencies, see Kenneth Dameron, "Cooperative Retail Buying of Apparel Goods," *HBR* 6 (July 1928): 444; on the number of factories in 1921, see "New Garment Center Reflects Power of Cooperative Effort in Industry," *DGE* (June 18, 1921), p. 112. On the general economic purpose of the district, see Crawford, *The Ways of Fashion*; American Guide Series, *New York City Guide*

(New York, 1970), pp. 160–62; Florence S. Richards, *The Ready-to-Wear Industry, 1900–1950* (New York, 1951), pp. 9, 22; New York University Graduate School of Public Administration, *The Garment Center: A Design Proposal* (New York, 1966), p. 111; Jeannette A. Jarnow and Beatrice Judelle, *Inside the Fashion Business* (New York, 1964); and Murray Sices, *Seventh Avenue* (New York, 1953).

116.   Crawford, *The Ways of Fashion*, pp. 264–65.

117.   Ibid., p. 165; *New York City Guide*, pp. 160–61.

118.   On the evolution of luxury in Western thought, see John Sekora, *Luxury: The Concept in Western Thought, Eden to Smollett* (Baltimore, 1977); and Carle C. Zimmerman, *Consumption and Standards of Living* (New York, 1936), pp. 278–305.

119.   Edwin R. A. Seligman, *The Economics of Installment Selling*, vol. 1 (New York, 1927), pp. 218–20.

120.   Samuel Strauss, *American Opportunity* (New York, 1935), pp. 156–62. This is not to say, however, that the debate over luxury disappeared. See, for competing positions, "The Appraisal of Luxuries," in *American Standards and Planes of Living*, Thomas D. Eliot, ed. (New York, 1931), pp. 427–68.

121.   Seligman, *The Economics of Installment Selling*, p. 221.

122.   See on the "living wage," John Ryan, *The Living Wage* (New York, 1906); on the interchangeability of these terms in early literature, see Zimmerman, *Consumption and Standards of Living*, pp. 462–65.

123.   On the history and character of the standard of living as a concept, see Zimmerman, *Consumption and the Standards of Living*, pp. 278–478.

124.   Chicago Standard Budget, Table XXXIX, "Cost of Minimum Requirements for the Necessities of Life by Individual Members of Families," quoted in Paul Nystrom, *Economic Principles of Consumption* (New York, 1929), p. 208. The quotations here also come from Nystrom, pp. 54–56. See also Hazel Kyrk, *A Theory of Consumption* (New York, 1923); Thomas D. Eliot, ed., *Introduction to American Standards of Living and Planes of Living* (Boston, 1931); L.L. Bernard, "Standards and Planes of Living," *Social Forces*, vol. 7 (1928): pp. 190–202; Werner Sombart, *Why Is There No Socialism in the United States?* (New York, 1976; orig. pub. 1906), esp. pp. 58–114; Robert and Helen Lynd, *Middletown* (New York, 1929); and Seligman, *The Economics of Installment Selling*, pp. 214–20.

125.   Thomas D. Eliot, ed., "American Standards and Planes of Living," in Introduction, p. 11.

126.   William Graham Sumner and Albert Galloway Keller, *The Science of Society* (New Haven, 1927), vol. I, pp. 71–79; and Edward Devine, *The Normal Life* (New York, 1917), pp. 1–8, 193–94. These sources are also cited in Eliot, ed., *Introduction to American Standards*, which supplies an excellent overview of the debate on the standard of living up to 1930.

127.   Zimmerman, *Consumption and Standards of Living*, pp. 136, 285, 563–64; and Eliot, ed., "American Standards and Planes of Living," pp. 13–14.

128.   Zimmerman, *Consumption and Standards of Living*, pp. 477–78, 567. Although Zimmerman wrote this book in 1936, many of his ideas had earlier been developed in his *Principles of Rural-Urban Sociology* (New York, 1929), which he co-wrote with Peter Sorokin. For a brief discussion of Zimmerman, see Christopher Lasch, *Haven in a Heartless World* (New York, 1977), pp.44–49. Lasch here compares Zimmerman unfavorably to sociologist Willard Waller who, unlike the "conservative" Zimmerman, espoused a "leftist position that harked back to Veblen and the best of populism" (p.50). But Zimmerman, too, owed a great deal to Veblen and to populism, as the 1936 book shows.

129.   Zimmerman, *Consumption and Standards of Living*, pp. 564, 580.

130.   Ibid, p.580.

131.   On the increased number of securities dealers in the twenties, see Ronald Chernow, *The House of Morgan*, p. 303; and for the 1990 figures on securities dealers and brokers, see Grace Toto, ed., *The Security Industry of the '80s*, SIA Fact Book (New York, 1990), p. 6.

132.   On numbers in credit agencies, see *PRL* (January 17, 1923): 12; and on the ad agencies, see William Leiss et al., *Social Communication in Advertising* (London, 1986), pp. 82–84, 97–145.

133.   Herbert Hoover, *The New Day: Campaign Speeches of Herbert Hoover, 1926* (Palo Alto, Calif., 1928), p. 82; and "Service Industries Creating Occupations for Men Replaced by Machinery," *DC* 2 (October 23, 1928): 1: "Since 1920 our factories have decreased their employees by more than 900,000." At the same time, due to the production of "automobiles, radios, telephones, motion pictures, and other contributions to comfort," a new group of workers have appeared—"more than 1,280,000 men . . . as chauffeurs or truck drivers," servicemen of automobiles, and repairmen for "electric refrigerators, oil heaters, and similar household appliances."

Chapter 10

1.   Helen Landon Cass, *PRL* (June 6, 1923): 6.

2.   Evans Clark, *Financing the Consumer* (New York, 1930), pp. 27–30.

3.   Rolf Nugent, *Consumer Credit and Economic Stability* (New York, 1939), p. 101.

4.   Ibid.

5.   "A Big Store's Advertising," *MRSW* 47 (November 1920): 5, 48; *MRSW* 79 (November 1936): 3.

6.   These percentages were reported by Alfred W. Miles, vice president of Best and Company, to NRA hearings in 1934; see "Proceeding—Hearing in the Matter of a Complaint Filed with the Retail Code Authority—City of New York by Best and Co., Inc., against R. H. Macy and Co., Inc." (April 2, 1934), NRA Transcripts of Hearings, Box 7289, Record Group 69, NA.

7. Nugent, *Consumer Credit*, p. 100.

8. Ibid., p. 96.

9. Evans, *Financing the Consumer*, pp. 212–13.

10. Daniel Bloomfield, manager of the Boston Retail Board of Trade, "Customer Returns of Merchandise Great Economic Waste," address before the NRDGA, New York City (February 6, 1929), Records of the BFDC, RG 151, file 751, "Conventions—NRDGA," NA.

11. Retail Trade Board, Boston Chamber of Commerce, "Report on Returned Merchandise," BFDC, RG 151, General Records, 402.300, "Domestic Commerce—Retail—Returned Merchandise," NA.

12. *DC* (Department of Commerce publication) (July 29, 1929), p. 45.

13. Bloomfield, "Customer Returns of Merchandise."

14. Grover Whalen, *Report of the Proceedings of the 12th Annual Controllers' Congress of the NRDGA*, Washington, D.C., May 25–28, 1931 (New York, 1931), pp. 265–66.

15. "Analysis and Control of Returns," *DC* (April 29, 1929), p. 7.

16. William Wales, assistant professor of merchandising, New York University School of Retailing, to Gordon James, Domestic Commerce Division (May 9, 1929), file 402.300, "Domestic Commerce—Retail—Returned Merchandise, 1925–27," Box 1956, RG 151, NA.

17. *NYT* (March 20, 1927), pt. II, p. 4; *NYT* (January 30, 1928), p. 25.

18. Adolph Zukor, "Influence of the Motion Picture," in *Broadway: The Grand Canyon of American Business* (New York, 1926), pp. 109–14.

19. "Market for Air Conditioning," *DC* (December 10, 1937), p. 311.

20. B. Franklin Miller, "Creating Indoor Weather," *The Journal of Retailing*, New York University 5 (April 1929): 21.

21. "Cool Shopping in Summer Is Macy Leaf from Movies," *NYT* (March 31, 1929), pt. II, p. 16; on other stores, see *MRSW* (August 1934): 26 and *MRSW* (October 1934): 15.

22. Herbert Hoover, "Advertising Is a Vital Force in Our National Life" repr. in *Advertising World* 30 (August 1925): 1–2; *PRL* (Second May Issue, 1925): 7.

23. Daniel Pope, *The Making of Modern Advertising* (New York, 1983), pp. 180–81.

24. Constance Rourke, *Charles Scheeler* (New York, 1938), p. 117.

25. Edward Bernays, *Biography of an Idea: Memoirs of Public Relations Counsel Edward L. Bernays* (New York, 1962), pp. 306–7.

26. Douglas Allan and Douglas Allan, Sr., with foreword by Paul Horgan and introduction by Richard Layton, *N. C. Wyeth: The Collected Paintings, Illustra-*

tions, and Murals (New York, 1972), pp. 161, 171. Wyeth did his first commercial mural, *Moods*, for the Hotel Utica Corporation, painting four large panels of American Indians in the different seasons of the year (*Indian Fisherman, Indian Fighter*, and so on), for the grillroom of the Hotel Utica, p. 157.

27. Ring Lardner used "Urbanesque" as a word to signify luxury; see "The Love Nest," in *The Best Short Stories of Ring Lardner* (New York, 1957), p. 168.

28. Howard Mandelbaum and Eric Myers, *Screen Deco* (New York, 1985), pp. 139–40.

29. Otto Teegan, "Joseph Urban's Philosophy of Color," Deems Taylor, "The Scenic Art of Joseph Urban," and Teegan, "Joseph Urban," *Architecture* 69 (May 1934): 258, 272, 256. See also Otto Teegan, lead typescript in collection catalog, Urban Papers, Butler Library, Columbia University.

30. Joseph Urban and Thomas Lamb, "The Ziegfeld Theater, New York," *Good Furniture* 46 (May 1927): 415–19; *Arts and Decoration* 21 (January 1927): 43, clipping in scrapbook, Urban portfolio no. 37, pt. 2, Urban Papers; and Ely J. Kahn, "The Ziegfeld Theater," *The Architectural Record* 61 (May 1927): 385–93.

31. Thomas Hibben, ed., "An Exhibition of the Mural Paintings of Boardman Robinson" (New York: The Gallery of the Art Students' League, New York City, 1929), Publicity Department, Kaufmann's Department Store, Pittsburgh, Pa.

32. Lloyd Goodrich, "Mural Paintings of Boardman Robinson," *The Arts* 16 (February 1930): 390–93, 498; Albert Christ-Janer, *Boardman Robinson* (Chicago: University of Chicago Press, 1946), pp. 15–31, 52.

33. Bureau of Labor Statistics, U.S. Department of Labor, "Productivity of Labor in the Glass Industry" (Washington, D.C., 1927), p. 170; Warren C. Scoville, *Revolution in Glassmaking* (Cambridge, Mass., 1948), p. 259.

34. "National Back to School Week," *MRSW* 69 (July 1931): 31.

35. Frederick Kiesler, *Contemporary Art Applied to the Store and Its Display* (New York, 1930), pp. 80, 82; "Productivity of Labor in the Glass Industry," p. 15.

36. "Mannikins Featured at Macy's," *MRSW* 61 (October 1927): 76; *MRSW* 61 (November 1927): 66; *WWD* (December 24, 1927), p. 17.

37. "Notes from New York," *MRSW* 61 (July 1927): 30; Kiesler, *Contemporary Art*, p. 103.

38. *DW* 3 (October 1923): 49. See also on Fraser, author interview with Dana O'Clare, displayman at Lord & Taylor in the 1930s (June 11, 1985); Arthur Fraser, "Lloyd Lewis Interviews," MFA; *MRSW* 79 (November 1936): 3.

39. Cecily Staples, *DW* 49 (August 1946): 90.

40. Quoted in Leonard Marcus, *The American Store Window* (Chicago, 1979), pp. 20–21.

41. On the spread of "modernist marketing" from the 1920s, see James Sloan

Allen, *The Romance of Commerce and Culture: Capitalism, Modernism, and the Chicago-Aspen Crusade for Cultural Reform* (Chicago, 1983), pp. 1–76.

42.   Kiesler, *Contemporary Art*, pp. 24–25.

43.   Lee Simonson, *Journal of The American Institute of Architects* 15 (July 1927): 231.

44.   Kenneth Reid, *Masters of Design* (New York, 1937), pp. 3–6; Norman Bel Geddes, *Miracle in the Evening: An Autobiography* (New York, 1960), pp. 10–92.

45.   Bel Geddes, *Miracle*, pp. 160–63.

46.   Norman Bel Geddes, *Horizons* (New York, 1932, 1977), p. 6.

47.   Norman Bel Geddes, "The Store Window a Stage; Merchandise the Actors," *WWD* (November 19, 1927), p. 1. This piece became the basis for Bel Geddes's more extended discussion of window display in *Horizons*, pp. 259–71.

48.   Bel Geddes, *Horizons*, p. 261.

49.   *WWD* (November 19, 1927), pp. 1–2, 18; *MRSW* 61 (July 1927): 33; *MRSW* 61 (October 1927): 30–31; *MRSW* 63 (July 1928): 44; Bel Geddes, *Miracle*, pp. 160, 259–67, 278–93, and *Horizons*, pp. 259–71.

50.   *WWD* (November 26, 1927), p. 1; *MRSW* 55 (August 1925): 12.

51.   Johan Huizinga, *America*, trans. with introduction and notes by Herbert Rowen (New York, 1972; orig. pub. 1927), pp. 232–33.

52.   On style changes, see *PRL* (First May Issue, 1928); Estelle Hamburger, *It's a Woman's Business* (New York, 1939), pp. 240–56. On the importance of style in advertising and industry, see Roland Marchand, *Advertising the American Dream: Making Way for Modernity, 1920–1940* (Berkeley, Calif., 1985), pp. 122–49; and Jeffrey Meikle, *Twentieth Century Limited: Industrial Design in America, 1925–1939* (Philadelphia, 1983).

53.   John Robert Powers, *The Power Girls: The Story of Models and Modeling* (New York, 1941), pp. 19–21, 23.

54.   For the 1923 figure, see "An Almost Perfect Thirty-Four," *Saturday Evening Post*, November 10, 1923: 22; and, for the 1930 figure, see John B. Kennedy, "Model Maids," *Collier's*, February 8, 1930: 61.

55.   Quoted in Kennedy, "Model Maids": 61.

56.   Powers, *The Power Girls*, pp. 21, 23–24, 45; Clyde M. Dessner, *So You Want to Be a Model* (Chicago, 1943), pp. 29, 80.

57.   "*Modes and Manners*—a New Magazine," J. Walter Thompson, *News Letter* 1 (January 17, 1924): 1–2, J. Walter Thompson Archives; *Business Week* (May 20, 1931), p. 13. On Bamberger's *Charm* magazine, see John E. O'Connor and Charles F. Cummings, "Bamberger's Department Store, *Charm* Magazine, and the Culture of Consumption in New Jersey, 1924–1932," *New Jersey History* 101 (Fall/Winter 1984): 1–33.

58. *Modes and Manners* (February 1925): 5; *Modes and Manners* (June 1924): 11–17.

59. *Amos Parrish Magazine* (hereafter APM) (June 1928): 11; *APM* (April 1925): 1; *APM* (January 1926): 13; *APM* (June 1928): 6; *WWD* (February 8, 1928); Elizabeth Hawes, *Fashion Is Spinach* (New York, 1938), p. 113; *MRSW* 69 (December 1931): 37.

60. *APM* (February 1929), p. 11; *APM* (August 28, 1928), pp. 8–9.

61. Elaine Jabenis, *The Fashion Director: What She Does and How to Be One* (New York, 1972), p. 371.

62. *WWD* (February 3, 1928): 1–2; *HBR* 1 (October 1927): 93.

63. *PRL* (First December Issue, 1926): 9; Frances Fisher Dubuc, "Women Wanted by Department Stores," *The Saturday Evening Post*, no. 200 (June 23, 1928): 130, 132, 134.

64. On Rose Van Sant, see *MRSW* 66 (January 1930): 43 and *Retailing* (July 31, 1933): 5; on Polly Pettit, see *MRSW* 64 (February 1929): 58 and *MRSW* 78 (April 1936): 32.

65. Frances Anne Allen, "Lady Buyers," *The American Mercury* 8 (February 1928): 138–44.

66. Julia Coburn, oral interview conducted by Mid Semple (April 30, 1984), p. 11, transcript in possession of author; Jabenis, *The Fashion Director*, p. 33. See also Estelle Hamburger, *It's a Woman's Business* (New York, 1939), p. 211; *WWD* (December 6, 1927): 1; *MRSW* 75 (February 1935): 30; and *Sheldon's Retail Trade in the United States* (New York, 1924), pp. 1–9.

67. Quoted in *MRSW* 69 (August 1931): 40.

68. Quoted in *PRL* (Second February Issue, 1927): 1.

69. SC, "The Magic of Color," a paper given before the Annual Meeting of the Textile Color Card Association of the United States (February 18, 1925), repr. in *The Brooklyn Museum Quarterly* (April 1925), SC; the Textile Color Card Association to Stewart Culin (April 20, 1928), SCP. See also "Color Standardization," *DGE* (April 13, 1918): 33; "Color Cards Help Sell Through Correct Matching," *DGE* (March 11, 1922): 24; "1933 Spring Hosiery Colors," *MRSW* 72 (January 1933): 17; "World Color Chart Urged as Trade Aid," *WWD* (July 20, 1928): 6; and *WWD* (February 25, 1926): 1.

70. On the show at Marshall Field's, see "1922 Arts and Industries Exhibit—Retail," the Field's scrapbook, Publicity XB-1, MFA.

71. William H. Baldwin, "Modern Art and the Machine Age," *The Independent* (July 9, 1927): 39; and "Art in Trade Glorified by Macy's," *The Bulletin (May 1927)*, exposition publicity, MA.

72. Repard Leirum, *The New Yorker* (May 14, 1927), Macy's scrapbook, MA.

73.   Macy's advertisement, *The New York Times* (May 28, 1928), Macy's scrapbook, MA.

74.   *The New York Times* (May 13, 1928), Macy's scrapbook, MA.

75.   On all these stores, see *WWD* (March 3, 1928): 1–2; *MRSW* 63 (November 1928): 7 and 63 (March 1928): 119; and N. C. Sanford, "An International Exhibit of Modern Art," *Good Furniture Magazine* (July 1928), Macy's scrapbook, MA.

76.   Richard Bach to Henry Kent (August 16, 1927), reported on the "season's work," "Bach, Richard F.," Correspondence, etc., relating to the Industrial Arts," Archives of the Metropolitan Museum of Art, New York City (hereafter MMAA); Mayor W. Freeland Kendrick to Henry Kent (June 27, 1927), "Bach, Richard F." Ellis Gimbel to Henry Kent (June 23, 1927), "Bach, Richard F." On the competition among museums, fairs, and department stores over which institution was most influencing public taste in the twenties, see Neil Harris, "Museums, Merchandising, and Popular Taste: The Struggle for Influence," in *Material Culture and the Study of American Life*, ed. Ian G. Quimby (New York, 1978), pp. 140–74.

77.   Metropolitan Museum of Art, attendance figures (1917–1929), file, "Exhibitions—Manufacturers and Designers," MMAA; for list of participants, catalog, "Sixth Exhibition of American Industrial Art" (January 15–February 26, 1922), MMAA; and Richard Bach, "Manufacturers, Merchants, and the Museum of Art," copy of article written for Marshall Field's *Fashions of the Hour*, in "Bach, Richard F.," MMAA. See also on Bach, Jay Cantor, "Art and Industry: Reflections on the Role of the American Museum in Encouraging Innovation in the Decorative Arts," ed. Ian Quimby and Polly Ann Earl in *Technological Innovation in the Decorative Arts* (Winterthur, Del., 1973): 332–54.

78.   Author interview with Marjorie Pleshette, buyer at Macy's and Bonwit Teller's in the 1930s (May 6, 1985).

79.   Samuel Reyburn, quoted in *The Independent* (a contemporary feminist magazine for businesswomen) (December 1924), p. 1; and for the best published sketch of Shaver's life, see Allene Talmey, "Dorothy Shaver of Lord & Taylor, Unorthodox Store Strategist," *Vogue* (February 1, 1946), Dorothy Shaver Papers, Costume Division, National Museum of American History, Washington, D.C.

80.   Talmey, "Dorothy Shaver."

81.   Quoted in *The Christian Science Monitor* (July 28, 1931) and in *Retailing* (February 14, 1931), newspaper clippings, Shaver Papers; and Mildred Custin to Dorothy Shaver (April 23, 1958), Shaver Papers.

82.   Stanley McCandless to Dorothy Shaver (March 10, 1928), Shaver Papers; Helen Appleton Read, "An Exposition of Modern French Decorative Art," vol. 6, scrapbook, Shaver Papers.

83.   Jeanne Perkins, "No. 1 Career Woman," *Life* (May 12, 1947), transcript in Shaver Papers, vol. 6; Edward L. Bernays, *Biography of an Idea: Memoirs of Public Relations Counsel Edward L. Bernays* (New York, 1962), p. 225; Shaver, quoted by Florence Yoder Wilson, "That Elusive Thing Called 'In Style' " (1931), p. 16,

in Shaver Papers; and Shaver, transcript talk given in the mid-1930s, vol. 3, Shaver Papers. On "closer alignment," see *WWD* (March 3, 1928): 1. And on the 1925 modernistic room, see Dorothy Shaver, "Principles and Practices in the Decorating Service of a Retailer," *House and Garden* (February 1928): 7, scrapbook on the Exposition of Modern French Decorative Art, Shaver Papers. On the showing of the "first ensembles," see Read, "An Exposition," scrapbook, Shaver Papers.

84.   Albert Camus, quoted in R. Jeffrey Lustig, *Corporate Liberalism: The Origins of Modern American Political Theory, 1890–1920* (Berkeley, Calif., 1982), p. 46; and Dorothy Shaver, "Excerpts from Miss Dorothy Shaver's Broadcast over the Radio on . . . 'Clothes are Really Different This Spring?' " (1937), transcript, Shaver Papers.

85.   Priscilla Whiley to Dorothy Shaver (March 2, 1928), Shaver Papers.

86.   For Adler quote, see *PRL* (July 16, 1924): 5; and also, on Adler, see "Growth of Color Interest," *Color News* 2 (June 1925): 5. On the NRDGA committee, see *DC* (August 10, 1930): 45; and on the Filene colorscope, see "Color Notes," *Color News* 1 (1924): 20.

87.   *MRSW* 56 (January 1925): 1. The quote belongs to Charles Morton, displayman for Weinstock, Lubin (Sacramento, Calif). For the Woodward and Lothrop ad, see *The Washington Evening Star* (December 12, 1921): 15.

88.   Clare Wilson, "Lloyd Lewis Interviews" (1946), MA.

89.   *DW* 3 (August 23, 1913): 7; *PRL* 28 (April 1933): 10.

90.   "Wanamaker Rearranges Old Stewart Store to Facilitate Buying and Selling," *DGE* (October 15, 1921): 47. "The changes which have taken place," this article says of New York's Wanamaker's, "have been largely in the nature of rearrangement of departments to accomplish a definite end—consolidating and correlating departments in such a way as to make both buying and selling easier."

91.   The museum fostered the current fashion for "American Colonial" by granting special morning tours to merchants and buyers; one winter morning in 1925, an army of Macy's buyers trooped through the "new addition under expert guidance." See *Sparks* (the Macy's employee magazine), vol. 7 (February 1925), p. 7; on the American Wing, see Marshall B. Davidson and Elizabeth Stillinger, *The American Wing at the Metropolitan Museum of Art* (New York, 1985).

92.   "L. Bamberger and Co. Build Ideal Home," *Decorative Furnisher* 44 (April 1923): 91; "Nottingham House, Demonstration House Furnished by Bamberger's Newark," *Good Furniture Magazine* 29 (August 1927): 54. On Macy's executive council decision, see "Minutes of the Executive Council," (February 20, 1924), MA.

93.   "All Glass Room," *NYT* (May 8, 1928), in Macy's album, "International Exposition of Art in Industry," MA. On Weber's rooms, see photograph no. 11 in Macy's album, and "Art in Industry Exposition at R. H. Macy and Co.," *House Furnishing Review* (June 1928), Macy's scrapbook, MA.

94.   Quoted in J. Walter Thompson and Co., *News Letter* 1 (February 6, 1924):

1–2; *MRSW* (1924) (see notebook 33); and "The Minutes of the Executive Council" (December 22, 1927), MA. On appointment of "interior display manager" to Lord & Taylor, see *DW* 5 (November 1924): 41.

95.   Bernays, *Biography of an Idea*, p. 77.

96.   Ibid., pp. 75, 87.

97.   Ibid., pp. 3–155.

98.   Edward L. Bernays, *Propaganda* (New York, 1928), pp. 27, 58; and Bernays, *Biography of an Idea*, pp. 155–72.

99.   Edward L. Bernays, *Crystallizing Public Opinion* (New York, 1925), pp. 14, 34, 125–26, 173; Bernays, *Biography of an Idea*, pp. 287–300; and interview with author (June 21, 1988), Cambridge, Mass.

100.   Bernays, *Crystallizing Public Opinion*, pp. 61–63, 95, 162.

101.   Bernays, *Biography of an Idea*, pp. 316–18.

102.   Ibid., p. 240; Daniel Boorstin, *The Image: A Guide to History of Pseudo-Events* (New York, 1964).

Chapter 11

1.   F. Scott Fitzgerald, "Absolution," in *Babylon Revisited and Other Stories* (New York, 1960), pp. 136–51.

2.   F. Scott Fitzgerald, *The Great Gatsby* (New York, 1925), p. 120.

3.   SC, address on the Rainbow House (December 8, 1926), typescript, SCP, Brooklyn Museum, Brooklyn, N. Y.; SC, *Art News* (December 19, 1925), Folder 6, "Extra-Museum Activities," and SC to Edward Lyman (February 16, 1926), SCP.

4.   SC to Edward Lyman (February 16, 1926), SCP; SC, *Men's Wear* (June 9, 1925), copy, SCP, and *NYT* (August 7, 1927), p. 23.

5.   John Wanamaker and Co., "The Sesquicentennial International Exposition" (Philadelphia, 1926), pp. 3–33, WA.

6.   F. Christopher Meyer, "Wherein Will Be Glorified the Things of Dress," *The Sesquicentennial Newsogram* 1 (December 1925): 12–13, SCP; on the architectural style, see *Sesquicentennial News Bulletin* 3 (June 1, 1926–December 1, 1926): 1, SCP.

7.   *Sesquicentennial News Bulletin* 1 (June 1–December 1, 1926), SCP; Ben Howe, director of the Fashion Exposition, to SC (February 18, 1926), memorandum on the exposition, in "Extra-Museum Activities," Folder 6 (1925–26), SCP; *The Philadelphia Inquirer* (November 24, 1925), scrapbook, textiles, SCP.

8.   *WWD* (December 7, 1925), scrapbook, textiles, SCP.

9.   SC to Ben Howe (October 21, 1925), Folder 6 (1925), "Extra-Museum Activities," Philadelphia Exposition, SCP.

10. SC, *Art News* (December 19, 1925), "Extra-Museum Activities," Folder 6, SCP.

11. For contributors, see Roy Schaeffer, advertising manager, "list of those participating in State Street Celebration," Marshall Field, MFA.

12. *Chicago Tribune* (October 15, 1926), *Chicago American* (October 8, 1926), *Chicago Herald Examiner* (October 15, 1926), and *Chicago Post* (October 15, 16, 1926)—all clippings in scrapbook, MFA.

13. Oral interview with George McAnery by Allen Nevins and Dean Albertson (1949), CUOHP, p. 94.

14. F. Scott Fitzgerald, "May Day," in *Babylon Revisited and Other Stories*, p. 25; and "May Day," Mayor's Papers, John Hylan (1918–22), Box 22, p. 332, departmental letters received, Municipal Archives, Manhattan; Grover Whalen to Reisenweber's Restaurant (April 2, 1919), Mayor's Papers, Hylan, Box 42, p. 32, file "Mayor's Committee on Welcome of Homecoming Troops," Municipal Archives; and Grover Whalen, *Mr. New York: The Autobiography of Grover Whalen* (New York, 1955), p. 82. See also Frederick Lewis Allen, *Only Yesterday* (New York, 1930), for the first description of New York's Welcome Home Celebration.

15. Oral interview with Arthur Wallender by Owen Bompard (January 1950), CUOHP, p. 14.

16. Emma Kidd Hulburt, "Every Child Needs a Playroom," *Children: The Magazine for Parents* 3 (November 1928): 45; Persis Leger, "Christmas Toys," *Child Welfare* 23 (December 1928): 184.

17. "Keynote for 1929," *Toy World* 25 (December 1928): 18; U.S. Department of Commerce, "International Trade in Toys," Trade Information Bulletin no. 449 (Washington, D.C., December 1926). For the European comparison, see Carle Zimmerman, *Consumption and Standards of Living* (New York, 1936), p. 11.

18. Laurence Hansen, "Measuring a Retail Market," Trade Information Bulletin no. 272 (Washington, D.C., October 13, 1924), p. 4.

19. *TN* 52 (June 1928): 64; *TN* 52 (August 1928): 82; *TN* 53 (January 1929): 330.

20. *TN* 53 (January 1929): 329; Joseph Jastrow, *Keeping Fit Mentally* (New York, 1928); Jastrow, *Character and Temperament* (New York, 1915).

21. For biographical material on Gruenberg, see Sidonie Gruenberg, unpublished autobiography (c. 1962), pp. 16–17, 44, 93, Box 64, Sidonie Gruenberg Papers, LC.

22. Sidonie Gruenberg, *Your Child Today and Tomorrow* (New York, 1910), pp. 32, 43–46; *Sons and Daughters* (New York, 1916), pp. 145, 235, 312; and unpublished autobiography, pp. 121–23.

23. On the performance of Baum's fairy tale, see *PRL* 21 (January 1923): 118.

24. On the Wanamaker's and Bloomingdale's shorts, see *WWD* (May 28, 1928), p. 7. On Gimbels and other store policies, see *PRL* (December 1924 Issue): 87; *PRL* (December Issue, 1925): 9; and *PRL* (First November Issue 1925): 1. On

"radio Santas," see NRDGA, *Radio Broadcasting Manual: The Radio as Publicity Medium in America* (New York, 1935), p. 43; and *Toy World* 2 (December 1928): 35.

25.   William Dean Howells, *Through the Eye of the Needle* (New York, 1907), p. 308; and Frank Weitenkampf, *Manhattan Kaleidoscope* (New York, 1947), p. 11.

26.   "Parading Thanksgiving Ragamuffins Except Out Where City Subway Lines End," *NYT* (November 28, 1930), p. 4; Al Smith, *Up to Now: An Autobiography* (New York, 1929), p. 30.

27.   On Thompson, see "Monster Militant at Panama Fair," *PT* 7 (June 1914): 72; "Toyland at the Panama Fair," *PT* 7 (July 1914): 76; and for the police interview, see *NYT* (November 22, 1930): 4.

28.   Interview with "Miss Clark," grocery buyer, by Ralph Hower (1930), RG 10, Harvard History Project, Box 4 of 4, p. 73, MA.

29.   Ralph Hower, *History of Macy's of New York, 1858–1919* (Cambridge, Mass., 1943, repr. 1967), pp. 336–69.

30.   Author's interview (May 6, 1985).

31.   Lecture by PS (January–April 1929), "History of the Training Department," RG 10, Harvard History Project (1934), MA.

32.   Author's interview (May 17, 1985).

33.   Interview with Dr. V. V. Anderson, employment manager, by Ralph Hower (1930), RG 10, Harvard History Project (1934), pp. 107–8, MA; G. Cowles, "How We Check Our Employment Tests," *System Magazine* 47 (May 1925): 131–33; "Psychiatrist Ministers to Macy Workers' Mental Health," *WWD* (October 19, 1927), p. 4; and Macy's buyer Dora Sanders, author interview (April 10, 1986), Manhattan. Sanders administered the tests in the early 1930s. Also see on the tests *WWD* (November 1, 1927): 4.

34.   "Minutes of the Council" (July 26, 1923), MA; the *PRL* (November 7, 1923): 3.

35.   *Business Week* (January 28, 1931), p. 11; *Business Week* (November 10, 1934), p. 14.

36.   On the Straus brothers' commitment to institutional service, see "Institutional Ad Series Relates 'Human Interests' Facts of Macy Store and Goods," *WWD* (October 22, 1927): 14; and Kenneth Collins (executive vice president of Macy's), "Institutionalizing Macy's," *Executive Training Course*, Series I, Lecture 3 (January–April 1929), p. 1, Record Group 22, Corporate Documentation, Management, Personnel Training Material (1929–49), MA. Summarizing the position, Collins said that "Macy's is anxious to be known as an institution in the community. A store becomes an institution when it succeeds in rendering services that are unique, absolutely distinctive."

37.   On this permission, see "The Marvels of Macyland," *PT* (December 1924):

246. On the month-by-month progress toward getting the parade underway, see "Minutes of the Executive Council" (June 12, 1924), p. 66; (August 7, 1924), pp. 78, 84; (September 4, 1924), p. 87; (September 25, 1924), p. 91; (October 9, 1924), p. 101; (November 6, 1924), p. 110; and "Macy's Christmas Parade," "Advertising—Special Events," p. 173, MA.

38. Sarg, quoted in Fred J. McIsaac, "Tony Sarg," *The Drama* (December 1921): 83, in "Clippings," Tony Sarg, Robinson Locke Collection, scrapbook, Sal-Swin, Lincoln Center Theater Collection, New York City. See also on Sarg, Jon Monk Saunders, "Tony Sarg Has Never Done a Stroke of Work in His Life," *The American Magazine* 1 (May 1926): 26–28, 100, 103–4, 106, 108.

39. Jameson Sewell, "The Marionette: The Movie of the Past," *Shadowland* (September 1919), pp. 15–18; obituary, *New York Herald Tribune* (March 17 and 21, 1942); *New York Herald* (Sunday, March 15, 1931); *The Villager* (March 12, 1942); *New York Sun* (February 28, 1942); Anne Stoddard, "The Renaissance of the Puppet Play," *Century Magazine* (June 1918), pp. 173–86, Sarg "Clippings."

40. On Bel Geddes, see *MRSW* 59 (December 1926): 22, and *Sparks* (the Macy's employee magazine) (December 1926): 15. On the management choice of Sarg to design the floats, see "Minutes of the Executive Council" (September 25, 1924), p. 91; and on his poster advertising, see *PRL* (November 2, 1925).

41. *Sparks* (November 1928): 4.

42. "Macy's Toy Circus Outshines the Glory of Last Year," *PRL* (December 1, 1924): 10; on the "large police force," see *NYT* (November 28, 1924), p. 15.

43. "The Marvels of Macyland": 10; *PT* (December 1924): 246; *MRSW* 55 (December 1924): 24. *MRSW* later reported that the parade was a unique one. Macy's, the journal said, was "the only department store of the kind in our recollection" to present a parade "marching from upper New York to the store"; see *MRSW* 56 (January 1925): 1.

44. "Santa Claus Exhibits," *NYT* (December 19, 1926), pt. II: 19.

45. *PRL* (Second December Issue, 1924): 1.

46. William H. Baldwin, "Like Topsy, We 'Just Growed,' The Case History of a Public Relations Counselor," *Public Relations Journal* 14 (September 1958): 9–10, 12.

47. *WWD* (November 23, 1927): 2; *WWD* (November 26, 1927): 17; *PRL* (First December Issue, 1927): 11; *MRSW* 56 (December 1927): 18.

48. Frances E. Fox, director of Drama Division of the Department of Recreation, Houston, to the Children's Bureau (October 9, 1930), Children's Bureau Papers, Folder 5-8-1, "Holiday Celebrations," RG 101, NA.

49. *Toy World* 3 (November 1929): 88–89.

50. *MRSW* (January 9, 1929): 36–37; "The Great Toystore Tableaux," Howard Kratz, Wanamaker's Philadelphia display manager, photo album (1927–31), WA; John Wanamaker and Co., "The Enchanted Forest" (Philadelphia, 1927), WA; *TN*

(January 1930): 197; *TN* (November 1930): 88–89; *PRL* (September 1933): 17.

51.   NYT (November 28, 1930), p. 4.

52.   See Betsy Blackmar, "Uptown Real Estate and the Creation of Times Square," in *Inventing Times Square*, ed. William R. Taylor (New York, 1991), pp. 51–66.

53.   "Grover Whalen Has New Plans to Speed Traffic," *NYT* (May 19, 1929), pt. X: 10; F. George Fredericks, *Adventuring in New York* (New York, 1923) p. 38; *ST* (March 1927): 60.

54.   David Schulte, real estate developer, quoted in NYT (April 30, 1925), p. 1.

55.   On the increase in expenditure, see Clyde Thompson of J. Walter Thompson, "The Trend in Outdoor Advertising," *The Advertising World* 35 (August 1930): 71–77; on Bullock's, see *The Advertising World* 31 (November 1926): 22–23.

56.   Thorstein Veblen, *Absentee Ownership and Business Enterprise in Recent Times: The Case of America* (New York, 1923), p. 315. On the zoning laws, see Jerome Charyn, *Metropolis: New York as Myth, Marketplace, and Magical Land* (New York, 1985), pp. 43–44.

57.   For an ordinary advertising day in the district in 1922, see ST (February 1922): 11; and for 1924, see ST (February 1924): 35. According to ST, automobile advertising began to dominate district advertising by 1924 (see "Automobile Advertising Leads Survey of Electric Signs Being Used," ST [February 1924]: 35). See also *The WPA Guide to New York City*, with introduction by William H. Whyte (New York, 1982; orig. pub. 1939), p. 170.

58.   Fredericks, *Adventuring in New York*, p. 38.

59.   ST (February 1925): 48.

60.   ST (January 1923): 45; ST (September 1920): 1.

61.   ST (April 1925): 48; ST (August 1924): 27.

62.   Quoted in Joseph Urban, "Wedding Theatre Beauty to Ballyhoo," *NYT* (August 19, 1928), pt. IV: 10.

63.   Edward L. Bernays to SC (January 26, 1928), SCP; Bernays, *Biography of an Idea* (New York, 1962), pp. 403–18; NYT (February 2, 1928): 5.

64.   NYT (November 11, 1929): 55.

65.   "Broadway's Colors," NYT (June 23, 1929), pt. V: 21; on Georges Claude, see ST (March 1927): 60.

66.   On the all-day advertising advantages of neon, see ST (March 1927): 60; and "Luminous Tube Signs Rapidly Developing in Popularity," ST (May 1926): 52.

67.   "Broadway's Colors": 21.

68.   Christopher Isherwood, quoted in Alex de Jonge, *The Weimar Chronicle: Prelude to Hitler* (New York, 1972), p. 125; Friedrich Sieburg, quoted in *The Paris We Remember*, ed. and trans. Elisabeth Finley Thomas, with introduction by Elliot Paul (New York, 1942), pp. 117–18; Henry Haynie, *Paris Past and Present* (New

York, 1902), vol. 1, pp. 339–41. On the six thousand neon signs in Paris, see *ST* (March 1927): 60; and Edith Wharton, *A Backward Glance* (New York, 1934), p. 320.

69.   *NYT* (June 18, 1928), editorial, p. 18. "What consternation would greet that order," said the *Times*, "if Mayor Walker were to promulgate it here? . . . Cigarette and motorcar advertisements would have to go, along with Tex Rickard's electric pointer."

70.   On the "battle" between the Fifth Avenue and Broadway associations, see *ST* (April 1922): 54; *ST* (June 1922): 38; *ST* (July 1922): 48; and *NYT* (February 12, 1928), pt. II: 5. On the Gude Company's membership in the Fifth Avenue Association, see *The Annual Report of the Fifth Avenue Association* (New York, 1919): 33.

71.   SC to Edward Bernays (January 26, 1928), SCP; Ezra Pound, *Patria Mia* (Chicago, 1950; written c. 1913), pp. 32–33.

72.   Veblen, *Absentee Ownership and Business Enterprise in Recent Times* (New York, 1923), pp. 321–22.

73.   Lang, quoted in Mandelbaum and Myers, *Screen Deco*, p. 166.

74.   Lewis Mumford, "The City," in *Civilization in the United States*, ed. Harold Stearns (New York, 1923), pp. 8–9.

75.   G. K. Chesterton, "A Meditation in Broadway," in *What I Saw in America*, in *The Collected Works of G. K. Chesterton*, ed. Robert Royal, vol. 21 (San Francisco, 1990), pp. 66–72.

76.   Chesterton, "A Meditation in Broadway," p. 68; "The Rituals of Christmas," *Illustrated London News* (December 24, 1927), in *The Collected Works of G. K. Chesterton*, ed. Lawrence J. Clipper, pp. 26, 438–39.

77.   *The Collected Works*, ed. Robert Royal, Chesterton, "What Is America?," vol. 21, pp. 47–48.

78.   Ibid., p. 48.

79.   Chesterton, "A Meditation in Broadway," p. 70.

Chapter 12

1.   R. L. Duffus, "A New National Symbol in Stone," *NYT* (May 15, 1932), sec. 5, magazine; *NYT* (June 4, 1929): 28.

2.   Herman Melville, *The Confidence Man* (New York, 1955), p. 12.

3.   *NYT* (December 26, 1931): 14.

4.   *NYT* (June 9, 1929), pt. III: 4.

5.   Duffus, "A New National Symbol in Stone": 11.

6.   Carroll H. Wooddy, *The Growth of the Federal Government, 1915–1932* (New

York, 1934), pp. 549–54. This study was actually prepared under the direction of President Herbert Hoover's Research Committee on Social Trends.

7.   The following biographical sketch has been drawn largely from David Burner's biography of Hoover, *Herbert Hoover: A Public Life* (New York, 1979) and from George H. Nash's massive two-volume study of Hoover's early years, *The Life of Herbert Hoover: The Engineer, 1874–1914* and *The Life of Herbert Hoover: The Humanitarian, 1914–1917* (New York, 1983, 1988).

8.   Herbert Hoover, "Message to the National Federation of Men's Bible Classes" (May 5, 1929), in *Herbert Hoover: Public Papers of the Presidents of the United States* (Washington, D.C., 1974), p. 136.

9.   Quoted in Burner, *Herbert Hoover*, p. 54. The reference to the passport policies of Turkey and Russia appears in Hoover's *Memoirs* as quoted in Burner, p. 73; and Nash, *The Life of Herbert Hoover: The Engineer*, pp. 245–83, 348–78, 384–475.

10.   Craig Lloyd, *Aggressive Introvert: A Study of Herbert Hoover and Public Relations Management, 1912–32* (Columbus, O., 1972), pp. 21–28.

11.   Robert Sobel, *The Great Bull Market: Wall Street in the 1920s* (New York, 1968), pp. 24–26.

12.   HH to JK (May 23, 1925), BFDC, Record Group 151, 402.1. General Files, NA, Washington, D.C. See also, for clear summations of the problems focused on by Commerce throughout the twenties, Frank Surface, assistant director of Domestic Commerce, *DC* 2 (February 3, 1928): 4; and "Report on the Census of Distribution," BFDC, 151, 024, General Files (1933–34), NA.

13.   On this compromise, see Ellis Hawley, "Herbert Hoover and Economic Stabilization, 1921–22," in *Herbert Hoover as Secretary of Commerce*, ed. Ellis Hawley (Iowa City, Ia., 1981), pp. 43–80; Hawley, essay in *Herbert Hoover and the Crisis of American Capitalism*, ed. Joseph Huthmacher and Warren Susman (Cambridge, Eng., 1970), pp. 3–33; David Burner, *Herbert Hoover*, pp. 158–89; Joseph Brandes, *Herbert Hoover and Economic Diplomacy* (Pittsburgh, Pa., 1962); Daniel Fox, *The Discovery of Abundance: Simon Patten and the Transformation of Social Theory* (Ithaca, N.Y., 1967), p. 164; Carolyn Grin, "The Unemployment Conference of 1921: An Experiment in National Cooperative Planning," *Mid-America* 55 (April 1973): 83–107; Guy Alchon, *The Invisible Hand of Planning: Capitalism, Social Science, and the State in the 1920s* (Princeton, N.J., 1985), pp. 3–15; and R. Jeffrey Lustig, *Corporate Liberalism: The Origins of Modern Political Theory, 1890–1920* (Berkeley, Calif., 1986). Not all of these historians agree, however, on the exact character of the compromise Hoover developed. Most see Hoover principally as a corporate liberal. For an excellent recent discussion of corporate liberalism and statism as ideologies, see Mary O. Furner, "Knowing Capitalism: Public Investigation and the Labor Question in the Long Progressive Era," in *The State and Economic Knowledge: The American and British Experiences*, ed. Mary O. Furner and Barry Supple (Cambridge, Eng., 1990), pp. 241–86.

14.   HH, *American Individualism* (New York, 1922), pp. 1–33.

15. On the impact of the "new economics" on Hoover, see esp. William J. Barber, *From New Era to New Deal* (Cambridge, Eng., 1985), pp. 7–77; and Alchon, *The Invisible Hand of Planning.*

16. HH, *American Individualism*, p. 33.

17. *Recent Economic Changes*, p. xviii.

18. *DC* (May 13, 1929), p. 6.

19. HH, *The Memoirs of Herbert Hoover: The Cabinet and the Presidency, 1920–1933*, vol. 2 (New York, 1952), p. 167.

20. Ibid.

21. HH, *The New Day: Campaign Speeches of Herbert Hoover* (Palo Alto, Calif., 1928), pp. 77–78; and HH, *Memoirs*, pp. 169–70.

22. A. Lincoln Filene to LK (April 23, 1921), Box 65, "Filene, A. Lincoln," LKP, Baker Library, Harvard Business School.

23. HH, *Memoirs*, pp. 168–173; and Burner, *Herbert Hoover*, pp. 172–73.

24. HH, *American Individualism*, p. 40.

25. HH, *The New Day*, pp. 10–23. On the relation of state power to "knowledge production," see Mary O. Furner and Barry Supple, "Ideas, Institutions, and State in the United States and Britain: An Introduction," in *The State and Economic Knowledge*, pp. 3–39; and Michael Lacy and Mary O. Furner, "Social Investigation and Public Discourse," in *State and Social Investigation in Britain and U.S.*, ed. Lacy and Furner (Cambridge, Eng., forthcoming). See also, on the emergence of centralized statistical agencies in Washington during World War I, Robert Cuff, "Creating Control Systems: Edwin F. Gay and the Central Bureau of Planning and Statistics, 1917–1919," *Business History Review* 63 (Autumn 1989): 588–613.

26. Wesley Clair Mitchell, "Economic Resources and Their Employment," in *Studies in Economics and Industrial Relations* (Philadelphia, 1941), p. 2.

27. Cuff, "Creating Control Systems," pp. 609–13.

28. Burner, *Herbert Hoover*, pp. 161–62.

29. HH, *New Day*, p. 74 (speech at Newark), p. 120 (speech at Boston), and p. 187 (Speech at St. Louis). For list of businessmen hired by Hoover to head his commodity divisions, see Will Kennedy, "Business Experts Make Sacrifices to Help Put the Hoover Plan Across," *The Washington Evening Star* (December 25, 1921), Editorial Sec.: 1. See also, on these divisions, Hawley, "Herbert Hoover and Economic Stabilization," pp. 52–53.

30. Dr. Frank Surface, assistant director of BFDC, quoted in *DC* (January 30, 1931), 27; JK, *Frontiers of Trade* (New York, 1929), pp. 120, 141.

31. JK to Bernays (December 9, 1929), General Files, 402.1, General (1927–49), BFDC, NA.

32. On this new "section," see S. L. Kedsierski, Costs and Operations Analysis,

Merchandising Research Division, to Max Kelley (November 28, 1930), RG 151, BFDC, entry 1 NE-27, General Records, 402.301, DC, Retail, Consumers, NA. On the overall structure, see Hancock Adams, "Our New Commerce Building," *National Republic* 19 (November 11, 1931): 5–6.

33.   Quoted in Joseph Dorfman, *The Economic Mind in American Civilization*, vol. 4 (New York, 1959), p. 367; Wesley Clair Mitchell, *Business Cycles* (Berkeley, Calif., 1913), p. 599; and Alchon, *The Invisible Hand of Planning*, p. 19.

34.   Quoted in Robert Seidel, "Progressive Pan Americanism: Development and United States Policy Toward South America, 1906–1931," Ph.D. diss., Cornell University (1973), p. 185; see also Seidel, pp. 169, 278; and JK to Edwin Gay (June 24, 1915), Edwin Gay Papers, Manuscripts and Archives, Baker Library, HBS.

35.   Melvin Copeland, *And Mark the Era: The Story of the Harvard Business School* (Boston, 1958), pp. 16–25, 214–16, 431; Edwin Gay, quoted in Herbert Heaton, *A Scholar in Action: Edwin F. Gay* (Cambridge, Mass., 1952), pp. 18, 38–49, 62–70, 80, 98–99.

36.   JK to Edwin Gay (September 27, 1915, October 3, 1915, and September 27, 1915); and Edwin Gay to A. Lawrence Lowell (February 15, 1912, and April 6, 1912), Gay Papers.

37.   JK, *The Mesta: A Study in Spanish Economic History, 1273–1836* (Cambridge, Mass., 1920), pp. vii–xi, 9–22, 28–42, 52; JK to Edwin Gay (September 7, 1917), Gay Papers.

38.   Franklin Johnston to JK (August 8, 1928), RG 151, BFDC, Criticism, NA; Julius Klein, biographical sketch in *Who's Who in Government* (New York, 1930), vol. 1, p. 312.

39.   Wesley Clair Mitchell, "Economic Resources and Their Employment," in *Studies in Economics and Industrial Relations* (Philadelphia, 1941), p. 2; Willford I. King, "Trade Cycles and Factory Production," and Francis Walker, "New Data Needed for Forecasting," in *The Problems of Business Forecasting*, ed. Warren Persons et al. (Boston, 1924), pp. 13–16, 27, 35, 85–91.

40.   JK, *Frontiers of Trade*, pp. 187–88.

41.   U.S. Department of Commerce, *Tenth Annual Report of the Secretary of Commerce* (Washington, D.C., 1922), p. 135.

42.   Ibid., pp. 96–98, 107–10.

43.   JK to Congresswoman Edith Rogers (October 16, 1928), BFDC, RG 151, 402.10, New England General, NA; A. Heath Onthank to the Chamber of Commerce, Cleveland, Ohio (May 6, 1925), 402.1, General Files, BFDC, NA; "The Retailer and the Consumer in New England," *Trade Information Bulletin* no. 575 (Washington, D.C., October 1925), pp. 1–3; and Irving Paull to John C. Rink, N. W. Ayer and Sons (August 22, 1923), RG 151, 402.4.7, BFDC, NA.

44.   On the retail credit survey, see *DC* (May 24, 1928): 2, and *DC* (July 9, 1928): 2. On retail distribution surveys, see John C. Rink of N. W. Ayer and Sons to I.

S. Paull (August 21, 1923), BFDC, RG 151, 402.4, Conferences on Retail Distribution, NA; and H. C. Dunn, chief of DC Division, to J. W. Roedel (October 9, 1929), 402.4, Returned Goods, RG 151, BFDC, NA.

45. Victor Cutter to JK (July 30, 1929), RG 151, "Domestic Commerce—Distribution—Surveys—New England," BFDC, NA.

46. "Resolution of the Association of National Advertisers," in convention at Detroit (May 11, 1927), RG 151, 402.1, General, 1927–29, General Files, BFDC, NA.

47. C. B. Clark, J. L. Hudson and Co., to Irving S. Paull, chief of Domestic Commerce Division (June 1, 1923), RG 151, 402.4 General, "Domestic Conferences—Conferences—General—1923–29," BFDC, NA.

48. Frederick M. Feiker to HH (January 7, 1925), RG 151, General Files, 402.1, General, 1925, BFDC, NA.

49. Robert P. Lamont, secretary of commerce, radio address (December 1, 1929), General Files, 0024, 1930, Census; "Philadelphia and the Census of Distribution" (May 3, 1930), 024, General (1930), Census, pp. 1–4; and "What the Census of Distribution Is," General, 024 (1933–34), Census, pp. 1–2, BFDC, NA. On the first British census, see Margaret Hall, John Knapp, and Christopher Winston, *Distribution in Great Britain and North America* (London, 1961), pp. 1–5.

50. *DC* (May 13, 1929): 6.

51. For a sample of BFDC publications, see "Retail Store Planning," *Trade Information Bulletin* 291 (Washington, D.C., 1924), pp. 2–3; "Cooperative Retail Advertising," *Trade Information Bulletin* 302 (Washington, D.C., January 1925); "Measuring a Retail Market," *Trade Information Bulletin* 272 (Washington, D.C., October 13, 1924); "Planning Salesman's Territories," *Trade Information Bulletin* 214 (Washington, D.C., 1924); and Domestic Commerce Series, "Retail Store Problems" (Washington, D.C., 1926).

52. JK, *Frontiers of Trade*, pp. 90–91, 210; and C. J. North to Chester Jones, Paris, commercial attaché (February 5, 1927), 400.2, France, RG 151, Trade Promotion, BFDC, NA.

53. JK, "Fundamental Basis of Our Prosperity," NYT (December 15, 1929), sec. XI: 3, 20.

54. HH, *Memoirs*, vol. 2, p. 79; Donald Breed to O. P. Hopkins (April 25, 1932), RG 151, 101.1, Criticism, BFDC, NA; JK, radio address, NYT (November 25, 1929), p. 4.

55. JK, report on CBS radio show, NYT (January 20, 1930), p. 9.

56. For Klein's radio show on industrial design, see "Beauty as a Business Builder," MRSW 66 (June 1930): 7–9; on show windows, "Art in Industry Pays Dividends," MRSW 61 (March 1930): 4, 13–17, and DC (March 1930): 98; and on advertising, NYT (October 14, 1929): 41.

57. NYT (October 14, 1929): 41.

58. *NYT* (October 22, 1929), editorial: 28; Bernays, *The Biography of an Idea,* (New York, 1962) pp. 445–59.

59. On Insull, see Forrest MacDonald, *Insull* (Chicago, 1962); and for the best account of the "jubilee" to celebrate Edison, see Matthew Josephson, *Edison* (New York, 1959), pp. 432–56.

60. See Grin, "The Unemployment Conference of 1921," pp. 83–107.

61. HH, *Memoirs*, vol. 2, p. 7.

62. On Hoover's Division of Building and Housing and the Better Homes Movement, see HH, *Memoirs*, vol. 2, pp. 92–94.

63. Lloyd, *Aggressive Introvert*, pp. 122–33. Lloyd provides a fine discussion of Hoover's publicity role on pp. 20–33, 45–55, 131–43, and 152–63. See also Gwendolyn Wright, *Building the Dream: A Social History of Housing in America* (New York, 1981), pp. 195–98.

64. John Gries and James Ford, ed., *Housing Objectives and Programs*, vol. 11 of *The President's Conference on Home Building and Home Ownership* (Washington, D.C., 1932), pp. 150–201.

65. HH, *Memoirs*, vol. 2, pp. 97, 99.

66. White House Conference on Child Health and Protection, *The Home and the Child: Housing, Furnishing, Management, Income, and Clothing* (New York, 1931), pp. 13–17.

67. Ibid., pp. 39–55.

68. Prentiss Terry, district manager, Louisville, Ky., to R. J. Croghan, Division of Current Information (April 21, 1932), 101.1, Criticism, RG 151, BFDC, NA; and ed., *Bulletin of the International Management Institute* [Geneva, Switz.] 7 (March 1933): 46.

69. Ernest DuBrul, general manager of National Machine Tool Builders' Association, to W. H. Rastall, chief of Industrial Machinery Division (January 30, 1928), RG 151, 402-10, Domestic Commerce—Conferences—General—1923–29," BFDC, NA.

70. JK, memorandum to Frank Surface (August 13, 1928); H. B. Dorsey, secretary of the Texas Grain Dealers' Association, to B. S. Culler, chief of the BFDC (May 20, 1919); Franklin Johnston, editor of *The American Economist*, to JK (August 8, 1928); R. J. Croghan to Prentiss Terry (April 21, 1932); M. J. Hart, congressman from Michigan, to E. Kent Hubbard, Connecticut Manufacturers' Association (June 10, 1932), 101.0, Criticism, RG 151, BFDC, NA.

71. Donald Breed, *The Freeport Journal Standard*, Freeport, Ill. (April 2, 1931), editorial: 8; Breed to O. P. Hopkins, assistant director of the BFDC (April 25, 1932), 101.0, Criticism, BFDC, NA.

72. *DC* (September 3, 1928): 1.

73. HH, "Advertising Is a Vital Force in Our National Life," repr. in *Advertising World* 30 (August 1925): 1–2. See also *PRL* (Second May Issue, 1925): 7.

74.   HH, "Addresses During the Campaign" (August 21, 1928), in *Public Papers of the Presidents* (Washington, 1958) pp. 521–24.

75.   Ibid., p. 524.

76.   On these writers, see Richard H. Pells, *Radical Visions and American Dreams: Culture and Social Thought in the Depression Years* (Middletown, Conn., 1984), pp. 96–105.

Conclusion

1.   Edmund Wilson, "The Literary Consequences of the Crash" (March 23, 1932), repub. in *The Shores of Light: A Literary Chronicle of the Twenties and Thirties*, ed. Edmund Wilson (Boston, 1985; orig. pub. 1952), p. 498.

2.   Edmund Wilson, "An Appeal to Progressives," orig. pub. 1930 and repub. in Edmund Wilson, ed., *The Shores of Light* (New York, 1961), pp. 518–27. All quotes in this paragraph are from this text.

3.   Sidonie and Benjamin Gruenberg, *Parents, Children, and Money* (New York, 1933), pp. 172–75.

4.   Quoted in Richard Pells, *Radical Visions and American Dreams* (Middletown, Conn., 1984), p. 108. Pells presents an excellent discussion of the thinking of these men, pp. 69–150.

5.   Quoted in Pells, pp. 99, 107.

6.   For the Dewey quote, see Pells, p. 120; on the quest for "wholeness," see Pells, pp. 97–102; and on Mumford's critique of constant growth, see Pells, p. 110.

7.   See, on dimensions of this search for a "shared American culture," Warren Susman, *Culture as History: The Transformation of American Society in the Twentieth Century* (New York, 1984), chap. 9, "The Culture of the Thirties," pp. 150–83.

8.   Samuel Strauss, *American Opportunity* (New York, 1935), pp. 23–25.

9.   On government modernization programs, see "Store Improvement Planned and Is Greatly on the Increase," *MRSW* 76 (April 1935): 37, 78 (April 1936): 1; and *DC* (November 30, 1936): 311. On *The New Republic* and *The Nation*, see Pells, pp. 81–86.

10.   James Rorty, *Where Life Is Better: The Unsentimental American Journey* (New York, 1936), pp. 103–110, p. 157, p. 169, p. 287, 380–81.

11.   Robert Heilbroner, *The Nature and Logic of Capitalism* (New York, 1985), pp. 104–5.

12.   James Grant, *Money on the Mind: Borrowing and Lending in America from the Civil War to Michael Milken* (New York, 1992), p. 5.

13.   Leroy C. Schwarz Kopf, *Government Reference Serials* (Englewood, Colo.: Libraries Unlimited, 1988); and Donna Andriot, ed., *Guide to U.S. Government Publications* (McLean, Va., 1990). I want to make clear here that this discussion

is not intended as an attack on the public sector; rather, it is meant to indicate how much business is dependent on the public sector for its existence. Businessmen who argue otherwise are, at the very least, disingenuous. Moreover, the private and public sectors are today so deeply intertwined that only ideologues can construe them as divorced from or contradicatory to one another.

14.   U.S. Government, *Budget of the United States Government, Fiscal Year 1990* (Washington, D.C., 1990), I-F7-F10.

15.   On the Kuwait service, see *NYT* (March 22, 1991): D1; and on the export licenses, see *The Wall Street Journal* (July 31, 1992): A14.

16.   "Selling to the World," *The Wall Street Journal* (August 27, 1992): 1.

17.   Michael Schudson, *Advertising, the Uneasy Persuasion: Its Dubious Impact on American Society* (New York, 1984).

18.   "Germans Sigh and Say 'Charge It,' " *NYT* (April 13, 1991): L37.

19.   "New Fashion School in India Draws from a Rich Heritage," *NYT* (June 21, 1989): C14.

20.   Anne Hollander, "Dragtime," *The New Republic* (August 31, 1992): 41.

21.   On the Nike advertising, see *NYT* (December 27, 1991): D5; and on the Indonesian factory, see letter to the editor, *NYT* (August 15, 1992): 18.

22.   Samuel Strauss, "The Future," *The Villager* 6 (April 28, 1923): 119.

23.   "American Culture Examined as a Force That Groups the World," *NYT* (March 11, 1992): C17.

24.   Deborah Levenson, *Death Into Life: Trade Unions and Terror in Guatemala, 1954–1985* (Chapel Hill, N.C., forthcoming).

25.   Robert E. Reich, "Who Is Them?," *Harvard Business Review* (March–April 1991): 82; and "For Coke, World Is Its Oyster," *NYT* (November 21, 1991): D1.

26.   The Marriott Hotel Corporation and its president, J. W. Marriott, Jr., provide a good example of this disregard. In ten years, from 1980 to 1990, they increased the number of their hotels from 75 to 650—a tremendously wasteful overbuilding that resulted only in numerous empty buildings and in the need to sell off one hotel after another. *NYT* (March 22, 1991): D1.

27.   Robert E. Litan, Robert Z. Lawrence, and Charles L. Schultze, eds. *American Living Standards: Threats and Challenges* (Washington, 1988), p. 14, 116–31; and Christopher Lasch, *The True and Only Heaven. Progress and Its Critics* (New York, 1991), pp. 412–532.

INDEX